MW00781654

PLATO
III

LCL 166

PLATO

LYSIS
SYMPOSIUM
PHAEDRUS

EDITED AND TRANSLATED BY

CHRIS EMLYN-JONES

AND

WILLIAM PREDDY

HARVARD UNIVERSITY PRESS
CAMBRIDGE, MASSACHUSETTS
LONDON, ENGLAND
2022

LOEB CLASSICAL LIBRARY® is a registered trademark
of the President and Fellows of Harvard College

Library of Congress Control Number 2021945892
CIP data available from the Library of Congress

ISBN 978-0-674-99743-1

*Composed in ZephGreek and ZephText by
Technologies 'N Typography, Merrimac, Massachusetts.
Printed on acid-free paper and bound by
Maple Press, York, Pennsylvania*

CONTENTS

GENERAL INTRODUCTION

1. INTRODUCTION

Plato's *Lysis*, *Symposium*, and *Phaedrus* were written at different periods of his long productive life, ranging from his early period to the late middle, roughly the late 390s/ early 380s to the 370s BC (see Chronology of Plato's Life and Works).[1] Although differing widely from each other in setting and approach, the works are grouped together here by virtue of their principal subject matter, a study of the relationship between two people known as love (*erōs*) or friendship (*philia*). As with almost all of Plato's works, they are in dialogue form, the central character in all three being Socrates. They are set (one might say "staged") during the last period of Socrates' life, ca. 416– 399. The first two, *Lysis* and *Symposium*, take place in Athenian upper-class male social institutions: in *Lysis* Socrates meets youths exercising in a *palaestra* (wrestling school) on the occasion of a religious festival; in the *Symposium* he attends a *sumposion* (drinking party) together

[1] For detailed discussion of the evidence for the supposed dramatic dates at which the dialogues are set and the dates of composition, see the Appendix at the end of the Introduction to each of the three dialogues. Throughout this volume, all dates are BC unless otherwise stated.

with a number of his distinguished friends, celebrating the victory of the host, the tragic playwright Agathon, in the competition of plays at a dramatic festival in the theater of Dionysus. In contrast, *Phaedrus* has a more intimate atmosphere: Socrates and his younger friend Phaedrus have a conversation in high summer on the banks of the river Ilissus outside the walls of Athens, accompanied by the background chirping of crickets. But even here we are made aware of the outside world: a presentation of speeches on the subject of love delivered by both Phaedrus and Socrates leads to a critical discussion of the current state of the theory and practice of rhetoric, a key aspect of Athenian political, social, and intellectual discourse.

2. LOVING RELATIONSHIPS IN FIFTH- AND FOURTH-CENTURY ATHENIAN SOCIETY

"Love," the English word for the personal attraction that Socrates and his friends are exploring in these three works, in Greek covers, like its English equivalent, a correspondingly wide range of relationships between individuals, from political and personal friendships and alliances or family attachments (e.g., parents for children and vice-versa) at one end of the spectrum to intense emotion and erotic desire at the other. But while the Greek *philia*, "friendship" (adjective *philos* = dear), usually represents the former, and *erōs*, "love," "desire" (*erastēs* = lover) the latter, their uses can overlap. For example, *philia* (and cognates) is a broad category that is used for love and friendship in the relationship between, e.g., political allies, friends, and family, but it is also used in a context where it can refer to love in a close relationship that may be sexual.[2] *Erōs*, however, is generally narrower in application and usually indicates erotic love, but it can on occasion also indicate the intensity of nonsexual desire or attraction.[3] In these dialogues, the word *epithumia* (desire), and cognates, is also found; this word has the broad meaning of desire in general, e.g., appetite for food or drink; but the word can also have the narrower meaning of the strong emotional attraction associated with love for another person.[4]

The assumption underlying the love relationship explored in the dialogues is that it was homoerotic, between males. This was taken for granted among the more well-to-do groups in Athenian society, within which Plato's dialogues are set. The subordinate and secluded position of women in families prosperous enough to preclude the necessity of the movement of female members outside the home made a liaison with a married citizen woman

[2] See Dover, *GPM*, 212. In these three dialogues there are occasions where *philia* and *erōs* can be found used interchangeably.

[3] There is a striking example of *erōs* used in a nonsexual context in *Symposium* 173b3–4, where, in describing the intensity of the emotional and intellectual devotion to Socrates of his follower Aristodemus, the narrator refers to him as Socrates' *erastēs* (lover), where a sexual implication is unlikely (Dover, 4, suggests it is "half a joke"—"fan" might be an appropriate translation, see *Protagoras* 317c). See also *Phaedrus* 266b3, where the word indicates Socrates' serious devotion to a philosophical theory.

[4] In *Phaedrus* 237dff. Socrates distinguishes the different applications of *epithumia*.

extremely difficult and dangerous.[5] Therefore, for sexual gratification, apart from casual encounters with prostitutes and slaves, and also for a more permanent and meaningful liaison, unmarried Athenian men and youths turned to younger members of their own sex. A typical relationship was between an active older male (*erastēs*) and a younger boy entering puberty (*erōmenos* or *paidika* = "loved one"). The older partner, the *erastēs*, typically felt erotic desire and pursued the passive younger one, the *erōmenos*, who accepted (or refused) his advances. The initial pursuit of the *erōmenos* by the *erastēs* frequently reflected society's double standards: the lover gained prestige if he succeeded in his seduction, while the *erōmenos*, carefully guarded by *paidagōgoi* (attendants), was censured by contemporaries and friends for submitting to his lover's advances. This relationship, however, when successful, was as much educative as erotic; the role of the older and more socially experienced lover was to initiate the younger boy into the values associated with *aretē*, meaning "excellence" or "virtue"—a broad indication of the positive moral qualities that would be expected of him as he grew into a mature citizen. This association should not, however, be confused with modern homosexuality. This choice was rarely an exclusive or lifelong sexual preference.[6] Both partners typically went on to enter into heterosexual relationships within marriage. Socrates himself

---

[5] An adulterer could be prosecuted or even killed by an offended husband if caught in the act of seducing a married woman (see Dover, *GPM*, 209).

[6] Agathon and Pausanias in the *Symposium* as lifelong same-sex partners (see, e.g., *Symposium* 193c) appear to have been an exception to the rule.

appears to have moved within the atmosphere of same-sex erotic byplay and humor (and possibly activity) while at the same time being married with three sons.[7]

A number of Plato's characters in the dialogues make us aware of this everyday background: see in particular, in the present context, the speeches of Phaedrus and Pausanias in praise of the god Eros in the *Symposium* (180c–85c) and Phaedrus' recitation of the speech-writer Lysias' (or possibly Plato's) speech on Love (*erōtikos logos*) in *Phaedrus* (230e–34c); these all give a detailed insight into the conventional relationship from different points of view.

3. LOVE AS A SUBJECT FOR PHILOSOPHY IN THE THREE DIALOGUES

At first sight, the idea that the emotional attraction known as friendship or love (*philia, erōs*)—and especially the latter, on which the *Symposium* and *Phaedrus* chiefly concentrate—should be a subject for philosophical study seems unexpected and inappropriate, especially for a post-Freudian society where relationships based on emotion are often seen as notoriously difficult to reconcile with rational thought. However, for Socrates the ultimate key to living the good life is the search for the acquisition of knowledge through self-examination.[8] In this endeavor,

---

[7] See *Phaedo* 60a, 116a–b. On the relationship generally, see Dover, *Greek Homosexuality*; Davidson, *Courtesans and Fishcakes*.

[8] See Socrates in Plato's version of his trial speech (*Apology*) 38a 5–6: ". . . the unexamined life is not fit for a man to live. . . ."

love plays a key role. Running through the dialogues is the idea that the perfect loving relationship between two people depends on their coming together to acquire knowledge of what goodness and beauty really are and how these relate to the desires of the individual human soul (*psuchē*).

We can see the seeds of this philosophical endeavor in the statements and questions arising out of the commonplace educational aims and objectives expressed by Socrates' interlocutors, based as these are on varied degrees of social awareness. For example, in *Lysis*, Socrates, conversing in the *palaestra* with his young friends, addresses an immediate question: how should the love-besotted young man Hippothales address his *erōmenos*, Lysis, and what are his underlying thoughts and aims? This initial question develops, under the direction of Socrates, into a discussion of the nature of the relationship involved in friendship or love (*philia* or *erōs*): in *Lysis* the emphasis is chiefly on the former, although both are involved and at times no clear distinction is made between the two. Socrates suggests in a somewhat schematic manner a number of possible relationships as candidates for friendship, e.g., like to like, good to good, neither bad nor good to good, etc.[9] Typically, as with other dialogues of this early period, some of these suggestions appear more promising than others. Nevertheless, when they have reached a number of dead ends, the dialogue concludes in a somewhat contrived *aporia* (impasse) with no apparent solution to the main question.

[9] On these choices and the underlying rationale of Plato's procedure in the argument, see Introduction to *Lysis*, §§3 and 4.

In contrast, the more elaborate *Symposium* (in the modern era undoubtedly the best known of the three dialogues)[10] takes as its starting point rhetorical display speeches (*epideixeis*) in honor of the god Love (Eros), delivered by a number of well-known Athenian citizens; these speeches explore the poetic, mythical, and scientific aspects of the love relationship. Socrates in his speech, guided, he says, by a discussion he once had with a priestess called Diotima (almost definitely a transparent fiction for Socrates himself), takes what he sees as the limitations of these earlier speeches as a basis for his own much more profound and wide-ranging exploration of the subject. He starts from the idea that Eros, far from being the embodiment of Love, as popularly supposed and as Agathon, the host, has just suggested in his speech, is actually a needy figure, seeking what he lacks; Love passionately desires to possess goodness and beauty, his ultimate goal being *eudaimonia* (happiness).[11] All humans, and even animals, are motivated by *erōs* in the desire to attain this goal, to perpetuate themselves by producing offspring, or in the case of creative people, for example, poets and lawgivers, to satisfy a desire for *kleos* (fame, reputation) by producing memorable works. But the lover in particular, being pregnant in his soul, desires to produce, together with his beloved, offspring in the form of goodness, beauty,

---

[10] A version of the *Symposium* was adapted and directed for UK BBC TV in 1965 by Jonathan Miller and Leo Aylen as "The Drinking Party," starring Leo McKern as Socrates. The production is available online.

[11] The aim of living the good life, not merely a psychological state; better translated as "fulfillment," "flourishing."

and wisdom, an "immortality" that, under the guidance of Diotima, ultimately leads to the "final mysteries." The lover leaves behind his preoccupation with the individual beauty of his beloved and all other physical beauty and intellectual excellence in an ascent toward the contemplation of absolute beauty and wisdom.[12] This is the end that the last speaker, the notorious Alcibiades, has conspicuously failed to attain, on his own admission.

Phaedrus takes as its starting point a speech on the love relationship allegedly written by the contemporary orator Lysias and delivered by the speech-besotted Phaedrus, who has just met Socrates by the city wall after a riveting session since daybreak with the orator. The socially conventional basis of Lysias' argument is somewhat disguised by the deliberately paradoxical thesis being presented, namely the social advantages of gratifying a lover who is not actually in love,[13] and Socrates is persuaded against his better judgment to compete with a similar effort. He then strongly repudiates his previous speech, to avoid the wrath of the gods, by composing a *palinode* (recantation) in which he completely abandons the competitive and sterile rhetorical moves of his and Phaedrus' earlier speeches and elaborates a picture of the nature of true love as a species of divinely-inspired madness and reveals its heavenly and

[12] On the emphasis on the desires, wishes, and activities of the *erastēs* in the *erastēs/erōmenos* relationship, see Introduction to *Symposium*, §3 (end).

[13] Plato's skill in stylistic imitation leaves it uncertain whether Phaedrus' speech is a version of a genuine *logos erōtikos* by Lysias or Plato's own invention.

earthly manifestations. Of the three dialogues *Phaedrus* explores most thoroughly, in this second speech of Socrates, the metaphysical aspect of Love, concentrating on the nature and activities of the human soul. Socrates depicts the soul as a self-moving entity, having wings that convey the lover upward toward the heavens to contemplate the Forms, supernatural manifestations of absolute and unchanging goodness, beauty, and wisdom. However, there is tension and conflict in the human soul that causes it to sink away from the heavens and prevents it from permanently contemplating the Forms, which leads to its progress through a number of reincarnations.[14] The psychological detail of this conflict is most memorably described in what is probably the best-known passage in the dialogue, the myth of the charioteer; the conflict is represented by a charioteer and his attempt to control his two horses, representing, respectively, good and honorable impulses toward the beloved and base desire, where the disorderly conduct of the latter threatens to overpower the charioteer's control of the other, obedient, horse and to lead to disaster. The second half of the dialogue consists of a discussion of the current state of speech-making, in which Socrates advocates a transformed rhetoric as concerned entirely with truth speaking to the soul rather than

---

[14] The idea of reincarnation of the soul also features, elaborately described, in *Republic* (10.614ff.). On the significance of Plato's exploration of the journey and behavior of the soul in relation to the arguments of *Meno*, *Phaedo*, and *Republic* for dating the composition of the dialogue, see further Introduction to *Phaedrus*, Appendix.

with mere persuasion, which is concerned with what is plausible; the delivery of a speech concerned with what is true leads to a kind of *psychagōgia* (leading of the soul), which draws the individual toward knowledge of goodness and beauty. This rhetoric advocates living speech over the unchanging written word as a flexible medium—a seed capable of bearing fruit in the soul of the hearer. The work concludes with a brief allusion to Isocrates, a prominent speechwriter and Plato's contemporary and rival in the practice of *philosophia*.

Despite their obvious diversity, the three dialogues contain certain themes in common. The emphasis on choices by the individual, briefly outlined in *Lysis*, becomes in the later dialogues a central element in Socrates' description of the lover's attempt to attain real knowledge of goodness and beauty. The *erastēs*, far from having this knowledge, is seen as needy, lacking those qualities that, as an aspiring lover, he needs to possess. In both *Symposium* and *Phaedrus*, Plato develops the idea of the lover as someone poised between knowledge and ignorance who nevertheless should aim to possess the knowledge of what is good and beautiful so that he can ascend (in *Phaedrus*, literally) to attain happiness in contemplation of the vision of absolute goodness and beauty.[15]

Socrates' engagement with rhetoric, with which the second half of *Phaedrus* is concerned, represents, at first sight, an anticlimax, following Socrates' elevated descrip-

[15] An idea brought out most strongly in the latter two dialogues, but anticipated, to a limited extent, in *Lysis* 219cff., with Socrates' proposal (not contradicted) that there is a "first friend" (*to prōton philon*), the ultimate object of love.

tion of the journey of the soul.[16] However, preoccupation with the role of dialectic in the development of Socrates' philosophical theories about love and friendship is not confined to *Phaedrus*, but is also revealed in the step-by-step examination of *Lysis* and the competing display speeches of the *Symposium*. This is not simply dramatic background. In each of the latter two works in particular, Socrates is expected to demonstrate, in competition with others, his rhetorical skill (*technē* = "art/expertise"). However, for Socrates, this *technē*, in contrast with that displayed by the others, is not basically competitive, but is closely related to attempts to attain knowledge of absolute goodness and beauty.

It may also be significant that none of the dialogues ends with a clear resolution in the sense of unequivocal acceptance of what Socrates imparts, and in none of them is Socrates' exposition the climax of the dialogue: *Lysis* ends on a downbeat, an apparently contrived *aporia* (failure to discover the nature of the relationship between *philoi*), any further investigation being disrupted by the youths' *paidagōgoi* (attendants) ordering them to go home. In *Symposium*, Socrates' exposition is followed by moderate applause overshadowed by the noisy irruption of the notorious Alcibiades, whose subsequent admission of his failure to secure Socrates as a lover is perhaps meant to demonstrate his distance from the ideal that Socrates seeks to impart. In *Phaedrus*, on the surface, Socrates' companion appears completely won over at the end of their conversation. However, taking the dialogue as a

---

[16] See, for the detailed argument, the Introduction to *Phaedrus*, §§4 and 5.

whole, it is debatable whether Socrates actually succeeds at the end in his aim of *psychagōgia*, the leading of his friend's soul to a full understanding of the truth.

4. THE HISTORICAL SOCRATES AND PLATO'S SOCRATES

In all three dialogues Plato places his chief character, Socrates (469–399), in dramatic scenes that are represented as taking place toward the end of the fifth century, when Socrates would have been getting on toward old age. He himself wrote nothing as far as we know, and his personality and philosophical ideas come to us largely through some twenty-five dialogues of his follower and pupil Plato, in almost all of which Socrates is the chief character. All of these were composed after Socrates' death, between the late 390s and Plato's death in 347 (see Chronology of Plato's Life and Works).

In 399 Socrates was prosecuted for impiety (*asebeia*) and condemned to death by the drinking of hemlock. A near-contemporary account of Socrates and his teaching is an arguably fictitious, or at least comically exaggerated, portrait in Aristophanes' comedy *Clouds* (staged in 423, revised 418), which connected the philosopher with a fantastic version of philosophical and scientific speculation that was around at the time, and that, according to Plato's version of Socrates' trial speech, his *Apology*, accounted for the *diabolē* (slander, prejudice) against him at his trial, which, he claims, played a large part in his condemnation (*Apology* 18bff.)

There are also a number of works by a wealthy soldier

and associate, Xenophon (428–ca. 354), who composed reminiscences of Socrates, including a *Symposium*, which probably postdated Plato's and resembles the latter in dramatic structure and form. In his other Socratic works, an *Apology* (his own version of the trial speech) and in his *Memorabilia* (*Memoirs of Socrates*), Xenophon puts forward a version of Socrates' personality and thought that, while having some themes in common with Plato, differs significantly from him in both content and tone.

There are also a number of philosophical dialogues and memoirs by friends and associates of Socrates, surviving only in fragments and recognized by Aristotle (384–322) in the *Poetics* (1447b11) as a literary genre, the "Socratic dialogues" (*Sōkratikoi logoi*).[17]

Aristotle, for some years a member of Plato's Academy, makes a distinction in his *Metaphysics* (1078b9–32) between the contribution of Socrates and that of Plato, based on the search for universal definitions: according to Aristotle, the former did not regard these as having a separate existence, whereas Plato did separate them and referred to them as "Ideas" or "Forms."[18] The question still remains, however, how far the doctrines Aristotle attributes to "Socrates" are actually those that were expressed by the historical Socrates.

Plato's portrait of Socrates, through its power and originality, has been largely accepted as *the* definitive version and has been a major influence on numerous thinkers (not

[17] These are collected in Giannantoni, *Socratis et Socraticorum Reliquiae.*

[18] See, e.g., *Symposium* 211ff. and *Phaedrus* 247ff.

to mention artists) through the ages. It had been generally accepted that at some point in his philosophical development Plato ceases to represent the historical character and creates for his own philosophical purposes the scenarios in which he places Socrates and his associates. A striking example of this occurs in *Symposium* where one of the guests, Aristophanes, the perpetrator of the "slander" of *Clouds* (see above), appears to be on the best of terms with his alleged victim, to the extent that Plato is able to develop a witty and sympathetic portrait of the comic dramatist. Whether in historical fact there was personal animosity between Socrates and Aristophanes over the play, and Plato is inventing their camaraderie in the *Symposium*, the evidence does not allow us to decide.[19]

Exactly where Socrates ends and Plato begins, and how much of the philosophy, eccentric character, and habits of the historical Socrates remain in Plato at any point has been a matter of much controversy.[20] For purposes of this volume, however, we propose to regard this as a side issue. While not ignoring the fact that distinctive features of the historical Socrates' personality and eccentric behavior are undoubtedly present in Plato's affectionate, and often

---

[19] The dramatic date of the *Symposium*, 416 (see Introduction to *Symposium*, §1(i)), is close to Aristophanes' (unsuccessful) production of *Clouds* (423, revised but not performed, ca. 418). It is perhaps worth noting that, alone of the participants in the *Symposium*, Aristophanes (d. ca. 386) may still have been alive when Plato composed the dialogue.

[20] See Vlastos, *Socrates: Ironist and Moral Philosopher*, 45–106 (a detailed case for the view that we can establish a distinct Socratic phase in Plato's early dialogues), and, for a more skeptical view, see Stokes, "Socrates' Mission."

moving portraits, references to "Socrates" will mean "Plato's Socrates," unless otherwise stated.

5. THE TEXT

The text printed in this edition is the Oxford Classical Text (OCT), edited by J. Burnet: *Platonis Opera*, vol. 3, 1909 [1903] (*Lysis*); vol. 2, 1910 [1901] (*Symposium* and *Phaedrus*) (Oxford: Oxford University Press).

The system of reference to sections and lines of Plato's Greek text is by page, letter, and number of the sixteenth-century edition of Henri Estienne (Stephanus), which is standard in all modern editions of Plato. Divisions within the numbered sections are indicated at every fifth line by a vertical stroke (|); where the original lineation splits a word, the stroke appears after that word.

The variant readings flagged in the notes to the text have been kept to a bare minimum and are confined to the few instances where a divergence in the Greek text significantly affects translation and/or interpretation of the Greek and a footnote is required.

The following late medieval manuscripts of the dialogues (taken from OCT) are cited in the textual notes:

B	cod. Bodleianus MS E. D. Clarke 39
T	cod. Venetus app. cl. 4.1
W	cod. Vindobonensis 54, suppl. phil. Gr. 7
V	cod. Vindobonensis 109
P.Oxy.	Oxyrhynchus Papyrus (Grenfell and Hunt, V, pp. 243ff.)

We have also included, where appropriate, ancient testimonia and modern editorial conjectures.

6. PLATO'S DIALOGUE FORM
AND TRANSLATION

It is likely that Plato's dialogue form originated in the oral method of the historical Socrates, who wrote nothing but appears to have believed that progress in philosophy is made through mutual discussion between two or more individuals rather than through a philosophical treatise, as in the Presocratics and Sophists, and later, Aristotle in his surviving works. The dialogue form in Plato is in no way an ornamental façade, but rather an essential part of his creative purpose. This is reflected in his style; in "staging"[21] his dialogues he makes full use of the intricacies and nuances of Greek prose style to convey not only ideas but also emotions and relationships between characters.

There are a number of translations of all three dialogues, aiming primarily at readers without knowledge of, or access to, the Greek (see General Bibliography). Our purpose is different: we operate on the assumption that our readers will be interested in being able to refer across from translation to text (or from text to translation).[22] We therefore aim to keep closer to the Greek than the average standalone translation, consistent with clarity of meaning and acceptable English style. In particular, we have generally endeavored to explain the English equivalents

[21] There is no evidence of any of the dialogues ever actually being performed in Plato's Academy or elsewhere; for a hypothetical reconstruction, see Ryle, *Plato's Progress*.

[22] See also editions of the Greek text with facing literal translation and detailed commentary by C. J. Rowe in the Aris & Phillips Classical Texts Series: *Symposium* (1998) and *Phaedrus* (1986).

of complex words that in context do not always translate straightforwardly from the Greek, such as *philia* and *erōs* (friendship, love), *kalos* (beautiful, fine, noble), *technē* (art, skill, craft), and their cognates.[23]

In the footnotes we aim to give the reader the basic background information necessary for an informed appreciation of Plato's text. Citations from Plato appear with name of work only; other ancient authors are cited by author and work. Modern scholarly works appear in the footnotes with name or short title, the full details to be found in the General Bibliography.

[23] Fuller explanations of these words will be given in footnotes, as appropriate. On the assumption that not all users of this volume may wish to read all three dialogues, information concerning key words and subjects is frequently duplicated in Introductions and footnotes.

CHRONOLOGY OF PLATO'S
LIFE AND WORKS

The dates and order of composition of Plato's dialogues cannot be established with certainty. The events of his life, and, in particular, details of his visits to Sicily, depend to a large extent on the *7th Letter*, which may or may not be genuine. On the order of dialogues, the following represents a general, but not universal, consensus that they can be divided into three broad periods: Early, Middle, and Late (omitting dialogues sometimes attributed to Plato, but generally regarded as not genuine). For differing approaches to questions of the chronology of Plato's dialogues, see, e.g., Brandwood, *Chronology of Plato's Dialogues*; Kahn, "On Platonic Chronology"; Ledger, *Recounting Plato*; Thesleff, *Studies in Platonic Chronology*; Vlastos, *Socrates*.

ca. 429	Birth of Plato from an old and wealthy Athenian family.
404	Defeat of Athens in the war with Sparta (the Peloponnesian War).
403	The rule of an oligarchic junta in Athens (the "Thirty Tyrants"), involving Plato's relatives, followed by the restoration of the democracy.

CHRONOLOGY OF PLATO'S LIFE AND WORKS

399	The trial, condemnation, and execution of Socrates on a charge of impiety: "not acknowledging the gods that the city acknowledges, but introducing new divinities and corrupting the youth."
390s–early 380s	Following the death of Socrates, Plato and other followers of Socrates withdraw from Athens to the nearby city of Megara. Plato travels extensively. Composition of the short Early Period dialogues: *Apology*, *Crito*, *Charmides*, *Euthyphro*, *Hippias Minor*, *Ion*, *Laches*, *Lysis*.
389/8	Plato visits Italy and Sicily, probably in order to make contact with Pythagorean philosophers.
ca. 387	Plato founds the Academy on the site of the shrine of the hero Academus in the northwest district of Athens.
380s	The later Early Period dialogues ("transitional"): *Gorgias*, *Menexenus*, *Protagoras*.
Late 380s	The Middle Period Dialogues: *Cratylus*, *Euthydemus*, *Meno*, *Phaedo*, *Symposium*.
370s	The later Middle Period dialogues: *Parmenides*, *Phaedrus*, *Republic*, *Theaetetus*.
367	Plato visits Sicily for the second time at the invitation of Dion, uncle of the young Dionysius, ruler of Syracuse, possibly in the hope of influencing the government of the city. The attempt is unsuccessful.

CHRONOLOGY OF PLATO'S LIFE AND WORKS

360s–350s	The Late Period dialogues: *Critias*, *Philebus*, *Sophist*, *Statesman*, *Timaeus*.
361	Final visit to Sicily, ending again in failure to influence Dionysius.
Late 350s	Final dialogue: *Laws*.
347	Death of Plato.

REFERENCES

Denniston Denniston, J. D. *The Greek Particles*. 2nd ed. Oxford: Oxford University Press, 1950.

DK Diels, H., and W. Kranz, eds. *Die Fragmente der Vorsokratiker*. 3 vols. 7th ed. Berlin: Weidmannsche Verlagsbuchhandlung, 1961.

GPM Dover, K. J. *Greek Popular Morality in the Time of Plato and Aristotle*. 2nd ed. Indianapolis: Hackett, 1994.

LSJ Liddell, H. G., and R. Scott, rev. H. S. Jones. *A Greek-English Lexicon*. 9th ed. Oxford: Oxford University Press, 1968.

OCD[3] Hornblower, S., and A. Spawforth, eds. *Oxford Classical Dictionary*. 3rd ed. Oxford: Oxford University Press, 1996.

GENERAL BIBLIOGRAPHY

TEXTS, TRANSLATIONS, AND COMMENTARIES

Lysis

Bolotin, D. *Plato's Dialogue on Friendship: An Interpretation of the* Lysis *with a New Translation*. Ithaca, NY: Cornell University Press, 1979.

Bordt, M. *Lysis. Übersetzung und Kommentar*. Göttingen: Vandenhoek & Ruprecht, 1998.

Lamb, W. R. M. *Lysis*. Text and translation, Loeb Classical Library. Vol. 3 (with *Symposium* and *Gorgias*). Cambridge, MA: Harvard University Press, 1925.

Lombardo, S. *Lysis*. Translated in C. D. C. Reeve, *Plato on Love*. Indianapolis/Cambridge: Hackett, 2006.

Penner, T., and C. J. Rowe. *Plato's* Lysis. [See under *Lysis* in Modern Scholarship, Individual Dialogues, Penner and Rowe.]

Waterfield, R. *Lysis*. Translated with a general introduction, in *Plato: Meno and Other Dialogues*. Oxford World's Classics. Oxford: Oxford University Press, 2005.

Watt, D. *Lysis*. Translated with introduction, in T. J. Saunders, ed. *Early Socratic Dialogues*. Harmondsworth: Penguin Books, 1987.

GENERAL BIBLIOGRAPHY

Symposium

Allen, R. E. *The Symposium.* In *The Dialogues of Plato.* Vol. 2. Translated with comment. New Haven: Yale University Press, 1991.

Bury, R. G. *The Symposium of Plato.* Edited with introduction, critical notes, and commentary. Cambridge: W. Heffer and Sons, 1932 [1909]. (Bury)

Dover, K. J. *Plato Symposium.* Edited with introduction and commentary. Cambridge Greek and Latin Classics. Cambridge: Cambridge University Press, 1982. (Dover)

Gill, C. *Plato: The Symposium.* Introduction, translation, and notes. Harmondsworth: Penguin Classics, 1999.

Hamilton, W. *Plato: The Symposium.* Introduction, translation, and notes. Harmondsworth: Penguin Classics, 1951.

Howatson, M. C. *The Symposium.* Translation and notes, edited with introduction by Howatson and F. C. C. Sheffield. *Cambridge Texts in the History of Philosophy.* Cambridge: Cambridge University Press, 2008.

Lamb, W. R. M. *Symposium.* Text and translation. Loeb Classical Library. Vol. 3 (with *Lysis* and *Gorgias*). Cambridge, MA: Harvard University Press, 1925.

Nehemas, A., and P. Woodruff. *Plato: Symposium.* Translation with introduction and notes. Indianapolis: Hackett, 1989.

Robin, L. *Platon. Oeuvres Complètes.* IV.2, *Le banquet.* Paris: Phèdre, 1966 [1935].

Rowe, C. J. *Plato Symposium.* Text, edited with introduction, translation, and commentary. Warminster: Aris & Phillips, 1998. (Rowe)

Waterfield, R. *Plato, Symposium.* Translated with introduction and notes. Oxford World's Classics. Oxford: Oxford University Press, 1994.

Phaedrus

De Vries, G. J. *A Commentary on the Phaedrus of Plato*. Amsterdam: Hakkert, 1969. (De Vries)

Fowler, H. N. *Phaedrus*. Text and translation. Loeb Classical Library. Vol. 1 (with *Euthyphro, Apology, Crito*, and *Phaedo*). Cambridge, MA: Harvard University Press, 1914.

Hackforth, R. *Plato's Phaedrus*. Translated with an introduction and commentary. Cambridge: Cambridge University Press, 1952. (Hackforth)

Nehemas, A., and P. Woodruff. *Plato, Phaedrus*. Translated with introduction and notes. Indianapolis: Hackett, 1995.

Robin, P. *Platon, Oeuvres Complètes* IV.3. Paris: Phèdre, 1950 [1933].

Rowe, C. J. *Plato, Phaedrus*. Edited with introduction, translation, and commentary. Warminster: Aris & Phillips, 1998 [1986]. (Rowe)

Ryan, P. *Plato's Phaedrus: A Commentary for Greek Readers*. With Introduction by M. L. Gill. Oklahoma Series in Classical Culture. Vol. 47. Norman: University of Oklahoma Press, 2012.

Waterfield, R. *Plato, Phaedrus*. Translation with introduction and notes. Oxford World's Classics. Oxford: Oxford University Press, 2002.

Yunis, H. *Plato, Phaedrus*. Edited with introduction and commentary. Cambridge Greek and Latin Classics. Cambridge: Cambridge University Press, 2011. (Yunis)

GENERAL BIBLIOGRAPHY

OTHER PRIMARY SOURCES

Campbell, D. A. *Greek Lyric*. Loeb Classical Library. Cambridge, MA: Harvard University Press, 1982. (Campbell)

Davies, M., ed. *Poetarum Melicorum Graecorum Fragmenta*. Oxford: Oxford University Press, 1991. (Davies)

Edmonds, J. M. *Elegy and Iambus*. Vol. 1. Loeb Classical Library. Cambridge, MA: Harvard University Press, 1961. (Edmonds *Elegy and Iambus*)

———. *Lyra Graeca*. Vol. 2. Loeb Classical Library. Cambridge, MA: Harvard University Press, 1964. (Edmonds *Lyra Graeca*)

Giannantoni, G. *Socratis et Socraticorum Reliquiae*. 4 vols. Naples: Edizioni del' Ateneo, 1990.

Kern, O. *Orphicorum Fragmenta*. Berlin: Weidmann, 1922. (Kern)

Kirk, G. S., J. E. Raven, and R. Schofield. *The Presocratic Philosophers: A Critical History with a Selection of Texts*. 2nd ed. Cambridge University Press: Cambridge, 1983. (Kirk–Raven)

Merkelbach, R., and M. L. West. *Hesiodi, Fragmenta Selecta*. Oxford: Oxford University Press, 1970. (Merkelbach-West)

Nauk, J. A. *Tragicorum Graecorum Fragmenta*. 2nd ed. Leipzig: Teubner, 1983 [1889]. (Nauk)

Snell, B. *Pindari Carmina cum Fragmentis*. 8th ed. Edited by H. Maehler. Leipzig: Teubner, 1989. (Snell)

Waterfield, R. *The First Philosophers: The Presocratics and the Sophists*. Translation with introduction and commentary. Oxford World's Classics. Oxford: Oxford University Press, 2000. (Waterfield)

GENERAL BIBLIOGRAPHY

MODERN SCHOLARSHIP

General

Blondell, R. *The Play of Character in Plato's Dialogues.* Cambridge: Cambridge University Press, 2002.

Brandwood, L. *The Chronology of Plato's Dialogues.* Cambridge: Cambridge University Press, 1990.

Buxton, R., ed. *From Myth to Reason: Studies in the Development of Greek Thought.* Oxford: Oxford University Press, 1999.

Crombie, I. M. *An Examination of Plato's Doctrines.* London: Routledge and Kegan Paul, 1963.

Davidson, J. *Courtesans and Fishcakes: The Consuming Passions of Classical Athens.* London: St Martin's Press, 1998.

Dover, K. J. *Greek Homosexuality.* London: Duckworth, 1978.

Fine, G. *Oxford Readings in Philosophy, Plato 2: Ethics, Politics, Religion and the Soul.* Oxford: Oxford University Press, 1999.

———. *The Oxford Handbook of Plato.* Oxford: Oxford University Press, 2008.

Guthrie, W. K. C. *A History of Greek Philosophy. Vol. 1, The Early Presocratics and the Pythagoreans.* Cambridge: Cambridge University Press, 1962.

———. *A History of Greek Philosophy. Vol. IV, Plato, the Man and His Dialogues: Earlier Period.* Cambridge: Cambridge University Press, 1975.

Harte, V. "Plato's Metaphysics." In Fine, *The Oxford Handbook of Plato*, 191–216.

Kahn, C. H. "On Platonic Chronolgy." In *New Perspec-*

tives on Plato, Modern and Ancient, edited by J. Annas and C. J. Rowe, 93–127. Washington, DC: Center for Hellenic Studies, 2002.

Kerferd, G. B. *The Sophistic Movement*. Cambridge: Cambridge University Press, 1981.

Konstan, D. *Friendship in the Classical World*. Cambridge: Cambridge University Press, 1997.

Kraut, R. "Plato on Love." In Fine, *The Oxford Handbook of Plato*, 286–310.

Ledger, G. R. *Recounting Plato: A Computer Analysis of Plato's Style*. Oxford: Oxford University Press, 1989.

McCabe, M. M. "Form and the Platonic Dialogues." In *A Companion to Plato. Blackwell Companions to Philosophy*, edited by H. H. Benson, 39–54. Oxford: Wiley-Blackwell, 2009.

Nails, D. *The People of Plato: A Prosopography of Plato and Other Socratics*. Indianopolis/Cambridge: Hackett, 2002. (Nails)

Nightingale, A. W. *Genres in Dialogue: Plato and the Construct of Philosophy*. Cambridge: Cambridge University Press, 1995.

Nussbaum, M. *The Fragility of Goodness: Luck and Ethics in Greek Tragedy and Philosophy*. Cambridge: Cambridge University Press, 1986.

Price, A. W. *Love and Friendship in Plato and Aristotle*. Oxford: Oxford University Press, 1997 [1989].

Rutherford, R. B. *The Art of Plato: Ten Essays in Platonic Interpretation*. London: Duckworth, 1995.

Ryle, G. *Plato's Progress*. Cambridge: Cambridge University Press, 1966.

Stokes, M. C. "Socrates Mission." In *Socratic Questions: New Essays on the Philosophy of Socrates and its Sig-*

nificance, edited by B. S. Gower and M. C. Stokes, 26–81. London: Routledge, 1992.

Thesleff, H. *Studies in Platonic Chronology.* (Commentationes humanarum litterarum, 70.) Helsinki: Societas Scientiarum Fennica, 1982.

Vlastos, G. "The Individual as an Object of Love in Plato." In "Socratic Studies," 3–34. Princeton: Princeton University Press, 1973. Reprinted in Fine, *Oxford Readings in Philosophy, Plato 2*, 137–63.

———. *Socrates: Ironist and Moral Philosopher.* Cambridge: Cambridge University Press, 1991.

INDIVIDUAL DIALOGUES

Lysis

Glidden, D. K. "The *Lysis* on Loving One's Own." *Classical Quarterly* 31 (1981): 39–59.

Guthrie, W. K. C. "The *Lysis*." In Guthrie, *A History of Philosophy, Vol. 4*, 134–54.

Hoerber, R. G. "Character Portrayal in Plato's *Lysis*." *Classical Journal* 41 (1945): 271–78.

———. "Plato's *Lysis*." *Phronesis* 4 (1959): 15–28.

Penner, T., and C. J. Rowe. *Plato's Lysis*. A critical study/commentary, concluding with a literal translation, pp. 326–51. Cambridge Studies in the Dialogues of Plato, edited by M. M. McCabe. Cambridge, Cambridge University Press, 2005. (Penner and Rowe)

Robinson, D. B. "Plato's *Lysis*: The Structural Problem." *Illinois Classical Studies* 11 (1986): 63–83.

Roth, M. D. "Did Plato Nod? Some Conjectures on Egoism and Friendship in the *Lysis*." *Archiv für Geschichte der Philosophie* 77 (1995): 1–20.

Rudebusch, G. "Socratic Love." In *A Companion to Socrates*, edited by S. Ahbel-Rappe and R. Kamtekar, 186–99. Chichester-Oxford: Wiley-Blackwell, 2009.

Versenyi, L. "Plato's *Lysis*." *Phronesis* 20 (1975): 185–98.

Symposium

Belfiore, E. "Dialectic with the Reader in Plato's *Symposium*." *Maia* 36 (1984): 137–49.

Blankenhagen, P. H. von. "Stage and Actors in Plato's *Symposium*." *Greek, Roman and Byzantine Studies* 33 (1) (1992): 51–68.

Csapo, E., and W. J. Slater. *The Context of Ancient Drama*. Ann Arbor: The University of Michigan Press, 1994.

Destrée, P., and Z. Giannopoulou, eds. *Plato's Symposium: A Critical Guide*. Cambridge Critical Studies. Cambridge: Cambridge University Press, 2017.

Dorter, K. "The Significance of the Speeches in Plato's *Symposium*." *Philosophy and Rhetoric* 2 (1969): 215–34.

Dover, K. J. "Eros and Nomos (Plato, *Symposium* 182a–185c)." *Bulletin of the Institute of Classical Studies* 11 (1964): 31–42.

Edelstein, L. "The role of Eryximachus in Plato's *Symposium*." *Transactions of the American Philological Association* 76 (1945): 85–103.

Emlyn-Jones, C. J. "The Dramatic Poet and His Audience: Agathon and Socrates in Plato's *Symposium*. *Hermes* 132 (4) (2004): 389–405.

Hobbs, A. "Female Imagery in Plato." In Lesher et al., *Plato's Symposium*, 252–71.

Hunter, R. *Plato's Symposium*. Oxford: Oxford University Press, 2004.

Lesher, J. H., D. Nails, and F. C. C. Sheffield, eds. *Plato's Symposium: Issues in Interpretation and Reception*. Hellenic Studies 22. Washington: Center for Hellenic Studies, 2006.

Mattingly, H. B. "The Date of Plato's *Symposium*." *Phronesis* 3 (1958): 31–39.

McPherran, M. "Medicine, Magic, and Religion in Plato's *Symposium*." In Lesher et al., *Plato's Symposium*, 71–95.

Murray, O., ed. *Sympotica: A Symposium on the Symposion*. Oxford: Oxford University Press, 1990.

Nails, D. "Tragedy Off-Stage." In Lesher et al., *Plato's Symposium*, 179–207.

Rowe, C. J. "*The Symposium* as a Socratic Dialogue." In Lesher et al., *Plato's Symposium*, 9–22.

Sheffield, F. C. C. "Alcibiades' Speech: A Satyric Drama." *Greece and Rome* 48 (2001): 193–209.

———. "Psychic Pregnancy and Platonic Epistemology." *Oxford Studies in Ancient Philosophy* 20 (2001): 1–35.

———. *Plato's Symposium: the Ethics of Desire*. Oxford Classical Monographs. Oxford: Oxford University Press, 2006.

———. "The Role of the Earlier Speeches in the *Symposium*: Plato's Endoxic Method?" In Lesher et al., *Plato's Symposium*, 23–46.

Stokes, M. "Socrates and a Tragic Poet." Chap. 3 in *Plato's Socratic Conversations*. Baltimore/London: The Athlone Press, 1986, 114–82.

Trivigno, F. V. "A Doctor's Folly: Diagnosing the Speech of Eryximachus." In Destrée and Giannopoulou, *Plato's Symposium*, 48–69.

GENERAL BIBLIOGRAPHY

Phaedrus

Bett, R. "Immortality and the Nature of the Soul in the *Phaedrus.*" *Phronesis* 31 (1986): 1–26. Reprinted in Fine, *Oxford Readings in Philosophy, Plato* 2, 425–49.

Blyth, D. "The Ever-moving Soul in Plato's *Phaedrus.*" *American Journal of Philology* 118 (1997): 185–217.

Dover, K. J. *Lysias and the Corpus Lysiacum.* Sather Classical Lectures 39. Berkley/Los Angeles: University of California Press, 1968.

Ferrari, G. R. F. *Listening to the Cicadas: A Study of Plato's Phaedrus.* Cambridge: Cambridge University Press, 1987.

Heath, M. "The Unity of Plato's *Phaedrus.*" *Oxford Studies in Ancient Philosophy* 7 (1989): 151–73.

Lloyd, G. E. R. *Methods and Problems in Greek Science.* Cambridge: Cambridge University Press, 1991.

Rowe, C. J. "The Charioteer and His Horses: An Example of Platonic Myth-Making." In *Plato's Myths*, edited by C. Partenie, 134–47. Cambridge: Cambridge University Press, 2009.

Werner, D. "Plato's *Phaedrus* and the Problem of Unity." *Oxford Studies in Ancient Philosophy* 32 (2007): 91–137.

Wycherley, R. E. "The Scene of Plato's *Phaidros.*" *Phoenix* 17 (1963): 88–98.

Yunis, H. "Dialectic and the Purpose of Rhetoric in Plato's *Phaedrus.*" *Proceedings of the Boston Area Colloquium in Ancient Philosophy* 24 (2009): 229–48.

LYSIS

INTRODUCTION

1. THE SUBJECT OF THE DIALOGUE

Lysis is the earliest in order of composition of the three works in this volume. It is usually included among those of Plato's "Early Period," written during the fifteen to twenty years following the death of Socrates (see Chronology of Plato's Life and Works).[1] These feature Socrates making inquiry about particular values: in *Laches*, how does one define a quality such as that required of a soldier in battle, namely courage (*andreia*), or in *Euthyphro*, the relationship between humans and gods described as "the holy" (*to hosion*). In *Lysis*, Socrates is on the same quest, exploring the erotic and social relationship between males: "love" (*erōs*) and "friendship" (*philia*).[2] He professes ignorance (feigned or real, see below §4) and speaks to two Athenian boys, Lysis and Menexenus, from whom he is anxious to obtain the necessary knowledge. Since

[1] On the relationship between the historical Socrates and the character presented in the dialogues, see General Introduction, §4.

[2] For the range of these two terms, the overlap and distinction between them, see General Introduction, §2.

3

they are friends, he assumes that they know what love is, or that an understanding of this relationship will result from rigorous and progressive logical argument. He addresses Menexenus: "But I am so far from having the possession that I don't know in what manner one individual becomes a friend (*philos*) of another. But these are the very questions I want to ask you about, in that you are experienced" (212a4–7).

Philia and *erōs*, like the English "love," cover a wide range of relationships, from political alliances, personal associations, and parental love at one end through to romantic and sexual relationships at the other. The adjective *philos* has itself a further ambiguity in English translation; it is usually passive, as in "friend" (someone/thing liked or loved or dear), but it also has an active sense, as in "philosopher," "philhellene" (e.g., *philetairos*, "friend-lover," 211e8), and it also functions as a verb, e.g., "x *philei* (loves) y" and vice-versa.[3] For more intense relationships, usually of an erotic or sexual nature, Greek tends to use *erōs*, which features prominently in the *Symposium* in its personified form as the god Eros, whom the participants in that dialogue celebrate in speeches. There is, however, considerable overlap in meaning between *philia* and *erōs*, which *Lysis* demonstrates right at the start of the dialogue, where Socrates turns the spotlight in turn on two examples of "love": Hippothales' erotic desire for Lysis and the mutual camaraderie of Lysis and Menexenus.

[3] The ambiguity of *philos* as both active and passive is particularly relevant to the argument at 212a8–13d2.

2. THE CONTEXT

Socrates, as the narrator, tells us that he was traveling southeast from the Academy to the Lyceum along the east city wall of Athens, when he was waylaid by a group of young men and invited to join them in a recently-built wrestling ground (*palaestra*), in which activities associated with the festival of the Hermaea were taking place. So the discussion that follows arises naturally out of a chance encounter, in this case between Socrates and individuals whose age, gender, and social position predispose them to be intimately involved in relationships that involve friendship and love. His first encounter is with an older youth, Hippothales, who is being severely teased by a contemporary, Ctesippus, for the way, as a potential lover (*erastēs*), he is conducting his love affair with a younger boy, the handsome and wellborn Lysis, the object of his affections (*erōmenos*), a relationship Socrates quickly recognizes and criticizes (204c2ff.).

So, as an introduction to the subject, Socrates, having persuaded Hippothales that he is going about his wooing in the wrong way (205dff.),[4] goes into the wrestling school along with Hippothales and the rest, and gets to question Menexenus, Ctesippus' cousin, joined by Lysis, who comes over to sit with Menexenus. Socrates' questioning of Lysis and Menexenus, which takes up most of the rest

---

[4] See Socrates' point to Hippothales that his wooing of Lysis is misguided, in that his underlying "intention," "thought" (*dianoia*, 205b2) is different from what he imagines and says that it is (205eff.).

of the dialogue (on the details of which see below, §3), gains dramatic impact from the presence of the listening Hippothales, hidden so as not to upset his beloved (207b4–7).

We are returned to the dramatic background again at the abrupt conclusion of the dialogue, when Socrates, admitting defeat in his quest to pin down *philia/erōs*, is prevented from exploring the subject further by the drunk attendants of the boys (*paidagōgoi*), who, "speaking their rather barbarian (*hupobarbarizontes*) Greek," hustle them off and bring the inquiry to an inconclusive end (223a–end).[5]

3. THE ARGUMENTS OF THE DIALOGUE: WHAT SORT OF RELATIONSHIP IS *PHILIA* AND WHAT KIND OF PEOPLE ARE *PHILOI*?

In the course of the dialogue, Socrates, apparently for most of the time subsuming *erōs* under the broader heading of *philia* (love/friendship) in general, appears to be exploring with his young companions, Lysis and Menexenus, two apparently separate questions: (1) a number of possible definitions of what kinds of people are friends (*philoi*) and (2) what is it that loves *to philon* (a loved or desired object). Hippothales' *erōs* can be contrasted with the mutual *philia* that the two boys admit to feeling for each other. However, Socrates' initial examination of the

[5] For a similar somewhat downbeat conclusion, compare *Symposium* 223bff.

6

nature of *philia* through his questioning of Lysis (207d5–10d8) is clearly intended to be at least in part an object lesson also for Hippothales; this becomes clear when Socrates prevents himself at the last moment from lecturing the hidden Hippothales and thereby exposing him to embarrassment in front of his beloved (210e).[6]

In attempting to chart a path through the argument, Socrates and the boys are continually taking what Socrates describes as wrong turnings requiring a fresh start.[7] At the end, having ostensibly gone down all possible alternative paths, they finally reach a dead end, *aporia* (impasse, inability to find a way through). The failure of their basic aim, and the assumption of Plato's Socrates that in order to enjoy genuine friendship they have to reach a correct understanding of it, is emphasized by Socrates' parting remark at the end of the dialogue: "Now then Lysis and Menexenus, we've become a laughingstock, I, an old man, and you. For when these people go away, they'll say that we think we are each other's friend—for I consider myself to be one of you—but we've not yet been able to discover what the friend is" (223b4–8).

Whether the *aporia* as stated by Socrates at 222e is intended by Plato as a genuine conclusion or whether there is a more positive outcome to be discovered somewhere in the dialogue is one question associated with this dialogue as with others of similar type that also end in *aporia*.

[6] On the relevance of the argument of 207d5–10d8 to Hippothales' situation, see immediately below, §3(i).

[7] See 213c9, e3, 4; 215c3; 216c4–5; 218c4f.

But the basic underlying issue, unique to *Lysis*, which has proved controversial, is the degree to which Socrates' argument as a whole is to be taken seriously as a coherent philosophical exploration of the subject.

(i) Questioning of Lysis: under what circumstances do his parents and others love him? (207d5–10d8)

This first passage of sustained questioning, which is directed toward Lysis, precedes the asking of the key question of who are *philoi*, and appears to be, at first sight, a preliminary to the main inquiry. At this point, Socrates' aim is to establish, with an extensive series of examples, that Lysis' parents' love involves wanting him to be happy, which means preventing him from doing and controlling things of which he does not yet have the requisite knowledge and allowing him to do things of which he does. Being happy (*eudaimōn*)[8] is dependent on having understanding. And being loved, by friends and relations as well as parents, and being a friend to the wider community, depends on Lysis being useful and of benefit; to be in this state, and to be "happy," he has to have knowledge of the things he controls. Controversially (at least to us—despite Lysis' apparent emphatic agreement at 210c7), if Lysis is of no benefit in this regard, he will not be regarded as a

---

[8] "Happy," not merely in a psychological sense, but a permanent state of being = "fulfilled," having a good *daimon* = "fortune," "destiny").

friend or be loved (*philos*) by anyone. This section, demonstrating the importance of knowledge in the love relationship, serves as a potential object lesson for the distressed and bewildered Hippothales, offstage, as it were (e5). His role should be to instruct his beloved in understanding, not to pander to his conceit.

(ii) Is it the lover/friend or the person/thing loved or both, who are philoi? (212a8–13d2)

At Lysis' request, Menexenus replaces him as Socrates' respondent, in Lysis' expectation that S. will cut the (supposedly) combative (*eristikos*) Menexenus down to size (211b3–c3).[9] Socrates' initial approach is typical: he treats Menexenus as someone who must have knowledge about *philia* since he and Lysis have what Socrates longs to possess, namely friendship with each other; it is this mutual relationship that Socrates wishes to explore with someone who is "experienced" (*empeiros*) and so must know what it is.[10]

His initial question generates the discussion: in the relationship, which of the two is *philos*—the lover of the loved one or the loved one of the lover? This question

---

[9] Assertion in argument on Menexenus' part is not a quality that appears at all in the subsequent dialogue with Socrates (211d6–13d2).

[10] Compare, for example, *Euthyphro* 5a2ff; there, Socrates assumes that, as the so-called religious expert, Euthyphro must know what he, Socrates, is looking for.

appears to play on the ambiguity of *philos* in Greek, in that both are *philoi*, but in different senses: the lover is *philos* in the subjective sense (he is friendly/loves), the loved one is *philos* in the objective sense (he is the object of friendship/is loved).[11] Menexenus' reply, that there is no difference between the two, seems the obvious answer from his point of view, especially since in his and Lysis' relationship they both share both roles, that is, they are to each other both subjectively and objectively friends (*philoi*). However, his next answer to Socrates, that both are *philoi* even if only one loves the other, exposes the ambiguity: they are both *philoi*, the lover in a subjective, the loved in an objective sense. But, as Socrates immediately observes, maybe the *philos* (loved one) does not reciprocate; maybe he does not love, or even hates, the *philos* (lover), which might be the case with parents who love small children who hate them. But can one who hates be described as *philos*, and in these circumstances are they then on both sides still *philoi*? The logical conclusion of this argument—that many are loved by their enemies and hated by those who are their friends and vice-versa (213a6–b2)—is "quite absurd" (*pollē alogia*), or rather impossible, as Socrates says. This argument appears to be going nowhere, and it is obvious that they need to find another route.[12]

---

[11] See above, §1. The whole issue of the relationship of *philoi* is analyzed and clarified by Aristotle at *Nichomachean Ethics* 8.2.3–3.6.

[12] That this section has more significance than Socrates simply pulling a pointless (and overelaborate) sophistic trick on an unsuspecting youth is argued in detail by Penner and Rowe, 58ff.

(iii) Is like always a friend/dear (philos) *to like?*
(213d6–15c3)

To answer this Socrates (resuming with Lysis in the place of Menexenus) invokes Homer and the "wisest men" who "talk and write about both nature and the universe" (214b2–5).[13] Half of the statement is true, says Socrates: bad men cannot be *philoi*, as they do each other wrong and are unstable,[14] whereas good men are like each other and therefore are *philoi*. Yet Socrates is still unhappy about this: are like men *philoi* in as far as they are like one another? But what benefit can a *philos* who is like another render to that other person which he cannot do for himself? How could two beings be *philoi* when they are of no service to each other, that is, self-sufficient?

In this argument Socrates seems to be using "like" (*homoios*) in the sense of "alike in every way," that is, two alike persons are completely identical, effectively "the same" (*ho autos*), and are self-sufficient, so not needing the other precisely because each has everything the other has. So, if they do not need each other in any way, they are of no benefit to each other, and therefore could not be *philoi*. Moreover, the good, in so far as they are good, are to that extent self-sufficient and, being like one another (in Socrates' understanding of *homoios*), would not lack anything the other has and so would not need the friendship of the other. Socrates appears to ignore the possibility that two

13 Plato is probably referring here to theories of natural philosophers and scientists such as Democritus and Empedocles.

14 Cf. *Republic* 1.351c7–52d2.

people might be alike or good only in some respects, that is, similar; if this is the case, they could be friends, since one might supply the deficiencies of the other. As it is, it appears again that they have been "led astray" (215c3).

(iv) So, is the reverse the case: that like is hostile to like and the unlike friendly to the unlike? (215c4–16b9)

Once again, Socrates cites poetry, on this occasion Hesiod, to illustrate hostile competition between those who are like one another in that they are engaged in the same activity. However, the unlike are naturally friendly to the unlike for the aid to be gained: the poor with the rich, the weak with the strong to gain help, the sick with the doctor for the sake of health, the ignorant with someone who has knowledge, etc. Again, Socrates draws on natural science and medicine to illustrate a harmony of opposites: dry desires wet; cold, hot; bitter, sweet; fullness, emptiness.[15] As Socrates puts it, "Opposite is food for its opposite" (215e8–9). Once again, we might note the assumption that absence of *philia* between those who are alike is supposed to validate its direct opposite, hostility, and, correspondingly, being opposite equals friendship. But Socrates sees another snag; surely, as the "antilogicians"[16] have it, is not

[15] See also the speech of Eryximachus in *Symposium* 186d–e, where he praises the god Eros for producing harmony between opposites.

[16] "The antilogicians" refers to a group of sophists whose main aim was to argue (and persuade others to accept) contradictory

the hostile the opposite of the friendly: for example, just
and unjust, temperate and intemperate, good and bad
(216b1–5)? Socrates confesses to having become dizzy
from *aporia* in the argument (c5). However, this problem
might perhaps contain the key to a way out . . .

(v) Is it the neither-good-nor-bad that is a friend to/loving the good? (216c1–18c3)

Having eliminated all other (as he sees it) alternatives
of possible combinations of *philia*—good/good, bad/bad,
good/bad—put forward in previous arguments, Socrates
fixes on a neutral, the neither-good-nor-bad, as the only
possible friend of the good. This looks like a more promising avenue of inquiry and gains plausibility from the following scenario: the human body which is neutral (i.e.,
neither-good-nor-bad) is sick from the presence of illness
(i.e., bad) in it, and so is a friend to/loves the doctor/med-
ical treatment (good) in order to gain health (217aff.).
Socrates characterizes the activity of the neither-good-
nor-bad in this three-way relationship by analogy with a
substance smeared with a particular color, as opposed to
something that is intrinsically that color. So the body is not
yet intrinsically bad (i.e., fatally sick), but has badness
smeared, as it were, on it, which still allows it to desire the
good (i.e., health-giving medicine). For example, Socrates
says that the wise no longer love wisdom (it can confer no

---

positions. For examples see the *Dissoi Logoi* (Double Arguments): DK 90; Waterfield, 285–99; and on antilogic, Kerferd,
The Sophistic Movement, 63–64.

benefit on those who already have it) nor do those love it who are so ignorant of it as to be bad, but those in the middle (the neither-good-nor-bad) who are not yet made ignorant, but have ignorance, smeared as it were, on them, "still are aware that they don't know what they don't know" (218a8).[17] Socrates and his friends think they have got there. But . . .

(vi) But the good must be philon because of/on account of something (dia ti) and for the sake of something (heneka tinos) (218d6–20b5)

For example, in the case of health: the sick individual is *philos*, loving (in the active sense) the good because of (on account of) the bad (sickness) for the sake of obtaining what is *philon* (in the passive sense—something loved), that is, health.[18] But health, in its turn, must be *philon* for the sake of something. So we are in danger here of an infinite regress: if everything is being loved for the sake of something else (Socrates gives some vivid examples [219d5ff.]), we must reach an end point, a *proton philon* (d1), an object of love, "that first one which is truly the friend" (*ho hōs alēthōs esti philon* (d4–5). This is where all

---

[17] See Socrates' characterization of himself in *Apology* as one of this middle group, those who are aware of their ignorance, in language strikingly reminiscent of this passage of *Lysis* (*Apology* 21d3ff., esp. 5–7). See also *Symposium* 204b. This idea of the lover as someone intermediate between ignorance and knowledge is a recurring theme in the *Symposium* and the *Phaedrus*.

[18] Note the shift of *philos* from active to passive sense, and vice-versa in this section.

these friendships end up. In these last two sections, (v) and (vi), in his use of *philon* in the passive sense, i.e., "what is loved," e.g., medicine for the sake of health, Plato's Socrates appears to be shifting the argument from an examination of a mutual relationship between those (actively) "loving" toward the idea of the pursuit of a loved object ("that which is loved"), the ultimate one being the *prōton philon*.

(vii) But what if bad went out of the way and no longer affected anything? (220c1–21d1)

But is the good a real friend? If bad were not present, good would not be at all useful to the neither-bad-nor-good. "If nothing were to do us harm any longer we would not need any help . . . But if there is no illness, there's no need for a cure" (i.e., the good would be of no benefit to us). So it appears that the good was not loved for itself but for the sake of the bad (220c7–d4). But if the bad is destroyed, would desire (*epithumia*) affecting the neither-good-nor-bad, hunger, thirst, etc. still exist? Yes, but surely in a beneficial way (221aff.) This could not be the case if the bad were the cause of something being *philon* (i.e., health being a friend because of sickness).

(viii) So, are we left with desire (which the neither-good-nor-bad feels) as a cause of philia, *and is he who has (not harmful) desires a friend to that which he desires? (221d–22b2)*

That which desires is a friend of what it is in need of, and whatever becomes needy, has something taken away from

PLATO

it which belongs (is *oikeios*) to it. So the object of love, friendship, and desire is in fact, it seems, what naturally belongs to it. So a genuine lover (*erastēs*) must be loved by his loved one (221e1–22a7). The reciprocal nature of the relationship is made clear. If Lysis and Menexenus are *oikeioi* (i.e., belong together), then they must love each other—note Hippothales' silent but expressive reaction.

(ix) Conclusion (222b3–end)

Have they reached their goal, successfully saying what a friend is? Yes, if there is a difference between being like (*homoios*) and belonging to (*oikeios*), since it was established ((§iii) above) that like cannot be a friend to like. If belonging to and being like are not the same, can we assume *either* (1) that the good belongs (is *oikeios*) to everything (good, bad, and neither-good-nor-bad) and the bad is alien to everything *or* (2) does the bad belong to the bad, the good to the good, and what is neither good-nor-bad to what is neither-good-nor-bad? Lysis and Menexenus, having accepted the second of Socrates' alternatives presented at c3–7—having agreed that the good belongs to the good, and that the good man is friend only to the good man (222c5–6)—are choosing an alternative that has already been dismissed earlier in §3(iii) (that the good cannot be a friend to good). All possibilities now seem exhausted (222e). Socrates' desire to continue is thwarted by the breakup of the meeting, and the end is *aporia*.

4. CRITICAL ANALYSIS OF *LYSIS*

Despite its modest proportions in comparison with the other two dialogues on love/friendship in this volume, the

16

Symposium and *Phaedrus*, Lysis proves, as it progresses, a difficult dialogue to read and understand. It gets off to an impressive start, as effectively dramatic as any composed by Plato in this early period, with lively interaction between characters. Moreover the initial discussion with Lysis (207d5–10d8) establishes a key Socratic argument connecting love, happiness, and knowledge. But the subsequent argument with Menexenus, almost halfway through the dialogue when Socrates finally gets down to it, seems to get bogged down as a result of inadvertent or deliberate confusion caused by failure to make distinctions in ambiguous terms: for example, *philos* ("dear": subjective or objective?), or *homoios* ("like" or "identical to"?).[19] It also appears that Plato's Socrates is confusing, or at least combining two separate investigations: first, investigating *philia* as a loving mutual relationship (see §§3(ii)–(iv)) and then moving toward the consideration of *philia* as the search for the ultimate object of love, *to (prōton) philon* (3(v)–(vii)), and then back to the initial investigation again at 221dff. (3(viii)–(ix)).[20]

Is there confusion and, if so, who is confused? If there is confusion, is Plato's Socrates the victim or the perpetrator? Assuming the latter, is Plato allowing his Socrates consciously to develop a sophistic line of argument, playing on the ambiguity of terms and practicing this skill on his young pupils, very much in the mold of the sophists Euthydemus and Dionysidorus on the youthful Cleinias in *Euthydemus*?[21] This is, however, hard to reconcile with

19 See 212dff., 215a.

20 See Robinson, "Plato's *Lysis*"; Watt, *Lysis*, Introduction, 123.

21 For example, *Euthydemus* 276ff., where Dionysidorus admits to Socrates that their questions are designed specifically to trap unsuspecting victims.

Plato's Socrates' expressed desire to take part in serious cooperative philosophical exploration, in direct or indirect opposition to the sophists, who were portrayed as deliberately using ambiguous arguments on unsuspecting and naïve associates in order to win an adversarial debate.[22]

Since, therefore, it seems inherently unlikely that Plato would have presented Socrates as, on the one hand, naively confused, or as, on the other, deliberately sophistical, we are left to explore the idea that, despite the surface appearance of confusion, Plato's Socrates' argument in *Lysis* has a coherence and a serious purpose.[23]

We might start by looking at the end of the dialogue, the so-called *aporia*. At 221e Socrates argues that love involves need and that whatever is needy has something taken away from it, which naturally belongs (is *oikeos*) to it; so Menexenus and Lysis are *philoi* and *oikeioi* to each other, that is, they supply a need in each other, which looks like a genuine solution to Socrates original problem (how to acquire a friend). However, this will not work, says Socrates, if "like" and "belonging to" are the same (see §3(iii) above). So Plato/Socrates, in allowing the boys to choose

---

[22] See Guthrie, *A History of Greek Philosophy*, 4:143ff., for a summary of (pre-1975) scholarly views of *Lysis*, and for his conclusion (143) that Socrates "appears to be completely at the mercy of the ambiguities of the Greek word for [friendship]"; or, however, see Crombie, *An Examination of Plato's Doctrines*, 1:20, characterizing Socrates' stance as that of "intellectual teasing."

[23] The most significant case for *Lysis* as a serious, seminal philosophical text has been put in a long, complex, and wide-ranging study by Penner and Rowe (2005). Limitations of space here make it impossible to give this work the detailed study it deserves.

this "dead end," already refuted alternative (222c7–d1), appears, as in other "Early" dialogues (e.g., in *Euthyphro* 14e10ff.), at the last minute to be throwing away a genuine solution: "the thing that naturally belongs to us has shown itself to us as something we must love" (222a5–6).

It is arguable that, despite the apparent sophistries in Plato/Socrates' argument in *Lysis*, a serious underlying purpose is detectable. There is a clue in the initial preliminary discussion between Socrates and Lysis (207d–10c), where Socrates argues that since wisdom or knowledge leads to happiness, Lysis' parents and others will love him when, and in as much as, he has acquired wisdom. So the apparently logically suspect point of "the good not loving the good" is understood when one realizes that desire to acquire the good must occur in someone who lacks it ("what is neither good nor bad is the friend of the beautiful and the good" [216d3–4]). Wanting to acquire knowledge (being neither good nor bad) is a state between wisdom and ignorance. Loving and being friends (*philoi*) requires that the partner derives benefit and has a *philos* as a possession (*ktēma*—see Socrates at 211e), which will lead the "needy" lovers to the "first friend" (*prōton philon:* 219c8), which is the ultimate "good," and for which no further arguments are needed. This is the vital link between the search for the nature of the active loving relationship and that ultimate thing that is loved, *to philon.*

Those, like Menexenus and Lysis, who aspire in their different ways to be *philoi*, should have the same goal: to aspire to the *proton philon*—knowledge of the good, which will lead to their ultimate happiness, since in Socratic ethical theory, "virtue is knowledge" (to know what is good is to do it). Hippothales also needs to direct his attention to acquiring knowledge so that he and Lysis may together not only belong to each other (be *oikeioi*) but also aspire to the knowledge of the ultimate good that will lead to happiness. In this way, the search of the active "lovers/ friends" for their "other half" (to use an image from Aristophanes in *Symposium*),[24] with which Socrates' initial search is concerned, is closely linked with the search for the ultimate "thing which is loved," *to philon.*

In this way, *Lysis* contains the essentials that look forward to the more elaborate pictures of *erōs*, *philia*, and desire, which are explored in the *Symposium* and the *Phaedrus*.[25]

APPENDIX: DRAMATIC DATE AND DATE OF COMPOSITION OF *LYSIS*

Plato gives no clue as to the dramatic date at which we are to suppose that the dialogue is taking place.[26] Furthermore, *Lysis* contains no reference to external events that might provide a clue as to its date of composition.[27] Xen-

[24] See *Symposium* 191d–93d, where in his speech in praise of Eros, the comic poet Aristophanes describes a lover as a half of an originally separated whole, searching for his other half.

[25] For the relationship between need, desire, goodness, and knowledge in and between *Lysis, Symposium, and Phaedrus*, see General Introduction, §3.

[26] Socrates refers to himself as an "old man" at 223b5, but this is clearly intended as a semijoking reference for the sake of his young audience.

[27] Reference to the Persian king Darius (209d) and his gold (211e6) might refer to Darius II (king of Persia, 424–405) but might simply be a general reference to the proverbial wealth of the Persian kings.

ophon, *Memorabilia* 2.6, outlines various possible relationships of *philoi* (friends), which bears some similarity to those discussed and rejected in *Lysis* 214–16, but no date can be given for either work. However, *Lysis*, in structure and aims, clearly belongs with other comparatively short "definition" dialogues that were composed shortly after Socrates' death (399), dating from the 390s to early 380s. *Lysis* is also similar to those other dialogues in being concerned with the search for general definitions as such, rather than super-worldly "Forms."[28] As such, it clearly precedes the *Symposium* and the *Phaedrus* (see Chronology of Plato's Life and Works).

[28] The *"proton philon"* (220a–b) as representing the ultimate friend, is perhaps a precursor of the Forms, which are featured in the *Symposium* and the *Phaedrus*.

ΛΥΣΙΣ

ΣΩΚΡΑΤΗΣ

203   Ἐπορευόμην μὲν ἐξ Ἀκαδημείας εὐθὺ Λυκείου τὴν
ἔξω τείχους ὑπ᾽ αὐτὸ τὸ τεῖχος· ἐπειδὴ δ᾽ ἐγενόμην
κατὰ τὴν πυλίδα ᾗ ἡ Πάνοπος κρήνη, ἐνταῦθα συν-
έτυχον Ἱπποθάλει τε τῷ Ἱερωνύμου καὶ Κτησίππῳ τῷ
Παιανιεῖ καὶ ἄλλοις μετὰ |τούτων νεανίσκοις ἀθρόοις
συνεστῶσι. καί με προσιόντα ὁ Ἱπποθάλης ἰδών, Ὦ
Σώκρατες, ἔφη, ποῖ δὴ πορεύῃ καὶ πόθεν;

b   Ἐξ Ἀκαδημείας, ἦν δ᾽ ἐγώ, πορεύομαι εὐθὺ Λυκείου.

Δεῦρο δή, ἦ δ᾽ ὅς, εὐθὺ ἡμῶν. οὐ παραβάλλεις;
ἄξιον μέντοι. |

Ποῖ, ἔφην ἐγώ, λέγεις, καὶ παρὰ τίνας τοὺς ὑμᾶς;

---

1 Socrates is walking from the Academy (northwest Athens,
ca. three-quarters of a mile outside the city wall, established as
Plato's "Academy" ca. 385) along the east side of the Themisto-
clean wall of the Acropolis, due south toward the Lyceum (a
sanctuary of Apollo Lycaeus, later famous as the site of Aristotle's
school). The gathering to which Socrates is diverted is a celebration of the festival of the Hermaea (206d1).

LYSIS

SOCRATES

I was making my way from the Academy straight to the Lyceum along the road outside the wall at the foot of the wall itself.[1] When I got to the little gate where Panops'[2] spring is, there I happened to meet Hippothales, Hieronymus' son and Ctesippus from the deme of Paiania and other young men standing with them all together.[3] Hippothales saw me approaching and said: "Socrates, where are you going and where have you come from?"

"From the Academy," I said, "I'm on my way straight to the Lyceum."

"Well, come over here," he said, "straight to us. Won't you come over? It'll really be worth it."

"Where do you mean," I said, "and who are the 'us' I'm coming over to?"

[2] Panops was a minor local deity.

[3] Ctesippus reveals his combative personality (see 204c4ff.) and also features in *Euthydemus* (274cff., 298bff.). Plato also has him and his cousin Menexenus (see below, 206dff.) present as nonspeaking characters at the death of Socrates (*Phaedo* 59b). Nothing for certain is known of Hippothales beyond the role that Plato gives him in *Lysis* (on all three, see Nails, 119, 202, 174).

Δεῦρο, ἔφη, δείξας μοι ἐν τῷ καταντικρὺ τοῦ τείχους περίβολόν τέ τινα καὶ θύραν ἀνεῳγμένην. δια-
τρίβομεν δέ, ἦ δ' ὅς, αὐτόθι ἡμεῖς τε αὐτοὶ καὶ ἄλλοι
πάνυ πολλοὶ καὶ καλοί.

204   Ἔστιν δὲ δὴ τί τοῦτο, καὶ τίς ἡ διατριβή;

Παλαίστρα, ἔφη, νεωστὶ ᾠκοδομημένη· ἡ δὲ δια-
τριβὴ τὰ πολλὰ ἐν λόγοις, ὧν ἡδέως ἄν σοι μεταδι-
δοῖμεν.

Καλῶς γε, ἦν δ' ἐγώ, ποιοῦντες· διδάσκει δὲ τίς
αὐτόθι; |

Σὸς ἑταῖρός γε, ἦ δ' ὅς, καὶ ἐπαινέτης, Μίκκος.

Μὰ Δία, ἦν δ' ἐγώ, οὐ φαῦλός γε ἀνήρ, ἀλλ' ἱκανὸς
σοφιστής.

Βούλει οὖν ἕπεσθαι, ἔφη, ἵνα καὶ ἴδῃς τοὺς ὄντας
αὐτόθι [αὐτοῦ];

b   Πρῶτον ἡδέως ἀκούσαιμ' ἂν ἐπὶ τῷ καὶ εἴσειμι καὶ
τίς ὁ καλός.

Ἄλλος, ἔφη, ἄλλῳ ἡμῶν δοκεῖ, ὦ Σώκρατες.

Σοὶ δὲ δὴ τίς, ὦ Ἱππόθαλες; τοῦτό μοι εἰπέ. |

Καὶ ὃς ἐρωτηθεὶς ἠρυθρίασεν. καὶ ἐγὼ εἶπον· Ὦ
παῖ Ἱερωνύμου Ἱππόθαλες, τοῦτο μὲν μηκέτι εἴπῃς,
εἴτε ἐρᾷς του εἴτε μή· οἶδα γὰρ ὅτι οὐ μόνον ἐρᾷς,
ἀλλὰ καὶ πόρρω ἤδη εἶ πορευόμενος τοῦ ἔρωτος.

---

4 *Hikanos* (a term perhaps better rendered "adequate").
Sophistēs, often given a pejorative connotation in Plato, is here
probably neutral (= "professional," "master of his art"). Miccus is
otherwise unknown (see Nails, 206).

"Over here," he said, pointing out me a sort of enclosure right opposite the wall with its door open; "we spend our time there, those of us here and quite a lot of other fellows, and good looking ones too."

"So what is this place, and how do you spend your time here?"   204

"It's a wrestling school," he said, "built recently. We spend most of our time in discussions, which we would be glad to share with you."

"Fine that you do that," I said, "but who teaches here?"

"Actually a friend and admirer of yours," he said, "Miccus."

"By Zeus," I said, "he's no mean fellow; indeed a competent[4] teacher of wisdom."

"So do you want to follow us," he said, "to see those who are there?"

"First I'd really like to hear what I'm going in for and who is the handsome one."[5]   b

"One seems handsome to one of us and another to another, Socrates," he said.

"But who is your choice, Hippothales? Tell me that."

He blushed at the question. And I said: "Son of Hieronymus, Hippothales, you don't need to tell me this any longer, whether you are in love with someone or not: for I know that not only are you in love, but are already pretty

---

[5] "Handsome" = *kalos*. The word has a significant range of meaning: = "beautiful" in a physical sense, but also indicating an ethical value = "fine, noble, honorable," often close or identical to *agathos* = "good." Cf. the adverb "fine" (*kalōs*) as a general term of approval, as in 204a4 above.

c εἰμὶ δ' ἐγὼ τὰ μὲν ἄλλα φαῦλος καὶ ἄχρηστος, τοῦτο
δέ μοί πως ἐκ θεοῦ δέδοται, ταχὺ οἵῳ τ' εἶναι γνῶναι
ἐρῶντά τε καὶ ἐρώμενον.

Καὶ ὃς ἀκούσας πολὺ ἔτι μᾶλλον ἠρυθρίασεν. ὁ
οὖν Κτήσιππος, Ἀστεῖόν γε, ἦ δ' ὅς, ὅτι ἐρυθριᾷς, ὦ
Ἱππόθαλες, | καὶ ὀκνεῖς εἰπεῖν Σωκράτει τοὔνομα· ἐὰν
δ' οὗτος καὶ σμικρὸν χρόνον συνδιατρίψῃ σοι, παρα-
ταθήσεται ὑπὸ σοῦ ἀκούων θαμὰ λέγοντος. ἡμῶν
γοῦν, ὦ Σώκρατες, ἐκκεκώφωκε τὰ ὦτα καὶ ἐμπέπληκε
d Λύσιδος· ἂν μὲν δὴ καὶ ὑποπίῃ, εὐμαρία ἡμῖν ἐστιν
καὶ ἐξ ὕπνου ἐγρομένοις Λύσιδος οἴεσθαι τοὔνομα
ἀκούειν. καὶ ἃ μὲν καταλογάδην διηγεῖται, δεινὰ
ὄντα, οὐ πάνυ τι δεινά ἐστιν, ἀλλ' ἐπειδὰν τὰ ποιή-
ματα ἡμῶν | ἐπιχειρήσῃ κατανταλεῖν καὶ συγγράμ-
ματα. καὶ ὅ ἐστιν τούτων δεινότερον, ὅτι καὶ ᾄδει εἰς
τὰ παιδικὰ φωνῇ θαυμασίᾳ, ἣν ἡμᾶς δεῖ ἀκούοντας
ἀνέχεσθαι. νῦν δὲ ἐρωτώμενος ὑπὸ σοῦ ἐρυθριᾷ.

e Ἔστιν δέ, ἦν δ' ἐγώ, ὁ Λύσις νέος τις, ὡς ἔοικε·
τεκμαίρομαι δέ, ὅτι ἀκούσας τοὔνομα οὐκ ἔγνων.

Οὐ γὰρ πάνυ, ἔφη, τὶ αὐτοῦ τοὔνομα λέγουσιν, ἀλλ'
ἔτι πατρόθεν ἐπονομάζεται διὰ τὸ σφόδρα τὸν πατέρα
γιγνώσκεσθαι | αὐτοῦ. ἐπεὶ εὖ οἶδ' ὅτι πολλοῦ δεῖς τὸ
εἶδος ἀγνοεῖν τοῦ παιδός· ἱκανὸς γὰρ καὶ ἀπὸ μόνου
τούτου γιγνώσκεσθαι.

Λεγέσθω, ἦν δ' ἐγώ, οὗτινος ἔστιν.

far gone in an affair. I am feeble and useless in other mat- c
ters, but this has been given me from a god, somehow—to
be able to recognize quickly both a lover and a loved one."[6]

And when he heard this he blushed more deeply than
ever. Then Ctesippus said: "Oh, quite charming that you
should blush, Hippothales, and shrink from telling Socrates his name. But if he spends even a short time with you,
he'll be worn out hearing you say it again and again. Certainly he's deafened our ears, Socrates, and filled them full
of Lysis. And even if he drinks just a little, the chances are d
we wake up from sleep thinking we can hear the name of
Lysis. And as for the things he talks about in everyday
conversation, they're dreadful enough, but not that dreadful, except when he tries to inundate us with his poems
and prose pieces. And what's even more dreadful than
these, is that he even sings to his beloved in an amazing
voice which we have to listen to and put up with. But now
when you ask him the question he blushes."

"Lysis is someone young, I imagine," I said. "I'm as- e
suming this as I didn't recognize the name when I heard
it."

"Yes, that's because people don't use his own name very
much," he said, "but he's still called by his father's name
on account of his father being very well known; since I'm
very sure there is little chance of your not knowing the boy
from his appearance. It's enough to recognize him from
that alone."

"Let me be told," I said "whose son he is."

[6] "In love" (204b6): the Greek uses the verbal form of *erōs*;
for this and other terms for "love" and the relationship between
"lover" and "loved one," see General Introduction, §2.

PLATO

Δημοκράτους, ἔφη, τοῦ Αἰξωνέως ὁ πρεσβύτατος
υός.

Εἶεν, ἦν δ᾽ ἐγώ, ὦ Ἱππόθαλες, ὡς γενναῖον καὶ
νεανικὸν | τοῦτον τὸν ἔρωτα πανταχῇ ἀνηῦρες· καί μοι
ἴθι ἐπίδειξαι ἃ καὶ τοῖσδε ἐπιδείκνυσαι, ἵνα εἰδῶ εἰ
ἐπίστασαι ἃ χρὴ ἐραστὴν περὶ παιδικῶν πρὸς αὐτὸν
ἢ πρὸς ἄλλους λέγειν.

205   Τούτων δέ τι, ἔφη, σταθμᾷ, ὦ Σώκρατες, ὧν ὅδε
λέγει;

Πότερον, ἦν δ᾽ ἐγώ, καὶ τὸ ἐρᾶν ἔξαρνος εἶ οὗ
λέγει ὅδε; |

Οὐκ ἔγωγε, ἔφη, ἀλλὰ μὴ ποιεῖν εἰς τὰ παιδικὰ
μηδὲ συγγράφειν.

Οὐχ ὑγιαίνει, ἔφη ὁ Κτήσιππος, ἀλλὰ ληρεῖ τε καὶ
μαίνεται.

Καὶ ἐγὼ εἶπον· Ὦ Ἱππόθαλες, οὔ τι τῶν μέτρων
δέομαι ἀκοῦσαι οὐδὲ μέλος εἴ τι πεποίηκας εἰς τὸν
b   νεανίσκον, ἀλλὰ τῆς διανοίας, ἵνα εἰδῶ τίνα τρόπον
προσφέρῃ πρὸς τὰ παιδικά.

Ὅδε δήπου σοι, ἔφη, ἐρεῖ· ἀκριβῶς γὰρ ἐπίσταται
καὶ | μέμνηται, εἴπερ, ὡς λέγει, ὑπ᾽ ἐμοῦ ἀεὶ ἀκούων
διατεθρύληται.

Νὴ τοὺς θεούς, ἔφη ὁ Κτήσιππος, πάνυ γε. καὶ γάρ
ἐστι καταγέλαστα, ὦ Σώκρατες. τὸ γὰρ ἐραστὴν ὄντα
καὶ διαφερόντως τῶν ἄλλων τὸν νοῦν προσέχοντα τῷ

---

7 Aexone is the family's deme (district of Athens). On the family of Lysis, see Nails, 195–97.

"Democrates," he said, "from Aexone; he's his eldest son."[7]

"Well, Hippothales," I said, "what a noble and high-spirited love this is you have discovered, in every respect. So come on and put on a show for me, as you have done for these others here, so that I may know if you understand what a lover must say about his loved one to his face or to others."

"Do you place any value on the things this fellow here   205
says, Socrates?"

"Do you deny that you're actually in love with the one this fellow mentions?" I said.

"No I don't," he said, "but I do deny writing poems and prose pieces to my beloved."

"He's not well," said Ctesippus; "he's talking rubbish and is mad."

And I said, "Hippothales, I don't want to hear any of your poems, nor if you have written a song to the young man, but I do about your intention[8] so I may know in what   b
way you approach your beloved."

"I expect this man will tell you" he said, "for he understands exactly and remembers if, as he says, he's being made deaf through always listening to me."

"By the gods," said Ctesippus, "very much so. And in fact the things he says are ridiculous too, Socrates. You see, since he's a lover and turns his attention far more than

---

[8] *Dianoia*: "(real) intention" or "thought" (behind what Hippothales is saying), which Socrates immediately argues is different from his expressed motive (whether he's conscious of it or not).

παιδὶ ἴδιον μὲν μηδὲν ἔχειν λέγειν ὃ οὐχὶ κἂν παῖς
c εἴποι, πῶς οὐχὶ καταγέλαστον; ἃ δὲ ἡ πόλις ὅλη ᾄδει
περὶ Δημοκράτους καὶ Λύσιδος τοῦ πάππου τοῦ παιδὸς καὶ πάντων πέρι τῶν προγόνων, πλούτους τε καὶ
ἱπποτροφίας καὶ νίκας Πυθοῖ καὶ Ἰσθμοῖ καὶ Νεμέᾳ
τεθρίπποις τε καὶ κέλησι, ταῦτα ποιεῖ τε καὶ λέγει,
πρὸς δὲ τούτοις ἔτι τούτων κρονικώτερα. τὸν γὰρ τοῦ
Ἡρακλέους ξενισμὸν πρῴην ἡμῖν ἐν ποιήματί τινι
διῄει, ὡς διὰ τὴν τοῦ Ἡρακλέους συγγένειαν ὁ πρό-
d γονος αὐτῶν ὑποδέξαιτο τὸν Ἡρακλέα, γεγονὼς αὐτὸς ἐκ Διός τε καὶ τῆς τοῦ δήμου ἀρχηγέτου θυγα-
τρός, ἅπερ αἱ γραῖαι ᾄδουσι, καὶ ἄλλα πολλὰ τοιαῦτα,
ὦ Σώκρατες· ταῦτ' ἐστὶν ἃ οὗτος λέγων τε καὶ ᾄδων
ἀναγκάζει καὶ ἡμᾶς ἀκροᾶσθαι. |

Καὶ ἐγὼ ἀκούσας εἶπον· Ὦ καταγέλαστε Ἱππόθαλες, πρὶν νενικηκέναι ποιεῖς τε καὶ ᾄδεις εἰς σαυτὸν
ἐγκώμιον;

Ἀλλ' οὐκ εἰς ἐμαυτόν, ἔφη, ὦ Σώκρατες, οὔτε ποιῶ
οὔτε ᾄδω.

Οὐκ οἴει γε, ἦν δ' ἐγώ. |

Τὸ δὲ πῶς ἔχει; ἔφη.

e Πάντων μάλιστα, εἶπον, εἰς σὲ τείνουσιν αὗται
αἱ ᾠδαί. ἐὰν μὲν γὰρ ἕλῃς τὰ παιδικὰ τοιαῦτα ὄντα,
κόσμος σοι ἔσται τὰ λεχθέντα καὶ ᾀσθέντα καὶ τῷ
ὄντι ἐγκώμια ὥσπερ νενικηκότι, ὅτι τοιούτων παιδι-
κῶν ἔτυχες· ἐὰν δέ σε διαφύγῃ, | ὅσῳ ἂν μείζω σοι

anyone else's on the boy, and has nothing particular to say that even a boy couldn't say: how is that not ridiculous? But what the whole city sings about Democrates and Lysis, the boy's grandfather, and about all his ancestors, their wealth, their horse rearing and their victories at the Pythian, Isthmian and Nemean games[9] in the four-horse chariot and single-horse races, that's what he composes poetry about and recites, and some things that are even more out of date than that. For example, he was going through the entertaining of Heracles for us in some poem or other the day before yesterday and how, because of their kinship with Heracles, their ancestor had received Heracles, as he, the ancestor, was himself descended from Zeus and the daughter of the deme's founder; things the old women sing about, and a lot of other such stuff, Socrates. It's these things this fellow here recites and sings and forces us to listen to as well."

When I heard this, I said: "You silly boy, Hippothales, are you writing poems and singing your own praises before you've won?"

"Oh no, Socrates," he said. "It's not to myself that I write or sing poems."

"You don't think you do, at any rate," I said.

"How is that so?" he said.

"Most of all, I said, these songs point toward yourself. For if you catch a beloved, if he is such as you describe, what you have said and sung will be an ornament and, in reality, a song of praise to yourself as if you were a winner because you have succeeded with such a beloved. But if he eludes you, the greater the praises you have uttered

9 Held in Delphi, Corinth, and the Argolid, respectively.

εἰρημένα ἢ ἐγκώμια περὶ τῶν παιδικῶν, τοσούτῳ μει-
ζόνων δόξεις καλῶν τε καὶ ἀγαθῶν ἐστερημένος
206 καταγέλαστος εἶναι. ὅστις οὖν τὰ ἐρωτικά, ὦ φίλε,
σοφός, οὐκ ἐπαινεῖ τὸν ἐρώμενον πρὶν ἂν ἕλῃ, δεδιὼς
τὸ μέλλον ὅπῃ ἀποβήσεται. καὶ ἅμα οἱ καλοί, ἐπειδάν
τις αὐτοὺς ἐπαινῇ καὶ αὔξῃ, φρονήματος ἐμπίμπλαν-
ται καὶ μεγαλαυχίας· ἢ οὐκ οἴει; |

Ἔγωγε, ἔφη.

Οὐκοῦν ὅσῳ ἂν μεγαλαυχότεροι ὦσιν, δυσαλωτό-
τεροι γίγνονται;

Εἰκός γε.

Ποῖός τις οὖν ἄν σοι δοκεῖ θηρευτὴς εἶναι, εἰ ἀνα-
σοβοῖ | θηρεύων καὶ δυσαλωτοτέραν τὴν ἄγραν ποιοῖ;

b Δῆλον ὅτι φαῦλος.

Καὶ μὲν δὴ λόγοις τε καὶ ᾠδαῖς μὴ κηλεῖν ἀλλ'
ἐξαγριαίνειν πολλὴ ἀμουσία· ἢ γάρ;

Δοκεῖ μοι. |

Σκόπει δή, ὦ Ἱππόθαλες, ὅπως μὴ πᾶσι τούτοις
ἔνοχον σαυτὸν ποιήσεις διὰ τὴν ποίησιν· καίτοι οἶμαι
ἐγὼ ἄνδρα ποιήσει βλάπτοντα ἑαυτὸν οὐκ ἄν σε ἐθέλειν ὁμολογῆσαι ὡς ἀγαθός ποτ' ἐστὶν ποιητής, βλα-
βερὸς ὢν ἑαυτῷ.

Οὐ μὰ τὸν Δία, ἔφη· πολλὴ γὰρ ἂν ἀλογία εἴη.
c ἀλλὰ διὰ ταῦτα δή σοι, ὦ Σώκρατες, ἀνακοινοῦμαι,
καὶ εἴ τι ἄλλο ἔχεις, συμβούλευε τίνα ἄν τις λόγον
διαλεγόμενος ἢ τί πράττων προσφιλὴς παιδικοῖς γένοιτο.

Οὐ ῥᾴδιον, ἦν δ' ἐγώ, εἰπεῖν· ἀλλ' εἴ μοι ἐθελήσαις

32

about your beloved, the greater will be the fine and good things you will appear to have been deprived of, and you will appear ridiculous. So he who is wise in the matters of love, my friend, does not praise his beloved before he has caught him, out of fear of how the future will turn out. And at the same time, the handsome ones, whenever someone praises and extols them, are filled with disdain and arrogance. Or do you not think so?" 206

"I do," he said.

"And so the more arrogant they get, the harder they are to win over?"

"Yes, it looks like it."

"What sort of person do you think a hunter would be, if he went hunting and scared his quarry and made it harder to catch?"

"A poor one, clearly." b

"And furthermore to use words and songs not to charm, but to drive mad would suggest a great absence of musical talent, wouldn't it?"

"I think so."

"So, Hippothales, see that you're careful and don't make yourself liable to all this through your poetry. And yet I think myself that you would not want to concede that a man who harms himself with his poetry is ever a good poet, in that he is harmful to himself."

"Certainly not, by Zeus," he said, "that would be quite absurd. But it's for just this reason that I'm sharing with c you what I think, Socrates, and if you have anything else to say, advise me what sort of thing one should say in conversation or do to become pleasing to a loved one."

"It's not easy to say," I said, "but if you were willing to

αὐτὸν | ποιῆσαι εἰς λόγους ἐλθεῖν, ἴσως ἂν δυναίμην σοι ἐπιδεῖξαι ἃ χρὴ αὐτῷ διαλέγεσθαι ἀντὶ τούτων ὧν οὗτοι λέγειν τε καὶ ᾄδειν φασί σε.

Ἀλλ᾽ οὐδέν, ἔφη, χαλεπόν. ἂν γὰρ εἰσέλθῃς μετὰ Κτησίππου τοῦδε καὶ καθεζόμενος διαλέγῃ, οἶμαι μὲν καὶ | αὐτός σοι πρόσεισι—φιλήκοος γάρ, ὦ Σώκρα-
d τες, διαφερόντως ἐστίν, καὶ ἅμα, ὡς Ἑρμαῖα ἄγουσιν, ἀναμεμειγμένοι ἐν ταὐτῷ εἰσιν οἵ τε νεανίσκοι καὶ οἱ παῖδες—πρόσεισιν οὖν σοι. εἰ δὲ μή, Κτησίππῳ συν-ήθης ἐστὶν διὰ τὸν τούτου ἀνεψιὸν Μενέξενον· Μενε-ξένῳ μὲν γὰρ δὴ πάντων μάλιστα ἑταῖρος | ὢν τυγ-χάνει. καλεσάτω οὖν οὗτος αὐτόν, ἐὰν ἄρα μὴ προσίῃ αὐτός.

Ταῦτα, ἦν δ᾽ ἐγώ, χρὴ ποιεῖν. Καὶ ἅμα λαβὼν τὸν Κτήσιππον προσῇα εἰς τὴν παλαίστραν· οἱ δ᾽ ἄλλοι ὕστεροι ἡμῶν ἦσαν.

e Εἰσελθόντες δὲ κατελάβομεν αὐτόθι τεθυκότας τε τοὺς παῖδας καὶ τὰ περὶ τὰ ἱερεῖα σχεδόν τι ἤδη πε-ποιημένα, | ἀστραγαλίζοντάς τε δὴ καὶ κεκοσμημέ-νους ἅπαντας. οἱ μὲν οὖν πολλοὶ ἐν τῇ αὐλῇ ἔπαιζον ἔξω, οἱ δέ τινες τοῦ ἀποδυτηρίου ἐν γωνίᾳ ἠρτίαζον ἀστραγάλοις παμπόλλοις, ἐκ φορμίσκων τινῶν προ-αιρούμενοι· τούτους δὲ περιέστασαν ἄλλοι θεωροῦν-

---

[10] Hermaea, a festival celebrating the god Hermes as patron of sport and gymnastics, often, as here, featuring athletic competitions in gymnasia involving young men and boys.

get him to come to have a conversation with me, perhaps I'd be able to show you what you should talk to him about instead of those things which these fellows claim you say and sing."

"Well, nothing difficult in that," he said, "for if you go in with Ctesippus here and sit down and start a conversation I think he will actually come to you by himself—you see, he's particularly fond of listening, Socrates, and besides, as they are celebrating the Hermaea, the young men and the boys are assembled together; so he will come to you.[10] But if he doesn't, he is familiar with Ctesippus through Ctesippus' cousin Menexenus.[11] In fact he happens to be a particular friend of Menexenus. Let Ctesippus call him over, if he doesn't actually come over himself."

"That's what we must do," I said, and saying this I took hold of Ctesippus and went into the wrestling school and the rest went in behind us.

When we went in we encountered the boys there who had made their sacrifices and the performance of the rituals was already almost over, and, all dressed up, they were playing knucklebones. Now most of them were playing in the courtyard outside, but some were playing at odds and evens in a corner of the changing room with a large number of knucklebones which they were selecting out of some little baskets.[12] Others stood around watching them.

d

e

[11] Menexenus, a young adolescent contemporary and friend of Lysis, features as an adult speaker with Socrates in the dialogue bearing his name (see also above, n. 3).

[12] "Knucklebones" (e5): a game similar to dice. "Odds and evens" (e7): probably some game of chance.

207 τες. ὧν δὴ καὶ ὁ Λύσις ἦν, καὶ εἱστήκει ἐν τοῖς παισί
τε καὶ νεανίσκοις ἐστεφανωμένος καὶ τὴν ὄψιν διαφέ-
ρων, οὐ τὸ καλὸς εἶναι μόνον ἄξιος ἀκοῦσαι, ἀλλ' ὅτι
καλός τε κἀγαθός. καὶ ἡμεῖς εἰς τὸ καταντικρὺ ἀπο-
χωρήσαντες ἐκαθεζόμεθα—ἦν γὰρ αὐτόθι ἡσυχία—
καί τι ἀλλήλοις | διελεγόμεθα. περιστρεφόμενος οὖν
ὁ Λύσις θαμὰ ἐπεσκοπεῖτο ἡμᾶς, καὶ δῆλος ἦν ἐπιθυμῶν προσελθεῖν. τέως μὲν οὖν ἠπόρει τε καὶ ὤκνει
b μόνος προσιέναι, ἔπειτα ὁ Μενέξενος ἐκ τῆς αὐλῆς
μεταξὺ παίζων εἰσέρχεται, καὶ ὡς εἶδεν ἐμέ τε καὶ τὸν
Κτήσιππον, ᾔει παρακαθιζησόμενος· ἰδὼν οὖν αὐτὸν
ὁ Λύσις εἵπετο καὶ συμπαρεκαθέζετο μετὰ τοῦ Μενεξένου. προσῆλθον δὴ καὶ οἱ ἄλλοι, καὶ δὴ καὶ ὁ Ἱπ-
ποθάλης, | ἐπειδὴ πλείους ἑώρα ἐφισταμένους, τού-
τους ἐπηλυγισάμενος προσέστη ᾗ μὴ ᾤετο κατόψεσθαι
τὸν Λύσιν, δεδιὼς μὴ αὐτῷ ἀπεχθάνοιτο· καὶ οὕτω
προσεστὼς ἠκροᾶτο.

Καὶ ἐγὼ πρὸς τὸν Μενέξενον ἀποβλέψας, Ὦ παῖ
Δημοφῶντος, ἦν δ' ἐγώ, πότερος ὑμῶν πρεσβύτερος;

c Ἀμφισβητοῦμεν, ἔφη.

Οὐκοῦν καὶ ὁπότερος γενναιότερος, ἐρίζοιτ' ἄν, ἦν
δ' ἐγώ.

Πάνυ γε, ἔφη. |

Καὶ μὴν ὁπότερός γε καλλίων, ὡσαύτως.

Ἐγελασάτην οὖν ἄμφω.

Now one of these was actually Lysis and he was standing 207
among the boys and the young men with a garland round
his head and distinguished by his appearance, worth comment not only for his beauty, but also because he was
handsome and well-bred.[13] We moved across to the opposite side and sat down—for it was quiet there—and
began discussing something among ourselves. So then Lysis turned round frequently and looked at us, and it was
obvious that he was keen to come over to us. While he was
undecided and hesitating to come over alone, at that mo- b
ment Menexenus came in from the courtyard between
games and, when he saw me and Ctesippus, he came to sit
down beside us. So when Lysis saw him, he followed and
sat down beside us with Menexenus. Then the others also
approached us and notably Hippothales, who, when he
saw quite a number of them standing by, stood with them
as a screen where he thought Lysis wouldn't catch sight of
him, afraid that he would annoy him. Standing thus he
listened.

I looked over at Menexenus and said: "Son of Demo-
phon, which of you two is the elder?"

"We have a dispute about that," he said. c

"And so likewise you would dispute as to which of you
is the nobler," I said.

"Very much so," he said.

"And again it would be the same over which is the more
handsome."

Accordingly they both burst out laughing.

[13] "Handsome and well-bred" (*kalos k'agathos*), an indication
not only of appearance but also of social status (see Dover, *GPM*,
41–45).

Οὐ μὴν ὁπότερός γε, ἔφην, πλουσιώτερος ὑμῶν, οὐκ ἐρήσομαι· φίλω γάρ ἐστον. ἦ γάρ;

Πάνυ γ᾽, ἐφάτην. |

Οὐκοῦν κοινὰ τά γε φίλων λέγεται, ὥστε τούτῳ γε οὐδὲν διοίσετον, εἴπερ ἀληθῆ περὶ τῆς φιλίας λέγετον.

Συνεφάτην.

d   Ἐπεχείρουν δὴ μετὰ τοῦτο ἐρωτᾶν ὁπότερος δικαιότερος καὶ σοφώτερος αὐτῶν εἴη. μεταξὺ οὖν τις προσελθὼν ἀνέστησε τὸν Μενέξενον, φάσκων καλεῖν τὸν παιδοτρίβην· ἐδόκει γάρ μοι ἱεροποιῶν τυγχάνειν. ἐκεῖνος μὲν οὖν ᾤχετο· | ἐγὼ δὲ τὸν Λύσιν ἠρόμην, Ἦ που, ἦν δ᾽ ἐγώ, ὦ Λύσι, σφόδρα φιλεῖ σε ὁ πατὴρ καὶ ἡ μήτηρ;

Πάνυ γε, ἦ δ᾽ ὅς.

Οὐκοῦν βούλοιντο ἄν σε ὡς εὐδαιμονέστατον εἶναι;

e   Πῶς γὰρ οὔ;

Δοκεῖ δέ σοι εὐδαίμων εἶναι ἄνθρωπος δουλεύων τε καὶ ᾧ μηδὲν ἐξείη ποιεῖν ὧν ἐπιθυμοῖ;

Μὰ Δί᾽ οὐκ ἔμοιγε, ἔφη.

Οὐκοῦν εἴ σε φιλεῖ ὁ πατὴρ καὶ ἡ μήτηρ καὶ εὐδαίμονά σε ἐπιθυμοῦσι γενέσθαι, τοῦτο παντὶ | τρόπῳ δῆλον ὅτι προθυμοῦνται ὅπως ἂν εὐδαιμονοίης.

---

14 The key question for the following section of the dialogue is prepared by getting Lysis on his own (Introduction, §3(i)).

15 "Love" here uses the verbal form of *philos* (dear), a term generally used of nonsexual (e.g., family) relationships, as op-

"Naturally, I won't ask which of you is the richer," I said. "After all, you're both friends, aren't you?"

"Very much so," they both said.

"Well it's said that what friends have they have in common; so in this respect at least there's no dispute between the two of you, if what you say about your friendship is true."

They both agreed.

After this I was setting out to ask which of the two was juster and wiser. Then in the middle of this someone came over and made Menexenus get up, saying that the trainer was calling him, for I gathered he was involved in preparing some sacrifice.[14] So off he went, and I questioned Lysis. "I imagine, Lysis," I said, "that your father and mother love you very much."[15] d

"Very much," he said.

"Therefore they would want you to be as happy as possible."[16]

"Of course." e

"Do you think a person is happy who is a slave and is prevented from doing any of the things he desires to do?"

"No, by Zeus, I don't," he said.

"Therefore if your father and mother love you and desire you to become happy, then clearly in every way they are earnest in the wish that you should be happy."

posed to *erōs*, as used by Socrates of Hippothales (see above 204c2 and n. 6), but, for the overlap between the usage of the two words and with *epithumia* = "desire" (e2ff.), see General Introduction, §2.   [16] On the question of what exactly Socrates means in the course of this argument by happiness and parental love, see 210bff. below.

Πῶς γὰρ οὐχί; ἔφη.

Ἐῶσιν ἄρα σε ἃ βούλει ποιεῖν, καὶ οὐδὲν ἐπιπλήτ-
τουσιν οὐδὲ διακωλύουσι ποιεῖν ὧν ἂν ἐπιθυμῇς;

Ναὶ μὰ Δία ἐμέ γε, ὦ Σώκρατες, καὶ μάλα γε πολλὰ
κωλύουσιν.

Πῶς λέγεις; ἦν δ᾽ ἐγώ. βουλόμενοί σε μακάριον
208 εἶναι διακωλύουσι τοῦτο ποιεῖν ὃ ἂν βούλῃ; ὧδε δέ
μοι λέγε. ἦν ἐπιθυμήσῃς ἐπί τινος τῶν τοῦ πατρὸς
ἁρμάτων ὀχεῖσθαι λαβὼν τὰς ἡνίας, ὅταν ἁμιλλᾶται,
οὐκ ἂν ἐῷέν σε ἀλλὰ διακωλύοιεν;

Μὰ Δί᾽ οὐ μέντοι ἄν, ἔφη, ἐῷεν. |

Ἀλλὰ τίνα μήν;

Ἔστιν τις ἡνίοχος παρὰ τοῦ πατρὸς μισθὸν φέ-
ρων.

Πῶς λέγεις; μισθωτῷ μᾶλλον ἐπιτρέπουσιν ἢ σοὶ
ποιεῖν ὅτι ἂν βούληται περὶ τοὺς ἵππους, καὶ προσέτι
αὐτοῦ τούτου ἀργύριον τελοῦσιν;

b   Ἀλλὰ τί μήν; ἔφη.

Ἀλλὰ τοῦ ὀρικοῦ ζεύγους οἶμαι ἐπιτρέπουσίν σοι
ἄρχειν, κἂν εἰ βούλοιο λαβὼν τὴν μάστιγα τύπτειν,
ἐῷεν ἄν.

Πόθεν, ἦ δ᾽ ὅς, ἐῷεν;

Τί δέ; ἦν δ᾽ ἐγώ· οὐδενὶ ἔξεστιν | αὐτοὺς τύπτειν;

Καὶ μάλα, ἔφη, τῷ ὀρεοκόμῳ.

Δούλῳ ὄντι ἢ ἐλευθέρῳ;

Δούλῳ, ἔφη.

Καὶ δοῦλον, ὡς ἔοικεν, ἡγοῦνται περὶ πλείονος ἢ
σὲ τὸν ὑόν, καὶ ἐπιτρέπουσι τὰ ἑαυτῶν μᾶλλον ἢ σοί,

40

"Of course," he said.

"Then do they let you do whatever you want? Do they not rebuke you at all and prevent you from doing whatever you desire to do?"

"Yes they certainly do, Socrates, by Zeus; they prevent me doing a great number of things."

"How do you mean?" I said. "In wanting to make you content do they stop you doing whatever you want? Tell me this: if you are keen to take the reins and ride on one of your father's chariots when there's a race, they wouldn't let you, but stop you?" 208

"By Zeus," he said, "they certainly wouldn't let me."

"Well who would they let then?"

"There's a driver in my father's employment."

"What do you mean? They entrust an employee rather than you to do whatever he wants regarding the horses, and in addition to that they pay him money?"

"Yes of course," he said. b

"But I imagine they leave you to drive the yoked mules and would allow you to take a whip and beat them if you wanted to."

"Why ever would they let me?"

"What," I said, "is no one allowed to beat them?"

"Yes of course," he said, "the muleteer."

"Is he a slave, or free?"

"A slave," he said.

"And they think a slave is worth more than you, their son, it seems, and they entrust their possessions to him

c καὶ ἐῶσιν ποιεῖν ὅτι βούλεται, σὲ δὲ διακωλύουσι; καί
μοι ἔτι τόδε εἰπέ. σὲ αὐτὸν ἐῶσιν ἄρχειν σεαυτοῦ, ἢ
οὐδὲ τοῦτο ἐπιτρέπουσί σοι;

Πῶς γάρ, ἔφη, ἐπιτρέπουσιν;

Ἀλλ᾽ ἄρχει τίς σου;

Ὅδε, παιδαγωγός, ἔφη.

Μῶν δοῦλος ὤν;

Ἀλλὰ τί μήν; ἡμέτερός γε, ἔφη. |

Ἦ δεινόν, ἦν δ᾽ ἐγώ, ἐλεύθερον ὄντα ὑπὸ δούλου
ἄρχεσθαι. τί δὲ ποιῶν αὖ οὗτος ὁ παιδαγωγός σου
ἄρχει;

Ἄγων δήπου, ἔφη, εἰς διδασκάλου.

Μῶν μὴ καὶ οὗτοί σου ἄρχουσιν, οἱ διδάσκαλοι;

d Πάντως δήπου.

Παμπόλλους ἄρα σοι δεσπότας καὶ ἄρχοντας ἑκὼν
ὁ πατὴρ ἐφίστησιν. ἀλλ᾽ ἄρα ἐπειδὰν οἴκαδε ἔλθῃς
παρὰ τὴν μητέρα, ἐκείνη σε ἐᾷ ποιεῖν ὅτι ἂν βούλῃ,
ἵν᾽ αὐτῇ μακάριος ᾖς, ἢ περὶ τὰ ἔρια ἢ περὶ | τὸν
ἱστόν, ὅταν ὑφαίνῃ; οὔ τι γάρ που διακωλύει σε ἢ τῆς
σπάθης ἢ τῆς κερκίδος ἢ ἄλλου του τῶν περὶ ταλα-
σιουργίαν ὀργάνων ἅπτεσθαι.

e Καὶ ὃς γελάσας, Μὰ Δία, ἔφη, ὦ Σώκρατες, οὐ
μόνον γε διακωλύει, ἀλλὰ καὶ τυπτοίμην ἂν εἰ ἁπτοί-
μην.

rather than to you, and allow him to do what he wants, but stop you from doing so? And tell me this too: do they allow c you yourself to control yourself, or don't they even entrust this to you?"

"No, how would they do this?" he said.

"Well, someone controls you?"

"This man here, my tutor."[17]

"He's not a slave, surely?"

"Well of course he is. He's ours after all," he said.

"Why, that is strange," I said, "that a free man is under the control of a slave. But what does this tutor do to control you?"

"By escorting me to the schoolmaster's of course," he said.

"You surely don't mean they control you too, these schoolmasters?"

"I should say they do!" d

"So then your father deliberately puts a large number of masters and controllers in charge of you. But what about when you come home to your mother, does she allow you to do whatever you want with the wool or the loom when she's weaving, so that she can make you happy? For I can't imagine for a moment that she prevents you from touching the batten, the shuttle or any of the other implements used in weaving."

And he laughed and said: "by Zeus, Socrates, not only e does she prevent me, but also I'd get beaten if I touched them."

[17] "Tutor" = *paidagōgos*, a slave who acts as an escort/guardian.

Ἡράκλεις, ἦν δ' ἐγώ, μῶν μή τι ἠδίκηκας τὸν πατέρα ἢ τὴν μητέρα;

Μὰ Δί' οὐκ ἔγωγε, ἔφη.

Ἀλλ' ἀντὶ τίνος μὴν οὕτω σε δεινῶς διακωλύουσιν εὐδαίμονα | εἶναι καὶ ποιεῖν ὅτι ἂν βούλῃ, καὶ δι' ἡμέρας ὅλης τρέφουσί σε ἀεί τῳ δουλεύοντα καὶ ἑνὶ λόγῳ ὀλίγου ὧν ἐπιθυμεῖς οὐδὲν ποιοῦντα; ὥστε σοι, ὡς ἔοικεν, οὔτε τῶν χρημάτων τοσούτων ὄντων οὐδὲν ὄφελος, ἀλλὰ πάντες αὐτῶν μᾶλλον ἄρχουσιν ἢ σύ, 209 οὔτε τοῦ σώματος οὕτω γενναίου ὄντος, ἀλλὰ καὶ τοῦτο ἄλλος ποιμαίνει καὶ θεραπεύει· σὺ δὲ ἄρχεις οὐδενός, ὦ Λύσι, οὐδὲ ποιεῖς οὐδὲν ὧν ἐπιθυμεῖς.

Οὐ γάρ πω, ἔφη, ἡλικίαν ἔχω, ὦ Σώκρατες.

Μὴ οὐ | τοῦτό σε, ὦ παῖ Δημοκράτους, κωλύῃ, ἐπεὶ τό γε τοσόνδε, ὡς ἐγῷμαι, καὶ ὁ πατὴρ καὶ ἡ μήτηρ σοι ἐπιτρέπουσιν καὶ οὐκ ἀναμένουσιν ἕως ἂν ἡλικίαν ἔχῃς. ὅταν γὰρ βούλωνται αὐτοῖς τινα ἀναγνωσθῆναι ἢ γραφῆναι, σέ, ὡς ἐγῷμαι, πρῶτον τῶν ἐν τῇ οἰκίᾳ ἐπὶ τοῦτο τάττουσιν. ἢ γάρ;

b   Πάνυ γ', ἔφη.

Οὐκοῦν ἔξεστί σοι ἐνταῦθ' ὅτι ἂν βούλῃ πρῶτον τῶν γραμμάτων γράφειν καὶ ὅτι ἂν δεύτερον· καὶ ἀναγιγνώσκειν ὡσαύτως ἔξεστιν. καὶ ἐπειδάν, ὡς ἐγῷμαι, | τὴν λύραν λάβῃς, οὐ διακωλύουσί σε οὔτε ὁ πατὴρ οὔτε ἡ μήτηρ ἐπιτεῖναί τε καὶ ἀνεῖναι ἣν ἂν βούλῃ τῶν χορδῶν, καὶ ψῆλαι καὶ κρούειν τῷ πλήκτρῳ. ἢ διακωλύουσιν;

Οὐ δῆτα.

"Heracles!" I said, "yet surely you've done your father and mother no wrong?"

"No, I haven't, by Zeus," he replied.

"Well what is it in return for which they prevent you so strangely from being happy and doing whatever you want, and bring you up throughout the day always as a slave to someone and, in a word, doing almost none of the things you desire? As a result, it seems, you gain no benefit from their wealth which is in such great abundance, but everyone has more control of it than you do, nor do you get any benefit from your body, that's of such noble stock, but even this someone else tends and looks after. But you have no control over anything, Lysis, and you don't do any of the things you desire to do." 209

"Yes, but that's because I haven't yet come of age, Socrates," he said.

"My guess is that it's not that which is stopping you, son of Democrates, since there is, I imagine, at least a certain amount that your father and mother do entrust to you, and are not waiting until you come of age. For when they want something to be read to them, or written, you, I suppose, are the first in the household they choose for this task. Isn't that so?"

"Yes, certainly," he said. b

"In this respect then it is possible for you to write whichever of the letters you want first, and whichever you want second. And the same goes for reading. And whenever you take up the lyre, I imagine, neither your father nor your mother stops you from tightening or slackening whichever of the strings you want, and plucking the strings or striking them with the plectrum. Or do they stop you?"

"Not at all."

Τί ποτ᾽ ἂν οὖν εἴη, ὦ Λύσι, τὸ αἴτιον ὅτι ἐνταῦθα μὲν οὐ διακωλύουσιν, ἐν οἷς δὲ ἄρτι ἐλέγομεν κωλύουσι;

c ᾽Ότι οἶμαι, ἔφη, ταῦτα μὲν ἐπίσταμαι, ἐκεῖνα δ᾽ οὔ.

Εἶεν, ἦν δ᾽ ἐγώ, ὦ ἄριστε· οὐκ ἄρα τὴν ἡλικίαν σου περιμένει ὁ πατὴρ ἐπιτρέπειν πάντα, ἀλλ᾽ ᾗ ἂν ἡμέρᾳ ἡγήσηταί σε | βέλτιον αὑτοῦ φρονεῖν, ταύτῃ ἐπιτρέψει σοι καὶ αὑτὸν καὶ τὰ αὑτοῦ.

Οἶμαι ἔγωγε, ἔφη.

Εἶεν, ἦν δ᾽ ἐγώ· τί δέ; τῷ γείτονι ἆρ᾽ οὐχ ὁ αὐτὸς d ὅρος ὅσπερ τῷ πατρὶ περὶ σοῦ; πότερον οἴει αὐτὸν ἐπιτρέψειν σοι τὴν αὑτοῦ οἰκίαν οἰκονομεῖν, ὅταν σε ἡγήσηται βέλτιον περὶ οἰκονομίας ἑαυτοῦ φρονεῖν, ἢ αὐτὸν ἐπιστατήσειν;

᾽Εμοὶ ἐπιτρέψειν οἶμαι.

Τί δ᾽; Ἀθηναίους οἴει σοι οὐκ ἐπιτρέψειν τὰ αὑτῶν, ὅταν | αἰσθάνωνται ὅτι ἱκανῶς φρονεῖς;

῎Εγωγε.

Πρὸς Διός, ἦν δ᾽ ἐγώ, τί ἄρα ὁ μέγας βασιλεύς; πότερον τῷ πρεσβυτάτῳ ὑεῖ, οὗ ἡ τῆς Ἀσίας ἀρχὴ γίγνεται, μᾶλλον ἂν ἐπιτρέψειεν ἑψομένων κρεῶν [ἐμβάλλειν] ὅτι ἂν βούληται ἐμβαλεῖν εἰς τὸν ζωμόν, ἢ e ἡμῖν, εἰ ἀφικόμενοι παρ᾽ ἐκεῖνον ἐνδειξαίμεθα αὐτῷ ὅτι ἡμεῖς κάλλιον φρονοῦμεν ἢ ὁ ὑὸς αὐτοῦ περὶ ὄψου σκευασίας;

Ἡμῖν δῆλον ὅτι, ἔφη.

46

"Whatever could be the reason, Lysis, that in this they don't stop you, but in those activities we were talking about just now, they do?"

"Because I think," he said, "these I understand, but not c
the others."

"Well said, my excellent friend," I said. "In that case your father isn't waiting for you to become of age to entrust everything to you, but on the day he thinks your understanding is better than his, that's the day he'll entrust both himself and his possessions to you."

"Yes, that's what I think," he said.

"Good," I said; "but what about this? Won't your neighbor have the same rule as your father where you're concerned? Do you think he'll hand over his own household d
to you to run whenever he thinks you have a better understanding of running a household than he does, or will he stay in charge of it himself?"

"He'll hand it over to me, I think."

"And then what? Do you think the Athenians won't put you in charge of their affairs when they see that that your understanding is adequate?"

"I think they will."

"In the name of Zeus!" I said, "so what about the Great King?[18] Would he entrust his eldest son, destined to become ruler of Asia, with adding whatever he wants to the broth when the meat is cooking, rather than us, if on ar- e
riving at his court we were to show him that we had a much finer understanding of preparing a dish than his son?"

"Us clearly," he said.

[18] The ruler of the Persian Empire, that is, the person popularly regarded as the most powerful and influential in the world.

Καὶ τὸν μέν γε οὐδ' ἂν σμικρὸν ἐάσειεν ἐμβαλεῖν· ἡμᾶς | δέ, κἂν εἰ βουλοίμεθα δραξάμενοι τῶν ἁλῶν, ἐφη ἂν ἐμβαλεῖν.

Πῶς γὰρ οὔ;

Τί δ' εἰ τοὺς ὀφθαλμοὺς ὁ ὑὸς αὐτοῦ ἀσθενοῖ, ἆρα ἐφη ἂν αὐτὸν ἅπτεσθαι τῶν ἑαυτοῦ ὀφθαλμῶν, μὴ ἰατρὸν ἡγούμενος, ἢ κωλύοι ἄν;

210   Κωλύοι ἄν.

Ἡμᾶς δέ γε εἰ ὑπολαμβάνοι ἰατρικοὺς εἶναι, κἂν εἰ βουλοίμεθα διανοίγοντες τοὺς ὀφθαλμοὺς ἐμπάσαι τῆς τέφρας, οἶμαι οὐκ ἂν κωλύσειεν, ἡγούμενος ὀρθῶς φρονεῖν. |

Ἀληθῆ λέγεις.

Ἆρ' οὖν καὶ τἆλλα πάντα ἡμῖν ἐπιτρέποι ἂν μᾶλλον ἢ ἑαυτῷ καὶ τῷ ὑεῖ, περὶ ὅσων ἂν δόξωμεν αὐτῷ σοφώτεροι ἐκείνων εἶναι;

Ἀνάγκη, ἔφη, ὦ Σώκρατες.

b   Οὕτως ἄρα ἔχει, ἦν δ' ἐγώ, ὦ φίλε Λύσι· εἰς μὲν ταῦτα, ἃ ἂν φρόνιμοι γενώμεθα, ἅπαντες ἡμῖν ἐπιτρέψουσιν, Ἕλληνές τε καὶ βάρβαροι καὶ ἄνδρες καὶ γυναῖκες, ποιήσομέν τε ἐν τούτοις ὅτι ἂν βουλώμεθα, καὶ οὐδεὶς ἡμᾶς ἑκὼν εἶναι ἐμποδιεῖ, ἀλλ' αὐτοί τε ἐλεύθεροι ἐσόμεθα ἐν αὐτοῖς καὶ | ἄλλων ἄρχοντες, ἡμέτερά τε ταῦτα ἔσται—ὀνησόμεθα γὰρ ἀπ' αὐτῶν—

---

19 Plato possibly has in mind here the use of *tephra* (ash) as a treatment for eye disease (according to pseud. Aristotle, *Mira-*

"And he wouldn't allow him to add even the smallest amount, but he would allow us, even if we wished to take salt by the handful, and throw it in."

"Of course."

"But what if his son had some trouble with his eyes, would he allow him to touch his own eyes, if he didn't consider him to be trained in medicine, or would he prevent him?"

"He'd prevent him."

210

"But if he supposed *we* were medical experts, even if we wanted to open his eyes and sprinkle ashes on them, I don't think he'd stop us even then, because he would think we had the right idea."[19]

"You're right."

"So would he therefore entrust everything else to us rather than to himself and his son, in however many respects we would appear to him to be wiser than they were?"

"It must be so, Socrates," he said.

"Then that's how it is, my dear Lysis, I said. With regard to those things in which we develop our understanding, everybody will entrust them to us, both Greeks and non-Greeks, men and women, and in them we shall do whatever we wish and no one will deliberately get in our way, but we ourselves shall have a free hand in these matters, and be rulers of others: these things shall be ours—for we shall profit from them—but with regard to those things

b

bilia 834b30). The point of these examples from cookery and medicine is that they require expert application (involving knowledge and understanding) to be effective.

εἰς ἃ δ' ἂν νοῦν μὴ κτησώμεθα, οὔτε τις ἡμῖν ἐπι-
c τρέψει περὶ αὐτὰ ποιεῖν τὰ ἡμῖν δοκοῦντα, ἀλλ' ἐμπο-
διοῦσι πάντες καθ' ὅτι ἂν δύνωνται, οὐ μόνον οἱ
ἀλλότριοι, ἀλλὰ καὶ ὁ πατὴρ καὶ ἡ μήτηρ καὶ εἴ τι
τούτων οἰκειότερόν ἐστιν, αὐτοί τε ἐν αὑτοῖς ἐσόμεθα
ἄλλων ὑπήκοοι, καὶ ἡμῖν ἔσται ἀλλότρια· οὐδὲν γὰρ
ἀπ' αὐτῶν ὀνησόμεθα. συγχωρεῖς | οὕτως ἔχειν;

Συγχωρῶ.

Ἆρ' οὖν τῳ φίλοι ἐσόμεθα καί τις ἡμᾶς φιλήσει
ἐν τούτοις, ἐν οἷς ἂν ὦμεν ἀνωφελεῖς;

Οὐ δῆτα, ἔφη.

Νῦν ἄρα οὐδὲ σὲ ὁ πατὴρ οὐδὲ ἄλλος ἄλλον οὐδένα
φιλεῖ, καθ' ὅσον ἂν ᾖ ἄχρηστος.

Οὐκ ἔοικεν, ἔφη.

d Ἐὰν μὲν ἄρα σοφὸς γένῃ, ὦ παῖ, πάντες σοι φίλοι
καὶ πάντες σοι οἰκεῖοι ἔσονται—χρήσιμος γὰρ καὶ
ἀγαθὸς ἔσῃ—εἰ δὲ μή, σοὶ οὔτε ἄλλος οὐδεὶς οὔτε ὁ
πατὴρ φίλος ἔσται οὔτε ἡ μήτηρ οὔτε οἱ οἰκεῖοι. οἷόν
τε οὖν ἐπὶ τούτοις, | ὦ Λύσι, μέγα φρονεῖν, ἐν οἷς τις
μήπω φρονεῖ;

Καὶ πῶς ἄν; ἔφη.

Εἰ δ' ἄρα σὺ διδασκάλου δέῃ, οὔπω φρονεῖς.

Ἀληθῆ.

Οὐδ' ἄρα μεγαλόφρων εἶ, εἴπερ ἄφρων ἔτι.

---

[20] "Belong to you," "be close to you" = *oikeios* (*oikeioi* = in
conventional Greek, "relations"). For the move in the argument

where we do not acquire understanding, no one will hand them over to us to do with them what we think is right, but all will obstruct us, as far as they can, not only strang- c ers, but also our father and mother, and anything else in a closer relationship to us than these ; in fact in these cases we ourselves will be subjects of others, and these things will be foreign to us, for we shall gain no advantage from them. Do you agree that this is the case?"

"Yes, I do."

"Shall we then be friends to anyone, and will anyone love us in those things in which we are of no benefit?"

"Certainly not," he said.

"So in that case, neither does your father love you, nor does anybody else love anyone else in as far as he is useless."

"It doesn't look like it," he said.

"If then you become wise, my boy, all will be your d friends and all will belong to you—for you will be useful and good—but if not, no one else will be your friend (*philos*), neither your father, nor your mother, nor those that belong to you.[20] Therefore is it possible, Lysis, to have serious thoughts about those things in which one does not yet have any understanding?"

"How could it be?" he said.

"If then you need a teacher, you don't yet have any understanding."

"True."

"Then you're not a serious thinker, if you are still thoughtless."

closely linking love and friendship with benefit (210c6–d8), see Introduction, §3(i).

PLATO

Μὰ Δία, ἔφη, ὦ Σώκρατες, οὔ μοι δοκεῖ.

e   Καὶ ἐγὼ ἀκούσας αὐτοῦ ἀπέβλεψα πρὸς τὸν Ἱπ-
ποθάλη, καὶ ὀλίγου ἐξήμαρτον· ἐπῆλθε γάρ μοι εἰπεῖν
ὅτι Οὕτω χρή, ὦ Ἱππόθαλες, τοῖς παιδικοῖς διαλέγεσθαι, ταπεινοῦντα καὶ συστέλλοντα, ἀλλὰ μὴ ὥσπερ
σὺ χαυνοῦντα καὶ διαθρύπτοντα. | κατιδὼν οὖν αὐτὸν
ἀγωνιῶντα καὶ τεθορυβημένον ὑπὸ τῶν λεγομένων,
ἀνεμνήσθην ὅτι καὶ προσεστὼς λανθάνειν τὸν Λύσιν
ἐβούλετο· ἀνέλαβον οὖν ἐμαυτὸν καὶ ἐπέσχον τοῦ λό-
211 γου. καὶ ἐν τούτῳ ὁ Μενέξενος πάλιν ἦκεν, καὶ ἐκαθέ-
ζετο παρὰ τὸν Λύσιν, ὅθεν καὶ ἐξανέστη. ὁ οὖν Λύσις
μάλα παιδικῶς καὶ φιλικῶς, λάθρα τοῦ Μενεξένου,
σμικρὸν πρός με λέγων ἔφη· Ὦ Σώκρατες, ἅπερ καὶ
ἐμοὶ | λέγεις, εἰπὲ καὶ Μενεξένῳ.

Καὶ ἐγὼ εἶπον, Ταῦτα μὲν σὺ αὐτῷ ἐρεῖς, ὦ Λύσι·
πάντως γὰρ προσεῖχες τὸν νοῦν.

Πάνυ μὲν οὖν, ἔφη.

Πειρῶ τοίνυν, ἦν δ' ἐγώ, ἀπομνημονεῦσαι αὐτὰ ὅτι
b   μάλιστα, ἵνα τούτῳ σαφῶς πάντα εἴπῃς· ἐὰν δέ τι
αὐτῶν ἐπιλάθῃ, αὖθίς με ἀνερέσθαι ὅταν ἐντύχῃς
πρῶτον.

Ἀλλὰ ποιήσω, ἔφη, ταῦτα, ὦ Σώκρατες, πάνυ σφόδρα, εὖ ἴσθι. ἀλλά τι ἄλλο αὐτῷ λέγε, ἵνα καὶ ἐγὼ
ἀκούω, | ἕως ἂν οἴκαδε ὥρα ᾖ ἀπιέναι.

Ἀλλὰ χρὴ ποιεῖν ταῦτα, ἦν δ' ἐγώ, ἐπειδή γε καὶ
σὺ κελεύεις. ἀλλὰ ὅρα ὅπως ἐπικουρήσεις μοι, ἐάν με
ἐλέγχειν ἐπιχειρῇ ὁ Μενέξενος· ἢ οὐκ οἶσθα ὅτι ἐρι-
στικός ἐστιν;

"By Zeus Socrates," he said, "I don't think I am."

Hearing him, I looked across at Hippothales and nearly e
made a blunder. For it occurred to me to say that "this is
how you must converse with a beloved, Hippothales, hum-
bling and putting him down, but not the way you do, filling
him with conceit and spoiling him." Well, noticing that he
was distressed and bewildered by what we had been saying, I remembered that he didn't want Lysis to notice even
that he was standing there. So I pulled myself together and
held back what I was about to say. Meanwhile Menexenus 211
had come back again and sat down from where he had got
up, next to Lysis. Then Lysis in a very playful and friendly
way, unobserved by Menexenus, said in a low voice to me:
"Socrates, tell Menexenus as well what you are saying to
me."

And I said: "you'll tell him that yourself, Lysis; after all
you were paying full attention."

"I certainly was," he said.

"So then," I said, "try to recall it as best you can, so that
you can tell him everything clearly. But if you forget any- b
thing, you can ask me again next time you happen to meet
me."

"Well I shall do that, Socrates, most certainly: be well
assured. But tell him something else so that I too can hear
it, until it's time to go back home."

"Well I must do this," I said, "since it's you who are
telling me to. But see that you'll come to my aid if Menexenus tries to refute me. Or don't you know that he's disputatious."

Ναὶ μὰ Δία, ἔφη, σφόδρα γε· διὰ ταῦτά τοι καὶ
βούλομαί σε αὐτῷ διαλέγεσθαι.

c   "Ινα, ἦν δ' ἐγώ, καταγέλαστος γένωμαι;

Οὐ μὰ Δία, ἔφη, ἀλλ' ἵνα αὐτὸν κολάσῃς.

Πόθεν; ἦν δ' ἐγώ. οὐ ῥᾴδιον· δεινὸς γὰρ ὁ ἄνθρω-
πος, | Κτησίππου μαθητής. πάρεστι δέ τοι αὐτός—
οὐχ ὁρᾷς;—Κτήσιππος.

Μηδενός σοι, ἔφη, μελέτω, ὦ Σώκρατες, ἀλλ' ἴθι
διαλέγου αὐτῷ.

Διαλεκτέον, ἦν δ' ἐγώ. |

Ταῦτα οὖν ἡμῶν λεγόντων πρὸς ἡμᾶς αὐτούς, Τί
ὑμεῖς, ἔφη ὁ Κτήσιππος, αὐτὼ μόνω ἑστιᾶσθον, ἡμῖν
δὲ οὐ μεταδίδοτον τῶν λόγων;

d   Ἀλλὰ μήν, ἦν δ' ἐγώ, μεταδοτέον. ὅδε γάρ τι ὧν
λέγω οὐ μανθάνει, ἀλλά φησιν οἴεσθαι Μενέξενον
εἰδέναι, καὶ κελεύει τοῦτον ἐρωτᾶν. |

Τί οὖν, ἦ δ' ὅς, οὐκ ἐρωτᾷς;

Ἀλλ' ἐρήσομαι, ἦν δ' ἐγώ. καί μοι εἰπέ, ὦ Μενέξενε,
ὃ ἄν σε ἔρωμαι. τυγχάνω γὰρ ἐκ παιδὸς ἐπιθυμῶν
κτήματός του, ὥσπερ ἄλλος ἄλλου. ὁ μὲν γάρ τις
ἵππους ἐπιθυμεῖ κτᾶσθαι, ὁ δὲ κύνας, ὁ δὲ χρυσίον, ὁ
e δὲ τιμάς· ἐγὼ δὲ πρὸς μὲν ταῦτα πρᾴως ἔχω, πρὸς δὲ
τὴν τῶν φίλων κτῆσιν πάνυ ἐρωτικῶς, καὶ βουλοίμην
ἄν μοι φίλον ἀγαθὸν γενέσθαι μᾶλλον ἢ τὸν ἄριστον
ἐν ἀνθρώποις ὄρτυγα ἢ | ἀλεκτρυόνα, καὶ ναὶ μὰ Δία
ἔγωγε μᾶλλον ἢ ἵππον τε καὶ κύνα—οἶμαι δέ, νὴ τὸν

---

21 Note the assumption by Lysis that the discussion is adver-

"Yes I do, by Zeus," he said, "very much so. That's precisely why I want you to talk to him."

"For me to make a fool of myself?" I said.   c

"No, by Zeus," he said, "but so you can give him a thrashing."[21]

"How come?" I said. "It's not easy. You see he's a formidable fellow, a student of Ctesippus. But here's the man himself: can't you see him?—Ctesippus."

"Don't worry about anyone, Socrates," he said. "Just go and talk to him."

"I must talk to him," I said.

Now while we were talking to each other, Ctesippus said: "Why are you two celebrating alone and not sharing your discussion with us?"

"Of course, I said, you must join in. You see there's   d something of what we're saying that this lad here doesn't understand, but he says he thinks Menexenus knows about it and is telling me to ask him."

"So," he said, "why don't you ask him?"

"Well I shall," I said. "Now do tell me, Menexenus, whatever I ask you. You see, ever since I was a boy it so happens that I've had a desire to have a certain possession, just as one person desires one thing, another something else. For example one person desires to possess horses, another dogs, another money, another honors; but I'm not   e very keen on these things, but I am very passionate about acquiring friends and I would rather wish for a good friend than have the best quail or cock in the world, and, by Zeus, even more than a horse or a dog—and I think, by the Dog,

sarial and the primary aim is to defeat an opponent in argument. Characterization of Menexenus as "disputatious" (*eristikos*: 211b8) is not borne out by his role in the subsequent discussion.

κύνα, μᾶλλον ἢ τὸ Δαρείου χρυσίον κτήσασθαι δε-
ξαίμην πολὺ πρότερον ἑταῖρον, μᾶλλον ⟨δὲ⟩ ἢ αὐτὸν
212   Δαρεῖον[1]—οὕτως ἐγὼ φιλέταιρός τίς εἰμι. ὑμᾶς οὖν
ὁρῶν, σέ τε καὶ Λύσιν, ἐκπέπληγμαι καὶ εὐδαιμονίζω
ὅτι οὕτω νέοι ὄντες οἷοί τ' ἐστὸν τοῦτο τὸ κτῆμα ταχὺ
καὶ ῥᾳδίως κτᾶσθαι, καὶ σύ τε τοῦτον οὕτω φίλον
ἐκτήσω ταχύ τε καὶ σφόδρα, καὶ αὖ οὗτος σέ· ἐγὼ δὲ
οὕτω πόρρω εἰμὶ | τοῦ κτήματος, ὥστε οὐδ' ὅντινα
τρόπον γίγνεται φίλος ἕτερος ἑτέρου οἶδα, ἀλλὰ
ταῦτα δὴ αὐτά σε βούλομαι ἐρέσθαι ἅτε ἔμπειρον.

Καί μοι εἰπέ· ἐπειδάν τίς τινα φιλῇ, πότερος ποτέ-
b   ρου φίλος γίγνεται, ὁ φιλῶν τοῦ φιλουμένου ἢ ὁ φιλούμενος τοῦ φιλοῦντος· ἢ οὐδὲν διαφέρει;

Οὐδέν, ἔφη, ἔμοιγε δοκεῖ διαφέρειν.

Πῶς λέγεις; ἦν δ' ἐγώ· ἀμφότεροι ἄρα ἀλλήλων
φίλοι γίγνονται, ἐὰν μόνος ὁ ἕτερος τὸν ἕτερον | φιλῇ;

Ἔμοιγε, ἔφη, δοκεῖ.

---

[1] μᾶλλον ἢ αὐτὸν Δαρεῖον secl. Schanz

---

[22] This final phrase has been suspected as an interpolation
(see textual note), but Penner and Rowe point out (42n10) that
getting possession of an individual fits well into the context of
acquiring friends at 211d6ff. "By the Dog" (e6) is a favorite oath
of Socrates, also found in Old Comedy, possibly related to the
dog-headed Egyptian god Anubis (see *Gorgias* 482b5).

[23] An admission of ignorance in the face of the interlocutor's
alleged expertise is a common Socratic ploy as a preliminary to
an *elenchus* (see, e.g., *Euthyphro* 5cff.).

[24] In order to understand why Menexenus thinks it reasonable
to reply in the way he does and to follow the subsequent argu-

rather than acquire Darius' gold I would much rather get a companion, more than getting Darius himself[22]—I'm such a lover of a friend. That's why on seeing you, both you and Lysis, I am astounded and count you happy because being so young the two of you are able to acquire this possession quickly and easily, and you have got such a friend as this one so quickly and assuredly, and moreover he has you. But I am so far from having the possession that I don't know in what manner one individual becomes a friend (*philos*) of another. But these are the very questions I want to ask you about, in that you are experienced.[23]

212

"So tell me: when anyone is in love with someone, which one becomes a friend of which? The lover of the loved one, or the loved one of the lover, or is there no difference?"

b

"It seems to me," he said, "that there is no difference."

"What do you mean?" I said. "Do both then become friends of each other, if only one of the two loves the other?"

"It seems so to me," he said.[24]

ment, we need to appreciate that, for him (and for the average contemporary Greek), if x loves, or feels friendly toward y, the term *philos* will apply to both x and y, but operating in two ways: (1) the "subjective:" x is *philos* because he loves (feels friendly toward) y; (2) the "objective:" y is *philos* because he (the object of friendship) is loved by x, whether he loves (feels friendly) in return or not. In addition, *philos* may indicate a mutual relationship: both are *philoi* because they love (feel friendly toward) each other. See Introduction, §3(ii) on how this potentially confusing ambiguity in the meaning of *philos* relates to the argument of 212a8–13d2. For the range of words in Greek denoting "friendship/love/erotic desire," see General Introduction, §2.

Τί δέ; οὐκ ἔστιν φιλοῦντα μὴ ἀντιφιλεῖσθαι ὑπὸ τούτου ὃν ἂν φιλῇ;

Ἔστιν.

Τί δέ; ἆρα ἔστιν καὶ μισεῖσθαι φιλοῦντα; οἷόν που ἐνίοτε δοκοῦσι καὶ οἱ ἐρασταὶ πάσχειν πρὸς τὰ παιδικά· φιλοῦντες γὰρ ὡς οἷόν τε μάλιστα οἱ μὲν οἴονται οὐκ ἀντιφιλεῖσθαι, οἱ δὲ καὶ μισεῖσθαι. ἢ οὐκ ἀληθὲς δοκεῖ σοι τοῦτο;

Σφόδρα γε, ἔφη, ἀληθές.

Οὐκοῦν ἐν τῷ τοιούτῳ, ἦν δ᾽ ἐγώ, ὁ μὲν φιλεῖ, ὁ δὲ φιλεῖται;

Ναί.

Πότερος οὖν αὐτῶν | ποτέρου φίλος ἐστίν; ὁ φιλῶν τοῦ φιλουμένου, ἐάντε καὶ ἀντιφιλῆται ἐάντε καὶ μισῆται, ἢ ὁ φιλούμενος τοῦ φιλοῦντος; ἢ οὐδέτερος αὖ ἐν τῷ τοιούτῳ οὐδετέρου φίλος ἐστίν, ἂν μὴ ἀμφότεροι ἀλλήλους φιλῶσιν;

Ἔοικε γοῦν οὕτως ἔχειν.

Ἀλλοίως ἄρα νῦν ἡμῖν δοκεῖ ἢ πρότερον ἔδοξεν. τότε μὲν γάρ, εἰ ὁ ἕτερος φιλοῖ, φίλω εἶναι ἄμφω· νῦν δέ, ἂν μὴ ἀμφότεροι φιλῶσιν, οὐδέτερος φίλος.

Κινδυνεύει, ἔφη.

Οὐκ ἄρα ἔστιν φίλον τῷ φιλοῦντι οὐδὲν μὴ | οὐκ ἀντιφιλοῦν.

Οὐκ ἔοικεν.

---

[25] *Erastai: erastēs* here having the same function as *ho philōn* (b1) in sense (1) in the previous note.

"What then? Isn't it possible for a lover not to be loved in return by the one he loves?"

"It is."

"And what then? Is it also possible for the one who loves to be hated even? The sort of thing I imagine lovers[25] seem to suffer sometimes at the hands of their loved one. For while loving to the extent of their ability, some lovers think they are not loved in return, others that they are even hated. Or do you not think that this is true?"   c

"It's very true," he said.

"Therefore in such a situation," I said, "the one loves and the other is loved, isn't he?"

"Yes."

"Then which one of them is the friend (*philos*) of which? The one who loves with the one who is loved, whether he is loved in return, or is even hated, or is the one who is loved the friend of the one who loves? Or again in such a situation is neither the friend of the other, unless both of them love each other?"

"That seems to be the case, at any rate."

"So now it certainly seems different from before. For   d previously if one of the two was in love, they were both friends. But now unless both are in love, neither is a friend."

"Quite possibly," he said.

"Then nothing is actually a friend to the one loving if it does not love in return."[26]

"It doesn't seem so."

[26] Note that in discussing in this section the argument of the relationships of those who are and are not *philoi*, Socrates appears to shift without warning from masculine to neuter: "loved one" and "loved thing" (as in d4ff.).

Οὐδ' ἄρα φίλιπποί εἰσιν οὓς ἂν οἱ ἵπποι μὴ ἀντι-
φιλῶσιν, οὐδὲ φιλόρτυγες, οὐδ' αὖ φιλόκυνές γε καὶ
φίλοινοι καὶ φιλογυμνασταὶ καὶ φιλόσοφοι, ἂν μὴ ἡ
e σοφία αὐτοὺς ἀντιφιλῇ. ἢ φιλοῦσι μὲν ταῦτα ἕκαστοι, οὐ μέντοι φίλα ὄντα, ἀλλὰ ψεύδεθ' ὁ ποιητής,
ὃς ἔφη

ὄλβιος, ᾧ παῖδές τε φίλοι καὶ μώνυχες ἵπποι
καὶ κύνες ἀγρευταὶ καὶ ξένος ἀλλοδαπός; |

Οὐκ ἔμοιγε δοκεῖ, ἦ δ' ὅς.
Ἀλλ' ἀληθῆ δοκεῖ λέγειν σοι;
Ναί.

Τὸ φιλούμενον ἄρα τῷ φιλοῦντι φίλον ἐστίν, ὡς
ἔοικεν, ὦ Μενέξενε, ἐάντε φιλῇ ἐάντε καὶ μισῇ· οἷον
καὶ τὰ νεωστὶ γεγονότα παιδία, τὰ μὲν οὐδέπω φιλοῦντα, τὰ δὲ καὶ μισοῦντα, ὅταν κολάζηται ὑπὸ τῆς
213 μητρὸς ἢ ὑπὸ τοῦ πατρός, ὅμως καὶ μισοῦντα ἐν
ἐκείνῳ τῷ χρόνῳ πάντων μάλιστά ἐστι τοῖς γονεῦσι
φίλτατα.

Ἔμοιγε δοκεῖ, ἔφη, οὕτως ἔχειν.
Οὐκ ἄρα ὁ φιλῶν φίλος ἐκ τούτου τοῦ λόγου, | ἀλλ'
ὁ φιλούμενος.
Ἔοικεν.
Καὶ ὁ μισούμενος ἐχθρὸς ἄρα, ἀλλ' οὐχ ὁ μισῶν.
Φαίνεται.

Πολλοὶ ἄρα ὑπὸ τῶν ἐχθρῶν φιλοῦνται, ὑπὸ δὲ τῶν
φίλων μισοῦνται, καὶ τοῖς μὲν ἐχθροῖς φίλοι εἰσίν,
b τοῖς δὲ φίλοις ἐχθροί, εἰ τὸ φιλούμενον φίλον ἐστὶν

"Then there are no horse lovers whom the horses don't love in return, nor quail lovers, nor again dog lovers and wine lovers and exercise lovers and wisdom lovers, if wisdom does not love them in return. Or do they each love   e these things, though these things are not friends, but did the poet lie, who said:

Blessed is he who has as his friends (*philoi*) children
    and hoofed horses
And hunting dogs and a host abroad?"[27]

"I don't think so," he said.
"But do you think he's telling the truth?"
"Yes."
"In that case, that which is loved is a friend to the one loving, it seems, Menexenus, whether it loves him or even if it hates him. For example, recently born children some of whom do not yet love and some also who actually hate when they are punished by their mother or by their father, nevertheless even at that time when they hate are espe-   213 cially most loved by their parents."

"It seems to be so to me," he said.
"Then by this argument it's not the one loving who is a friend but the one loved."
"It seems so."
"And it's the one hated who is an enemy then, not he who hates."
"He appears to be"
"Then many are loved by their enemies, but hated by those who are their friends, and they are friendly to their enemies and hostile to their friends, if that which is loved   b

27 Solon fr. 23 Edmonds (*Elegy and Iambus*).

PLATO

ἀλλὰ μὴ τὸ φιλοῦν. καίτοι πολλὴ ἀλογία, ὦ φίλε
ἑταῖρε, μᾶλλον δὲ οἶμαι καὶ ἀδύνατον, τῷ τε φίλῳ
ἐχθρὸν καὶ τῷ ἐχθρῷ φίλον εἶναι.

Ἀληθῆ, ἔφη, | ἔοικας λέγειν, ὦ Σώκρατες.

Οὐκοῦν εἰ τοῦτ᾽ ἀδύνατον, τὸ φιλοῦν ἂν εἴη φίλον
τοῦ φιλουμένου.

Φαίνεται.

Τὸ μισοῦν ἄρα πάλιν ἐχθρὸν τοῦ μισουμένου.

Ἀνάγκη.

Οὐκοῦν ταὐτὰ ἡμῖν συμβήσεται ἀναγκαῖον εἶναι
c ὁμολογεῖν, ἅπερ ἐπὶ τῶν πρότερον, πολλάκις φίλον
εἶναι μὴ φίλου, πολλάκις δὲ καὶ ἐχθροῦ, ὅταν ἢ μὴ
φιλοῦν τις φιλῇ ἢ καὶ μισοῦν φιλῇ· πολλάκις δ᾽
ἐχθρὸν εἶναι μὴ ἐχθροῦ ἢ καὶ φίλου, ὅταν ἢ <μὴ>
μισοῦν τις μισῇ ἢ καὶ φιλοῦν μισῇ. |

Κινδυνεύει, ἔφη.

Τί οὖν δὴ χρησώμεθα, ἦν δ᾽ ἐγώ, εἰ μήτε οἱ φιλοῦντες φίλοι ἔσονται μήτε οἱ φιλούμενοι μήτε οἱ φιλοῦν-
τές τε καὶ φιλούμενοι; ἀλλὰ καὶ παρὰ ταῦτα ἄλλους
τινὰς ἔτι φήσομεν εἶναι φίλους ἀλλήλοις γιγνομέ-
νους;

Οὐ μὰ τὸν Δία, ἔφη, ὦ Σώκρατες, οὐ πάνυ εὐπορῶ
ἔγωγε.

d Ἆρα μή, ἦν δ᾽ ἐγώ, ὦ Μενέξενε, τὸ παράπαν οὐκ
ὀρθῶς ἐζητοῦμεν;

Οὐκ ἔμοιγε δοκεῖ, ὦ Σώκρατες, ἔφη, ὁ Λύσις, καὶ
ἅμα εἰπὼν ἠρυθρίασεν· ἐδόκει γάρ μοι ἄκοντ᾽ αὐτὸν
ἐκφεύγειν τὸ λεχθὲν διὰ τὸ σφόδρα προσέχειν τὸν

62

is the friend, but not that which loves. Yet this is quite absurd, my dear friend, or rather I think it's actually impossible to be an enemy to a friend and friend to an enemy."

"You appear to be telling the truth, Socrates."

"If this then is impossible, it is that which loves which would be friend of what is loved."

"It appears so."

"Then conversely that which hates would be enemy of what is hated."

"It must be so."

"Therefore it will turn out that we must be in agreement with the same things as we did before: often one is   c
a friend of what is not a friend, often of an enemy too, when someone either loves what does not love, or one loves that which even hates. And often one can be an enemy of what is not an enemy, or even a friend, when one hates that which does not hate, or hates that which is actually a friend."

"Possibly so," he said

"What then shall we make of it," I said, "if neither those who love will be friends, nor those who are loved, nor those who love and are loved? But are there any others also in addition to this who we shall still say become friends with each other?"

"No, by Zeus, Socrates," he said, "I really can't see my way out of it."

"Can it be, Menexenus," I said, "that we were not ac-   d
tually making our inquiry in the right way at all?"

"I don't think we were, Socrates," said Lysis. And as he spoke he blushed. For it seemed to me that the words escaped him involuntarily on account of his intense atten-

νοῦν | τοῖς λεγομένοις, δῆλος δ᾽ ἦν καὶ ὅτε ἠκροᾶτο οὕτως ἔχων.

Ἐγὼ οὖν βουλόμενος τόν τε Μενέξενον ἀναπαῦσαι καὶ ἐκείνου ἡσθεὶς τῇ φιλοσοφίᾳ, οὕτω μεταβαλὼν πρὸς τὸν Λύσιν ἐποιούμην τοὺς λόγους, καὶ εἶπον· e   Ὦ Λύσι, ἀληθῆ μοι δοκεῖς λέγειν ὅτι εἰ ὀρθῶς ἡμεῖς ἐσκοποῦμεν, οὐκ ἄν ποτε οὕτως ἐπλανώμεθα.

Ἀλλὰ ταύτῃ μὲν μηκέτι ἴωμεν—καὶ γὰρ χαλεπή τίς μοι φαίνεται ὥσπερ ὁδὸς ἡ σκέψις—ᾗ | δὲ ἐτράπημεν, δοκεῖ μοι χρῆναι ἰέναι, σκοποῦντα [τὰ] κατὰ 214   τοὺς ποιητάς· οὗτοι γὰρ ἡμῖν ὥσπερ πατέρες τῆς σοφίας εἰσὶν καὶ ἡγεμόνες. λέγουσι δὲ δήπου οὐ φαύλως ἀποφαινόμενοι περὶ τῶν φίλων, οἳ τυγχάνουσιν ὄντες· ἀλλὰ τὸν θεὸν αὐτόν φασιν ποιεῖν φίλους αὐτούς, ἄγοντα παρ᾽ ἀλλήλους. | λέγουσι δέ πως ταῦτα, ὡς ἐγῷμαι, ὡδί,

αἰεί τοι τὸν ὁμοῖον ἄγει θεὸς ὡς τὸν ὁμοῖον

καὶ ποιεῖ γνώριμον· ἢ οὐκ ἐντετύχηκας τούτοις τοῖς ἔπεσιν;

b   Ἔγωγ᾽, ἔφη.

Οὐκοῦν καὶ τοῖς τῶν σοφωτάτων συγγράμμασιν ἐντετύχηκας ταῦτα αὐτὰ λέγουσιν, ὅτι τὸ ὅμοιον τῷ ὁμοίῳ ἀνάγκη ἀεὶ φίλον εἶναι; εἰσὶν δέ που οὗτοι οἱ περὶ | φύσεώς τε καὶ τοῦ ὅλου διαλεγόμενοι καὶ γράφοντες.

---

[28] An adaptation of Homer, *Odyssey* 17.218. Reference to

tion to what was being said. It was clear this was so too, all the while he was listening.

As I wanted therefore to give Menexenus a break, and being delighted by Lysis' interest in philosophy, for that reason I changed tack and directed my remarks to Lysis and said: "Lysis, I think you are right in saying that if we e were conducting our inquiry correctly, we would never have gone so far astray as we have now.

"Well let's not go down that route any more—for the inquiry seems to me difficult, like a rough road—I think we ought to go to where we turned off; we must look at things as the poets see them. For these are like fathers and 214 leaders to us in their wisdom. They speak, I suppose, in no insignificant way in what they reveal about friends, who they really are; but they do say it's god himself who makes them friends, by bringing them together. They express this, I think, something like as follows:

God always leads like to like[28]

and makes them known to each other. Or have you not come across these lines?"

"Yes, I have," he said. b

"So have you also come across the writings of the wisest men saying these same things: that like is of necessity always a friend to like? These are the ones, I believe, who talk and write about both nature and the universe."[29]

"god" is nonspecific ("a deity"). For the two arguments of 213d6–16b9, see Introduction, §§3(iii) and (iv).

[29] For example, Democritus, DK 68B164, quoted by Sextus Empiricus, *adv. math.* VII 117 (see Waterfield, 184–85). Also, if we include writers in verse, Empedocles' *Philia* (Love) is a divine force that unites similars, see DK 68B20ff. (Waterfield, 147–49).

Ἀληθῆ, ἔφη, λέγεις.

Ἆρ᾽ οὖν, ἦν δ᾽ ἐγώ, εὖ λέγουσιν;

Ἴσως, ἔφη.

Ἴσως, ἦν δ᾽ ἐγώ, τὸ ἥμισυ αὐτοῦ, ἴσως δὲ καὶ πᾶν, ἀλλ᾽ ἡμεῖς οὐ συνίεμεν. δοκεῖ γὰρ ἡμῖν ὅ γε πονηρὸς τῷ πονηρῷ, ὅσῳ ἂν ἐγγυτέρω προσίῃ καὶ μᾶλλον c ὁμιλῇ, τοσούτῳ ἐχθίων γίγνεσθαι. ἀδικεῖ γάρ· ἀδικοῦντας δὲ καὶ ἀδικουμένους ἀδύνατόν που φίλους εἶναι. οὐχ οὕτως;

Ναί, ἦ δ᾽ ὅς.

Ταύτῃ μὲν ἂν τοίνυν τοῦ λεγομένου τὸ ἥμισυ οὐκ | ἀληθὲς εἴη, εἴπερ οἱ πονηροὶ ἀλλήλοις ὅμοιοι.

Ἀληθῆ λέγεις.

Ἀλλά μοι δοκοῦσιν λέγειν τοὺς ἀγαθοὺς ὁμοίους εἶναι ἀλλήλοις καὶ φίλους, τοὺς δὲ κακούς, ὅπερ καὶ λέγεται περὶ αὐτῶν, μηδέποτε ὁμοίους μηδ᾽ αὐτοὺς d αὐτοῖς εἶναι, ἀλλ᾽ ἐμπλήκτους τε καὶ ἀσταθμήτους· ὃ δὲ αὐτὸ αὑτῷ ἀνόμοιον εἴη καὶ διάφορον, σχολῇ γέ τῳ ἄλλῳ ὅμοιον ἢ φίλον γένοιτ᾽ ἄν. ἢ οὐ καὶ σοὶ δοκεῖ οὕτως;

Ἔμοιγ᾽, ἔφη.

Τοῦτο τοίνυν αἰνίττονται, ὡς ἐμοὶ δοκοῦσιν, ὦ ἑταῖρε, οἱ τὸ ὅμοιον | τῷ ὁμοίῳ φίλον λέγοντες, ὡς ὁ ἀγαθὸς τῷ ἀγαθῷ μόνος μόνῳ φίλος, ὁ δὲ κακὸς οὔτε ἀγαθῷ οὔτε κακῷ οὐδέποτε εἰς ἀληθῆ φιλίαν ἔρχεται. συνδοκεῖ σοι;

---

[30] See Plato, *Republic* 9.588cff. citing the complex many-

"What you say is true," he said.

"And are they correct then?" I said.

"Perhaps," he said.

"Perhaps half of it; perhaps all of it too," I said, "only we're not understanding it. For it seems to us that in fact the evil person, the closer he approaches an evil person and the more he has dealings with him, the more he becomes his enemy. You see he does him wrong. It is, I imagine, impossible for those who do wrong and those who are wronged to be friends. Is that not so?" c

"Yes," he said.

"Looked at like this, then, half of what's been said would not be true, if evil people are like each other."

"What you say is true."

"But to me they seem to be saying that the good are like each other, and are friends, but the bad, as a saying also goes about them, can never be alike, not even to themselves, but are capricious and unstable.[30] And what is itself unlike and at variance with itself would hardly become like, or a friend to anything else. Or does it not seem to be so to you?" d

"It does to me," he said.

"This then is what they are saying in a riddling way, as it seems to me my friend, those who say that like is a friend to like: that the good person alone is only friend to the good person alone, while a bad person never enters into a true friendship with either the good or the bad person. Do you agree?"

headed mythical beast, the Chimera, as an image of the instability of the evil man (in this case the tyrant). For the statement that like is friend to like, and bad never makes friends with bad, see *Phaedrus* 255b1–2.

Κατένευσεν.

Ἔχομεν ἄρα ἤδη τίνες εἰσὶν οἱ φίλοι· ὁ γὰρ λόγος
ἡμῖν σημαίνει ὅτι οἳ ἂν ὦσιν ἀγαθοί.

e   Πάνυ γε, ἔφη, δοκεῖ.

Καὶ ἐμοί, ἦν δ᾽ ἐγώ. καίτοι δυσχεραίνω τί γε ἐν
αὐτῷ· φέρε οὖν, ὦ πρὸς Διός, ἴδωμεν τί καὶ ὑποπτεύω.
ὁ ὅμοιος τῷ ὁμοίῳ καθ᾽ ὅσον ὅμοιος φίλος, καὶ ἔστιν
χρήσιμος ὁ | τοιοῦτος τῷ τοιούτῳ; μᾶλλον δὲ ὧδε·
ὁτιοῦν ὅμοιον ὁτῳοῦν ὁμοίῳ τίνα ὠφελίαν ἔχειν ἢ τίνα
βλάβην ἂν ποιῆσαι δύναιτο, ὃ μὴ καὶ αὐτὸ αὑτῷ; ἢ
215   τί ἂν παθεῖν, ὃ μὴ καὶ ὑφ᾽ αὑτοῦ πάθοι; τὰ δὴ τοιαῦτα
πῶς ἂν ὑπ᾽ ἀλλήλων ἀγαπηθείη, μηδεμίαν ἐπικουρίαν
ἀλλήλοις ἔχοντα; ἔστιν ὅπως;

Οὐκ ἔστιν.

Ὁ δὲ μὴ ἀγαπῷτο, πῶς φίλον;

Οὐδαμῶς.

Ἀλλὰ δὴ ὁ μὲν ὅμοιος τῷ ὁμοίῳ οὐ φίλος· ὁ δὲ
ἀγαθὸς τῷ ἀγαθῷ | καθ᾽ ὅσον ἀγαθός, οὐ καθ᾽ ὅσον
ὅμοιος, φίλος ἂν εἴη;

Ἴσως.

Τί δέ; οὐχ ὁ ἀγαθός, καθ᾽ ὅσον ἀγαθός, κατὰ τοσοῦτον ἱκανὸς ἂν εἴη αὑτῷ;

---

31 Socrates, here and in the subsequent argument (215a3–c2),
appears to be assuming that *homoios* = "similar" = *ho autos* = "the
same" = "identical"), the underlying assumption being that one
would only "love" (*philein*) someone/something who/which had
something of benefit to offer, i.e., what one lacked. Consequently, on Socrates' interpretation of the word, those who are

He nodded in agreement.

"Then we have now got the idea who friends are. For our discussion indicates to us that it's whoever are good."

"That seems to be very much the case," he said.   e

"And to me too," I said. "And yet I'm unhappy at something that's in it. Come on then, in the name of Zeus, let's see what my suspicion is about. Is the like person a friend to the like person in as far as he is like him, and is such a person useful to such a person? Or put it like this: when something, whatever it is, is like something else whatever, what benefit can it have for that other thing, or what harm could it do to it, which it couldn't do to itself? Or what could be done to it which could not also be done to it by itself? Indeed how could such things be welcomed by each   215 other when they are of no service to each other? Is there a way?"[31]

"No there isn't."

"And that which was not welcomed, how would that be a friend?"

"It wouldn't in any way."

"But in that case the like is not a friend to the like; but could the good be a friend of the good in as far as he is good, not in as far as he is like him?"

"Perhaps."

"What then? Wouldn't the good person in as far as he is good, to that extent be sufficient for himself?"

good, in as far as they are like (the same as) each other in being self-sufficient, would not lack anything the other good person has, and so would have no need to love or cherish anybody else (on the dependence of love on personal benefit, see above, 210c5–6). See further, Introduction §3(iii).

Ναί.

Ὁ δέ γε ἱκανὸς οὐδενὸς δεόμενος κατὰ τὴν ἱκανότητα.

Πῶς γὰρ οὔ;

Ὁ δὲ μή του δεόμενος οὐδέ τι ἀγαπῴη ἄν.

Οὐ γὰρ οὖν.

Ὁ δὲ μὴ ἀγαπῴη, οὐδ' ἂν φιλοῖ.

Οὐ δῆτα.

b   Ὁ δὲ μὴ φιλῶν γε οὐ φίλος.

Οὐ φαίνεται.

Πῶς οὖν οἱ ἀγαθοὶ τοῖς ἀγαθοῖς ἡμῖν φίλοι ἔσονται τὴν ἀρχήν, οἳ μήτε ἀπόντες ποθεινοὶ ἀλλήλοις—ἱκανοὶ γὰρ ἑαυτοῖς καὶ χωρὶς ὄντες—μήτε παρόντες χρείαν αὑτῶν ἔχουσιν; τοὺς δὴ τοιούτους τίς μηχανὴ περὶ πολλοῦ ποιεῖσθαι ἀλλήλους;

Οὐδεμία, ἔφη.

Φίλοι δέ γε οὐκ ἂν εἶεν μὴ περὶ πολλοῦ ποιούμενοι ἑαυτούς.

c   Ἀληθῆ.

Ἄθρει δή, ὦ Λύσι, πῇ παρακρουόμεθα. ἆρά γε ὅλῳ τινὶ ἐξαπατώμεθα;

Πῶς δή; ἔφη.

Ἤδη ποτέ του ἤκουσα λέγοντος, καὶ ἄρτι ἀναμιμνῄσκομαι, ὅτι τὸ μὲν ὅμοιον τῷ ὁμοίῳ καὶ οἱ ἀγαθοὶ τοῖς ἀγαθοῖς πολεμιώτατοι εἶεν· καὶ δὴ καὶ τὸν Ἡσίοδον ἐπήγετο μάρτυρα, λέγων ὡς ἄρα

"Yes."

"But the self-sufficient lacks nothing because of his sufficiency?"

"Of course."

"But he who is not lacking in anything would not welcome anything."

"No in truth."

"And he who does not welcome anything would not love anything."

"No indeed."

"And the one who does not love is not a friend."   b

"It doesn't seem so."

"How therefore can we say the good will be friends with the good from the start, who neither long for each other when absent—for they are self-sufficient even they live apart—nor when they are present do they need each other? Indeed in the case of such people what way is there to make them have a high regard for each other?"

"None," he said.

"If they didn't have much regard for each other, they wouldn't be friends."

"True."   c

"Then look, Lysis, how we've been led astray. Can it be that we've been deceived in the whole of this?"

"How so?" he said.

"I once heard someone say somewhere, and I've just remembered it, that the like is most hostile to the like, and the good to the good. And what's more he cited Hesiod as a witness, saying in fact:

καὶ κεραμεὺς κεραμεῖ κοτέει καὶ ἀοιδὸς ἀοιδῷ

d καὶ πτωχὸς πτωχῷ,

καὶ τἆλλα δὴ πάντα οὕτως ἔφη ἀναγκαῖον εἶναι μάλιστα τὰ ὁμοιότατα ⟨πρὸς⟩ ἄλληλα φθόνου τε καὶ
φιλονικίας καὶ ἔχθρας ἐμπίμπλασθαι, τὰ δ' ἀνομοιό-
τατα φιλίας· τὸν γὰρ | πένητα τῷ πλουσίῳ ἀναγκάζε-
σθαι φίλον εἶναι καὶ τὸν ἀσθενῆ τῷ ἰσχυρῷ τῆς ἐπι-
κουρίας ἕνεκα, καὶ τὸν κάμνοντα τῷ ἰατρῷ, καὶ πάντα
e δὴ τὸν μὴ εἰδότα ἀγαπᾶν τὸν εἰδότα καὶ φιλεῖν. καὶ
δὴ καὶ ἔτι ἐπεξῄει τῷ λόγῳ μεγαλοπρεπέστερον, λέγων ὡς ἄρα παντὸς δέοι τὸ ὅμοιον τῷ ὁμοίῳ φίλον
εἶναι, ἀλλ' αὐτὸ τὸ ἐναντίον εἴη τούτου· τὸ γὰρ ἐναν-
τιώτατον τῷ ἐναντιωτάτῳ εἶναι μάλιστα φίλον. ἐπιθυ-
μεῖν γὰρ τοῦ | τοιούτου ἕκαστον, ἀλλ' οὐ τοῦ ὁμοίου·
τὸ μὲν γὰρ ξηρὸν ὑγροῦ, τὸ δὲ ψυχρὸν θερμοῦ, τὸ δὲ
πικρὸν γλυκέος, τὸ δὲ ὀξὺ ἀμβλέος, τὸ δὲ κενὸν πλη-
ρώσεως, καὶ τὸ πλῆρες δὲ κενώσεως, καὶ τἆλλα οὕτω
κατὰ τὸν αὐτὸν λόγον. τροφὴν γὰρ εἶναι τὸ ἐναντίον
τῷ ἐναντίῳ· τὸ γὰρ ὅμοιον τοῦ ὁμοίου οὐδὲν ἂν ἀπο-
216 λαῦσαι. καὶ μέντοι, ὦ ἑταῖρε, καὶ κομψὸς ἐδόκει εἶναι
ταῦτα λέγων· εὖ γὰρ ἔλεγεν. ὑμῖν δέ, ἦν δ' ἐγώ, πῶς
δοκεῖ λέγειν;

Εὖ γε, ἔφη ὁ Μενέξενος, ὥς γε οὑτωσὶ ἀκοῦσαι.

---

32 Hesiod, *Works and Days* 25–26 (adapted; the original:
"And potter is angry with potter and craftsman with craftsman,
and beggar is envious of beggar, and bard of bard").

And potter is angry with potter, bard with bard
and beggar with beggar[32]   d

and in all other cases too he said it was inevitable that it
was like this: things that are most like each other are filled
with envy, contentiousness and enmity with each other,
and the most unlike filled with friendship. For the poor
person is forced to be friends with the rich, and the weak
with the strong for the sake of gaining help, and the sick
with the doctor, and indeed every ignorant person has affection for him who has knowledge, and loves him. And in   e
addition he developed the argument even further more
impressively saying that the like was so far from being
friends with like, that it was the very opposite of that; for
it is the most opposite which is the best friend to the most
opposite. You see each has a desire for something of that
sort, but not for its like. For example dry for wet, cold for
hot, bitter for sweet, sharp for blunt, and empty for filling
and full for emptying, and so with everything else on the
same principle.[33] For the opposite is food for its opposite;
for the like would get no benefit from the like. And you   216
know, my friend, I thought he was rather clever saying
this, for he did speak well. But what do you both think of
what he said?" I asked.

"He definitely spoke well," said Menexenus, "at least
hearing it put like this."

[33] See the resemblance of Socrates' theory here to that of
Eryximachus in *Symposium*, 186d–e.

Φῶμεν ἄρα τὸ ἐναντίον τῷ ἐναντίῳ μάλιστα | φίλον εἶναι;

Πάνυ γε.

Εἶεν, ἦν δ᾽ ἐγώ· οὐκ ἀλλόκοτον, ὦ Μενέξενε; καὶ ἡμῖν εὐθὺς ἄσμενοι ἐπιπηδήσονται οὗτοι οἱ πάσσοφοι ἄνδρες, οἱ ἀντιλογικοί, καὶ ἐρήσονται εἰ οὐκ ἐναν-
b τιώτατον ἔχθρα φιλίᾳ; οἷς τί ἀποκρινούμεθα; ἢ οὐκ ἀνάγκη ὁμολογεῖν ὅτι ἀληθῆ λέγουσιν;

Ἀνάγκη.

Ἆρ᾽ οὖν, φήσουσιν, τὸ ἐχθρὸν τῷ φίλῳ φίλον ἢ τὸ φίλον τῷ ἐχθρῷ;

Οὐδέτερα, ἔφη.

Ἀλλὰ τὸ δίκαιον τῷ ἀδίκῳ, ἢ τὸ | σῶφρον τῷ ἀκολάστῳ, ἢ τὸ ἀγαθὸν τῷ κακῷ;

Οὐκ ἄν μοι δοκεῖ οὕτως ἔχειν.

Ἀλλὰ μέντοι, ἦν δ᾽ ἐγώ, εἴπερ γε κατὰ τὴν ἐναντιότητά τί τῳ [φίλῳ] φίλον ἐστίν, ἀνάγκη καὶ ταῦτα φίλα εἶναι.

Ἀνάγκη.

Οὔτε ἄρα τὸ ὅμοιον τῷ ὁμοίῳ οὔτε τὸ ἐναντίον τῷ ἐναντίῳ φίλον.

Οὐκ ἔοικεν.

c Ἔτι δὲ καὶ τόδε σκεψώμεθα, μὴ ἔτι μᾶλλον ἡμᾶς λανθάνει τὸ φίλον ὡς ἀληθῶς οὐδὲν τούτων ὄν, ἀλλὰ τὸ μήτε ἀγαθὸν μήτε κακὸν φίλον οὕτω ποτὲ γιγνόμενον τοῦ ἀγαθοῦ.

Πῶς, ἦ δ᾽ ὅς, λέγεις;

"Then are we to say that the opposite is particularly friendly to the opposite?"

"Very much so."

"Well then," I said, "isn't it strange, Menexenus? Won't those very clever men, the antilogicians, gladly spring on us straight away and ask if hostility is not the extreme opposite of friendship?[34] What will be our answer to them? Or do we not have to agree that they are telling the truth?"   b

"We must."

"Will they then say that the hostile is friendly to a friend, or the friend is friend to the hostile?"

"Neither," he said.

"But is the just a friend to the unjust, or the temperate to the intemperate, or the good to the bad?"

"I don't think it's like that."

"But yet," I said, "if something is a friend to something, in respect of their opposition, then these must be friends."

"Yes it must be so."

"Then neither is the like a friend of the like, nor the opposite a friend of the opposite."

"It doesn't seem to be."

"But still let's look at the following too, whether the   c friend is not escaping us still further, being in truth none of these things, but something which is neither good nor bad, for that reason perhaps, becoming the friend of the good."

"How do you mean?" he said.

[34] "The antilogicians" refers to a group of sophists whose main aim was to argue (and persuade others to accept) contradictory arguments (see Waterfield, 285ff.).

Ἀλλὰ μὰ Δία, ἦν δ' ἐγώ, οὐκ | οἶδα, ἀλλὰ τῷ ὄντι αὐτὸς εἰλιγγιῶ ὑπὸ τῆς τοῦ λόγου ἀπορίας, καὶ κινδυνεύει κατὰ τὴν ἀρχαίαν παροιμίαν τὸ καλὸν φίλον εἶναι. ἔοικε γοῦν μαλακῷ τινι καὶ λείῳ καὶ λιπαρῷ· διὸ καὶ ἴσως ῥᾳδίως διολισθαίνει καὶ διαδύεται ἡμᾶς,
d ἅτε τοιοῦτον ὄν. λέγω γὰρ τἀγαθὸν καλὸν εἶναι· σὺ δ' οὐκ οἴει;

Ἔγωγε.

Λέγω τοίνυν ἀπομαντευόμενος, τοῦ καλοῦ τε καὶ ἀγαθοῦ φίλον εἶναι τὸ μήτε ἀγαθὸν μήτε κακόν· | πρὸς ἃ δὲ λέγων μαντεύομαι, ἄκουσον. δοκεῖ μοι ὡσπερεὶ τρία ἄττα εἶναι γένη, τὸ μὲν ἀγαθόν, τὸ δὲ κακόν, τὸ δ' οὔτ' ἀγαθὸν οὔτε κακόν· τί δὲ σοί;

Καὶ ἐμοί, ἔφη.

Καὶ οὔτε τἀγαθὸν τἀγαθῷ οὔτε τὸ κακὸν τῷ κακῷ οὔτε τἀγαθὸν τῷ κακῷ φίλον εἶναι, ὥσπερ οὐδ' ὁ ἔμ-
e προσθεν λόγος ἐᾷ· λείπεται δή, εἴπερ τῴ τί ἐστιν φίλον, τὸ μήτε ἀγαθὸν μήτε κακὸν φίλον εἶναι ἢ τοῦ ἀγαθοῦ ἢ τοῦ τοιούτου οἷον αὐτό ἐστιν. οὐ γὰρ ἄν που τῷ κακῷ φίλον ἄν τι γένοιτο. |

Ἀληθῆ.

Οὐδὲ μὴν τὸ ὅμοιον τῷ ὁμοίῳ ἔφαμεν ἄρτι· ἢ γάρ;

Ναί.

Οὐκ ἄρα ἔσται τῷ μήτε ἀγαθῷ μήτε κακῷ τὸ τοιοῦτον φίλον οἷον αὐτό.

"By Zeus," I said, "I don't know, but in reality I've become dizzy from the impasse in the argument, and it's likely, according to the old proverb, the beautiful is a friend. At any rate it resembles something delicate, smooth and sleek; and that is the reason perhaps why it gives us the slip and escapes from us, inasmuch as it's that kind of thing. For I say that the good is beautiful, but you, don't you think so?"[35]   d

"I do think so."

"Now I say, and I'm prophesying, that what is neither good nor bad is the friend of the beautiful and the good; but hear my reasons for making my prediction. It seems to me as if there are some three classes: the good, the bad and the neither good nor bad: what do you think?"

"I agree," he said.

"And neither is the good a friend to the good, nor the bad a friend to the bad, nor the good a friend to the bad, just as our previous discussion also didn't allow. It then   e remains that if anything is a friend to anything, that which is neither good nor bad is a friend to either the good, or the one that is of the kind that it is itself. For I can't imagine that anything could become a friend to the bad."

"True."

"Nor again, as we said a little while ago, would the like be a friend to the like. Isn't that so?"

"Yes."

"Indeed then what is neither good nor bad will not be a friend to the same sort as itself."

[35] For the close relationship of *to agathon* and *to kalon*, see above, n. 5. For the argument of 216c1–18c3, see Introduction, §3(v).

Οὐ φαίνεται.

Τῷ ἀγαθῷ ἄρα τὸ μήτε ἀγαθὸν μήτε κακὸν μόνῳ μόνον συμβαίνει γίγνεσθαι φίλον.

217 Ἀνάγκη, ὡς ἔοικεν.

Ἆρ᾽ οὖν καὶ καλῶς, ἦν δ᾽ ἐγώ, ὦ παῖδες, ὑφηγεῖται ἡμῖν τὸ νῦν λεγόμενον; εἰ γοῦν θέλοιμεν ἐννοῆσαι τὸ ὑγιαῖνον | σῶμα, οὐδὲν ἰατρικῆς δεῖται οὐδὲ ὠφελίας· ἱκανῶς γὰρ ἔχει, ὥστε ὑγιαίνων οὐδεὶς ἰατρῷ φίλος διὰ τὴν ὑγίειαν. ἦ γάρ;

Οὐδείς.

Ἀλλ᾽ ὁ κάμνων οἶμαι διὰ τὴν νόσον.

b   Πῶς γὰρ οὔ;

Νόσος μὲν δὴ κακόν, ἰατρικὴ δὲ ὠφέλιμον καὶ ἀγαθόν.

Ναί.

Σῶμα δέ γέ που κατὰ τὸ σῶμα εἶναι οὔτε ἀγαθὸν οὔτε κακόν.

Οὕτως

Ἀναγκάζεται δέ γε σῶμα διὰ νόσον ἰατρικὴν ἀσπάζεσθαι καὶ φιλεῖν.

Δοκεῖ μοι.

Τὸ μήτε | κακὸν ἄρα μήτ᾽ ἀγαθὸν φίλον γίγνεται τοῦ ἀγαθοῦ διὰ κακοῦ παρουσίαν.

Ἔοικεν.

Δῆλον δέ γε ὅτι πρὶν γενέσθαι αὐτὸ κακὸν ὑπὸ τοῦ

"It doesn't appear so."

"In that case it turns out that only that which is neither good nor bad can become a friend of the good, and of that alone."

"It must be so, it seems," he said.   217

"Well then, boys," I said, "is what is now being said also guiding us well? At any rate if we should wish to think about the healthy body, it needs no medical expertise and no kind of help. For it is self-sufficient, so that no one in good health is a friend of the doctor because of his health.[36] Isn't that so?"

"No, no one."

"But I think a sick man is, because of his illness."

"Of course."   b

"Illness is a bad thing, but the practice of medicine is something beneficial and good."

"Yes."

"Whereas the body, I suppose, as a body, is neither good nor bad."

"That is so."

"But a body has to welcome and love medical treatment because of illness."

"I think so."

"Then in that case that which is neither bad nor good becomes a friend of the good because of the presence of bad."

"It seems so."

"But clearly this is before it itself becomes bad as a

[36] This follows from the argument at 215a–b that the self-sufficient cannot be friends with that from which it can derive no benefit.

κακοῦ οὗ ἔχει. οὐ γὰρ δή γε κακὸν γεγονὸς ἔτι ἄν τι
c τοῦ ἀγαθοῦ [οὗ] ἐπιθυμοῖ καὶ φίλον εἴη· ἀδύνατον γὰρ
ἔφαμεν κακὸν ἀγαθῷ φίλον εἶναι.

Ἀδύνατον γάρ.

Σκέψασθε δὴ ὃ λέγω. λέγω γὰρ ὅτι ἔνια μέν, οἷον
ἂν ᾖ τὸ παρόν, τοιαῦτά ἐστι καὶ αὐτά, ἔνια δὲ οὔ.
ὥσπερ εἰ | ἐθέλοι τις χρώματί τῳ ὁτιοῦν [τι] ἀλεῖψαι,
πάρεστίν που τῷ ἀλειφθέντι τὸ ἐπαλειφθέν.

Πάνυ γε.

Ἆρ᾽ οὖν καὶ ἔστιν τότε τοιοῦτον τὴν χρόαν τὸ
ἀλειφθέν, οἷον τὸ ἐπόν;

d Οὐ μανθάνω, ἦ δ᾽ ὅς.

Ἀλλ᾽ ὧδε, ἦν δ᾽ ἐγώ. εἴ τίς σου ξανθὰς οὔσας τὰς
τρίχας ψιμυθίῳ ἀλείψειεν, πότερον τότε λευκαὶ εἶεν ἢ
φαίνοιντ᾽ ἄν;

Φαίνοιντ᾽ ἄν, ἦ δ᾽ ὅς.

Καὶ μὴν παρείη γ᾽ ἂν αὐταῖς λευκότης.

Ναί.

Ἀλλ᾽ ὅμως | οὐδέν τι μᾶλλον ἂν εἶεν λευκαί πω,
ἀλλὰ παρούσης λευκότητος οὔτε τι λευκαὶ οὔτε μέ-
λαιναί εἰσιν.

Ἀληθῆ.

Ἀλλ᾽ ὅταν δή, ὦ φίλε, τὸ γῆρας αὐταῖς ταὐτὸν
τοῦτο χρῶμα ἐπαγάγῃ, τότε ἐγένοντο οἷόνπερ τὸ παρόν, λευκοῦ παρουσίᾳ λευκαί.

e Πῶς γὰρ οὔ;

Τοῦτο τοίνυν ἐρωτῶ νῦν δή, εἰ ᾧ ἄν τι παρῇ,

result of the badness which it has. For, having become bad, it certainly would no longer at all desire, and be a friend of, the good. For we said it's impossible for the bad c to be a friend of the good."

"Yes, it's impossible."

"Have a look, then, at what I'm saying. For I'm saying that some things are themselves of the same kind as whatever is present in them, others are not. For example if one wished to smear something whatever with a certain color, the color applied is there, I suppose, with the material that was smeared."

"Very much so."

"Therefore at that point is that which has been smeared of such a kind in its color as that which has been applied?"

"I don't understand," he said. d

"Well it's like this," I said: "if someone were to smear your hair, which is fair, with white lead, would it be white, or would it appear to be white?"

"It would appear to be white," he said.

"And yet whiteness would be actually present in it."

"Yes."

"Nevertheless it would still not any more than before *be* white; though whiteness is present, in no way is it white any more than black."

"True."

"But when old age, my friend, brings this very same color to it, then it would become as what is present, white through the presence of white."

"Of course." e

"Therefore that is the question I'm asking you now: if something has something or other present within it, will it

81

τοιοῦτον ἔσται τὸ ἔχον οἷον τὸ παρόν· ἢ ἐὰν μὲν κατά
τινα τρόπον παρῇ, ἔσται, ἐὰν δὲ μή, οὔ;

Οὕτω μᾶλλον, ἔφη.

Καὶ τὸ μήτε κακὸν ἄρα μήτ᾽ ἀγαθὸν ἐνίοτε | κακοῦ
παρόντος οὔπω κακόν ἐστιν, ἔστιν δ᾽ ὅτε ἤδη τὸ
τοιοῦτον γέγονεν.

Πάνυ γε.

Οὐκοῦν ὅταν μήπω κακὸν ᾖ κακοῦ παρόντος, αὕτη
μὲν ἡ παρουσία ἀγαθοῦ αὐτὸ ποιεῖ ἐπιθυμεῖν· ἡ δὲ
κακὸν ποιοῦσα ἀποστερεῖ αὐτὸ τῆς τε ἐπιθυμίας ἅμα
καὶ τῆς φιλίας τοῦ ἀγαθοῦ. οὐ γὰρ ἔτι ἐστὶν οὔτε
218 κακὸν οὔτε ἀγαθόν, ἀλλὰ κακόν· φίλον δὲ ἀγαθῷ κακὸν οὐκ ἦν.

Οὐ γὰρ οὖν.

Διὰ ταῦτα δὴ φαῖμεν ἂν καὶ τοὺς ἤδη σοφοὺς
μηκέτι φιλοσοφεῖν, εἴτε θεοὶ εἴτε ἄνθρωποί εἰσιν οὗ-
τοι· οὐδ᾽ αὖ ἐκείνους φιλοσοφεῖν τοὺς οὕτως ἄγνοιαν
| ἔχοντας ὥστε κακοὺς εἶναι· κακὸν γὰρ καὶ ἀμαθῆ
οὐδένα φιλοσοφεῖν. λείπονται δὴ οἱ ἔχοντες μὲν τὸ
κακὸν τοῦτο, τὴν ἄγνοιαν, μήπω δὲ ὑπ᾽ αὐτοῦ ὄντες
ἀγνώμονες μηδὲ ἀμαθεῖς, ἀλλ᾽ ἔτι ἡγούμενοι μὴ εἰδέ-
b ναι ἃ μὴ ἴσασιν. διὸ δὴ καὶ φιλοσοφοῦσιν οἱ οὔτε
ἀγαθοὶ οὔτε κακοί πω ὄντες, ὅσοι δὲ κακοὶ οὐ φιλοσοφοῦσιν, οὐδὲ οἱ ἀγαθοί· οὔτε γὰρ τὸ ἐναντίον τοῦ
ἐναντίου οὔτε τὸ ὅμοιον τοῦ ὁμοίου φίλον | ἡμῖν ἐφάνη
ἐν τοῖς ἔμπροσθεν λόγοις. ἢ οὐ μέμνησθε;

be of the same sort as what is present; or will it be so if it is present in a certain way, and not if not?"

"More likely the latter," he said.

"And so then that which is neither bad nor good is sometimes not yet bad, though bad is present, and there are times when it has already become so."

"Very much so."

"Therefore whenever something is not yet bad, though bad is present, this presence makes it desire the good, but the presence which makes it bad deprives it at the same time both of its desire and its friendship for the good. For it is no longer neither bad nor good, but bad. And we es- 218 tablished that bad was not a friend to the good."

"Indeed no."

"For just these reasons we would say also that those who are already wise no longer love wisdom, whether these are gods or mortals. Nor again, that those people are lovers of wisdom who are so ignorant as to be bad, for no bad and ignorant person loves wisdom. That then leaves those who possess this bad trait, ignorance, but who are not yet made senseless nor ignorant by it, but still are aware that they don't know what they don't know.[37] For b this reason indeed those who love wisdom are those who are neither yet good or bad, while all those who are bad don't love wisdom, nor do the good. For it was shown by us earlier in our discussion that opposite is not a friend of opposite, nor is like friend of like.[38] Or do you not remember?"

[37] Cf. Socrates characterizing himself as one of these in *Apology*, 21d5–6. For the intermediate state between ignorance and wisdom, see also *Symposium*, 204aff.
[38] At 214e–16b.

Πάνυ γε, ἐφάτην.

Νῦν ἄρα, ἦν δ' ἐγώ, ὦ Λύσι τε καὶ Μενέξενε, παντὸς μᾶλλον ἐξηυρήκαμεν ὃ ἔστιν τὸ φίλον καὶ οὔ. φαμὲν γὰρ αὐτό, καὶ κατὰ τὴν ψυχὴν καὶ κατὰ τὸ c σῶμα καὶ πανταχοῦ, τὸ μήτε κακὸν μήτε ἀγαθὸν διὰ κακοῦ παρουσίαν τοῦ ἀγαθοῦ φίλον εἶναι.

Παντάπασιν ἐφάτην τε καὶ συνεχωρείτην οὕτω τοῦτ' ἔχειν.

Καὶ δὴ καὶ αὐτὸς ἐγὼ πάνυ ἔχαιρον, ὥσπερ θηρευτής τις, | ἔχων ἀγαπητῶς ὃ ἐθηρευόμην. κἄπειτ' οὐκ οἶδ' ὁπόθεν μοι ἀτοπωτάτη τις ὑποψία εἰσῆλθεν ὡς οὐκ ἀληθῆ εἴη τὰ ὡμολογημένα ἡμῖν, καὶ εὐθὺς ἀχθεσθεὶς εἶπον· Βαβαῖ, ὦ Λύσι τε καὶ Μενέξενε, κινδυνεύομεν ὄναρ πεπλουτηκέναι.

d Τί μάλιστα; ἔφη ὁ Μενέξενος.

Φοβοῦμαι, ἦν δ' ἐγώ, μὴ ὥσπερ ἀνθρώποις ἀλαζόσιν λόγοις τισὶν τοιούτοις [ψευδέσιν] ἐντετυχήκαμεν περὶ τοῦ φίλου. |

Πῶς δή; ἔφη.

Ὧδε, ἦν δ' ἐγώ, σκοπῶμεν· φίλος ὃς ἂν εἴη, πότερόν ἐστίν τῳ φίλος ἢ οὔ;

Ἀνάγκη, ἔφη.

Πότερον οὖν οὐδενὸς ἕνεκα καὶ δι' οὐδέν, ἢ ἕνεκά του καὶ διά τι;

Ἕνεκά του καὶ διά τι.

Πότερον φίλου ὄντος ἐκείνου τοῦ πράγματος, οὗ |

"Of course we do," they both replied.

"So now," I said, "Lysis and Menexenus, we have conclusively discovered what is the friend and what isn't. For we are saying that with respect to the soul and with respect to the body and everywhere, that which is neither bad nor good is a friend of the good owing to the presence of the bad."

"Absolutely," they both said, and agreed that this was the case.

And what's more I myself was very pleased too, like a huntsman, at satisfactorily getting what I was hunting for. And then, I don't know where it came from, a very strange suspicion came over me that what we had agreed on was not true and straight away in annoyance I said: "Damn it, Lysis and Menexenus, we were in danger there of merely creating a fabulous dream!"

"In what particular way?" asked Menexenus.

"I'm afraid, I said, we have encountered arguments about the friend of a sort which are, as it were, imposters."

"How can that be?" he said.

"Let's look at it this way," I said: "he who would be a friend, is a friend to something,[39] or not?"

"He must be," he said.

"Would that then be for the sake of nothing and because of nothing, or would it be for the sake of something and because of something?"

"For the sake of something and because of something."

"And that something for the sake of which the friend is

[39] Or "to someone" (*tōi* can be masculine or neuter); for example, the sick man can be *philos* to the doctor (*iatros*), e.g., 217a5–6, or to medical expertise (*iatrikē*), b4.

85

ἕνεκα φίλος ὁ φίλος τῷ φίλῳ, ἢ οὔτε φίλου οὔτε
ἐχθροῦ;

e   Οὐ πάνυ, ἔφη, ἕπομαι.

Εἰκότως γε, ἦν δ' ἐγώ· ἀλλ' ὧδε ἴσως ἀκολουθήσεις,
οἶμαι δὲ καὶ ἐγὼ μᾶλλον εἴσομαι ὅτι λέγω. ὁ κάμνων,
νυνδὴ ἔφαμεν, τοῦ ἰατροῦ φίλος· οὐχ οὕτως;

Ναί.

Οὐκοῦν διὰ νόσον ἕνεκα ὑγιείας τοῦ ἰατροῦ| φίλος;

Ναί.

Ἡ δέ γε νόσος κακόν;

Πῶς δ' οὔ;

Τί δὲ ὑγίεια; ἦν δ' ἐγώ· ἀγαθὸν ἢ κακὸν ἢ οὐδέτερα;

Ἀγαθόν, ἔφη.

219   Ἐλέγομεν δ' ἄρα, ὡς ἔοικεν, ὅτι τὸ σῶμα, οὔτε
ἀγαθὸν οὔτε κακὸν ⟨ὄν⟩, διὰ τὴν νόσον, τοῦτο δὲ διὰ
τὸ κακόν, τῆς ἰατρικῆς φίλον ἐστίν, ἀγαθὸν δὲ ἰα-
τρική· ἕνεκα δὲ τῆς ὑγιείας τὴν φιλίαν ἡ ἰατρικὴ
ἀνῄρηται, ἡ δὲ ὑγίεια ἀγαθόν.| ἦ γάρ;

Ναί.

Φίλον δὲ ἢ οὐ φίλον ἡ ὑγίεια;

Φίλον.

Ἡ δὲ νόσος ἐχθρόν.

Πάνυ γε.

b   Τὸ οὔτε κακὸν οὔτε ἀγαθὸν ἄρα διὰ τὸ κακὸν καὶ
τὸ ἐχθρὸν τοῦ ἀγαθοῦ φίλον ἐστὶν ἕνεκα τοῦ ἀγαθοῦ
καὶ φίλου.

---

40 Note that the introduction of the distinction, *dia* (because

a friend to the friend—is it a friend or neither a friend nor an enemy?"

"I don't quite follow you," he said.　　　　　　　　　　　　　e

"That's natural enough," I said; "well perhaps you'll follow if I put it like this, and I think I too will understand more of what I'm saying. The sick man, we said a little while ago is a friend of the doctor; is that not so?"

"Yes."

"So that means that it's because of his illness for the sake of his health that he is a friend of the doctor?"

"Yes."

"But the illness is a bad thing?"

"Of course."

"What about health?" I said, "is it good, bad, or neither?"

"Good," he said.

"We were saying then, it seems, that the body, being　219 neither good nor bad, because of its illness, that is, because of the bad, is a friend of medicine, and medicine is a good thing; but that it is for the sake of health that medicine has gained the friendship, and health is a good thing, is that not so?"

"Yes."

"And is health a friend or not a friend?"

"A friend."

"And illness is an enemy."

"Very much so."

"So then what is neither good nor bad, because of the　b bad and the hostile, is a friend of the good for the sake of good and a friend."[40]

of) and *heneka* (for the sake of), sets the agenda for the argument that started at 218d6; see Introduction, §3(vi).

Φαίνεται.

Ἕνεκα ἄρα τοῦ φίλου ⟨τοῦ φίλου⟩ τὸ φίλον φίλον διὰ τὸ ἐχθρόν.

Ἔοικεν. |

Εἶεν, ἦν δ᾽ ἐγώ. ἐπειδὴ ἐνταῦθα ἥκομεν, ὦ παῖδες, πρόσσχωμεν τὸν νοῦν μὴ ἐξαπατηθῶμεν. ὅτι μὲν γὰρ φίλον τοῦ φίλου τὸ φίλον γέγονεν, ἐῶ χαίρειν, καὶ τοῦ ὁμοίου γε τὸ ὅμοιον φίλον γίγνεται, ὅ φαμεν ἀδύνα-τον εἶναι· ἀλλ᾽ ὅμως τόδε σκεψώμεθα, μὴ ἡμᾶς ἐξ-
c ἀπατήσῃ τὸ νῦν λεγόμενον. ἡ ἰατρική, φαμέν, ἕνεκα τῆς ὑγιείας φίλον.

Ναί.

Οὐκοῦν καὶ ἡ ὑγίεια φίλον;

Πάνυ γε.

Εἰ ἄρα φίλον, ἕνεκά του.

Ναί.

Φίλου γέ τινος δή, εἴπερ ἀκολουθήσει τῇ πρόσθεν ὁμολογίᾳ.

Πάνυ γε.

Οὐκοῦν καὶ ἐκεῖνο φίλον αὖ | ἔσται ἕνεκα φίλου;

Ναί.

Ἆρ᾽ οὖν οὐκ ἀνάγκη ἀπειπεῖν ἡμᾶς οὕτως ἰόντας ἢ ἀφικέσθαι ἐπί τινα ἀρχήν, ἢ οὐκέτ᾽ ἐπανοίσει ἐπ᾽ ἄλλο φίλον, ἀλλ᾽ ἥξει ἐπ᾽ ἐκεῖνο ὅ ἐστιν πρῶτον φί-λον, οὗ ἕνεκα καὶ τὰ ἄλλα φαμὲν πάντα φίλα εἶναι;

---

41 The translation omits OCT's unnecessary addition of ⟨τοῦ φίλου⟩.

"It appears to be."

"So it's for the sake of the friend[41] that the friend is a friend, because of the hostile."

"It seems to be."

"Well, I said, since we have reached this point, boys, let's turn our attention to making sure we're not deceiving ourselves. For indeed, that the friend has become a friend of a friend, I'm dismissing, and that like becomes friend of like, which we said is impossible. But nevertheless let's look at the following in case what is now being said deceives us. Medicine, we say, is a friend for the sake of   c health."

"Yes."

"Therefore health is a friend too?"

"Very much so."

"So if it's a friend, it's for the sake of something."

"Yes."

"It must be for the sake of some friend then, if it's going to follow from our previous agreement."

"Very much so."

"Therefore that in its turn will be a friend for the sake of a friend?"

"Yes."

"Is it not inevitable, therefore, that we'll tire ourselves out going on in this way, or must we not reach some starting point which will no longer bring us back to another friend, but will come to that point which is that first friend for whose sake we say all other things are friends too?"[42]

---

[42] The *prōton philon* (primary/first friend) is the "final friend" in the sense that it is not friend for the sake of (*heneka*) any more basic *philon*; see below, 220b3ff.

d   Ἀνάγκη.

Τοῦτο δή ἐστιν ὃ λέγω, μὴ ἡμᾶς τἆλλα πάντα ἃ εἴπομεν ἐκείνου ἕνεκα φίλα εἶναι, ὥσπερ εἴδωλα ἄττα ὄντα αὐτοῦ, ἐξαπατᾷ, ᾗ δ᾽ ἐκεῖνο τὸ πρῶτον, ὃ ὡς | ἀληθῶς ἐστι φίλον. ἐννοήσωμεν γὰρ οὑτωσί· ὅταν τίς τι περὶ πολλοῦ ποιῆται, οἱόνπερ ἐνίοτε πατὴρ υἱὸν ἀντὶ πάντων τῶν ἄλλων χρημάτων προτιμᾷ, ὁ δὴ τοιοῦτος ἕνεκα τοῦ τὸν υἱὸν περὶ παντὸς ἡγεῖσθαι ἆρα

e   καὶ ἄλλο τι ἂν περὶ πολλοῦ ποιοῖτο; οἷον εἰ αἰσθά-νοιτο αὐτὸν κώνειον πεπωκότα, ἆρα περὶ πολλοῦ ποι-οῖτ᾽ ἂν οἶνον, εἴπερ τοῦτο ἡγοῖτο τὸν υἱὸν σώσειν;

Τί μήν; ἔφη.

Οὐκοῦν καὶ τὸ ἀγγεῖον, ἐν ᾧ ὁ | οἶνος ἐνείη;

Πάνυ γε.

Ἆρ᾽ οὖν τότε οὐδὲν περὶ πλείονος ποιεῖται, κύλικα κεραμέαν ἢ τὸν υἱὸν τὸν αὑτοῦ, οὐδὲ τρεῖς κοτύλας οἴνου ἢ τὸν υἱόν; ἢ ὧδέ πως ἔχει· πᾶσα ἡ τοιαύτη σπουδὴ οὐκ ἐπὶ τούτοις ἐστὶν ἐσπουδασμένη, ἐπὶ τοῖς ἕνεκά του παρασκευαζομένοις, ἀλλ᾽ ἐπ᾽ ἐκείνῳ

220   οὗ ἕνεκα πάντα τὰ τοιαῦτα παρασκευάζεται. οὐχ ὅτι πολλάκις λέγομεν ὡς περὶ πολλοῦ ποιούμεθα χρυ-σίον καὶ ἀργύριον· ἀλλὰ μὴ οὐδέν τι μᾶλλον οὕτω τό γε ἀληθὲς ἔχῃ, ἀλλ᾽ ἐκεῖνό ἐστιν ὃ περὶ παντὸς ποι-ούμεθα, ὃ ἂν φανῇ ὄν, ὅτου ἕνεκα καὶ | χρυσίον καὶ πάντα τὰ παρασκευαζόμενα παρασκευάζεται. ἆρ᾽ οὕ-τως φήσομεν;

Πάνυ γε.

Οὐκοῦν καὶ περὶ τοῦ φίλου ὁ αὐτὸς λόγος; ὅσα γὰρ

"We must."   d

"This then is what I'm saying: make sure that all those
things we said are friends for the sake of that one[43] do not
mislead us like so many false images of it, when it is that
first one which is truly a friend. Let's think of it in this way:
when someone values something highly, such as when
sometimes a father values his son above all his other possessions, then for the sake of valuing his son highly would
such a person value anything else very highly? For exam-   e
ple, if he realized he had drunk some hemlock, would he
value wine highly if he thought this would save his son?"

"Of course," he said.

"And the container the wine was in?"

"Very much so."

"Therefore does he value nothing more highly at that
moment: an earthenware wine cup more than his son,
three measures of wine more than his son? Or is it something like this? All such concern is not lavished on those
things that are provided for the sake of something, but on
that for the sake of which all things like this are provided.
Not that we don't often say that we value gold and silver   220
highly, but that doesn't get us any nearer to the truth. But
what we do value highly, whatever it may prove to be, is
that for the sake of which gold and all such goods which
are procured are procured. Is that how we shall put it?"

"Very much so."

"And does the same argument apply to the friend also?

---

[43] That is, the "first friend" (c7).

φαμεν φίλα εἶναι ἡμῖν ἕνεκα φίλου τινὸς ἑτέρου, ῥή-
b ματι φαινόμεθα λέγοντες αὐτό· φίλον δὲ τῷ ὄντι κινδυνεύει ἐκεῖνο αὐτὸ εἶναι, εἰς ὃ πᾶσαι αὗται αἱ λεγό-
μεναι φιλίαι τελευτῶσιν.

Κινδυνεύει οὕτως, ἔφη, ἔχειν.

Οὐκοῦν τό γε τῷ ὄντι φίλον οὐ φίλου τινὸς ἕνεκα
φίλον | ἐστίν;

Ἀληθῆ.

Τοῦτο μὲν δὴ ἀπήλλακται, μὴ φίλου τινὸς ἕνεκα
τὸ φίλον φίλον εἶναι· ἀλλ' ἆρα τὸ ἀγαθόν ἐστιν φίλον;

Ἔμοιγε δοκεῖ.

Ἆρ' οὖν διὰ τὸ κακὸν τὸ ἀγαθὸν φιλεῖται, καὶ ἔχει
c ὧδε· εἰ τριῶν ὄντων ὧν νυνδὴ ἐλέγομεν, ἀγαθοῦ καὶ
κακοῦ καὶ μήτε ἀγαθοῦ μήτε κακοῦ, τὰ δύο λειφθείη,
τὸ δὲ κακὸν ἐκποδὼν ἀπέλθοι καὶ μηδενὸς ἐφάπτοιτο
μήτε σώματος μήτε ψυχῆς μήτε τῶν ἄλλων, ἃ δή φα-
μεν αὐτὰ | καθ' αὑτὰ οὔτε κακὰ εἶναι οὔτε ἀγαθά, ἆρα
τότε οὐδὲν ἂν ἡμῖν χρήσιμον εἴη τὸ ἀγαθόν, ἀλλ'
ἄχρηστον ἂν γεγονὸς εἴη; εἰ γὰρ μηδὲν ἡμᾶς ἔτι
d βλάπτοι, οὐδὲν ἂν οὐδεμιᾶς ὠφελίας δεοίμεθα, καὶ
οὕτω δὴ ἂν τότε γένοιτο κατάδηλον ὅτι διὰ τὸ κακὸν
τἀγαθὸν ἠγαπῶμεν καὶ ἐφιλοῦμεν, ὡς φάρμακον ὂν
τοῦ κακοῦ τὸ ἀγαθόν, τὸ δὲ κακὸν νόσημα· νοσήματος
δὲ μὴ ὄντος οὐδὲν δεῖ φαρμάκου. ἆρ' οὕτω | πέφυκέ τε
καὶ φιλεῖται τἀγαθὸν διὰ τὸ κακὸν ὑφ' ἡμῶν, τῶν
μεταξὺ ὄντων τοῦ κακοῦ τε καὶ τἀγαθοῦ, αὐτὸ δ' ἑαυτοῦ ἕνεκα οὐδεμίαν χρείαν ἔχει;

For the things we say are friends to us for the sake of some other friend—we appear to be saying it simply as a phrase. But the real friend is likely to be that very thing where all b these friendships we speak of end up."

"It seems likely that that is how it is," he said.

"Therefore what is the real friend isn't a friend for the sake of some friend, is it?"

"True."

"Then we have got rid of this idea that it is for the sake of some friend that the friend is a friend; but is the good a friend?"

"I think so."

"Then is it because of the bad that the good is loved, and does it go as follows: if, of the three types we were c talking about just now, good, bad and the neither good nor bad, two were left and bad went off out of the way, and it affected nothing, neither body nor soul, nor any of the other things which we say taken by themselves are neither bad nor good, then would the good actually be of no use to us, but would have become useless? You see, if nothing were to do us harm any longer we would not need any d help, and so in this way then it would become clear that we welcomed and loved the good on account of the bad, the good being like a cure for the bad, and bad being an illness. But if there is no illness, there's no need for a cure. Is this then the nature of the good, to be loved by us because of the bad, placed as we are between the bad and the good, but by itself it is of no use at all for its own sake?"

Ἔοικεν, ἦ δ' ὅς, οὕτως ἔχειν.

Τὸ ἄρα φίλον ἡμῖν ἐκεῖνο, εἰς ὃ ἐτελεύτα πάντα τὰ
e ἄλλα—ἕνεκα ἑτέρου φίλου φίλα ἔφαμεν εἶναι ἐκεῖνα—
οὐδὲν [δὲ] τούτοις ἔοικεν. ταῦτα μὲν γὰρ φίλου ἕνεκα
φίλα κέκληται, τὸ δὲ τῷ ὄντι φίλον πᾶν τοὐναντίον
τούτου φαίνεται πεφυκός· φίλον γὰρ ἡμῖν ἀνεφάνη ὂν
ἐχθροῦ ἕνεκα, εἰ δὲ τὸ | ἐχθρὸν ἀπέλθοι, οὐκέτι, ὡς
ἔοικ', ἔσθ' ἡμῖν φίλον.

Οὔ μοι δοκεῖ, ἔφη, ὥς γε νῦν λέγεται.

Πότερον, ἦν δ' ἐγώ, πρὸς Διός, ἐὰν τὸ κακὸν ἀπόληται, οὐδὲ πεινῆν ἔτι ἔσται οὐδὲ διψῆν οὐδὲ ἄλλο
221 οὐδὲν τῶν τοιούτων; ἢ πείνη μὲν ἔσται, ἐάνπερ ἄνθρωποί τε καὶ τἆλλα ζῷα ᾖ, οὐ μέντοι βλαβερά γε; καὶ
δίψα δὴ καὶ αἱ ἄλλαι ἐπιθυμίαι, ἀλλ' οὐ κακαί, ἅτε
τοῦ κακοῦ ἀπολωλότος; ἢ γελοῖον τὸ ἐρώτημα, ὅτι
ποτ' | ἔσται τότε ἢ μὴ ἔσται; τίς γὰρ οἶδεν; ἀλλ' οὖν
τόδε γ' ἴσμεν, ὅτι καὶ νῦν ἔστιν πεινῶντα βλάπτε-
σθαι, ἔστιν δὲ καὶ ὠφελεῖσθαι. ἦ γάρ;

Πάνυ γε.

b   Οὐκοῦν καὶ διψῶντα καὶ τῶν ἄλλων τῶν τοιούτων
πάντων ἐπιθυμοῦντα ἔστιν ἐνίοτε μὲν ὠφελίμως ἐπιθυμεῖν, ἐνίοτε δὲ βλαβερῶς, ἐνίοτε δὲ μηδέτερα;

---

44 At 219cff.

45 That is, if the bad disappeared, the good would no longer
be of any benefit to us as a remedy for the bad. Penner and Rowe
(134), against most other commentators, argue that "for the sake
of (heneka) [an enmity]" in e4 is not a simple confusion or mistake
for "because of" (dia), but intentional: "If it were true that the

"It seems to be so," he said.

"Then that friend of ours, where all the rest end up—we said they were friends for the sake of another friend[44]—doesn't resemble any of them. You see these are called friends for the sake of a friend, but the real friend appears to be naturally the complete opposite of this, for it was clearly shown to us as being a friend for the sake of an enmity, but if the enmity should go away, we no longer have it as a friend, it seems."[45]

"It seems that we don't, he said, at least as it's now being expressed."

"In the name of Zeus, I said, if the bad is destroyed, will hunger, or even thirst, or anything else of this kind no longer exist? Or if there are humans and the other animals, will there be hunger, though not a harmful sort? And will there be thirst and other desires, but they will not be bad, inasmuch as the bad has been destroyed? Or is it a silly question on whatever will be then, or won't be? For who knows? But what we do know is this much at least, that as it is now it's possible for a man to feel hunger and to be harmed by it, and it's also possible for him to be benefited. Is that not so?"

"Very much so."

"Likewise with someone who is thirsty and is desiring any other things of this sort, is it possible to have that desire sometimes in a beneficial way, sometimes in a harmful way, and sometimes neither?"

good would no longer be a friend if the bad disappeared, then, if there is always a something for the sake of which in 'friendship,' that something in this case must be (getting rid of) the bad— hence love *is*, on this view, 'for the sake of the bad.'"

Σφόδρα γε.

Οὐκοῦν ἐὰν ἀπολλύηται τὰ κακά, ἅ γε μὴ τυγχάνει ὄντα κακά, τί προσήκει τοῖς κακοῖς | συναπόλλυσθαι;

Οὐδέν.

Ἔσονται ἄρα αἱ μήτε ἀγαθαὶ μήτε κακαὶ ἐπιθυμίαι καὶ ἐὰν ἀπόληται τὰ κακά.

Φαίνεται.

Οἷόν τε οὖν ἐστιν ἐπιθυμοῦντα καὶ ἐρῶντα τούτου οὗ ἐπιθυμεῖ καὶ ἐρᾷ μὴ φιλεῖν;

Οὐκ ἔμοιγε δοκεῖ.

Ἔσται ἄρα καὶ τῶν κακῶν ἀπολομένων, ὡς ἔοικεν, φίλ᾽ ἄττα.

c   Ναί.

Οὐκ ἄν, εἴ γε τὸ κακὸν αἴτιον ἦν τοῦ φίλον τι εἶναι, οὐκ ἂν ἦν τούτου ἀπολομένου φίλον ἕτερον ἑτέρῳ. αἰτίας γὰρ ἀπολομένης ἀδύνατόν που ἦν ἔτ᾽ ἐκεῖνο εἶναι, οὗ ἦν αὕτη ἡ | αἰτία.

Ὀρθῶς λέγεις.

Οὐκοῦν ὡμολόγηται ἡμῖν τὸ φίλον φιλεῖν τι καὶ διά τι· καὶ ᾠήθημεν τότε γε διὰ τὸ κακὸν τὸ μήτε ἀγαθὸν μήτε κακὸν τὸ ἀγαθὸν φιλεῖν;

Ἀληθῆ.

d   Νῦν δέ γε, ὡς ἔοικε, φαίνεται ἄλλη τις αἰτία τοῦ φιλεῖν τε καὶ φιλεῖσθαι.

Ἔοικεν.

Ἆρ᾽ οὖν τῷ ὄντι, ὥσπερ ἄρτι ἐλέγομεν, ἡ ἐπιθυμία τῆς φιλίας αἰτία, καὶ τὸ ἐπιθυμοῦν φίλον ἐστὶν τούτῳ

"Most certainly."

"So if bad things are destroyed, why does it belong to those things which are not actually bad to be destroyed along with the bad things?"

"It doesn't at all."

"Then the desires that are neither good nor bad will exist even if the bad things are destroyed."

"It appears so."

"Therefore is it possible for someone desiring and feeling passion for the thing he desires and feels passion for, not to love it?"

"I don't think so."

"Then some things that are friends will exist, it seems, even when bad things have been destroyed?"

"Yes."   c

"That would not be possible if the bad were actually the cause of something being a friend, that when this (the bad) had been destroyed one thing couldn't be a friend to another. For when the cause has been removed, it would be impossible, I imagine, for that still to exist of which this was the cause."

"You're right."

"Then it has been agreed by us that the friend loves something, and because of something; and we thought then that it was because of the bad that the neither good nor bad loved the good, didn't we?"

"True."

"But now, it seems, there appears to be another cause   d of loving and being loved."

"It seems so."

"Therefore is it in fact, as we were saying just now, that desire is the cause of friendship, and that which desires is

οὗ ἐπιθυμεῖ καὶ τότε ὅταν ἐπιθυμῇ, ὃ δὲ | τὸ πρότερον
ἐλέγομεν φίλον εἶναι, ὕθλος τις ἦν, ὥσπερ ποίημα
μακρὸν² συγκείμενον;

Κινδυνεύει, ἔφη.

Ἀλλὰ μέντοι, ἦν δ' ἐγώ, τό γε ἐπιθυμοῦν, οὗ ἂν
ἐνδεὲς ᾖ, τούτου ἐπιθυμεῖ. ἢ γάρ;

e   Ναί.

Τὸ δ' ἐνδεὲς ἄρα φίλον ἐκείνου οὗ ἂν ἐνδεὲς ᾖ;

Δοκεῖ μοι.

Ἐνδεὲς δὲ γίγνεται οὗ ἄν τι ἀφαιρῆται.

Πῶς δ' οὔ;

Τοῦ οἰκείου δή, ὡς ἔοικεν, ὅ τε ἔρως καὶ ἡ φιλία
καὶ ἡ ἐπιθυμία τυγχάνει οὖσα, ὡς φαίνεται, | ὦ Με-
νέξενέ τε καὶ Λύσι.

Συνεφάτην.

Ὑμεῖς ἄρα εἰ φίλοι ἐστὸν ἀλλήλοις, φύσει πῃ οἰ-
κεῖοί ἐσθ' ὑμῖν αὐτοῖς.

Κομιδῇ, ἐφάτην.

222   Καὶ εἰ ἄρα τις ἕτερος ἑτέρου ἐπιθυμεῖ, ἦν δ' ἐγώ,
ὦ παῖδες, ἢ ἐρᾷ, οὐκ ἄν ποτε ἐπεθύμει οὐδὲ ἤρα οὐδὲ
ἐφίλει, εἰ μὴ οἰκεῖός πῃ τῷ ἐρωμένῳ ἐτύγχανεν ὢν ἢ

---

² Ποίημα μακρὸν Burnet: ποίημα μάτην Ast: ποίημα
Κρόνῳ Madvig: ποίημα κακῶς Penner-Rowe

---

46 This translates the OCT reading (see textual note), which
is likely to be corrupt (*length* is not the key quality of what is
admitted to be nonsense). Of various conjectures, the most prom-

a friend to that which it desires and at that time when it may desire it, but what we said previously about being a friend, was a nonsense, like a poem that has been put together for mere length?"[46]

"That is probable," he said.

"But there again," I said, "that which desires, desires what it is in need of. Isn't that so?"

"Yes."   e

"So then would whatever is needy be a friend of that which it is in need of?"

"I think so."

"And whatever becomes needy, then, is whatever has something taken away from it."

"Of course."

"So it's of something that belongs to us, it seems, Menexenus and Lysis, which the passionate love and the friendship and the desire[47] are actually directed toward."

They both agreed.

"Then in that case, if you two are friends with each other, in some way you naturally belong to each other."

"Exactly," they both said.

"And if then one person desires another, boys, I said,   222
or feels passion, then he would never long for, nor even love, nor be a friend, unless in some way he really be-

---

ising seems to be that of Penner and Rowe, 153n149 (admittedly not presented with much conviction): *poiēma* <u>*kakōs*</u> *sunkeimenon* (a poem *badly* put together).

[47] "Passionate love" = *erōs*, "friendship"= *philia*, "desire" = *epithumia*.

κατὰ τὴν ψυχὴν ἢ κατά τι τῆς ψυχῆς ἦθος ἢ τρόπους
ἢ εἶδος.

Πάνυ γε, ἔφη ὁ Μενέξενος· ὁ δὲ Λύσις ἐσίγησεν.

Εἶεν, | ἦν δ' ἐγώ. τὸ μὲν δὴ φύσει οἰκεῖον ἀναγκαῖον
ἡμῖν πέφανται φιλεῖν.

Ἔοικεν, ἔφη.

Ἀναγκαῖον ἄρα τῷ γνησίῳ ἐραστῇ καὶ μὴ προσ-
ποιήτῳ φιλεῖσθαι ὑπὸ τῶν παιδικῶν.

b   Ὁ μὲν οὖν Λύσις καὶ ὁ Μενέξενος μόγις πως ἐπε-
νευσάτην, ὁ δὲ Ἱπποθάλης ὑπὸ τῆς ἡδονῆς παντοδαπὰ ἠφίει χρώματα.

Καὶ ἐγὼ εἶπον, βουλόμενος τὸν λόγον ἐπισκέψα-
σθαι, Εἰ μέν τι τὸ οἰκεῖον τοῦ ὁμοίου διαφέρει, λέγοι-
μεν ἄν τι, ὡς | ἐμοὶ δοκεῖ, ὦ Λύσι τε καὶ Μενέξενε,
περὶ φίλου, ὃ ἔστιν· εἰ δὲ ταὐτὸν τυγχάνει ὂν ὅμοιόν
τε καὶ οἰκεῖον, οὐ ῥᾴδιον ἀποβαλεῖν τὸν πρόσθεν λόγον, ὡς οὐ τὸ ὅμοιον τῷ ὁμοίῳ κατὰ τὴν ὁμοιότητα
ἄχρηστον· τὸ δὲ ἄχρηστον φίλον ὁμολογεῖν πλημμε-
c   λές. βούλεσθ' οὖν, ἦν δ' ἐγώ, ἐπειδὴ ὥσπερ μεθύομεν
ὑπὸ τοῦ λόγου, συγχωρήσωμεν καὶ φῶμεν ἕτερόν τι
εἶναι τὸ οἰκεῖον τοῦ ὁμοίου;

Πάνυ γε.

Πότερον οὖν καὶ τἀγαθὸν οἰκεῖον θήσομεν παντί,

---

48 The ambiguity of *eidos*, "form" (of soul and/or body), may
be dramatically significant for the concealed listening Hippothales, as well as for the other participants (note Hippothales'
reaction graphically described at 222b2). On the gap between

longed to the loved one, either in his soul, either some character of the soul, or habits, or form."[48]

"Very much so," said Menexenus; but Lysis kept silent.[49]

"Well then," I said, "the thing that naturally belongs to us has shown itself to us as something we must love."

"It seems so," he said.

"Then it is necessary for a genuine lover and not a pretend one to be loved by his beloved."

Now Lysis and Menexenus scarcely managed some   b
kind of nod, but Hippothales turned all sorts of colors out of delight.

As I wanted to inspect the argument, I said: "if there is a difference between belonging and being like, it seems to me, Lysis and Menexenus, we would have something to say about what a friend is; but if it actually is the case that like and belonging are the same, it's not easy to dismiss the previous argument that the like is useless to the like in respect of its likeness, and to agree that the useless is a friend is to commit an error.[50] Since we are, as it were,   c
intoxicated by our argument, I said, would you like us to agree and say that that which belongs to something is other than being like."

"Very much so."

"Shall we then establish that the good belongs to ev-

Hippothales' likely understanding (see above, 204–6) and what Socrates is actually arguing here, see Penner and Rowe, 166–70.

[49] Why should Lysis keep silence here? Are we meant to infer something about his side of the relationship with Hippothales?

[50] For the "previous argument" (b7), see 214b–15c.

τὸ δὲ κακὸν ἀλλότριον | εἶναι; ἢ τὸ μὲν κακὸν τῷ κακῷ
οἰκεῖον, τῷ δὲ ἀγαθῷ τὸ ἀγαθόν, τῷ δὲ μήτε ἀγαθῷ
μήτε κακῷ τὸ μήτε ἀγαθὸν μήτε κακόν;

Οὕτως ἐφάτην δοκεῖν σφίσιν ἕκαστον ἑκάστῳ οἰκεῖον εἶναι.

d Πάλιν ἄρα, ἦν δ' ἐγώ, ὦ παῖδες, οὓς τὸ πρῶτον
λόγους ἀπεβαλόμεθα περὶ φιλίας, εἰς τούτους εἰσ-
πεπτώκαμεν· ὁ γὰρ ἄδικος τῷ ἀδίκῳ καὶ ὁ κακὸς τῷ
κακῷ οὐδὲν ἧττον φίλος ἔσται ἢ ὁ ἀγαθὸς τῷ ἀγαθῷ. |

Ἔοικεν, ἔφη.

Τί δέ; τὸ ἀγαθὸν καὶ τὸ οἰκεῖον ἂν ταὐτὸν φῶμεν
εἶναι, ἄλλο τι ἢ ὁ ἀγαθὸς τῷ ἀγαθῷ μόνον φίλος;

Πάνυ γε.

Ἀλλὰ μὴν καὶ τοῦτό γε ᾠόμεθα ἐξελέγξαι ἡμᾶς
αὐτούς· ἢ οὐ μέμνησθε;

Μεμνήμεθα.

e Τί οὖν ἂν ἔτι χρησαίμεθα τῷ λόγῳ; ἢ δῆλον ὅτι
οὐδέν; δέομαι οὖν, ὥσπερ οἱ σοφοὶ ἐν τοῖς δικαστηρίοις, τὰ εἰρημένα ἅπαντα ἀναπεμπάσασθαι. εἰ γὰρ
μήτε οἱ φιλούμενοι μήτε οἱ φιλοῦντες μήτε οἱ ὅμοιοι
μήτε οἱ ἀνόμοιοι μήτε οἱ ἀγαθοὶ | μήτε οἱ οἰκεῖοι μήτε
τὰ ἄλλα ὅσα διεληλύθαμεν—οὐ γὰρ ἔγωγε ἔτι μέμνημαι ὑπὸ τοῦ πλήθους—ἀλλ᾽ εἰ μηδὲν τούτων φίλον
ἐστίν, ἐγὼ μὲν οὐκέτι ἔχω τί λέγω.

---

51 For the significance of Socrates' alternatives in 222c3–7
and Menexenus' and Lysis' choice in c7–d1, see Introduction, §4.

eryone, but the bad is alien, or does the bad belong to the bad, and the good to the good, and the neither good nor bad to the neither good nor bad?"

They both said that it seemed to them that each belongs to each.[51]

"In that case, boys, I said, we have again fallen back on d the arguments about friendship which we rejected at the beginning, for the unjust man will be a friend to the unjust man, and the bad man to the bad man no less than the good man to the good man."

"It seems so," he said.

"But then what? If we are to say that the good and that which belongs are the same, is it any different from saying that the good man is friend only to the good man?"

"No it isn't."

"But there again we thought that we ourselves had refuted this one too, or don't you remember?"[52]

"Yes we do."

"What further use, then, could we make of the argu- e ment? Or is it clear that there isn't any? Therefore like the clever men in the jury courts, I need[53] to go back over all that has been said. For if neither those who are loved, nor those who love, nor the like nor the unlike, nor the good, nor those who belong, nor the other things that we discussed—for I myself no longer remember: there were so many of them—but if none of these is a friend, I no longer have anything I can say."[54]

---

[52] At 215b
[53] Or ". . . I ask you if I may . . ."
[54] On the *aporia* ending, see Introduction §4.

223 Ταῦτα δ' εἰπὼν ἐν νῷ εἶχον ἄλλον ἤδη τινὰ τῶν
πρεσβυτέρων κινεῖν· κᾆτα, ὥσπερ δαίμονές τινες,
προσελθόντες οἱ παιδαγωγοί, ὅ τε τοῦ Μενεξένου καὶ
ὁ τοῦ Λύσιδος, ἔχοντες αὐτῶν τοὺς ἀδελφούς, παρ-
εκάλουν καὶ ἐκέλευον αὐτοὺς οἴκαδ' | ἀπιέναι· ἤδη γὰρ
ἦν ὀψέ. τὸ μὲν οὖν πρῶτον καὶ ἡμεῖς καὶ οἱ περι-
εστῶτες αὐτοὺς ἀπηλαύνομεν· ἐπειδὴ δὲ οὐδὲν ἐφρόν-
τιζον ἡμῶν, ἀλλ' ὑποβαρβαρίζοντες ἠγανάκτουν τε
b καὶ οὐδὲν ἧττον ἐκάλουν, ἀλλ' ἐδόκουν ἡμῖν ὑποπεπω-
κότες ἐν τοῖς Ἑρμαίοις ἄποροι εἶναι προσφέρεσθαι,
ἡττηθέντες οὖν αὐτῶν διελύσαμεν τὴν συνουσίαν.
ὅμως δ' ἔγωγε ἤδη ἀπιόντων αὐτῶν, Νῦν μέν, ἦν δ'
ἐγώ, ὦ Λύσι τε καὶ Μενέξενε, καταγέλαστοι | γεγόνα-
μεν ἐγώ τε, γέρων ἀνήρ, καὶ ὑμεῖς. ἐροῦσι γὰρ οἵδε
ἀπιόντες ὡς οἰόμεθα ἡμεῖς ἀλλήλων φίλοι εἶναι—καὶ
ἐμὲ γὰρ ἐν ὑμῖν τίθημι—οὔπω δὲ ὅτι ἔστιν ὁ φίλος
οἷοί τε ἐγενόμεθα ἐξευρεῖν.

Having said this, I had it in mind at that point to arouse   223
some other of the older people there, and then like some
divine spirits, the attendants of Menexenus and Lysis
came forward with the boys' brothers and called them and
ordered them to go home. For by now it was late. Now, to
start with we and those standing around began to drive
them away, but when they paid no attention to us, but
grew angry speaking their rather barbarian Greek, and
kept calling the boys all the same; and they seemed to us   b
to have drunk a bit too much at the Hermaea and would
be difficult to deal with—so, admitting defeat, we broke
up the gathering. Nevertheless, as they were going away,
I did say: "Now then Lysis and Menexenus, we've become
a laughing stock, I, an old man, and you. For as these
people go away, they'll say that we think we are each other's friend—for I consider myself to be one of you—but
we've not yet been able to discover what the friend is."

SYMPOSIUM

INTRODUCTION

1. THE SETTING OF THE DIALOGUE

(i) The Context

The *Symposium* departs from the largely interrogatory format of most of Plato's works in featuring a drinking party (*sumposion*) to which Socrates is invited along with a number of other guests, who, in the course of the party, are all asked to deliver speeches praising the god Eros (Ἔρως = Love).[1] The party is given by the tragic playwright Agathon, and, whether an invention of Plato or a real event, it is fixed to an unusually precise date, since we are told (173a5–7) that it takes place the day after a sacrificial feast to celebrate Agathon's first victory in the dra-

---

[1] The speeches delivered at the party are formally in praise of the God Eros. In the *Symposium* as a whole, however, it is frequently a matter of interpretation in individual cases whether the speakers are praising aspects of the god or speaking about love as an abstract force or emotion, or even whether a conscious distinction is always made between the two aspects. Classical Greek did not distinguish between upper- and lowercase letters, and the Greek text that is adopted for this edition uses either, as and when the editor felt appropriate in the context. Accordingly, we will generally translate Ἔρως/ἔρως as "Love" (the God)/"love" (the emotion).

matic competition of tragedies at Athens at the Lenaia festival (January–February 416).[2]

The question of whether the party actually happened, and whether the particular individuals attending actually came together at this date, or whether the whole occasion is an invention of Plato, is less important than it might seem: we should note rather the choice of an event for which there is a precise date for the background to the dialogue, Agathon's victory, and in particular, the presentation of the party in an unusually complex way. The occasion is retold many years afterward by a follower of Socrates, Apollodorus, who is replying to a request from an unnamed acquaintance representing others, to tell him all about it; he informs him about a similar request he has had previously from a friend, Glaucon,[3] who hailed him while he was walking from his house in Phalerum up to Athens. Glaucon had heard about the party from others and wanted a clearer report, only to learn that it happened much longer ago than he thought. Apollodorus was too young to have been there himself and had his report of it principally from another follower of Socrates, Aristodemus, who had been present at the party in circumstances, initially embarrassing, that we learn about in the dialogue itself (174a3–75c2, and see below, §1(iii)). That Plato intends his audience to remain aware throughout of the ele-

[2] Agathon's victory is recorded by Athenaeus 5.217a–b (ca. AD 200). The ascription to the Lenaia is problematic (Csapo and Slater, *The Context of Ancient Drama*, 3A i. 70A and B), but Plato obviously envisages a winter event (see "the nights were long" at 223c1).

[3] Possibly Plato's brother or half brother (for the complexities of this identification, see Nails, 154–56).

ment of reportage is clear from the persistent use in the dialogue of double indirect speech (he said he said).[4]

As for the date at which Apollodorus is supposed to be relating the event: Agathon had long departed from Athens for the court of Archelaus, ruler of Macedonia. He is presumed still alive, "Agathon hasn't lived here for many years" (172c3–5), and he died probably before 399.[5] Socrates, whose devoted follower Apollodorus has been for less than three years (172c3–6), was tried on an charge of impiety and executed in 399; so a dramatic date set by Plato some few years before 400 seems likely.[6] (On the question of the date of the actual composition of the *Symposium* in relation to *Lysis* and *Phaedrus*, see the Appendix at the end of this Introduction).

Why so complex a narrative framework? Several other dialogues feature conversations that portray Socrates conversing with friends and associates, reported to those anxious to know about their content: notably *Phaedo*, Socrates' last conversation in prison before his death, and two later more technical dialogues, *Theaetetus* and *Parmenides*. These latter two both resemble the *Symposium*

[4] See 175a3, etc. Clumsy in translation and used sparingly in this edition.

[5] The scholion to Aristophanes' *Frogs* 83 (produced 405) comments on the statement that Agathon has gone "to the banquet of the blessed" as supposedly referring either to his departure to the Macedonian court or, less likely, to his death (see Csapo and Slater, *The Context of Ancient Drama*, IA i. 26A).

[6] On the dramatic date of the dialogue, see further Bury, lxvi–lxviii. For the suggestion (there is no direct evidence) that Plato may have intended Socrates' indictment actually to have been the stimulus to recall the party, see Nails, "Tragedy Off-Stage," 205 and n. 70. See also below, §5.

to the limited extent that they relate conversations told at
secondhand that allegedly took place many years previously. However, the *Symposium* is distinguished, first, by
featuring not, like *Parmenides* and *Theaetetus*, complex
and theoretical subjects (discussions concerning the Theory of Forms and the epistemological status of knowledge
and perception) but rather a celebration around a notable
public event (Antiphon's victory) involving praise speeches
(*enkōmia*) in honor of the god Love. Second, the subject
of Love or love (see n. 1) bridges ethical and social issues
likely to be of interest to a wide range of people; third, the
guests are not, as in *Parmenides*, long-dead visiting philosophers, but some of the most prominent figures in the
intellectual, artistic, and political life of later fifth century
Athens, including, among others, the comic playwright
Aristophanes, the tragedian Agathon, and a late drunk
gate-crasher, the politician and playboy Alcibiades. Finally, and most significant, the pressing desire of a number
of people to know from Apollodorus about a comparatively distant private event, initially surprising, and their
perseverance in the face of the difficulty in acquiring
an accurate account, serve to emphasize its importance.
Apollodorus' continuing devotion to Socrates (172c4ff.)
serves to draw our attention to the ongoing influence of
the latter as a teacher and foreshadows his key role in the
work.

(ii) The Symposium

The tradition of the aristocratic male drinking party, dating back to its military and political origins in the archaic period, was by the fifth and fourth centuries in Athens a largely social bonding of men that took place in the *andrōn*, the main room in the men's section of the private house. Underlying the symposium's activities was the demonstration, transmission, and reinforcement of social and ethical values appropriate to the gender and class of the participants.

More formal than a modern dinner party, the symposium consisted of a clear separation of activities: eating was followed by the ritual washing of hands, libations to the gods, and (often hard) drinking accompanied by poems and songs provided by the guests. Young men and all women were absent, apart from slaves of both sexes to wait on the guests and provide musical entertainment and other services.[7] The guests lay on a number of couches in an open square around the room, usually two to a couch, reclining on their left side and eating and drinking with the right hand. As we shall see in the *Symposium* (e.g., 185c, 222d–23b), Plato uses the placing of the guests to dramatic effect.

Plato roughly follows the traditional procedure for the gathering, with the proviso that the latter part is to be a relatively sober affair, as they had all had too much to drink the previous day at Agathon's victory celebration. It

---

[7] An example of the activities of a symposium from the archaic period (somewhat sanitized) is provided by an elegiac poem of the pre-Socratic philosopher Xenophanes, DK 2B1, Edmonds fr.1 (*Elegy and Iambus*), also translated by Guthrie, *A History of Greek Philosophy*, 1:360. On the symposium in general, see Murray, *Sympotica*.

is proposed to send the entertainer, a flute girl, away, and the time is to be filled with discussion of a serious subject, namely a series of speeches praising the god Eros (Love). The speeches that follow, despite their manifest diversity in style and content, mostly adhere fairly closely to a succession of themes that were traditionally laid down as suitable for an *encomion* (a speech of praise) to a deity, including the origins of the god, his nature and qualities, his achievements, and the benefits bestowed on mortals.[8]

(iii) Plato's Dramatic Sense and Platonic Philosophy

The *Symposium* is delicately balanced between the comic and the serious. The mixture of formality and spontaneous humor in *Symposium* is handled by Plato with great dexterity and lightness of touch. Aristodemus, Socrates' follower (and Apollodorus' source), ends up at the party almost by accident, having been invited by Socrates rather than by the host; when he arrives, his obvious embarrassment at a social *faux pas* is smoothed over by Agathon, who claims (pretends?) he was meaning to invite him anyway (174e). Socrates himself has no worries about such social niceties and behaves in a characteristically eccentric manner: absorbed in some philosophical problem, he stands becalmed in a neighboring porch and arrives late, Aristodemus having assured an anxious Agathon that there

[8] The rules for *encomia* were codified later in the fourth century by the author of the *Rhetorica ad Alexandrum*, on which see Dover, 11–12.

was no point in trying to fetch him, "this is a habit of his" (175b1–2).[9]

The speeches that make up the bulk of the work are interspersed with comic episodes: Aristophanes unable to take his turn because of hiccups, and two abrupt and unexpected interruptions, the first by a drunk Alcibiades (212c6ff.), the second right at the end of the dialogue (223b), when a sudden influx of revelers breaks up the relatively calm atmosphere and leads to the end, when only Socrates, still talking (and never, apparently, the worse for drink), Agathon, and Aristophanes are still (just) awake. Plato also exploits the traditional element of competition, open or disguised, between speakers, in the exchanges that occur in the interludes between speeches, for example, Eryximachus and Aristophanes at 189a–c, Agathon and Socrates at 193d6–94e3. Plato draws attention to his own gift of stylistic parody by having his characters intersperse sly comments on individual speakers' idiosyncrasies, for example, Apollodorus as narrator on Pausanias (185c4–5), and, more extensively, Socrates on Agathon (198c3–5).

2. THE FIRST FIVE SPEECHES

The *Symposium* contains seven speeches on Love, presided over by a self-appointed "master of ceremonies" (*sumposiarchos*), the medical and scientific Eryximachus,

[9] For a further example of Socrates' absorption in a philosophical problem, in an even more improbable situation, see below, 220c–d.

and delivered in turn in the order of guests on the couches, from left to right (177d3). Here for purposes of discussion, we separate them into three main groups, representing significant shifts in the argument and mood: the first five, Phaedrus, Pausanias, Eryximachus, Aristophanes, and Agathon; second, Socrates/Diotima; third, Alcibiades. They were the ones, Aristodemus tells us, "worth remembering" (178a3–4); the party also had other unidentified guests, omission of whose speeches Aristodemus (or Apollodorus) explains by stating that he could not properly remember all the details (178a1–5). Moreover, we have no speech from Aristodemus himself, who, once he has prevented Agathon from fetching Socrates in at 175c, is confined to the role of reporter, effectively "disappearing" as a character in the dialogue until just before the end (223cff.).[10]

The first five speeches belong together as *encomia* praising the workings and effects of Love (Eros). Each speaker, either explicitly or by implication, aims to correct, expand, or change the emphasis of his predecessor. The speeches as a whole articulate in a variety of ways the aims and benefits of Love from a number of viewpoints.

(i) The Speeches of Phaedrus and Pausanias (178a6–85c3)

These two belong naturally together as expressing an Athenian social perspective on upper-class Athenian erotic relationships. Eryximachus tells us that Phaedrus is the

---

[10] The elaborate narrative frame that starts the dialogue has no corresponding conclusion: at 223d we are not returned to Apollodorus and his listening audience.

originator of the theme (177a3–c5), and, as the speeches proceed *epi dexia* (from left to right around the couches), he goes first (177d3–4). His starting point is a conventional one: mythology as set out by the traditional teachers, the poets. He celebrates Love as being among the oldest of the gods according to the genealogy found in Hesiod (*Theogony* 116–20) and others. Love, presiding over the conventional homoerotic relationship between an older man (*erastēs*) and an adolescent boy, (*erōmenos*) represents, he claims, a powerful inducement for them both to be seen as avoiding shameful deeds and acting honorably and bravely in each other's eyes (178d), an inducement much greater than the attitude of family or society in general.[11] In a relatively superficial and orthodox exposition relying on poetic authority, Phaedrus uses mythological examples to prove that love leads to great sacrifices: Alcestis dying for her husband, Admetus; Achilles avenging Patroclus. Any more searching exploration of the nature of the relationship beyond these simple aims is left for subsequent speeches.

In the following much longer speech (180c2ff.), Pausanias also starts with mythological precedent, but in his case to discriminate between different types of Love. In a speech that is more complex in argument than that of Phaedrus (see esp. 182d5ff.), he distinguishes "Heavenly" love (Aphrodite as the daughter of Uranus, without a mother) and "Common" love (a younger Aphrodite as the daughter of Zeus and Dione). An activity associated with the former is fine (*kalon*), concerned with *aretē* (virtue,

---

[11] On this relationship in Classical Athens, see General Introduction, §2. On "shameful deeds," see the following note.

excellence); with the latter, concentrated on the body, it is shameful (*aischron*).[12] As a lover of Agathon, a partnership unusual in being apparently lifelong,[13] Pausanias betrays his exclusively homoerotic outlook in denigrating heterosexual relationships, along with other exclusively sensual partnerships, as an indication of "Common" love in favor of what he sees as the "Heavenly" ideal: an exclusively male partnership (Aphrodite born without a mother) between a man and an adolescent boy, combining a physical and an intellectual relationship, in which the older man influences the younger by tuition and example. In contrast to the lack of discrimination in other societies, Athens has a complex convention (*nomos*) in which considerable moral license is allowed to the partners provided that their ultimate goal is the pursuit of a higher love, involving *aretē* (excellence).

In his speech he expands on Phaedrus' blanket approval of Love, yet going one better than Phaedrus, by accurately pinpointing the double standards involved in the approval/disapproval of the *erastēs*/*erōmenos* relationship (183cff.). In his broad references to *aretē* and the soul, it remains unclear what the *erastēs* has to do to cultivate in the *erōmenos* qualities associated with goodness and wisdom (*sophia*), beyond what is generally accepted as the ethical norm (*nomos*): the excellence (*aretē*) associated with an educated Athenian citizen.

12 *Kalos* (fine, beautiful, noble) and its opposite *aischros* (shameful) were the most powerful terms of general approval/ disapproval in the Greek ethical vocabulary.

13 See Xenophon, *Symposium* 8.32.

(ii) The Speech of Eryximachus (185e6–88e4)

The next speaker, Eryximachus, like Pausanias, distinguishes a double aspect of Love, but with a medical/scien-
tific dimension: as a medical man familiar with Hippocratic medicine and the pre-Socratic philosophers, his
authority derives not from mythological tradition but from
science, in which he distinguishes Pausanias' Common
Love and the Heavenly Love as sickness and health,
respectively, in the human body.[14] It is fine (*kalon*) to
gratify what is healthy but shameful (*aischron*) to do this
with regard to what is sick. The job of the expert medical
practitioner is to harmonize the opposites, cold/hot, sweet/
bitter, dry/wet, etc. Eryximachus extends the pre-Socratic/
Hippocratic theory of the harmonization of opposites into
such diverse human pursuits as gymnastic activity, agriculture, and music, where the expert's job is to help to create
prosperity and health through the gratification of an orderly (*kosmios*), as opposed to a violent, love. In this way,
by maintaining moderation and justice, mortals maintain
good relationships with each other and with the gods.

Eryximachus' broadening of the subject into the scientific realm makes an advance on the previous speeches to
the extent that it outlines a general theory of human activity that represents a step up from Pausanias' *nomos* in that
it claims to be based on scientific knowledge. However, it
takes the reader no further on the subject of love as a human emotion, and it still remains as unclear as it did with

[14] For pre-Socratic and medical authority for Eryximachus'
theories, see *Symposium* translation nn. 48–52.

Pausanias how Eryximachus' exposition, in his case in terms of the body, relates to the emotional aspect of the relationship of love between individuals.

It is not immediately obvious either how seriously Plato intends us to take Eryximachus' speech. The learned, rather pompous style suggests elements of parody in Plato's portrayal. It may also be significant that Plato has placed Eryximachus out of turn ahead of Aristophanes, who was prevented from speaking by hiccups (185c–e). This may suggest that we are to see Plato's disruption of the designated speech order by couches as a deliberate dramatic device to imagine Eryximachus' prescribed cure for Aristophanes as a chance for the latter to do his comic turn: the gargling and sneezing going on at least for part of Eryximachus' speech as a background to the doctor's lofty exposition.[15]

(iii) The Speech of Aristophanes (189c2–93d5)

At all events Eryximachus' cure works, and with Aristophanes' speech we enter a different world. Set loosely in the tradition of speculation about human origins,[16] Aristophanes' account is an invented story with the characteristics

[15] Eryximachus' name could be punned on as "burp-" or "hiccup fighter." There are different opinions on how seriously we are to take Eryximachus' speech: on the positive side, see Edelstein, "The Role of Eryximachus in Plato's Symposium," and McPherran, "Medicine, Magic, and Religion in Plato's *Symposium*"; on the negative, see Trivigno, "A Doctor's Folly."

[16] See especially Empedocles, DK B31.57–62, on the grotesque appearance of the earliest humans (Waterfield, 152–53)

of a folk tale or fairy story in a "once upon a time" tradition that explains how people are now. Once upon a time,
he says, humans had two opposite fronts, four limbs, and
were any one of three sexes: wholly male, male-female
(hermaphrodite), and wholly female. They proved to be
violent and threatened (like the giants of mythology
Ephialtes and Otus) to attack the gods.[17] In order to prevent this, Zeus cut them in half, threatening to repeat the
process if they caused any more trouble. This splitting of
the original body in half serves to explain why each individual, half of a severed whole, seeks his or her particular
other half; if this other half is found, there is an innate
desire for a union beyond mere sexual intercourse, which
will restore their original wholeness, fused by the god Hephaestus into one being.

Like previous speakers, Aristophanes is celebrating the
workings of Love, but unlike their conception his myth
focuses more on Love as an emotional need for an attach-
ment to a particular individual as an explanation of an
exclusive and lifelong relationship (with an incidental reference to Agathon and Pausanias, 193b7). There is a single
"other" out there to which we belong (our *oikeios*), to
which Love leads us (191d2ff). Aristophanes moves us
from a generalized discussion of the social context of love
in the other speeches toward a closer focus on the emotional impulse behind the relationship. And, to the extent
that his treatment of Love demonstrates a lack in the in-

---

and Protagoras, DK 80C1, speaking of the origins of humans in
Plato, *Protagoras* 320c8ff. (Waterfield, 217–19).

[17] On Ephialtes and Otus, see Homer, *Odyssey* 11.307–20.

dividual, Aristophanes goes some way toward anticipating Diotima's argument at 203ff.[18] But where Aristophanes stops is where, in a sense, Socrates/Diotima later picks up.

(iv) The Speech of Agathon (194e4–97e8)

Agathon, reflecting perhaps his own youthful demeanor and good looks, claims the key aspects of Love as youth and beauty. Continuing the competitive element inherent in the succession of speeches by directly contradicting Phaedrus' mythology in *his* speech (see above, §2(i)), Agathon says that Love, far from being involved in the violent activities of the oldest of the gods, is the youngest (195–96b3). Agathon proceeds to couple the god Love to qualities such as beauty, gentleness, and grace, and to virtues such as justice, moderation, and courage. Exhibiting the highly stylized and balanced sentence structure and florid language of the sophist and rhetorician Gorgias, especially toward the end (as Socrates humorously observes, 198b–c), Agathon's speech is a victory of manner over matter, a rhetorical tour de force. It is closely followed by Socrates' public demolition of his argument in the only passage of Socratic cross-examination (*elenchus*: "examination" or "scrutiny") in the whole dialogue.

Of the first five speeches, Agathon's is the one, Aris-

---

[18] Aristophanes' idea of lovers "belonging" to each other finds an echo in Socrates' (Diotima's) speech; however, Aristophanes is Diotima's obvious target at 205e, when she says that love is not a search for the other half that "belongs," unless it is a search for the good (see Aristophanes recognition of this implicit correction at 212c5–6).

todemus tells us, where "all those present . . . broke into thunderous applause" (*anathorubēsai*) (198a2), in marked contrast, we may note, to the "praise" that later greets Socrates' speech (212c4). This audience reception of Agathon's speech suggests that Plato is portraying it as a kind of theatrical performance, following their host's public success the previous day. Plato prepares us for this in advance in the interlude before Agathon's speech (193d6–94e3), where Socrates appears to be sending up Agathon by feigning stage fright at the prospect of having to follow what he fears is going to be a fine display (194a2ff.). This is followed by what threatens to develop into a deadly Socratic *elenchus* in which Agathon is saved by the bell, as it were, by Phaedrus, who puts a stop to Socrates' disruption of proceedings (194c–d).[19] But after Agathon's speech and in the preliminaries to his own, Socrates reveals his real feelings, in which he includes all the other speeches, when he says:

> I think you (*plural*) are digging up everything you can say and ascribing it to Love . . . in order that he may appear to be the finest and the best possible, obviously for people who do not know him—for it surely couldn't be for those who do—and the eulogy is certainly delivered in a fine and impressive manner. (198e4–99a3)

[19] On the conversational play between Agathon and Socrates at 193d4–94e3, cut short by Phaedrus, see Emlyn-Jones, "The Dramatic Poet and His Audience," 397–402. Note also Agathon's characterization of his own speech as combining play/entertainment (*paidias*) and moderate seriousness (*spoudēs metrias*, 197e7–8).

This is an immediate preliminary to his close examination of Agathon's central thesis, the beauty and the goodness of Love, with a characteristically disarming "just a few little questions" (199b8–9).

In this way Plato prepares us for the radical contrast to be drawn between these speeches and Socrates' original and profound treatment of the subject. However, despite Socrates' damaging criticisms, the contributions of the preceding speakers, which take up more than a third of the whole work, amount to something more than simply a foil to Socratic exploration. Their obvious individual limitations may perhaps be seen by us, the external audience, as those of men of social standing, intellect, and learning who contribute a broad and interesting range of perspectives that give a context to Socrates/Diotima's argument.[20]

3. THE SPEECH OF SOCRATES/DIOTIMA

(i) The Nature of Love (199c3–204c8)

In his dialectic with Agathon (a mini *elenchus*), in working with "love" as a relational term, that is, love must be love *of* something, Socrates establishes that Love must be love of what he does not possess: so, if Love is love of the beautiful (*to kalon*), Love cannot, as Agathon maintained in his speech, be beautiful; and if good things are beautiful, he would also be lacking in good things (201a–c). Socrates develops a logical argument that, whatever its ambiguities

[20] See especially Sheffield, "The Role of the Earlier Speeches in the *Symposium*, 23–46. On the speeches as an intertextual structured development, see Rowe, 8–10.

and flaws, lays the foundation for the subsequent theory of the nature and aims of Love (love).[21] At the end of his *elenchus* with Agathon, in reply to the latter's admission that he cannot argue against Socrates, in a brief phrase Socrates disclaims any independent knowledge: "No . . . it is rather the truth that you cannot argue against . . . since there's nothing difficult about arguing against Socrates" (201c8–9).

At this point Socrates hands over the argument, so to speak, to Diotima, a woman from Mantinea whom he once spoke to as a wise woman, an "expert" (*sophē*) in love (201d–e), with Socrates taking the unusual role of respondent. Both at the end of the previous *elenchus* (see immediately above) and in what follows, it appears that Plato is placing Socrates dramatically in the position of an ignorant learner whose possession of the truth comes from an authoritative source outside himself, so perhaps lessening the impact of his previous criticism of Antiphon and the others.[22]

The other speakers have almost all, in different ways,

[21] For a close analysis of the argument, see Stokes, *Plato's Socratic Conversations*, chap. 3 (114–82), and Rowe, n. on 199c5ff; see also Dover, 133ff., Waterfield, n. on 201b. For the relationship of "good" and "beautiful," see below, n. 24.

[22] Diotima = "honored by (or "honoring") Zeus"; she is almost definitely a Platonic fiction, both sides of the conversation representing Socrates himself, which is certainly what Aristophanes assumes (see 212c4–6). Her place of origin, Mantinea, resembles the word *mantis* = "seer." The story of the postponement of the plague may be modeled on the story (*Laws* 642d) of Epimenides the Cretan, brought to Athens to prophesy that the Persian invasion would not happen for ten years (see Dover, n. on 201d3). For Socrates' self-confessed "ignorance," see *Apology* 21d).

concentrated on the *aims* of Love, not what his *nature* is, which is, according to Socrates, an essential first step: to know exactly what it is you are talking about.[23] Agathon, despite being the most directly criticized of the symposiasts, alone followed the rule (195ff.), and it is from his assertion that Love is the most beautiful (195a7ff.) that Diotima starts out. Love, she claims, is neither beautiful nor ugly, neither good nor bad, but something in between; not a god or a mortal but a "spirit" (*daimōn*), an intermediary between gods and men. In the following (203bff.) myth of Penia (Poverty) and Porus (Resource, Contrivance), Love, living with characteristics of both, is in constant need, scheming to acquire what he lacks (203b–4c6).

(ii) The Aim of Love (204d1–6a13)

Socrates earlier linked *to agathon* (the good) with *to kalon* (the beautiful), in the cross-examination of Agathon at 201c2; from this point on they are closely identified as a fundamental basis of the argument. The possibility that not all that is *kalon* is necessarily *agathon* is not considered. This close identification of *kalon* and *agathon* is less problematic in Greek, given the spectrum of meaning of *kalos*: not just "aesthetically beautiful," but "fine, noble, honorable"—often close in meaning to *agathos* = ethically "good."[24] The lover of the beautiful will love good

---

[23] Socrates forcibly makes the same point at *Phaedrus*, e.g., 237cff.: the need to establish right at the beginning the nature of what is being discussed.

[24] "It might be near the truth to say that τὸ καλόν is neither less nor more than τὸ ἀγαθόν in its external aspect, 'goodness' as apprehended by the aesthetic faculty, or goodness *qua* attractive and soul-stirring" (Bury, n. on 201c1–2).

things, which will result in happiness (*eudaimonia*). The attainment of *eudaimonia* in the *Symposium* appears to assume the Socratic ethical principal that all basically want what is good as a route to happiness, and wrongdoing comes from ignorance (as in *Apology* and other early dialogues):

> DIOTIMA: "Do you think this wish and this love are common to all people, and do they all wish for good things always for themselves, or what do you say?"

> SOCRATES: "Just as you say," I said, "it's common to everyone." (205a5–8)[25]

(iii) The Activity of Love (206b1–9e4)

The activity of Love between the *erastēs* and the *erōmenos* is centered on the image of pregnancy, the desire to give birth in the beautiful (206bff.).[26] There are those (by implication males) who are pregnant in their soul even more than in the body, whether poets, politicians, or lovers, wishing to bring forth, with their beloved, wisdom: those associating in this way give birth to "offspring" more beautiful and immortal than the result of any physical union between a man and a woman.

Behind all this is the desire for immortality, common to all living creatures, human and animal. Plato's Socrates builds on the common Greek aspiration of *kleos* (immortal

[25] On the Socratic aspect of knowledge and desire in the *Symposium*, see Rowe, "The *Symposium* as a Socratic Dialogue," 9–22.

[26] See Hobbs, "Female Imagery in Plato," 252–71.

fame), taking to a new level the mythical examples of the power of Love in the speech of Phaedrus (179b–80b). For Socrates this is, in its highest form, the production of mental "children" in a relationship with a beautiful loved one. As she develops her description of the needs of the *erastēs* in terms of love, Diotima broadens description of the conventional erotic situation, using sexual language metaphorically to describe the creation of "children," offspring in the form of wisdom and virtue, with widening reference to the "offspring" of the great poets and lawgivers (209c–e).

(iv) The "Final Mysteries" (209e5–12c3)

Diotima goes on to reveal the ultimate goal, established at an earlier stage, where it was stated that being happy (*eudaimōn*) "seems to contain the end (*telos*) of the inquiry" (205a3). But how is this final goal reached? *Eudaimonia* is the key: as Diotima stated earlier, it is a state that makes life completely worthwhile; this, Diotima now says, can come only ultimately from an encounter with absolute beauty. To have what really leads to a flourishing life, we need to listen to the final section of the speech, a revelation of the final mysteries. This section (210aff.) uses the imagery of initiation into secret religious rites such as the Eleusinian Mysteries to depict the ascent of the lover, led by his guide, from attachments to beautiful individuals, toward the realization that one beautiful body is much like another, and from that position to the study of beauty in souls, and from there to the "great ocean of beauty" contained in knowledge (210d4), and finally to initiation into the final goal, eternal beauty that "alone by itself with itself . . . is an eternal single form" (211b1–2). This beauty is essentially one of Plato's unchanging Forms, the absolutes, imperfectly reflected in the changing things of our world.[27]

From early in the speech, the goal of Love, *eudaimonia*, has been seen in terms of a search for "possession" (*ktēsis*) of "good things" (*agatha*) for himself by the *erastēs*, which will lead to his happiness. It seems to follow that, right from the beginning of the exposition, the main perspective on Love (love) is that of the needs and desires of the *erastēs*. Diotima says, "It seems to me, judging by what you're telling me, you thought that Love was what is loved, not that which loves. This is the reason I think Love appeared to be most beautiful to you. Indeed it is that which is loved which is in reality beautiful, gentle, perfect and regarded as most blessed" (204c4–5). This perspective appears to underlie the whole speech.

A much-debated issue arises from this: if love is defined in terms of the needs and the desires of the aspirant *erastēs*, does concern for the *erōmenos* get left behind as the *erastēs* ascends through the stages of loving in his approach toward the final mysteries and the Form of Beauty (211bff.)? In *Nichomachean Ethics* Books 8 and 9, in a discussion of different types of friendship, Aristotle distinguishes one type of friend as "one who wishes, and promotes by action, the real or apparent good of another for

---

[27] The Form is described in language more or less identical to that in, e.g., *Phaedo* (78d5–6), where Socrates attempts to prove that the immortal soul acquires knowledge of the Forms before birth. The argument for personal immortality (set out in *Meno* 81aff., *Phaedo* 72eff., and *Phaedrus* 249c) does not occur unambiguously in the *Symposium*.

that other's sake" (1166a3–5). If, for Plato's Socrates, the ultimate goal of the loving relationship is for the lover to gain personal *eudaimonia* through contemplation of the Form of Beauty, is the good of the loved one for his own sake lost sight of in this ascent? However, could it be argued that for someone who has succeeded in reaching the ultimate goal, a loving relationship must involve caring for another and acting as a guide (as Diotima does for Socrates) as an integral part of perfecting the flourishing life? If this is the case, part of the duty of the initiate philosopher—an expression of his love and fulfillment of his *eudaimonia*—is to descend from the highest mysteries to assist those aspirants at a lower level. One might perhaps make a comparison with the philosopher rulers in *Republic* 540aff., who descend from contemplation of the Form of the Good back into the Cave to take their turn in ruling and assist those in the everyday world.[28]

4. THE SPEECH OF ALCIBIADES

The entry of Alcibiades, immediately following the philosophical climax of Diotima's speech, is the dramatic masterstroke of the work. His inebriated and noisy gate-

---

[28] The whole issue was raised by Vlastos, "The Individual as an Object of love in Plato," 137–63. Vlastos argues that the crucial flaw in Plato's theory of love was that it was compatible with a view that the love of beautiful individuals was used by the lover "instrumentally," as means of his own ascension to the contemplation of the Forms. For a dissenting view, see Price, *Love and Friendship in Plato and Aristotle*, 45–49, and for a judicious

crashing abruptly returns us from the elevated heights to rowdy semidrunken reality (212cff.). Following humorous byplay involving suggestive innuendo between Socrates, Alcibiades, and Agathon (213a–e), Alcibiades delivers his speech, which stands out from the others as an encomium not of Love but of Socrates himself. It follows the form of the *enkomion*: a description of the subject's nature, followed by his fine qualities (*aretē*), and his achievements. Socrates (notoriously ugly) is compared superficially to a sculptured figurine of Silenus that opens up to reveal a statue of a god inside; his words have an emotional effect on Alcibiades more powerful than the *aulos*-player Marsyas (215bff.). As a youth, Alcibiades had tried unsuccessfully to seduce Socrates (effectively reversing the roles of *erastēs* and *erōmenos*), thereby demonstrating the latter's moderation and self-control (217aff.). Socrates' physical endurance and bravery were amply demonstrated when on campaign in the Peloponnesian War he rescued a wounded Alcibiades (220ff.). Finally, Alcibiades reverts to what he said at the beginning: underneath a superficially mundane manner of speech, once opened up, Socrates reveals a divinely inspired wisdom.

Alcibiades has not, of course, heard Socrates' speech; yet the positioning of his speech *after* that of Socrates is significant and suggests from its content that Plato intends Alcibiades unconsciously to provide a commentary on key points in Socrates' speech, though its total

---

analysis of both sides of the argument, see Sheffield, *Plato's Symposium*, chap. 5, 154–82 ("Socrates' Speech: Concern for Others?", and bibliography cited there).

significance in this respect remains for the reader/listener to perceive. Like Socrates, Alcibiades undertakes to tell the truth, which he undoubtedly does, according to his lights (215a). In recounting a situation in which he attempted to seduce Socrates in exchange for instruction in virtue (218d), it becomes clear that what he actually wanted is something not far from the conventional homoerotic relationship (not unlike that outlined by Pausanias earlier, see §3(i)), in which he, as beautiful *erōmenos*, is seduced by the older man who would give, in exchange for sex, instruction in *aretē* (virtue, excellence), the possession of which Socrates, with characteristic *eironea* (mock modesty), disclaimed. It becomes clear that Socrates would have regarded this as a one-sided bargain, if he really did possess the wisdom Alcibiades seeks (he would be giving away "gold for bronze" (218e7).[29]

Yet Alcibiades is depicted by Plato as a torn character. He has a glimpse of something beyond the conventional, but he demonstrates that, despite being bitten by the "madness and frenzy of philosophy" (218b), he is ambivalent about the effort it would take to reform his way of life and make a joint inquiry with Socrates that might be the beginning of an ascent toward the knowledge of love, beauty, and goodness. He is ultimately unwilling or unable to follow Socrates even beyond the basic stages of the relationship.

[29] Socrates' positioning of himself in his own speech earlier as someone ignorant and desiring wisdom from Diotima (206b5–6) suggests that he wishes to present himself as a seeker rather than a possessor of what Alcibiades imagines he is looking for.

5. CONCLUSION

The whole work ends on a lighter note: humorously erotic byplay between Alcibiades, Socrates, and Agathon (222cff.) is followed by a rowdy invasion of revelers, and eventually most of the partygoers either leave or fall asleep. Socrates eventually goes off to spend the day in his usual manner and then goes home to rest.

Abrupt alternation of serious philosophical discussion, humorous byplay, and comic knockabout pervade the whole work; this may well lie behind the claim by Socrates, still arguing at cockcrow with Aristophanes and Agathon (the only remaining partygoers left half-awake), that the accomplished poet should know how to write comedy and tragedy (223d2–6). Exactly what Plato intended us to imagine lay behind this claim is unclear, since Aristodemus woke up to find Socrates in full flow. Yet the personality of Socrates himself may have embodied both genres: external comic ugliness combined with inner beauty, as Alcibiades had been at pains to emphasize in his speech (215a–16c). This contrast is reflected in Socrates' customary way of speaking, in which ordinary prose and homely images are used to reveal divinely inspired truths, as Alcibiades points out (221e–22a).

Yet a tragic (in our sense) subtext in the relationship between Socrates and Alcibiades may perhaps be intended by Plato, looking back in retrospect from the fourth century. On the one hand, there is Plato's choice of a precise historical context, the public festival of the Lenaia and Agathon's dramatic triumph (early in 416). This event shortly preceded the ill-fated Athenian expedition to Sicily (spring 415), in which Alcibiades was involved as one of the military leaders. We learn from Thucydides (6.27–29) that one night during the preparations for this expedition religious sacrilege was committed involving desecration of images of the god Hermes and profanation of the sacred mysteries. Accusations were made against several of those whom Plato portrays as having attended Agathon's party, particularly Alcibiades (Thuc. 6.28), but also Phaedrus and Eryximachus (Phaedrus, and possibly Eryximachus, fleeing into exile and avoiding trial).[30]

Between the date of the party and the likely intended dramatic date of the frame conversation (see §1(i)), Athens suffered defeat at the hands of the Spartans in the Peloponnesian War (404), followed by a period of political upheaval. Alcibiades died at about this time, but earlier, following his prominent involvement in the religious sacrilege and debacle of the Athenian expedition to Sicily, he had played a dubious role in subsequent events, at one point deserting to the Spartan side to avoid prosecution in connection with the above-mentioned religious sacrilege (Thuc. 6.60–61). It is possible that in the *Symposium* (whether recording a real or fictional event) Plato wished to present the conduct and attitudes of Alcibiades and the others in the light of the subsequent political upheaval and witch hunt.

On the other hand, there is the other key dramatic date, that of the *Symposium* frame conversation itself. Its date, close to Socrates' trial and execution in 399, may possibly explain the urgency of the desire of Socrates' devotee, Apollodorus, and his friends to hear about the

---

30 See Nails (n. 6), 202–3.

party (see above, §1(i)). In reflecting on the trial and death of his master, Plato may have been using the drama of the *Symposium*, and the desire of others to hear it, to lead his audience to reflect on why Socrates' pursuit of the fulfilled life based on an erotic relationship aiming at *eudaimonia*, advocated in his speech, appeared to have so little effect on some of his listeners. This question emerges sharply in the case of Alcibiades. In Socrates' 399 trial on a charge of *asebeia* (impiety), the most serious accusation, Plato tells us, was corruption of the young (*Apology* 24b8–c1). Alcibiades is not mentioned by Plato's Socrates in the *Apology* (he had died in 404), but one of the allegations behind this charge was thought to be Socrates' earlier corrupting relationship with him (Xenophon, *Memorabilia* 1.2.12ff.). Alcibiades' role in the *Symposium* is perhaps being used as an example of this inability to follow Socrates in his quest for wisdom in the face of the competing desire for fame and personal honor. In this he appears to be quite unlike the speakers in the frame dialogue, Apollodorus and Aristodemus, devoted followers, for whom Socrates represented *the* route to the fulfilled life.

The setting, the structure, and above all the abrupt changes of mood characteristic of *Symposium* have practically no parallels within the Platonic corpus, a fact that renders conclusions as to its meaning and its purpose difficult to draw. The *Symposium* as Plato's apologia for Socrates? Perhaps through Alcibiades' speech we are to see Socrates' own tragedy: his failure, as an *erastēs* searching to attain *eudaimonia*, to take his potential *erōmenos*, or for that matter his whole audience, with him, the endpoint of this failure being his trial and execution.

APPENDIX: DRAMATIC DATE
AND DATE OF COMPOSITION
OF THE *SYMPOSIUM*

The dramatic date at which the actual *Symposium* and the later reporting of it is set is discussed in detail at §1(i) above, and so needs no further amplification here.

As to the date of composition, there are three references in the dialogue to external events: (1) at 178e–79b3, one of the speakers, Phaedrus, refers to an army of lovers and loved ones, which may be a reference to the "sacred band" of Thebans, dated to ca. 379/8; (2) at 182b6ff., another of the speakers, Pausanias, speaks of "Ionia and many other places elsewhere . . . under foreign rule," which suggests composition after The King's Peace of 387/6, which recognized Persian claims to rule the cities in Asia (i.e., Asia Minor Greeks) that had previously been under Greek rule; (3) at 193a2ff., Aristophanes in his speech refers to the splitting up of the Arcadians by the Lacedaemonians, which occurred in 385 (for discussion of the significance of this reference for the dating of the composition of the *Symposium*, see Mattingly, "The Date of Plato's *Symposium*").

Internal evidence from Plato's supposed philosophical development does not provide precise dating. Assuming a developmental model of Early-Middle-Late dialogues, a model not universally accepted (see Chronology of Plato's Life and Works), the *Symposium* fits into the Middle period, along with *Meno* and *Phaedo*, in its clear reference to the theory of Forms; but it almost definitely precedes *Republic* and *Phaedrus* in apparently assuming a "Socratic psychology"—that all desire the good (see, e.g., 205a),

involving the absence of reference in the individual soul
to an element of desire conflicting with the reasoning part
(see the tripartite model in *Republic* 439b4ff. and *Phaedrus* 253cff.).[31]

The evidence, external and internal, suggests a date in
the late 380s for composition of the *Symposium*, that is,
the "Middle Period."

[31] The absence of evidence in the *Symposium* of a view that
the individual can experience personal immortality as indicated
in the *Republic* and the *Phaedrus* (rather than "immortality"
through reproduction, or *kleos* [immortal fame] through the creation of laws, poetic works, etc.) has also been cited as evidence
that the *Symposium* precedes those dialogues, but the value of
this evidence for dating is inconclusive. See, for example, Rowe,
n. on 206e8–7a2 (184–85), for a discussion of the evidence.

ΣΥΜΠΟΣΙΟΝ

ΑΠΟΛΛΟΔΩΡΟΣ   ΕΤΑΙΡΟΣ

172   ΑΠΟΛΛΟΔΩΡΟΣ Δοκῶ μοι περὶ ὧν πυνθάνεσθε οὐκ
ἀμελέτητος εἶναι. καὶ γὰρ ἐτύγχανον πρῴην εἰς ἄστυ
οἴκοθεν ἀνιὼν Φαληρόθεν· τῶν οὖν γνωρίμων τις ὄπισθεν κατιδών με πόρρωθεν ἐκάλεσε, καὶ παίζων ἅμα
τῇ κλήσει, "Ὦ Φαληρεύς," ἔφη, | "οὗτος Ἀπολλόδω-
ρος, οὐ περιμένεις;" Κἀγὼ ἐπιστὰς περιέμεινα. Καὶ
ὅς, "Ἀπολλόδωρε," ἔφη, "καὶ μὴν καὶ ἔναγχός σε ἐζήτουν βουλόμενος διαπυθέσθαι τὴν Ἀγάθωνος συνουσίαν καὶ Σωκράτους καὶ Ἀλκιβιάδου καὶ τῶν ἄλλων
b   τῶν τότε ἐν τῷ συνδείπνῳ παραγενομένων, περὶ τῶν
ἐρωτικῶν λόγων τίνες ἦσαν· ἄλλος γάρ τίς μοι διηγεῖτο ἀκηκοὼς Φοίνικος τοῦ Φιλίππου, ἔφη δὲ καὶ σὲ
εἰδέναι. ἀλλὰ γὰρ οὐδὲν εἶχε | σαφὲς λέγειν. σὺ οὖν

---

[1] Apollodorus addresses his recital of the whole event to a
friend who is the spokesperson for a number of enquirers (plural at a1 and 173c–e). On the dramatic date of the dialogue, its
significance, and the complexity of the dialogue frame detailed
in 172a–73b8, see Introduction, §1(i). The devotion of Apollodorus to Socrates, as well as his emotional nature, is also dem-

SYMPOSIUM

APOLLODORUS   COMPANION

APOLLODORUS: I think I'm not unprepared for what   172
you're inquiring about.[1] For I happened to be going up to
town the other day from my house in Phalerum.[2] One of
my acquaintances caught sight of me from behind and
hailed me from some distance, and jokingly called out:
"Hey, Phalerian, you, Apollodorus, wait, won't you?"[3] And
I stopped and waited. And he said: "Apollodorus, why, it
was only just now I was looking for you as I wanted to find
out all about Agathon's party, that time when Socrates and
Alcibiades and the others had gathered for dinner, and   b
about what they said in their speeches on love. You see
someone else was recounting it to me, having heard it
from Phoenix, Philippus' son,[4] but he said you knew about
it too. But the truth is he had nothing precise to say. So

onstrated in his reaction to Socrates' imminent death in *Phaedo*
117d3–6.

[2] Phalerum was the main harbor of nearby Athens until the
fifth century, when it was displaced by Piraeus.

[3] The joke probably lies in the mock formality of addressing
Apollodorus with the name of his deme (district of Athens), Phalerum (see previous note).

[4] Otherwise unknown.

μοι διήγησαι· δικαιότατος γὰρ εἶ τοὺς τοῦ ἑταίρου
λόγους ἀπαγγέλλειν. πρότερον δέ μοι," ἦ δ' ὅς, "εἰπέ,
σὺ αὐτὸς παρεγένου τῇ συνουσίᾳ ταύτῃ ἢ οὔ;" Κἀγὼ
εἶπον ὅτι "Παντάπασιν ἔοικέ σοι οὐδὲν διηγεῖσθαι
σαφὲς ὁ διηγούμενος, εἰ νεωστὶ ἡγῇ τὴν συνουσίαν
γεγονέναι ταύτην ἣν ἐρωτᾷς, ὥστε καὶ ἐμὲ παραγενέ-
c σθαι." "Ἐγώ γε δή," ἔφη. "Πόθεν, ἦν δ' ἐγώ, ὦ Γλαύ-
κων; οὐκ οἶσθ' ὅτι πολλῶν ἐτῶν Ἀγάθων ἐνθάδε οὐκ
ἐπιδεδήμηκεν, ἀφ' οὗ δ' | ἐγὼ Σωκράτει συνδιατρίβω
καὶ ἐπιμελὲς πεποίημαι ἑκάστης ἡμέρας εἰδέναι ὅτι
173 ἂν λέγῃ ἢ πράττῃ, οὐδέπω τρία ἔτη ἐστίν; πρὸ τοῦ δὲ
περιτρέχων ὅπῃ τύχοιμι καὶ οἰόμενος τὶ ποιεῖν ἀθλιώ-
τερος ἦ ὁτουοῦν, οὐχ ἧττον ἢ σὺ νυνί, οἰόμενος δεῖν
πάντα μᾶλλον πράττειν ἢ φιλοσοφεῖν." Καὶ ὅς, "Μὴ
σκῶπτ'," ἔφη, "ἀλλ' εἰπέ μοι πότε ἐγένετο ἡ συνουσία
| αὕτη." Κἀγὼ εἶπον ὅτι "Παίδων ὄντων ἡμῶν ἔτι, ὅτε
τῇ πρώτῃ τραγῳδίᾳ ἐνίκησεν Ἀγάθων, τῇ ὑστεραίᾳ ἢ
ἧ τὰ ἐπινίκια ἔθυεν αὐτός τε καὶ οἱ χορευταί." "Πάνυ,"
ἔφη, "ἄρα πάλαι, ὡς ἔοικεν. ἀλλὰ τίς σοι διηγεῖτο; ἢ
b αὐτὸς Σωκράτης;" "Οὐ μὰ τὸν Δία," ἦν δ' ἐγώ, "ἀλλ'
ὅσπερ Φοίνικι. Ἀριστόδημος ἦν τις, Κυδαθηναιεύς,
σμικρός, ἀνυπόδητος ἀεί· παρεγεγόνει δ' ἐν τῇ συνουσίᾳ, Σωκράτους ἐραστὴς ὢν ἐν τοῖς μάλιστα τῶν

---

[5] That is, Socrates.

[6] Possibly the half brother of Plato, a major respondent of
Socrates in *Republic* (see further Nails, 154–56).

you tell me about it, for you're just the right person to report the words of your companion.[5] But before that," he said, "tell me, were you yourself present at that gathering, or not?" And I replied: "it looks as if your informant got absolutely nothing clear, if you think this party you're asking about took place recently enough for me to have been there too." "Well, that's indeed what I thought," he said. "Where did you get that from, Glaucon?"[6] I said, "don't you know that Agathon hasn't lived here for many years, and it's not yet three years I've spent with Socrates and made it my business every day to know what he was saying or doing? Previously, I was running about at random, thinking I was achieving something, but in a more miserable state than anyone else you might mention, no less than you right now, and thinking I should be doing anything rather than philosophy." And he said: "Don't mock me, but tell me when this gathering took place." And I said: "When we were still boys, when Agathon won with his first tragedy, the day after he and his choral dancers celebrated their victory with the sacrificial feast."[7] "It seems it really was a long time ago then," he said, "but who described it to you? Or was it Socrates himself?" "Oh no, by Zeus," I said, "but the person who told Phoenix. Someone called Aristodemus, from Cydatheneum, a small man, always going around barefoot. He was at the gathering, being a lover of Socrates, as much as any, I think, of those

c

173

b

---

[7] The "sacrificial feast" for chorus and actors was a thanksgiving for victory in the dramatic competition held at one of the festivals in the year, in this case the Lenaia (Winter) festival, 416. On the evidence for the festival and the (unusually) precise dramatic date, see Introduction, §1(i).

τότε, ὡς ἐμοὶ δοκεῖ. οὐ μέντοι ἀλλὰ καὶ | Σωκράτη γε
ἔνια ἤδη ἀνηρόμην ὧν ἐκείνου ἤκουσα, καί μοι ὡμο-
λόγει καθάπερ ἐκεῖνος διηγεῖτο." "Τί οὖν," ἔφη, "οὐ
διηγήσω μοι; πάντως δὲ ἡ ὁδὸς ἡ εἰς ἄστυ ἐπιτηδεία
πορευομένοις καὶ λέγειν καὶ ἀκούειν."

Οὕτω δὴ ἰόντες ἅμα τοὺς λόγους περὶ αὐτῶν ἐποιούμεθα, ὥστε, ὅπερ ἀρχόμενος εἶπον, οὐκ ἀμελετήτως
c ἔχω. εἰ οὖν δεῖ καὶ ὑμῖν διηγήσασθαι, ταῦτα χρὴ ποιεῖν. καὶ γὰρ ἔγωγε καὶ ἄλλως, ὅταν μέν τινας περὶ
φιλοσοφίας λόγους ἢ αὐτὸς ποιῶμαι ἢ ἄλλων ἀκούω,
χωρὶς τοῦ οἴεσθαι ὠφελεῖσθαι | ὑπερφυῶς ὡς χαίρω·
ὅταν δὲ ἄλλους τινάς, ἄλλως τε καὶ τοὺς ὑμετέρους
τοὺς τῶν πλουσίων καὶ χρηματιστικῶν, αὐτός τε
ἄχθομαι ὑμᾶς τε τοὺς ἑταίρους ἐλεῶ, ὅτι οἴεσθε τὶ
d ποιεῖν οὐδὲν ποιοῦντες. καὶ ἴσως αὖ ὑμεῖς ἐμὲ ἡγεῖσθε
κακοδαίμονα εἶναι, καὶ οἴομαι ὑμᾶς ἀληθῆ οἴεσθαι·
ἐγὼ μέντοι ὑμᾶς οὐκ οἴομαι ἀλλ' εὖ οἶδα.

ΕΤΑΙΡΟΣ Ἀεὶ ὅμοιος εἶ, ὦ Ἀπολλόδωρε· ἀεὶ γὰρ
σαυτόν | τε κακηγορεῖς καὶ τοὺς ἄλλους, καὶ δοκεῖς
μοι ἀτεχνῶς πάντας ἀθλίους ἡγεῖσθαι πλὴν Σωκράτους, ἀπὸ σαυτοῦ ἀρξάμενος. καὶ ὁπόθεν ποτὲ ταύτην

---

8 Cydathenaeum, is Aristodemus' deme, near the center of
Athens. He is otherwise unknown in Plato; his small size is also
noted in Xenophon, *Memorabilia* 1.4.2. "Lover" translates *erastēs*,
most usually found in erotic contexts, but here denotes his passionate devotion to Socrates and his teaching; he is barefoot
(173b2) in imitation of Socrates (see 174a4). On the meaning of

around at the time,[8] but mind you, afterward I asked Socrates about some of the things I heard from Aristodemus, and he confirmed it just as the other had related it." "So why don't you recount it to me?" he said. "At all events the road into town is convenient for us to talk and listen as we go along."

So as he suggested we went along and at the same time talked about the occasion so that, as I said when I started, I am not unprepared. If therefore I am to recount it to you all too that's what I must do. You see in any case when either I myself have any discussion about philosophy, or I listen to others, quite apart from thinking I am benefiting from it, it's extraordinary how delighted I am. But whenever it's any other kind of discussion, especially the talk of those of you who are rich and into moneymaking, I get bored and feel sorry for you, my companions, because you think you're doing something, when you're achieving nothing. And you in your turn think perhaps I'm the one who is a wretched fellow,[9] and I believe you are right to think so. However, I don't just think you are wretched, I know full well you are.

COMPANION: You're always the same, Apollodorus, for you're always running yourself and others down, and you seem to me to think that all are miserable without exception, apart from Socrates, beginning with yourself. And where on earth you got this nickname from, being

words for "love," "friendship," "desire" (*erōs, philia, epithumia*), see General Introduction §2.

[9] "Wretched" = *kakodaimōn*, the opposite of *eudaimōn* (happy, fulfilled), objective states and not merely psychological.

τὴν ἐπωνυμίαν ἔλαβες τὸ μαλακὸς[1] καλεῖσθαι, οὐκ
οἶδα ἔγωγε· ἐν μὲν γὰρ τοῖς λόγοις ἀεὶ τοιοῦτος εἶ,
σαυτῷ τε καὶ τοῖς ἄλλοις ἀγριαίνεις | πλὴν Σωκρά-
τους.

e   ΑΠ. Ὦ φίλτατε, καὶ δῆλόν γε δὴ ὅτι οὕτω διανο-
ούμενος καὶ περὶ ἐμαυτοῦ καὶ περὶ ὑμῶν μαίνομαι καὶ
παραπαίω;

    ΕΤ. Οὐκ ἄξιον περὶ τούτων, Ἀπολλόδωρε, νῦν ἐρί-
ζειν· | ἀλλ' ὅπερ ἐδεόμεθά σου, μὴ ἄλλως ποιήσῃς,
ἀλλὰ διήγησαι τίνες ἦσαν οἱ λόγοι.

    ΑΠ. Ἦσαν τοίνυν ἐκεῖνοι τοιοίδε τινές—μᾶλλον δ'
ἐξ ἀρχῆς ὑμῖν ὡς ἐκεῖνος διηγεῖτο καὶ ἐγὼ πειράσομαι διηγήσασθαι.

174   Ἔφη γάρ οἱ Σωκράτη ἐντυχεῖν λελουμένον τε καὶ
τὰς βλαύτας ὑποδεδεμένον, ἃ ἐκεῖνος ὀλιγάκις ἐποίει·
καὶ ἐρέσθαι | αὐτὸν ὅποι ἴοι οὕτω καλὸς γεγενημένος.

    Καὶ τὸν εἰπεῖν ὅτι Ἐπὶ δεῖπνον εἰς Ἀγάθωνος. χθὲς
γὰρ αὐτὸν διέφυγον τοῖς ἐπινικίοις, φοβηθεὶς τὸν
ὄχλον· ὡμολόγησα δ' εἰς τήμερον παρέσεσθαι. ταῦτα
δὴ ἐκαλλωπισάμην, ἵνα καλὸς παρὰ καλὸν ἴω. ἀλλὰ
σύ, ἦ δ' ὅς, πῶς ἔχεις πρὸς τὸ ἐθέλειν ἂν ἰέναι ἄκλητος ἐπὶ δεῖπνον;

---

[1] μαλακὸς B: μανικὸς TW

---

    [10] The textual variant *manikos* (mad) (see textual note), would
not make sense of the following sentence.

called "Softy,"[10] for my part I don't know. For you are always like this in our discussions; you get angry with both yourself and others, apart from Socrates.

A. Oh my dearest fellow, so it's obvious, is it, that in   e thinking in this way about myself and all of you, I'm mad and out of my wits?

C. It's not worth squabbling about these things now, Apollodorus, but please, do what we were asking you to do, just recount what the speeches were.

A. Well now, they went something like this:—but rather, just as he did,[11] so too I'll try to recount them to you from the beginning.

So he told him that he came across Socrates bathed and   174 wearing his sandals, a thing he rarely did, and he asked him where he was going, to have made himself so smart.

And he replied: "To dinner at Agathon's. For yesterday I kept out of his way at the victory celebrations, afraid of the crowd; but I agreed to be there today. So I have smartened myself up like this in order to go as one smart fellow to another smart fellow.[12] But what about you, he said, how would you feel about being willing to come to a dinner uninvited?"

[11] That is, Aristodemus, who was present at the party.

[12] "Smart" is how we are translating *kalos* here, a term with a wide range of meaning, but basically indicating strong approval (fine, beautiful, noble, good) with an overlap between aesthetic and moral meaning (often = *agathos*, "good"). *To kalon* (the beautiful) is a key concept in Socrates' speech later in the dialogue (204bff.).

b   Κἀγώ, ἔφη, εἶπον ὅτι Οὕτως ὅπως ἂν σὺ κελεύῃς.

Ἕπου τοίνυν, ἔφη, ἵνα καὶ τὴν παροιμίαν διαφθεί-
ρωμεν μεταβαλόντες, ὡς ἄρα καὶ

Ἀγάθων'[2] ἐπὶ δαῖτας ἴασιν | αὐτόματοι ἀγαθοί.

Ὅμηρος μὲν γὰρ κινδυνεύει οὐ μόνον διαφθεῖραι
ἀλλὰ καὶ ὑβρίσαι εἰς ταύτην τὴν παροιμίαν· ποιήσας
γὰρ τὸν Ἀγαμέμνονα διαφερόντως ἀγαθὸν ἄνδρα τὰ
c   πολεμικά, τὸν δὲ Μενέλεων "μαλθακὸν αἰχμητήν," θυ-
σίαν ποιουμένου καὶ ἑστιῶντος τοῦ Ἀγαμέμνονος
ἄκλητον ἐποίησεν ἐλθόντα τὸν Μενέλεων ἐπὶ τὴν θοί-
νην, χείρω ὄντα ἐπὶ τὴν τοῦ ἀμείνονος. |

Ταῦτ' ἀκούσας εἰπεῖν ἔφη Ἴσως μέντοι κινδυνεύσω
καὶ ἐγὼ οὐχ ὡς σὺ λέγεις, ὦ Σώκρατες, ἀλλὰ καθ'
Ὅμηρον φαῦλος ὢν ἐπὶ σοφοῦ ἀνδρὸς ἰέναι θοίνην
ἄκλητος. ὅρα οὖν ἄγων με τί ἀπολογήσῃ, ὡς ἐγὼ μὲν
οὐχ ὁμολογήσω ἄκλητος ἥκειν, ἀλλ' ὑπὸ σοῦ κεκλη-
μένος.

d   "Σύν τε δύ'," ἔφη, "ἐρχομένω πρὸ ὁδοῦ" βουλευσό-
μεθα ὅτι ἐροῦμεν. ἀλλ' ἴωμεν.

---

2 Ἀγάθων' Lachmann: ἀγαθῶν BTW

---

13 This double-reported speech, Apollodorus reporting what
Aristodemus told him (for reasons of readability often omitted
here in translation) frequently though not consistently used, is a
deliberate feature of the dialogue, doubtless to keep reminding
us of the frame of the narrator and the audience. The element of
reportage is also frequently indicated in the Greek by extended
passages governed by the accusative + infinitive of indirect
speech.

And I said, he said,[13] "just whatever you say."　　　　　　　b

"Then follow," said Socrates, "so that we can also spoil the proverb by changing it, so then actually it's:

'Good men go of their own accord to dinner at
　　Agathon's.'[14]

For it looks as if Homer not only undermines, but also does violence to this proverb for having made Agamemnon an outstandingly good man in warfare, but Menelaus　c a 'fainthearted spearman,' when Agamemnon was making a sacrifice and feasting, he made Menelaus go to the feast uninvited, as an inferior going to the feast of a superior."

When he heard this, Aristodemus said he replied: "But perhaps I too shall run the risk, Socrates, and not as you say, but according to Homer, I, an undistinguished man, shall be going to an accomplished man's feast uninvited. So consider what excuse you'll make if you take me, as I shall not confess to going uninvited, but invited by you."

"While the two of us make our way together along the　d road,"[15] he said, "we'll discuss what we're going to say. Well, let's go."

---

[14] The point of the saying lies in the pun on Agathon's name (*agathos* = "good"), and the "undermining" of Homer, where it is the *inferior* Menelaus ("fainthearted spearman," *Il.* 17.587–88) who goes of his own accord to Agamemnon's feast at *Iliad* 2.408. The MSS (see textual note) translate as: "Good men go uninvited to good men's feasts." We follow the reading of Burnet in OCT (see textual note), which follows a modern conjecture and arguably gives more point to the pun.

[15] A quotation loosely based on Homer, *Iliad* 10.222–26, suggesting that when two travel together, one looks out to see what's best—in this case, Socrates leaves it to Aristodemus!

147

Τοιαῦτ᾽ ἄττα σφᾶς ἔφη διαλεχθέντας ἰέναι. τὸν οὖν
| Σωκράτη ἑαυτῷ πως προσέχοντα τὸν νοῦν κατὰ τὴν
ὁδὸν πορεύεσθαι ὑπολειπόμενον, καὶ περιμένοντος οὗ
e κελεύειν προϊέναι εἰς τὸ πρόσθεν. ἐπειδὴ δὲ γενέσθαι
ἐπὶ τῇ οἰκίᾳ τῇ Ἀγάθωνος, ἀνεῳγμένην καταλαμβάνειν τὴν θύραν, καί τι ἔφη αὐτόθι γελοῖον παθεῖν. οἱ
μὲν γὰρ εὐθὺς παῖδά τινα τῶν ἔνδοθεν ἀπαντήσαντα
ἄγειν οὗ κατέκειντο οἱ ἄλλοι, καὶ καταλαμβάνειν ἤδη
μέλλοντας δειπνεῖν· εὐθὺς δ᾽ οὖν ὡς | ἰδεῖν τὸν Ἀγά-
θωνα, Ὦ, φάναι, Ἀριστόδημε, εἰς καλὸν ἥκεις ὅπως
συνδειπνήσῃς· εἰ δ᾽ ἄλλου τινὸς ἕνεκα ἦλθες, εἰς αὖθις ἀναβαλοῦ, ὡς καὶ χθὲς ζητῶν σε ἵνα καλέσαιμι,
οὐχ οἷός τ᾽ ἦ ἰδεῖν. ἀλλὰ Σωκράτη ἡμῖν πῶς οὐκ
ἄγεις;

Καὶ ἐγώ, ἔφη, μεταστρεφόμενος οὐδαμοῦ ὁρῶ Σω-
κράτη | ἑπόμενον· εἶπον οὖν ὅτι καὶ αὐτὸς μετὰ Σω-
κράτους ἥκοιμι, κληθεὶς ὑπ᾽ ἐκείνου δεῦρ᾽ ἐπὶ δεῖπνον.

Καλῶς γ᾽, ἔφη, ποιῶν σύ· ἀλλὰ ποῦ ἔστιν οὗτος;

175   Ὄπισθεν ἐμοῦ ἄρτι εἰσῄει· ἀλλὰ θαυμάζω καὶ
αὐτὸς ποῦ ἂν εἴη.

Οὐ σκέψῃ, ἔφη, παῖ, φάναι τὸν Ἀγάθωνα, καὶ εἰ-
σάξεις Σωκράτη; σὺ δ᾽, ἦ δ᾽ ὅς, Ἀριστόδημε, παρ᾽
Ἐρυξίμαχον | κατακλίνου.

Καὶ ἓ μὲν ἔφη ἀπονίζειν τὸν παῖδα ἵνα κατακέοιτο·
ἄλλον δέ τινα τῶν παίδων ἥκειν ἀγγέλλοντα ὅτι "Σωκράτης οὗτος ἀναχωρήσας ἐν τῷ τῶν γειτόνων προ-
θύρῳ ἕστηκεν, κἀμοῦ καλοῦντος οὐκ ἐθέλει εἰσιέναι." |

After talking about such things as this he said they went on their way. Then Socrates was somehow absorbed by his own thoughts and while making his way along the road he was falling behind, and when Aristodemus stopped to wait for him, he told him to go on ahead. When he arrived at e Agathon's house, he discovered the door open, and there, he said, he found himself in a ridiculous position. For one of the slaves of those inside immediately met him and led him to where the others were reclining and he found them already about to eat. Anyway as soon as Agathon saw him: "Aristodemus," he said, "you have come just at the right moment to join us in a meal. If you've come for some other reason, leave it for another time, as I came looking for you yesterday in order to invite you, but I wasn't able to see you. But how come you're not bringing Socrates to us?"

And I turned round, he said, and nowhere could I see Socrates following. So I said that it was in fact I who was coming with Socrates, at *his* invitation to come here for dinner.

"Well done you," he said, "but where is the man himself?"

"He was coming in behind me just now, but I'm won- 175 dering myself where he might be."

"Won't you go and look for Socrates, boy," said Agathon, "and bring him here? But you, Aristodemus," he said, "lie down beside Eryximachus."

And he said the slave boy washed him so he could lie down. Another of the slave boys came and announced that "Socrates is here but has gone back and is just standing in the neighbors' porch, and when I called him he was un- willing to come in."

Ἄτοπόν γ᾽, ἔφη, λέγεις· οὔκουν καλεῖς αὐτὸν καὶ μὴ ἀφήσεις;

b Καὶ ὃς ἔφη εἰπεῖν Μηδαμῶς, ἀλλ᾽ ἐᾶτε αὐτόν. ἔθος γάρ τι τοῦτ᾽ ἔχει· ἐνίοτε ἀποστὰς ὅποι ἂν τύχῃ ἔστηκεν. ἥξει δ᾽ αὐτίκα, ὡς ἐγὼ οἶμαι. μὴ οὖν κινεῖτε, ἀλλ᾽ ἐᾶτε.

Ἀλλ᾽ οὕτω χρὴ ποιεῖν, εἰ σοὶ δοκεῖ, ἔφη φάναι τὸν Ἀγάθωνα. ἀλλ᾽ ἡμᾶς, ὦ παῖδες, τοὺς ἄλλους ἑστιᾶτε. πάντως παρατίθετε ὅτι ἂν βούλησθε, ἐπειδάν τις ὑμῖν μὴ ἐφεστήκῃ—ὃ ἐγὼ οὐδεπώποτε ἐποίησα—νῦν οὖν, νομίζοντες καὶ ἐμὲ ὑφ᾽ ὑμῶν κεκλῆσθαι ἐπὶ δεῖπνον καὶ τούσδε τοὺς ἄλλους, θεραπεύετε, ἵν᾽ ὑμᾶς ἐπαινῶμεν.

c Μετὰ ταῦτα ἔφη σφᾶς μὲν δειπνεῖν, τὸν δὲ Σωκράτη οὐκ εἰσιέναι. τὸν οὖν Ἀγάθωνα πολλάκις κελεύειν μεταπέμψασθαι τὸν Σωκράτη, ἓ δὲ οὐκ ἐᾶν. ἥκειν οὖν αὐτὸν οὐ πολὺν χρόνον ὡς εἰώθει διατρίψαντα, ἀλλὰ μάλιστα σφᾶς μεσοῦν δειπνοῦντας. τὸν οὖν Ἀγάθωνα—τυγχάνειν γὰρ ἔσχατον κατακείμενον μόνον—Δεῦρ᾽, ἔφη φάναι, Σώκρατες, παρ᾽ ἐμὲ κατάκεισο, ἵνα καὶ τοῦ σοφοῦ ἁπτόμενός σου ἀπολαύσω, d ὅ σοι προσέστη ἐν τοῖς προθύροις. δῆλον γὰρ ὅτι ηὗρες αὐτὸ καὶ ἔχεις· οὐ γὰρ ἂν προαπέστης.

Καὶ τὸν Σωκράτη καθίζεσθαι καὶ εἰπεῖν ὅτι Εὖ ἂν ἔχοι, φάναι, ὦ Ἀγάθων, εἰ τοιοῦτον εἴη ἡ σοφία ὥστ᾽ ἐκ τοῦ πληρεστέρου εἰς τὸ κενώτερον ῥεῖν ἡμῶν, ἐὰν ἁπτώμεθα ἀλλήλων, ὥσπερ τὸ ἐν ταῖς κύλιξιν ὕδωρ τὸ διὰ τοῦ ἐρίου ῥέον ἐκ τῆς πληρεστέρας εἰς τὴν

"That's odd what you're saying," he said. "Won't you call him and not let him go?"

And, said Aristodemus, he replied: "No way, but let b him be. You see, this is a habit of his. Sometimes he turns aside wherever he happens to be and just stands there. He'll come presently, I think. Don't disturb him then, just let him be."

"Well that's what we must do if you think so," Agathon replied. "But you, slaves, entertain the rest of us. In any case, you bring us entirely what you like when there's no one supervising you (which I've never ever done) so now, just imagine that I too have been invited by you for dinner as well as the rest of these people, and look after us, so that we may sing your praises."

After this, he said, they had their meal, but Socrates c did not come in. So Agathon ordered Socrates to be sent for several times, but Aristodemus did not allow it. Then not long afterward he did come in having spent time in his usual manner; but by then they were about halfway through the meal. Then Agathon,—for he happened to be reclining alone on the last couch—said: "come over here, Socrates, and recline beside me so that being in contact with you I too can enjoy the piece of wisdom that came to you in the porch. For it's clear you have found it, and have d a hold on it, for otherwise you wouldn't have stopped searching."

So Socrates sat himself down, and said: "It would be a good thing, Agathon, if wisdom were such a thing as to flow from the fuller one of us into the emptier if we were touching each other, like the water in wine cups that flows through the strand of wool from the fuller into the emptier

κενωτέραν. εἰ γὰρ οὕτως ἔχει καὶ ἡ σοφία, πολλοῦ
e τιμῶμαι τὴν παρὰ σοὶ κατάκλισιν· οἶμαι γάρ με παρὰ
σοῦ πολλῆς καὶ καλῆς σοφίας πληρωθήσεσθαι. ἡ
μὲν γὰρ ἐμὴ φαύλη τις ἂν εἴη, ἢ καὶ ἀμφισβητήσι-
μος ὥσπερ ὄναρ οὖσα, ἡ δὲ σὴ λαμπρά τε καὶ πολ-
λὴν ἐπίδοσιν ἔχουσα, ἥ γε | παρὰ σοῦ νέου ὄντος
οὕτω σφόδρα ἐξέλαμψεν καὶ ἐκφανὴς ἐγένετο πρῴην
ἐν μάρτυσι τῶν Ἑλλήνων πλέον ἢ τρισμυρίοις.

Ὑβριστὴς εἶ, ἔφη, ὦ Σώκρατες, ὁ Ἀγάθων. καὶ
ταῦτα μὲν καὶ ὀλίγον ὕστερον διαδικασόμεθα ἐγώ τε
καὶ σὺ περὶ τῆς σοφίας, δικαστῇ χρώμενοι τῷ Διο-
νύσῳ· νῦν δὲ πρὸς τὸ | δεῖπνον πρῶτα τρέπου.

176 Μετὰ ταῦτα, ἔφη, κατακλινέντος τοῦ Σωκράτους
καὶ δειπνήσαντος καὶ τῶν ἄλλων, σπονδάς τε σφᾶς
ποιήσασθαι, καὶ ᾁσαντας τὸν θεὸν καὶ τἆλλα τὰ νο-
μιζόμενα, τρέπεσθαι πρὸς τὸν πότον· τὸν οὖν Παυσα-
νίαν ἔφη λόγου τοιούτου | τινὸς κατάρχειν. Εἶεν, ἄν-
δρες, φάναι, τίνα τρόπον ῥᾷστα πιόμεθα; ἐγὼ μὲν οὖν
λέγω ὑμῖν ὅτι τῷ ὄντι πάνυ χαλεπῶς ἔχω ὑπὸ τοῦ
χθὲς πότου καὶ δέομαι ἀναψυχῆς τινος—οἶμαι δὲ καὶ
ὑμῶν τοὺς πολλούς· παρῆστε γὰρ χθές—σκοπεῖσθε
οὖν τίνι τρόπῳ ἂν ὡς ῥᾷστα πίνοιμεν.

b Τὸν οὖν Ἀριστοφάνη εἰπεῖν, Τοῦτο μέντοι εὖ λέ-

---

16 A deliberately teasing wild exaggeration (recognized as
such by Agathon in the following line); the Theater of Dionysus,
where Agathon's play was performed, may have held up to 14,000

one. For if this is the case with wisdom too, I think highly
of reclining next to you, for I think I'll be filled with much e
fine wisdom from you. For mine would be an inferior
thing, or even debatable, being like a dream, but yours is
both bright and shows much promise, seeing that only the
day before yesterday it shone out from you so vividly,
young as you are, and displayed with more than thirty
thousand Greeks as witnesses."[16]

"You are outrageous, Socrates," said Agathon. "We'll
sort out our claims to wisdom, you and I, in court a little
later, with Dionysus as our judge.[17] But now first turn your
attention to your dinner."

After this, he said, when Socrates had reclined and 176
eaten his food along with the others, they made their liba-
tion, sang a hymn to the god and carried out the rest of
the customary rituals and turned to the drink. Then Pausanias, he said, began with a speech that went something
like this: "Well now, gentlemen, he said, what will be the
easiest way for us to drink? From my point of view I tell
you I'm really in a pretty bad way after yesterday's drinking
and I need a break—as I think most of you do too; for you
were there yesterday—so consider in what way we can
drink that is easiest on us."

Then Aristophanes spoke: "That's a good idea, Pausa- b

spectators (31,000 was roughly the number of citizens in early
fourth century Athens), and the Lenaia would have attracted
mainly a local audience.

[17] That is, when they've all had plenty of wine. However: "In
the end, it is logic, not drunken confidence or sentimentality
which helps the reader to decide the question (199c3–201c9),"
Dover, n. ad loc.

γεις, ὦ Παυσανία, τὸ παντὶ τρόπῳ παρασκευάσασθαι
ῥαστώνην τινὰ τῆς πόσεως· καὶ γὰρ αὐτός εἰμι τῶν
χθὲς βεβαπτισμένων. |

Ἀκούσαντα οὖν αὐτῶν ἔφη Ἐρυξίμαχον τὸν Ἀκου-
μενοῦ Ἦ καλῶς, φάναι, λέγετε. καὶ ἔτι ἑνὸς δέομαι
ὑμῶν ἀκοῦσαι πῶς ἔχει πρὸς τὸ ἐρρῶσθαι πίνειν,
Ἀγάθων‹ος›.

Οὐδαμῶς, φάναι, οὐδ᾽ αὐτὸς ἔρρωμαι.

c   Ἕρμαιον ἂν εἴη ἡμῖν, ἦ δ᾽ ὅς, ὡς ἔοικεν, ἐμοί τε
καὶ Ἀριστοδήμῳ καὶ Φαίδρῳ καὶ τοῖσδε, εἰ ὑμεῖς οἱ
δυνατώτατοι πίνειν νῦν ἀπειρήκατε· ἡμεῖς μὲν γὰρ ἀεὶ
ἀδύνατοι. Σωκράτη δ᾽ ἐξαιρῶ λόγου· ἱκανὸς γὰρ καὶ
ἀμφότερα, ὥστ᾽ | ἐξαρκέσει αὐτῷ ὁπότερ᾽ ἂν ποιῶμεν.
ἐπειδὴ οὖν μοι δοκεῖ οὐδεὶς τῶν παρόντων προθύμως
ἔχειν πρὸς τὸ πολὺν πίνειν οἶνον, ἴσως ἂν ἐγὼ περὶ
τοῦ μεθύσκεσθαι οἷόν ἐστι τἀληθῆ λέγων ἧττον ἂν
εἴην ἀηδής. ἐμοὶ γὰρ δὴ τοῦτό γε οἶμαι κατάδηλον
γεγονέναι ἐκ τῆς ἰατρικῆς, ὅτι χαλεπὸν τοῖς ἀνθρώ-
d ποις ἡ μέθη ἐστίν· καὶ οὔτε αὐτὸς ἑκὼν εἶναι πόρρω
ἐθελήσαιμι ἂν πιεῖν οὔτε ἄλλῳ συμβουλεύσαιμι, ἄλ-
λως τε καὶ κραιπαλῶντα ἔτι ἐκ τῆς προτεραίας. |

Ἀλλὰ μήν, ἔφη φάναι ὑπολαβόντα Φαῖδρον τὸν
Μυρρινούσιον, ἔγωγέ σοι εἴωθα πείθεσθαι ἄλλως τε
καὶ ἅττ᾽ ἂν περὶ ἰατρικῆς λέγῃς· νῦν δ᾽, ἂν εὖ βουλεύ-
e ωνται, καὶ οἱ λοιποί. ταῦτα δὴ ἀκούσαντας συγχωρεῖν
πάντας μὴ διὰ μέθης ποιήσασθαι τὴν ἐν τῷ παρόντι
συνουσίαν, ἀλλ᾽ οὕτω πίνοντας πρὸς ἡδονήν.

Ἐπειδὴ τοίνυν, φάναι τὸν Ἐρυξίμαχον, τοῦτο μὲν

154

nias, to devise in any way some sort of relief from drinking: for I was myself one of those who got a good soaking yesterday."

Now when he heard them, he said, Eryximachus, Acumenus' son, joined in: "That's certainly a good idea. And yet I still need to hear from one of you, namely Agathon, how he feels about his ability to cope with the drink."

"There's no way I can cope with it either," Agathon said.

"I think it would be a godsend for us," Eryximachus said, "both for me and Aristodemus and Phaedrus, and these people here, if you, the people most able to hold your drink, have now renounced it, for we're always incapable. I'm leaving Socrates out of account, for he is all right either way and it'll be fine with him whatever we do. Since then I get the impression that no one here is keen to drink a lot of wine, perhaps I would be less of a bore if I say what the truth is about getting oneself intoxicated. You see I think this has become quite evident to me from my medical calling: that being drunk is bad for people. I myself wouldn't willingly go on drinking if I could help it, nor would I advise anyone else to, especially someone with a hangover from the day before."

"Very well," said Phaedrus from the deme of Myrrhinous, joining in, "I myself am used to doing what you say, especially in anything connected with medicine, and on this occasion, if they are well advised, so should the rest." When they heard this, they all agreed in the present circumstances not to conduct the party by getting drunk, but drinking simply to enjoy themselves.

"Well then," said Eryximachus, "since this has been

155

δέδοκται, | πίνειν ὅσον ἂν ἕκαστος βούληται, ἐπάναγ-
κες δὲ μηδὲν εἶναι, τὸ μετὰ τοῦτο εἰσηγοῦμαι τὴν μὲν
ἄρτι εἰσελθοῦσαν αὐλητρίδα χαίρειν ἐᾶν, αὐλοῦσαν
ἑαυτῇ ἢ ἂν βούληται ταῖς γυναιξὶ ταῖς ἔνδον, ἡμᾶς
δὲ διὰ λόγων ἀλλήλοις συνεῖναι τὸ τήμερον· καὶ δι'
οἵων λόγων, εἰ βούλεσθε, ἐθέλω ὑμῖν | εἰσηγήσασθαι.

177   Φάναι δὴ πάντας καὶ βούλεσθαι καὶ κελεύειν αὐτὸν
εἰσηγεῖσθαι. εἰπεῖν οὖν τὸν Ἐρυξίμαχον ὅτι Ἡ μέν
μοι ἀρχὴ τοῦ λόγου ἐστὶ κατὰ τὴν Εὐριπίδου Μελα-
νίππην· οὐ γὰρ ἐμὸς ὁ μῦθος, ἀλλὰ Φαίδρου τοῦδε, ὃν
μέλλω λέγειν. | Φαῖδρος γὰρ ἑκάστοτε πρός με ἀγα-
νακτῶν λέγει Οὐ δεινόν, φησίν, ὦ Ἐρυξίμαχε, ἄλλοις
μέν τισι θεῶν ὕμνους καὶ παίωνας εἶναι ὑπὸ τῶν ποιητῶν πεποιημένους, τῷ δὲ Ἔρωτι, τηλικούτῳ ὄντι καὶ
τοσούτῳ θεῷ, μηδὲ ἕνα πώποτε τοσούτων γεγονότων
b   ποιητῶν πεποιηκέναι μηδὲν ἐγκώμιον; εἰ δὲ βούλει αὖ
σκέψασθαι τοὺς χρηστοὺς σοφιστάς, Ἡρακλέους μὲν
καὶ ἄλλων ἐπαίνους καταλογάδην συγγράφειν, ὥσπερ
ὁ βέλτιστος Πρόδικος—καὶ τοῦτο μὲν ἧττον καὶ θαυ-
μαστόν, ἀλλ' ἔγωγε | ἤδη τινὶ ἐνέτυχον βιβλίῳ ἀν-

---

[18] An allusion to a lost play of Euripides, *Melanippe the Wise*
(fr. 488 Nauk²). The heroine prefaces a speech about the origin
of the world with the words "The story is not mine, but from my
mother."

[19] Probably not strictly true, or at least a rhetorical exaggeration; a fragment of the sixth-century lyric poet Alcaeus (fr. 327
Campbell) appears to come from a hymn to Love.

agreed, that each will drink only as much as he wishes, and
there's to be no compulsion, as for what happens next I
propose that we dismiss the flute girl who has just arrived;
she can play to herself, or if she wishes to the women inside, while for today we occupy each other in talk and, if
you wish, I'm willing to propose to you what kind of talk
we should have."

They all said they were willing and told him to make   177
his proposal. Then Eryximachus said: "the beginning of
my speech is after the manner of Euripides' Melanippe.
For it is not my story I intend to tell, but one of Phaedrus'
here.[18] You see all the time Phaedrus complains to me and
says: Isn't it strange, Eryximachus, he says, that there are
hymns and paeans composed by the poets to some of the
other gods, but to Love, a god of such age and so great,
not one of the great number of our poets that have ever
been has ever yet written anything in his praise?[19] But   b
again, if you care to consider the worthy sophists,[20] that
they write eulogies of Heracles and others in prose, such
as the excellent Prodicus—and that is not so very surprising, but a while ago I came across some book by a clever

[20] "Worthy" (*chrēstos* = "deserving," close to "good") sophists,
possibly with an ironical connotation here (the term *sophistēs* has
a generally pejorative or condescending connotation in Plato); or
he may be representing Phaedrus' own view, or perhaps contrasting the older sophists, e.g., Prodicus (a near contemporary of
Socrates who wrote a "Choice of Heracles," DK 84B2, Waterfield,
246–49), from a more recent generation. *Encomia* on salt (b5):
see Isocrates *Helen* 12, referring to those who praise "bumble-
bees, salt and suchlike."

δρὸς σοφοῦ, ἐν ᾧ ἐνῆσαν ἅλες ἔπαινον θαυμάσιον
ἔχοντες πρὸς ὠφελίαν, καὶ ἄλλα τοιαῦτα συχνὰ ἴδοις
c ἂν ἐγκεκωμιασμένα—τὸ οὖν τοιούτων μὲν πέρι πολλὴν σπουδὴν ποιήσασθαι, Ἔρωτα δὲ μηδένα πω ἀνθρώπων τετολμηκέναι εἰς ταυτηνὶ τὴν ἡμέραν ἀξίως
ὑμνῆσαι· ἀλλ' οὕτως ἠμέληται τοσοῦτος θεός. ταῦτα
δή μοι δοκεῖ εὖ | λέγειν Φαῖδρος. ἐγὼ οὖν ἐπιθυμῶ
ἅμα μὲν τούτῳ ἔρανον εἰσενεγκεῖν καὶ χαρίσασθαι,
ἅμα δ' ἐν τῷ παρόντι πρέπον μοι δοκεῖ εἶναι ἡμῖν τοῖς
d παροῦσι κοσμῆσαι τὸν θεόν. εἰ οὖν συνδοκεῖ καὶ ὑμῖν,
γένοιτ' ἂν ἡμῖν ἐν λόγοις ἱκανὴ διατριβή· δοκεῖ γάρ
μοι χρῆναι ἕκαστον ἡμῶν λόγον εἰπεῖν ἔπαινον Ἔρωτος ἐπὶ δεξιὰ ὡς ἂν δύνηται κάλλιστον, ἄρχειν δὲ
Φαῖδρον πρῶτον, ἐπειδὴ καὶ πρῶτος κατάκειται καὶ
ἔστιν | ἅμα πατὴρ τοῦ λόγου.

Οὐδείς σοι, ὦ Ἐρυξίμαχε, φάναι τὸν Σωκράτη,
ἐναντία ψηφιεῖται. οὔτε γὰρ ἄν που ἐγὼ ἀποφήσαιμι,
ὃς οὐδέν φημι ἄλλο ἐπίστασθαι ἢ τὰ ἐρωτικά, οὔτε
e που Ἀγάθων καὶ Παυσανίας, οὐδὲ μὴν Ἀριστοφάνης,
ᾧ περὶ Διόνυσον καὶ Ἀφροδίτην πᾶσα ἡ διατριβή,
οὐδὲ ἄλλος οὐδεὶς τουτωνὶ ὧν ἐγὼ ὁρῶ. καίτοι οὐκ ἐξ
ἴσου γίγνεται ἡμῖν τοῖς ὑστάτοις κατακειμένοις· ἀλλ'
ἐὰν οἱ πρόσθεν ἱκανῶς καὶ καλῶς | εἴπωσιν, ἐξαρκέσει
ἡμῖν. ἀλλὰ τύχῃ ἀγαθῇ καταρχέτω Φαῖδρος καὶ ἐγ-
κωμιαζέτω τὸν Ἔρωτα.

---

[21] The speakers go in the order they are reclining, from left
to right. For the organization of couches, see Introduction, §1(ii).

fellow in which salt was lauded in a remarkable way for its usefulness and you can see many other things like that extolled—to think that they have devoted much serious   c
effort to such things, but no human being to this day has ever yet ventured to sing the praises of Love in worthy fashion! Yet this is how far such a great god has been ne-glected. That's the reason I think Phaedrus is right. There-fore I am keen to make my contribution to the feast and gratify him, and at the same time in the present circum-stances it seems to me fitting for us who are here to honor the god. If then you also think the same, there would be   d
enough time to keep us busy with speeches: for I think each of us should make a speech in praise of the god from left to right, the finest he can, and Phaedrus should be the first to start, since he is in first place and at the same time he is father of the speech."[21]

"Nobody, Eryximachus," said Socrates, "is going to vote against you. For I don't think I would say no either, seeing that I claim to understand nothing but the affairs of love, nor I think would Agathon and Pausanias, nor even   e
Aristophanes who spends all his time on Dionysus and Aphrodite, nor anyone else of these people who I see here.[22] Yet it isn't fair on those of us reclining on the last couches; but if those who speak first do it adequately and well, it will be good enough for us. Well, let Phaedrus begin and praise Love and good luck to him."

[22] The special sense in which Socrates understands "affairs of love" (*ta erōtica*) becomes clear in his exchange with Diotima (201d1ff.) and with Alcibiades (215a5ff.). Agathon and Pausanias were lifelong same-sex partners (193b–c); the reference to Aris-tophanes the writer of comedy jokingly implies that his plays were exclusively devoted to wine and love (Dionysus and Aphrodite).

Ταῦτα δὴ καὶ οἱ ἄλλοι πάντες ἄρα συνέφασάν τε
178 καὶ ἐκέλευον ἅπερ ὁ Σωκράτης. πάντων μὲν οὖν ἃ
ἕκαστος εἶπεν, οὔτε πάνυ ὁ Ἀριστόδημος ἐμέμνητο
οὔτ᾽ αὖ ἐγὼ ἃ ἐκεῖνος ἔλεγε πάντα· ἃ δὲ μάλιστα καὶ
ὧν ἔδοξέ μοι ἀξιομνημόνευτον, τούτων ὑμῖν ἐρῶ ἑκά-
στου τὸν | λόγον.

Πρῶτον μὲν γάρ, ὥσπερ λέγω, ἔφη Φαῖδρον ἀρξάμε-
νον ἐνθένδε ποθὲν λέγειν, ὅτι μέγας θεὸς εἴη ὁ Ἔρως
καὶ θαυμαστὸς ἐν ἀνθρώποις τε καὶ θεοῖς, πολλαχῇ
μὲν καὶ ἄλλη, οὐχ ἥκιστα δὲ κατὰ τὴν γένεσιν. τὸ
γὰρ ἐν τοῖς πρεσβύτατον εἶναι τὸν θεὸν τίμιον, ἦ δ᾽
b ὅς, τεκμήριον δὲ τούτου· γονῆς γὰρ Ἔρωτος οὔτ᾽ εἰσὶν οὔτε λέγονται ὑπ᾽ οὐδενὸς οὔτε ἰδιώτου οὔτε ποιητοῦ, ἀλλ᾽ Ἡσίοδος πρῶτον μὲν Χάος φησὶ γενέ-
σθαι |

αὐτὰρ ἔπειτα
Γαῖ᾽ εὐρύστερνος, πάντων ἕδος ἀσφαλὲς αἰεί,
ἠδ᾽ Ἔρος

Ἡσιόδῳ δὲ καὶ Ἀκουσίλεως σύμφησιν μετὰ τὸ Χάος
δύο τούτω γενέσθαι, Γῆν τε καὶ Ἔρωτα. Παρμενίδης
δὲ τὴν | γένεσιν λέγει—

πρώτιστον μὲν Ἔρωτα θεῶν μητίσατο πάντων.

c οὕτω πολλαχόθεν ὁμολογεῖται ὁ Ἔρως ἐν τοῖς πρε-

All the rest then agreed and repeated Socrates' instruction. Now Aristodemus didn't recall entirely everything   178
that each person said, nor could in I in my turn remember
everything that he told me, but of the speeches he remembered best and of the ones which seemed to me to contain
what was worth remembering, of these I shall recount
each man's speech to you.

The Speech of Phaedrus

So first, as I say, Phaedrus spoke beginning at roughly this
point, saying that Love is a great god, a wonder to both
men and gods in many different ways, but not least in his
birth. For the god is honored for being among the oldest
among them, he said, and there is proof of this: there are   b
no parents of Love and none are mentioned by writers in
prose or verse, but Hesiod says that Chaos first came into
being:

> . . . but then
> Broad-bosomed Earth, the secure abode of all forever
> And Love . . .

and Acusilaus agrees with Hesiod and says after Chaos
these two were born: Earth and Love. Parmenides says of
his birth:

> Love was devised first of all the gods.[23]

Thus from many sources Love is agreed to be among the   c

[23] References are to Hesiod, *Theogony* 116–17, 120; Acusilaus (? 5th century); Parmenides, DK B13 and 14 (Waterfield, 63–64).

σβύτατος εἶναι. πρεσβύτατος δὲ ὢν μεγίστων ἀγαθῶν ἡμῖν αἴτιός ἐστιν. οὐ γὰρ ἔγωγ᾽ ἔχω εἰπεῖν ὅτι
μεῖζόν ἐστιν ἀγαθὸν εὐθὺς νέῳ ὄντι ἢ ἐραστὴς χρη-
στὸς καὶ ἐραστῇ | παιδικά. ὃ γὰρ χρὴ ἀνθρώποις
ἡγεῖσθαι παντὸς τοῦ βίου τοῖς μέλλουσι καλῶς βιώ-
σεσθαι, τοῦτο οὔτε συγγένεια οἵα τε ἐμποιεῖν οὕτω
καλῶς οὔτε τιμαὶ οὔτε πλοῦτος οὔτ᾽ ἄλλο οὐδὲν ὡς

d ἔρως. λέγω δὲ δὴ τί τοῦτο; τὴν ἐπὶ μὲν τοῖς αἰσχροῖς
αἰσχύνην, ἐπὶ δὲ τοῖς καλοῖς φιλοτιμίαν· οὐ γὰρ ἔστιν
ἄνευ τούτων οὔτε πόλιν οὔτε ἰδιώτην μεγάλα καὶ καλὰ
ἔργα ἐξεργάζεσθαι. φημὶ τοίνυν ἐγὼ ἄνδρα ὅστις |
ἐρᾷ, εἴ τι αἰσχρὸν ποιῶν κατάδηλος γίγνοιτο ἢ πάσχων ὑπό του δι᾽ ἀνανδρίαν μὴ ἀμυνόμενος, οὔτ᾽ ἂν
ὑπὸ πατρὸς ὀφθέντα οὕτως ἀλγῆσαι οὔτε ὑπὸ ἑταίρων

e οὔτε ὑπ᾽ ἄλλου οὐδενὸς ὡς ὑπὸ παιδικῶν. ταὐτὸν δὲ
τοῦτο καὶ τὸν ἐρώμενον ὁρῶμεν, ὅτι διαφερόντως τοὺς
ἐραστὰς αἰσχύνεται, ὅταν ὀφθῇ ἐν αἰσχρῷ τινι ὤν. εἰ
οὖν μηχανή τις γένοιτο ὥστε πόλιν γενέσθαι ἢ στρα-
τόπεδον ἐραστῶν τε καὶ παιδικῶν, | οὐκ ἔστιν ὅπως
ἂν ἄμεινον οἰκήσειαν τὴν ἑαυτῶν ἢ ἀπεχόμενοι πάν-

179 των τῶν αἰσχρῶν καὶ φιλοτιμούμενοι πρὸς ἀλλήλους,
καὶ μαχόμενοί γ᾽ ἂν μετ᾽ ἀλλήλων οἱ τοιοῦτοι νικῷεν
ἂν ὀλίγοι ὄντες ὡς ἔπος εἰπεῖν πάντας ἀνθρώπους.
ἐρῶν γὰρ ἀνὴρ ὑπὸ παιδικῶν ὀφθῆναι ἢ λιπὼν τάξιν

---

24 *Kalos* (fine) and its opposite *aischros* (shameful) were the
most powerful terms of general approval/disapproval in the

oldest of them. Being very old he is the cause of the greatest good things for us. For I myself cannot say what is a greater good for someone, just as soon as he reaches boyhood, than a worthy lover, nor for a lover a boy to be loved. Now that which should guide men who intend to live well throughout their lives—this neither family, nor honor, nor wealth, nor anything else can implant as well as love can. So what is it I'm talking about? The shame that comes   d
from shameful deeds; and the love of honor that comes from those that are fine.[24] For without these no city or individual can accomplish great and noble deeds. Now I say if a man who is in love is palpably doing something shameful, or through cowardice does not defend himself when he is maltreated by someone, he wouldn't feel so much pain when he is seen by his father, or his comrades, or anyone else, as when he is seen by his beloved. We see   e
this same thing also in the loved one, that he especially feels shame toward his lovers when he is seen in a shameful situation. If therefore there were some means of creating a city, or an army of lovers and their loved ones, there cannot be a better way to organize their affairs than by abstaining from all things shameful, and competing with   179
each other in honor, and fighting alongside each other; such a force, even though few in number, would, so to speak, conquer all mankind.[25] For a man in love would be less inclined, I suppose, to be seen by his beloved either

Greek ethical vocabulary (also adverb καλῶς, "well"); see especialy Pausanias' speech at 181a. "Noble" in the following sentence (178d4) also translates *kalos*.

[25] Possibly an anachronistic reference to the Theban "Sacred Band" of the 380s (see Introduction, Appendix).

ἢ ὅπλα ἀποβαλὼν ἧττον ἂν δήπου δέξαιτο ἢ ὑπὸ
πάντων τῶν | ἄλλων, καὶ πρὸ τούτου τεθνάναι ἂν πολ-
λάκις ἕλοιτο. καὶ μὴν ἐγκαταλιπεῖν γε τὰ παιδικὰ ἢ
μὴ βοηθῆσαι κινδυνεύοντι—οὐδεὶς οὕτω κακὸς ὅντινα
οὐκ ἂν αὐτὸς ὁ Ἔρως ἔνθεον ποιήσειε πρὸς ἀρετήν,
ὥστε ὅμοιον εἶναι τῷ ἀρίστῳ φύσει· καὶ ἀτεχνῶς, ὃ
ἔφη Ὅμηρος, "μένος ἐμπνεῦσαι" ἐνίοις τῶν ἡρώων
b τὸν θεόν, τοῦτο ὁ Ἔρως τοῖς ἐρῶσι παρέχει γιγνόμενον παρ᾽ αὑτοῦ.

Καὶ μὴν ὑπεραποθνήσκειν γε μόνοι ἐθέλουσιν οἱ
ἐρῶντες, | οὐ μόνον ὅτι ἄνδρες, ἀλλὰ καὶ αἱ γυναῖκες.
τούτου δὲ καὶ ἡ Πελίου θυγάτηρ Ἄλκηστις ἱκανὴν
μαρτυρίαν παρέχεται ὑπὲρ τοῦδε τοῦ λόγου εἰς τοὺς
Ἕλληνας, ἐθελήσασα μόνη ὑπὲρ τοῦ αὑτῆς ἀνδρὸς
c ἀποθανεῖν, ὄντων αὐτῷ πατρός τε καὶ μητρός, οὓς
ἐκείνη τοσοῦτον ὑπερεβάλετο τῇ φιλίᾳ διὰ τὸν ἔρωτα,
ὥστε ἀποδεῖξαι αὐτοὺς ἀλλοτρίους ὄντας τῷ ὑεῖ καὶ
ὀνόματι μόνον προσήκοντας, καὶ τοῦτ᾽ ἐργασαμένη
τὸ ἔργον οὕτω καλὸν ἔδοξεν ἐργάσασθαι οὐ μόνον
ἀνθρώποις | ἀλλὰ καὶ θεοῖς, ὥστε πολλῶν πολλὰ καὶ
καλὰ ἐργασαμένων εὐαριθμήτοις δή τισιν ἔδοσαν
τοῦτο γέρας οἱ θεοί, ἐξ Ἅιδου ἀνεῖναι πάλιν τὴν ψυχήν, ἀλλὰ τὴν ἐκείνης ἀνεῖσαν ἀγασθέντες τῷ ἔργῳ·
d οὕτω καὶ θεοὶ τὴν περὶ τὸν ἔρωτα σπουδήν τε καὶ
ἀρετὴν μάλιστα τιμῶσιν. Ὀρφέα δὲ τὸν Οἰάγρου
ἀτελῆ ἀπέπεμψαν ἐξ Ἅιδου, φάσμα δείξαντες τῆς γυναικὸς ἐφ᾽ ἣν ἧκεν, αὐτὴν δὲ οὐ δόντες, ὅτι μαλθακί-

deserting the line, or throwing away his weapons, than by all others, and he would choose to die many times over rather than that. And again as for leaving his beloved in the lurch, or not running to his aid when in danger—no one is so cowardly that Love himself would not cause him to be inspired with courage, so that he becomes like a man who is supremely brave by nature, and it's exactly as Homer said: the god 'breathed might' into some of the heroes:[26] this is what Love produces, arising from his particular power, for those in love.

Furthermore it's only lovers who are willing to die for another, and I don't just mean men, but also women. And of that Peleas' daughter Alcestis offers adequate evidence among the Greeks in support of this argument, she who was the only one willing to die on behalf of her own husband, though he had a father and mother living, whom she so exceeded in devotion through her love as to show them up as strangers to their son, related only in name; and having performed such a deed as this, she seemed not only to men but also to the gods to have done such a fine deed that, although many have carried out many fine deeds, and it would be easy to count the number to whom the gods granted the prize of sending back their soul from Hades, they released hers in admiration of her deed.[27] Thus the gods too honor especially the zeal and courage associated with love. But they sent Orpheus, son of Oeagrus, out of Hades empty-handed, showing him an apparition of his wife for whom he had come, but not giving him the woman herself, because he was regarded as fainthearted in that

b

c

d

---

[26] A common Homeric formula for heroes preparing for combat.   [27] For the dramatized story, see Euripides, *Alcestis*.

ζεσθαι ἐδόκει, | ἅτε ὢν κιθαρῳδός, καὶ οὐ τολμᾶν
ἕνεκα τοῦ ἔρωτος ἀποθνῄσκειν ὥσπερ Ἄλκηστις,
ἀλλὰ διαμηχανᾶσθαι ζῶν εἰσιέναι εἰς Ἅιδου. τοιγάρ-
τοι διὰ ταῦτα δίκην αὐτῷ ἐπέθεσαν, καὶ ἐποίησαν τὸν
e θάνατον αὐτοῦ ὑπὸ γυναικῶν γενέσθαι, οὐχ ὥσπερ
Ἀχιλλέα τὸν τῆς Θέτιδος υὸν ἐτίμησαν καὶ εἰς μακάρων νήσους ἀπέπεμψαν, ὅτι πεπυσμένος παρὰ τῆς
μητρὸς ὡς ἀποθανοῖτο ἀποκτείνας Ἕκτορα, μὴ ποιή-
σας δὲ τοῦτο οἴκαδε ἐλθὼν γηραιὸς τελευτήσοι, |
ἐτόλμησεν ἑλέσθαι βοηθήσας τῷ ἐραστῇ Πατρόκλῳ
καὶ τιμωρήσας οὐ μόνον ὑπεραποθανεῖν ἀλλὰ καὶ
180 ἐπαποθανεῖν τετελευτηκότι· ὅθεν δὴ καὶ ὑπεραγασθέν-
τες οἱ θεοὶ διαφερόντως αὐτὸν ἐτίμησαν, ὅτι τὸν ἐραστὴν οὕτω περὶ πολλοῦ ἐποιεῖτο. Αἰσχύλος δὲ φλυα-
ρεῖ φάσκων Ἀχιλλέα Πατρόκλου| ἐρᾶν, ὃς ἦν καλλίων
οὐ μόνον Πατρόκλου ἀλλ' ἅμα καὶ τῶν ἡρώων ἁπάντων, καὶ ἔτι ἀγένειος, ἔπειτα νεώτερος πολύ, ὥς φησιν
Ὅμηρος. ἀλλὰ γὰρ τῷ ὄντι μάλιστα μὲν ταύτην τὴν
b ἀρετὴν οἱ θεοὶ τιμῶσιν τὴν περὶ τὸν ἔρωτα, μᾶλλον
μέντοι θαυμάζουσιν καὶ ἄγανται καὶ εὖ ποιοῦσιν ὅταν
ὁ ἐρώμενος τὸν ἐραστὴν ἀγαπᾷ, ἢ ὅταν ὁ ἐραστὴς τὰ
παιδικά. θειότερον γὰρ ἐραστὴς παιδικῶν· ἔνθεος γάρ
ἐστι. διὰ ταῦτα καὶ τὸν Ἀχιλλέα τῆς Ἀλκήστιδος |

---

28 The story of Orpheus and his wife Eurydice is most fully
available to us in Virgil, *Georgics* 4.453–527.

he was a cithara player and did not have the courage to die for love as Alcestis had done, but had contrived to enter Hades while alive. This is the reason therefore they punished him and caused his death to come about at the hands of women.[28] They did not honor him as they did Achilles,   e son of Thetis, whom they sent off to the Isles of the Blessed because when he had found out from his mother that he was to die after killing Hector, but if he didn't do this he would return home to die in old age, he had the courage to choose to come to the aid of his lover Patroclus and in avenging him not only to die for him, but also to add his own death when Patroclus himself had died.[29] Hence with   180 greatest admiration the gods gave him especial honor because he valued his lover so highly. But Aeschylus is talking nonsense in claiming that Achilles was the lover of Patroclus, because he was not only more handsome than Patroclus, but also more than all the other heroes, and still beardless as well as being far younger, as Homer says.[30] But the fact is in truth the gods honor this excellence the most, the kind that is related to love; however, they reserve   b greater wonder and admiration for the beloved and are more generous to him when he feels affection for his lover more than when the lover loves the beloved. For a lover is something more divine than a loved one, for he is inspired by a god. For these reasons they honored Achilles

[29] Achilles tells of his fated choice at *Iliad* 9.410–16, and makes his choice at 18.88–96.

[30] On Achilles' surpassing beauty, cf. *Iliad* 2.673ff. As the younger partner he would have been, according to normal Athenian practice, Patroclus' *erōmenos* (beloved) rather than his *erastēs*: hence, Phaedrus' comment on Aeschylus.

μᾶλλον ἐτίμησαν, εἰς μακάρων νήσους ἀποπέμψαν-
τες.

Οὕτω δὴ ἔγωγέ φημι Ἔρωτα θεῶν καὶ πρεσβύτατον καὶ τιμιώτατον καὶ κυριώτατον εἶναι εἰς ἀρετῆς
καὶ εὐδαιμονίας κτῆσιν ἀνθρώποις καὶ ζῶσι καὶ τε-
λευτήσασιν.

c   Φαῖδρον μὲν τοιοῦτόν τινα λόγον ἔφη εἰπεῖν, μετὰ δὲ
Φαῖδρον ἄλλους τινὰς εἶναι ὧν οὐ πάνυ διεμνημόνευε·
οὓς παρεὶς τὸν Παυσανίου λόγον διηγεῖτο.

Εἰπεῖν δ᾽ αὐτὸν ὅτι Οὐ καλῶς μοι δοκεῖ, ὦ Φαῖδρε,
προβεβλῆσθαι ἡμῖν | ὁ λόγος, τὸ ἁπλῶς οὕτως παρ-
ηγγέλθαι ἐγκωμιάζειν Ἔρωτα. εἰ μὲν γὰρ εἷς ἦν ὁ
Ἔρως, καλῶς ἂν εἶχε, νῦν δὲ οὐ γάρ ἐστιν εἷς· μὴ
ὄντος δὲ ἑνὸς ὀρθότερόν ἐστι πρότερον προρρηθῆναι
d   ὁποῖον δεῖ ἐπαινεῖν. ἐγὼ οὖν πειράσομαι τοῦτο ἐπαν-
ορθώσασθαι, πρῶτον μὲν Ἔρωτα φράσαι ὃν δεῖ ἐπαινεῖν, ἔπειτα ἐπαινέσαι ἀξίως τοῦ θεοῦ. πάντες γὰρ
ἴσμεν ὅτι οὐκ ἔστιν ἄνευ Ἔρωτος Ἀφροδίτη. μιᾶς μὲν
οὖν | οὔσης εἷς ἂν ἦν Ἔρως· ἐπεὶ δὲ δὴ δύο ἐστόν, δύο
ἀνάγκη καὶ Ἔρωτε εἶναι. πῶς δ᾽ οὐ δύο τὼ θεά; ἡ μέν
γέ που πρεσβυτέρα καὶ ἀμήτωρ Οὐρανοῦ θυγάτηρ,

---

31 Underlying Phaedrus' argument here is that traditionally
the lover (erastēs) as the active partner in the relationship is
"possessed" and so "more divine," whereas the beloved (erōmenos) being the passive recipient of love and only human (the word

more than Alcestis, and sent him to the Isles of the Blessed.[31]

Thus I declare that Love is the oldest and most honored and most powerful of the gods in enabling the acquisition of excellence and happiness by humans both living and dead.[32]

The Speech of Pausanias

Phaedrus made his speech along these lines, he said, but   c
after Phaedrus there were some others which he didn't quite remember. Passing over them he related Pausanias' speech. Pausanias said:

"I don't think the topic has been proposed well to us, Phaedrus, in that we have been instructed to praise Love and simply that; for if Love were one god, all would be well, but as it is, you see, he isn't one god; and since he isn't, it is more correct to state first which kind of Love we must praise. So I shall try to set this right and first make   d
clear the Love we must praise, and then praise the god in a manner worthy of him. For we all know there is no Aphrodite without Love. So, if she were one, there would be one Love, but since there are actually two, then there must be two Loves also. How can there not be two goddesses? The one, I take it, is older and daughter of Uranus

to express his love is *agapē* = [brotherly] love) has to make a greater sacrifice, and so is worthy of greater respect from the gods.

[32] "Excellence" = *aretē* (virtue, goodness, valor), the positive quality required of the man who wished to be generally well-thought of.

ἣν δὴ καὶ Οὐρανίαν ἐπονομάζομεν· ἡ δὲ νεωτέρα Διὸς
e   καὶ Διώνης, ἣν δὴ Πάνδημον καλοῦμεν. ἀναγκαῖον δὴ
καὶ Ἔρωτα τὸν μὲν τῇ ἑτέρᾳ συνεργὸν Πάνδημον ὀρθῶς καλεῖσθαι, τὸν δὲ Οὐράνιον. ἐπαινεῖν μὲν οὖν δεῖ
πάντας θεούς, ἃ δ᾽ οὖν ἑκάτερος εἴληχε πειρατέον εἰ-
πεῖν. πᾶσα γὰρ πρᾶξις ὧδ᾽ | ἔχει· αὐτὴ ἐφ᾽ ἑαυτῆς
181   πραττομένη οὔτε καλὴ οὔτε αἰσχρά. οἷον ὃ νῦν ἡμεῖς
ποιοῦμεν, ἢ πίνειν ἢ ᾄδειν ἢ διαλέγεσθαι, οὐκ ἔστι
τούτων αὐτὸ καλὸν οὐδέν, ἀλλ᾽ ἐν τῇ πράξει, ὡς ἂν
πραχθῇ, τοιοῦτον ἀπέβη· καλῶς μὲν γὰρ πραττόμενον
καὶ ὀρθῶς καλὸν γίγνεται, μὴ ὀρθῶς δὲ αἰσχρόν.
οὕτω δὴ | καὶ τὸ ἐρᾶν καὶ ὁ Ἔρως οὐ πᾶς ἐστι καλὸς
οὐδὲ ἄξιος ἐγκωμιάζεσθαι, ἀλλὰ ὁ καλῶς προτρέπων
ἐρᾶν.

Ὁ μὲν οὖν τῆς Πανδήμου Ἀφροδίτης ὡς ἀληθῶς
b   πάνδημός ἐστι καὶ ἐξεργάζεται ὅτι ἂν τύχῃ· καὶ οὗτός
ἐστιν ὃν οἱ φαῦλοι τῶν ἀνθρώπων ἐρῶσιν. ἐρῶσι δὲ
οἱ τοιοῦτοι πρῶτον μὲν οὐχ ἧττον γυναικῶν ἢ παίδων,
ἔπειτα ὧν καὶ ἐρῶσι τῶν σωμάτων μᾶλλον ἢ τῶν ψυ-
χῶν, ἔπειτα ὡς ἂν | δύνωνται ἀνοητοτάτων, | πρὸς τὸ
διαπράξασθαι μόνον βλέποντες, ἀμελοῦντες δὲ τοῦ
καλῶς ἢ μή· ὅθεν δὴ συμβαίνει αὐτοῖς ὅτι ἂν τύχωσι
τοῦτο πράττειν, ὁμοίως μὲν ἀγαθόν, ὁμοίως δὲ τοὐναντίον. ἔστι γὰρ καὶ ἀπὸ τῆς θεοῦ νεωτέρας τε οὔσης

---

33 There were two version of the birth of Aphrodite: (1) she
was formed from the foam from the genitals of the castrated
Uranus, cf. Hesiod, *Theogony* 188–202 (hence, Uranian); (2) she

without a mother, whom in fact we call Uranian. The younger is daughter of Zeus and Dione, whom we call Pandemus. So necessarily the one Love, coworker with the latter   e
goddess, must rightly be called Common and the other one Heavenly.[33] On the one hand then we must praise all gods, but for now we must try and say what each Love has been allotted to do. For every activity is like this: performed in and by itself it is neither fine nor shameful, such   181
as what we are now doing: drinking, or singing, or having a discussion; of these none is in itself fine, but it is the nature of the activity, the way it is performed, which determines the way it turns out. If it's performed well and correctly, it becomes fine; if not it's shameful. So too also with loving and Love: it is not all fine or worth praising, but only the one who urges us toward loving well.

"Now the Love who belongs to Common Aphrodite is truly common and acts at random, and this is the one ordinary people love. Firstly these sorts of people love   b
women no less than boys, secondly, they love those they love more for their bodies than their souls, and thirdly, they love those who have the least possible understanding, looking only to achieve their aim,[34] with no concern for whether it's done well or not. Hence it turns out for them that they do whatever they chance on, irrespective of whether it's good or the opposite. For this love comes not only from the goddess who is much younger than the

was born more naturally from Zeus and Dione, cf. Homer, *Iliad* 5.370ff. (Pandemus)—translated as, respectively, "Heavenly" and "Common."

[34] One of a number of euphemisms for sexual activity (*dia-prassō* = "accomplish [one's purpose]").

PLATO

πολὺ ἢ τῆς ἑτέρας, καὶ μετεχούσης ἐν τῇ γενέσει καὶ
c θήλεος καὶ ἄρρενος. ὁ δὲ τῆς Οὐρανίας πρῶτον μὲν
οὐ μετεχούσης θήλεος ἀλλ᾽ ἄρρενος μόνον—καὶ ἔστιν
οὗτος ὁ τῶν παίδων ἔρως—ἔπειτα πρεσβυτέρας,
ὕβρεως ἀμοίρου· ὅθεν | δὴ ἐπὶ τὸ ἄρρεν τρέπονται οἱ
ἐκ τούτου τοῦ ἔρωτος ἔπιπνοι, τὸ φύσει ἐρρωμενέστε-
ρον καὶ νοῦν μᾶλλον ἔχον ἀγαπῶντες. καί τις ἂν
γνοίη καὶ ἐν αὐτῇ τῇ παιδεραστίᾳ τοὺς εἰλικρινῶς
d ὑπὸ τούτου τοῦ ἔρωτος ὡρμημένους· οὐ γὰρ ἐρῶσι
παίδων, ἀλλ᾽ ἐπειδὰν ἤδη ἄρχωνται νοῦν ἴσχειν,
τοῦτο δὲ πλησιάζει τῷ γενειάσκειν. παρεσκευασμένοι
γὰρ οἶμαί εἰσιν οἱ ἐντεῦθεν ἀρχόμενοι ἐρᾶν ὡς τὸν
βίον ἅπαντα συνεσόμενοι | καὶ κοινῇ συμβιωσόμενοι,
ἀλλ᾽ οὐκ ἐξαπατήσαντες, ἐν ἀφροσύνῃ λαβόντες ὡς
νέον, καταγελάσαντες οἰχήσεσθαι ἐπ᾽ ἄλλον ἀποτρέ-
e χοντες. χρῆν δὲ καὶ νόμον εἶναι μὴ ἐρᾶν παίδων, ἵνα
μὴ εἰς ἄδηλον πολλὴ σπουδὴ ἀνηλίσκετο· τὸ γὰρ τῶν
παίδων τέλος ἄδηλον οἷ τελευτᾷ κακίας καὶ ἀρετῆς
ψυχῆς τε πέρι καὶ σώματος. οἱ μὲν οὖν ἀγαθοὶ τὸν
νόμον τοῦτον αὐτοὶ αὑτοῖς ἑκόντες τίθενται, χρῆν δὲ
καὶ τούτους | τοὺς πανδήμους ἐραστὰς προσαναγκά-
ζειν τὸ τοιοῦτον, ὥσπερ καὶ τῶν ἐλευθέρων γυναικῶν
προσαναγκάζομεν αὐτοὺς καθ᾽ ὅσον δυνάμεθα μὴ

---

35 That is, Dione and Zeus.   36 In Greek popular morality, violence was a characteristic of the young (see Dover, GPM,
103). For the general view that men were naturally more intelligent than women, see Dover, GPM, 98–102.

172

other, but also in her birth has a share of both female and male.[35] But the Love who accompanies the Heavenly goddess firstly has no share of the female, but only the male— and this is the love of boys—secondly, she being the elder, has no share of lawless violence (*hubris*). Hence those who are inspired by this kind of love turn to the male, attracted to that which is naturally stronger and more intelligent.[36] And one is able to recognize, within the love of boys itself, those who are aroused purely by this kind of love. For they don't love boys except at the point when they begin to develop the mind, and this comes on when they are near to growing a beard. For I think those who begin to love them from that point are prepared to be with them for the whole of their lives, and share their lives with them, and not deceive them by taking advantage of their simple mindedness as a youngster, and then, mocking them, go running off to someone else.[37] There should actually be a law against loving young boys in order to prevent serious attention being paid to something with unclear outcome: for it's not clear where boys will end up with regard to badness and excellence in both soul and body. Now those who are good voluntarily apply this law to themselves, but it's necessary to compel those commonplace lovers also to adopt such behavior, just as we compel them as far as we can not to make love to freeborn women.[38]

c

d

e

[37] For the unusual state in Athens of a lifelong exclusively same-sex partnership, as advocated here (Pausanias and Agathon being an example), see General Introduction, §2.

[38] For the distinction in sexual freedom between freeborn and slave women, see General Introduction, §2.

182 ἐρᾶν. οὗτοι γάρ εἰσιν οἱ καὶ τὸ ὄνειδος πεποιηκότες,
ὥστε τινὰς τολμᾶν λέγειν ὡς αἰσχρὸν χαρίζεσθαι
ἐρασταῖς· λέγουσι δὲ εἰς τούτους ἀποβλέποντες,
ὁρῶντες αὐτῶν τὴν ἀκαιρίαν καὶ ἀδικίαν, ἐπεὶ οὐ δή-
που | κοσμίως γε καὶ νομίμως ὁτιοῦν <πρᾶγμα> πρατ-
τόμενον ψόγον ἂν δικαίως φέροι.

Καὶ δὴ καὶ ὁ περὶ τὸν ἔρωτα νόμος ἐν μὲν ταῖς
ἄλλαις πόλεσι νοῆσαι ῥᾴδιος, ἁπλῶς γὰρ ὥρισται· ὁ
b δ' ἐνθάδε καὶ ἐν Λακεδαίμονι ποικίλος.[3] ἐν Ἤλιδι μὲν
γὰρ καὶ ἐν Βοιωτοῖς, καὶ οὗ μὴ σοφοὶ λέγειν, ἁπλῶς
νενομοθέτηται καλὸν τὸ χαρίζεσθαι ἐρασταῖς, καὶ
οὐκ ἄν τις εἴποι οὔτε νέος οὔτε παλαιὸς ὡς αἰσχρόν,
ἵνα οἶμαι μὴ πράγματ' | ἔχωσιν λόγῳ πειρώμενοι πεί-
θειν τοὺς νέους, ἅτε ἀδύνατοι λέγειν· τῆς δὲ Ἰωνίας
καὶ ἄλλοθι πολλαχοῦ αἰσχρὸν νενόμισται, ὅσοι ὑπὸ
βαρβάροις οἰκοῦσιν. τοῖς γὰρ βαρβάροις διὰ τὰς τυ-
ραννίδας αἰσχρὸν τοῦτό γε καὶ ἥ γε φιλοσοφία καὶ
c ἡ φιλογυμναστία· οὐ γὰρ οἶμαι συμφέρει τοῖς ἄρ-
χουσι φρονήματα μεγάλα ἐγγίγνεσθαι τῶν ἀρχομέ-
νων, οὐδὲ φιλίας ἰσχυρὰς καὶ κοινωνίας, ὃ δὴ μάλιστα φιλεῖ τά τε ἄλλα πάντα καὶ ὁ ἔρως ἐμποιεῖν.

---

[3] καὶ ἐν Λακεδαίμονι secl. Winckelmann vel post γὰρ transp.

---

39 An editorial suggestion (see textual note) is to delete the
reference to Lacedaemon (Sparta) or move it to the next sentence
after "in Elis . . . ," on the grounds that inarticulateness was a
notorious characteristic of Sparta. But see Xenophon, *Constitution of Sparta* 1.12ff., where Sparta is contrasted with Boeotia and

174

For these are the men who have brought about the re-   182
proach which makes some venture to say that it's shameful
to grant favors to lovers, and they say it with these people
in mind, seeing their importunity and injustice, since I
imagine doing anything whatsoever in a decent and lawful
way would surely not justly incur censure.

"And in particular, the convention about love in other
cities is easy to grasp for it has been defined in simple
terms. But here and in Lacedaemon it is complicated.[39]
You see in Elis and among the Boeotians and where they   b
are not skilled in speaking it is simply laid down that it is
a fine thing to grant favors to lovers and no one, young or
old, would say it is shameful, in order, I suppose, that they
should have no problems trying to persuade the young
verbally, inasmuch as they are not capable of making
speeches. But in Ionia and many other places elsewhere,
for as many as live under foreign rule, it is considered
shameful.[40] For it is owing to their tyrannies that foreigners think this is shameful, along with the pursuit of philosophy and of physical exercise; for I don't think it's in the   c
rulers' interest that big ideas should be engendered among
their subjects, nor strong friendships and associations,
which all the other activities, but especially love, tend to

Elis with respect to acceptable and unacceptable same-sex relations.

[40] At the supposed dramatic date of Agathon's dinner party
(416), the Ionians were still part of the Athenian empire; they
were later ceded to Persia to be "under foreign rule" (b7) by a
peace treaty of 387/6. For this anachronism as an indication of
the date when the dialogue was written, see Introduction, Appendix.

ἔργῳ δὲ | τοῦτο ἔμαθον καὶ οἱ ἐνθάδε τύραννοι· ὁ γὰρ
Ἀριστογείτονος ἔρως καὶ ἡ Ἁρμοδίου φιλία βέβαιος
γενομένη κατέλυσεν αὐτῶν τὴν ἀρχήν. οὕτως οὗ μὲν
d αἰσχρὸν ἐτέθη χαρίζεσθαι ἐρασταῖς, κακίᾳ τῶν θεμένων κεῖται, τῶν μὲν ἀρχόντων πλεονεξίᾳ, τῶν δὲ ἀρ-
χομένων ἀνανδρίᾳ· οὗ δὲ καλὸν ἁπλῶς ἐνομίσθη, διὰ
τὴν τῶν θεμένων τῆς ψυχῆς ἀργίαν. ἐνθάδε δὲ πολὺ
τούτων κάλλιον νενομοθέτηται, καὶ | ὅπερ εἶπον, οὐ
ῥᾴδιον κατανοῆσαι. ἐνθυμηθέντι γὰρ ὅτι λέγεται κάλλιον τὸ φανερῶς ἐρᾶν τοῦ λάθρᾳ, καὶ μάλιστα τῶν
γενναιοτάτων καὶ ἀρίστων, κἂν αἰσχίους ἄλλων ὦσι,
καὶ ὅτι αὖ ἡ παρακέλευσις τῷ ἐρῶντι παρὰ πάντων
θαυμαστή, οὐχ ὥς τι αἰσχρὸν ποιοῦντι, καὶ ἑλόντι τε
e καλὸν δοκεῖ εἶναι καὶ μὴ ἑλόντι αἰσχρόν, καὶ πρὸς τὸ
ἐπιχειρεῖν ἑλεῖν ἐξουσίαν ὁ νόμος δέδωκε τῷ ἐραστῇ
θαυμαστὰ ἔργα ἐργαζομένῳ ἐπαινεῖσθαι, ἃ εἴ τις τολ-
μῴη ποιεῖν ἄλλ' ὁτιοῦν διώκων καὶ βουλόμενος δια-
183 πράξασθαι πλὴν τοῦτο, †φιλοσοφίας†[4] τὰ μέγιστα
καρποῖτ' ἂν ὀνείδη—εἰ γὰρ ἢ χρήματα βουλόμενος
παρά του λαβεῖν ἢ ἀρχὴν ἄρξαι ἤ τινα ἄλλην δύναμιν ἐθέλοι ποιεῖν οἷάπερ οἱ ἐρασταὶ πρὸς τὰ παιδικά,
ἱκετείας | τε καὶ ἀντιβολήσεις ἐν ταῖς δεήσεσιν ποι-

---

[4] secl. Schleiermacher

---

[41] See Thucydides 6.53–59. Harmodius and Aristogeiton had
been responsible in 514 for assassinating Hipparchus, brother of
the Athenian tyrant Hippias. The matching of the older partner
Aristogeiton's *erōs* (love) with the younger Harmodius' *philia*

bring about. Our tyrants here too learned this from experience, for it was Aristogeiton's love and Harmodius' friendship, when both grew steadfast, which destroyed their rule.[41] Thus where it has been laid down that it is shameful to gratify lovers, it is established by the bad character of those who made the laws, the greed of the rulers and the cowardliness of their subjects. But where it was simply considered fine (*kalon*) it was on account of the laziness of mind of the lawmakers. But here the convention is laid down in a much better way, and as I said, it's not easy to grasp. For when we think that it's said to be finer to love openly than in secret, and especially with the noblest and the best, even if they are more ill-favored than others; and again that the encouragement of the lover by all is extraordinary, not to be expected for someone doing anything shameful; and it is thought fine for him if he catches his love, and shameful for him if he doesn't, and that in his attempt to seduce his beloved, custom has given the lover the freedom to do, and be praised for doing, extraordinary deeds, for which, if anyone were to dare to do them in pursuit of anything else whatsoever, and wanting to accomplish anything except this,[42] he would incur the strongest reproaches—for if in wanting either to gain money from someone, or political office, or some other function, he were willing to do the sort of things lovers do for their loved ones, begging them by offering supplications and entreaties, and swearing oaths,

d

e

183

(friendship) precisely mirrors the asymmetry of the homosexual relationship (see General Introduction, §2).

[42] Note φιλοσοφίας (183a1), which Burnet (OCT) and all editors regard as an intrusive error (see textual note).

οὐμενοι, καὶ ὅρκους ὀμνύντες, καὶ κοιμήσεις ἐπὶ θύραις, καὶ ἐθέλοντες δουλείας δουλεύειν οἵας οὐδ᾽ ἂν
δοῦλος οὐδείς, ἐμποδίζοιτο ἂν μὴ πράττειν οὕτω τὴν
b πρᾶξιν καὶ ὑπὸ φίλων καὶ ὑπὸ ἐχθρῶν, τῶν μὲν ὀνει-
διζόντων κολακείας καὶ ἀνελευθερίας, τῶν δὲ νουθε-
τούντων καὶ αἰσχυνομένων ὑπὲρ αὐτῶν—τῷ δ᾽ ἐρῶντι
πάντα ταῦτα ποιοῦντι χάρις ἔπεστι, καὶ δέδοται ὑπὸ
τοῦ νόμου ἄνευ ὀνείδους πράττειν, ὡς πάγκαλόν τι
πρᾶγμα | διαπραττομένου· ὃ δὲ δεινότατον, ὥς γε λέ-
γουσιν οἱ πολλοί, ὅτι καὶ ὀμνύντι μόνῳ συγγνώμη
παρὰ θεῶν ἐκβάντι τῶν ὅρκων—ἀφροδίσιον γὰρ ὅρ-
c κον οὔ φασιν εἶναι· οὕτω καὶ οἱ θεοὶ καὶ οἱ ἄνθρωποι
πᾶσαν ἐξουσίαν πεποιήκασι τῷ ἐρῶντι, ὡς ὁ νόμος
φησὶν ὁ ἐνθάδε—ταύτῃ μὲν οὖν οἰηθείη ἄν τις πάγκαλον νομίζεσθαι ἐν τῇδε τῇ πόλει καὶ τὸ ἐρᾶν καὶ τὸ
φίλους γίγνεσθαι τοῖς ἐρασταῖς. ἐπειδὰν δὲ παιδα-
γωγοὺς | ἐπιστήσαντες οἱ πατέρες τοῖς ἐρωμένοις μὴ
ἐῶσι διαλέγεσθαι τοῖς ἐρασταῖς, καὶ τῷ παιδαγωγῷ
ταῦτα προστεταγμένα ᾖ, ἡλικιῶται δὲ καὶ ἑταῖροι
d ὀνειδίζωσιν ἐάν τι ὁρῶσιν τοιοῦτον γιγνόμενον, καὶ
τοὺς ὀνειδίζοντας αὖ οἱ πρεσβύτεροι μὴ διακωλύσωσι
μηδὲ λοιδορῶσιν ὡς οὐκ ὀρθῶς λέγοντας, εἰς δὲ ταῦτά
τις αὖ βλέψας ἡγήσαιτ᾽ ἂν πάλιν αἴσχιστον τὸ τοιοῦτον ἐνθάδε νομίζεσθαι. τὸ δὲ οἶμαι ὧδ᾽ ἔχει· οὐχ
ἁπλοῦν ἐστιν, ὅπερ ἐξ ἀρχῆς ἐλέχθη οὔτε καλὸν |

lying down to sleep at their doors and being willing to perform slavish tasks such as no slave would do, he would be prevented from doing anything like this both by his friends and by his enemies, the one group reproaching   b
him for his flattery and servility, the other telling him off and feeling ashamed of his activities—but a lover who does all these things finds favor and it is permitted by custom to do them without reproach on the grounds that he is doing a very fine thing.[43] But what is most extraordinary, at least as most people say, is that even in swearing oaths he alone is to be granted pardon by the gods when he breaks them—for they say a lover's oath is no oath. Thus both gods and men have given full license to the   c
lover, as the convention here says—and so from this one would think that in this city it's considered a very fine thing both to be in love and to show affection to lovers. But when fathers put attendants in charge of those who are loved, and do not allow them to speak to their lovers, and these are the instructions given to the attendant, and the boys' contemporaries and companions reproach them if they see anything like this happening, and again their   d
elders do not stop those who reproach them, and they do not abuse them for speaking out of turn; anyone looking at this would think that on the contrary such behavior is considered most shameful here.[44] But I think the situation is like this: it's no simple matter; as we said back at the

[43] The translation of this long, straggling sentence (with no main verb directly answering "For when we think . . ." [182d5]) is intended to reflect the loosely connected Greek syntax.

[44] For "double standards" in social attitudes to erotic relationships in Athenian society, see General Introduction, §2.

εἶναι αὐτὸ καθ᾽ αὑτὸ οὔτε αἰσχρόν, ἀλλὰ καλῶς μὲν
πραττόμενον καλόν, αἰσχρῶς δὲ αἰσχρόν. αἰσχρῶς
μὲν οὖν ἐστι πονηρῷ τε καὶ πονηρῶς χαρίζεσθαι,
καλῶς δὲ χρηστῷ τε καὶ καλῶς. πονηρὸς δ᾽ ἐστὶν
ἐκεῖνος ὁ ἐραστὴς ὁ πάνδημος, ὁ τοῦ σώματος μᾶλ-
e λον ἢ τῆς ψυχῆς ἐρῶν· καὶ γὰρ οὐδὲ μόνιμός ἐστιν,
ἅτε οὐδὲ μονίμου ἐρῶν πράγματος. ἅμα γὰρ τῷ τοῦ
σώματος ἄνθει λήγοντι, οὗπερ ἤρα, "οἴχεται ἀποπτά-
μενος," πολλοὺς λόγους καὶ ὑποσχέσεις καταισχύ-
νας· | ὁ δὲ τοῦ ἤθους χρηστοῦ ὄντος ἐραστὴς διὰ βίου
184 μένει, ἅτε μονίμῳ συντακείς. τούτους δὴ βούλεται ὁ
ἡμέτερος νόμος εὖ καὶ καλῶς βασανίζειν, καὶ τοῖς μὲν
χαρίσασθαι, τοὺς δὲ διαφεύγειν. διὰ ταῦτα οὖν τοῖς
μὲν διώκειν παρακελεύεται, τοῖς δὲ φεύγειν, ἀγωνοθε-
τῶν καὶ βασανίζων ποτέρων ποτέ ἐστιν ὁ ἐρῶν καὶ
ποτέρων ὁ | ἐρώμενος. οὕτω δὴ ὑπὸ ταύτης τῆς αἰτίας
πρῶτον μὲν τὸ ἁλίσκεσθαι ταχὺ αἰσχρὸν νενόμισται,
ἵνα χρόνος ἐγγένηται, ὃς δὴ δοκεῖ τὰ πολλὰ καλῶς
βασανίζειν, ἔπειτα τὸ ὑπὸ χρημάτων καὶ ὑπὸ πολιτικῶν δυνάμεων ἁλῶναι αἰσχρόν, ἐάν τε κακῶς πάσχων
b πτήξῃ καὶ μὴ καρτερήσῃ, ἄν τ᾽ εὐεργετούμενος εἰς
χρήματα ἢ εἰς διαπράξεις πολιτικὰς μὴ καταφρο-
νήσῃ· οὐδὲν γὰρ δοκεῖ τούτων οὔτε βέβαιον οὔτε μό-
νιμον εἶναι, χωρὶς τοῦ μηδὲ πεφυκέναι ἀπ᾽ αὐτῶν
γενναίαν | φιλίαν. μία δὴ λείπεται τῷ ἡμετέρῳ νόμῳ
ὁδός, εἰ μέλλει καλῶς χαριεῖσθαι ἐραστῇ παιδικά.

beginning, taken in isolation and by itself it is neither fine nor shameful, but if it is done well it is fine and if done badly, shameful. So if favors are granted to a worthless person in a worthless fashion, this is to act shamefully; to grant them to a decent person in a fine manner is to act in a fine way. Worthless is that lover, the common one, who loves the body more than the soul: for he is not constant either, in that he is not the lover of anything lasting. For as the bloom of the body which he loved fades away 'he flies off and is gone'[45] having dishonored many words and promises. But he who is a lover of worthy character remains so for life in that he has become joined intimately with something constant. It is these groups of people our custom wants to put well and truly to the test, and to grant favors to one group and shun the other. This is why therefore our rule encourages one group to pursue, the other to flee by setting up a competition and testing which group the lover and which one the beloved belongs to. So this is the reason why firstly it is considered shameful to be caught quickly, so that a period of time may intervene, which seems to test most things well; secondly, why it is considered disgraceful to be caught by money and political influence if, having been treated badly, one cringes and does not stand firm, or if in being offered favors with regard to money matters, or in the achievement of political aims, one does not despise the offers. For none of these things seems secure or lasting, quite apart from the fact that a noble friendship cannot not come from them. Indeed there is one way left according to our custom, if a loved one is going to grant his lover a favor in a fine way.

e

184

b

---

[45] Homer, *Iliad* 2.71.

ἔστι γὰρ ἡμῖν νόμος, ὥσπερ ἐπὶ τοῖς ἐρασταῖς ἦν
δουλεύειν ἐθέλοντα ἡντινοῦν δουλείαν παιδικοῖς μὴ
c κολακείαν εἶναι μηδὲ ἐπονείδιστον, οὕτω δὴ καὶ ἄλλη
μία μόνη δουλεία ἑκούσιος λείπεται οὐκ ἐπονείδιστος·
αὕτη δ' ἐστὶν ἡ περὶ τὴν ἀρετήν. νενόμισται γὰρ δὴ
ἡμῖν, ἐάν τις ἐθέλῃ τινὰ θεραπεύειν | ἡγούμενος δι'
ἐκεῖνον ἀμείνων ἔσεσθαι ἢ κατὰ σοφίαν τινὰ ἢ κατὰ
ἄλλο ὁτιοῦν μέρος ἀρετῆς, αὕτη αὖ ἡ ἐθελοδουλεία
οὐκ αἰσχρὰ εἶναι οὐδὲ κολακεία. δεῖ δὴ τὼ νόμω
τούτω συμβαλεῖν εἰς ταὐτόν, τόν τε περὶ τὴν παιδε-
ραστίαν καὶ τὸν περὶ τὴν φιλοσοφίαν τε καὶ τὴν ἄλ-
d λην ἀρετήν, εἰ μέλλει συμβῆναι καλὸν γενέσθαι τὸ
ἐραστῇ παιδικὰ χαρίσασθαι. ὅταν γὰρ εἰς τὸ αὐτὸ
ἔλθωσιν ἐραστής τε καὶ παιδικά, νόμον ἔχων ἑκάτε-
ρος, ὁ μὲν χαρισαμένοις παιδικοῖς | ὑπηρετῶν ὁτιοῦν
δικαίως ἂν ὑπηρετεῖν, ὁ δὲ τῷ ποιοῦντι αὐτὸν σοφόν
τε καὶ ἀγαθὸν δικαίως αὖ ὁτιοῦν ἂν ὑπουργῶν ⟨ὑπουρ-
γεῖν⟩, καὶ ὁ μὲν δυνάμενος εἰς φρόνησιν καὶ τὴν ἄλ-
e λην ἀρετὴν συμβάλλεσθαι, ὁ δὲ δεόμενος εἰς παίδευσιν καὶ τὴν ἄλλην σοφίαν κτᾶσθαι, τότε δὴ τούτων
συνιόντων εἰς ταὐτὸν τῶν νόμων μοναχοῦ ἐνταῦθα
συμπίπτει τὸ καλὸν εἶναι παιδικὰ ἐραστῇ χαρίσα-
σθαι, ἄλλοθι δὲ οὐδαμοῦ. ἐπὶ | τούτῳ καὶ ἐξαπατηθῆ-
ναι οὐδὲν αἰσχρόν· ἐπὶ δὲ τοῖς ἄλλοις πᾶσι καὶ ἐξ-
185 απατωμένῳ αἰσχύνην φέρει καὶ μή. εἰ γάρ τις ἐραστῇ
ὡς πλουσίῳ πλούτου ἕνεκα χαρισάμενος ἐξαπατηθείη

For we have a convention, just as it was possible for lovers to carry out voluntarily any servile acts whatever for their loved one without it being regarded as flattery or worthy of reproach, so there is left also only one other kind of c voluntary enslavement that is irreproachable: this is enslavement which relates to excellence.[46] For we take the view that, if one wishes to cultivate someone with the idea that through that person he will be better either in terms of some kind of wisdom, or any other aspect whatever of excellence, then this voluntary servitude is neither shameful nor is it flattery. We must then combine these two conventions into one: the one concerning loving of boys and the other concerning love of wisdom and other kinds of excellence, if it is to turn out that it is a fine thing for a d beloved to gratify his lover. For when a lover and his beloved come together, each with his own rule, the one believing that in serving in whatever way the beloved who has granted him his favor, he is right to serve, and the other who thinks that submitting to the person making him wise and good, he is right to submit in any way whatsoever, the one being able to contribute to his good judgment and his excellence in general, and the other wanting to acquire it e for his education and wisdom in general: then it is when these principles come together into one, and here alone, that it turns out to be fine for a beloved to gratify his lover; otherwise in no other circumstances. And in this situation even to have been misled is nothing to be ashamed of: but in all other instances it brings shame upon someone whether one has been misled or not. For if someone were 185 to gratify his lover in the belief that he's rich, for the sake

---

46 "Excellence" or "virtue" = *aretē.*

PLATO

καὶ μὴ λάβοι χρήματα, ἀναφανέντος τοῦ ἐραστοῦ πέ-
νητος, οὐδὲν ἧττον αἰσχρόν· δοκεῖ γὰρ ὁ τοιοῦτος τό
γε αὑτοῦ ἐπιδεῖξαι, ὅτι ἕνεκα χρημάτων ὁτιοῦν ἂν
ὁτῳοῦν ὑπηρετοῖ, | τοῦτο δὲ οὐ καλόν. κατὰ τὸν αὐτὸν
δὴ λόγον κἂν εἴ τις ὡς ἀγαθῷ χαρισάμενος καὶ αὐτὸς
ὡς ἀμείνων ἐσόμενος διὰ τὴν φιλίαν ἐραστοῦ ἐξαπατηθείη, ἀναφανέντος ἐκείνου κακοῦ καὶ οὐ κεκτημένου
b ἀρετήν, ὅμως καλὴ ἡ ἀπάτη· δοκεῖ γὰρ αὖ καὶ οὗτος
τὸ καθ' αὑτὸν δεδηλωκέναι, ὅτι ἀρετῆς γ' ἕνεκα καὶ
τοῦ βελτίων γενέσθαι πᾶν ἂν παντὶ προθυμηθείη,
τοῦτο δὲ αὖ πάντων κάλλιστον· οὕτω πᾶν πάντως γε
καλὸν | ἀρετῆς γ' ἕνεκα χαρίζεσθαι. οὗτός ἐστιν ὁ τῆς
οὐρανίας θεοῦ ἔρως καὶ οὐράνιος καὶ πολλοῦ ἄξιος
καὶ πόλει καὶ ἰδιώταις, πολλὴν ἐπιμέλειαν ἀναγκάζων
ποιεῖσθαι πρὸς ἀρετὴν τόν τε ἐρῶντα αὐτὸν αὑτοῦ
c καὶ τὸν ἐρώμενον· οἱ δ' ἕτεροι πάντες τῆς ἑτέρας, τῆς
πανδήμου. ταῦτά σοι, ἔφη, ὡς ἐκ τοῦ παραχρῆμα, ὦ
Φαῖδρε, περὶ Ἔρωτος συμβάλλομαι.

Παυσανίου δὲ παυσαμένου—διδάσκουσι γάρ με
ἴσα λέγειν | οὑτωσὶ οἱ σοφοί—ἔφη ὁ Ἀριστόδημος

---

47 The two words *Pausaniou . . . pausamenou* (When Pausanias had paused) balance as two similar-sounding four-syllable
words. The narrator, Apollodorus, speaking in his own person
(and incidentally reminding us that he is still recounting the
whole event to his companion as they walk toward Athens), refers
by implication to Pausanias' somewhat convoluted style and the

of his money, and was misled and received none when his lover was revealed to be poor, it would be no less shameful. For such a person seems to be showing himself up for what he is, in that he would do any service whatever for anyone whatever for the sake of money, and this would not be a fine thing. By the same argument, even if one were to grant favors to an apparently good man, in order to be a better person oneself through the affection of the lover, and were to be deceived when that man had been exposed as bad and not in possession of any virtue, nevertheless the deception would be a fine thing. For this person too in his   b turn seems to have revealed his own character, that for the sake of excellence and becoming a better person he would be eager to do anything for anyone and that, moreover, would be the finest motive of all. Therefore it is entirely fine to grant every favor in all circumstances, provided that it is for the sake of excellence. This is the love of the heavenly goddess, itself heavenly and of great value both to the state and to individuals, compelling both the lover to take every care of himself with regard to his virtue, and the loved one also. But as for all the rest they belong to   c the other goddess, the common love. This then, he said, is what I am contributing to you, on the spur of the moment, Phaedrus, on the subject of Love."

When Pausanias had paused—you see the experts teach me to speak in this balanced manner[47]—Aristode-

highly wrought rhetoric practiced by the "experts," the sophists, undercutting, incidentally, Pausanias' claim to be speaking "on the spur of the moment" [c3]).

δεῖν μὲν Ἀριστοφάνη λέγειν, τυχεῖν δὲ αὐτῷ τινα ἢ
ὑπὸ πλησμονῆς ἢ ὑπό τινος ἄλλου λύγγα ἐπιπεπτω-
κυῖαν καὶ οὐχ οἷόν τε εἶναι λέγειν, ἀλλ᾽ εἰπεῖν αὐτόν—
ἐν τῇ κάτω γὰρ αὐτοῦ τὸν ἰατρὸν Ἐρυξίμαχον κατα-
d κεῖσθαι—"Ὦ Ἐρυξίμαχε, δίκαιος εἶ ἢ παῦσαί με τῆς
λυγγὸς ἢ λέγειν ὑπὲρ ἐμοῦ, ἕως ἂν ἐγὼ παύσωμαι."
καὶ τὸν Ἐρυξίμαχον εἰπεῖν "Ἀλλὰ ποιήσω ἀμφότερα
ταῦτα· | ἐγὼ μὲν γὰρ ἐρῶ ἐν τῷ σῷ μέρει, σὺ δ᾽ ἐπει-
δὰν παύσῃ, ἐν τῷ ἐμῷ. ἐν ᾧ δ᾽ ἂν ἐγὼ λέγω, ἐὰν μέν
σοι ἐθέλῃ ἀπνευστὶ ἔχοντι πολὺν χρόνον παύεσθαι ἡ
e λύγξ· εἰ δὲ μή, ὕδατι ἀνακογχυλίασον. εἰ δ᾽ ἄρα πάνυ
ἰσχυρά ἐστιν, ἀναλαβών τι τοιοῦτον οἵῳ κινήσαις ἂν
τὴν ῥῖνα, πτάρε· καὶ ἐὰν τοῦτο ποιήσῃς ἅπαξ ἢ δίς,
καὶ εἰ πάνυ ἰσχυρά ἐστι, παύσεται." "Οὐκ ἂν φθάνοις
λέγων," φάναι τὸν Ἀριστοφάνη· "ἐγὼ | δὲ ταῦτα ποι-
ήσω."

Εἰπεῖν δὴ τὸν Ἐρυξίμαχον·

Δοκεῖ τοίνυν μοι ἀναγκαῖον εἶναι, ἐπειδὴ Παυσανίας ὁρμήσας ἐπὶ τὸν λόγον καλῶς οὐχ ἱκανῶς ἀπε-
τέλεσε, δεῖν ἐμὲ πειρᾶσθαι τέλος ἐπιθεῖναι τῷ λόγῳ.
186 τὸ μὲν γὰρ διπλοῦν εἶναι τὸν Ἔρωτα δοκεῖ μοι καλῶς
διελέσθαι· ὅτι δὲ οὐ μόνον ἐστὶν ἐπὶ ταῖς ψυχαῖς τῶν
ἀνθρώπων πρὸς τοὺς καλοὺς ἀλλὰ καὶ πρὸς ἄλλα
πολλὰ | καὶ ἐν τοῖς ἄλλοις, τοῖς τε σώμασι τῶν πάν-
των ζῴων καὶ τοῖς ἐν τῇ γῇ φυομένοις καὶ ὡς ἔπος
εἰπεῖν ἐν πᾶσι τοῖς οὖσι, καθεωρακέναι μοι δοκῶ ἐκ

mus said that it was Aristophanes' turn to speak, but it happened that either from eating too much or from some other cause he had an attack of the hiccups and not being able to make his speech, he said: "Eryximachus"—the doctor Eryximachus was lying on the couch below him—"you're just the right man either to stop my hiccups, d or speak in my place until I can stop them myself." And Eryximachus said, "Well, I shall do both of these things: I shall speak in your place, and when you stop, you can speak in mine. And while I'm speaking, if you hold your breath for a long time, your hiccups may be inclined to stop; but if not, gargle with some water. But if they actually e take a strong hold of you, take something you can tickle your nose with and sneeze; and if you do this once or twice, even if they are quite persistent, they will stop." "So the sooner you start speaking the better" said Aristophanes, "and I shall do what you advise."

The Speech of Eryximachus

So Eryximachus began to speak:

"I think it's incumbent upon me, since Pausanias embarked on his speech well, but didn't bring it to a satisfactory conclusion, to attempt to round off what he said. That 186 Love has a double aspect seems to me to show good discernment: but that it's not only in the souls of men reacting to those who are beautiful, but also in relation to many other things and in other things, the bodies of all animals and the things that grow in the earth and, so to speak, in all that exists, this I think I have observed from medical

b τῆς ἰατρικῆς, τῆς ἡμετέρας τέχνης, ὡς μέγας καὶ θαυμαστὸς καὶ ἐπὶ πᾶν ὁ θεὸς τείνει καὶ κατ᾿ ἀνθρώπινα
καὶ κατὰ θεῖα πράγματα. ἄρξομαι δὲ ἀπὸ τῆς ἰατρικῆς λέγων, ἵνα καὶ πρεσβεύωμεν τὴν τέχνην. ἡ γὰρ
φύσις τῶν σωμάτων τὸν διπλοῦν Ἔρωτα τοῦτον ἔχει·
| τὸ γὰρ ὑγιὲς τοῦ σώματος καὶ τὸ νοσοῦν ὁμολογου-
μένως ἕτερόν τε καὶ ἀνόμοιόν ἐστι, τὸ δὲ ἀνόμοιον
ἀνομοίων ἐπιθυμεῖ καὶ ἐρᾷ. ἄλλος μὲν οὖν ὁ ἐπὶ τῷ
ὑγιεινῷ ἔρως, ἄλλος δὲ ὁ ἐπὶ τῷ νοσώδει. ἔστιν δή,
ὥσπερ ἄρτι Παυσανίας ἔλεγεν τοῖς μὲν ἀγαθοῖς καλὸν χαρίζεσθαι τῶν ἀνθρώπων, τοῖς δ᾿ ἀκολάστοις

c αἰσχρόν, οὕτω καὶ ἐν αὐτοῖς τοῖς σώμασιν τοῖς μὲν
ἀγαθοῖς ἑκάστου τοῦ σώματος καὶ ὑγιεινοῖς καλὸν
χαρίζεσθαι καὶ δεῖ, καὶ τοῦτό ἐστιν ᾧ ὄνομα τὸ ἰατρι-
κόν, τοῖς δὲ κακοῖς καὶ νοσώδεσιν αἰσχρόν τε καὶ δεῖ
ἀχαριστεῖν, | εἰ μέλλει τις τεχνικὸς εἶναι. ἔστι γὰρ
ἰατρική, ὡς ἐν κεφαλαίῳ εἰπεῖν, ἐπιστήμη τῶν τοῦ
σώματος ἐρωτικῶν πρὸς πλησμονὴν καὶ κένωσιν, καὶ
ὁ διαγιγνώσκων ἐν τούτοις τὸν καλόν τε καὶ αἰσχρὸν

d ἔρωτα, οὗτός ἐστιν ὁ ἰατρικώτατος, καὶ ὁ μεταβάλλειν
ποιῶν, ὥστε ἀντὶ τοῦ ἑτέρου ἔρωτος τὸν ἕτερον κτᾶσθαι, καὶ οἷς μὴ ἔνεστιν ἔρως, δεῖ δ᾿ ἐγγενέσθαι, ἐπιστάμενος ἐμποιῆσαι καὶ ἐνόντα ἐξελεῖν, ἀγαθὸς ἂν

---

48 For Eros (Love) as a cosmic force, and its opposing counterpart, Eris (Strife), see the Pre-Socratic philosopher Empedocles (DK 31B17, Waterfield, 147–48).

practice, my profession, seeing how the god, great and   b
marvelous, reaches into everything, the affairs of men and
gods alike.[48] I shall begin my speech from medicine so that
we may also give pride of place to that profession. You see
it is the nature of our bodies to have this double Love; for
the healthy part of the body and the sick part are by common agreement separate and unlike each other, and the
unlike craves for and loves what is unlike.[49] So love in the
one who is healthy is one thing and love in the sick is another. Indeed just as Pausanias was saying just now, that it
is fine to gratify those among men who are good, and
shameful to gratify those who are licentious, so too in bod-   c
ies themselves it is fine to gratify the good and healthy
parts of each body, and one should do so, and this is what
the term medical expertise relates to; but indulging those
parts which are bad and sickly is shameful, and they must
not be favored if one is going to be proficient. For the art
of medicine, to put it concisely, is the understanding of the
erotic desires of the body in respect of repletion and depletion,[50] and the one who distinguishes in these the fine
love and the shameful love, that man is supremely expert   d
in medicine, and the one who brings about changes so as
to obtain one kind of love in place of the other, and needs
to generate it where there is no love, knowing how to
implant it, and remove it when it is present, would be a

[49] For appetites in the sick and the healthy body, see the Hippocratic *On Ancient Medicine* 20.

[50] "Repletion and depletion": the idea of health as a balance
of elements in the body by the careful operation of *plēsmonē* and
kenōsis and the right balance of opposites (see d6–e1) was a basic
assumption of Greek medical theory.

PLATO

εἴη | δημιουργός. δεῖ γὰρ δὴ τὰ ἔχθιστα ὄντα ἐν τῷ
σώματι φίλα οἷόν τ᾽ εἶναι ποιεῖν καὶ ἐρᾶν ἀλλήλων.
ἔστι δὲ ἔχθιστα τὰ ἐναντιώτατα, ψυχρὸν θερμῷ, πι-
e κρὸν γλυκεῖ, ξηρὸν ὑγρῷ, πάντα τὰ τοιαῦτα· τούτοις
ἐπιστηθεὶς ἔρωτα ἐμποιῆσαι καὶ ὁμόνοιαν ὁ ἡμέτερος
πρόγονος Ἀσκληπιός, ὥς φασιν οἵδε οἱ ποιηταὶ καὶ
ἐγὼ πείθομαι, συνέστησεν τὴν ἡμετέραν τέχνην. ἥ τε
οὖν ἰατρική, ὥσπερ λέγω, πᾶσα διὰ τοῦ θεοῦ τούτου
κυβερνᾶται, ὡσαύτως δὲ καὶ γυμναστικὴ καὶ γεωρ-
187 γία· μουσικὴ δὲ καὶ παντὶ κατάδηλος τῷ καὶ σμικρὸν
προσέχοντι τὸν νοῦν ὅτι κατὰ ταὐτὰ ἔχει τούτοις,
ὥσπερ ἴσως καὶ Ἡράκλειτος βούλεται λέγειν, ἐπεὶ
τοῖς γε ῥήμασιν οὐ καλῶς λέγει. τὸ | ἓν γάρ φησι
"διαφερόμενον αὐτὸ αὑτῷ συμφέρεσθαι," "ὥσπερ ἁρμονίαν τόξου τε καὶ λύρας." ἔστι δὲ πολλὴ ἀλογία
ἁρμονίαν φάναι διαφέρεσθαι ἢ ἐκ διαφερομένων ἔτι
εἶναι. ἀλλὰ ἴσως τόδε ἐβούλετο λέγειν, ὅτι ἐκ διαφερομένων πρότερον τοῦ ὀξέος καὶ βαρέος, ἔπειτα
ὕστερον ὁμολογησάντων γέγονεν ὑπὸ τῆς μουσικῆς
b τέχνης. οὐ γὰρ δήπου ἐκ διαφερομένων γε ἔτι τοῦ
ὀξέος καὶ βαρέος ἁρμονία ἂν εἴη· ἡ γὰρ ἁρμονία συμ-
φωνία ἐστίν, συμφωνία δὲ ὁμολογία | τις—ὁμολογίαν
δὲ ἐκ διαφερομένων, |ἕως ἂν διαφέρωνται, ἀδύνατον
εἶναι· διαφερόμενον δὲ αὖ καὶ μὴ ὁμολογοῦν ἀδύνατον

---

[51] The legendary founder of medicine. "These poets here"
include Agathon and Aristophanes.

good practitioner. For what he must do is to make the most hostile elements in the body benign and love each other. The most hostile are the most opposite: cold to hot, bitter to sweet, dry to wet: all such things. With his understanding of implanting love and harmony in these elements, our ancestor Asclepius established our profession, as these poets here say and as I am persuaded.[51] Therefore, as I say, all medicine is guided by means of this god, and, in the same sort of way, so are gymnastics and agriculture. It's clear to everyone too, even if they are paying little attention, that music belongs with these on the same principles, just as perhaps Heraclitus also means when he expresses it, though by his actual wording not very well. You see he says that the one 'being at variance with itself is in agreement,' 'just like the harmony of a bow and a lyre.'[52] It is quite illogical to say that a harmony is at variance, or it still exists when being drawn in different directions. But perhaps what he meant to say was this, that it came to be from the high and the low note, being previously drawn apart, then brought into agreement later by the art of music. For surely there could not be harmony from the high and low when they are still drawn apart. For harmony is a sounding together, and sounding together is a kind of agreement—and it's impossible for agreement to come from elements which are at variance for as long as they are at variance, and again, impossible to harmonize that which is being drawn apart and is not in agreement—just as

e

187

b

[52] Heraclitus, DK B51 (Waterfield 40). Heraclitus (early 5th century) was notorious for the obscurity of his language, and his theory of the tension between opposites was generally misunderstood, as it certainly is by Eryximachus here.

ἁρμόσαι—ὥσπερ γε καὶ ὁ ῥυθμὸς ἐκ τοῦ ταχέος καὶ
βραδέος, ἐκ διενηνεγμένων πρότερον, ὕστερον δὲ ὁμο-
c λογησάντων γέγονε. τὴν δὲ ὁμολογίαν πᾶσι τούτοις,
ὥσπερ ἐκεῖ ἡ ἰατρική, ἐνταῦθα ἡ μουσικὴ ἐντίθησιν,
ἔρωτα καὶ ὁμόνοιαν ἀλλήλων ἐμποιήσασα· καὶ ἔστιν
αὖ μουσικὴ περὶ | ἁρμονίαν καὶ ῥυθμὸν ἐρωτικῶν ἐπι-
στήμη. καὶ ἐν μέν γε αὐτῇ τῇ συστάσει ἁρμονίας τε
καὶ ῥυθμοῦ οὐδὲν χαλεπὸν τὰ ἐρωτικὰ διαγιγνώσκειν,
οὐδὲ ὁ διπλοῦς ἔρως ἐνταῦθά πω ἔστιν· ἀλλ᾽ ἐπειδὰν
δέῃ πρὸς τοὺς ἀνθρώπους καταχρῆσθαι ῥυθμῷ τε καὶ
d ἁρμονίᾳ ἢ ποιοῦντα, ὃ δὴ μελοποιίαν καλοῦσιν, ἢ
χρώμενον ὀρθῶς τοῖς πεποιημένοις μέλεσί τε καὶ μέ-
τροις, ὃ δὴ παιδεία ἐκλήθη, ἐνταῦθα δὴ καὶ χαλεπὸν
καὶ ἀγαθοῦ δημιουργοῦ δεῖ. πάλιν γὰρ ἥκει ὁ αὐτὸς
λόγος, ὅτι τοῖς μὲν | κοσμίοις τῶν ἀνθρώπων, καὶ ὡς
ἂν κοσμιώτεροι γίγνοιντο οἱ μήπω ὄντες, δεῖ χαρίζεσθαι καὶ φυλάττειν τὸν τούτων ἔρωτα, καὶ οὗτός ἐστιν
ὁ καλός, ὁ οὐράνιος, ὁ τῆς Οὐρανίας μούσης Ἔρως·
e ὁ δὲ Πολυμνίας ὁ πάνδημος, ὃν δεῖ εὐλαβούμενον
προσφέρειν οἷς ἂν προσφέρῃ, ὅπως ἂν τὴν μὲν ἡδονὴν αὐτοῦ καρπώσηται, ἀκολασίαν δὲ μηδεμίαν ἐμ-
ποιήσῃ, ὥσπερ ἐν τῇ ἡμετέρᾳ τέχνῃ μέγα ἔργον ταῖς
περὶ τὴν ὀψοποιικὴν | τέχνην ἐπιθυμίαις καλῶς χρῆ-
σθαι, ὥστ᾽ ἄνευ νόσου τὴν ἡδονὴν καρπώσασθαι. καὶ
ἐν μουσικῇ δὴ καὶ ἐν ἰατρικῇ καὶ ἐν τοῖς ἄλλοις πᾶσι

rhythm too, comes about from the quick and the slow, elements having been at variance previously, coming later into agreement. So agreement in all these things, just as c
in the previous example medicine, is supplied here by music, by putting in them love and unanimity with each other. Music is, in its turn, the understanding of the elements of love in relation to harmony and rhythm. And there is no difficulty in distinguishing the element of love in the structure of both harmony and rhythm itself, nor does twofold love yet exist here. But when it is necessary to apply both rhythm and harmony to human beings, either by creating it, which they call composing music, or d
using correctly tunes and rhythms already composed, which is called education, this is really where it is difficult and needs a good practitioner. For the same argument as before returns, that it is to the people who are orderly[53] that one must grant favors, and in such a way that those who are not yet so may become more orderly, and one must protect the love of these people. This is the beautiful Love, the heavenly one, the Love which comes from the heavenly Muse. But the commonplace Love is from e
Polymnia,[54] and he should be applied with care to those to whom one applies him, so that the pleasure coming from him may be enjoyed, but that he may not implant any intemperance, just as in our profession it is a big task to deal well with the desires relating to cookery, so that the pleasure may be enjoyed without sickness. Both in music, then, and in medicine and in all the other human and di-

---

[53] "Orderly" = *kosmios*, that is, having the right balance of elements.   [54] The name suggests multiplicity. Polymnia is listed by Hesiod as one of the Muses (*Theogony* 75–79).

καὶ τοῖς ἀνθρωπείοις καὶ τοῖς θείοις, καθ᾽ ὅσον παρεί-
κει, φυλακτέον ἑκάτερον τὸν Ἔρωτα· ἔνεστον γάρ.
188 ἐπεὶ καὶ ἡ τῶν ὡρῶν τοῦ ἐνιαυτοῦ σύστασις μεστή
ἐστιν ἀμφοτέρων τούτων, καὶ ἐπειδὰν μὲν πρὸς ἄλληλα τοῦ κοσμίου τύχῃ ἔρωτος ἃ νυνδὴ ἐγὼ ἔλεγον,
τά τε θερμὰ καὶ τὰ ψυχρὰ καὶ ξηρὰ καὶ ὑγρά, καὶ
ἁρμονίαν καὶ κρᾶσιν λάβῃ | σώφρονα, ἥκει φέροντα
εὐετηρίαν τε καὶ ὑγίειαν ἀνθρώποις καὶ τοῖς ἄλλοις
ζῴοις τε καὶ φυτοῖς, καὶ οὐδὲν ἠδίκησεν· ὅταν δὲ ὁ
μετὰ τῆς ὕβρεως Ἔρως ἐγκρατέστερος περὶ τὰς τοῦ
ἐνιαυτοῦ ὥρας γένηται, διέφθειρέν τε πολλὰ καὶ ἠδί-
b κησεν. οἵ τε γὰρ λοιμοὶ φιλοῦσι γίγνεσθαι ἐκ τῶν
τοιούτων καὶ ἄλλα ἀνόμοια πολλὰ νοσήματα καὶ τοῖς
θηρίοις καὶ τοῖς φυτοῖς· καὶ γὰρ πάχναι καὶ χάλαζαι
καὶ ἐρυσῖβαι ἐκ πλεονεξίας καὶ ἀκοσμίας περὶ ἄλ-
ληλα τῶν τοιούτων γίγνεται | ἐρωτικῶν, ὧν ἐπιστήμη
περὶ ἄστρων τε φορὰς καὶ ἐνιαυτῶν ὥρας ἀστρονομία
καλεῖται. ἔτι τοίνυν καὶ αἱ θυσίαι πᾶσαι καὶ οἷς μαντικὴ ἐπιστατεῖ—ταῦτα δ᾽ ἐστὶν ἡ περὶ θεούς τε καὶ
c ἀνθρώπους πρὸς ἀλλήλους κοινωνία—οὐ περὶ ἄλλο
τί ἐστιν ἢ περὶ Ἔρωτος φυλακήν τε καὶ ἴασιν. πᾶσα
γὰρ ἀσέβεια φιλεῖ γίγνεσθαι ἐὰν μή τις τῷ κοσμίῳ
Ἔρωτι χαρίζηται μηδὲ τιμᾷ τε αὐτὸν καὶ πρεσβεύῃ
ἐν παντὶ ἔργῳ, | ἀλλὰ τὸν ἕτερον, καὶ περὶ γονέας
καὶ ζῶντας καὶ τετελευτηκότας καὶ περὶ θεούς· ἃ δὴ
προστέτακται τῇ μαντικῇ ἐπισκοπεῖν τοὺς ἐρῶντας
d καὶ ἰατρεύειν, καὶ ἔστιν αὖ ἡ μαντικὴ φιλίας θεῶν καὶ
ἀνθρώπων δημιουργὸς τῷ ἐπίστασθαι τὰ κατὰ ἀν-

vine pursuits, as far as circumstances permit, we must look
out for each kind of Love. For both are present. Take note   188
that even the seasons of the year are in their composition
full of both of these Loves, and when those elements I was
talking about just now, hot and cold, dry and wet, come
together under the influence of the orderly love and take
on a temperate harmony and combination, they come
bringing prosperity and health to men and other animals
and plants, and do no harm. But when the Love combined
with violence becomes more powerful in relation to the
seasons of the year, he destroys and damages a great deal.
For plagues usually come about as a result of such things,   b
as do many other kinds of abnormal illness, afflicting both
animals and plants. For frost and hail and blight come
about as a result of excess and disorderliness among such
kinds of erotic influences in relation to each other, the
understanding of which, relating to the courses of the stars
and the seasons of the year is called astronomy. There
again, all sacrifices and those things divination has control
over—that is the association of gods and men with each
other—are about nothing other than what relates to the   c
guarding and the healing power relating to Love. For all
impiety usually occurs if one does not gratify the orderly
Love and does not honor him and give him precedence in
every action, but favors the other one, both as regards
parents, alive or dead, and the gods. This is what has been
ordained for divination, to oversee lovers and heal them,
and again divination is a worker for friendship between   d
gods and men through its understanding of the affairs of

θρώπους ἐρωτικά, ὅσα τείνει πρὸς θέμιν καὶ εὐσέβειαν.[5]

Οὕτω πολλὴν καὶ μεγάλην, μᾶλλον δὲ πᾶσαν δύ-
ναμιν ἔχει | συλλήβδην μὲν ὁ πᾶς Ἔρως, ὁ δὲ περὶ
τἀγαθὰ μετὰ σωφροσύνης καὶ δικαιοσύνης ἀποτε-
λούμενος καὶ παρ᾽ ἡμῖν καὶ παρὰ θεοῖς, οὗτος τὴν
μεγίστην δύναμιν ἔχει καὶ πᾶσαν ἡμῖν εὐδαιμονίαν
παρασκευάζει καὶ ἀλλήλοις δυναμένους ὁμιλεῖν καὶ
e φίλους εἶναι καὶ τοῖς κρείττοσιν ἡμῶν θεοῖς. ἴσως μὲν
οὖν καὶ ἐγὼ τὸν Ἔρωτα ἐπαινῶν πολλὰ παραλείπω,
οὐ μέντοι ἑκών γε. ἀλλ᾽ εἴ τι ἐξέλιπον, σὸν ἔργον, ὦ
Ἀριστόφανες, ἀναπληρῶσαι· ἢ εἴ πως ἄλλως ἐν νῷ
ἔχεις ἐγκωμιάζειν τὸν θεόν, ἐγκωμίαζε, ἐπειδὴ καὶ τῆς
λυγγὸς πέπαυσαι.

189   Ἐκδεξάμενον οὖν ἔφη εἰπεῖν τὸν Ἀριστοφάνη ὅτι
Καὶ μάλ᾽ ἐπαύσατο, οὐ μέντοι πρίν γε τὸν πταρμὸν
προσενεχθῆναι αὐτῇ, ὥστε με θαυμάζειν εἰ τὸ κό-
σμιον τοῦ σώματος ἐπιθυμεῖ τοιούτων ψόφων καὶ
γαργαλισμῶν, οἷον καὶ ὁ πταρμός | ἐστιν· πάνυ γὰρ
εὐθὺς ἐπαύσατο, ἐπειδὴ αὐτῷ τὸν πταρμὸν προσ-
ήνεγκα.

Καὶ τὸν Ἐρυξίμαχον, Ὠγαθέ, φάναι, Ἀριστόφανες,
ὅρα τί ποιεῖς. γελωτοποιεῖς μέλλων λέγειν, καὶ φύ-

---

[5] εὐσέβειαν Stobaeus: ἀσέβειαν BTW

human love as far as they tend toward right and rever-ence.[55]

"Love has so much and such great power, or rather total power taken as a whole, but the Love which is con-cerned with the good and accomplished with moderation and justice both among us and among the gods—this is the one that has the greatest power and provides all happiness for us and enables us to get along with each other and be friends, and so too with those greater than us, the gods. Now, perhaps I too have left out a great deal in my praise of Love; certainly however, I've not done it deliberately. But if I have left something out, then it's your job, Aris-tophanes, to fill in the gap; or if you intend to praise the god in some other way, then praise him, since you have stopped hiccupping." *e*

So then, he said, Aristophanes took over and said: "the hiccups certainly have stopped, though not before apply-ing the sneeze cure to them, which leaves me amazed that it's the orderly part of the body which is keen on such noises and ticklings, such as the sneeze actually is.[56] You see they stopped straight away when I applied the sneeze to it." *189*

And Eryximachus said: "My dear Aristophanes, look at what you're doing: in getting ready to speak you're raising

---

[55] Right = *themis*, "good order, sanction" (personified as a goddess in Hesiod, *Theogony* 135 as daughter of Gaia and Oura-nos). Reverence = *eusebeia* (the MSS have a variant *asebeia* = "impiety" [see textual note], which would also fit the context).

[56] "The orderly part" = *to kosmion*: a sly dig at Eryximachus' speech (cf. 187d5).

λακά με τοῦ λόγου ἀναγκάζεις γίγνεσθαι τοῦ σεαυτοῦ, ἐάν τι γελοῖον εἴπῃς, ἐξόν σοι ἐν εἰρήνῃ λέγειν.

b   Καὶ τὸν Ἀριστοφάνη γελάσαντα εἰπεῖν Εὖ λέγεις,
ὦ Ἐρυξίμαχε, καί μοι ἔστω ἄρρητα τὰ εἰρημένα.
ἀλλὰ μή με | φύλαττε, ὡς ἐγὼ φοβοῦμαι περὶ τῶν
μελλόντων ῥηθήσεσθαι, οὔ τι μὴ γελοῖα εἴπω—τοῦτο
μὲν γὰρ ἂν κέρδος εἴη καὶ τῆς ἡμετέρας μούσης ἐπι-
χώριον—ἀλλὰ μὴ καταγέλαστα.

Βαλών γε, φάναι, ὦ Ἀριστόφανες, οἴει ἐκφεύξε-
σθαι· ἀλλὰ πρόσεχε τὸν νοῦν καὶ οὕτως λέγε ὡς δώ-
σων λόγον. ἴσως μέντοι, ἂν δόξῃ μοι, ἀφήσω σε.

c   Καὶ μήν, ὦ Ἐρυξίμαχε, εἰπεῖν τὸν Ἀριστοφάνη, ἄλλῃ
γέ πῃ ἐν νῷ ἔχω λέγειν ἢ ᾗ σύ τε καὶ Παυσανίας
εἰπέτην. ἐμοὶ γὰρ δοκοῦσιν ἄνθρωποι παντάπασι τὴν
τοῦ ἔρωτος | δύναμιν οὐκ ᾐσθῆσθαι, ἐπεὶ αἰσθανόμε-
νοί γε μέγιστ' ἂν αὐτοῦ ἱερὰ κατασκευάσαι καὶ βω-
μούς, καὶ θυσίας ἂν ποιεῖν μεγίστας, οὐχ ὥσπερ νῦν
τούτων οὐδὲν γίγνεται περὶ αὐτόν, δέον πάντων μάλι-

d   στα γίγνεσθαι. ἔστι γὰρ θεῶν φιλανθρωπότατος, ἐπί-
κουρός τε ὢν τῶν ἀνθρώπων καὶ ἰατρὸς τούτων ὧν
ἰαθέντων μεγίστη εὐδαιμονία ἂν τῷ ἀνθρωπείῳ γένει
εἴη. ἐγὼ οὖν πειράσομαι ὑμῖν εἰσηγήσασθαι τὴν δύναμιν αὐτοῦ, ὑμεῖς δὲ τῶν ἄλλων διδάσκαλοι ἔσεσθε.
| δεῖ δὲ πρῶτον ὑμᾶς μαθεῖν τὴν ἀνθρωπίνην φύσιν
καὶ τὰ παθήματα αὐτῆς. ἡ γὰρ πάλαι ἡμῶν φύσις

a laugh and forcing me to keep an eye on your speech in case you say something ridiculous when you could speak in peace."

Aristophanes laughed and said: "You're right, Eryxima-   b
chus; let what I've said be unsaid. But don't keep an eye on me, because my fear of what I'm about to say is not that I say something humorous—for this would be to my advantage and in the territory of my Muse—but in case I shall say something ridiculous."

"Aristophanes," he replied, "you fired away at me, and think you're going to get away with it! Well, pay attention and talk as if you're going to be held to account. You never know, perhaps I'll let you off, if I feel like it."

The Speech of Aristophanes

"Well now, Eryximachus," said Aristophanes, "I do intend   c
to speak differently from the way both you and Pausanias spoke. You see it seems to me that people have completely failed to perceive the power of love, since if they had realized it, they would have built the biggest temples and altars in his name, and performed the biggest sacrifices, not as now when none of these is done for him, though he deserves it most of all. For he is the most benevolent of gods, being man's ally and healer of those ills which, when   d
cured, would be the source of the greatest happiness for the human race. Therefore I shall try to explain his power to you, and you shall be the teachers of others. First you must understand the nature of human beings and what has happened to it. For once upon a time our natural form was

οὐχ αὐτὴ ἦν ἥπερ νῦν, ἀλλ᾽ ἀλλοία. πρῶτον μὲν γὰρ
τρία ἦν τὰ γένη τὰ τῶν ἀνθρώπων, οὐχ ὥσπερ νῦν
e δύο, ἄρρεν καὶ θῆλυ, ἀλλὰ καὶ τρίτον προσῆν κοινὸν
ὂν ἀμφοτέρων τούτων, οὗ νῦν ὄνομα λοιπόν, αὐτὸ δὲ
ἠφάνισται· ἀνδρόγυνον γὰρ ἓν τότε μὲν ἦν καὶ εἶδος
καὶ ὄνομα ἐξ ἀμφοτέρων κοινὸν τοῦ τε ἄρρενος καὶ
θήλεος, νῦν δὲ οὐκ ἔστιν ἀλλ᾽ ἢ ἐν ὀνείδει | ὄνομα
κείμενον. ἔπειτα ὅλον ἦν ἑκάστου τοῦ ἀνθρώπου τὸ
εἶδος στρογγύλον, νῶτον καὶ πλευρὰς κύκλῳ ἔχον,
χεῖρας δὲ τέτταρας εἶχε, καὶ σκέλη τὰ ἴσα ταῖς χερ-
σίν, καὶ πρόσωπα δύ᾽ ἐπ᾽ αὐχένι κυκλοτερεῖ, ὅμοια
190 πάντῃ· κεφαλὴν δ᾽ ἐπ᾽ ἀμφοτέροις τοῖς προσώποις
ἐναντίοις κειμένοις μίαν, καὶ ὦτα τέτταρα, καὶ αἰδοῖα
δύο, καὶ τἆλλα πάντα ὡς ἀπὸ τούτων ἄν τις εἰκάσειεν.
ἐπορεύετο δὲ καὶ ὀρθὸν ὥσπερ | νῦν, ὁποτέρωσε βου-
ληθείη· καὶ ὁπότε ταχὺ ὁρμήσειεν θεῖν, ὥσπερ οἱ
κυβιστῶντες καὶ εἰς ὀρθὸν τὰ σκέλη περιφερόμενοι
κυβιστῶσι κύκλῳ, ὀκτὼ τότε οὖσι τοῖς μέλεσιν ἀπ-
b ερειδόμενοι ταχὺ ἐφέροντο κύκλῳ. ἦν δὲ διὰ ταῦτα
τρία τὰ γένη καὶ τοιαῦτα, ὅτι τὸ μὲν ἄρρεν ἦν τοῦ
ἡλίου τὴν ἀρχὴν ἔκγονον, τὸ δὲ θῆλυ τῆς γῆς, τὸ δὲ
ἀμφοτέρων μετέχον τῆς σελήνης, ὅτι καὶ ἡ σελήνη
ἀμφοτέρων μετέχει· περιφερῆ δὲ δὴ ἦν καὶ αὐτὰ καὶ
ἡ πορεία αὐτῶν διὰ τὸ τοῖς γονεῦσιν | ὅμοια εἶναι. ἦν
οὖν τὴν ἰσχὺν δεινὰ καὶ τὴν ῥώμην, καὶ τὰ φρονήματα μεγάλα εἶχον, ἐπεχείρησαν δὲ τοῖς θεοῖς, καὶ ὃ
λέγει Ὅμηρος περὶ Ἐφιάλτου τε καὶ Ὤτου, περὶ ἐκείνων λέγεται, τὸ εἰς τὸν οὐρανὸν ἀνάβασιν ἐπιχειρεῖν

not the same as we have now, but different. First of all
there were three kinds of human being, not two as now,
male and female, but in addition there was a third one   e
which combined the nature of both of these, whose name
still exists, but the kind itself has disappeared. For at that
time there was one kind which was androgynous in form
and had a name common to both male and female, but the
name no longer exists except as a term of reproach. Secondly the form of each human being was completely
round, its back and sides being formed in a circle, and it
had four hands and the same number of legs as hands, and
two faces, alike in every way, on a circular neck; a single   190
head for the two faces which faced in opposite directions,
and four ears, and two sets of genitals and all the rest as
you might guess from all this. It walked upright, as now,
in whichever direction was required; and when it started
to run quickly, just as tumblers bringing their legs round
upright turn head over heels in a circle, they were quickly
carried round in circular motion, supporting themselves
on what were then eight limbs. The reason that there were   b
three kinds and of this sort, was that the male was originally a descendant of the sun, the female of the earth, and
the one which shared both was from the moon, because
the moon also shares in both kinds. They themselves and
the way they moved were circular owing to their resemblance to their parents. Now in their strength and power
they were formidable and they had big ideas; they made
an attempt on the gods, and what Homer says about Ephialtes and Otus is said about them, that they tried to make

c ποιεῖν, ὡς ἐπιθησομένων τοῖς θεοῖς. ὁ οὖν Ζεὺς καὶ
οἱ ἄλλοι θεοὶ ἐβουλεύοντο ὅτι χρὴ αὐτοὺς ποιῆσαι,
καὶ ἠπόρουν· οὔτε γὰρ ὅπως ἀποκτείναιεν εἶχον καὶ
ὥσπερ τοὺς γίγαντας κεραυνώσαντες τὸ γένος ἀφα-
νίσαιεν—αἱ τιμαὶ | γὰρ αὐτοῖς καὶ ἱερὰ τὰ παρὰ τῶν
ἀνθρώπων ἠφανίζετο—οὔτε ὅπως ἐῷεν ἀσελγαίνειν.
μόγις δὴ ὁ Ζεὺς ἐννοήσας λέγει ὅτι "Δοκῶ μοι," ἔφη,
"ἔχειν μηχανήν, ὡς ἂν εἶέν τε ἄνθρωποι καὶ παύ-
d σαιντο τῆς ἀκολασίας ἀσθενέστεροι γενόμενοι. νῦν
μὲν γὰρ αὐτούς, ἔφη, διατεμῶ δίχα ἕκαστον, καὶ ἅμα
μὲν ἀσθενέστεροι ἔσονται, ἅμα δὲ χρησιμώτεροι ἡμῖν
διὰ τὸ πλείους τὸν ἀριθμὸν γεγονέναι· καὶ βαδιοῦνται
ὀρθοὶ ἐπὶ δυοῖν σκελοῖν. ἐὰν δ' ἔτι δοκῶσιν ἀσελγαί-
νειν | καὶ μὴ 'θέλωσιν ἡσυχίαν ἄγειν, πάλιν αὖ, ἔφη,
τεμῶ δίχα, ὥστ' ἐφ' ἑνὸς πορεύσονται σκέλους ἀσκω-
λιάζοντες." ταῦτα εἰπὼν ἔτεμνε τοὺς ἀνθρώπους δίχα,
ὥσπερ οἱ τὰ ὄα τέμνοντες καὶ μέλλοντες ταριχεύειν,
e ἢ ὥσπερ οἱ τὰ ᾠὰ ταῖς θριξίν· ὅντινα δὲ τέμοι, τὸν
Ἀπόλλω ἐκέλευεν τό τε πρόσωπον μεταστρέφειν καὶ
τὸ τοῦ αὐχένος ἥμισυ πρὸς τὴν τομήν, ἵνα θεώμενος
τὴν αὑτοῦ τμῆσιν κοσμιώτερος | εἴη ὁ ἄνθρωπος, καὶ
τἆλλα ἰᾶσθαι ἐκέλευεν. ὁ δὲ τό τε πρόσωπον μετ-
έστρεφε, καὶ συνέλκων πανταχόθεν τὸ δέρμα ἐπὶ τὴν
γαστέρα νῦν καλουμένην, ὥσπερ τὰ σύσπαστα βαλ-
λάντια, ἐν στόμα ποιῶν ἀπέδει κατὰ μέσην τὴν γα-
191 στέρα, ὃ δὴ τὸν ὀμφαλὸν καλοῦσι. καὶ τὰς μὲν ἄλλας
ῥυτίδας τὰς πολλὰς ἐξελέαινε καὶ τὰ στήθη διήρθρου,
ἔχων τι τοιοῦτον ὄργανον οἷον οἱ σκυτοτόμοι περὶ τὸν

a path up to the sky in order to attack the gods.[57] Zeus c
therefore and the rest of the gods took counsel on what to
do with them and were at a loss, for they had no way of
killing them and destroying their race with thunderbolts,
as they had done with the giants—for the honors and sacrifices they received from humans would disappear—nor
could they allow them to behave outrageously. After some
difficult reflection Zeus spoke and said: 'I think I have a
scheme for humans to exist and cease from their wanton
behavior by making them weaker. For now, he said, I shall d
cut each of them in half with the result that they will be
weaker, and at the same time they will become more useful to us on account of there being more of them, and they
will walk upright on two legs. And if they still appear to be
acting wantonly and unwilling to hold their peace, then I'll
cut them in half again,' he said, 'so that they'll go around
hopping on one leg.' Having said this he proceeded to cut
the humans in half, like people who cut up sorb apples
intending to preserve them, or like those who cut up eggs
with hairs. For each one he cut he ordered Apollo to turn e
the face and the half of the neck round toward the cut so
that the person when looking at his own cut might act in
a more orderly fashion, and he ordered him to heal their
other wounds. Apollo then turned the face around and
drew the skin together from all sides to what is now called
the belly, like purses with drawstrings, and making one
opening he fastened it off over the middle of the belly,
which they call the navel. He smoothed out the many 191
other wrinkles and constructed the chest using the sort of
tool shoemakers use for smoothing out wrinkles in the

[57] Homer, *Iliad* 5.385ff.; *Odyssey* 11.307–20.

καλάποδα λεαίνοντες τὰς τῶν σκυτῶν ῥυτίδας· ὀλίγας
δὲ κατέλιπε, τὰς περὶ αὐτὴν τὴν γαστέρα καὶ τὸν ὀμ-
φαλόν, μνημεῖον | εἶναι τοῦ παλαιοῦ πάθους. ἐπειδὴ
οὖν ἡ φύσις δίχα ἐτμήθη, ποθοῦν ἕκαστον τὸ ἥμισυ
τὸ αὑτοῦ συνῄει, καὶ περιβάλλοντες τὰς χεῖρας καὶ
συμπλεκόμενοι ἀλλήλοις, ἐπιθυμοῦντες συμφῦναι,
ἀπέθνῃσκον ὑπὸ λιμοῦ καὶ τῆς ἄλλης ἀργίας διὰ τὸ
b μηδὲν ἐθέλειν χωρὶς ἀλλήλων ποιεῖν. καὶ ὁπότε τι
ἀποθάνοι τῶν ἡμίσεων, τὸ δὲ λειφθείη, τὸ λειφθὲν
ἄλλο ἐζήτει καὶ συνεπλέκετο, εἴτε γυναικὸς τῆς ὅλης
ἐντύχοι ἡμίσει—ὃ δὴ νῦν γυναῖκα καλοῦμεν—εἴτε |
ἀνδρός· καὶ οὕτως ἀπώλλυντο. ἐλεήσας δὲ ὁ Ζεὺς ἄλλην μηχανὴν πορίζεται, καὶ μετατίθησιν αὐτῶν τὰ
αἰδοῖα εἰς τὸ πρόσθεν—τέως γὰρ καὶ ταῦτα ἐκτὸς εἶχον, καὶ ἐγέννων καὶ ἔτικτον οὐκ εἰς ἀλλήλους ἀλλ᾽
c εἰς γῆν, ὥσπερ οἱ τέττιγες—μετέθηκέ τε οὖν οὕτω
αὐτῶν εἰς τὸ πρόσθεν καὶ διὰ τούτων τὴν γένεσιν ἐν
ἀλλήλοις ἐποίησεν, διὰ τοῦ ἄρρενος ἐν τῷ θήλει,
τῶνδε ἕνεκα, ἵνα ἐν τῇ συμπλοκῇ | ἅμα μὲν εἰ ἀνὴρ
γυναικὶ ἐντύχοι, γεννῷεν καὶ γίγνοιτο τὸ γένος, ἅμα
δ᾽ εἰ καὶ ἄρρην ἄρρενι, πλησμονὴ γοῦν γίγνοιτο τῆς
συνουσίας καὶ διαπαύοιντο καὶ ἐπὶ τὰ ἔργα τρέποιντο
d καὶ τοῦ ἄλλου βίου ἐπιμελοῖντο. ἔστι δὴ οὖν ἐκ τόσου
ὁ ἔρως ἔμφυτος ἀλλήλων τοῖς ἀνθρώποις καὶ τῆς ἀρ-
χαίας φύσεως συναγωγεὺς καὶ ἐπιχειρῶν ποιῆσαι ἓν
ἐκ δυοῖν καὶ ἰάσασθαι τὴν φύσιν τὴν ἀνθρωπίνην.
ἕκαστος οὖν ἡμῶν ἐστιν ἀνθρώπου σύμβολον, ἅτε

hides on their last, but he left a few behind, those in the area around the belly itself, that is the navel, to be a reminder of what they went through long ago. So when their original form had been cut in half, each half came together in longing for its respective half, and throwing their arms around each other they embraced in their yearning to grow together, and died of hunger and general inactivity because they were unwilling to do anything separated from each other. Whenever one of the halves died and the other was left behind, the one left behind sought and embraced another one, whether it encountered half of what had been wholly woman—that is what we now call a woman—or man. And so they perished. Out of pity Zeus devised another scheme and moved their genitals to the front—for until then they had these too on the outside and they conceived and gave birth not by the penetration of the one into the another but in the ground like cicadas[58]—and thus he moved the genitals to the front and by this means caused their reproduction inside each other through the male being inside the female, for this reason: that if a man and a woman came together in intercourse, they would reproduce and the race would continue. And at the same time even if a male met up with a male, at any rate they would have the satisfaction of their intercourse and take a rest and turn to their work and look after the other aspects of their life. So it is that from that far back in time love of one another has been innate in human beings and is what restores our old natural state and attempts to make one out of two and to heal our human nature. Thus each of us is a token of a human being in as much as

b

c

d

[58] On the reproductive habits of cicadas, see Dover, n. ad loc.

τετμημένος ὥσπερ αἱ ψῆτται, | ἐξ ἑνὸς δύο· ζητεῖ δὴ
ἀεὶ τὸ αὑτοῦ ἕκαστος σύμβολον. ὅσοι μὲν οὖν τῶν
ἀνδρῶν τοῦ κοινοῦ τμῆμά εἰσιν, ὃ δὴ τότε ἀνδρόγυνον
ἐκαλεῖτο, φιλογύναικές τέ εἰσι καὶ οἱ πολλοὶ τῶν μοι-
χῶν ἐκ τούτου τοῦ γένους γεγόνασιν, καὶ ὅσαι αὖ
γυναῖκες φίλανδροί τε καὶ μοιχεύτριαι ἐκ τούτου τοῦ
e γένους γίγνονται. ὅσαι δὲ τῶν γυναικῶν γυναικὸς
τμῆμά εἰσιν, οὐ πάνυ αὗται τοῖς ἀνδράσι τὸν νοῦν
προσέχουσιν, ἀλλὰ μᾶλλον πρὸς τὰς γυναῖκας τε-
τραμμέναι | εἰσί, καὶ αἱ ἑταιρίστριαι ἐκ τούτου τοῦ
γένους γίγνονται. ὅσοι δὲ ἄρρενος τμῆμά εἰσι, τὰ
ἄρρενα διώκουσι, καὶ τέως μὲν ἂν παῖδες ὦσιν, ἅτε
τεμάχια ὄντα τοῦ ἄρρενος, φιλοῦσι τοὺς ἄνδρας καὶ
χαίρουσι συγκατακείμενοι καὶ συμπεπλεγμένοι τοῖς
192 ἀνδράσι, καί εἰσιν οὗτοι βέλτιστοι τῶν παίδων καὶ
μειρακίων, ἅτε ἀνδρειότατοι ὄντες φύσει. φασὶ δὲ δή
τινες αὐτοὺς ἀναισχύντους εἶναι, ψευδόμενοι· οὐ γὰρ
ὑπ' ἀναισχυντίας τοῦτο δρῶσιν ἀλλ' ὑπὸ θάρρους καὶ
ἀνδρείας | καὶ ἀρρενωπίας, τὸ ὅμοιον αὑτοῖς ἀσπαζό-
μενοι. μέγα δὲ τεκμήριον· καὶ γὰρ τελεωθέντες μόνοι
ἀποβαίνουσιν εἰς τὰ πολιτικὰ ἄνδρες οἱ τοιοῦτοι.
b ἐπειδὰν δὲ ἀνδρωθῶσι, παιδεραστοῦσι καὶ πρὸς γά-
μους καὶ παιδοποιίας οὐ προσέχουσι τὸν νοῦν φύσει,
ἀλλ' ὑπὸ τοῦ νόμου ἀναγκάζονται· ἀλλ' ἐξαρκεῖ αὐτοῖς
μετ' ἀλλήλων καταζῆν ἀγάμοις. πάντως μὲν οὖν ὁ
τοιοῦτος παιδεραστής τε καὶ φιλεραστὴς γίγνεται, |
ἀεὶ τὸ συγγενὲς ἀσπαζόμενος. ὅταν μὲν οὖν καὶ αὐτῷ
ἐκείνῳ ἐντύχῃ τῷ αὑτοῦ ἡμίσει καὶ ὁ παιδεραστὴς καὶ

he has been split like flatfish, two out of one. Each is then constantly looking for his matching token. Moreover those men who are a segment of the shared gender which was called androgynous at that time, are lovers of women and the majority of adulterers come from this kind, and in turn those women who are lovers of men and adulteresses come from this kind. Such women, on the other hand, as   e are a segment of the wholly woman don't pay much attention to men, but are oriented rather toward women, and females loving females come from this kind. Those who are a segment of the male pursue the male, and while they are boys, in that they are segments of the male, they are affectionate toward men and enjoy intercourse with men and embracing them, and these are the best of boys and   192 youths in that they are naturally the most manly. Indeed some say these are shameless, but this is a lie; for they do this not out of shamelessness, but out of courage and bravery and manliness, embracing that which is of their kind. There is significant proof of this: for such men are indeed the only ones who, on reaching maturity, turn out to be the real men in politics. When they reach manhood they   b become lovers of boys, and pay attention to marriage and the fathering of children not by nature, but they are compelled to by convention; but it's sufficient for them to live their lives out with each other unmarried. So, in short, such a person becomes a lover of boys and, as a boy fond of lovers, always welcoming his own kind. Now whenever the lover of boys, and anyone else, encounters that actual

ἄλλος πᾶς, τότε καὶ θαυμαστὰ ἐκπλήττονται φιλίᾳ τε
c καὶ οἰκειότητι καὶ ἔρωτι, οὐκ ἐθέλοντες ὡς ἔπος εἰπεῖν
χωρίζεσθαι ἀλλήλων οὐδὲ σμικρὸν χρόνον. καὶ οἱ
διατελοῦντες μετ' ἀλλήλων διὰ βίου οὗτοί εἰσιν, οἳ
οὐδ' ἂν ἔχοιεν εἰπεῖν ὅτι βούλονται σφίσι παρ' ἀλλή-
λων γίγνεσθαι. οὐδενὶ | γὰρ ἂν δόξειεν τοῦτ' εἶναι ἡ
τῶν ἀφροδισίων συνουσία, ὡς ἄρα τούτου ἕνεκα ἕτερος ἑτέρῳ χαίρει συνὼν οὕτως ἐπὶ μεγάλης σπουδῆς·
d ἀλλ' ἄλλο τι βουλομένη ἑκατέρου ἡ ψυχὴ δήλη ἐστίν,
ὃ οὐ δύναται εἰπεῖν, ἀλλὰ μαντεύεται ὃ βούλεται, καὶ
αἰνίττεται. καὶ εἰ αὐτοῖς ἐν τῷ αὐτῷ κατακειμένοις
ἐπιστὰς ὁ Ἥφαιστος, ἔχων τὰ ὄργανα, ἔροιτο· "Τί
ἔσθ' ὃ βούλεσθε, ὦ ἄνθρωποι, ὑμῖν παρ' ἀλλήλων
γενέσθαι;" | καὶ εἰ ἀποροῦντας αὐτοὺς πάλιν ἔροιτο·
"Ἆρά γε τοῦδε ἐπιθυμεῖτε, ἐν τῷ αὐτῷ γενέσθαι ὅτι
μάλιστα ἀλλήλοις, ὥστε καὶ νύκτα καὶ ἡμέραν μὴ
ἀπολείπεσθαι ἀλλήλων; εἰ γὰρ τούτου ἐπιθυμεῖτε,
θέλω ὑμᾶς συντῆξαι καὶ συμφυσῆσαι εἰς τὸ αὐτό,
e ὥστε δύ' ὄντας ἕνα γεγονέναι καὶ ἕως τ' ἂν ζῆτε, ὡς
ἕνα ὄντα, κοινῇ ἀμφοτέρους ζῆν, καὶ ἐπειδὰν ἀπο-
θάνητε, ἐκεῖ αὖ ἐν Ἅιδου ἀντὶ δυοῖν ἕνα εἶναι κοινῇ
τεθνεῶτε· ἀλλ' ὁρᾶτε εἰ τούτου ἐρᾶτε καὶ | ἐξαρκεῖ ὑμῖν
ἂν τούτου τύχητε." ταῦτ' ἀκούσας ἴσμεν ὅτι οὐδ' ἂν
εἷς ἐξαρνηθείη οὐδ' ἄλλο τι ἂν φανείη βουλόμενος,
ἀλλ' ἀτεχνῶς οἴοιτ' ἂν ἀκηκοέναι τοῦτο ὃ πάλαι ἄρα
ἐπεθύμει, συνελθὼν καὶ συντακεὶς τῷ ἐρωμένῳ ἐκ δυ-

other half of his, both of them are struck in an extraordinary way with affection, belonging[59] and love, in a word, unwilling to be separated from one another even for a short time. These then are the ones who spend the rest of their lives with each other, though they would be unable even to say what they want for themselves from each other. For no one would think it was just for making love, that it was because of this that each enjoys being with the other with such great enthusiasm. But clearly it is something else that the soul of each wants which it cannot express, but it intuitively grasps and hints at what it wants. And if Hephaestus were to stand over them as they lie together his tools at the ready and ask: 'What is it, you people, that you want for yourselves from each other?' And if they were stuck for an answer and he were to ask again: 'Is this then what you are after, to be together with each other as much as you possibly can, so you will not be left without each other night and day? If this is what you are keen to have, I am willing to melt you down and weld you together so that the two of you become one and pass your life so long as you live sharing with each other as a single being, and when you die, down there in Hades too you will be one instead of two, having died together. Well, consider whether this is what you desire and whether it will satisfy you if you achieve this.' We know that on hearing this not a single person would refuse nor would it become apparent that they wanted anything else, but would simply think that he had heard what he had all along been yearning for, to come together and be fused with his loved one, from

c

d

e

---

[59] "Belonging" = *oikeiotēs* (as a key element in the love relationship, see esp. *Lysis*, 221dff.).

οἷν εἰς γενέσθαι. τοῦτο γάρ ἐστι τὸ αἴτιον, ὅτι ἡ ἀρ-
χαία φύσις | ἡμῶν ἦν αὕτη καὶ ἦμεν ὅλοι· τοῦ ὅλου
193 οὖν τῇ ἐπιθυμίᾳ καὶ διώξει ἔρως ὄνομα. καὶ πρὸ τοῦ,
ὥσπερ λέγω, ἓν ἦμεν, νυνὶ δὲ διὰ τὴν ἀδικίαν διῳκί-
σθημεν ὑπὸ τοῦ θεοῦ, καθάπερ Ἀρκάδες ὑπὸ Λακεδαι-
μονίων· φόβος οὖν ἔστιν, ἐὰν μὴ κόσμιοι ὦμεν πρὸς
τοὺς θεούς, ὅπως μὴ καὶ αὖθις | διασχισθησόμεθα,
καὶ περίιμεν ἔχοντες ὥσπερ οἱ ἐν ταῖς στήλαις κατα-
γραφὴν ἐκτετυπωμένοι, διαπεπρισμένοι κατὰ τὰς ῥῖ-
νας, γεγονότες ὥσπερ λίσπαι. ἀλλὰ τούτων ἕνεκα
πάντ᾽ ἄνδρα χρὴ ἅπαντα παρακελεύεσθαι εὐσεβεῖν
περὶ θεούς, ἵνα τὰ μὲν ἐκφύγωμεν, τῶν δὲ τύχωμεν,
b   ὡς ὁ Ἔρως ἡμῖν ἡγεμὼν καὶ στρατηγός. ᾧ μηδεὶς
ἐναντία πραττέτω—πράττει δ᾽ ἐναντία ὅστις θεοῖς
ἀπεχθάνεται—φίλοι γὰρ γενόμενοι καὶ διαλλαγέντες
τῷ θεῷ ἐξευρήσομέν τε καὶ | ἐντευξόμεθα τοῖς παιδι-
κοῖς τοῖς ἡμετέροις αὐτῶν, ὃ τῶν νῦν ὀλίγοι ποιοῦσι.
καὶ μή μοι ὑπολάβῃ Ἐρυξίμαχος, κωμῳδῶν τὸν λόγον, ὡς Παυσανίαν καὶ Ἀγάθωνα λέγω—ἴσως μὲν
γὰρ καὶ οὗτοι τούτων τυγχάνουσιν ὄντες καὶ εἰσὶν
c   ἀμφότεροι τὴν φύσιν ἄρρενες—λέγω δὲ οὖν ἔγωγε
καθ᾽ ἁπάντων καὶ ἀνδρῶν καὶ γυναικῶν, ὅτι οὕτως ἂν
ἡμῶν τὸ γένος εὔδαιμον γένοιτο, εἰ ἐκτελέσαιμεν τὸν
ἔρωτα καὶ τῶν παιδικῶν τῶν | αὑτοῦ ἕκαστος τύχοι εἰς
τὴν ἀρχαίαν ἀπελθὼν φύσιν. εἰ δὲ τοῦτο ἄριστον,

---

[60] Most probably an anachronistic reference to the Spartan

two beings into one. You see this is the cause, that our original nature was like this and we were wholes. So the desire and pursuit of the whole has the name of love. Before this, as I say, we were one, but now because of our 193 wrongdoing we have been dispersed by the god just as the Arcadians were by the Lacedaemonians.[60] Our fear therefore is if we do not behave in an orderly fashion toward the gods, we may be cut in two again, and go around just like those who have been carved in profile on gravestones sawn in half down the nose, ending up like dice cut in half.[61] Well, for these reasons every man must encourage reverence in relation to the gods in all things in order to avoid the one fate and achieve the other, according as Love is our leader and commander. Let no one oppose b him in this—he does the opposite of this who is hateful to the gods—for having become friends and having reconciled ourselves with the god, we shall discover and meet a loved one who is our own, which few of those around today achieve. And I hope Eryximachus isn't going to come back at me and treat my speech as a comedy on the grounds that I mean Pausanias and Agathon—for perhaps it may well be that they really are among these and are both male by nature—what *I'm* saying is with reference to all, both c men and women, that the way to happiness for our race would be this: if we find love in the end, and each of us finds his own beloved, reverting to our original nature. If this is best, then what is nearest to this, given our current

dispersal of the Mantineans in Arcadia in 385 (Xenophon, *Hellenica* 5.2.5–7). See Introduction, Appendix.

[61] See 191d4. *Lispai* = "dice cut in two by friends . . . each of whom kept half as a tally" (LSJ).

211

ἀναγκαῖον καὶ τῶν νῦν παρόντων τὸ τούτου ἐγγυτάτω
ἄριστον εἶναι· τοῦτο δ' ἐστὶ παιδικῶν τυχεῖν κατὰ
νοῦν αὐτῷ πεφυκότων· οὗ δὴ τὸν αἴτιον θεὸν ὑμνοῦν-
d τες δικαίως ἂν ὑμνοῖμεν Ἔρωτα, ὃς ἔν τε τῷ παρόντι
ἡμᾶς πλεῖστα ὀνίνησιν εἰς τὸ οἰκεῖον ἄγων, καὶ εἰς τὸ
ἔπειτα ἐλπίδας μεγίστας παρέχεται, ἡμῶν παρεχομέ-
νων πρὸς θεοὺς εὐσέβειαν, καταστήσας ἡμᾶς εἰς τὴν
ἀρχαίαν φύσιν καὶ | ἰασάμενος μακαρίους καὶ εὐδαί-
μονας ποιῆσαι.

Οὗτος, ἔφη, ὦ Ἐρυξίμαχε, ὁ ἐμὸς λόγος ἐστὶ περὶ
Ἔρωτος, ἀλλοῖος ἢ ὁ σός. ὥσπερ οὖν ἐδεήθην σου,
μὴ κωμῳδήσῃς αὐτόν, ἵνα καὶ τῶν λοιπῶν ἀκούσωμεν
e τί ἕκαστος ἐρεῖ, μᾶλλον δὲ τί ἑκάτερος· Ἀγάθων γὰρ
καὶ Σωκράτης λοιποί.

Ἀλλὰ πείσομαί σοι, ἔφη φάναι τὸν Ἐρυξίμαχον·
καὶ γάρ μοι ὁ λόγος ἡδέως ἐρρήθη. καὶ εἰ μὴ συνῄδη
Σωκράτει | τε καὶ Ἀγάθωνι δεινοῖς οὖσι περὶ τὰ ἐρω-
τικά, πάνυ ἂν ἐφοβούμην μὴ ἀπορήσωσι λόγων διὰ
τὸ πολλὰ καὶ παντοδαπὰ εἰρῆσθαι· νῦν δὲ ὅμως
θαρρῶ.

194 Τὸν οὖν Σωκράτη εἰπεῖν Καλῶς γὰρ αὐτὸς ἠγώνι-
σαι, ὦ Ἐρυξίμαχε· εἰ δὲ γένοιο οὗ νῦν ἐγώ εἰμι, μᾶλλον δὲ ἴσως οὗ ἔσομαι ἐπειδὰν καὶ Ἀγάθων εἴπῃ εὖ,
καὶ μάλ' ἂν φοβοῖο καὶ ἐν παντὶ εἴης ὥσπερ ἐγὼ νῦν.|

Φαρμάττειν βούλει με, ὦ Σώκρατες, εἰπεῖν τὸν
Ἀγάθωνα, ἵνα θορυβηθῶ διὰ τὸ οἴεσθαι τὸ θέατρον
προσδοκίαν μεγάλην ἔχειν ὡς εὖ ἐροῦντος ἐμοῦ.

circumstances, must also be best. And this is to meet up with a beloved who is in his way of thinking congenial to oneself. Indeed in singing the praises of the god who is the cause of this, we would rightly sing the praises of Love who in the present circumstances benefits us the most by leading us to what belongs to us, and gives us the greatest expectations for the future, that if we offer reverence toward the gods, having established us in our original nature and having healed us, he will make us blessed and happy.

"This, Eryximachus, he said, is my speech about Love, of a different kind from yours. Therefore, as I asked you, don't make fun of it in order that we may hear what each of those who are left will say, or rather what each of the two will say. For Agathon and Socrates are the ones left."[62]

"Well I shall obey you," he said Eryximachus replied. "For indeed I enjoyed the speech. And if I didn't know full well that Socrates and Agathon are experts in matters of love, I'd be very much afraid they would be stuck for words because much has been said in all sorts of ways. But as it is I am confident nevertheless."

So Socrates said: "Yes, because you yourself have competed well, Eryximachus. If you were where I am now, or rather perhaps where I shall be when Agathon too makes a good speech, you'd be as terrified and at your wits end as I am now."

"You want to put the evil eye on me, Socrates, said Agathon, to throw me into confusion at the thought that the spectators have high expectations that I shall make a good speech."

---

[62] It is actually the turn of Aristodemus, lying with Eryximachus (cf. 175a4–5), but he leaves himself out.

Ἐπιλήσμων μεντἂν εἴην, ὦ Ἀγάθων, εἰπεῖν τὸν
b Σωκράτη, εἰ ἰδὼν τὴν σὴν ἀνδρείαν καὶ μεγαλοφρο-
σύνην ἀναβαίνοντος ἐπὶ τὸν ὀκρίβαντα μετὰ τῶν
ὑποκριτῶν, καὶ βλέψαντος ἐναντία τοσούτῳ θεάτρῳ,
μέλλοντος ἐπιδείξεσθαι σαυτοῦ λόγους, καὶ οὐδ' ὁπω-
στιοῦν ἐκπλαγέντος, νῦν | οἰηθείην σε θορυβήσεσθαι
ἕνεκα ἡμῶν ὀλίγων ἀνθρώπων.

Τί δέ, ὦ Σώκρατες; τὸν Ἀγάθωνα φάναι, οὐ δήπου
με οὕτω θεάτρου μεστὸν ἡγῇ ὥστε καὶ ἀγνοεῖν ὅτι
νοῦν ἔχοντι ὀλίγοι ἔμφρονες πολλῶν ἀφρόνων φοβε-
ρώτεροι;

c Οὐ μεντἂν καλῶς ποιοίην, φάναι, ὦ Ἀγάθων, περὶ
σοῦ τι ἐγὼ ἄγροικον δοξάζων· ἀλλ' εὖ οἶδα ὅτι εἴ
τισιν ἐντύχοις οὓς ἡγοῖο σοφούς, μᾶλλον ἂν αὐτῶν
φροντίζοις ἢ τῶν πολλῶν. ἀλλὰ μὴ οὐχ οὗτοι ἡμεῖς
ὦμεν—ἡμεῖς μὲν γὰρ | καὶ ἐκεῖ παρῆμεν καὶ ἦμεν
τῶν πολλῶν—εἰ δὲ ἄλλοις ἐντύχοις σοφοῖς, τάχ' ἂν
αἰσχύνοιο αὐτούς, εἴ τι ἴσως οἴοιο αἰσχρὸν ὂν ποιεῖν·
ἢ πῶς λέγεις;

Ἀληθῆ λέγεις, φάναι.

Τοὺς δὲ πολλοὺς οὐκ ἂν αἰσχύνοιο εἴ τι οἴοιο αἰ-
σχρὸν ποιεῖν; |

d Καὶ τὸν Φαῖδρον ἔφη ὑπολαβόντα εἰπεῖν Ὦ φίλε
Ἀγάθων, ἐὰν ἀποκρίνῃ Σωκράτει, οὐδὲν ἔτι διοίσει

---

63 Socrates is referring to the *Proagon*, the occasion in advance of the performance when plays were advertised. He is here

"Yes, but Agathon," said Socrates, "I'd have to be for- b
getful if, on seeing your confidence and self-assurance
when you mounted the platform with the actors, and
looked such a large audience straight in the eye, not the
slightest bit panic-stricken as you prepared to deliver your
compositions, I should now think you are about to be
thrown into confusion on account a few people like us."[63]

"What, Socrates?" said Agathon, "surely you don't
think, do you, that I'm so crammed full of the theater that
I'm unaware that for a man of intelligence, a few sensible
people are more intimidating than the many who are
senseless?"

"I would of course not be behaving well, Agathon," he c
said, "if I entertained any boorish thoughts about *you*, but
I am well aware that if you came across any people you
considered to be wise, you would hold them in higher
esteem than the general public. But maybe we're not
these people—for we were there and were part of the
mass—but if you were to meet others who are wise, maybe
you would be ashamed in their presence if you thought
perhaps you were doing something that is shameful. Or
what do you say?"

"What you say is true," he said.

"But you wouldn't be ashamed in front of the general
public if you thought you were doing something shameful?"

Now Phaedrus, he said, interrupted and said: "Agathon, d
my friend, if you answer Socrates' question, after that it

"setting up" Agathon, in advance of his speech, as a public theatrical performer (see above, 175e5, and for the context see Introduction, §2(iv)).

αὐτῷ ὁπηοῦν τῶν ἐνθάδε ὁτιοῦν γίγνεσθαι, ἐὰν μόνον
ἔχῃ ὅτῳ διαλέγηται, ἄλλως τε καὶ καλῷ. ἐγὼ δὲ ἡδέως
μὲν ἀκούω | Σωκράτους διαλεγομένου, ἀναγκαῖον δέ
μοι ἐπιμεληθῆναι τοῦ ἐγκωμίου τῷ Ἔρωτι καὶ ἀπο-
δέξασθαι παρ' ἑνὸς ἑκάστου ὑμῶν τὸν λόγον· ἀποδοὺς
οὖν ἑκάτερος τῷ θεῷ οὕτως ἤδη διαλεγέσθω.

e   Ἀλλὰ καλῶς λέγεις, ὦ Φαῖδρε, φάναι τὸν Ἀγάθωνα, καὶ οὐδέν με κωλύει λέγειν· Σωκράτει γὰρ καὶ
αὖθις ἔσται πολλάκις διαλέγεσθαι.

Ἐγὼ δὲ δὴ βούλομαι πρῶτον μὲν εἰπεῖν ὡς χρή με
εἰπεῖν, | ἔπειτα εἰπεῖν. δοκοῦσι γάρ μοι πάντες οἱ
πρόσθεν εἰρηκότες οὐ τὸν θεὸν ἐγκωμιάζειν ἀλλὰ
τοὺς ἀνθρώπους εὐδαιμονίζειν τῶν ἀγαθῶν ὧν ὁ θεὸς
αὐτοῖς αἴτιος· ὁποῖος δέ τις αὐτὸς ὢν ταῦτα ἐδωρή-
195 σατο, οὐδεὶς εἴρηκεν. εἷς δὲ τρόπος ὀρθὸς παντὸς
ἐπαίνου περὶ παντός, λόγῳ διελθεῖν οἷος οἵων αἴτιος
ὢν τυγχάνει περὶ οὗ ἂν ὁ λόγος ᾖ. οὕτω δὴ τὸν
Ἔρωτα καὶ ἡμᾶς δίκαιον ἐπαινέσαι πρῶτον αὐτὸν
οἷός ἐστιν, ἔπειτα | τὰς δόσεις. φημὶ οὖν ἐγὼ πάντων
θεῶν εὐδαιμόνων ὄντων Ἔρωτα, εἰ θέμις καὶ ἀνεμέ-
σητον εἰπεῖν, εὐδαιμονέστατον εἶναι αὐτῶν, κάλλιστον ὄντα καὶ ἄριστον. ἔστι δὲ κάλλιστος ὢν τοιόσδε. πρῶτον μὲν νεώτατος θεῶν, ὦ Φαῖδρε. μέγα δὲ

---

[64] "Happy" = *eudaimōn* (see above, n. 9).

won't matter to him one bit how what is going on here will end up, as long as he has someone to discuss it with, especially if he's good-looking. I'm happy to hear Socrates in discussion, but I must keep my mind on the praise of Love and get a speech out of each one of you. Therefore only after each of you two has paid his due to the god, *then* you can have your discussion."

"Quite right, Phaedrus," said Agathon, "and there's e nothing to stop me speaking. Why, Socrates will have plenty of chances to have the discussion another time.

The Speech of Agathon

"Now first I want to say how I ought to speak, and then make my speech. For all those who have spoken already seem to me not to be praising the god, but to show how fortunate people are to have the good things for which the god is responsible. But no one has said what kind of being he is who has bestowed these gifts upon us. There is one 195 correct way for every kind of praise on any topic: to explain in the speech, whoever the speech is about, what kind of being he really is, and what kind of things he is responsible for. In this way then it is right that we too praise Love himself for what he is and then for his gifts. I therefore claim that while all the gods are happy,[64] Love, if it is right to say this without causing them offense, is the most happy as he is the most beautiful and the best. He's the most beautiful on these grounds: firstly he's the youngest of the gods, Phaedrus.[65] He himself provides substantial proof

[65] Phaedrus claimed Eros was among the oldest of the gods (178a9–b1).

b τεκμήριον τῷ λόγῳ αὐτὸς παρέχεται, φεύγων φυγῇ τὸ
γῆρας, ταχὺ ὂν δῆλον ὅτι· θᾶττον γοῦν τοῦ δέοντος
ἡμῖν προσέρχεται. ὃ δὴ πέφυκεν Ἔρως μισεῖν καὶ
οὐδ' ἐντὸς πολλοῦ πλησιάζειν. μετὰ δὲ νέων ἀεὶ σύν-
εστί τε καὶ ἔστιν· | ὁ γὰρ παλαιὸς λόγος εὖ ἔχει, ὡς
ὅμοιον ὁμοίῳ ἀεὶ πελάζει. ἐγὼ δὲ Φαίδρῳ πολλὰ ἄλλα
ὁμολογῶν τοῦτο οὐχ ὁμολογῶ, ὡς Ἔρως Κρόνου καὶ
Ἰαπετοῦ ἀρχαιότερός ἐστιν, ἀλλά φημι νεώτατον
c αὐτὸν εἶναι θεῶν καὶ ἀεὶ νέον, τὰ δὲ παλαιὰ πράγματα περὶ θεούς, ἃ Ἡσίοδος καὶ Παρμενίδης λέγουσιν, Ἀνάγκῃ καὶ οὐκ Ἔρωτι γεγονέναι, εἰ ἐκεῖνοι
ἀληθῆ ἔλεγον· οὐ γὰρ ἂν ἐκτομαὶ οὐδὲ δεσμοὶ ἀλλή-
λων ἐγίγνοντο καὶ ἄλλα | πολλὰ καὶ βίαια, εἰ Ἔρως
ἐν αὐτοῖς ἦν, ἀλλὰ φιλία καὶ εἰρήνη, ὥσπερ νῦν, ἐξ
οὗ Ἔρως τῶν θεῶν βασιλεύει. νέος μὲν οὖν ἐστι,
πρὸς δὲ τῷ νέῳ ἁπαλός· ποιητοῦ δ' ἔστιν ἐνδεὴς οἷος
d ἦν Ὅμηρος πρὸς τὸ ἐπιδεῖξαι θεοῦ ἁπαλότητα. Ὅμηρος γὰρ Ἄτην θεόν τέ φησιν εἶναι καὶ ἁπαλήν—τοὺς
γοῦν πόδας αὐτῆς ἁπαλοὺς εἶναι—λέγων

    τῆς μένθ' ἁπαλοὶ πόδες· οὐ γὰρ ἐπ' οὔδεος |
    πίλναται, ἀλλ' ἄρα ἥ γε κατ' ἀνδρῶν κράατα
    βαίνει.

καλῶ οὖν δοκεῖ μοι τεκμηρίῳ τὴν ἁπαλότητα ἀποφαί-
νειν, ὅτι οὐκ ἐπὶ σκληροῦ βαίνει, ἀλλ' ἐπὶ μαλθακοῦ.
τῷ αὐτῷ δὴ καὶ ἡμεῖς χρησόμεθα τεκμηρίῳ περὶ
e Ἔρωτα ὅτι ἁπαλός. οὐ γὰρ ἐπὶ γῆς βαίνει οὐδ' ἐπὶ
κρανίων, ἅ ἐστιν οὐ πάνυ μαλακά, ἀλλ' ἐν τοῖς μαλα-

for what I say: by flight he shuns old age, although that is b
clearly swift: at any rate it approaches us quicker than it
should. Indeed Love naturally hates it and comes nowhere
near it. He always associates with the young, and is young:
for the old saying holds true, that like always draws near
to like. But while agreeing with Phaedrus on many other
points, on this one I do not agree with him, that Love is
more ancient than Cronus and Iapetus; on the contrary I
claim that he is the youngest of the gods and is always c
young, but the old activities involving the gods, which Hesiod and Parmenides speak of, happened through Necessity, not Love, if they were telling the truth: for there
would have been no castrations and chaining up of each
other and many other violent acts if Love was among
them, but there would have been friendship and peace, as
now, from the time Love has been ruling the gods. So he's
young then and gentle as well as young; but he lacks a poet
such as was Homer to demonstrate the gentleness of the
god. For Homer says Ate was a goddess and gentle too—at d
least her feet were gentle—when he says:

> Yet her feet are gentle, for she does not approach
> Over the ground, but walks upon the heads of men.[66]

So he seems to me to reveal excellent evidence of her
gentleness: that she does not walk on something hard, but
something soft. We will use the same proof about Love
being gentle, for he does not walk on the ground, nor even e
on skulls which are not at all soft, but he both walks and

[66] Homer, *Iliad* 19.92–93.

κωτάτοις τῶν ὄντων καὶ βαίνει καὶ οἰκεῖ. ἐν γὰρ ἤθεσι
καὶ ψυχαῖς θεῶν καὶ ἀνθρώπων τὴν | οἴκησιν ἵδρυται,
καὶ οὐκ αὖ ἑξῆς ἐν πάσαις ταῖς ψυχαῖς, ἀλλ' ᾗτινι ἂν
σκληρὸν ἦθος ἐχούσῃ ἐντύχῃ, ἀπέρχεται, ᾗ δ' ἂν μα-
λακόν, οἰκίζεται. ἁπτόμενον οὖν ἀεὶ καὶ ποσὶν καὶ
πάντῃ ἐν μαλακωτάτοις τῶν μαλακωτάτων, ἁπαλώτα-
196 τον ἀνάγκη εἶναι. νεώτατος μὲν δή ἐστι καὶ ἁπαλώ-
τατος, πρὸς δὲ τούτοις ὑγρὸς τὸ εἶδος. οὐ γὰρ ἂν οἷός
τ' ἦν πάντῃ περιπτύσσεσθαι οὐδὲ διὰ πάσης ψυχῆς
καὶ εἰσιὼν τὸ πρῶτον λανθάνειν καὶ ἐξιών, εἰ σκλη-
ρὸς ἦν. συμμέτρου δὲ καὶ | ὑγρᾶς ἰδέας μέγα τεκμή-
ριον ἡ εὐσχημοσύνη, ὃ δὴ διαφερόντως ἐκ πάντων
ὁμολογουμένως Ἔρως ἔχει· ἀσχημοσύνη γὰρ καὶ
Ἔρωτι πρὸς ἀλλήλους ἀεὶ πόλεμος. χρόας δὲ κάλλος
b ἡ κατ' ἄνθη δίαιτα τοῦ θεοῦ σημαίνει· ἀνανθεῖ γὰρ
καὶ ἀπηνθηκότι καὶ σώματι καὶ ψυχῇ καὶ ἄλλῳ
ὁτῳοῦν οὐκ ἐνίζει Ἔρως, οὗ δ' ἂν εὐανθής τε καὶ εὐώ-
δης τόπος ᾖ, ἐνταῦθα δὲ καὶ ἵζει καὶ μένει.

Περὶ μὲν οὖν κάλλους τοῦ θεοῦ καὶ ταῦτα ἱκανὰ
καὶ ἔτι | πολλὰ λείπεται, περὶ δὲ ἀρετῆς Ἔρωτος μετὰ
ταῦτα λεκτέον, τὸ μὲν μέγιστον ὅτι Ἔρως οὔτ' ἀδικεῖ
οὔτ' ἀδικεῖται οὔτε ὑπὸ θεοῦ οὔτε θεόν, οὔτε ὑπ' ἀνθρώπου οὔτε ἄνθρωπον. οὔτε γὰρ αὐτὸς βίᾳ πάσχει,
εἴ τι πάσχει—βία γὰρ Ἔρωτος οὐχ ἅπτεται· οὔτε
c ποιῶν ποιεῖ—πᾶς γὰρ ἑκὼν Ἔρωτι πᾶν ὑπηρετεῖ, ἃ
δ' ἂν ἑκὼν ἑκόντι ὁμολογήσῃ, φασὶν "οἱ πόλεως βα-

---

[67] "Virtue" here translates *aretē* (see above, n. 32).

dwells in the softest things. For he has fixed his dwelling place among the characters and souls of gods and men, and again not in all souls one after another, but when he comes upon one with a hard character, he steers away from it and finds his home in one that is soft. Therefore always fastening himself onto the softest of their softest parts, both with his feet and all over, he is necessarily the most gentle. He is, then, the youngest and the most gentle and, in addition to these he is fluid in form. You see, he would not be able to wind himself around someone completely nor would he be able to enter through the whole soul first, then leave it without our noticing it, if he were hard. Substantial proof of his well-proportioned and supple form is his gracefulness, in which indeed Love is by common consent outstanding, for there is always conflict between gracelessness and Love. The dwelling of the god among flowers shows beauty of complexion; for Love does not settle in a body, in a soul or in anything else whatever that is without flower and has not bloomed, but wherever there is a place full of blossom and perfume, there he settles and remains.

196

b

"On the beauty of the god this then will be enough, even though there still remains a lot to be said. But following this we must talk about the virtue[67] of Love. The most important point is that Love neither does any wrong to any god or any human being, nor is he wronged by any god or any human being. You see if anything is done to him he does not himself suffer violence—for violence does not touch Love; nor in his dealings does he commit any violence—for everyone willingly serves Love in all things: whatever terms one party willingly agrees with another,

c

σιλῆς νόμοι" δίκαια εἶναι. πρὸς δὲ τῇ δικαιοσύνῃ σωφροσύνης πλείστης μετέχει. εἶναι γὰρ ὁμολογεῖται
σωφροσύνη | τὸ κρατεῖν ἡδονῶν καὶ ἐπιθυμιῶν, Ἔρω-
τος δὲ μηδεμίαν ἡδονὴν κρείττω εἶναι· εἰ δὲ ἥττους,
κρατοῖντ᾽ ἂν ὑπὸ Ἔρωτος, ὁ δὲ κρατοῖ, κρατῶν δὲ
ἡδονῶν καὶ ἐπιθυμιῶν ὁ Ἔρως διαφερόντως ἂν σω-
φρονοῖ. καὶ μὴν εἴς γε ἀνδρείαν Ἔρωτι "οὐδ᾽ Ἄρης
d ἀνθίσταται." οὐ γὰρ ἔχει Ἔρωτα Ἄρης, ἀλλ᾽ Ἔρως
Ἄρη—Ἀφροδίτης, ὡς λόγος—κρείττων δὲ ὁ ἔχων τοῦ
ἐχομένου· τοῦ δ᾽ ἀνδρειοτάτου τῶν ἄλλων κρατῶν
πάντων ἂν ἀνδρειότατος εἴη. περὶ μὲν οὖν δικαιοσύ-
νης καὶ σωφροσύνης | καὶ ἀνδρείας τοῦ θεοῦ εἴρηται,
περὶ δὲ σοφίας λείπεται· ὅσον οὖν δυνατόν, πειρατέον
μὴ ἐλλείπειν. καὶ πρῶτον μέν, ἵν᾽ αὖ καὶ ἐγὼ τὴν ἡμετέραν τέχνην τιμήσω ὥσπερ Ἐρυξίμαχος τὴν αὑτοῦ,
e ποιητὴς ὁ θεὸς σοφὸς οὕτως ὥστε καὶ ἄλλον ποιῆσαι·
πᾶς γοῦν ποιητὴς γίγνεται, "κἂν ἄμουσος ᾖ τὸ πρίν,"
οὗ ἂν Ἔρως ἅψηται. ᾧ δὴ πρέπει ἡμᾶς μαρτυρίῳ
χρῆσθαι, ὅτι ποιητὴς ὁ Ἔρως ἀγαθὸς ἐν κεφαλαίῳ |
πᾶσαν ποίησιν τὴν κατὰ μουσικήν· ἃ γάρ τις ἢ μὴ
ἔχει ἢ μὴ οἶδεν, οὔτ᾽ ἂν ἑτέρῳ δοίη οὔτ᾽ ἂν ἄλλον
197 διδάξειεν. καὶ μὲν δὴ τήν γε τῶν ζῴων ποίησιν πάντων τίς ἐναντιώσεται μὴ οὐχὶ Ἔρωτος εἶναι σοφίαν,
ᾗ γίγνεταί τε καὶ φύεται πάντα τὰ ζῷα; ἀλλὰ τὴν τῶν

---

68 Sophocles fr. 235 Nauck². 69 A probable allusion to
Homer, *Odyssey* 8.266–366, in which the god Hephaestus traps
Ares and Aphrodite when they are making love.

'the kings of the city, the laws,' say are just. In addition
to justice he has a very great measure of moderation. For
it is agreed that moderation is the control of pleasures and
desires; and that no pleasure is greater than Love. But
if they are weaker, they will be controlled by Love and
he will control them, and in controlling pleasures and desires Love will be supreme in moderation. Furthermore,
regarding courage, 'not even Ares offers resistance' to
Love.[68] For Ares does not possess Love, but Love pos-   d
sesses Ares—lover of Aphrodite, so the story goes[69]—he
who possesses is stronger than the one who is being possessed, and he who masters the one who is the bravest out
of the rest would be the bravest of them all. So now that
we have spoken about the justice, moderation and courage
of the god, it remains to speak of his wisdom; so as far as
possible we must try not to fall short. Firstly then, in order
that I too pay tribute to my craft, as Eryximachus did to
his, the god is so skilled a poet as to make another a poet   e
also; for in truth everyone whom Love gets in his grasp
becomes a poet, 'even if he were uninspired by the Muse
before.'[70] Indeed the evidence it is right for us to use is
that, in short, Love is a good creator in all creation associated with the arts:[71] for one could not pass on to someone
else, nor teach another what one doesn't have or know.
Now as for the creation of all living creatures, who will   197
argue against the idea that it is the wisdom of Love by
which all living creatures come into being and are born?

[70] Euripides fr. 663 Nauk[2] (*Stheneboea*).

[71] "Creator" = *poiētēs* ("creation" = *poiēsis*). "The arts," translates the wide range of *mousikē* (all activity associated with the
Muses).

τεχνῶν δημιουργίαν οὐκ ἴσμεν, ὅτι οὗ μὲν ἂν ὁ θεὸς
οὗτος διδάσκαλος γένηται, | ἐλλόγιμος καὶ φανὸς
ἀπέβη, οὗ δ' ἂν Ἔρως μὴ ἐφάψηται, σκοτεινός; τοξι-
κήν γε μὴν καὶ ἰατρικὴν καὶ μαντικὴν Ἀπόλλων
ἀνηῦρεν ἐπιθυμίας καὶ ἔρωτος ἡγεμονεύσαντος, ὥστε
b καὶ οὗτος Ἔρωτος ἂν εἴη μαθητής, καὶ Μοῦσαι μουσικῆς καὶ Ἥφαιστος χαλκείας καὶ Ἀθηνᾶ ἱστουργίας
καὶ "Ζεὺς κυβερνᾶν θεῶν τε καὶ ἀνθρώπων." ὅθεν δὴ
καὶ κατεσκευάσθη τῶν θεῶν τὰ πράγματα Ἔρωτος
ἐγγενομένου, | δῆλον ὅτι κάλλους—αἴσχει γὰρ οὐκ
ἔπι ἔρως—πρὸ τοῦ δέ, ὥσπερ ἐν ἀρχῇ εἶπον, πολλὰ
καὶ δεινὰ θεοῖς ἐγίγνετο, ὡς λέγεται, διὰ τὴν τῆς
Ἀνάγκης βασιλείαν· ἐπειδὴ δ' ὁ θεὸς οὗτος ἔφυ, ἐκ
τοῦ ἐρᾶν τῶν καλῶν πάντ' ἀγαθὰ γέγονεν καὶ θεοῖς
καὶ ἀνθρώποις.

c   Οὕτως ἐμοὶ δοκεῖ, ὦ Φαῖδρε, Ἔρως πρῶτος αὐτὸς
ὢν κάλλιστος καὶ ἄριστος μετὰ τοῦτο τοῖς ἄλλοις ἄλλων τοιούτων αἴτιος εἶναι. ἐπέρχεται δέ μοί τι καὶ
ἔμμετρον εἰπεῖν, ὅτι οὗτός ἐστιν ὁ ποιῶν |

εἰρήνην μὲν ἐν ἀνθρώποις, πελάγει δὲ γαλήνην
νηνεμίαν, ἀνέμων κοίτην ὕπνον τ' ἐνὶ κήδει.

d οὗτος δὲ ἡμᾶς ἀλλοτριότητος μὲν κενοῖ, οἰκειότητος
δὲ πληροῖ, τὰς τοιάσδε συνόδους μετ' ἀλλήλων πά-
σας τιθεὶς συνιέναι, ἐν ἑορταῖς, ἐν χοροῖς, ἐν θυσίαισι

As for the skill of handicrafts, do we not know that of whoever this god becomes the teacher, he will turn out with a high reputation and distinction, but whoever Love does not lay his hands on will be obscure? Moreover Apollo invented archery, medicine and prophecy under the guidance of desire and love, so that he too will be a pupil of Love, and the Muses in the arts, Hephaestus in   b
metalwork, and Athene in weaving and 'Zeus in the government of both gods and men.'[72] Hence then the activities of the gods were actually established after Love had been born among them, love of beauty, clearly—for there is no love for ugliness—but before this, as I said at the beginning, many terrible things happened among the gods, so it is said, on account of the rule of Necessity. But when this god was born, from his love of the beautiful all good things came into being for gods and men.

"Thus I think, Phaedrus, Love, being himself the first   c
to be most beautiful and best, after this was the cause of other such things for others. I feel the urge coming over me to say something in verse: that he is the one who creates

> Peace among men and a windless calm upon the sea
> A lulling of the winds and sleep in anxiety.[73]

This is he who empties us of our estrangement and fills us   d
with a sense of belonging together, having ordained that we come together at all gatherings such as this, becoming our leader at festivals, dances and sacrifices; giving us

[72] A quotation, possibly from Aeschylus, from Agathon's own work or made up by Plato.

[73] Source unknown, possibly by Agathon himself or by Plato.

γιγνόμενος ἡγεμών· πρᾳότητα μὲν πορίζων, ἀγριό-
τητα δ' ἐξορίζων· φιλόδωρος | εὐμενείας, ἄδωρος δυσ-
μενείας· ἵλεως ἀγαθός· θεατὸς σοφοῖς, ἀγαστὸς θεοῖς·
ζηλωτὸς ἀμοίροις, κτητὸς εὐμοίροις· τρυφῆς, ἁβρότη-
τος, χλιδῆς, χαρίτων, ἱμέρου, πόθου πατήρ· ἐπιμελὴς
ἀγαθῶν, ἀμελὴς κακῶν· ἐν πόνῳ, ἐν φόβῳ, ἐν πόθῳ,
e ἐν λόγῳ κυβερνήτης, ἐπιβάτης, παραστάτης τε καὶ
σωτὴρ ἄριστος, συμπάντων τε θεῶν καὶ ἀνθρώπων
κόσμος, ἡγεμὼν κάλλιστος καὶ ἄριστος, ᾧ χρὴ
ἕπεσθαι πάντα ἄνδρα ἐφυμνοῦντα καλῶς, ᾠδῆς μετ-
έχοντα ἣν ᾄδει θέλγων πάντων θεῶν | τε καὶ ἀνθρώ-
πων νόημα.

Οὗτος, ἔφη, ὁ παρ' ἐμοῦ λόγος, ὦ Φαῖδρε, τῷ θεῷ
ἀνακείσθω, τὰ μὲν παιδιᾶς, τὰ δὲ σπουδῆς μετρίας,
καθ' ὅσον ἐγὼ δύναμαι, μετέχων.

198 Εἰπόντος δὲ τοῦ Ἀγάθωνος πάντας ἔφη ὁ Ἀριστόδημος ἀναθορυβῆσαι τοὺς παρόντας, ὡς πρεπόντως
τοῦ νεανίσκου εἰρηκότος καὶ αὑτῷ καὶ τῷ θεῷ. τὸν οὖν
Σωκράτη εἰπεῖν βλέψαντα εἰς τὸν Ἐρυξίμαχον, Ἆρά
σοι δοκῶ, φάναι, ὦ | παῖ Ἀκουμενοῦ, ἀδεὲς πάλαι δέος
δεδιέναι, ἀλλ' οὐ μαντικῶς ἃ νυνδὴ ἔλεγον εἰπεῖν, ὅτι
Ἀγάθων θαυμαστῶς ἐροῖ, ἐγὼ δ' ἀπορήσοιμι;

Τὸ μὲν ἕτερον, φάναι τὸν Ἐρυξίμαχον, μαντικῶς
μοι δοκεῖς εἰρηκέναι, ὅτι Ἀγάθων εὖ ἐρεῖ· τὸ δὲ σὲ
ἀπορήσειν, | οὐκ οἶμαι.

gentleness, banishing fierceness, a generous giver of goodwill, no giver of ill will; graciously kind, to be gazed at by
the wise, admired by the gods, to be envied by those who
do not have a share of him, a treasured possession for
those who have a generous share; the father of delicacy,
luxuriousness, daintiness, charms, longing, yearning; one
to take care of good things, to be uncaring of bad things;
in toil, in fear, in yearning, in argument he is the best
helmsman, defender, comrade in arms, lifesaver; orna-   e
ment of all gods and men, finest and best leader whom
everyone must follow, singing his praises well, taking part
in the songs which he sings, enchanting the minds of all
gods and men.[74]

    "Let this speech of mine, Phaedrus, be dedicated to the
god with its share on the one hand of play and on the other
of a measure of seriousness, as far as I am able."

    When Agathon had said this, all those present, said   198
Aristodemus, broke into thunderous applause as the
young man had spoken so appropriately for himself and
the god. Then Socrates looked across at Eryximachus and
said: "Do you think, son of Acumenus, that the fear I expressed before was groundless, or was what I said a while
ago not prophetically spoken, that Agathon would give a
wonderful speech and I would be left stranded?"

    "On the one point," said Eryximachus, "I think you
spoke prophetically saying that Agathon would make a
good speech, but on the other, that you would left stranded,
I don't think so."

[74] 197dff. with balanced opposing clauses and absence of connectives is an obvious parody of the style of Gorgias, cf. Socrates'
ironic comment on this passage in particular at 198b4–5.

PLATO

b   Καὶ πῶς, ὦ μακάριε, εἰπεῖν τὸν Σωκράτη, οὐ μέλλω
ἀπορεῖν καὶ ἐγὼ καὶ ἄλλος ὁστισοῦν, μέλλων λέξειν
μετὰ καλὸν οὕτω καὶ παντοδαπὸν λόγον ῥηθέντα; καὶ
τὰ μὲν ἄλλα οὐχ ὁμοίως μὲν θαυμαστά· τὸ δὲ ἐπὶ
τελευτῆς τοῦ κάλλους | τῶν ὀνομάτων καὶ ῥημάτων
τίς οὐκ ἂν ἐξεπλάγη ἀκούων; ἐπεὶ ἔγωγε ἐνθυμούμε-
νος ὅτι αὐτὸς οὐχ οἷός τ᾽ ἔσομαι οὐδ᾽ ἐγγὺς τούτων
οὐδὲν καλὸν εἰπεῖν, ὑπ᾽ αἰσχύνης ὀλίγου ἀποδρὰς
c ᾠχόμην, εἴ πῃ εἶχον. καὶ γάρ με Γοργίου ὁ λόγος
ἀνεμίμνῃσκεν, ὥστε ἀτεχνῶς τὸ τοῦ Ὁμήρου ἐπε-
πόνθη· ἐφοβούμην μή μοι τελευτῶν ὁ Ἀγάθων Γοργίου κεφαλὴν δεινοῦ λέγειν ἐν τῷ λόγῳ ἐπὶ τὸν ἐμὸν
λόγον πέμψας αὐτόν | με λίθον τῇ ἀφωνίᾳ ποιήσειεν.
καὶ ἐνενόησα τότε ἄρα καταγέλαστος ὤν, ἡνίκα ὑμῖν
ὡμολόγουν ἐν τῷ μέρει μεθ᾽ ὑμῶν ἐγκωμιάσεσθαι τὸν
d Ἔρωτα καὶ ἔφην εἶναι δεινὸς τὰ ἐρωτικά, οὐδὲν εἰδὼς
ἄρα τοῦ πράγματος, ὡς ἔδει ἐγκωμιάζειν ὁτιοῦν. ἐγὼ
μὲν γὰρ ὑπ᾽ ἀβελτερίας ᾤμην δεῖν τἀληθῆ λέγειν
περὶ ἑκάστου τοῦ ἐγκωμιαζομένου, καὶ τοῦτο μὲν |
ὑπάρχειν, ἐξ αὐτῶν δὲ τούτων τὰ κάλλιστα ἐκλεγομέ-
νους ὡς εὐπρεπέστατα τιθέναι· καὶ πάνυ δὴ μέγα
ἐφρόνουν ὡς εὖ ἐρῶν, ὡς εἰδὼς τὴν ἀλήθειαν τοῦ
ἐπαινεῖν ὁτιοῦν. τὸ δὲ ἄρα, ὡς ἔοικεν, οὐ τοῦτο ἦν τὸ
καλῶς ἐπαινεῖν ὁτιοῦν, ἀλλὰ τὸ ὡς μέγιστα ἀνατιθέ-

---

75 See the previous note. Here Socrates is punning on the
similar sound of Gorgias and Gorgon, the Gorgon Medusa, a
dreadful monster the sight of whose gaze turned the looker to

"And how, my good fellow," said Socrates, "am I and   b
anyone else not going to be left at a loss when I'm about
to speak after a speech that has been delivered so beautifully and in so rich and varied a manner? The rest was not
quite as amazing, but toward the end who would not have
been astounded on hearing the beauty of the words and
expressions? Since I was thinking that I myself will not be
able to say anything anywhere near as fine as this, I almost
ran away out of shame, and was gone, if I'd had anywhere
to go. You see, the speech reminded me of Gorgias, that   c
what Homer described had really happened to me: I was
afraid that as he brought his speech to an end, Agathon
would send me the head of Gorgias the clever speaker to
deliver his speech against my speech and turn me to stone
and render me speechless.[75] And it was then I actually
realized I was being very silly when I agreed to sing the
praises of Love, taking my turn with you all, saying that I   d
was an expert on the subject of love, given that I actually
knew nothing of the subject, how one ought to praise
anything whatever. You see, in my simplemindedness I
thought I had to tell the truth about everything which was
being praised, and that was the basis, and from that we had
to choose the best of these aspects and set them out in the
most fitting way possible; and indeed I was really very
confident that I would speak well, as I assumed I knew the
true way to praise anything whatsoever. But the fact is, so
it seems, that this was not the way to praise anything whatsoever well, but to ascribe the greatest and finest details

stone. (Pindar, *Pythian Ode* 10.44–48). The Homeric reference:
in the *Odyssey* (11.633–35), Odysseus quits Hades in fear that if
he stayed he might encounter a monster such as the Gorgon.

ναι τῷ πράγματι καὶ ὡς κάλλιστα, ἐάν τε ᾖ οὕτως
e ἔχοντα ἐάν τε μή· εἰ δὲ ψευδῆ, οὐδὲν ἄρ᾽ ἦν πρᾶγμα.
προυρρήθη γάρ, ὡς ἔοικεν, ὅπως ἕκαστος ἡμῶν τὸν
Ἔρωτα ἐγκωμιάζειν δόξει, οὐχ ὅπως ἐγκωμιάσεται.
διὰ ταῦτα δὴ | οἶμαι πάντα λόγον κινοῦντες ἀνατίθετε
τῷ Ἔρωτι, καί φατε αὐτὸν τοιοῦτόν τε εἶναι καὶ τοσούτων αἴτιον, ὅπως ἂν φαίνηται ὡς κάλλιστος καὶ
199 ἄριστος, δῆλον ὅτι τοῖς μὴ γιγνώσκουσιν—οὐ γὰρ
δήπου τοῖς γε εἰδόσιν—καὶ καλῶς γ᾽ ἔχει καὶ σεμνῶς
ὁ ἔπαινος. ἀλλὰ γὰρ ἐγὼ οὐκ ᾔδη ἄρα τὸν τρόπον τοῦ
ἐπαίνου, οὐ δ᾽ εἰδὼς ὑμῖν ὡμολόγησα καὶ αὐτὸς | ἐν
τῷ μέρει ἐπαινέσεσθαι. "ἡ γλῶσσα οὖν ὑπέσχετο, ἡ
δὲ φρὴν οὔ·" χαιρέτω δή. οὐ γὰρ ἔτι ἐγκωμιάζω τοῦτον
τὸν τρόπον—οὐ γὰρ ἂν δυναίμην—οὐ μέντοι ἀλλὰ τά
b γε ἀληθῆ, εἰ βούλεσθε, ἐθέλω εἰπεῖν κατ᾽ ἐμαυτόν, οὐ
πρὸς τοὺς ὑμετέρους λόγους, ἵνα μὴ γέλωτα ὄφλω.
ὅρα οὖν, ὦ Φαῖδρε, εἴ τι καὶ τοιούτου λόγου δέῃ, περὶ
Ἔρωτος τἀληθῆ λεγόμενα ἀκούειν, ὀνομάσει δὲ καὶ
θέσει ῥημάτων τοιαύτη ὁποία δἄν | τις τύχῃ ἐπελ-
θοῦσα.

Τὸν οὖν Φαῖδρον ἔφη καὶ τοὺς ἄλλους κελεύειν
λέγειν, ὅπῃ αὐτὸς οἴοιτο δεῖν εἰπεῖν, ταύτῃ.

Ἔτι τοίνυν, φάναι, ὦ Φαῖδρε, πάρες μοι Ἀγάθωνα

---

76 Euripides, *Hippolytus* 612.

77 Plato's Socrates also makes this claim of spontaneity at the
beginning of his own trial speech in *Apology* (17c). See also the
same claim made by Pausanias on his speech at 185c3.

possible to the subject, whether they are really like this or not. But if they are false, then it's no matter. For it seems e it's been proposed how each of us should give the appearance of praising Love, not how we should actually praise him. For these reasons then I think you are digging up everything you can say and ascribing it to Love, and you claim that he is of such a kind and responsible for so many things in order that he may appear to be the finest and the best possible, obviously for people who do not know 199 him—for it surely couldn't be for those who do—and the eulogy is certainly delivered in a fine and impressive manner. But you see I was not actually aware of the method of the eulogy and in my ignorance I agreed with you that I too would praise him when it came to my turn. 'My tongue therefore made the promise, but not my mind.'[76] So much for that! You see I'm not making another eulogy in that style—well I couldn't—but all the same the truth I am willing, if you wish, to speak, in accordance with my own principles, not in reply to your speeches, so that I don't b incur ridicule. So, Phaedrus, consider whether there really is any need for such a speech as well, and to hear the truth spoken about Love with such wording and arrangement of phrases as might happen to come to mind."[77]

Accordingly, Aristodemus said, Phaedrus and the others told him to speak in whatever way he thought he ought to.

"In that case, Phaedrus," he said, "let me ask Agathon just a few little questions, so when I've got his agreement

σμίκρ᾽ ἄττα ἐρέσθαι, ἵνα ἀνομολογησάμενος παρ᾽
αὑτοῦ οὕτως ἤδη | λέγω.

c   Ἀλλὰ παρίημι, φάναι τὸν Φαῖδρον, ἀλλ᾽ ἐρώτα.
μετὰ ταῦτα δὴ τὸν Σωκράτη ἔφη ἐνθένδε ποθὲν ἄρξα-
σθαι.

Καὶ μήν, ὦ φίλε Ἀγάθων, καλῶς μοι ἔδοξας καθη-
γήσασθαι τοῦ λόγου, λέγων ὅτι πρῶτον μὲν δέοι
αὐτὸν ἐπιδεῖξαι | ὁποῖός τίς ἐστιν ὁ Ἔρως, ὕστερον
δὲ τὰ ἔργα αὐτοῦ. ταύτην τὴν ἀρχὴν πάνυ ἄγαμαι.
ἴθι οὖν μοι περὶ Ἔρωτος, ἐπειδὴ καὶ τἆλλα καλῶς καὶ
μεγαλοπρεπῶς διῆλθες οἷός ἐστι, καὶ τόδε εἰπέ· πότερόν ἐστι τοιοῦτος οἷος εἶναί τινος ὁ Ἔρως ἔρως, ἢ
d   οὐδενός; ἐρωτῶ δ᾽ οὐκ εἰ μητρός τινος ἢ πατρός
ἐστιν—γελοῖον γὰρ ἂν εἴη τὸ ἐρώτημα εἰ Ἔρως ἐστὶν
ἔρως μητρὸς ἢ πατρός—ἀλλ᾽ ὥσπερ ἂν εἰ αὐτὸ τοῦτο
πατέρα | ἠρώτων, ἆρα ὁ πατήρ ἐστι πατήρ τινος ἢ οὔ;
εἶπες ἂν δήπου μοι, εἰ ἐβούλου καλῶς ἀποκρίνασθαι,
ὅτι ἔστιν ὑέος γε ἢ θυγατρὸς ὁ πατὴρ πατήρ· ἢ οὔ;

Πάνυ γε, φάναι τὸν Ἀγάθωνα.

Οὐκοῦν καὶ ἡ μήτηρ ὡσαύτως; Ὁμολογεῖσθαι καὶ
e   τοῦτο. Ἔτι τοίνυν, εἰπεῖν τὸν Σωκράτη, ἀπόκριναι
ὀλίγῳ πλείω, ἵνα μᾶλλον καταμάθῃς ὃ βούλομαι. εἰ
γὰρ ἐροίμην, "Τί δέ; ἀδελφός, αὐτὸ τοῦθ᾽ ὅπερ ἔστιν,
ἔστι τινὸς ἀδελφὸς ἢ οὔ;" Φάναι εἶναι. |

Οὐκοῦν ἀδελφοῦ ἢ ἀδελφῆς; Ὁμολογεῖν.

---

[78] For ironic admiration and self-deprecation followed by a

I can then go ahead and then make my speech on that basis."[78]

"Well I'll let you do that," said Phaedrus; "go on and c ask him." After this, Aristodemus said, Socrates began from some point such as this:

"Well now, my dear Agathon, I thought you started off your speech well when you said one should show first what sort of being Love is, and after this his achievements. I very much admire an opening such as that. So, on the subject of Love, since you explained what sort he is in other respects in a fine and splendid way, come on then and tell me this too: is Love of the sort to be love of some- thing or of nothing? I'm not asking if he's (born) of some d mother or father—for it would be absurd to ask if Love is of a mother or father in that sense—but just as if I were asking that same question about a father: is the father a father of someone or not? I'm sure you'd tell me, if you wanted to give me the right answer that the father is father of a son or a daughter. Isn't that so?"

"Certainly," said Agathon.

"And therefore the same with the mother?" He agreed with this too. "Going on then," said Socrates, "answer a e few more questions, so you may understand better what I mean. If I were to ask: What about this point? A brother, in so far as he is so, is he brother of someone, or not?" He said he was.

"That is, of a brother or a sister?" He agreed.

disarming request to answer "a few little questions" as a prelude to a rigorous Socratic *elenchus* (examination of beliefs for pur- poses of refutation), see also *Protagoras* 328dff.

Πειρῶ δή, φάναι, καὶ τὸν ἔρωτα εἰπεῖν. ὁ Ἔρως ἔρως ἐστὶν οὐδενὸς ἢ τινός;

Πάνυ μὲν οὖν ἔστιν.

200 Τοῦτο μὲν τοίνυν, εἰπεῖν τὸν Σωκράτη, φύλαξον παρὰ σαυτῷ μεμνημένος ὅτου· τοσόνδε δὲ εἰπέ, πότερον ὁ Ἔρως ἐκείνου οὗ ἔστιν ἔρως, ἐπιθυμεῖ αὐτοῦ ἢ οὔ;

Πάνυ γε, φάναι. |

Πότερον ἔχων αὐτὸ οὗ ἐπιθυμεῖ τε καὶ ἐρᾷ, εἶτα ἐπιθυμεῖ τε καὶ ἐρᾷ, ἢ οὐκ ἔχων;

Οὐκ ἔχων, ὡς τὸ εἰκός γε, φάναι.

Σκόπει δή, εἰπεῖν τὸν Σωκράτη, ἀντὶ τοῦ εἰκότος εἰ ἀνάγκη οὕτως, τὸ ἐπιθυμοῦν ἐπιθυμεῖν οὗ ἐνδεές b ἐστιν, ἢ μὴ ἐπιθυμεῖν, ἐὰν μὴ ἐνδεὲς ᾖ; ἐμοὶ μὲν γὰρ θαυμαστῶς δοκεῖ, ὦ Ἀγάθων, ὡς ἀνάγκη εἶναι· σοὶ δὲ πῶς;

Κἀμοί, φάναι, δοκεῖ.

Καλῶς λέγεις. ἆρ᾽ οὖν βούλοιτ᾽ ἄν τις μέγας ὢν μέγας | εἶναι, ἢ ἰσχυρὸς ὢν ἰσχυρός;

Ἀδύνατον ἐκ τῶν ὡμολογημένων.

Οὐ γάρ που ἐνδεὴς ἂν εἴη τούτων ὅ γε ὤν.

Ἀληθῆ λέγεις.

Εἰ γὰρ καὶ ἰσχυρὸς ὢν βούλοιτο ἰσχυρὸς εἶναι, φάναι τὸν | Σωκράτη, καὶ ταχὺς ὢν ταχύς, καὶ ὑγιὴς ὢν ὑγιής—ἴσως γὰρ ἄν τις ταῦτα οἰηθείη καὶ πάντα τὰ τοιαῦτα τοὺς ὄντας τε τοιούτους καὶ ἔχοντας ταῦτα c τούτων ἅπερ ἔχουσι καὶ ἐπιθυμεῖν, ἵν᾽ οὖν μὴ ἐξαπατηθῶμεν, τούτου ἕνεκα λέγω—τούτοις γάρ, ὦ Ἀγά-

"Then try," he said, "and apply this to love also. Is Love love of nothing or of something?"

"Of something, certainly."

"Well then," said Socrates, "keep this in mind and re- 200 member what it is the love of.[79] Tell me this much: does Love desire that which he is the love of, or not?"

"Indeed he does," he replied.

"Does he desire and love what he desires and loves when he has it, or when he doesn't?"

"When he doesn't, as is likely, at least," he said.

"Consider then," said Socrates, "if, instead of that 'likely,' it must necessarily be like this: what desires desires what it lacks, or if it's not lacking it doesn't desire it? For b it seems extraordinary to me, Agathon, how compelling that is. How does it look to you?"

"It seems so to me too," he said.

"You're right. Would someone want to be big, if he was big, or strong, if he was strong?"

"It's impossible according to what we have agreed."

"Yes, for presumably he wouldn't be lacking these attributes if he had them."

"You're right."

"Yes, for if he wanted to be strong even when he was strong," said Socrates, "and he wanted to be quick when he was quick, and healthy when he was healthy—for perhaps one might think that in these and in all cases of this sort people who have these sort of qualities also desire what they have; the reason I mention them is in order that c

[79] Socrates is probably referring to his previous statement (Love is love of something) coupled with Agathon's previous assertions in his speech of the objects of Love (197d).

θων, εἰ ἐννοεῖς, ἔχειν μὲν ἕκαστα τούτων ἐν τῷ παρ-
όντι ἀνάγκη ἃ ἔχουσιν, ἐάντε βούλωνται | ἐάντε μή,
καὶ τούτου γε δήπου τίς ἂν ἐπιθυμήσειεν; ἀλλ' ὅταν
τις λέγῃ ὅτι ἐγὼ ὑγιαίνων βούλομαι καὶ ὑγιαίνειν,
καὶ πλουτῶν βούλομαι καὶ πλουτεῖν, καὶ ἐπιθυμῶ
αὐτῶν τούτων ἃ ἔχω, εἴποιμεν ἂν αὐτῷ ὅτι σύ, ὦ ἄν-
θρωπε, πλοῦτον κεκτημένος καὶ ὑγίειαν καὶ ἰσχὺν
βούλει καὶ εἰς τὸν ἔπειτα χρόνον ταῦτα κεκτῆσθαι,
d   ἐπεὶ ἐν τῷ γε νῦν παρόντι, εἴτε βούλει εἴτε μή, ἔχεις·
σκόπει οὖν, ὅταν τοῦτο λέγῃς, ὅτι ἐπιθυμῶ τῶν παρ-
όντων, εἰ ἄλλο τι λέγεις | ἢ τόδε, ὅτι βούλομαι τὰ νῦν
παρόντα καὶ εἰς τὸν ἔπειτα χρόνον παρεῖναι. ἄλλο τι
ὁμολογοῖ ἄν; Συμφάναι ἔφη τὸν Ἀγάθωνα.

Εἰπεῖν δὴ τὸν Σωκράτη, Οὐκοῦν τοῦτό γ' ἐστὶν
ἐκείνου ἐρᾶν, ὃ οὔπω ἕτοιμον αὐτῷ ἐστιν οὐδὲ ἔχει, τὸ
εἰς τὸν | ἔπειτα χρόνον ταῦτα εἶναι αὐτῷ σωζόμενα
καὶ παρόντα;

e   Πάνυ γε, φάναι.

Καὶ οὗτος ἄρα καὶ ἄλλος πᾶς ὁ ἐπιθυμῶν τοῦ μὴ
ἑτοίμου ἐπιθυμεῖ καὶ τοῦ μὴ παρόντος, καὶ ὃ μὴ ἔχει
καὶ ὃ μὴ ἔστιν αὐτὸς καὶ οὗ ἐνδεής ἐστι, τοιαῦτ' ἄττα
ἐστὶν ὧν ἡ ἐπιθυμία | τε καὶ ὁ ἔρως ἐστίν;

Πάνυ γ', εἰπεῖν.

Ἴθι δή, φάναι τὸν Σωκράτη, ἀνομολογησώμεθα τὰ
εἰρημένα. ἄλλο τι ἔστιν ὁ Ἔρως πρῶτον μὲν τινῶν,
ἔπειτα τούτων ὧν ἂν ἔνδεια παρῇ αὐτῷ;

201   Ναί, φάναι.

Ἐπὶ δὴ τούτοις ἀναμνήσθητι τίνων ἔφησθα ἐν τῷ

we should not be misled—you see, if you think about these people, Agathon, they must have each of these attributes that they do have at the present time, whether they want them or not, and I wonder who would desire this? But when someone says 'I am healthy and I wish also to be healthy, and I am rich, and wish to be rich and I desire these things which I have,' we would say to him: 'You, my friend, being in possession of wealth and health and strength, want to possess them for the future as well, since you have them now in the present, whether you want them or not.' Therefore consider, when you say 'I desire what I have at the present time,' if you mean something other than this, that 'I want what I have now at the present time to be there in the future too.' Surely he would agree?" Aristodemus said that Agathon assented.

Then Socrates said: "Therefore doesn't this mean to love that thing which is not yet available for him and he doesn't yet have, that is, for these things to be preserved and present for him in the future?"

"Very much so," he said.

"Then this person and everyone else also who desires, desires what is not available and is not to hand, and what he does not have and what he himself is not and what he is lacking: are these the kinds of thing for which there is desire and love?"

"Very much so," he said.

"Come on then," said Socrates, "let's summarize what we've agreed on. Firstly Love is surely love of certain things, and secondly for those things of which he has a lack?"

"Yes," he said.

"This being so, remember what you said in your speech

λόγῳ εἶναι τὸν Ἔρωτα· εἰ δὲ βούλει, ἐγώ σε ἀνα-
μνήσω. οἶμαι γάρ σε οὑτωσί πως εἰπεῖν, ὅτι τοῖς θε-
οῖς κατεσκευάσθη τὰ | πράγματα δι᾽ ἔρωτα καλῶν·
αἰσχρῶν γὰρ οὐκ εἴη ἔρως. οὐχ οὑτωσί πως ἔλεγες;

Εἶπον γάρ, φάναι τὸν Ἀγάθωνα.

Καὶ ἐπιεικῶς γε λέγεις, ὦ ἑταῖρε, φάναι τὸν Σω-
κράτη· καὶ εἰ τοῦτο οὕτως ἔχει, ἄλλο τι ὁ Ἔρως κάλ-
λους ἂν εἴη | ἔρως, αἴσχους δὲ οὔ; Ὡμολόγει.

b   Οὐκοῦν ὡμολόγηται, οὗ ἐνδεής ἐστι καὶ μὴ ἔχει,
τούτου ἐρᾶν;

Ναί, εἰπεῖν.

Ἐνδεὴς ἄρ᾽ ἐστὶ καὶ οὐκ ἔχει ὁ Ἔρως κάλλος. |
Ἀνάγκη, φάναι.

Τί δέ; τὸ ἐνδεὲς κάλλους καὶ μηδαμῇ κεκτημένον
κάλλος ἆρα λέγεις σὺ καλὸν εἶναι;

Οὐ δῆτα.

Ἔτι οὖν ὁμολογεῖς Ἔρωτα καλὸν εἶναι, εἰ ταῦτα
οὕτως | ἔχει;

Καὶ τὸν Ἀγάθωνα εἰπεῖν Κινδυνεύω, ὦ Σώκρατες,
οὐδὲν εἰδέναι ὧν τότε εἶπον.

c   Καὶ μὴν καλῶς γε εἶπες, φάναι, ὦ Ἀγάθων. ἀλλὰ
σμικρὸν ἔτι εἰπέ· τἀγαθὰ οὐ καὶ καλὰ δοκεῖ σοι εἶναι;

Ἔμοιγε.

---

80 See Agathon's speech, 197b.
81 At 200a9–b2.

were the objects of Love; if you wish, I will remind you. You see I think you said something like this: the activities of the gods were established through their love of beautiful things: for there is no love of ugly things.[80] Is this the sort of thing you said?"

"Yes, that's what I said," said Agathon.

"And what you say is quite reasonable, my friend, said Socrates; and if this is the case could Love be anything else but love of beauty, and not of ugliness?" He agreed it was love of beauty.

"Wasn't it then agreed that he loves what he lacks and doesn't have?"[81]   b

"Yes," he said.

"Then Love is lacking and does not possess beauty."

"That must be so," he said.

"What? Are you really saying that what lacks beauty and doesn't possess it in any way is beautiful?"

"No, not at all."

"Then do you still agree that Love is beautiful, if this is the case?"

Agathon said: "it rather looks, Socrates, as if I didn't understand anything about what I was saying then."[82]

"And yet you spoke beautifully, Agathon, he said. But   c still tell me just a little thing: do you not think good things are also beautiful?"

"I do."

[82] Agathon's immediate and total capitulation here is not typical of Plato's interlocutors under pressure, e.g., Protagoras in *Protagoras* 329dff., Thrasymachus in *Republic* 1.337ff. Plato clearly wants his Socrates to get on with the argument.

PLATO

Εἰ ἄρα ὁ Ἔρως τῶν καλῶν ἐνδεής ἐστι, τὰ δὲ
ἀγαθὰ | καλά, κἂν τῶν ἀγαθῶν ἐνδεὴς εἴη.

Ἐγώ, φάναι, ὦ Σώκρατες, σοὶ οὐκ ἂν δυναίμην
ἀντιλέγειν, ἀλλ᾽ οὕτως ἐχέτω ὡς σὺ λέγεις.

Οὐ μὲν οὖν τῇ ἀληθείᾳ, φάναι, ὦ φιλούμενε Ἀγάθων, δύνασαι ἀντιλέγειν, ἐπεὶ Σωκράτει γε οὐδὲν χα-
λεπόν.

d   Καὶ σὲ μέν γε ἤδη ἐάσω· τὸν δὲ λόγον τὸν περὶ τοῦ
Ἔρωτος, ὅν ποτ᾽ ἤκουσα γυναικὸς Μαντινικῆς Διοτί-
μας, ἣ ταῦτά τε σοφὴ ἦν καὶ ἄλλα πολλά—καὶ Ἀθη-
ναίοις ποτὲ θυσαμένοις πρὸ τοῦ λοιμοῦ δέκα ἔτη ἀνα-
βολὴν ἐποίησε τῆς | νόσου, ἣ δὴ καὶ ἐμὲ τὰ ἐρωτικὰ
ἐδίδαξεν—ὃν οὖν ἐκείνη ἔλεγε λόγον, πειράσομαι
ὑμῖν διελθεῖν ἐκ τῶν ὡμολογημένων ἐμοὶ καὶ Ἀγά-
θωνι, αὐτὸς ἐπ᾽ ἐμαυτοῦ, ὅπως ἂν δύνωμαι. δεῖ δή, ὦ
Ἀγάθων, ὥσπερ σὺ διηγήσω, διελθεῖν αὐτὸν πρῶτον,
τίς ἐστιν ὁ Ἔρως καὶ ποῖός τις, ἔπειτα τὰ ἔργα αὐτοῦ.
e   δοκεῖ οὖν μοι ῥᾷστον εἶναι οὕτω διελθεῖν, ὥς ποτέ με
ἡ ξένη ἀνακρίνουσα διῄει. σχεδὸν γάρ τι καὶ ἐγὼ
πρὸς αὐτὴν ἕτερα τοιαῦτα ἔλεγον οἷάπερ νῦν πρὸς ἐμὲ

---

[83] Socrates' "little thing," here, the association of "good" and
"beautiful" (c2), is a vital link in the chain of argument resurfacing
again at 204d–e and relies to some extent on the overlap in Greek
between these terms (*agathon* and *kalon*); see Introduction,
§3(ii).

240

"If then Love is lacking in beautiful things, and good things are beautiful, then he would be lacking in good things too."[83]

"I cannot argue against you, Socrates; well then, let it be as you say."

"No," he said, "it is rather the truth that you cannot argue against, my beloved Agathon," said Socrates, "since there's nothing difficult about arguing against Socrates.

The Speech of Socrates

"And now I'm going to let you be. But I want to take up d the account of Love which I once heard from a woman from Mantinea, Diotima, who was an expert in these and many other matters—once before the plague she caused a ten year delay in the sickness after the Athenians had performed sacrifices, and she it was who also taught me about love—now the account which she gave I shall try to go through with you all on my own in whatever way I can, on the basis of what Agathon and I agreed on.[84] Just as you led the way, Agathon, I myself must first explain about Love himself, who he is and what he is like and then what he does. So it seems to me easiest to go through it in the e following way, as once the stranger did when she examined me. For I was saying to her other things of pretty well the

---

[84] For Diotima as an invention of Plato, see Introduction §3(i) and n. 22. There is no clear evidence that the Athenians had reason to fear a plague ten years before it actually happened in 430.

| Ἀγάθων, ὡς εἴη ὁ Ἔρως μέγας θεός, εἴη δὲ τῶν καλῶν· ἤλεγχε δή με τούτοις τοῖς λόγοις οἷσπερ ἐγὼ τοῦτον, ὡς οὔτε καλὸς εἴη κατὰ τὸν ἐμὸν λόγον οὔτε ἀγαθός.

Καὶ ἐγώ, Πῶς λέγεις, ἔφην, ὦ Διοτίμα; αἰσχρὸς ἄρα ὁ Ἔρως ἐστὶ καὶ κακός; |

Καὶ ἥ, Οὐκ εὐφημήσεις; ἔφη· ἢ οἴει, ὅτι ἂν μὴ καλὸν ᾖ, ἀναγκαῖον αὐτὸ εἶναι αἰσχρόν;

202   Μάλιστά γε.

ᵔΗ καὶ ἂν μὴ σοφόν, ἀμαθές; ἢ οὐκ ᾔσθησαι ὅτι ἔστιν τι μεταξὺ σοφίας καὶ ἀμαθίας;

Τί τοῦτο; |

Τὸ ὀρθὰ δοξάζειν καὶ ἄνευ τοῦ ἔχειν λόγον δοῦναι οὐκ οἶσθ᾽, ἔφη, ὅτι οὔτε ἐπίστασθαί ἐστιν—ἄλογον γὰρ πρᾶγμα πῶς ἂν εἴη ἐπιστήμη;—οὔτε ἀμαθία—τὸ γὰρ τοῦ ὄντος τυγχάνον πῶς ἂν εἴη ἀμαθία;—ἔστι δὲ δήπου τοιοῦτον ἡ ὀρθὴ δόξα, μεταξὺ φρονήσεως καὶ ἀμαθίας. |

Ἀληθῆ, ἦν δ᾽ ἐγώ, λέγεις.

b   Μὴ τοίνυν ἀνάγκαζε ὃ μὴ καλόν ἐστιν αἰσχρὸν εἶναι, μηδὲ ὃ μὴ ἀγαθόν, κακόν. οὕτω δὲ καὶ τὸν Ἔρωτα ἐπειδὴ αὐτὸς ὁμολογεῖς μὴ εἶναι ἀγαθὸν μηδὲ καλόν, μηδέν τι μᾶλλον οἴου δεῖν αὐτὸν αἰσχρὸν καὶ κακὸν εἶναι, ἀλλά τι | μεταξύ, ἔφη, τούτοιν.

Καὶ μήν, ἦν δ᾽ ἐγώ, ὁμολογεῖται γε παρὰ πάντων μέγας θεὸς εἶναι.

sort Agathon said to me just now, how Love was a great god and was love of beautiful things; she examined me with those arguments with which I examined him: that he is neither beautiful according to my argument, nor good.

"So I said: 'What do you mean, Diotima? Is Eros actually ugly and bad?'

"And she said: 'Mind what you say![85] Or do you think that whatever is not beautiful must be ugly?'

"I certainly do.

202

"'Would that mean also that what is not wise is ignorant? Or haven't you realized that there is something between wisdom and ignorance?'

"'What is that?'

"'Do you not know,' she said, 'that to form correct beliefs, but without giving a rational account of them, is neither to have knowledge—for how could something irrational be knowledge? Nor could it be ignorance—for how could chancing upon what is true be ignorance? Correct belief, I suppose, would be the sort of thing which is in between understanding and ignorance.'

"'What you say is true,' I said.

"'Well then, don't insist that what is not beautiful has   b to be ugly, and that what is not good, bad. Thus with Love too, since you yourself admit that he is not good and not beautiful, do not think any more for that reason that he must be ugly and bad, but rather something between those two,' she said.

"'And yet,' I said, 'it's agreed by everyone that he's a great god.'

[85] Literally, "Won't you speak auspicious words?"

Τῶν μὴ εἰδότων, ἔφη, πάντων λέγεις, ἢ καὶ τῶν εἰδότων;

Συμπάντων μὲν οὖν. |

c Καὶ ἣ γελάσασα Καὶ πῶς ἄν, ἔφη, ὦ Σώκρατες, ὁμολογοῖτο μέγας θεὸς εἶναι παρὰ τούτων, οἵ φασιν αὐτὸν οὐδὲ θεὸν εἶναι;

Τίνες οὗτοι; ἦν δ᾽ ἐγώ.

Εἷς μέν, ἔφη, σύ, μία δ᾽ ἐγώ. |

Κἀγὼ εἶπον, Πῶς τοῦτο, ἔφην, λέγεις;

Καὶ ἥ, Ῥᾳδίως, ἔφη. λέγε γάρ μοι, οὐ πάντας θεοὺς φῂς εὐδαίμονας εἶναι καὶ καλούς; ἢ τολμήσαις ἄν τινα μὴ φάναι καλόν τε καὶ εὐδαίμονα θεῶν εἶναι;

Μὰ Δί᾽ οὐκ ἔγωγ᾽, ἔφην. |

Εὐδαίμονας δὲ δὴ λέγεις οὐ τοὺς τἀγαθὰ καὶ τὰ καλὰ κεκτημένους;

Πάνυ γε.

d Ἀλλὰ μὴν Ἔρωτά γε ὡμολόγηκας δι᾽ ἔνδειαν τῶν ἀγαθῶν καὶ καλῶν ἐπιθυμεῖν αὐτῶν τούτων ὧν ἐνδεής ἐστιν.

Ὡμολόγηκα γάρ. |

Πῶς ἂν οὖν θεὸς εἴη ὅ γε τῶν καλῶν καὶ ἀγαθῶν ἄμοιρος;

Οὐδαμῶς, ὥς γ᾽ ἔοικεν.

Ὁρᾷς οὖν, ἔφη, ὅτι καὶ σὺ Ἔρωτα οὐ θεὸν νομίζεις;

Τί οὖν ἄν, ἔφην, εἴη ὁ Ἔρως; θνητός;

Ἥκιστά γε. |

Ἀλλὰ τί μήν;

"'By everyone you mean by all those who do not know,' she said, 'or do you mean those who are in the know as well?'

"'I mean the whole lot.'

"And laughing she said: 'And how, Socrates, could it be admitted that he is a great god by those who say he's not a god at all?'

c

"'Who are these people?' I asked.

"'You're one of them,' she said, 'and I'm another.'

"And I replied: 'How can you say that?'

"'Easily,' she said. 'For instance, tell me, do you not say that all the gods are happy and beautiful? Or would you have the courage to deny that any one of the gods is beautiful and happy?'

"'I certainly would not, by Zeus.'

"'But don't you call happy those who possess what is beautiful and good?'

"'Very much so.'

"'And yet you have agreed that in the case of Love it's through a lack of good and beautiful things that he desires those very things he's lacking.'

d

"'Yes, I have agreed that.'

"'Then how could he be a god if he has no share of beautiful and good things?'

"'He can't be in any way, it seems.'

"'So do you see,' she said, 'that you too believe that Love is not a god?'

"'So then,' I said, 'what could Love be? Mortal?'

"'Not at all.'

"'Well what then?'

Ὥσπερ τὰ πρότερα, ἔφη, μεταξὺ θνητοῦ καὶ ἀθανάτου.

Τί οὖν, ὦ Διοτίμα;

Δαίμων μέγας, ὦ Σώκρατες· καὶ γὰρ πᾶν τὸ δαιμόνιον μεταξύ ἐστι θεοῦ τε καὶ θνητοῦ.

e   Τίνα, ἦν δ᾽ ἐγώ, δύναμιν ἔχον;

Ἑρμηνεῦον καὶ διαπορθμεῦον θεοῖς τὰ παρ᾽ ἀνθρώπων καὶ ἀνθρώποις τὰ παρὰ θεῶν, τῶν μὲν τὰς δεήσεις καὶ | θυσίας, τῶν δὲ τὰς ἐπιτάξεις τε καὶ ἀμοιβὰς τῶν θυσιῶν, ἐν μέσῳ δὲ ὂν ἀμφοτέρων συμπληροῖ, ὥστε τὸ πᾶν αὐτὸ αὑτῷ συνδεδέσθαι. διὰ τούτου καὶ ἡ μαντικὴ πᾶσα χωρεῖ καὶ ἡ τῶν ἱερέων τέχνη τῶν τε περὶ τὰς θυσίας καὶ τελετὰς καὶ τὰς ἐπῳδὰς καὶ τὴν 203 μαντείαν πᾶσαν καὶ γοητείαν. θεὸς δὲ ἀνθρώπῳ οὐ μείγνυται, ἀλλὰ διὰ τούτου πᾶσά ἐστιν ἡ ὁμιλία καὶ ἡ διάλεκτος θεοῖς πρὸς ἀνθρώπους, καὶ ἐγρηγορόσι καὶ καθεύδουσι· καὶ ὁ μὲν περὶ τὰ τοιαῦτα σοφὸς | δαιμόνιος ἀνήρ, ὁ δὲ ἄλλο τι σοφὸς ὢν ἢ περὶ τέχνας ἢ χειρουργίας τινὰς βάναυσος. οὗτοι δὴ οἱ δαίμονες πολλοὶ καὶ παντοδαποί εἰσιν, εἷς δὲ τούτων ἐστὶ καὶ ὁ Ἔρως.

Πατρὸς δέ, ἦν δ᾽ ἐγώ, τίνος ἐστὶ καὶ μητρός;

b   Μακρότερον μέν, ἔφη, διηγήσασθαι· ὅμως δέ σοι ἐρῶ. ὅτε γὰρ ἐγένετο ἡ Ἀφροδίτη, ἡστιῶντο οἱ θεοὶ οἵ τε ἄλλοι καὶ ὁ τῆς Μήτιδος ὑὸς Πόρος. ἐπειδὴ δὲ ἐδείπνησαν, προσαιτήσουσα οἷον δὴ εὐωχίας οὔσης

"'As in the previous cases,' she said, 'between mortal and immortal.'

"'So what is he, Diotima?'

"'A great spirit,[86] Socrates, for everything concerned with spirits lies between god and mortal.'

"'What function does it have?' I asked. e

"'To interpret and communicate the affairs of men to the gods and from the gods to men, the petitions and sacrifices of the former, and of the latter the commands and favors returned for the sacrifices, and, being in the middle of both, it fills the gap between them, so that the whole is bound together into one. Through this also all divination proceeds, the skill of priests and those engaged in sacrifice and ritual and incantations and the whole of prophecy and magic. God does not mix with humanity, but by this means 203 all exchange and communication from the gods to humans takes place both when they are awake and when asleep. The man who is wise in these matters is a man inspired spiritually, but he who is experienced in any other way about some kinds of skills and crafts is concerned with the material world.[87] These divine spirits, then, are many and of many different sorts, and one of these is Love.'

"'Who are his father and mother?' I asked.

"'It's rather a long haul to go through it, she said, but b nevertheless, I shall tell you. For when Aphrodite was born, all the gods celebrated, and among them was Porus the son of Metis. While they were feasting Penia arrived

[86] "Spirit" = *daimōn*, a semidivine being, offspring of gods or gods and mortals, who serves as intermediary between gods and mortals.   [87] "Concerned with the material world" (materialistic) = *banausos*, someone practicing manual occupations.

ἀφίκετο ἡ Πενία, καὶ | ἦν περὶ τὰς θύρας. ὁ οὖν Πόρος
μεθυσθεὶς τοῦ νέκταρος—οἶνος γὰρ οὔπω ἦν—εἰς τὸν
τοῦ Διὸς κῆπον εἰσελθὼν βεβαρημένος ηὗδεν. ἡ οὖν
Πενία ἐπιβουλεύουσα διὰ τὴν αὑτῆς ἀπορίαν παιδίον
ποιήσασθαι ἐκ τοῦ Πόρου, κατακλίνεταί τε παρ' αὐτῷ

c καὶ ἐκύησε τὸν Ἔρωτα. διὸ δὴ καὶ τῆς Ἀφροδίτης
ἀκόλουθος καὶ θεράπων γέγονεν ὁ Ἔρως, γεννηθεὶς
ἐν τοῖς ἐκείνης γενεθλίοις, καὶ ἅμα φύσει ἐραστὴς ὢν
περὶ τὸ καλὸν καὶ τῆς Ἀφροδίτης καλῆς οὔσης. | ἅτε
οὖν Πόρου καὶ Πενίας ὑὸς ὢν ὁ Ἔρως ἐν τοιαύτῃ
τύχῃ καθέστηκεν. πρῶτον μὲν πένης ἀεί ἐστι, καὶ
πολλοῦ δεῖ ἁπαλός τε καὶ καλός, οἷον οἱ πολλοὶ οἴονται, ἀλλὰ σκληρὸς καὶ αὐχμηρὸς καὶ ἀνυπόδητος καὶ

d ἄοικος, χαμαιπετὴς ἀεὶ ὢν καὶ ἄστρωτος, ἐπὶ θύραις
καὶ ἐν ὁδοῖς ὑπαίθριος κοιμώμενος, τὴν τῆς μητρὸς
φύσιν ἔχων, ἀεὶ ἐνδείᾳ σύνοικος. κατὰ δὲ αὖ τὸν πα-
τέρα ἐπίβουλός ἐστι τοῖς καλοῖς καὶ τοῖς | ἀγαθοῖς,
ἀνδρεῖος ὢν καὶ ἴτης καὶ σύντονος, θηρευτὴς δεινός,
ἀεί τινας πλέκων μηχανάς, καὶ φρονήσεως ἐπιθυμη-
τὴς καὶ πόριμος, φιλοσοφῶν διὰ παντὸς τοῦ βίου,

e δεινὸς γόης καὶ φαρμακεὺς καὶ σοφιστής· καὶ οὔτε ὡς
ἀθάνατος πέφυκεν οὔτε ὡς θνητός, ἀλλὰ τοτὲ μὲν τῆς
αὐτῆς ἡμέρας θάλλει τε καὶ ζῇ, ὅταν εὐπορήσῃ, τοτὲ

---

88 Porus = "Resource," Metis = "Cunning" (according to Hesiod, *Theogony* 886ff., the first wife of Zeus). Penia = "Poverty."

89 "In relation to," translates the preposition *peri*, a variation
on the usual genitive (cf. also 204b3).This usage may be signifi-

begging, as indeed happens when a party is in progress, and was around the doors.[88] Now Porus, drunk on nectar—for wine did not yet exist—had gone into the garden of Zeus and, overcome with drink, was fast asleep. So Penia through her lack of resource contrived a plan to have a child of Porus, and she lay with him and conceived Love. That is indeed why it was Aphrodite whose attendant and follower Love became, having been conceived on her birthday, and also because he is naturally a lover in relation to beauty,[89] and Aphrodite is beautiful. Inasmuch as he is the son of Porus and Penia this is the situation Love finds himself in: firstly he is always poor, and is far from being delicate and beautiful as most people think, but hard and squalid, unshod and homeless; he always sleeps on the ground without any bedding, he lies in doorways and by the roadside under the open sky; and, naturally taking after his mother, he lives with constant need. But again, taking after his father, he is a schemer for those things which are beautiful and good, being brave, impetuous and intense, a cunning huntsman, always weaving various schemes, desiring understanding and resourceful at acquiring it, a lover of wisdom all his life, a clever magician, a sorcerer, and a sophist.[90] And he has the nature neither of an immortal nor a mortal, but at one moment within the same day he is alive and flourishing when he's

cant in view of what Diotima goes on to say: Eros is, strictly speaking, not love of the beautiful, but of "giving birth in the beautiful" (206e5).

[90] "Sophist" (*sophistēs*) has positive or negative connotations; the name, like "magician, sorcerer," is ambivalent—a force for good or evil.

δὲ ἀποθνήσκει, πάλιν δὲ ἀναβιώσκεται διὰ τὴν τοῦ
πατρὸς φύσιν, τὸ δὲ ποριζόμενον ἀεὶ ὑπεκρεῖ, ὥστε
οὔτε ἀπορεῖ Ἔρως ποτὲ | οὔτε πλουτεῖ, σοφίας τε αὖ
204 καὶ ἀμαθίας ἐν μέσῳ ἐστίν. ἔχει γὰρ ὧδε. θεῶν οὐδεὶς
φιλοσοφεῖ οὐδ' ἐπιθυμεῖ σοφὸς γενέσθαι—ἔστι γάρ—
οὐδ' εἴ τις ἄλλος σοφός, οὐ φιλοσοφεῖ. οὐδ' αὖ οἱ
ἀμαθεῖς φιλοσοφοῦσιν οὐδ' ἐπιθυμοῦσι σοφοὶ γενέ-
σθαι· αὐτὸ γὰρ τοῦτό ἐστι χαλεπὸν ἀμαθία, τὸ μὴ |
ὄντα καλὸν κἀγαθὸν μηδὲ φρόνιμον δοκεῖν αὑτῷ εἶναι
ἱκανόν. οὔκουν ἐπιθυμεῖ ὁ μὴ οἰόμενος ἐνδεὴς εἶναι οὗ
ἂν μὴ οἴηται ἐπιδεῖσθαι.

Τίνες οὖν, ἔφην ἐγώ, ὦ Διοτίμα, οἱ φιλοσοφοῦντες,
εἰ μήτε οἱ σοφοὶ μήτε οἱ ἀμαθεῖς;

b Δῆλον δή, ἔφη, τοῦτό γε ἤδη καὶ παιδί, ὅτι οἱ
μεταξὺ τούτων ἀμφοτέρων, ὧν ἂν εἴη καὶ ὁ Ἔρως.
ἔστιν γὰρ δὴ τῶν καλλίστων ἡ σοφία, Ἔρως δ' ἐστὶν
ἔρως περὶ τὸ καλόν, ὥστε ἀναγκαῖον Ἔρωτα φιλόσο-
φον εἶναι, φιλόσοφον δὲ | ὄντα μεταξὺ εἶναι σοφοῦ
καὶ ἀμαθοῦς. αἰτία δὲ αὐτῷ καὶ τούτων ἡ γένεσις·
πατρὸς μὲν γὰρ σοφοῦ ἐστι καὶ εὐπόρου, μητρὸς δὲ
οὐ σοφῆς καὶ ἀπόρου. ἡ μὲν οὖν φύσις τοῦ δαίμονος,
ὦ φίλε Σώκρατες, αὕτη· ὃν δὲ σὺ ᾠήθης Ἔρωτα εἶναι,
c θαυμαστὸν οὐδὲν ἔπαθες. ᾠήθης δέ, ὡς ἐμοὶ δοκεῖ
τεκμαιρομένη ἐξ ὧν σὺ λέγεις, τὸ ἐρώμενον Ἔρωτα
εἶναι, οὐ τὸ ἐρῶν· διὰ ταῦτά σοι οἶμαι πάγκαλος ἐφαίνετο ὁ Ἔρως. καὶ γὰρ ἔστι τὸ ἐραστὸν τὸ τῷ ὄντι

doing well, at another he dies, but comes to life again because of the nature of his father, but his resources are always slowly ebbing away, so that Love is never without resources at any moment, but neither is he wealthy: again he is in between wisdom and ignorance. You see it's like this: none of the gods is a lover of wisdom and none of them desires to become wise, for they are so: nor, if anyone else is wise, does he love wisdom. Nor again do the ignorant love wisdom or desire to become wise. For this is the real difficulty with ignorance: in not being fine and good nor wise, one thinks oneself quite adequate. So he who does not think he is lacking has no desire for that which he does not think he lacks.'

"'Then who are they, Diotima,' I said, 'who love wisdom, if they are neither the wise nor the ignorant?'

"'Well, that's surely clear by now,' she said, even to a child, that it's those who are in between both of these groups, of whom Love will be one. For wisdom is one of the most beautiful things, and Love is love in relation to the beautiful, so that it must be that Love is a lover of wisdom, and being a lover of wisdom he is in between wise and ignorant. Again, the reason for this is his birth, for he comes from a father who is wise and resourceful, but from a mother who is not wise and has no resources. This then, my dear Socrates, is the nature of the spirit.[91] But as for whom you thought Love to be, there's nothing surprising in the impression you received. It seems to me, judging by what you're telling me, you thought that Love was what is loved, not that which loves. This is the reason I think Love appeared to be most beautiful to you. Indeed it is that

204

b

c

[91] The spirit (*daimōn*) is Love (*Erōs*).

καλὸν καὶ | ἁβρὸν καὶ τέλεον καὶ μακαριστόν· τὸ δέ
γε ἐρῶν ἄλλην ἰδέαν τοιαύτην ἔχον, οἵαν ἐγὼ διῆλ-
θον.

Καὶ ἐγὼ εἶπον, Εἶεν δή, ὦ ξένη, καλῶς γὰρ λέγεις·
τοιοῦτος ὢν ὁ Ἔρως τίνα χρείαν ἔχει τοῖς ἀνθρώποις;

d   Τοῦτο δὴ μετὰ ταῦτ᾽, ἔφη, ὦ Σώκρατες, πειράσομαί
σε διδάξαι. ἔστι μὲν γὰρ δὴ τοιοῦτος καὶ οὕτω γεγονὼς ὁ Ἔρως, ἔστι δὲ τῶν καλῶν, ὡς σὺ φῄς. εἰ δέ τις
ἡμᾶς ἔροιτο· Τί τῶν καλῶν ἐστιν ὁ Ἔρως, ὦ Σώκρα-
τές τε | καὶ Διοτίμα; ὧδε δὲ σαφέστερον· ἐρᾷ ὁ ἐρῶν
τῶν καλῶν· τί ἐρᾷ;

Καὶ ἐγὼ εἶπον ὅτι Γενέσθαι αὑτῷ.

Ἀλλ᾽ ἔτι ποθεῖ, ἔφη, ἡ ἀπόκρισις ἐρώτησιν τοιάνδε·
Τί ἔσται ἐκείνῳ ᾧ ἂν γένηται τὰ καλά; |

Οὐ πάνυ ἔφην ἔτι ἔχειν ἐγὼ πρὸς ταύτην τὴν ἐρώτησιν προχείρως ἀποκρίνασθαι.

e   Ἀλλ᾽, ἔφη, ὥσπερ ἂν εἴ τις μεταβαλὼν ἀντὶ τοῦ
καλοῦ τῷ ἀγαθῷ χρώμενος πυνθάνοιτο· Φέρε, ὦ Σώκρατες, ἐρᾷ ὁ ἐρῶν τῶν ἀγαθῶν· τί ἐρᾷ;

Γενέσθαι, ἦν δ᾽ ἐγώ, αὑτῷ. |

Καὶ τί ἔσται ἐκείνῳ ᾧ ἂν γένηται τἀγαθά;

Τοῦτ᾽ εὐπορώτερον, ἦν δ᾽ ἐγώ, ἔχω ἀποκρίνασθαι,
ὅτι εὐδαίμων ἔσται.

205   Κτήσει γάρ, ἔφη, ἀγαθῶν οἱ εὐδαίμονες εὐδαίμονες, καὶ οὐκέτι προσδεῖ ἐρέσθαι Ἵνα τί δὲ βούλεται

which is loved which is in reality beautiful, gentle, perfect and regarded as most blessed, but that which loves has a different form such as I have explained.'

"And I said: 'good enough, my friend, for you are right. But if this is what Love is like, what use is he to human beings?'

"'This is what I shall try to teach you next, Socrates,' d she said. 'For this is the kind of being Love is and he was born like this. He is, according to you, love of beautiful things. But if someone were to ask us: why is Love of beautiful things, Socrates and Diotima? Or to put it more clearly: the lover of beautiful things loves them; why does he love them?'

"And I said: 'So that he should possess them for himself.'

"'But that answer still requires the following question: what will he who possesses beautiful things gain by it?'

"I said that I didn't yet have a ready answer to this question.

"'Well,' she said, 'it's just as if someone were to make a e change and instead of the "the beautiful" substituted "the good" and inquired: "Come now, Socrates, the lover loves good things: why does he love them?"'

"'To possess them for himself,' I said.

"'And what will he gain if he possesses good things?'

"'That one is easier,' I said, 'I can answer that: he'll be happy.'[92]

"'Yes,' she said, 'for the happy are happy by their pos- 205 session of good things and there is no longer any further

[92] Being "happy" (*eudaimōn*) is an objective state ("fulfilled"); see above, n. 9.

εὐδαίμων εἶναι ὁ βουλόμενος; ἀλλὰ τέλος δοκεῖ ἔχειν
ἡ ἀπόκρισις.

Ἀληθῆ λέγεις, εἶπον ἐγώ. |

Ταύτην δὴ τὴν βούλησιν καὶ τὸν ἔρωτα τοῦτον
πότερα κοινὸν οἴει εἶναι πάντων ἀνθρώπων, καὶ πάντας τἀγαθὰ βούλεσθαι αὐτοῖς εἶναι ἀεί, ἢ πῶς λέγεις;

Οὕτως, ἦν δ' ἐγώ· κοινὸν εἶναι πάντων.

Τί δὴ οὖν, ἔφη, ὦ Σώκρατες, οὐ πάντας ἐρᾶν φαμεν,
εἴπερ γε πάντες τῶν αὐτῶν ἐρῶσι καὶ ἀεί, ἀλλά τινάς
φαμεν ἐρᾶν, τοὺς δ' οὔ;

b   Θαυμάζω, ἦν δ' ἐγώ, καὶ αὐτός.

Ἀλλὰ μὴ θαύμαζ', ἔφη· ἀφελόντες γὰρ ἄρα τοῦ
ἔρωτός | τι εἶδος ὀνομάζομεν, τὸ τοῦ ὅλου ἐπιτιθέντες
ὄνομα, ἔρωτα, τὰ δὲ ἄλλα ἄλλοις καταχρώμεθα ὀνόμασιν.

Ὥσπερ τί; ἦν δ' ἐγώ.

Ὥσπερ τόδε. οἶσθ' ὅτι ποίησίς ἐστί τι πολύ· ἡ γάρ
τοι ἐκ τοῦ μὴ ὄντος εἰς τὸ ὂν ἰόντι ὁτῳοῦν αἰτία πᾶσά
c ἐστι ποίησις, ὥστε καὶ αἱ ὑπὸ πάσαις ταῖς τέχναις
ἐργασίαι ποιήσεις εἰσὶ καὶ οἱ τούτων δημιουργοὶ πάντες ποιηταί.

Ἀληθῆ λέγεις.

Ἀλλ' ὅμως, ἦ δ' ἥ, οἶσθ' ὅτι οὐ καλοῦνται ποιηταὶ
ἀλλὰ | ἄλλα ἔχουσιν ὀνόματα, ἀπὸ δὲ πάσης τῆς ποι-
ήσεως ἓν μόριον ἀφορισθὲν τὸ περὶ τὴν μουσικὴν καὶ
τὰ μέτρα τῷ τοῦ ὅλου ὀνόματι προσαγορεύεται. ποί-

need to ask: To what end does he who wishes it wish to be happy? Well, the answer seems to contain the end of the inquiry.'

"'You're right,' I said.

"'Do you think this wish and this love are common to all people, and do they all wish for good things always for themselves, or what do you say?'

"'Just as you say,' I said, 'it's common to everyone.'

"'So, Socrates,' she said 'why then don't we say all people love, at any rate if, that is, they all love the same things and do so all the time, but we say some love and others don't?'

"'I'm wondering about that myself,' I said.   b

"'Well don't wonder about it,' she said. 'You see we have actually singled out a particular form of love and give it the name of the whole, love; but for other things we use other names.'

"'For example?' I said.

"'Take this case: you know that creation is a complex thing: for after all, that which is the cause of anything whatsoever, moving from nonbeing into being, is, all of it, creation, so that the procedures in all the crafts are cre-   c ative and all their craftsmen are creators.'[93]

"'You're right.'

"'But nevertheless, she said, you know that they are not called creators (poets), but have other names, and from all creativity one section is separated off: the one that deals with music and verse is referred to by the name of the

---

[93] Diotima's argument depends on Greek having the single word for "creation" and "poetry": "Creation" (poetry) = *poiēsis*; "creators (poets)" = *poiētai*; see also c4–9.

ησις γὰρ τοῦτο μόνον καλεῖται, καὶ οἱ ἔχοντες τοῦτο
τὸ μόριον τῆς ποιήσεως ποιηταί. |

Ἀληθῆ λέγεις, ἔφην.

d Οὕτω τοίνυν καὶ περὶ τὸν ἔρωτα. τὸ μὲν κεφάλαιόν
ἐστι πᾶσα ἡ τῶν ἀγαθῶν ἐπιθυμία καὶ τοῦ εὐδαιμονεῖν ὁ "μέγιστός τε καὶ δολερὸς ἔρως" παντί· ἀλλ' οἱ
μὲν ἄλλῃ τρεπόμενοι πολλαχῇ ἐπ' αὐτόν, ἢ κατὰ χρη-
ματισμὸν ἢ κατὰ | φιλογυμναστίαν ἢ κατὰ φιλοσο-
φίαν, οὔτε ἐρᾶν καλοῦνται οὔτε ἐρασταί, οἱ δὲ κατὰ
ἕν τι εἶδος ἰόντες τε καὶ ἐσπουδακότες τὸ τοῦ ὅλου
ὄνομα ἴσχουσιν, ἔρωτά τε καὶ ἐρᾶν καὶ ἐρασταί.

Κινδυνεύεις ἀληθῆ, ἔφην ἐγώ, λέγειν. |

Καὶ λέγεται μέν γέ τις, ἔφη, λόγος, ὡς οἱ ἂν τὸ
e ἥμισυ ἑαυτῶν ζητῶσιν, οὗτοι ἐρῶσιν· ὁ δ' ἐμὸς λόγος
οὔτε ἡμίσεός φησιν εἶναι τὸν ἔρωτα οὔτε ὅλου, ἐὰν
μὴ τυγχάνῃ γέ που, ὦ ἑταῖρε, ἀγαθὸν ὄν, ἐπεὶ αὑτῶν
γε καὶ πόδας καὶ χεῖρας ἐθέλουσιν ἀποτέμνεσθαι οἱ
ἄνθρωποι, ἐὰν αὑτοῖς δοκῇ τὰ | ἑαυτῶν πονηρὰ εἶναι.
οὐ γὰρ τὸ ἑαυτῶν οἶμαι ἕκαστοι ἀσπάζονται, εἰ μὴ εἴ
τις τὸ μὲν ἀγαθὸν οἰκεῖον καλεῖ καὶ ἑαυτοῦ, τὸ δὲ
κακὸν ἀλλότριον· ὡς οὐδέν γε ἄλλο ἐστὶν οὗ ἐρῶσιν
ἄνθρωποι ἢ τοῦ ἀγαθοῦ. ἢ σοὶ δοκοῦσιν;

206 Μὰ Δί' οὐκ ἔμοιγε, ἦν δ' ἐγώ.

---

94 A poetic quotation, source unknown. "Treacherous love,"
possibly because the desire for good things and happiness may be
misdirected.

whole. This is part alone is called poetry, and those who are occupied with this section of creativity are called poets.'

"'You're right,' I said.

"'The case is then similar too regarding love. In general   d every desire for good things and to be happy is "the greatest and treacherous love"[94] for everyone. But those who turn to it in all kinds of different ways, either by making money, or by a passion for physical exercise, or by philosophy, are neither said to be in love, nor are they called lovers, but others who pursue one particular form, and do so seriously, keep the terminology of the whole thing: "love," "to love," and "lovers."'

"'You're probably right,' I said.

"'And the story is told,' she said, 'that those who are seeking the other half of themselves are the ones who love; but my version of the story says love is not of the half, nor   e the whole, unless, my friend, it actually happens to be good, since people are even willing to have their own feet and hands cut off if they think their own are in a bad state. For I don't think that it's that which is their own which either group welcomes unless someone calls "the good" what belongs to him and is his own, and calls "the bad" what does not belong to him, since there is nothing else that people love except the good.[95] Or do you think there is?'

"'Certainly not, by Zeus,' I said.   206

[95] This looks like a critical allusion to Aristophanes' speech at 191d–93d (see Aristophanes' recognition of this at 212c4–6).

Ἆρ' οὖν, ἦ δ' ἥ, οὕτως ἁπλοῦν ἐστι λέγειν ὅτι οἱ ἄνθρωποι τἀγαθοῦ ἐρῶσιν;

Ναί, ἔφην.

Τί δέ; οὐ προσθετέον, ἔφη, ὅτι καὶ εἶναι τὸ ἀγαθὸν αὑτοῖς ἐρῶσιν;

Προσθετέον.

Ἆρ' οὖν, ἔφη, καὶ οὐ μόνον εἶναι, ἀλλὰ καὶ ἀεὶ εἶναι;

Καὶ τοῦτο προσθετέον.

Ἔστιν ἄρα συλλήβδην, ἔφη, ὁ ἔρως τοῦ τὸ ἀγαθὸν αὑτῷ εἶναι ἀεί.

Ἀληθέστατα, ἔφην ἐγώ, λέγεις.

b   Ὅτε δὴ τοῦτο ὁ ἔρως ἐστὶν ἀεί, ἦ δ' ἥ, τῶν τίνα τρόπον διωκόντων αὐτὸ καὶ ἐν τίνι πράξει ἡ σπουδὴ καὶ ἡ σύντασις ἔρως ἂν καλοῖτο; τί τοῦτο τυγχάνει ὂν τὸ ἔργον; ἔχεις εἰπεῖν;

Οὐ μεντἂν σέ, ἔφην ἐγώ, ὦ Διοτίμα, ἐθαύμαζον ἐπὶ σοφίᾳ καὶ ἐφοίτων παρὰ σὲ αὐτὰ ταῦτα μαθησόμενος.

Ἀλλὰ ἐγώ σοι, ἔφη, ἐρῶ. ἔστι γὰρ τοῦτο τόκος ἐν καλῷ καὶ κατὰ τὸ σῶμα καὶ κατὰ τὴν ψυχήν.

Μαντείας, ἦν δ' ἐγώ, δεῖται ὅτι ποτε λέγεις, καὶ οὐ μανθάνω.

c   Ἀλλ' ἐγώ, ἦ δ' ἥ, σαφέστερον ἐρῶ. κυοῦσιν γάρ, ἔφη, ὦ Σώκρατες, πάντες ἄνθρωποι καὶ κατὰ τὸ σῶμα καὶ κατὰ τὴν ψυχήν, καὶ ἐπειδὰν ἔν τινι ἡλικίᾳ γένωνται, τίκτειν ἐπιθυμεῖ ἡμῶν ἡ φύσις. τίκτειν δὲ ἐν μὲν αἰσχρῷ οὐ δύναται, ἐν δὲ τῷ καλῷ. ἡ γὰρ ἀνδρὸς

"'Can it be as simple as this then, she said, to say that people love what is good?'

"'Yes,' I said.

"'But should we not add, she said, that what they also love is that the good should be theirs?'

"'Yes, we must add that.'

"'And not just theirs, but theirs for ever?'

"'Yes, we must add that too.'

"'Then putting all that together, she said, love is desire to possess the good for ever.'

"'You're absolutely right,' I said.

"'Now since this is always what love is,' she said, 'in b what way and in what sphere of activity could the passion and supreme effort of those pursuing it be called love? What actually is this function which it has? Can you tell me?'

"'Well if I could, I assure you I wouldn't be admiring you for your wisdom, Diotima,' I said, 'and I wouldn't be coming here to see you to learn these very things.'

"'Well then I'll tell you, she said. For this activity is giving birth in the beautiful in respect of both the body and the soul.'

"'Whatever you can possibly mean, I said, needs divination and I don't understand.'

"'Well then, she said, I will speak more clearly. You see, c Socrates, she said, all human beings are pregnant both in body and in soul, and when we get to a certain age our nature is to yearn to produce offspring. But to give birth in what is ugly is not possible, but it is in what is beautiful.

καὶ γυναικὸς συνουσία τόκος ἐστίν. ἔστι δὲ τοῦτο
θεῖον τὸ πρᾶγμα, καὶ τοῦτο ἐν θνητῷ ὄντι τῷ ζῴῳ
ἀθάνατον ἔνεστιν, ἡ κύησις καὶ ἡ γέννησις. τὰ δὲ ἐν
τῷ ἀναρμόστῳ ἀδύνατον γενέσθαι. ἀνάρμοστον δ᾽
ἐστὶ τὸ αἰσχρὸν παντὶ τῷ θείῳ, τὸ δὲ καλὸν ἁρμότ-
d τον. Μοῖρα οὖν καὶ Εἰλείθυια ἡ Καλλονή ἐστι τῇ γενέσει. διὰ ταῦτα ὅταν μὲν καλῷ προσπελάζῃ τὸ κυ-
οῦν, ἵλεών τε γίγνεται καὶ εὐφραινόμενον διαχεῖται |
καὶ τίκτει τε καὶ γεννᾷ· ὅταν δὲ αἰσχρῷ, σκυθρωπόν
τε καὶ λυπούμενον συσπειρᾶται καὶ ἀποτρέπεται καὶ
ἀνείλλεται καὶ οὐ γεννᾷ, ἀλλὰ ἴσχον τὸ κύημα χαλεπῶς φέρει. ὅθεν δὴ τῷ κυοῦντί τε καὶ ἤδη σπαργῶντι
πολλὴ ἡ πτοίησις γέγονε περὶ τὸ καλὸν διὰ τὸ μεγά-
e λης ὠδῖνος ἀπολύειν τὸν ἔχοντα. ἔστιν γάρ, ὦ Σώκρατες, ἔφη, οὐ τοῦ καλοῦ ὁ ἔρως, ὡς σὺ οἴει.

Ἀλλὰ τί μήν; |

Τῆς γεννήσεως καὶ τοῦ τόκου ἐν τῷ καλῷ.

Εἶεν, ἦν δ᾽ ἐγώ.

Πάνυ μὲν οὖν, ἔφη. τί δὴ οὖν τῆς γεννήσεως; ὅτι
ἀειγενές ἐστι καὶ ἀθάνατον ὡς θνητῷ ἡ γέννησις.
207 ἀθανασίας δὲ ἀναγκαῖον ἐπιθυμεῖν μετὰ ἀγαθοῦ ἐκ
τῶν ὡμολογημένων, εἴπερ τοῦ ἀγαθοῦ ἑαυτῷ εἶναι ἀεὶ

---

96 Eileithyia was the goddess who oversaw childbirth, with
Moira (Fate) attending, here personified as Beauty (*Kallonē*).

For the intercourse between a man and a woman is a giving birth. This is a divine process, this pregnancy and procreation, and this is an immortal element in the living
creature, despite its mortality. It is impossible for this to
happen where there is discord. And what is in discord with
everything divine is what is ugly; but beauty is in harmony
with it. Now in the process of generation Beauty is Moira   d
and Eileithyia.[96] For these reasons whenever what is pregnant approaches the beautiful, it becomes gracious and
melts[97] with gladness, gives birth and procreates. But
when it comes near the ugly it contracts, sullen and distressed, turns away and shrivels up. It does not give birth
and, holding back the fetus, is much upset. Hence for the
one who is pregnant and already full to bursting, there
comes about much excitement around the beautiful because he who possesses it will release the pregnant one
from the great pangs of childbirth. For love, Socrates, she   e
said is not love of the beautiful, as you think.'

"'But what is it then?'

"'It's of procreation and giving birth in the beautiful.'

"'That may well be so,' I said.

"'Yes it certainly is so,' she said. 'Why then is the object
of love procreation? Because procreation is something
eternal and immortal, as far as can be the case for a mortal.
From what has been agreed[98] there must be a desire for   207
immortality along with the good, if love is always about

[97] Or "is poured out" (*diacheitai*); in the passage as a whole,
Diotima appears to be putting emphasis on the reactions of the
male or the female (or both) to sexual stimulus. See further Sheffield, "Psychic Pregnancy and Platonic Epistemology."

[98] At 206a9–13.

ἔρως ἐστίν. ἀναγκαῖον δὴ ἐκ τούτου τοῦ λόγου καὶ τῆς ἀθανασίας τὸν ἔρωτα εἶναι. |

Ταῦτά τε οὖν πάντα ἐδίδασκέ με, ὁπότε περὶ τῶν ἐρωτικῶν λόγους ποιοῖτο, καί ποτε ἤρετο Τί οἴει, ὦ Σώκρατες, αἴτιον εἶναι τούτου τοῦ ἔρωτος καὶ τῆς ἐπιθυμίας; ἢ οὐκ αἰσθάνῃ ὡς δεινῶς διατίθεται πάντα τὰ θηρία ἐπειδὰν γεννᾶν ἐπιθυμήσῃ, καὶ τὰ πεζὰ καὶ τὰ πτηνά, νοσοῦντά τε πάντα καὶ ἐρωτικῶς διατιθέμενα,

b πρῶτον μὲν περὶ τὸ συμμιγῆναι ἀλλήλοις, ἔπειτα περὶ τὴν τροφὴν τοῦ γενομένου, καὶ ἕτοιμά ἐστιν ὑπὲρ τούτων καὶ διαμάχεσθαι τὰ ἀσθενέστατα τοῖς ἰσχυροτάτοις καὶ ὑπεραποθνήσκειν, καὶ αὐτὰ τῷ | λιμῷ παρατεινόμενα ὥστ' ἐκεῖνα ἐκτρέφειν, καὶ ἄλλο πᾶν ποιοῦντα. τοὺς μὲν γὰρ ἀνθρώπους, ἔφη, οἴοιτ' ἄν τις ἐκ λογισμοῦ ταῦτα ποιεῖν· τὰ δὲ θηρία τίς αἰτία οὕτως

c ἐρωτικῶς διατίθεσθαι; ἔχεις λέγειν;

Καὶ ἐγὼ αὖ ἔλεγον ὅτι οὐκ εἰδείην· ἡ δ' εἶπεν, Διανοῇ οὖν δεινός ποτε γενήσεσθαι τὰ ἐρωτικά, ἐὰν ταῦτα μὴ ἐννοῇς; |

Ἀλλὰ διὰ ταῦτά τοι, ὦ Διοτίμα, ὅπερ νυνδὴ εἶπον, παρὰ σὲ ἥκω, γνοὺς ὅτι διδασκάλων δέομαι. ἀλλά μοι λέγε καὶ τούτων τὴν αἰτίαν καὶ τῶν ἄλλων τῶν περὶ τὰ ἐρωτικά.

Εἰ τοίνυν, ἔφη, πιστεύεις ἐκείνου εἶναι φύσει τὸν ἔρωτα, οὗ πολλάκις ὡμολογήκαμεν, μὴ θαύμαζε. ἐν-

d ταῦθα γὰρ τὸν αὐτὸν ἐκείνῳ λόγον ἡ θνητὴ φύσις ζητεῖ κατὰ τὸ δυνατὸν ἀεί τε εἶναι καὶ ἀθάνατος. δύ-

possession of the good for oneself. Indeed from this argument love must also be love of the eternal.'[99]

"So she taught me all this whenever she held a discussion about matters of love, and once she asked: 'What do you think, Socrates, is the cause of this love and this desire? Or don't you see how terribly all wild animals, both land animals and birds, are affected when they desire to procreate; all are sick and disposed to feel love, firstly   b
when they copulate with each other, and secondly over the feeding of their offspring; and they're prepared to fight it out in defense of them, even the weakest against the strongest, and to die for them, and themselves be worn out with hunger so that they can feed them, and do everything else they have to. One might assume that humans do this, she said, by reasoning, but what is the cause of wild animals becoming affected by love in such a way? Can you tell me?'   c

"Again I was saying I didn't know, but she said: 'Do you then consider one day becoming expert on the subject of love, if you don't think about these things?'

"'Well, that's the very reason, Diotima, as I was saying just now, that I have come to you, knowing that I need teachers. But tell me the reason for this and everything else on the subject of love.'

"'If then, she said, you believe love is by nature the love of that which we have often agreed on,[100] don't be surprised. For here, by the same argument as before,[101] our   d
mortal nature seeks as far as it's possible to exist for ever

[99] In this passage Diotima appears to be advancing the thesis that "immortality" occurs through reproduction and *kleos* ([immortal] "fame"); see also 212a6–7.

[100] For example, at 206e3–7a4.

[101] That is, as in the animal world (207a7–c1 above).

ναται δὲ ταύτῃ μόνον, τῇ γενέσει, ὅτι ἀεὶ καταλείπει
ἕτερον νέον ἀντὶ τοῦ παλαιοῦ, ἐπεὶ καὶ ἐν ᾧ ἓν ἕκα-
στον τῶν ζῴων ζῆν καλεῖται καὶ εἶναι | τὸ αὐτό—οἷον
ἐκ παιδαρίου ὁ αὐτὸς λέγεται ἕως ἂν πρεσβύτης γέ-
νηται· οὗτος μέντοι οὐδέποτε τὰ αὐτὰ ἔχων ἐν αὑτῷ
ὅμως ὁ αὐτὸς καλεῖται, ἀλλὰ νέος ἀεὶ γιγνόμενος, τὰ
δὲ ἀπολλύς, καὶ κατὰ τὰς τρίχας καὶ σάρκα καὶ ὀστᾶ
e καὶ αἷμα καὶ σύμπαν τὸ σῶμα. καὶ μὴ ὅτι κατὰ τὸ
σῶμα, ἀλλὰ καὶ κατὰ τὴν ψυχὴν οἱ τρόποι, τὰ ἤθη,
δόξαι, ἐπιθυμίαι, ἡδοναί, λῦπαι, φόβοι, τούτων ἕκαστα οὐδέποτε τὰ αὐτὰ πάρεστιν ἑκάστῳ, ἀλλὰ τὰ μὲν
γίγνεται, τὰ δὲ ἀπόλλυται. | πολὺ δὲ τούτων ἀτοπώτε-
ρον ἔτι, ὅτι καὶ αἱ ἐπιστῆμαι μὴ ὅτι αἱ μὲν γίγνονται,
208 αἱ δὲ ἀπόλλυνται ἡμῖν, καὶ οὐδέποτε οἱ αὐτοί ἐσμεν
οὐδὲ κατὰ τὰς ἐπιστήμας, ἀλλὰ καὶ μία ἑκάστη τῶν
ἐπιστημῶν ταὐτὸν πάσχει. ὃ γὰρ καλεῖται μελετᾶν,
ὡς ἐξιούσης ἐστὶ τῆς ἐπιστήμης· λήθη γὰρ | ἐπιστή-
μης ἔξοδος, μελέτη δὲ πάλιν καινὴν ἐμποιοῦσα ἀντὶ
τῆς ἀπιούσης μνήμην σῴζει τὴν ἐπιστήμην, ὥστε τὴν
αὐτὴν δοκεῖν εἶναι. τούτῳ γὰρ τῷ τρόπῳ πᾶν τὸ θνητὸν σῴζεται, οὐ τῷ παντάπασιν τὸ αὐτὸ ἀεὶ εἶναι
b ὥσπερ τὸ θεῖον, ἀλλὰ τῷ τὸ ἀπιὸν καὶ παλαιούμενον
ἕτερον νέον ἐγκαταλείπειν οἷον αὐτὸ ἦν. ταύτῃ τῇ μη-
χανῇ, ὦ Σώκρατες, ἔφη, θνητὸν ἀθανασίας μετέχει,
καὶ σῶμα καὶ τἆλλα πάντα· ἀθάνατον δὲ ἄλλῃ. μὴ
οὖν θαύμαζε εἰ τὸ αὑτοῦ | ἀποβλάστημα φύσει πᾶν
τιμᾷ· ἀθανασίας γὰρ χάριν παντὶ αὕτη ἡ σπουδὴ καὶ
ὁ ἔρως ἕπεται.

and be immortal. It's only possible by the following means: by generation, because it always leaves behind something else new in place of the old, since even during the time when each living creature is said to exist and to be the same—for example one is said to be the same person from childhood until becoming an old man; this individual is nevertheless called the same person despite never having the same properties in him, but always coming into new being and losing what he had: in his hair, his flesh, his bones, his blood and the whole of his body. And don't sup- e pose that this happens just in his body, but in his soul also, his ways, habits, beliefs, desires, pleasures, pains, fears: each of these is never present in each individual as the same, but some come into being and others pass away. It's still much stranger than this with our items of knowledge: it's not only that some come into being, and some pass away, and we are never the same, not even in what we 208 know, but also each one of the things we know undergoes the same process. For what is known as practice is so be- cause knowledge leaves us: for forgetting is a departure of knowledge, and practice, bringing back a fresh recollec- tion in place of what is going away, preserves our knowl- edge so that it appears to be the same. For in this way everything mortal is preserved, not by always being the same in every respect, like the divine, but by that which is b departing and aging leaving behind something else new of the same kind as was there before. By this means, Socra- tes,' she said, 'the mortal has share of the immortal, both body and everything else, but what is immortal does so by other means. Then don't be surprised if in nature every- thing values its own offspring, for it is for the sake of im- mortality that this passion and love attends on everything.'

Καὶ ἐγὼ ἀκούσας τὸν λόγον ἐθαύμασά τε καὶ εἶπον
Εἶεν, ἦν δ' ἐγώ, ὦ σοφωτάτη Διοτίμα, ταῦτα ὡς ἀληθῶς οὕτως ἔχει;

c   Καὶ ἥ, ὥσπερ οἱ τέλεοι σοφισταί, Εὖ ἴσθι, ἔφη, ὦ
Σώκρατες· ἐπεί γε καὶ τῶν ἀνθρώπων εἰ ἐθέλεις εἰς
τὴν φιλοτιμίαν βλέψαι, θαυμάζοις ἂν τῆς ἀλογίας
περὶ ἃ ἐγὼ εἴρηκα εἰ μὴ ἐννοεῖς, ἐνθυμηθεὶς ὡς δεινῶς
διάκεινται ἔρωτι | τοῦ ὀνομαστοὶ γενέσθαι "καὶ κλέος
ἐς τὸν ἀεὶ χρόνον ἀθάνατον καταθέσθαι," καὶ ὑπὲρ
τούτου κινδύνους τε κινδυνεύειν ἕτοιμοί εἰσι πάντας
ἔτι μᾶλλον ἢ ὑπὲρ τῶν παίδων, καὶ χρήματα ἀνα-
λίσκειν καὶ πόνους πονεῖν οὑστινασοῦν καὶ ὑπεραπο-
d θνῄσκειν. ἐπεὶ οἴει σύ, ἔφη, Ἄλκηστιν ὑπὲρ Ἀδμήτου
ἀποθανεῖν ἄν, ἢ Ἀχιλλέα Πατρόκλῳ ἐπαποθανεῖν, ἢ
προαποθανεῖν τὸν ὑμέτερον Κόδρον ὑπὲρ τῆς | βασι-
λείας τῶν παίδων, μὴ οἰομένους ἀθάνατον μνήμην
ἀρετῆς πέρι ἑαυτῶν ἔσεσθαι, ἣν νῦν ἡμεῖς ἔχομεν;
πολλοῦ γε δεῖ, ἔφη, ἀλλ' οἶμαι ὑπὲρ ἀρετῆς ἀθανάτου
καὶ τοιαύτης δόξης εὐκλεοῦς πάντες πάντα ποιοῦσιν,
e ὅσῳ ἂν ἀμείνους ὦσι, τοσούτῳ μᾶλλον· τοῦ γὰρ ἀθανάτου ἐρῶσιν. οἱ μὲν οὖν ἐγκύμονες, ἔφη, κατὰ τὰ
σώματα ὄντες πρὸς τὰς γυναῖκας μᾶλλον τρέπονται

---

102 "Accomplished" (*teleios* = "perfect") in the authoritative
tone of her reply, typical, Plato suggests, of sophists, though probably not entirely without the Socratic irony often surrounding this
term.   103 Source unknown.

104 "Valor" = *aretē* (also "immortal virtue," below at d7). Di-

"And when I heard this account I was surprised and I replied: 'Really, I said, most wise Diotima; are things truly like this?'

"And she, like the accomplished sophists, said:[102] 'rest c assured they are, Socrates: with humans too, if in fact you want to examine their love of honor, you would be surprised at their irrationality regarding what I've mentioned, unless you bear in mind, having thought about it, how strangely they are disposed by their love of becoming famous and "of establishing immortal fame for all of time,"[103] and for the sake of this are prepared to risk all dangers even more than in defense of their children, and to spend money and endure any suffering whatsoever and die for it. Do you imagine, she said, that Alcestis would have died d on behalf of Admetus, that Achilles would have followed Patroclus to his death, or your Codrus would have died an early death for the sake of his sons' succession to the kingship, unless they thought that the memory of their own valor would be immortal, which is how we regard it now?[104] Far from it in fact,' she said. 'But I think all do everything for the sake of immortal virtue and this sort of glorious reputation, and the better they are, the more they do this: you see, they are in love with what is immortal. So e those who are pregnant in body,' she said, 'turn rather to

otima (Socrates) implicitly corrects or extends Phaedrus' examples of Alcestis and Achilles (see 179d6–80a1) with reference to their motives for sacrificing their lives for a loved one. Codrus, a mythical king of Athens (Diotima speaks as an outsider), was said to have died to save his city from Dorian invaders, in order to fulfill an oracle that stated that they would only take Athens if they failed to kill the king.

καὶ ταύτῃ ἐρωτικοί εἰσιν, διὰ παιδογονίας ἀθανασίαν
καὶ μνήμην καὶ εὐδαιμονίαν, ὡς οἴονται, αὑτοῖς | εἰς
209 τὸν ἔπειτα χρόνον πάντα ποριζόμενοι· οἱ δὲ κατὰ τὴν
ψυχήν—εἰσὶ γὰρ οὖν, ἔφη, οἳ ἐν ταῖς ψυχαῖς κυοῦσιν
ἔτι μᾶλλον ἢ ἐν τοῖς σώμασιν, ἃ ψυχῇ προσήκει καὶ
κυῆσαι καὶ τεκεῖν· τί οὖν προσήκει; φρόνησίν τε καὶ
τὴν ἄλλην ἀρετήν—ὧν δή εἰσι καὶ οἱ ποιηταὶ πάντες
γεννήτορες καὶ | τῶν δημιουργῶν ὅσοι λέγονται εὑρε-
τικοὶ εἶναι· πολὺ δὲ μεγίστη, ἔφη, καὶ καλλίστη τῆς
φρονήσεως ἡ περὶ τὰ τῶν πόλεών τε καὶ οἰκήσεων
διακόσμησις, ᾗ δὴ ὄνομά ἐστι σωφροσύνη τε καὶ
δικαιοσύνη—τούτων δ᾽ αὖ ὅταν τις ἐκ νέου ἐγκύμων
b ᾖ τὴν ψυχήν, ἤθεος[6] ὢν καὶ ἡκούσης τῆς ἡλικίας,
τίκτειν τε καὶ γεννᾶν ἤδη ἐπιθυμῇ, ζητεῖ δὴ οἶμαι καὶ
οὗτος περιιὼν τὸ καλὸν ἐν ᾧ ἂν γεννήσειεν· ἐν τῷ γὰρ
αἰσχρῷ οὐδέποτε γεννήσει. τά τε οὖν σώματα τὰ |
καλὰ μᾶλλον ἢ τὰ αἰσχρὰ ἀσπάζεται ἅτε κυῶν, καὶ
ἂν ἐντύχῃ ψυχῇ καλῇ καὶ γενναίᾳ καὶ εὐφυεῖ, πάνυ
δὴ ἀσπάζεται τὸ συναμφότερον, καὶ πρὸς τοῦτον τὸν
ἄνθρωπον εὐθὺς εὐπορεῖ λόγων περὶ ἀρετῆς καὶ περὶ
οἷον χρὴ εἶναι τὸν ἄνδρα τὸν ἀγαθὸν καὶ ἃ ἐπιτηδεύ-

---

[6] ἤθεος Parmentier: θεῖος BTW P.Oxy.

---

[105] "Virtue" = *aretē*. Diotima's commendation of poets in a4
appears rather different from Plato's well-documented view of
poetry in general (see *Apology* 22a–c; *Republic* 2, 3, and 10). She
may be contrasting, by implication, present company with Homer
and Hesiod and "the rest of the good poets" who leave "immortal"

women and engage in lovemaking in this way to provide, so they think, immortality and memory and happiness for themselves for all future time through the production of children. But those who are pregnant in their souls—for indeed there are those,' she said, 'who are pregnant in their souls even more than in their bodies with the things which it is appropriate for the soul to conceive and give birth to. So what is "appropriate"? Practical wisdom and the rest of virtue—of which poets are all indeed procreators,[105] and those craftsmen who are said to be inventive. But by far the greatest and finest kind of wisdom,' she said, 'is that concerned with the regulation of cities and households, which has the name moderation and justice—moreover when someone is pregnant with these things in his soul from an early age, being unmarried[106] and just at the right age and is now eager to give birth and produce children, he too, I think, goes round searching for what is beautiful in which to procreate, for he will never do it in what is ugly. So he welcomes beautiful bodies rather than ugly ones, given that he is pregnant, and if he comes upon a soul that is beautiful, noble and gifted, he very much welcomes the combination of body and soul, and immediately he has an abundance of things to say to this individual about virtue and about what sort of thing the good man should be concerned with, and what pursuits he must

209

b

works (209d1–4), or intending "an ironic compliment to Agathon and Aristophanes," Rowe, n. ad loc.

[106] Or, on the MSS reading, "divinely inspired" (see textual note). Burnet (OCT) accepts the modern emendation; both readings are possible, the MSS reading being perhaps more appropriate to the context that follows.

c εἰν, καὶ ἐπιχειρεῖ παιδεύειν. ἁπτόμενος γὰρ οἶμαι τοῦ
καλοῦ καὶ ὁμιλῶν αὐτῷ, ἃ πάλαι ἐκύει τίκτει καὶ
γεννᾷ, καὶ παρὼν καὶ ἀπὼν μεμνημένος, καὶ τὸ γεν-
νηθὲν συνεκτρέφει κοινῇ μετ' ἐκείνου, | ὥστε πολὺ
μείζω κοινωνίαν τῆς τῶν παίδων πρὸς ἀλλήλους οἱ
τοιοῦτοι ἴσχουσι καὶ φιλίαν βεβαιοτέραν, ἅτε καλλι-
όνων καὶ ἀθανατωτέρων παίδων κεκοινωνηκότες. καὶ
πᾶς ἂν δέξαιτο ἑαυτῷ τοιούτους παῖδας μᾶλλον γεγο-
d νέναι ἢ τοὺς ἀνθρωπίνους, καὶ εἰς Ὅμηρον ἀποβλέψας καὶ Ἡσίοδον καὶ τοὺς ἄλλους ποιητὰς τοὺς ἀγαθοὺς ζηλῶν, οἷα ἔκγονα ἑαυτῶν καταλείπουσιν, ἃ
ἐκείνοις ἀθάνατον κλέος καὶ μνήμην παρέχεται αὐτὰ
τοιαῦτα ὄντα· εἰ δὲ βούλει, ἔφη, οἵους Λυκοῦργος |
παῖδας κατελίπετο ἐν Λακεδαίμονι σωτῆρας τῆς Λα-
κεδαίμονος καὶ ὡς ἔπος εἰπεῖν τῆς Ἑλλάδος. τίμιος δὲ
παρ' ὑμῖν καὶ Σόλων διὰ τὴν τῶν νόμων γέννησιν, καὶ
ἄλλοι ἄλλοθι πολλαχοῦ ἄνδρες, καὶ ἐν Ἕλλησι καὶ
e ἐν βαρβάροις, πολλὰ καὶ καλὰ ἀποφηνάμενοι ἔργα,
γεννήσαντες παντοίαν ἀρετήν· ὧν καὶ ἱερὰ πολλὰ ἤδη
γέγονε διὰ τοὺς τοιούτους παῖδας, διὰ δὲ τοὺς ἀνθρω-
πίνους οὐδενός πω. |

Ταῦτα μὲν οὖν τὰ ἐρωτικὰ ἴσως, ὦ Σώκρατες, κἂν

---

[107] Lycurgus, a semilegendary figure, was celebrated as the
creator of Spartan laws and institutions, his "immortal children."
The Spartans (and so, by implication, the laws, Lycurgus' "children") might be said to have "saved Greece" by playing a major
part in its defense against the invading Persians in the first quarter of the fifth century.

follow, and he tries to educate him. For I think in attaching   c
himself to what is beautiful and associating with it he con-
ceives and brings forth that with which he has long been
pregnant, and when he is both with him and mindful of
him when absent, he joins the other in bringing up the
offspring together, so that such people have a much
greater partnership with each other than the one that
comes from children, and a firmer friendship in that they
share more beautiful and more immortal children. And
everyone would prefer to have given birth to such offspring as these for himself rather than human ones, look-   d
ing with envy at Homer and Hesiod and the rest of the
good poets, and the kind of offspring that they have left
behind them, which bring them immortal fame and a me-
morial, in that they are themselves such [i.e. immortal].
And if you like,' she said, 'think of the kind of children
Lycurgus left behind in Lacedaemon [Sparta], who were
saviors of Lacedaemon and, so to speak, of Greece.[107]
Among you, Solon too is respected on account of his procreation of your laws,[108] and many other men in other
places everywhere, both in Greece and among foreigners,
who displayed many fine deeds and gave birth to all kinds   e
of virtue, for whom many shrines have been built because
of such children, but none as yet on account of human
children.

"'Now into these rites of love, Socrates, perhaps you

[108] Solon, an Athenian legislator of the early sixth century,
reshaped the Athenian constitution and remained a central figure
in Athenian social and political tradition.

210 σὺ μυηθείης· τὰ δὲ τέλεα καὶ ἐποπτικά, ὧν ἕνεκα καὶ
ταῦτα ἔστιν, ἐάν τις ὀρθῶς μετίῃ, οὐκ οἶδ᾽ εἰ οἷός τ᾽
ἂν εἴης. ἐρῶ μὲν οὖν, ἔφη, ἐγὼ καὶ προθυμίας οὐδὲν
ἀπολείψω· πειρῶ δὲ ἔπεσθαι, ἂν οἷός τε ᾖς. δεῖ γάρ,
ἔφη, τὸν ὀρθῶς | ἰόντα ἐπὶ τοῦτο τὸ πρᾶγμα ἄρχεσθαι
μὲν νέον ὄντα ἰέναι ἐπὶ τὰ καλὰ σώματα, καὶ πρῶτον
μέν, ἐὰν ὀρθῶς ἡγῆται ὁ ἡγούμενος, ἑνὸς αὐτὸν σώματος ἐρᾶν καὶ ἐνταῦθα γεννᾶν λόγους καλούς, ἔπειτα
δὲ αὐτὸν κατανοῆσαι ὅτι τὸ κάλλος τὸ ἐπὶ ὁτῳοῦν
b σώματι τῷ ἐπὶ ἑτέρῳ σώματι ἀδελφόν ἐστι, καὶ εἰ δεῖ
διώκειν τὸ ἐπ᾽ εἴδει καλόν, πολλὴ ἄνοια μὴ οὐχ ἕν τε
καὶ ταὐτὸν ἡγεῖσθαι τὸ ἐπὶ πᾶσιν τοῖς σώμασι κάλ-
λος· τοῦτο δ᾽ ἐννοήσαντα καταστῆναι πάντων τῶν
καλῶν σωμάτων | ἐραστήν, ἑνὸς δὲ τὸ σφόδρα τοῦτο
χαλάσαι καταφρονήσαντα καὶ σμικρὸν ἡγησάμενον·
μετὰ δὲ ταῦτα τὸ ἐν ταῖς ψυχαῖς κάλλος τιμιώτερον
ἡγήσασθαι τοῦ ἐν τῷ σώματι, ὥστε καὶ ἐὰν ἐπιεικὴς
c ὢν τὴν ψυχήν τις κἂν σμικρὸν ἄνθος ἔχῃ, ἐξαρκεῖν
αὐτῷ καὶ ἐρᾶν καὶ κήδεσθαι καὶ τίκτειν λόγους τοιούτους καὶ ζητεῖν, οἵτινες ποιήσουσι βελτίους τοὺς
νέους, ἵνα ἀναγκασθῇ αὖ θεάσασθαι τὸ ἐν τοῖς ἐπι-
τηδεύμασι καὶ τοῖς νόμοις καλὸν καὶ τοῦτ᾽ ἰδεῖν ὅτι
πᾶν αὐτὸ αὑτῷ | συγγενές ἐστιν, ἵνα τὸ περὶ τὸ σῶμα
καλὸν σμικρόν τι ἡγήσηται εἶναι· μετὰ δὲ τὰ ἐπιτηδεύματα ἐπὶ τὰς ἐπιστήμας ἀγαγεῖν, ἵνα ἴδῃ αὖ ἐπι-

too could be initiated. But into the final mysteries and   210
revelations, for which that foundation exists, if one approaches them in the right way, I don't know if you could
be initiated. Well now, she said, I will tell you, and I'll
spare no effort: you try and follow, if you can.[109] You see,'
she said, 'it's necessary for the one who is approaching this
undertaking in the right way to begin by turning to beautiful bodies when he's young and firstly, if his guide is
leading him in the right way, he must love one body and
with it procreate fine words, and then he must realize for
himself that the beauty that is in any body whatever is akin
to that in any other body, and if he is to pursue beauty in   b
appearance it would be very foolish not to think that the
beauty in all bodies is one and the same. With this in mind
he must make himself a lover of all beautiful bodies and
relax this intense feeling for the one, scorning it and regarding it as of no importance. Following this, he must
consider beauty in souls as of greater value than that in the
body, so that if someone is decent in his soul even though
his physical bloom is slight, it is enough for him to love   c
that person and care for him and give birth to and seek
out such words that will make young men better, in order
that he may in turn be compelled to view the beauty in
pursuits and laws, and perceive that all of this is inter-
related, so that he may consider that the beauty of the
body is something trivial. After these pursuits his guide
must lead him toward types of knowledge so that he can
further contemplate the beauty of its various branches

[109] Socrates/Diotima here uses the imagery of the Eleusinian
Mysteries; the "highest mysteries" represent the final step for the
initiate—the revelation of sacred objects.

d στημῶν κάλλος, καὶ βλέπων πρὸς πολὺ ἤδη τὸ καλὸν
μηκέτι τὸ παρ' ἑνί, ὥσπερ οἰκέτης, ἀγαπῶν παιδαρίου
κάλλος ἢ ἀνθρώπου τινὸς ἢ ἐπιτηδεύματος ἑνός, δουλεύων φαῦλος ᾖ καὶ σμικρολόγος, ἀλλ' ἐπὶ τὸ πολὺ
πέλαγος τετραμμένος τοῦ καλοῦ καὶ θεωρῶν πολλοὺς
| καὶ καλοὺς λόγους καὶ μεγαλοπρεπεῖς τίκτῃ καὶ δια-
νοήματα ἐν φιλοσοφίᾳ ἀφθόνῳ, ἕως ἂν ἐνταῦθα ῥω-
σθεὶς καὶ αὐξηθεὶς κατίδῃ τινὰ ἐπιστήμην μίαν τοι-
e αύτην, ἥ ἐστι καλοῦ τοιοῦδε. πειρῶ δέ μοι, ἔφη, τὸν
νοῦν προσέχειν ὡς οἷόν τε μάλιστα. ὃς γὰρ ἂν μέχρι
ἐνταῦθα πρὸς τὰ ἐρωτικὰ παιδαγωγηθῇ, θεώμενος
ἐφεξῆς τε καὶ ὀρθῶς τὰ καλά, πρὸς τέλος ἤδη ἰὼν τῶν
ἐρωτικῶν ἐξαίφνης κατόψεταί τι θαυμαστὸν | τὴν φύ-
σιν καλόν, τοῦτο ἐκεῖνο, ὦ Σώκρατες, οὗ δὴ ἕνεκεν καὶ
οἱ ἔμπροσθεν πάντες πόνοι ἦσαν, πρῶτον μὲν ἀεὶ ὂν
211 καὶ οὔτε γιγνόμενον οὔτε ἀπολλύμενον, οὔτε αὐξανό-
μενον οὔτε φθίνον, ἔπειτα οὐ τῇ μὲν καλόν, τῇ δ' αἰσχρόν, οὐδὲ τοτὲ μέν, τοτὲ δὲ οὔ, οὐδὲ πρὸς μὲν τὸ
καλόν, πρὸς δὲ τὸ αἰσχρόν, οὐδ' ἔνθα μὲν καλόν, ἔνθα
δὲ αἰσχρόν, ὡς | τισὶ μὲν ὂν καλόν, τισὶ δὲ αἰσχρόν·
οὐδ' αὖ φαντασθήσεται αὐτῷ τὸ καλὸν οἷον πρόσω-
πόν τι οὐδὲ χεῖρες οὐδὲ ἄλλο οὐδὲν ὧν σῶμα μετέχει,
οὐδέ τις λόγος οὐδέ τις ἐπιστήμη, οὐδέ που ὂν ἐν
ἑτέρῳ τινι, οἷον ἐν ζῴῳ ἢ ἐν γῇ ἢ ἐν οὐρανῷ ἢ ἔν τῳ
b ἄλλῳ, ἀλλ' αὐτὸ καθ' αὑτὸ μεθ' αὑτοῦ μονοειδὲς ἀεὶ
ὄν, τὰ δὲ ἄλλα πάντα καλὰ ἐκείνου μετέχοντα τρόπον

and, in looking at beauty now in its many forms, he may d
no longer, like a slave, fix on beauty in one thing, loving
the beauty of a boy, or some individual, or a particular
pursuit, worthless and small-minded in his slavery; but
having turned to the great ocean of beauty and contemplating it may engender many fine and indeed magnificent
words and thoughts in an unlimited love of wisdom, until
there, strengthened and increased in growth, he may catch
sight of a single kind of knowledge which is of a sort of
beauty I shall now describe. Try then,' she said, 'to pay e
attention as carefully as you can. For whoever has been
educated to this point in the subject of love by looking at
beautiful things in order and in the right way, will now
approach the final goal in matters of love, and will suddenly behold a beauty marvelous in its nature, that very
thing, Socrates, for the sake of which all previous efforts
were undertaken: firstly, being eternal, it neither comes
into being nor passes away, it does not increase, nor does 211
it diminish; secondly, it is not beautiful in one respect and
ugly in another; it is not beautiful at one moment and ugly
at another; nor beautiful by one standard and by another
ugly; nor is it beautiful here and ugly there because it is
beautiful to some, ugly to others. Again beauty will not
appear to him like a face or hands or anything else that a
body has a share of, nor like any discourse or piece of
knowledge. Nor do I think it exists in anything else, such
as in a living being either on the ground or in the sky, or
in any other thing, but alone by itself with itself it is an b
eternal single form,[110] but all other beautiful things share

[110] A characteristic Platonic description of the Beautiful and
other Forms (see, e.g., *Phaedo* 78d–e).

τινὰ τοιοῦτον, οἷον γιγνομένων τε τῶν ἄλλων καὶ
ἀπολλυμένων μηδὲν ἐκεῖνο μήτε τι πλέον μήτε ἔλατ-
τον γίγνεσθαι μηδὲ | πάσχειν μηδέν. ὅταν δή τις ἀπὸ
τῶνδε διὰ τὸ ὀρθῶς παιδεραστεῖν ἐπανιὼν ἐκεῖνο τὸ
καλὸν ἄρχηται καθορᾶν, σχεδὸν ἄν τι ἅπτοιτο τοῦ
τέλους. τοῦτο γὰρ δή ἐστι τὸ ὀρθῶς ἐπὶ τὰ ἐρωτικὰ
c ἰέναι ἢ ὑπ' ἄλλου ἄγεσθαι, ἀρχόμενον ἀπὸ τῶνδε τῶν
καλῶν ἐκείνου ἕνεκα τοῦ καλοῦ ἀεὶ ἐπανιέναι, ὥσπερ
ἐπαναβασμοῖς χρώμενον, ἀπὸ ἑνὸς ἐπὶ δύο καὶ ἀπὸ
δυοῖν ἐπὶ πάντα τὰ καλὰ σώματα, καὶ ἀπὸ τῶν καλῶν
| σωμάτων ἐπὶ τὰ καλὰ ἐπιτηδεύματα, καὶ ἀπὸ τῶν
ἐπιτηδευμάτων ἐπὶ τὰ καλὰ μαθήματα, καὶ ἀπὸ τῶν
μαθημάτων ἐπ' ἐκεῖνο τὸ μάθημα τελευτῆσαι, ὅ ἐστιν
οὐκ ἄλλου ἢ αὐτοῦ ἐκείνου τοῦ καλοῦ μάθημα, καὶ
d γνῷ αὐτὸ τελευτῶν ὃ ἔστι καλόν. ἐνταῦθα τοῦ βίου,
ὦ φίλε Σώκρατες, ἔφη ἡ Μαντινικὴ ξένη, εἴπερ που
ἄλλοθι, βιωτὸν ἀνθρώπῳ, θεωμένῳ αὐτὸ τὸ καλόν. ὃ
ἐάν ποτε ἴδῃς, οὐ κατὰ χρυσίον τε καὶ ἐσθῆτα καὶ
τοὺς καλοὺς παῖδάς τε καὶ νεανίσκους δόξει σοι | εἶ-
ναι, οὓς νῦν ὁρῶν ἐκπέπληξαι καὶ ἕτοιμος εἶ καὶ σὺ
καὶ ἄλλοι πολλοί, ὁρῶντες τὰ παιδικὰ καὶ συνόντες
ἀεὶ αὐτοῖς, εἴ πως οἷόν τ' ἦν, μήτ' ἐσθίειν μήτε πίνειν,
ἀλλὰ θεᾶσθαι μόνον καὶ συνεῖναι. τί δῆτα, ἔφη, οἰόμεθα, εἴ τῳ γένοιτο αὐτὸ τὸ καλὸν ἰδεῖν εἰλικρινές,
e καθαρόν, ἄμεικτον, ἀλλὰ μὴ ἀνάπλεων σαρκῶν τε
ἀνθρωπίνων καὶ χρωμάτων καὶ ἄλλης πολλῆς φλυα-
ρίας θνητῆς, ἀλλ' αὐτὸ τὸ θεῖον καλὸν δύναιτο μονο-
212 ειδὲς κατιδεῖν; ἆρ' οἴει, ἔφη, φαῦλον βίον γίγνεσθαι

in it in such a way that, while other things come into being and pass away, it does not become more or less in any way, nor is it affected at all. When someone, because he is a lover of boys in the right way, ascends from these stages and begins to catch sight of that beauty, he will have almost reached his goal. For this is the correct way to approach the subject of love, or to be led by another, starting c from these beautiful things here, forever passing upward for the sake of that beauty, using these as ascending steps from one to two, and from two to all beautiful bodies, and from beautiful bodies to beautiful pursuits, and from pursuits to beautiful kinds of learning and from learning ending with that form of learning which is the learning of nothing other than that beauty itself, so that he may finally know what beauty itself is. In this region of life, if anywhere, my dear Socrates, said the visitor from Mantinea, d a man should live, contemplating beauty itself. If you ever see this you will think there is no comparison with gold, clothing, the beautiful boys and youths who now leave you transfixed when you look at them, and you are ready, as are many others, so long as you can see your loved ones and be with them always, neither to eat nor drink if somehow it were possible, but only gaze at them and be with them. What do we think then, she said, if it happened that someone could see actual beauty, simple, pure, unalloyed, and not defiled by human flesh and color and all the rest e of mortal trivia, but he was able to behold divine beauty itself in its simple form? Do you think, she said, that it's a 212

PLATO

ἐκεῖσε βλέποντος ἀνθρώπου καὶ ἐκεῖνο ᾧ δεῖ θεωμέ-
νου καὶ συνόντος αὐτῷ; ἢ οὐκ ἐνθυμῇ, ἔφη, ὅτι ἐνταῦθα αὐτῷ μοναχοῦ γενήσεται, ὁρῶντι ᾧ ὁρατὸν τὸ
καλόν, τίκτειν οὐκ εἴδωλα ἀρετῆς, ἅτε οὐκ εἰδώλου
ἐφαπτομένῳ, | ἀλλὰ ἀληθῆ, ἅτε τοῦ ἀληθοῦς ἐφαπτο-
μένῳ· τεκόντι δὲ ἀρετὴν ἀληθῆ καὶ θρεψαμένῳ ὑπάρχει θεοφιλεῖ γενέσθαι, καὶ εἴπέρ τῳ ἄλλῳ ἀνθρώπων
ἀθανάτῳ καὶ ἐκείνῳ;

b   Ταῦτα δή, ὦ Φαῖδρέ τε καὶ οἱ ἄλλοι, ἔφη μὲν Διοτίμα, πέπεισμαι δ᾽ ἐγώ· πεπεισμένος δὲ πειρῶμαι καὶ
τοὺς ἄλλους πείθειν ὅτι τούτου τοῦ κτήματος τῇ ἀν-
θρωπείᾳ φύσει συνεργὸν ἀμείνω Ἔρωτος οὐκ ἄν τις
ῥᾳδίως λάβοι. διὸ δὴ | ἔγωγέ φημι χρῆναι πάντα ἄν-
δρα τὸν Ἔρωτα τιμᾶν, καὶ αὐτὸς τιμῶ τὰ ἐρωτικὰ καὶ
διαφερόντως ἀσκῶ, καὶ τοῖς ἄλλοις παρακελεύομαι,
καὶ νῦν τε καὶ ἀεὶ ἐγκωμιάζω τὴν δύναμιν καὶ ἀν-
c   δρείαν τοῦ Ἔρωτος καθ᾽ ὅσον οἷός τ᾽ εἰμί. τοῦτον οὖν
τὸν λόγον, ὦ Φαῖδρε, εἰ μὲν βούλει, ὡς ἐγκώμιον εἰς
Ἔρωτα νόμισον εἰρῆσθαι, εἰ δέ, ὅτι καὶ ὅπῃ χαίρεις
ὀνομάζων, τοῦτο ὀνόμαζε.

Εἰπόντος δὲ ταῦτα τοῦ Σωκράτους τοὺς μὲν ἐπαι-
νεῖν, τὸν | δὲ Ἀριστοφάνη λέγειν τι ἐπιχειρεῖν, ὅτι
ἐμνήσθη αὐτοῦ λέγων ὁ Σωκράτης περὶ τοῦ λόγου·
καὶ ἐξαίφνης τὴν αὔλειον θύραν κρουομένην πολὺν

111 That is, the soul (*psyche*) or the mind (*nous*).
112 See 205d10–e7 and n. 95 above for the indirect reference

278

worthless life if a man looks in that direction and contemplates it with the part with which he must contemplate it[111] and be in its company? Or do you not conclude, she said, that only there will it become possible for him, seeing beauty with the means that make it visible, to give birth not to images of virtue, in that he is not grasping an image, but to true virtue, because he is grasping the truth, and after bringing forth true virtue and nurturing it, it's possible to become one who is loved by the gods, and for that man too, if possible for any human, to be immortal?'

"This then, Phaedrus, and the rest of you, is what Diotima said, and I am convinced by it. Having been persuaded I try to persuade others too that in acquiring this possession one could not easily gain a better partner for human nature than Love. Therefore I declare that every man must honor Love and I myself respect all that is to do with love and practice it above all else, and I encourage everyone else to do so too; both now and always, I praise the power and courage of Love as much as I can. So, Phaedrus, consider this speech, if you will, delivered as my encomium of Love, or if not, call it whatever and in whatever way you like." ·

When Socrates had finished, Aristodemus said the others were praising him, but Aristophanes tried to say something because in his speech Socrates had made a reference to his own speech.[112] Suddenly a knocking on the court-

to Aristophanes' speech. It would appear from Aristophanes' comment here that Plato intends us (and probably his audience) to assume that what "Diotima" says is basically Socrates' own creation.

ψόφον παρασχεῖν ὡς κωμαστῶν, καὶ αὐλητρίδος φωνὴν ἀκούειν. τὸν οὖν Ἀγάθωνα, Παῖδες, φάναι, οὐ
d σκέψεσθε; καὶ ἐὰν μέν τις τῶν ἐπιτηδείων ᾖ, καλεῖτε·
εἰ δὲ μή, λέγετε ὅτι οὐ πίνομεν ἀλλ' ἀναπαυόμεθα
ἤδη.

Καὶ οὐ πολὺ ὕστερον Ἀλκιβιάδου τὴν φωνὴν ἀκούειν ἐν τῇ αὐλῇ σφόδρα μεθύοντος καὶ μέγα βοῶντος,
ἐρωτῶντος | ὅπου Ἀγάθων καὶ κελεύοντος ἄγειν παρ'
Ἀγάθωνα. ἄγειν οὖν αὐτὸν παρὰ σφᾶς τήν τε αὐλητρίδα ὑπολαβοῦσαν καὶ ἄλλους τινὰς τῶν ἀκολού-
θων, καὶ ἐπιστῆναι ἐπὶ τὰς θύρας ἐστεφανωμένον
e αὐτὸν κιττοῦ τέ τινι στεφάνῳ δασεῖ καὶ ἴων, καὶ ταινίας ἔχοντα ἐπὶ τῆς κεφαλῆς πάνυ πολλάς, καὶ εἰπεῖν·
Ἄνδρες, χαίρετε· μεθύοντα ἄνδρα πάνυ σφόδρα δέξε-
σθε συμπότην, ἢ ἀπίωμεν ἀναδήσαντες μόνον Ἀγά-
θωνα, | ἐφ' ᾧπερ ἤλθομεν; ἐγὼ γάρ τοι, φάναι, χθὲς
μὲν οὐχ οἷός τ' ἐγενόμην ἀφικέσθαι, νῦν δὲ ἥκω ἐπὶ
τῇ κεφαλῇ ἔχων τὰς ταινίας, ἵνα ἀπὸ τῆς ἐμῆς κεφαλῆς τὴν τοῦ σοφωτάτου καὶ καλλίστου κεφαλὴν
ἐὰν εἴπω οὑτωσὶ[7] ἀναδήσω. ἆρα καταγελάσεσθέ μου
ὡς μεθύοντος; ἐγὼ δέ, κἂν ὑμεῖς γελᾶτε, ὅμως εὖ οἶδ'
213 ὅτι ἀληθῆ λέγω. ἀλλά μοι λέγετε αὐτόθεν, ἐπὶ ῥητοῖς
εἰσίω ἢ μή; συμπίεσθε ἢ οὔ;

Πάντας οὖν ἀναθορυβῆσαι καὶ κελεύειν εἰσιέναι
καὶ κατακλίνεσθαι, καὶ τὸν Ἀγάθωνα καλεῖν αὐτόν.
καὶ τὸν | ἰέναι ἀγόμενον ὑπὸ τῶν ἀνθρώπων, καὶ περι-

[7] ἐὰν εἴπω οὑτωσὶ BT P.Oxy.: ἀνειπὼν οὑτωσὶ Winckelmann

yard door produced a great amount of noise as if there were revelers and they heard the voice of a flute girl. So Agathon said: "You slaves, won't you go and look? And if   d it's one of our circle, invite him in. And if it isn't, say we're not drinking, but going off to bed right now."

And not much after this they heard the voice of Alcibiades in the courtyard, very drunk and shouting loudly, asking where Agathon was and ordering them to take him to Agathon. So the flute girl who was propping him up, and several others of his attendants led him into the party and he stood by the doors crowned with a thick garland of ivy and violets and with a large bunch of ribbons on his   e head, and he said: "Greetings gentlemen: will you receive a very very drunken man as your fellow imbiber, or are we to go away after we've just tied a ribbon on Agathon's head, which is the reason we've come? You see, he said, I couldn't make it yesterday, but now I've come with ribbons on my head so that I may take them from my head and adorn the head of the wisest and most beautiful man, if I may speak of him thus.[113] So are you going to laugh at me because I'm drunk? Even if you are laughing, never mind, I know full well that I'm telling the truth. But tell me here   213 and now, am I to enter on my conditions or not? Will you drink with me or not?"

So everyone burst out shouting and bade him come in and find a place to recline, and Agathon called to him. He came in led by his fellows, and because he was unwinding

[113] Translating the MSS (Burnet's OCT). Most editors prefer Winkelmann's amendment (see textual note) "proclaiming him thus."

αἱρούμενον ἅμα τὰς ταινίας ὡς ἀναδήσοντα, ἐπίπρο-
σθε τῶν ὀφθαλμῶν ἔχοντα οὐ κατιδεῖν τὸν Σωκράτη,
ἀλλὰ καθίζεσθαι παρὰ τὸν Ἀγάθωνα ἐν μέσῳ Σωκράτους τε καὶ ἐκείνου· παραχωρῆσαι γὰρ τὸν Σωκράτη
b ὡς ἐκεῖνον κατιδεῖν. παρακαθεζόμενον δὲ αὐτὸν ἀσπά-
ζεσθαί τε τὸν Ἀγάθωνα καὶ ἀναδεῖν.

Εἰπεῖν οὖν τὸν Ἀγάθωνα Ὑπολύετε, παῖδες, Ἀλκι-
βιάδην, | ἵνα ἐκ τρίτων κατακέηται.

Πάνυ γε, εἰπεῖν τὸν Ἀλκιβιάδην· ἀλλὰ τίς ἡμῖν ὅδε
τρίτος συμπότης; καὶ ἅμα μεταστρεφόμενον αὐτὸν
ὁρᾶν τὸν Σωκράτη, ἰδόντα δὲ ἀναπηδῆσαι καὶ εἰπεῖν
Ὦ Ἡράκλεις, τουτὶ τί ἦν; Σωκράτης οὗτος; ἐλλοχῶν
αὖ με ἐνταῦθα κατέκεισο, ὥσπερ εἰώθεις ἐξαίφνης
c ἀναφαίνεσθαι ὅπου ἐγὼ ᾤμην ἥκιστά σε ἔσεσθαι. καὶ
νῦν τί ἥκεις; καὶ τί αὖ ἐνταῦθα κατεκλίνης; ὡς οὐ
παρὰ Ἀριστοφάνει οὐδὲ εἴ τις ἄλλος γελοῖος ἔστι τε
καὶ βούλεται, ἀλλὰ διεμηχανήσω ὅπως παρὰ | τῷ
καλλίστῳ τῶν ἔνδον κατακείσῃ.

Καὶ τὸν Σωκράτη, Ἀγάθων, φάναι, ὅρα εἴ μοι
ἐπαμύνεις· ὡς ἐμοὶ ὁ τούτου ἔρως τοῦ ἀνθρώπου οὐ
φαῦλον πρᾶγμα γέγονεν. ἀπ᾽ ἐκείνου γὰρ τοῦ χρόνου,
d ἀφ᾽ οὗ τούτου ἠράσθην, οὐκέτι ἔξεστίν μοι οὔτε
προσβλέψαι οὔτε διαλεχθῆναι καλῷ οὐδ᾽ ἑνί, ἢ οὑτοσὶ
ζηλοτυπῶν με καὶ φθονῶν θαυμαστὰ ἐργάζεται καὶ
λοιδορεῖταί τε καὶ τὼ χεῖρε μόγις ἀπέχεται. ὅρα οὖν
μή τι καὶ νῦν ἐργάσηται, ἀλλὰ διάλλαξον | ἡμᾶς, ἢ
ἐὰν ἐπιχειρῇ βιάζεσθαι, ἐπάμυνε, ὡς ἐγὼ τὴν τούτου
μανίαν τε καὶ φιλεραστίαν πάνυ ὀρρωδῶ.

the ribbons at the same time so he could adorn Agathon and was holding them in front of his eyes, he didn't notice Socrates, but sat down next to Agathon in between Socrates and him, for Socrates had moved over when he caught sight of him. So sitting there beside him he embraced b Agathon and tied the ribbons on him.

So Agathon said: "Slaves, take Alcibiades' shoes off so he can recline and make a third with us."

"Certainly," said Alcibiades, "but who is this third member of our drinking group?" And turning round as he said this he saw Socrates, and on seeing him he jumped up and said: "Heracles! What's this? Socrates here? You were there lying in ambush again, so you could suddenly appear, as you were accustomed to do, where I least thought you'd be. So why have you come now? What's more, why are you c lying here? It wasn't to be next to Aristophanes, nor indeed anyone else who is laughable and willing to be so, but you've wangled it so you're reclining next to the best looking of those in the room."[114]

Socrates said: "Agathon, see if you can defend me, as my love for this fellow has become no light matter. You see from that time when I fell in love with him it's no longer d been possible for me to cast a look at or talk to a single good-looking man at all without this fellow here getting jealous and resentful, and he does the most extraordinary things; he abuses me and can hardly keep his hands off me. See to it then that he doesn't do anything now, but reconcile us, or if he tries to resort to brute force, keep him off as I'm really terrified of his madness and passion for being loved."

---

[114] From this byplay (213a3–d6), we gather that Agathon's couch could hold three people (see also 222e3ff.).

Ἀλλ' οὐκ ἔστι, φάναι τὸν Ἀλκιβιάδην, ἐμοὶ καὶ σοὶ
διαλλαγή. ἀλλὰ τούτων μὲν εἰς αὖθίς σε τιμωρήσο-
e μαι· νῦν δέ μοι, Ἀγάθων, φάναι, μετάδος τῶν ταινιῶν,
ἵνα ἀναδήσω καὶ τὴν τούτου ταυτηνὶ τὴν θαυμαστὴν
κεφαλήν, καὶ μή μοι μέμφηται ὅτι σὲ μὲν ἀνέδησα,
αὐτὸν δὲ νικῶντα ἐν λόγοις πάντας ἀνθρώπους, οὐ
μόνον πρῴην ὥσπερ σύ, ἀλλ' ἀεί, | ἔπειτα οὐκ ἀνέ-
δησα. καὶ ἅμ' αὐτὸν λαβόντα τῶν ταινιῶν ἀναδεῖν τὸν
Σωκράτη καὶ κατακλίνεσθαι.

Ἐπειδὴ δὲ κατεκλίνη, εἰπεῖν· Εἶεν δή, ἄνδρες· δο-
κεῖτε γάρ μοι νήφειν. οὐκ ἐπιτρεπτέον οὖν ὑμῖν, ἀλλὰ
ποτέον· ὡμολόγηται γὰρ ταῦθ' ἡμῖν. ἄρχοντα οὖν
αἱροῦμαι τῆς | πόσεως, ἕως ἂν ὑμεῖς ἱκανῶς πίητε,
ἐμαυτόν. ἀλλὰ φερέτω, Ἀγάθων, εἴ τι ἔστιν ἔκπωμα
μέγα. μᾶλλον δὲ οὐδὲν δεῖ, ἀλλὰ φέρε, παῖ, φάναι,
τὸν ψυκτῆρα ἐκεῖνον, ἰδόντα αὐτὸν πλέον ἢ ὀκτὼ κο-
214 τύλας χωροῦντα. τοῦτον ἐμπλησάμενον πρῶτον μὲν
αὐτὸν ἐκπιεῖν, ἔπειτα τῷ Σωκράτει κελεύειν ἐγχεῖν καὶ
ἅμα εἰπεῖν· Πρὸς μὲν Σωκράτη, ὦ ἄνδρες, τὸ σόφισμά
μοι οὐδέν· ὁπόσον γὰρ ἂν κελεύῃ τις, τοσοῦτον | ἐκ-
πιὼν οὐδὲν μᾶλλον μή ποτε μεθυσθῇ.

Τὸν μὲν οὖν Σωκράτη ἐγχέαντος τοῦ παιδὸς πίνειν·
τὸν δ' Ἐρυξίμαχον Πῶς οὖν, φάναι, ὦ Ἀλκιβιάδη,
b ποιοῦμεν; οὕτως οὔτε τι λέγομεν ἐπὶ τῇ κύλικι οὔτε τι
ᾄδομεν, ἀλλ' ἀτεχνῶς ὥσπερ οἱ διψῶντες πιόμεθα;

Τὸν οὖν Ἀλκιβιάδην εἰπεῖν· Ὦ Ἐρυξίμαχε, βέλ-
τιστε βελτίστου πατρὸς καὶ σωφρονεστάτου, χαῖρε. |

"Well there's no reconciling me and you, said Alcibiades. But I shall get my revenge on you for this another time; but now, Agathon, give me back some of your ribbons so I can tie some on the wonderful head of this man too. And don't let him reproach me that I tied a ribbon on you, when he defeats all men with words, not only the day before yesterday as you did, but always—and despite that, I didn't crown him." And saying this he took some ribbons and tied them on Socrates and then lay down. e

When he had lain down, he said: "Well now gentlemen, you seem to me to be sober. Now this cannot be entrusted to you, but you must drink, for this was what we agreed. I therefore appoint as master of the drinks until you have drunk enough—myself. Well, Agathon, if you've got a large drinking cup, let it be brought out. Better still, there's no need; slave, fetch that wine cooler," he said, seeing that it had room for more than eight measures.[115] When this had been filled, he first drank it off himself and 214 then told them to fill it up for Socrates and at the same time he said: "Against Socrates, gentlemen, my trick is of no use, for however much anyone tells him to drink, that much he drinks without ever getting more drunk."

So when the slave filled it up, Socrates drank; and Eryximachus said: "so what are we doing, Alcibiades? Are b we not talking or singing anything over the wine cup, but are we simply going to drink like men with a thirst?"

At this, Alcibiades said: "Eryximachus! best son of the best and most temperate father, greetings!"

[115] Eight *kotulai* (i.e., almost two liters).

Καὶ γὰρ σύ, φάναι τὸν Ἐρυξίμαχον· ἀλλὰ τί ποιῶμεν;

Ὅτι ἂν σὺ κελεύῃς. δεῖ γάρ σοι πείθεσθαι·

ἰητρὸς γὰρ ἀνὴρ πολλῶν ἀντάξιος ἄλλων·

ἐπίταττε οὖν ὅτι βούλει.

Ἄκουσον δή, εἰπεῖν τὸν Ἐρυξίμαχον. ἡμῖν πρὶν σὲ
| εἰσελθεῖν ἔδοξε χρῆναι ἐπὶ δεξιὰ ἕκαστον ἐν μέρει
λόγον περὶ Ἔρωτος εἰπεῖν ὡς δύναιτο κάλλιστον, καὶ
c ἐγκωμιάσαι. οἱ μὲν οὖν ἄλλοι πάντες ἡμεῖς εἰρήκα-
μεν· σὺ δ᾽ ἐπειδὴ οὐκ εἴρηκας καὶ ἐκπέπωκας, δίκαιος
εἶ εἰπεῖν, εἰπὼν δὲ ἐπιτάξαι Σωκράτει ὅτι ἂν βούλῃ,
καὶ τοῦτον τῷ ἐπὶ δεξιὰ καὶ οὕτω | τοὺς ἄλλους.

Ἀλλά, φάναι, ὦ Ἐρυξίμαχε, τὸν Ἀλκιβιάδην, καλῶς μὲν λέγεις, μεθύοντα δὲ ἄνδρα παρὰ νηφόντων
λόγους παραβάλλειν μὴ οὐκ ἐξ ἴσου ᾖ. καὶ ἅμα, ὦ
d μακάριε, πείθει τί σε Σωκράτης ὧν ἄρτι εἶπεν; ἢ οἶσθα ὅτι τοὐναντίον ἐστὶ πᾶν ἢ ὃ ἔλεγεν; οὗτος γάρ,
ἐάν τινα ἐγὼ ἐπαινέσω τούτου παρόντος ἢ θεὸν ἢ ἄν-
θρωπον ἄλλον ἢ τοῦτον, οὐκ ἀφέξεταί μου τὼ χεῖρε. |

Οὐκ εὐφημήσεις; φάναι τὸν Σωκράτη.

Μὰ τὸν Ποσειδῶ, εἰπεῖν τὸν Ἀλκιβιάδην, μηδὲν
λέγε πρὸς ταῦτα, ὡς ἐγὼ οὐδ᾽ ἂν ἕνα ἄλλον ἐπαινέ-
σαιμι σοῦ παρόντος.

---

116 Homer, *Iliad* 11.514.
117 See above, 201e10 and n. 85.

"And to you too, said Eryximachus, but what are we to do?"

"Whatever you tell us. We must obey you, you know:"

> 'He who is a doctor is equal in worth to many
>   others'[116]

So arrange it as you will."

"Listen then, said Eryximachus. Before you arrived, we decided that starting from left to right each of us in turn should make the finest speech he could about Love and praise him. Now all the rest of us have made our speeches. But since you haven't spoken and have drained your cup, it's right that you make a speech, and when you've spoken, you can give to Socrates whatever orders you like and he to the next one on his right and so on with the others."   c

"Well, Eryximachus," said Alcibiades, "that's a great idea, but for a drunken man to match his words with sober men I'm afraid would not be fair. And at the same time, my dear friend, does any of what Socrates has just said convince you? Or do you know that everything is the op-   d posite of what he was saying? For this man, if I praise anyone else in his presence, either a god, or a man other than him, won't refrain from laying his hands on me."

"Watch what you're saying,"[117] said Socrates.

"By Poseidon,"[118] said Alcibiades, "don't argue against me on that, as there really isn't any other person I'd praise in your presence."

[118] Swearing by Poseidon is an oath frequently found in comedy, but only here in Plato; there is a suggestion of bullying overtones (see Dover, n. ad loc.).

Ἀλλ' οὕτω ποίει, φάναι τὸν Ἐρυξίμαχον, εἰ βούλει·
| Σωκράτη ἐπαίνεσον.

e Πῶς λέγεις; εἰπεῖν τὸν Ἀλκιβιάδην· δοκεῖ χρῆναι,
ὦ Ἐρυξίμαχε; ἐπιθῶμαι τῷ ἀνδρὶ καὶ τιμωρήσωμαι
ὑμῶν ἐναντίον;

Οὗτος, φάναι τὸν Σωκράτη, τί ἐν νῷ ἔχεις; ἐπὶ τὰ
| γελοιότερά με ἐπαινέσαι; ἢ τί ποιήσεις;

Τἀληθῆ ἐρῶ. ἀλλ' ὅρα εἰ παρίῃς.

Ἀλλὰ μέντοι, φάναι, τά γε ἀληθῆ παρίημι καὶ
κελεύω λέγειν.

Οὐκ ἂν φθάνοιμι, εἰπεῖν τὸν Ἀλκιβιάδην. καὶ μέν-
τοι | οὑτωσὶ ποίησον. ἐάν τι μὴ ἀληθὲς λέγω, μεταξὺ
ἐπιλαβοῦ, ἂν βούλῃ, καὶ εἰπὲ ὅτι τοῦτο ψεύδομαι·
215 ἑκὼν γὰρ εἶναι οὐδὲν ψεύσομαι. ἐὰν μέντοι ἀναμιμνησκόμενος ἄλλο ἄλλοθεν λέγω, μηδὲν θαυμάσῃς· οὐ
γάρ τι ῥᾴδιον τὴν σὴν ἀτοπίαν ὧδ' ἔχοντι εὐπόρως
καὶ ἐφεξῆς καταριθμῆσαι.

Σωκράτη δ' ἐγὼ ἐπαινεῖν, ὦ ἄνδρες, οὕτως ἐπιχει-
ρήσω, | δι' εἰκόνων. οὗτος μὲν οὖν ἴσως οἰήσεται ἐπὶ
τὰ γελοιότερα, ἔσται δ' ἡ εἰκὼν τοῦ ἀληθοῦς ἕνεκα,
οὐ τοῦ γελοίου. φημὶ γὰρ δὴ ὁμοιότατον αὐτὸν εἶναι
τοῖς σιληνοῖς τούτοις τοῖς ἐν τοῖς ἑρμογλυφείοις καθ-
b ημένοις, οὕστινας ἐργάζονται οἱ δημιουργοὶ σύριγ-
γας ἢ αὐλοὺς ἔχοντας, οἳ διχάδε διοιχθέντες φαίνον-
ται ἔνδοθεν ἀγάλματα ἔχοντες θεῶν. καὶ φημὶ αὖ

"Well do it this way, if you wish," said Eryximachus. "Praise Socrates."

"What do you mean?" said Alcibiades. "Do you think I e should, Eryximachus? Am I to set about the man and take my revenge in front of you all?"

"Hey you!" said Socrates, "what do you have in mind? Praise me to make me look even more ridiculous? Or what are you going to do?"

"I shall speak the truth. But see if you'll let me."

"Well, in that case," he replied, "I certainly permit you to tell the truth; indeed I order you to do so."

"I'll start straightaway," said Alcibiades. "Nevertheless do as follows: if I say something that isn't true, interrupt me, if you wish, and say that what I'm saying is false. For I will not knowingly tell a lie. If however in my recollection 215 I speak in a mixed-up fashion, don't be surprised. You see it's not at all easy for someone in my state to recount the details of your singular behavior fluently and in the right order."

The Speech of Alcibiades

"Socrates I shall attempt to praise in the following way, my friends, by means of images. Possibly he'll think it's to make him look more ridiculous, but the image will be in the interests of truth, not ridicule. For I declare that he most closely resembles those figurines of Silenus that sit in sculptors' workshops, the sort which the artists make b holding pipes or *auloi*, and when they are opened out into two halves they are revealed containing statues of gods

289

ἐοικέναι αὐτὸν τῷ σατύρῳ τῷ Μαρσύᾳ. ὅτι μὲν οὖν τό
γε | εἶδος ὅμοιος εἶ τούτοις, ὦ Σώκρατες, οὐδ᾽ αὐτὸς
ἄν που ἀμφισβητήσαις· ὡς δὲ καὶ τἆλλα ἔοικας, μετὰ
τοῦτο ἄκουε. ὑβριστὴς εἶ· ἢ οὔ; ἐὰν γὰρ μὴ ὁμολογῇς,
μάρτυρας παρέξομαι. ἀλλ᾽ οὐκ αὐλητής; πολύ γε θαυ-
μασιώτερος ἐκείνου. ὁ μέν γε δι᾽ ὀργάνων ἐκήλει τοὺς
c   ἀνθρώπους τῇ ἀπὸ τοῦ στόματος δυνάμει, καὶ ἔτι νυνὶ
ὃς ἂν τὰ ἐκείνου αὐλῇ—ἃ γὰρ Ὄλυμπος ηὔλει, Μαρσύου λέγω, τούτου διδάξαντος—τὰ οὖν ἐκείνου ἐάντε
ἀγαθὸς αὐλητὴς αὐλῇ ἐάντε φαύλη αὐλητρίς, | μόνα
κατέχεσθαι ποιεῖ καὶ δηλοῖ τοὺς τῶν θεῶν τε καὶ τελετῶν δεομένους διὰ τὸ θεῖα εἶναι. σὺ δ᾽ ἐκείνου τοσοῦτον μόνον διαφέρεις, ὅτι ἄνευ ὀργάνων ψιλοῖς λό-
d   γοις ταὐτὸν τοῦτο ποιεῖς. ἡμεῖς γοῦν ὅταν μέν του
ἄλλου ἀκούωμεν λέγοντος καὶ πάνυ ἀγαθοῦ ῥήτορος
ἄλλους λόγους, οὐδὲν μέλει ὡς ἔπος εἰπεῖν οὐδενί·
ἐπειδὰν δὲ σοῦ τις ἀκούῃ ἢ τῶν σῶν λόγων ἄλλου
λέγοντος, κἂν πάνυ φαῦλος ᾖ ὁ λέγων, | ἐάντε γυνὴ
ἀκούῃ ἐάντε ἀνὴρ ἐάντε μειράκιον, ἐκπεπληγμένοι
ἐσμὲν καὶ κατεχόμεθα. ἐγὼ γοῦν, ὦ ἄνδρες, εἰ μὴ
ἔμελλον κομιδῇ δόξειν μεθύειν, εἶπον ὀμόσας ἂν ὑμῖν

---

119 "Figurines of Silenus" (a7): Silenuses were portrayed in art
in a similar way to satyrs, as having snub noses and prominent,
bulging eyes, like portraits of Socrates. Marsyas (b4), a satyr (wild
naked creature, human, but with animal features), challenged
Apollo to a music competition and was flayed alive by the god
(Herodotus 7.26.3).

inside. I also claim he resembles the Satyr Marsyas.[119]
Now the fact that you resemble these creatures, at any rate
in appearance, Socrates, I don't think even you would dispute. But to learn how you are like them in other respects,
listen to the following. You treat people with insolence;[120]
is that not so? If you don't agree, I'll produce witnesses.
But you're not an *aulos* player? Yes, you are, and far more
remarkable than Marsyas. For he beguiled people through
instruments by the power which came from his mouth,
and even now whoever plays his *aulos* tunes—for the   c
tunes Olympus used to play I call Marsyas' music, since he
taught Olympus[121]—his tunes then, whether it's a good
aulos player who is playing, or some cheap *aulos* girl, are
the only ones which can hold you in their sway and, on
account of their being divine, reveal those in need of the
gods and their initiation rites. But you differ from him to
this extent only, that you achieve this very same effect in
plain prose without instruments. At any rate whenever we   d
hear someone else, even a very good orator, using words
of a different kind, practically none of us cares in the
slightest. But whenever someone hears you, or someone
else speaking your words, even if he is a very poor speaker,
whether it's a woman who hears you, or a man, or a youth,
we are stunned and spellbound. At any rate, my friends, if
I weren't going to appear to be completely intoxicated, I
would tell you on oath the sort of things I myself have

[120] Socrates is "*hybristēs*," that is, he treats people with insolence or outrageously in argument and in other ways, as Alcibiades goes on to claim in his speech.

[121] Olympus (c2–3) was a mythical figure associated with
Marsyas as inventing the *aulos* and its music.

PLATO

οἷα δὴ πέπονθα αὐτὸς ὑπὸ τῶν τούτου λόγων καὶ
e πάσχω ἔτι καὶ νυνί. ὅταν γὰρ ἀκούω, πολύ μοι μᾶλλον ἢ τῶν κορυβαντιώντων ἥ τε καρδία πηδᾷ καὶ
δάκρυα ἐκχεῖται ὑπὸ τῶν λόγων τῶν τούτου, ὁρῶ δὲ
καὶ ἄλλους παμπόλλους τὰ αὐτὰ πάσχοντας· Περι-
κλέους δὲ ἀκούων καὶ ἄλλων ἀγαθῶν | ῥητόρων εὖ μὲν
ἡγούμην λέγειν, τοιοῦτον δ' οὐδὲν ἔπασχον, οὐδ' ἐτε-
θορύβητό μου ἡ ψυχὴ οὐδ' ἠγανάκτει ὡς ἀνδραποδω-
δῶς διακειμένου, ἀλλ' ὑπὸ τουτουὶ τοῦ Μαρσύου πολλάκις δὴ οὕτω διετέθην ὥστε μοι δόξαι μὴ βιωτὸν
216 εἶναι ἔχοντι ὡς ἔχω. καὶ ταῦτα, ὦ Σώκρατες, οὐκ ἐρεῖς
ὡς οὐκ ἀληθῆ. καὶ ἔτι γε νῦν σύνοιδ' ἐμαυτῷ ὅτι εἰ
ἐθέλοιμι παρέχειν τὰ ὦτα, οὐκ ἂν καρτερήσαιμι ἀλλὰ
ταὐτὰ ἂν πάσχοιμι. ἀναγκάζει | γάρ με ὁμολογεῖν ὅτι
πολλοῦ ἐνδεὴς ὢν αὐτὸς ἔτι ἐμαυτοῦ μὲν ἀμελῶ, τὰ δ'
Ἀθηναίων πράττω. βίᾳ οὖν ὥσπερ ἀπὸ τῶν Σειρήνων
ἐπισχόμενος τὰ ὦτα οἴχομαι φεύγων, ἵνα μὴ αὐτοῦ
καθήμενος παρὰ τούτῳ καταγηράσω. πέπονθα δὲ
b πρὸς τοῦτον μόνον ἀνθρώπων, ὃ οὐκ ἄν τις οἴοιτο ἐν
ἐμοὶ ἐνεῖναι, τὸ αἰσχύνεσθαι ὁντινοῦν· ἐγὼ δὲ τοῦτον
μόνον αἰσχύνομαι. σύνοιδα γὰρ ἐμαυτῷ ἀντιλέγειν
μὲν οὐ δυναμένῳ ὡς οὐ δεῖ ποιεῖν ἃ οὗτος κελεύει,
ἐπειδὰν δὲ ἀπέλθω, | ἡττημένῳ τῆς τιμῆς τῆς ὑπὸ τῶν
πολλῶν. δραπετεύω οὖν αὐτὸν καὶ φεύγω, καὶ ὅταν

122 On powerfully emotional music as an element in religious
cults, associated with such groups as the Corybantes, originally
priests of the Phrygian goddess, Cybele, see *Crito* 54d4–5 and
Ion 534.   123 That is, as a politician and a general.

experienced under the influence of that man's words and that I still experience even now. For whenever I hear him, my heart leaps even more than the Corybantes[122] and the tears flow as a result of his words, and I see countless others undergoing the same. When I heard Pericles and other good orators speaking I thought they spoke well, but I experienced nothing like this, nor was my soul thrown into confusion or annoyed at thinking I was in the condition of a slave; but frequently I was indeed so much in this state under the influence of this Marsyas here, that it seemed to me my life was not worth living in the state I'm in. And this, Socrates, you will not deny as the truth. And even now I am aware that if I were willing to give ear to him, I would not be resolute, but I would experience the same again. For he compels me to admit that despite myself lacking in much it's still myself I neglect, and attend to the affairs of the Athenians.[123] Therefore I forcibly stop my ears and run away from him, as if from the Sirens, to prevent my sitting there and growing old beside him[124] I have experienced this only toward this person, something no one would think I had in me, to be made to feel ashamed in front of somebody, whoever it may be. It's only toward him I feel this. For I am aware that I cannot argue against him or deny that I have to do what he tells me to, and that whenever I leave him I am giving way to my desire for honor from the mass of the people. Therefore I desert him

[124] Just as in Homer, Odysseus' men had to bind Odysseus to the ship's mast as they rowed past the island of the Sirens to prevent him from being seduced and permanently immobilized by the beauty of their song (*Odyssey* 12.177–200), so Alcibiades had to stop his ears to Socrates' seductive words.

ἴδω, αἰσχύνομαι τὰ ὡμολογημένα. καὶ πολλάκις μὲν
c ἡδέως ἂν ἴδοιμι αὐτὸν μὴ ὄντα ἐν ἀνθρώποις· εἰ δ' αὖ
τοῦτο γένοιτο, εὖ οἶδα ὅτι πολὺ μεῖζον ἂν ἀχθοίμην,
ὥστε οὐκ ἔχω ὅτι χρήσωμαι τούτῳ τῷ ἀνθρώπῳ.

Καὶ ὑπὸ μὲν δὴ τῶν αὐλημάτων καὶ ἐγὼ καὶ ἄλλοι
πολλοὶ | τοιαῦτα πεπόνθασιν ὑπὸ τοῦδε τοῦ σατύρου·
ἄλλα δὲ ἐμοῦ ἀκούσατε ὡς ὅμοιός τ' ἐστὶν οἷς ἐγὼ
ἤκασα αὐτὸν καὶ τὴν δύναμιν ὡς θαυμασίαν ἔχει. εὖ
d γὰρ ἴστε ὅτι οὐδεὶς ὑμῶν τοῦτον γιγνώσκει· ἀλλὰ ἐγὼ
δηλώσω, ἐπείπερ ἠρξάμην. ὁρᾶτε γὰρ ὅτι Σωκράτης
ἐρωτικῶς διάκειται τῶν καλῶν καὶ ἀεὶ περὶ τούτους
ἐστὶ καὶ ἐκπέπληκται, καὶ αὖ ἀγνοεῖ πάντα καὶ οὐδὲν
οἶδεν. ὡς τὸ σχῆμα αὐτοῦ τοῦτο οὐ σιληνῶδες; | σφό-
δρα γε. τοῦτο γὰρ οὗτος ἔξωθεν περιβέβληται, ὥσπερ
ὁ γεγλυμμένος σιληνός· ἔνδοθεν δὲ ἀνοιχθεὶς πόσης
οἴεσθε γέμει, ὦ ἄνδρες συμπόται, σωφροσύνης; ἴστε
ὅτι οὔτε εἴ τις καλός ἐστι μέλει αὐτῷ οὐδέν, ἀλλὰ
e καταφρονεῖ τοσοῦτον ὅσον οὐδ' ἂν εἷς οἰηθείη, οὔτ' εἴ
τις πλούσιος, οὔτ' εἰ ἄλλην τινὰ τιμὴν ἔχων τῶν ὑπὸ
πλήθους μακαριζομένων· ἡγεῖται δὲ πάντα ταῦτα τὰ
κτήματα οὐδενὸς ἄξια καὶ ἡμᾶς οὐδὲν εἶναι—λέγω
ὑμῖν—εἰρωνευόμενος δὲ καὶ παίζων πάντα τὸν | βίον
πρὸς τοὺς ἀνθρώπους διατελεῖ. σπουδάσαντος δὲ αὐτοῦ καὶ ἀνοιχθέντος οὐκ οἶδα εἴ τις ἑώρακεν τὰ ἐντὸς

---

125 On Socrates' "ignorance," see *Apology* 21b–22e.

126 "Feigning ignorance" = *eironeia* ("mock modesty" or simply "deception"; not "irony" in the modern sense). See below

like a runaway slave, and whenever I see him I'm ashamed because of the agreements I made with him. Many times I would gladly see him no longer part of the human race, but again if this were to happen, I know very well that my grief would be much greater, so that I don't know how to handle this fellow.

"So this is the way both I and many others have been affected by this Satyr as a result of his *aulos* playing. Well, listen to me when I tell you other ways in which he is like those with whom I compared him, and how extraordinary is the power he has. Be well aware that none of you knows this man. But, seeing that I've started, I will show you. For you see that Socrates has erotic leanings toward handsome young men; he's always around them and is smitten by violent passion, and yet again he is ignorant of everything and knows nothing.[125] As for this appearance of his, isn't this just like Silenus? Every bit of it. You see this is what this man assumes for his outer wrapping, just like the carved Silenus. But inside, once you've opened him up, my fellow drinking partners, can you imagine how full of moderation he is? Let me tell you that if someone is handsome, it matters not a bit to him; on the contrary not a single person can imagine how great is his contempt for it. Nor if someone is wealthy, nor in possession of some other honor of those through which someone is counted as blessed by the majority of people. He considers all these possessions to be worthless and we are of no account—I'm telling you—and he spends his entire life feigning ignorance and playing with people.[126] But when he's serious and opened up, I don't know if anyone has seen the statues

(218d6) and, e.g., Thrasymachus to Socrates at *Republic* 337a. (See Vlastos, "Socratic Irony," in *Socrates*, 21–44).

ἀγάλματα· ἀλλ' ἐγὼ ἤδη ποτ' εἶδον, καί μοι ἔδοξεν
οὕτω θεῖα καὶ χρυσᾶ εἶναι καὶ πάγκαλα καὶ θαυ-
μαστά, ὥστε ποιητέον εἶναι ἔμβραχυ ὅτι κελεύοι Σω-
217 κράτης. ἡγούμενος δὲ αὐτὸν ἐσπουδακέναι ἐπὶ τῇ ἐμῇ
ὥρᾳ ἕρμαιον ἡγησάμην εἶναι καὶ εὐτύχημα ἐμὸν θαυ-
μαστόν, ὡς ὑπάρχον μοι χαρισαμένῳ Σωκράτει πάντ'
| ἀκοῦσαι ὅσαπερ οὗτος ᾔδει· ἐφρόνουν γὰρ δὴ ἐπὶ τῇ
ὥρᾳ θαυμάσιον ὅσον. ταῦτα οὖν διανοηθείς, πρὸ τοῦ
οὐκ εἰωθὼς ἄνευ ἀκολούθου μόνος μετ' αὐτοῦ γίγνεσθαι, τότε ἀποπέμπων τὸν ἀκόλουθον μόνος συνεγιγνόμην—δεῖ γὰρ πρὸς ὑμᾶς πάντα τἀληθῆ εἰπεῖν·
b ἀλλὰ προσέχετε τὸν νοῦν, καὶ εἰ ψεύδομαι, Σώκρατες,
ἐξέλεγχε—συνεγιγνόμην γάρ, ὦ ἄνδρες, μόνος μόνῳ,
καὶ ᾤμην αὐτίκα διαλέξεσθαι αὐτόν μοι ἅπερ ἂν |
ἐραστὴς παιδικοῖς ἐν ἐρημίᾳ διαλεχθείη, καὶ ἔχαιρον.
τούτων δ' οὐ μάλα ἐγίγνετο οὐδέν, ἀλλ' ὥσπερ εἰώθει
διαλεχθεὶς ἄν μοι καὶ συνημερεύσας ᾤχετο ἀπιών.
μετὰ ταῦτα συγγυμνάζεσθαι προυκαλούμην αὐτὸν
c καὶ συνεγυμναζόμην, ὥς τι ἐνταῦθα περανῶν. συνε-
γυμνάζετο οὖν μοι καὶ προσεπάλαιεν πολλάκις οὐδενὸς παρόντος· καὶ τί δεῖ λέγειν; οὐδὲν γάρ μοι πλέον
ἦν. ἐπειδὴ δὲ οὐδαμῇ ταύτῃ ἤνυτον, ἔδοξέ μοι | ἐπιθε-
τέον εἶναι τῷ ἀνδρὶ κατὰ τὸ καρτερὸν καὶ οὐκ ἀνετέον,
ἐπειδήπερ ἐνεκεχειρήκη, ἀλλὰ ἰστέον ἤδη τί ἐστι τὸ
πρᾶγμα. προκαλοῦμαι δὴ αὐτὸν πρὸς τὸ συνδειπνεῖν,
ἀτεχνῶς ὥσπερ ἐραστὴς παιδικοῖς ἐπιβουλεύων. καί
μοι οὐδὲ τοῦτο ταχὺ ὑπήκουσεν, ὅμως δ' οὖν χρόνῳ

within. I did see them once, and it seemed to me they were
so divine and golden, so utterly beautiful and marvelous
that, in brief, I had to do whatever Socrates told me to.
Thinking he was keen on my youthful beauty I thought   217
this was a godsend, and my remarkably good luck that if I
gratified Socrates I could hear everything that he knew. I
assure you I was proud of how wonderful my youthful
charms were. So with this in mind, whereas before this
time I was not in the habit of meeting up with him alone
without an attendant, at this point, dismissing the attendant, I started meeting up with him on my own—you see
I must tell you the whole truth; but you all pay attention   b
and, if I tell a lie, Socrates, tell me I'm wrong—yes, I was
meeting up with him one to one, my friends, and I thought
he would immediately talk to me as a lover would talk to
his loved one alone, and I was delighted. But none of this
happened at all, but he would talk to me as usual and after
spending the day together, he went on his way. After this
I invited him to go and take exercise with me and I exercised with him hoping to achieve something that way. So   c
he exercised and wrestled with me many times with no one
else there. And what must I say? I was no further forward.
Since I was not getting anywhere this way either, I decided
I'd have to go for him by direct assault and not give up,
since I'd started things off; I just had to see what the problem was. I invited him to supper with me, just like a lover
plotting to get his loved one.[127] And he didn't answer very
quickly, yet nevertheless in time he was persuaded to

[127] That is, the reverse of the normal relationship, where the
erastēs (lover) as the older man takes the initiative with the *paidika* (loved one), the younger.

PLATO

d ἐπείσθη. ἐπειδὴ δὲ ἀφίκετο τὸ πρῶτον, δειπνήσας
ἀπιέναι ἐβούλετο. καὶ τότε μὲν αἰσχυνόμενος ἀφῆκα
αὐτόν· αὖθις δ' ἐπιβουλεύσας, ἐπειδὴ ἐδεδειπνήκεμεν
διελεγόμην ἀεὶ πόρρω τῶν νυκτῶν, καὶ ἐπειδὴ | ἐβού-
λετο ἀπιέναι, σκηπτόμενος ὅτι ὀψὲ εἴη, προσηνάγ-
κασα αὐτὸν μένειν. ἀνεπαύετο οὖν ἐν τῇ ἐχομένῃ ἐμοῦ
κλίνῃ, ἐν ᾗπερ ἐδείπνει, καὶ οὐδεὶς ἐν τῷ οἰκήματι
e ἄλλος καθηῦδεν ἢ ἡμεῖς. μέχρι μὲν οὖν δὴ δεῦρο τοῦ
λόγου καλῶς ἂν ἔχοι καὶ πρὸς ὁντινοῦν λέγειν· τὸ δ'
ἐντεῦθεν οὐκ ἄν μου ἠκούσατε λέγοντος, εἰ μὴ πρῶτον
μέν, τὸ λεγόμενον, οἶνος ἄνευ τε παίδων καὶ μετὰ παί-
δων ἦν ἀληθής, ἔπειτα ἀφανίσαι Σωκράτους | ἔργον
ὑπερήφανον εἰς ἔπαινον ἐλθόντα ἄδικόν μοι φαίνεται.
ἔτι δὲ τὸ τοῦ δηχθέντος ὑπὸ τοῦ ἔχεως πάθος κἄμ'
ἔχει. φασὶ γάρ πού τινα τοῦτο παθόντα οὐκ ἐθέλειν
λέγειν οἷον ἦν πλὴν τοῖς δεδηγμένοις, ὡς μόνοις γνω-
σομένοις τε καὶ συγγνωσομένοις εἰ πᾶν ἐτόλμα δρᾶν
218 τε καὶ λέγειν ὑπὸ τῆς ὀδύνης. ἐγὼ οὖν δεδηγμένος τε
ὑπὸ ἀλγεινοτέρου καὶ τὸ ἀλγεινότατον ὧν ἄν τις δη-
χθείη—τὴν καρδίαν γὰρ ἢ ψυχὴν ἢ ὅτι δεῖ αὐτὸ ὀνο-
μάσαι πληγείς τε καὶ δηχθεὶς | ὑπὸ τῶν ἐν φιλοσοφίᾳ
λόγων, οἳ ἔχονται ἐχίδνης ἀγριώτερον, νέου ψυχῆς μὴ
ἀφυοῦς ὅταν λάβωνται, καὶ ποιοῦσι δρᾶν τε καὶ λέγειν ὁτιοῦν—καὶ ὁρῶν αὖ Φαίδρους, Ἀγάθωνας, Ἐρυ-
ξιμάχους, Παυσανίας, Ἀριστοδήμους τε καὶ Ἀριστο-

128 An obscure phrase: there was a proverb "truth comes from

298

come. But when he came the first time, he wanted to leave   d
after the meal. On that occasion I let him go out of shame;
but I came up with another ruse and when we had eaten
dinner I kept talking far into the night, and when he
wanted to go I prevailed upon him to stay, on the excuse
that it was late. So he prepared to take his rest on the
couch next to me where he had taken his meal, and no one
else slept in the room except us. Well up to this point in   e
the story it would have been all right to tell it to anyone,
no matter who. But you wouldn't have heard me recount
what followed, if first of all, as the saying goes, wine didn't
reveal the truth, without and with slaves present,[128] and
secondly, to me it seems wrong to suppress Socrates'
splendidly disdainful treatment, when I've embarked on
my praise of him; and what's more, the feeling you have
when bitten by a snake has got hold of me. For they say, I
think, that someone who has suffered this is unwilling to
say what it was like except to those who have been bitten,
as they would be the only ones who would understand and
excuse him if he brought himself to do and say anything
because of the pain. So for myself, having been bitten by   218
something more painful, and in the most painful place
where one can be bitten—for I was struck and bitten in
the heart or the soul, or whatever we ought to call it, by
words talked about in philosophy which cling much more
savagely than a viper when they seize the soul of a young
man not lacking in natural talent and make him do and
say anything whatever—and moreover seeing people like
Phaedrus, Agathon, Eryximachus, Pausanias, Aristode-

wine and children," and Alcibiades may be somehow playing on
the double meaning of *pais* ="child" and "slave."

299

b φάνας· Σωκράτη δὲ αὐτὸν τί δεῖ λέγειν, καὶ ὅσοι ἄλλοι; πάντες γὰρ κεκοινωνήκατε τῆς φιλοσόφου μανίας τε καὶ βακχείας—διὸ πάντες ἀκούσεσθε· συγγνώσεσθε γὰρ τοῖς τε | τότε πραχθεῖσι καὶ τοῖς νῦν λεγομένοις. οἱ δὲ οἰκέται, καὶ εἴ τις ἄλλος ἐστὶν βέβηλός τε καὶ ἄγροικος, πύλας πάνυ μεγάλας τοῖς ὠσὶν ἐπίθεσθε.

c Ἐπειδὴ γὰρ οὖν, ὦ ἄνδρες, ὅ τε λύχνος ἀπεσβήκει καὶ οἱ παῖδες ἔξω ἦσαν, ἔδοξέ μοι χρῆναι μηδὲν ποικίλλειν πρὸς αὐτόν, ἀλλ᾽ ἐλευθέρως εἰπεῖν ἅ μοι ἐδόκει· καὶ εἶπον κινήσας αὐτόν, Σώκρατες, καθεύδεις;

Οὐ δῆτα, ἦ δ᾽ ὅς. |

Οἶσθα οὖν ἅ μοι δέδοκται;

Τί μάλιστα, ἔφη.

Σὺ ἐμοὶ δοκεῖς, ἦν δ᾽ ἐγώ, ἐμοῦ ἐραστὴς ἄξιος γεγονέναι μόνος, καί μοι φαίνῃ ὀκνεῖν μνησθῆναι πρός με. ἐγὼ δὲ οὑτωσὶ ἔχω· πάνυ ἀνόητον ἡγοῦμαι εἶναι σοὶ μὴ οὐ καὶ | τοῦτο χαρίζεσθαι καὶ εἴ τι ἄλλο ἢ τῆς

d οὐσίας τῆς ἐμῆς δέοιο ἢ τῶν φίλων τῶν ἐμῶν. ἐμοὶ μὲν γὰρ οὐδέν ἐστι πρεσβύτερον τοῦ ὡς ὅτι βέλτιστον ἐμὲ γενέσθαι, τούτου δὲ οἶμαί μοι συλλήπτορα οὐδένα κυριώτερον εἶναι σοῦ. ἐγὼ δὴ τοιούτῳ ἀνδρὶ πολὺ μᾶλλον ἂν μὴ χαριζόμενος αἰσχυνοίμην | τοὺς φρονίμους, ἢ χαριζόμενος τούς τε πολλοὺς καὶ ἄφρονας.

Καὶ οὗτος ἀκούσας μάλα εἰρωνικῶς καὶ σφόδρα ἑαυτοῦ τε καὶ εἰωθότως ἔλεξεν Ὦ φίλε Ἀλκιβιάδη, κινδυνεύεις τῷ ὄντι οὐ φαῦλος εἶναι, εἴπερ ἀληθῆ τυγ-

mus and Aristophanes: and do I have to mention Socrates   b
himself and the rest of you? For you have all participated
in the madness and frenzy of philosophy—so all of you will
hear me out, for you will forgive what was done then and
what is being said now. But you household slaves, and
anyone else uninitiated and vulgar, put pretty large doors
over your ears.

"So then, gentlemen, when the lamp had been extin-
guished and the slave boys were out of the room, I re-   c
solved not to try anything fancy with him, but to declare
openly what I had decided. I nudged him and said: Socrates, are you asleep?"

"Indeed no," he said.

"So do you know what I have decided?"

"What in particular?" he replied.

I said "I think you are the only lover I've had worthy of
me and you appear to be holding back from mentioning it
to me. This is where I stand: I think it is very foolish not
to grant you this favor, or if there is anything else you need
from my property or that of my friends. For nothing is   d
more important to me than for me to become as good as
possible, and in this I don't think anyone is a more capable
partner for me than you. Indeed I would be much more
ashamed in the presence of intelligent people for not
granting my favors to such a man as you than I would if I
did so in front of the very many people who have no
sense."

When he heard this, with his great mock modesty[129]
and in his usual manner so very characteristic of him, he
said: "my dear Alcibiades, it looks as if in actual fact you

[129] See above, n. 126.

e χάνει ὄντα ἃ λέγεις περὶ ἐμοῦ, καί τις ἔστ' ἐν ἐμοὶ
δύναμις δι' ἧς ἂν σὺ γένοιο ἀμείνων· ἀμήχανόν τοι
κάλλος ὁρῴης ἂν ἐν ἐμοὶ καὶ τῆς παρὰ σοὶ εὐμορφίας
πάμπολυ διαφέρον. εἰ δὴ καθορῶν αὐτὸ κοινώσασθαί
τέ μοι ἐπιχειρεῖς καὶ ἀλλάξασθαι κάλλος | ἀντὶ κάλ-
λους, οὐκ ὀλίγῳ μου πλεονεκτεῖν διανοῇ, ἀλλ' ἀντὶ
δόξης ἀλήθειαν καλῶν κτᾶσθαι ἐπιχειρεῖς καὶ τῷ ὄντι
219 "χρύσεα χαλκείων" διαμείβεσθαι νοεῖς. ἀλλ', ὦ μακάριε, ἄμεινον σκόπει, μή σε λανθάνω οὐδὲν ὤν. ἤ τοι
τῆς διανοίας ὄψις ἄρχεται ὀξὺ βλέπειν ὅταν ἡ τῶν
ὀμμάτων τῆς ἀκμῆς λήγειν ἐπιχειρῇ· σὺ δὲ τούτων ἔτι
πόρρω. |

Κἀγὼ ἀκούσας, Τὰ μὲν παρ' ἐμοῦ, ἔφην, ταῦτά
ἐστιν, ὧν οὐδὲν ἄλλως εἴρηται ἢ ὡς διανοοῦμαι· σὺ δὲ
αὐτὸς οὕτω βουλεύου ὅτι σοί τε ἄριστον καὶ ἐμοὶ
ἡγῇ.

Ἀλλ', ἔφη, τοῦτό γ' εὖ λέγεις· ἐν γὰρ τῷ ἐπιόντι
χρόνῳ βουλευόμενοι πράξομεν ὃ ἂν φαίνηται νῷν
περί τε τούτων καὶ περὶ τῶν ἄλλων ἄριστον.

b Ἐγὼ μὲν δὴ ταῦτα ἀκούσας τε καὶ εἰπών, καὶ ἀφεὶς
ὥσπερ βέλη, τετρῶσθαι αὐτὸν ᾤμην· καὶ ἀναστάς γε,
οὐδ' | ἐπιτρέψας τούτῳ εἰπεῖν οὐδὲν ἔτι, ἀμφιέσας τὸ
ἱμάτιον τὸ ἐμαυτοῦ τοῦτον—καὶ γὰρ ἦν χειμών—ὑπὸ
τὸν τρίβωνα κατακλινεὶς τὸν τουτουί, περιβαλὼν τὼ
χεῖρε τούτῳ τῷ δαιμονίῳ ὡς ἀληθῶς καὶ θαυμαστῷ,

---

130 At Homer, Iliad 6.232–36 the Trojan Glaucus gives his

are not worthless if what you're saying about me is actually true, and there is in me some ability to make you better; you would see in me an extraordinary beauty, far superior to the beauty of form that you have. If then in looking at this you are attempting to strike a bargain with me and exchange beauty for beauty, you're thinking of gaining the advantage over me in no small way and are trying to obtain truly beautiful things instead of apparent ones, and you have it in mind to make an exchange which is in reality 'gold for bronze.'[130] Well, my dear boy, have a better look in case you haven't noticed that I'm worthless. I tell you, the sight of the mind begins to see distinctly when that of the eyes starts to decline from its high point. But you're still a long way from there."

When I heard this, I said: "these are my feelings; nothing has been said contrary to my purpose; so it's for you yourself to decide what you think is the best way for both you and me."

"Well, you're right there," he said, "for in the future we shall take counsel and do what appears best to us, both in these and in other matters."

When I'd had my say and heard his reply, having let fly my arrows, as it were, I thought he had been wounded. I got up and without letting him say another word I wrapped this cloak of mine around him—for it was winter—and laid myself down under the threadbare cloak of this man here, and throwing my arms round this godlike and truly mag-

Greek enemy Diomedes golden armor in exchange for bronze. Socrates is saying that, if he actually did possess the qualities Alcibiades attributes to him, this would be gold in exchange for his possession of Alcibiades' beauty, which would be mere bronze.

c κατεκείμην τὴν νύκτα ὅλην. καὶ οὐδὲ ταῦτα αὖ, ὦ Σώκρατες, ἐρεῖς ὅτι ψεύδομαι. ποιήσαντος δὲ δὴ ταῦτα
ἐμοῦ οὗτος τοσοῦτον περιεγένετό τε καὶ κατεφρόνη-
σεν καὶ κατεγέλασεν τῆς ἐμῆς ὥρας καὶ | ὕβρισεν—
καὶ περὶ ἐκεῖνό γε ᾤμην τὶ εἶναι, ὦ ἄνδρες δικασταί·
δικασταὶ γάρ ἐστε τῆς Σωκράτους ὑπερηφανίας—εὖ
γὰρ ἴστε μὰ θεούς, μὰ θεάς, οὐδὲν περιττότερον κατα-
δεδαρθηκὼς ἀνέστην μετὰ Σωκράτους, ἢ εἰ μετὰ πατρὸς καθηῦδον ἢ ἀδελφοῦ πρεσβυτέρου.

d   Τὸ δὴ μετὰ τοῦτο τίνα οἴεσθέ με διάνοιαν ἔχειν,
ἡγούμενον μὲν ἠτιμάσθαι, ἀγάμενον δὲ τὴν τούτου
φύσιν τε καὶ | σωφροσύνην καὶ ἀνδρείαν, ἐντετυχη-
κότα ἀνθρώπῳ τοιούτῳ οἵῳ ἐγὼ οὐκ ἂν ᾤμην ποτ᾽
ἐντυχεῖν εἰς φρόνησιν καὶ εἰς καρτερίαν; ὥστε οὔθ᾽
ὅπως οὖν ὀργιζοίμην εἶχον καὶ ἀποστερηθείην τῆς
τούτου συνουσίας, οὔτε ὅπῃ προσαγαγοίμην αὐτὸν
e ηὐπόρουν. εὖ γὰρ ἤδη ὅτι χρήμασί γε πολὺ μᾶλλον
ἄτρωτος ἦν πανταχῇ ἢ σιδήρῳ ὁ Αἴας, ᾧ τε ᾤμην
αὐτὸν μόνῳ ἁλώσεσθαι, διεπεφεύγει με. ἠπόρουν δή,
καταδεδουλωμένος τε ὑπὸ τοῦ ἀνθρώπου ὡς οὐδεὶς
ὑπ᾽ οὐδενὸς | ἄλλου περιῄα. ταῦτά τε γάρ μοι ἅπαντα
προυγεγόνει, καὶ μετὰ ταῦτα στρατεία ἡμῖν εἰς Πο-
τείδαιαν ἐγένετο κοινὴ καὶ συνεσιτοῦμεν ἐκεῖ. πρῶτον
μὲν οὖν τοῖς πόνοις οὐ μόνον ἐμοῦ περιῆν, ἀλλὰ καὶ

---

131 In 432–430 (i.e., about sixteen to fourteen years before the
dramatic date of the party: Potidaea in Northern Greece was a

nificent man I lay there the whole night through. Now c
you're not going to say I'm telling lies here either, Socrates. So although I had done this, he so much got the better
of me, and scorned and mocked my beauty and treated it
outrageously—and in that respect I really thought I was
something, you gentlemen of the jury; for you are the
judges of Socrates' disdain—for know full well, by the
gods and the goddesses, I got up with nothing out of the
ordinary having happened after I'd slept with Socrates
than if I'd slept with my father or elder brother.

"As to what came after that, what frame of mind do you d
think I was in, on the one hand thinking I had been
snubbed, but on the other admiring the nature of this man
and his self-control and courage, having come upon such
a man with such wisdom and steadfastness as I thought I
would never meet? The result was that there was no way
I could be angry and be deprived of his company, nor
could I find a way to win him over. For I knew perfectly e
well that he was much more completely untouchable by
money than Ajax was by the sword and as for the only way
by which I thought he would be caught, he had escaped
me. Indeed I was at a loss; I went around enslaved by the
fellow as no one had been by any other. For after all this
had happened to me we went on campaign together to
Potidaea and shared the same mess there.[131] Firstly, in
putting up with hardships he was superior not only to me

key strategic city in the lead-up to the Peloponnesian War). Mess-
ing together in this instance seems to have implied personal
friendship, as Alcibiades and Socrates were from different Athenian tribes.

τῶν ἄλλων ἁπάντων—ὁπότ᾽ ἀναγκασθεῖμεν ἀποlη-
φθέντες που, οἷα δὴ ἐπὶ στρατείας, ἀσιτεῖν, οὐδὲν
220 ἦσαν οἱ ἄλλοι πρὸς τὸ καρτερεῖν—ἔν τ᾽ αὖ ταῖς εὐω-
χίαις μόνος ἀπολαύειν οἷός τ᾽ ἦν τά τ᾽ ἄλλα καὶ πίνειν οὐκ ἐθέλων, ὁπότε ἀναγκασθείη, πάντας ἐκράτει,
καὶ ὃ πάντων θαυμαστότατον, Σωκράτη μεθύοντα οὐ-
δεὶς πώποτε | ἑώρακεν ἀνθρώπων. τούτου μὲν οὖν μοι
δοκεῖ καὶ αὐτίκα ὁ ἔλεγχος ἔσεσθαι. πρὸς δὲ αὖ τὰς
τοῦ χειμῶνος καρτερήσεις—δεινοὶ γὰρ αὐτόθι χειμῶ-
νες—θαυμάσια ἠργάζετο τά τε ἄλλα, καί ποτε ὄντος
b πάγου οἵου δεινοτάτου, καὶ πάντων ἢ οὐκ ἐξιόντων
ἔνδοθεν, ἢ εἴ τις ἐξίοι, ἠμφιεσμένων τε θαυμαστὰ δὴ
ὅσα καὶ ὑποδεδεμένων καὶ ἐνειλιγμένων τοὺς πόδας
εἰς πίλους καὶ ἀρνακίδας, οὗτος δ᾽ ἐν τούτοις ἐξῄει |
ἔχων ἱμάτιον μὲν τοιοῦτον οἷόνπερ καὶ πρότερον εἰώθει φορεῖν, ἀνυπόδητος δὲ διὰ τοῦ κρυστάλλου ῥᾷον
ἐπορεύετο ἢ οἱ ἄλλοι ὑποδεδεμένοι, οἱ δὲ στρατιῶται
c ὑπέβλεπον αὐτὸν ὡς καταφρονοῦντα σφῶν. καὶ ταῦτα
μὲν δὴ ταῦτα·

οἷον δ᾽ αὖ τόδ᾽ ἔρεξε καὶ ἔτλη καρτερὸς ἀνὴρ

ἐκεῖ ποτε ἐπὶ στρατιᾶς, ἄξιον ἀκοῦσαι. συννοήσας
γὰρ αὐτόθι ἕωθέν τι εἱστήκει σκοπῶν, καὶ ἐπειδὴ οὐ
προυχώρει | αὐτῷ, οὐκ ἀνίει ἀλλὰ εἱστήκει ζητῶν. καὶ
ἤδη ἦν μεσημβρία, καὶ ἄνθρωποι ᾐσθάνοντο, καὶ
θαυμάζοντες ἄλλος ἄλλῳ ἔλεγεν ὅτι Σωκράτης ἐξ ἕω-

but also to all the rest—whenever we were forced to go without food after being cut off somewhere, as happens on campaign, the rest were nothing when it came to endurance; on the other hand, when it came to feasting he 220 was uniquely able to enjoy it, and in particular, though he was unwilling to drink, yet when forced to do so he used to beat the lot of us, and the most amazing thing: no one alive has ever seen Socrates drunk. Well, of that, I think, there will be proof any time now. Again as for his endurance of winter weather—for the winters are terrible up there—he managed some remarkable feats, and in particular one day when there was a frost as terrible as it could be, and with everyone either not going out from under b cover or if anyone did go out they were remarkably well wrapped up, with their shoes on and with their feet swathed in felt and fleeces: this man went out among them wearing the sort of cloak he had been accustomed to wear before and made his way across the ice in bare feet more easily than the rest with their shoes on, and the soldiers looked askance at him, thinking he was showing contempt for them. So much, then, for that; but: c

'What a thing this was again which the stalwart man
    did and endured'[132]

there once on campaign was an event worth hearing about. For from daybreak he had been standing in meditation on the spot contemplating something, and when he was making no progress at it, he didn't give up, but stood there searching. By now it was midday and people were noticing him and in their amazement said to one another that Soc-

[132] Based on Homer, *Odyssey* 4.242, 271.

θινοῦ φροντίζων τι ἔστηκε. τελευτῶντες δέ τινες τῶν
d Ἰώνων, ἐπειδὴ ἑσπέρα ἦν, δειπνήσαντες—καὶ γὰρ
θέρος τότε γ᾽ ἦν—χαμεύνια ἐξενεγκάμενοι ἅμα μὲν ἐν
τῷ ψύχει καθηῦδον, ἅμα δ᾽ ἐφύλαττον αὐτὸν εἰ καὶ
τὴν νύκτα ἑστήξοι. ὁ δὲ εἱστήκει μέχρι ἕως ἐγένετο
καὶ ἥλιος ἀνέσχεν· ἔπειτα ᾤχετ᾽ ἀπιὼν προσευξάμε-
νος τῷ | ἡλίῳ. εἰ δὲ βούλεσθε ἐν ταῖς μάχαις—τοῦτο
γὰρ δὴ δίκαιόν γε αὐτῷ ἀποδοῦναι—ὅτε γὰρ ἡ μάχη
ἦν ἐξ ἧς ἐμοὶ καὶ τἀριστεῖα ἔδοσαν οἱ στρατηγοί,
e οὐδεὶς ἄλλος ἐμὲ ἔσωσεν ἀνθρώπων ἢ οὗτος, τετρω-
μένον οὐκ ἐθέλων ἀπολιπεῖν, ἀλλὰ συνδιέσωσε καὶ τὰ
ὅπλα καὶ αὐτὸν ἐμέ. καὶ ἐγὼ μέν, ὦ Σώκρατες, καὶ
τότε ἐκέλευον σοὶ διδόναι τἀριστεῖα τοὺς στρατηγούς,
καὶ τοῦτό γέ μοι οὔτε μέμψῃ οὔτε ἐρεῖς ὅτι ψεύδομαι·
| ἀλλὰ γὰρ τῶν στρατηγῶν πρὸς τὸ ἐμὸν ἀξίωμα
ἀποβλεπόντων καὶ βουλομένων ἐμοὶ διδόναι τἀριστεῖα, αὐτὸς προθυμότερος ἐγένου τῶν στρατηγῶν
ἐμὲ λαβεῖν ἢ σαυτόν. ἔτι τοίνυν, ὦ ἄνδρες, ἄξιον ἦν
θεάσασθαι Σωκράτη, ὅτε ἀπὸ Δηλίου φυγῇ ἀνεχώρει
221 τὸ στρατόπεδον· ἔτυχον γὰρ παραγενόμενος ἵππον
ἔχων, οὗτος δὲ ὅπλα. ἀνεχώρει οὖν ἐσκεδασμένων
ἤδη τῶν ἀνθρώπων οὗτός τε ἅμα καὶ Λάχης· καὶ ἐγὼ
περιτυγχάνω, καὶ ἰδὼν εὐθὺς παρακελεύομαί τε αὐτοῖν
θαρρεῖν, | καὶ ἔλεγον ὅτι οὐκ ἀπολείψω αὐτώ. ἐνταῦθα
δὴ καὶ κάλλιον ἐθεασάμην Σωκράτη ἢ ἐν Ποτειδαίᾳ—

---

133 For the Athenian defeat at Delium (424), see Thucydides

rates had been standing there thinking about something since daybreak. Finally when evening came, some of the Ionians, having had their supper, brought out some pallet beds—for it was summer at the time—and slept in the cool and at the same time watched him to see if he would stand there all night as well. And he did stand there until it was dawn and the sun rose; then he went off after praying to the sun. If you want to hear about him in the battles—for indeed it's right to pay him this tribute—when there was a battle after which the commanders actually gave me an award for bravery, no other man rescued me but this man, who refused to leave me behind wounded, but also saved my armor as well as myself. And on that occasion, Socrates, I was actually telling the commanders to give you the award for bravery, and on that point you will not blame me, nor say that I'm telling lies. But the fact is that when the commanders were taking into account my own standing and wanted to give me the award for bravery, you were keener than the commanders that I should take it rather than you yourself. And yet again, gentlemen, it was worth looking at Socrates when the army withdrew from Delium in flight. You see I happened to be there, I with a horse, he with his arms.[133] So when the men had already scattered, he withdrew along with Laches. I happened to meet them and as soon as I saw them I shouted to both of them to keep their courage up and said I would not abandon the two of them. It was then I got an even better view of Socrates than at Potidaea—for I was less

d

e

221

4.89–101. Alcibiades was a cavalryman and Socrates a hoplite (heavy-armed foot soldier). For Socrates' conduct, see *Laches* 181b, and for his military service in general, *Apology* 28e.

αὐτὸς γὰρ ἧττον ἐν φόβῳ ᾖ διὰ τὸ ἐφ' ἵππου εἶναι—
πρῶτον μὲν ὅσον περιῆν Λάχητος τῷ ἔμφρων εἶναι·
b ἔπειτα ἔμοιγ' ἐδόκει, ὦ Ἀριστόφανες, τὸ σὸν δὴ τοῦτο,
καὶ ἐκεῖ διαπορεύεσθαι ὥσπερ καὶ ἐνθάδε, "βρενθυό-
μενος καὶ τὠφθαλμὼ παραβάλλων," ἠρέμα παρασκο-
πῶν καὶ τοὺς φιλίους καὶ τοὺς πολεμίους, | δῆλος ὢν
παντὶ καὶ πάνυ πόρρωθεν ὅτι εἴ τις ἅψεται τούτου τοῦ
ἀνδρός, μάλα ἐρρωμένως ἀμυνεῖται. διὸ καὶ ἀσφαλῶς
ἀπῄει καὶ οὗτος καὶ ὁ ἑταῖρος· σχεδὸν γάρ τι τῶν
οὕτω διακειμένων ἐν τῷ πολέμῳ οὐδὲ ἅπτονται, ἀλλὰ
τοὺς προτροπάδην φεύγοντας διώκουσιν.

c   Πολλὰ μὲν οὖν ἄν τις καὶ ἄλλα ἔχοι Σωκράτη
ἐπαινέσαι καὶ θαυμάσια· ἀλλὰ τῶν μὲν ἄλλων ἐπιτηδευμάτων τάχ' ἄν τις καὶ περὶ ἄλλου τοιαῦτα εἴποι,
τὸ δὲ μηδενὶ ἀνθρώπων | ὅμοιον εἶναι, μήτε τῶν πα-
λαιῶν μήτε τῶν νῦν ὄντων, τοῦτο ἄξιον παντὸς θαύ-
ματος. οἷος γὰρ Ἀχιλλεὺς ἐγένετο, ἀπεικάσειεν ἄν τις
καὶ Βρασίδαν καὶ ἄλλους, καὶ οἷος αὖ Περικλῆς, καὶ
Νέστορα καὶ Ἀντήνορα—εἰσὶ δὲ καὶ ἕτεροι—καὶ τοὺς
d ἄλλους κατὰ ταῦτ' ἄν τις ἀπεικάζοι· οἷος δὲ οὑτοσὶ
γέγονε τὴν ἀτοπίαν ἄνθρωπος, καὶ αὐτὸς καὶ οἱ λόγοι
αὐτοῦ, οὐδ' ἐγγὺς ἂν εὕροι τις ζητῶν, οὔτε τῶν νῦν
οὔτε τῶν παλαιῶν, εἰ μὴ ἄρα εἰ οἷς ἐγὼ λέγω ἀπεικά-

---

134 An adapted quotation from Aristophanes' comedy *Clouds*
362, where the Chorus is satirizing Socrates' allegedly absurd
meteorological speculation.

fearful on account of my being on horseback—firstly how superior he was to Laches in having his wits about him, and then it seemed to me, Aristophanes, after all this is one of yours, he made his way there just as he does here, 'swaggering and casting his eyes sideways'[134] calmly observing friend and foe, making it plain to all, even if they were some distance away, that if anyone attacked this man, he would defend himself with the utmost vigor. That's the reason he and his comrade got away safely. You see as a rule in war people don't lay a finger on those who behave like this, but pursue those who are fleeing headlong.

"Now one could find many other things to say in praise of Socrates, and remarkable ones too; and with regard to his other activities perhaps one could say such things about someone else too, but the fact that he is unlike any other human being, both from the past and the present— *that* is worthy of our total wonder. For the kind of person Achilles was, one could compare Brasidas and others; again for Pericles we have Nestor and Antenor—and there are others too—and one could make other comparisons along the same lines.[135] But as for the sort of man this fellow is in his extraordinary nature, both in himself and what he says, one wouldn't get close to finding anyone if one searched among people of today or people of the past, unless perhaps one were to compare him to the figures I'm

135 Brasidas was a Spartan general in the Peloponnesian War, killed fighting at Amphipolis in 422 (Thucydides 5.10), compared to Homeric Achilles, the most prominent Greek fighter at Troy. Pericles, the Athenian leader, is compared to Homeric Nestor, renowned for oratory (Homer, *Iliad* 1.248), and Antenor for wisdom (*Iliad* 7.347).

ζοι τις αὐτόν, | ἀνθρώπων μὲν μηδενί, τοῖς δὲ σιλη-
νοῖς καὶ σατύροις, αὐτὸν καὶ τοὺς λόγους.

Καὶ γὰρ οὖν καὶ τοῦτο ἐν τοῖς πρώτοις παρέλιπον,
ὅτι καὶ οἱ λόγοι αὐτοῦ ὁμοιότατοί εἰσι τοῖς σιληνοῖς
e τοῖς διοιγομένοις. εἰ γὰρ ἐθέλοι τις τῶν Σωκράτους
ἀκούειν λόγων, φανεῖεν ἂν πάνυ γελοῖοι τὸ πρῶτον·
τοιαῦτα καὶ ὀνόματα καὶ ῥήματα ἔξωθεν περιαμπέχον-
ται, σατύρου δή τινα ὑβριστοῦ δοράν. ὄνους γὰρ καν-
θηλίους λέγει καὶ χαλκέας τινὰς | καὶ σκυτοτόμους
καὶ βυρσοδέψας, καὶ ἀεὶ διὰ τῶν αὐτῶν τὰ αὐτὰ φαίνεται λέγειν, ὥστε ἄπειρος καὶ ἀνόητος ἄνθρωπος
222 πᾶς ἂν τῶν λόγων καταγελάσειεν. διοιγομένους δὲ
ἰδὼν ἄν τις καὶ ἐντὸς αὐτῶν γιγνόμενος πρῶτον μὲν
νοῦν ἔχοντας ἔνδον μόνους εὑρήσει τῶν λόγων, ἔπειτα
θειοτάτους καὶ πλεῖστα ἀγάλματ᾽ ἀρετῆς ἐν αὑτοῖς
ἔχοντας καὶ ἐπὶ πλεῖστον | τείνοντας, μᾶλλον δὲ ἐπὶ
πᾶν ὅσον προσήκει σκοπεῖν τῷ μέλλοντι καλῷ κἀ-
γαθῷ ἔσεσθαι.

Ταῦτ᾽ ἐστίν, ὦ ἄνδρες, ἃ ἐγὼ Σωκράτη ἐπαινῶ· καὶ
αὖ ἃ μέμφομαι συμμείξας ὑμῖν εἶπον ἅ με ὕβρισεν.
b καὶ μέντοι οὐκ ἐμὲ μόνον ταῦτα πεποίηκεν, ἀλλὰ καὶ
Χαρμίδην τὸν Γλαύκωνος καὶ Εὐθύδημον τὸν Διοκλέ-
ους καὶ ἄλλους πάνυ πολλούς, οὓς οὗτος ἐξαπατῶν ὡς
ἐραστὴς παιδικὰ μᾶλλον αὐτὸς καθίσταται ἀντ᾽ ἐρα-

---

136 "Fine and good" = *kalos k'agathos*, combining goodness,
nobility, and physical courage: all the ideal qualities required of
the Athenian male (see Dover, *GPM*, 41–45).

137 Charmides, a young man who gives his name to the title of

talking about, not to any human beings, but to the Silenuses and Satyrs, both him and what he says.

"And yes, there is this I left out at the beginning, that
his conversations are also most like the Silenus figures that
you open up. For if one were willing to listen to what Soc-   e
rates says, it would appear to be quite ridiculous at first.
Such are the words and phrases it is clothed in on the
outside, just like the skin of some naughty Satyr. For he
talks of pack asses and people like smiths and cobblers and
tanners, and he always seems to be talking about the same
things in the same terms, so that every person unused to
him and foolish would laugh at what he says. But anyone   222
who sees his words opened up and gets inside them will
discover firstly they are the only kinds of speech that contain any meaning within them, secondly that they are to
the highest degree divinely inspired and have within them
very many images of virtue which reach out over the greatest area, or rather over everything that it is fitting to consider for the person whose ambition it is to be fine and
good.[136]

"So, my friends, this is my speech in praise of Socrates.
And I have also mixed in with it and told you the things I
reproach him for and the occasions when he has abused
me. And yet I'm not the only one he's done this to: there's   b
also Charmides, Glaucon's son, and Euthydemus, son of
Diocles, and very many others whom this man has deceived into thinking of him as a lover while making himself
more the loved one rather than the lover.[137] And what I'm

Plato's *Charmides.* Euthydemus (not the sophist who is the main
speaker in Plato's dialogue of that name) is a young man mentioned in Xenophon, *Memorabilia* 1.2.29, 4.2.1. See further Nails,
90–94, 151.

στοῦ. ἃ δὴ καὶ σοὶ | λέγω, ὦ Ἀγάθων, μὴ ἐξαπατᾶ-
σθαι ὑπὸ τούτου, ἀλλ' ἀπὸ τῶν ἡμετέρων παθημάτων
γνόντα εὐλαβηθῆναι, καὶ μὴ κατὰ τὴν παροιμίαν
ὥσπερ νήπιον παθόντα γνῶναι.

c   Εἰπόντος δὴ ταῦτα τοῦ Ἀλκιβιάδου γέλωτα γενέσθαι ἐπὶ τῇ παρρησίᾳ αὐτοῦ, ὅτι ἐδόκει ἔτι ἐρωτικῶς
ἔχειν τοῦ Σωκράτους. τὸν οὖν Σωκράτη, Νήφειν μοι
δοκεῖς, φάναι, ὦ Ἀλκιβιάδη. οὐ γὰρ ἄν ποτε οὕτω
κομψῶς κύκλῳ περιβαλλόμενος | ἀφανίσαι ἐνεχείρεις
οὗ ἕνεκα ταῦτα πάντα εἴρηκας, καὶ ὡς ἐν παρέργῳ δὴ
λέγων ἐπὶ τελευτῆς αὐτὸ ἔθηκας, ὡς οὐ πάντα τούτου
d ἕνεκα εἰρηκώς, τοῦ ἐμὲ καὶ Ἀγάθωνα διαβάλλειν, οἰόμενος δεῖν ἐμὲ μὲν σοῦ ἐρᾶν καὶ μηδενὸς ἄλλου, Ἀγάθωνα δὲ ὑπὸ σοῦ ἐρᾶσθαι καὶ μηδ' ὑφ' ἑνὸς ἄλλου.
ἀλλ' οὐκ ἔλαθες, ἀλλὰ τὸ σατυρικόν σου δρᾶμα τοῦτο
καὶ σιληνικὸν κατάδηλον ἐγένετο. ἀλλ', ὦ | φίλε Ἀγά-
θων, μηδὲν πλέον αὐτῷ γένηται, ἀλλὰ παρασκευάζου
ὅπως ἐμὲ καὶ σὲ μηδεὶς διαβαλεῖ.

   Τὸν οὖν Ἀγάθωνα εἰπεῖν, Καὶ μήν, ὦ Σώκρατες,
e κινδυνεύεις ἀληθῆ λέγειν. τεκμαίρομαι δὲ καὶ ὡς
κατεκλίνη ἐν μέσῳ ἐμοῦ τε καὶ σοῦ, ἵνα χωρὶς ἡμᾶς
διαλάβῃ. οὐδὲν οὖν πλέον αὐτῷ ἔσται, ἀλλ' ἐγὼ παρὰ
σὲ ἐλθὼν κατακλινήσομαι.

---

138 See Homer, *Iliad* 17.32; Hesiod, *Works and Days* 218;
Aeschylus, *Agamemnon* 177.

telling you too, Agathon, is don't be deceived by this man, but learning from what we have experienced take care and don't, like the proverb, learn it, like a fool, from suffering."[138]

When Alcibiades had said this, there was laughter at c his frankness because it seemed he was still in love with Socrates. "So," Socrates said: "I think you're sober, Alcibiades, for otherwise, as you cast your cloak around you so elegantly,[139] you would never have tried to conceal why you have said all this and put it in at the end as a side issue, as if it were not all said for this reason, to set me and Ag- d athon against each other, thinking that I must love you and none other, and that Agathon must be loved by you and no one else at all. But you didn't fool me; the purpose of this Satyric and Silenic play of yours has become very clear.[140] Well, my dear Agathon, don't let him gain anything by it, but make sure that no one sets you and me against each other."

Then Agathon said: "well, you could be right, Socrates. I take it as evidence that he reclined between me and you e in order to keep us apart. But he won't gain any advantage; I'll come and recline beside you."

[139] That is, "you'd have never been so ingenious (in trying to conceal) . . ."

[140] The satyr play, comic in tone and featuring a chorus of satyrs, rounded off the set of three tragedies at the festival of the Great Dionysia. Alcibiades' speech is the comic "Satyric" speech following Socrates' serious *encomium*. It is also "Silenic" in that a comic exterior, opened up, conceals a serious purpose (see 215b6ff.).

Πάνυ γε, φάναι τὸν Σωκράτη, δεῦρο ὑποκάτω ἐμοῦ
| κατακλίνου.

Ὦ Ζεῦ, εἰπεῖν τὸν Ἀλκιβιάδην, οἷα αὖ πάσχω ὑπὸ
τοῦ ἀνθρώπου. οἴεταί μου δεῖν πανταχῇ περιεῖναι.
ἀλλ᾽ εἰ μή τι ἄλλο, ὦ θαυμάσιε, ἐν μέσῳ ἡμῶν ἔα
Ἀγάθωνα κατακεῖσθαι. |

Ἀλλ᾽ ἀδύνατον, φάναι τὸν Σωκράτη. σὺ μὲν γὰρ
ἐμὲ ἐπῄνεσας, δεῖ δὲ ἐμὲ αὖ τὸν ἐπὶ δεξί᾽ ἐπαινεῖν. ἐὰν
οὖν ὑπὸ σοὶ κατακλινῇ Ἀγάθων, οὐ δήπου ἐμὲ πάλιν
ἐπαινέσεται, πρὶν ὑπ᾽ ἐμοῦ μᾶλλον ἐπαινεθῆναι; ἀλλ᾽
223 ἔασον, ὦ δαιμόνιε, καὶ μὴ φθονήσῃς τῷ μειρακίῳ ὑπ᾽
ἐμοῦ ἐπαινεθῆναι· καὶ γὰρ πάνυ ἐπιθυμῶ αὐτὸν ἐγκωμιάσαι.

Ἰοῦ ἰοῦ, φάναι τὸν Ἀγάθωνα, Ἀλκιβιάδη, οὐκ ἔσθ᾽
ὅπως ἂν ἐνθάδε μείναιμι, ἀλλὰ παντὸς μᾶλλον μετα-
ναστήσομαι, | ἵνα ὑπὸ Σωκράτους ἐπαινεθῶ.

Ταῦτα ἐκεῖνα, φάναι τὸν Ἀλκιβιάδην, τὰ εἰωθότα·
Σωκράτους παρόντος τῶν καλῶν μεταλαβεῖν ἀδύνατον ἄλλῳ. καὶ νῦν ὡς εὐπόρως καὶ πιθανὸν λόγον
ηὗρεν, ὥστε παρ᾽ ἑαυτῷ τουτονὶ κατακεῖσθαι.

b   Τὸν μὲν οὖν Ἀγάθωνα ὡς κατακεισόμενον παρὰ τῷ
Σωκράτει ἀνίστασθαι· ἐξαίφνης δὲ κωμαστὰς ἥκειν

---

141 Plato takes the original idea of speeches to be delivered in
order of reclining on couches to stage a humorously erotic byplay.
Agathon ("the youngster," 223a1) is the supposed object of the
competitive attentions of Socrates and Alcibiades. The proposals

"Certainly," said Socrates, "come over here and lie down below me."

"Zeus!" said Alcibiades, "the things I suffer again at this man's hands! He thinks he must get the better of me in everything. Well, if nothing else, my good friend, let Agathon recline between us."

"But that's impossible," said Socrates. "You see you sang my praises, so I must therefore in turn praise the man on my right. So if Agathon reclines below you, won't he praise me again rather than being praised by me? Well let him be, like a good fellow, and don't begrudge the youngster being praised by me. You see I'm very keen to sing his 223 praises."

"Hey hey, Alcibiades!" said Agathon, "there's no way I can remain here, but, come what may, I'm going to change places so I can be praised by Socrates."

"There we go again as usual," said Alcibiades. "When Socrates is around it's impossible for anyone else to get a share of the handsome ones. And now how easily he's found a plausible reason for this one to recline beside himself."

So Agathon got up to recline beside Socrates.[141] But b suddenly a large crowd of revelers arrived at the doors,

are that the original order on their couch, Alcibiades between Agathon and Socrates (213a7–c5), should be changed around, first, on Agathon's proposal, to Alcibiades-Socrates-Agathon (222e3–4), then, on Alcibiades' proposal to Alcibiades-Agathon-Socrates (e8–9), and Agathon then agrees (on Socrates' proposal) that he should move to the other side of Socrates (223b1); it's not clear that any of these moves, except possibly the last, actually happens.

παμπόλλους ἐπὶ τὰς θύρας, καὶ ἐπιτυχόντας ἀνεῳγ-
μέναις ἐξιόντος τινὸς εἰς τὸ ἄντικρυς πορεύεσθαι
παρὰ σφᾶς καὶ κατακλίνεσθαι, | καὶ θορύβου μεστὰ
πάντα εἶναι, καὶ οὐκέτι ἐν κόσμῳ οὐδενὶ ἀναγκάζε-
σθαι πίνειν πάμπολυν οἶνον. τὸν μὲν οὖν Ἐρυξίμαχον
καὶ τὸν Φαῖδρον καὶ ἄλλους τινὰς ἔφη ὁ Ἀριστόδημος οἴχεσθαι ἀπιόντας, ἓ δὲ ὕπνον λαβεῖν, καὶ κατα-
c δαρθεῖν πάνυ πολύ, ἅτε μακρῶν τῶν νυκτῶν οὐσῶν,
ἐξεγρέσθαι δὲ πρὸς ἡμέραν ἤδη ἀλεκτρυόνων ἀ̣δόν-
των, ἐξεγρόμενος δὲ ἰδεῖν τοὺς μὲν ἄλλους καθεύδον-
τας καὶ οἰχομένους, Ἀγάθωνα δὲ καὶ Ἀριστοφάνη καὶ
Σωκράτη ἔτι | μόνους ἐγρηγορέναι καὶ πίνειν ἐκ φιά-
λης μεγάλης ἐπὶ δεξιά. τὸν οὖν Σωκράτη αὐτοῖς δια-
λέγεσθαι· καὶ τὰ μὲν ἄλλα ὁ Ἀριστόδημος οὐκ ἔφη
d μεμνῆσθαι τῶν λόγων—οὔτε γὰρ ἐξ ἀρχῆς παραγε-
νέσθαι ὑπονυστάζειν τε—τὸ μέντοι κεφάλαιον, ἔφη,
προσαναγκάζειν τὸν Σωκράτη ὁμολογεῖν αὐτοὺς τοῦ
αὐτοῦ ἀνδρὸς εἶναι κωμῳδίαν καὶ τραγῳδίαν ἐπίστα-
σθαι | ποιεῖν, καὶ τὸν τέχνῃ τραγῳδοποιὸν ὄντα ⟨καὶ⟩
κωμῳδοποιὸν εἶναι. ταῦτα δὴ ἀναγκαζομένους αὐτοὺς
καὶ οὐ σφόδρα ἑπομένους νυστάζειν, καὶ πρότερον
μὲν καταδαρθεῖν τὸν Ἀριστοφάνη, ἤδη δὲ ἡμέρας γι-
γνομένης τὸν Ἀγάθωνα. τὸν οὖν Σωκράτη, κατακοιμί-
σαντ’ ἐκείνους, ἀναστάντα ἀπιέναι, | καὶ ⟨ἓ⟩ ὥσπερ
εἰώθει ἕπεσθαι, καὶ ἐλθόντα εἰς Λύκειον, ἀπονιψάμε-
νον, ὥσπερ ἄλλοτε τὴν ἄλλην ἡμέραν διατρίβειν, καὶ
οὕτω διατρίψαντα εἰς ἑσπέραν οἴκοι ἀναπαύεσθαι.

and finding them open as somebody went out, they proceeded straight on in to join the group and lay down on the couches. Everywhere was full of uproar, and with nothing any longer in any kind of order they were forced to drink a great quantity of wine. So, said Aristodemus, Eryximachus, Phaedrus and several others went off, but he himself went to sleep and slept on for quite a long time, since the nights were long,[142] and woke up when it was c almost daylight and the cocks were already crowing. Having woken up he saw the rest were asleep or had gone away, but Agathon, Aristophanes and Socrates were the only ones still awake and were drinking from a large bowl from left to right. Socrates was then having a conversation with them. Aristodemus said he didn't remember the rest of what was said—for he hadn't been there from the beginning and in fact he was nodding off to sleep—however the main thing was Socrates was pressing them to agree that the same man should know how to write comedy and tragedy, and that he who is a skillful writer of tragedy is also a skillful writer of comedy.[143] Being pressed to agree about this and not following very much, they were nodding off, and Aristophanes fell asleep first and then Agathon when day was already breaking. Having seen them off to sleep, Socrates got up and left, and he, Aristodemus, as usual followed. Socrates went to the Lyceum and had a wash and spent the rest of the day as on other days, and toward evening he went home to rest.

[142] The Lenaia festival, at which Agathon's play was performed, took place in midwinter.

[143] This discussion was possibly intended to reflect the mix of comic and tragic elements in the dialogue and in Plato's portrayal of Socrates himself (see Introduction, §5).

PHAEDRUS

INTRODUCTION

1. THE SETTING

In *Phaedrus*, as in *Lysis* and *Symposium*, we find Socrates involved in a philosophical discussion on the subject of love (*erōs*). However, unlike the other two dialogues, which involve social groups meeting in the city, this one consists of a conversation *tête-à-tête* between Socrates and a younger friend, Phaedrus, and takes place in the countryside outside Athens. The dialogue begins with a chance encounter by the city wall near the temple of Olympian Zeus. In response to an opening abrupt question from Socrates as to his movements, Phaedrus reveals that he has been captivated since early morning by the up-and-coming speechwriter Lysias and has been practicing a speech on the subject of love that Lysias has just composed.[1]

Phaedrus' naïve enthusiasm, his "Corybantic passion" (228b7), for Lysias' speeches, and the fact that he has the speech with him under his cloak, is teased out by Socrates' humorous leg-pulling—Socrates claims (somewhat im-

---

[1] The choice of Phaedrus as Socrates' partner in the dialogue might suggest a link with the *Symposium*, which also features speeches on the subject of Love, a topic introduced there by Phaedrus (*Symposium* 177a–c).

probably) also to have this passion, to be "sick with desire for listening to speeches" (228b6)—and they both walk to find a suitable spot from which Phaedrus can deliver the speech. The two friends walk barefoot downstream in the cold, refreshing water of the river Ilissus.[2]

When they have found a suitable spot by the river, Socrates embarks, uncharacteristically, on what amounts to a formal *ekphrasis* (a lyrical description, 230b2–c5), waxing eloquent on the shade of the overhanging trees, the lush grass, and the continuous chorus of cicadas.[3] Teased by Phaedrus for behaving like a stranger in the countryside, he replies, "The countryside and trees don't want to teach me anything, but people in town do" (230c–d).[4]

Despite this denial, the unaccustomed atmosphere of the countryside, with the continual background of the chattering cicadas (230c2), appears to have a marked effect on Socrates. The tone of much of the conversation between the two friends matches this atmosphere: it is multilayered, frequently balanced between open humor, irony, and seriousness. Socrates in particular seems, on the surface, to be transformed from his customary rational self by the unaccustomed magic of the place: he indulges in allegory, particularly fanciful allusions to myth, poetic quotation often possibly invented on the spot, and later on

[2] For discussion of the route taken by Socrates and Phaedrus, see Wycherley, "The Scene of Plato's *Phaidros*."

[3] Socrates' *ekphrasis* and the whole of the scene became a key reference point for the *locus amoenus* (pleasant, delightful place), a literary display piece common to Hellenistic pastoral poetry.

[4] For Socrates' reputed disinclination to travel outside the city of Athens, see, e.g., *Crito* 52b.

in the dialogue he elevates the madness of love into a prized possession sent by the gods (245c). However, the ending of the dialogue is as abrupt and unassuming as the beginning, with Socrates' casual "Let's go" (279c8).

2. THE STRUCTURAL PROBLEM: THE UNITY OF THE DIALOGUE

The question of the formal unity of the dialogue is an issue that has preoccupied commentators since Antiquity. The speeches on love delivered by Phaedrus and Socrates come to a climax with Socrates' monumental second speech, in which he develops in detail the mythical, metaphysical, psychological, and emotional aspects of the topic. This speech, drawing on themes developed in other dialogues, such as *Meno*, *Phaedo*, and *Republic*, arguably represents (together with the *Symposium*) Plato's most profound exploration of the nature and the effects of love.

These three speeches, together with the introduction, take up rather more than half the dialogue. However, the second half appears, at first sight, to change the subject and the mood abruptly from the elevated heights of Platonic metaphysics—developing into a closely argued discussion of the contribution of rhetoric and dialectic—to the practice of philosophical teaching and discussion. Socrates indulges in sharply humorous criticism of current practice in speechwriting and ironically praises some of its most famous contemporary exponents. *Erōs* (love), hitherto the key subject of the dialogue, now appears incidentally as "one of the things we argue about" (263c7ff.), the nature of which must be clearly understood by anyone who wishes to master the rhetorical art.[5] The question of what links the two halves and whether the dialogue actually has a unified subject is, therefore, an important one, which will be explored below (§5).

3. THE SPEECHES

(i) Introductory (229c–30e)

When they arrive at their destination, Socrates shows himself to be unexpectedly familiar with local mythology (229c1ff.). The topic is introduced at this point to emphasize his attitude to mythological stories; he is not a skeptic rationalist like the sophists, but his agnostic attitude toward interpretation of the stories leaves the way open for his own idiosyncratic introduction of myth in his main (second) speech. Moreover, his emphasis on the priority of self-examination (229e4ff.) may be intended to point forward to his emphasis on the human soul later in the dialogue.

(ii) Lysias' Speech (230e6–34c5)

This takes the form of a conventional *logos erōtikos*, a display speech (*epideixis*) on the subject of love. It is a tribute to Plato's remarkable ability at imitating and parodying different styles of prose writing elsewhere that there

[5] As in the *Symposium*, *Erōs* (the god Love) appears along with *erōs* (the emotion); for the difficulty of distinguishing between them in Greek, see the *Symposium*, Introduction, n. 1.

has never been consensus on whether on this occasion we have a genuine speech of Lysias or a clever imitation.[6] However, whichever way the argument goes, Plato's clear purpose is to put up the speech as a target for criticism on stylistic, structural, and, ultimately, moral grounds.

The speech is a *paignion*, or *jeu d'esprit*, an attempt to oppose the conventional belief about love; Lysias argues that, paradoxically, a relationship between a man and a boy is more satisfactory, fulfilling, and long-lasting if the older partner (conventionally the *erastēs*) is not actually in love with the younger (the *erōmenos*), openly confesses this to his partner, and conducts the relationship on this basis. The underlying quality the nonlover possesses is "soundness of mind" (*sōphrosune*), the ability calmly to organize the relationship for the mutual enjoyment and benefit of both parties. Being in love is, however, a deluded madness in which lovers themselves admit that they are "sick rather than sound in mind" and have no judgment or self-control (231d2–4). Consequently, the relationship with a lover has consequences that will harm rather than help his partner.

Addressing the *erōmenos* (loved one), Lysias goes on to list the disadvantages of being in love and the corresponding benefits of the opposite state. The nonlover is free from the unreliability of the lover: the lover's emotions are fickle and his attitude to his partner changes if/when he

---

[6] Stylistic arguments do not rule out a genuine speech of Lysias (see, e.g., Dover, *Lysias and the Corpus Lysiacum*, 69–71); insistent repetition of characteristic Lysianic connectives could take the argument either way (see *Phaedrus* translation, nn. 20 and 21). In subsequent references to this speech, "Lysias" is shorthand for "Lysias or Plato."

falls out of love and contracts a later relationship, whereas
the nonlover maintains long-lasting friendship. The lover,
because of his sickness, is prone to be jealous of others'
possible influence over his beloved and steers the latter
away from his friends. Furthermore, the lover may be
indiscreet, because he cannot keep the affair secret, and
so he exposes his younger partner to public censure.[7] The
nonlover is more frank and honest with the beloved, because he lacks the fear of offending him. And so on, and
so on.

In the Interlude that follows, Socrates, after excessive
and obviously ironic praise for Lysias' style, concentrates
his criticism on the random order in which the points of
the argument were made, joined by such repetitious connectives as "again," "and another point"; Lysias is "behaving like some swaggering youth, showing off the fact that
he can say the same thing in this way and in that " (235a6–
8), and in no particular logical order.[8]

(iii) Socrates' First Speech (237b7–41d1)

After a passage of lighthearted banter and characteristically ironic disclaimers, Socrates agrees under protest to
put up a competing speech on the same subject, defending
the same position: the advantages to the boy of having a

[7] For the Athenian "double standards" involved in such ex-
posure—admiration for the lover in contracting, and shame on
the beloved for allowing the relationship—see General Introduction, §2.

[8] Socrates makes a somewhat similar criticism of previous
speeches in *Symposium* 198e5ff.

nonlover as partner, but in his case making the (vital) qualification that the "nonlover" is really in love, but actually pretending not to be (237b3–5).[9] This fundamental difference between Socrates' speech and that of Lysias is established right at the beginning, and at the same time Socrates also introduces a major theme of the dialogue: the need, by means of division, to define exactly what is being argued about, its essential nature.[10] This organized structure, in contrast to Lysias' random list of points, is established right from the start. Arguing that love is a kind of desire, Socrates divides desire into two opposed categories: pleasure versus acquired judgment aiming at what is best; the former category, pleasure, can itself be further subdivided into desire for food, drink, or bodily beauty (237d–38c). Love, corresponding on this analysis to desire for bodily beauty, is placed firmly on this side of the division: an emotion in which "a desire without reason which has taken control of a judgment which is urging toward what is right . . . having gained its name from its own strength, is called love" (238b8–c4). The spurious etymological connection of "love" (*erōs*) with "strength" (*rhōmē*), one of a number of fanciful etymologies in the dialogue, clearly indicates Socrates' underlying attitude toward the thesis he is defending, which, of course, his second speech, his *palinode* (recantation), totally repudiates.

[9] "There is a clear progression through the three speeches, from Lysias' non-lover, to Socrates' secret lover here, to the open lover of his final speech" (Waterfield, *Phaedrus*, n. on 237b.).

[10] An anticipation of the fundamental analysis of the division of madness into different types at the beginning of Socrates' second speech (244aff.).

Before embarking on his speech, Socrates had conceded that he could not build his argument by making points entirely different from those of Lysias (235e2–5). But Socrates' argumentative points against the lover are not only much more coherently put together but also more sharply focused on the lover's motivation, based on his previous analysis of love as a subspecies of desire. The need to satisfy this desire underlies the whole relationship with the beloved, in which the lover is entirely concerned with himself and his desires at the beloved's expense. The destructive effect this relationship has on the younger partner is pithily summed up in Socrates' final sentence: "as wolves delight in lambs, so is lovers' affection for a boy" (241d1).

(iv) Socrates' Second Speech (244a1–57b6)

Having shown that he is perfectly capable of playing Lysias' rhetorical game, Socrates resists Phaedrus' protest that he now needs to argue the nonlover's side of the case. He is aware that there are other forces at work: through his speech he is already in danger of offending the god of love Eros: "A silly one [speech] and verging on the impious. What speech could be more terrible than that?" (242d7). So he needs to make amends as quickly as possible to avoid the fate of the archaic lyric poet Stesichorus (ca. 600–550), whose calumny against Helen of Troy as the cause of the Trojan War aroused the wrath of the gods and caused him to be struck blind (243a–b). But Socrates, following the example of Stesichorus and in obedience to his own warning sign, far from wanting to expound the corresponding virtues of the nonlover, prepares to deliver a

329

palinode (recantation) of his previous speech. Phaedrus, still apparently under the impression that they are engaged in a contest, Socrates versus Lysias, reacts with pleasurable anticipation (243b8).

Socrates begins by taking up a key point from his previous speech—that the lover is in some sense mad, because overcome by desire. He resorts once again to the method of division (see above, on his first speech, 237b7ff.), by separating out madness as a human ailment from madness as divine possession, and then the latter into four categories, which are a divine gift. The first three are the gift of prophecy (as with the priestesses at Delphi and Dodona), purification from madness through prayers and worship, and poetic frenzy. Socrates' task is to demonstrate that the fourth category, sent as a gift from the gods, the madness of love, is "for our greatest good fortune" (245b7).

Socrates' argument in favor of the true lover takes the discussion entirely away from the weighing up of practical options and personal interest, which underlay the arguments of the previous two speeches, and bases it on exploration of the nature and behavior of the human soul, which, he claims, is immortal and lies at the heart of all human activity. Plato's discussion of the activity of the soul, especially in relation to the body, can be found in other Platonic dialogues, principally *Phaedo*, the *Symposium*, and the *Republic*.[11] However, *Phaedrus* takes the

[11] See especially *Phaedo* 64eff., *Symposium* 201dff., *Republic* 614bff. On the soul in *Phaedrus*, see Bett, "Immortality and the Nature of the Soul in the *Phaedrus*." It is assumed here that the composition of *Phaedrus* postdates *Phaedo* and the *Republic* as well as the *Symposium* (see Appendix). On distinctions between

topic in a new direction and goes into much more detail.
Socrates' particular argument here for the soul's immortality is based, first, on its nature as a prime mover, that
is, something that moves other things but is itself self-
moving—the proof of which is demonstrated in a tightly-
structured argument (245c5–46a2).[12] Second, the soul is
a complex entity: for an explanation of conflicts within it,
we have the famous myth of the charioteer and his chariot
(246aff. and 253dff.), in which the charioteer, representing reason aiming at what is good, attempts to control a
pair of horses, the disorderly conduct of one threatening
to overpower the charioteer's control of the other, obedient horse. This resembles the conflict between desire, the
spirited element, and reason in the theory of the tripartite
soul in *Republic* 4. The third key element in Plato's myth
is the Theory of Recollection, introduced in *Meno* and
Phaedo, but argued out here in more detail: the human
soul has a memory, however imperfect, of what it saw
before birth when traveling outside the heavens, namely,
the Forms: perfect, timeless, nonspatial, and immutable
entities, unchanging models of absolute beauty, justice,
wisdom, temperance, which we dimly perceive in our
world of sensible changing things.[13]

In *Phaedrus* the soul is imagined as having wings that

---

the conception of soul developed in *Phaedrus* and that of the
earlier dialogues, see Bett, *op. cit.*, 442ff.

[12] This argument for the soul's immortality appears to be developed from an account by the pre-Socratic Alcmaeon of Croton,
as reported in Aristotle, *De Anima* 405a29–b1.

[13] For the tripartite soul, see *Republic* 4.439ff; for the Theory
of Recollection, see *Meno* 81–86, *Phaedo* 73b–76e.

naturally move it upward toward the realm of the gods and beyond (246bff.). The chariots of the gods routinely travel round outside the heavens and are free to contemplate the Forms. The soul, which inhabits the human body, unlike those of the gods, catches only glimpses of the Forms, hampered by a chariot drawn by disorderly horses that pull it down to earth. Human souls are ranked by the degree to which they are able to ascend to the region outside the heavens and view reality, ranging from the philosopher, whose perception of reality is the clearest, through to sophists and tyrants, who have the least perception (248a–e). Each life is followed, after death, by a punishment or a reward, after which the soul is reincarnated and chooses the form of its next earthly existence. The philosopher alone, who loves wisdom, has the opportunity to rejoin the heavenly procession after traveling through three philosophical lives in succession.[14]

"Now it is to this point that the whole of my argument about the fourth kind of madness has been coming" (249d4–5). Here, about halfway through his speech, Socrates reveals that the mythical/metaphysical picture of the journey of the soul that he has been painting is essentially a preliminary to his central argument concerning the activity of the "mad" lover. The lover is mad because the sight of a loved one brings a direct recollection of the absolute beauty that his soul when winged once saw in his journey above the heavens. Of the senses, sight is unique in affording a direct recollection of this absolute beauty (250d1–e1). Those who have lived earthly lives that have

[14] For the theory of successive lives, punishment, and reincarnation, see also *Republic* 10.615–21.

caused them to sink down and to be forgetful of what they saw above and have allowed their senses to be contaminated, surrender to crude desire for sexual pleasure. But for those newly initiated, the sight of an image of a loved one recalls directly the Form of absolute beauty. This memory, combined with the direct visual experience of the beauty of his beloved, initiates a change in the lover with the symptoms that Socrates describes vividly and in particularly precise physical detail: sweating, fever, and a melting of the hard area around the soul's wing, long since closed, and the consequent effect, a mixture of joy and pain that the sprouting of the opening wing causes the lover, which Socrates strikingly compares, in a characteristically homely simile, to the cutting of teeth (251a–e). While under this influence, he is unable to give his attention to anything or anybody else, family or friends, despises his past life, and is unable to live apart from his beloved. The lover experiences the need to grow wings and rise with his beloved to a contemplation of absolute beauty.

Each lover reacts to his beloved according to the god to whom he has been attached, Zeus, Ares, Hera, etc.; the lover is in effect an initiate into the mysteries of his particular god, and his one desire is that the one he loves should become like the god he follows (253a1–c6). His aim is to persuade and train the beloved in the god's image.

The remainder of the speech is mainly taken up with a very vivid and lengthy description (253c–56e) of the interaction of the charioteer and his two horses, a conflict that precipitates the sinking of the soul again into the mortal state. Here we are treated to a dramatic description of the conflicting emotions of the soul, seen as a tension between a charioteer (who represents the memory that the soul has of absolute beauty), attempting to control a good horse (one who is imbued with a sense of shame or respect), and a bad horse, who wishes to give in to sexual desires. Provided the good side wins, the lover and his beloved live an ordered life with philosophy, having control of the evil part and giving the virtuous part free rein, and after death the winged soul rises to the heavens. A love of honor, though not raising the lover to the level of the philosopher's search for knowledge, still raises him above the level of the masses, and although at death he leaves the body wingless, he still aspires to regain the soul's wings.

The final paragraph of the palinode returns to the basic purpose of the speech: to emphasize the superiority of the friendship (*philia*) of the lover over the relationship of the nonlover, based as it is on "worldly temperance, dispensing gifts of a mortal and sparing kind" (256e4–5). Socrates' argument is based, as he has just shown, on an extensive and profound exploration of the experiences of the soul, both in the mortal body and in its journey in the spiritual realm.

4. SPEECHMAKING, WRITING, AND TRUTH

(i) Rhetoric and Dialectic (257b7–74c4)

There is at this stage, approximately the halfway point in the dialogue, an abrupt change of mood and, apparently, subject (257b7ff.). Ignoring the totally different content of Socrates' second speech, Phaedrus reveals his limitations by commenting merely on its superiority to the first in terms of its aesthetic qualities and reverts to the aspect of competition in rhetoric in which he imagines Socrates and Lysias are still engaging. The conversation turns around the social and intellectual status of speechwriting and speechwriters (*logographoi*) in general and what constitutes a good speech. In targeting politicians who abused Lysias as a speechwriter,[15] Socrates makes it clear that he is not simply aiming his criticisms at him but is including politicians in his attack on the whole basis of the popular practice of rhetoric. Making speeches is not in itself bad; the question is whether the composer of a speech needs to know the truth of what he is arguing about or simply requires the power to persuade those whom he is addressing (259eff.). Without knowledge of the truth, Socrates argues, oratorical skill is useless; in arguing a particular case and then the reverse, in the course of deceiving others the orator is able to avoid being taken in himself only if he understands precisely the degree of resemblance or difference between things, and he can only do that if he knows the truth about them (262aff.).[16] This is a trivial question in the case of knowledge of simple objects, such as "iron" or "silver," where agreement is obvious, but less so in the case of concepts, such as love, as the previous speeches (arguing opposite sides of the case) illustrate.[17]

However, Socrates is far from arguing that the ability

[15] For the professional limitations arising from Lysias' status as a metic (resident alien) in Athens, see *Phaedrus* translation, n. 85.

[16] "Persuasion versus truth" in oratory is a major concern of Socrates in the earlier dialogue *Gorgias*, e.g., 451–57.

[17] On opposed arguments, see Kerferd, *The Sophistic Movement*, 59–66.

to persuade is irrelevant. Indeed, he gets Phaedrus to re-
read the beginning of Lysias' speech in order to demonstrate that its failure to demonstrate a logical sequence
makes it ineffective, even on its own terms, as a vehicle of
persuasion. Whereas both of Socrates' speeches, despite
being totally different in almost every way, in defining
different kinds of love by the method of Collection and
Division (see above, §3(iii)), formed a sound basis for the
argument.

So what is left for rhetoric? Socrates runs through a
(tongue-in-cheek) survey of the main techniques of persuasion employed by orators of Plato's day (266c–67e),
only to show that, by analogy with professional arts such
as medicine, they are like people able to master the techniques of treating a diseased body without knowing to
whom or when they should apply them, or in the case of
tragedy, how to make speeches of a different type and
length, or of a musician, how to play high and low notes
without having any understanding of how to use the art in
question. They understand the preliminaries to their art
but not the art itself. Without knowledge of the truth,
there is no genuine art (*technē*).[18]

Up to this point Plato appears to be rehearsing arguments already explored in his *Gorgias*. However, here he
goes further. Rhetoric on its own treats the soul as a passive recipient. But the orator, to be a true master of dialectic, needs to have a knowledge of the mind (soul) of the

[18] The Greek *technē* = "art" ("skill" or "craft") indicates an
activity characterized by knowledge, here (260e5), and in *Gorgias*
(463b3–4), contrasted with an "artless routine" (*atechnos tribē*).
For the reasons for the choice of "art" to translate *technē*, see
Phaedrus translation, n. 93.

individual recipient, just as the medical expert needs to know about the nature of the individual body; by a "leading of the soul" (*psychagōgia*) progressively by means of dialectic, the teacher of rhetoric can, through an active and reciprocal relationship with his pupil, bring the recipient to the understanding of ultimate truths. In a particularly densely-written passage, Socrates explains that this process must be addressed to the individual, and, since there is a wide variety of human souls and ways of addressing them, it is no easy task, as Phaedrus recognizes (272b5–6).

(ii) Writing and Speech (274c5–78e3)

The previous argument, highlighting the importance of the interactive relationship, leads naturally into a discussion of the superior merits of the spoken word as a medium for this kind of individual discourse. Socrates places the origins of this discovery in a so-called ancient Egyptian story (made up by him for the purpose, as Phaedrus clearly recognizes [275b3–4]) where a divinity, Theuth, attempts unsuccessfully to persuade god/king Thamous of the superior merits of the new discovery of writing for making Egyptians wiser and improving their memory (274e4–7). Thamous rejects Theuth's arguments on the grounds that reliance on writing will lead to neglect of the use of memory, but more vitally, to uncritical reception of what is written.[19] This is because, Socrates says, written words

[19] Socrates is here countering the inclusion of writing by, e.g., sophists as a discovery, similar to fire, which led to the progressive social and intellectual development of mankind (see, e.g., *Protagoras* 320dff.).

always say the same thing and present an imperviously silent front to any attempt to question them; they are unable to defend themselves in argument, in contrast to spoken interaction. The spoken word, as Socrates has already argued, speaks to the individual recipient's soul. This long-term advantage of the spoken word is emphasized by Socrates in a memorable agricultural image: Socrates depicts "the man who has knowledge" (276c3–5) as planting words in a soul capable of receiving them, as "a seed from which others grow in other habitats, capable of making it forever immortal" (277a1–2).

Socrates proceeds to sum up his argument: if words are delivered truthfully about important subjects and the composer is able to support them in dialectical argument and successfully aim them at an individual recipient's soul, he has a claim to be called a lover of wisdom, that is, a philosopher.

(iii) Socrates and Isocrates

The last few sections (278e4–79b3) look at first sight like an addendum to the main dialogue. In reply to Socrates' injunction that Phaedrus should pass on all this to his friend (*hetairos*) Lysias, Phaedrus retorts that Socrates should in his turn pass it on to *his* friend Isocrates. As the foremost author of written speeches in the mid-fourth century, who also laid claim to *philosophia*, Isocrates was an influential teacher of rhetoric. As such he can be seen as a rival to Plato and so a possible implied target of Socrates' criticisms, ostensibly of Lysias and other speechwriters: "a man who has nothing more to his credit than the things he has composed or written, twisting them this and that way in the course of time" (278d8–9), that is, *not* concerned with a meeting of souls in interactive dialectic as Socrates has been describing it. Therefore, the question of whether Socrates' subsequent commendation of Isocrates (279a3ff.) is sincere in the light of all this is, to say the least, debatable. Many commentators detect an ironic twist in Socrates' comments here.

Furthermore, in Socrates' cautiously expressed hopes for Isocrates' future, Plato may be exploiting a tension between the late fifth-century date in which the dialogue is set, at which point Isocrates (b. 436) might be seen as a promising up-and-coming young rhetorician, and the actual date of composition, when Isocrates would have been an established orator. Plato may well be using this casual exchange to aim a sideswipe at an eminent rival. This, Plato may be saying, is what Isocrates' "certain philosophical instinct" (279a9–b1) might have become.[20]

5. THE UNITY OF THE DIOLOGUE: LOVE AND/OR RHETORIC?

Finally, we return to the question that has been looming in the background throughout this Introduction: the unity of the dialogue and what exactly is its *skopos* (aim) or what, as a whole, it is about. This has been the subject of extensive discussion from as far back as the earliest extant commentary on *Phaedrus* by the Neoplatonist Hermias of Alexandria (5th century AD). Many Plato commentators have seen Socrates' second speech, the construction of a

[20] See De Vries, 15–18; Rowe, n. on 278e5ff. (pp. 215–16). Ryan, *Plato's Phaedrus* (n. on 279a9), comments on "[Socrates'] warm bath of condescension." Representing the view that Plato's commendation is sincere, see Hackforth, 168.

powerful myth of the journey of the winged soul and the effect of this experience on the lover and the loved one (244a1–57b6), as the emotional climax of the dialogue, only to be followed, for some reason, by an abrupt change of topic and mood.

Just to accept that the dialogue divides for some reason into two distinct parts is, however, to ignore the "necessary compositional rule" (*anankē logographikē* [see 264b7]), the fitting of words and parts together to form a coherent whole, which Socrates complains Lysias' speech lacked, and which, one would suppose, Plato would hardly be likely to ignore in his own composition. Moreover, if the second speech of Socrates is intended as a climax, his subsequent comment on it is, at first sight, difficult to understand. He describes it, "Mixing together a not altogether unpersuasive speech, we playfully sang a hymn in the form of a story (*muthikon tina humnon*) in appropriate and pious fashion to my master and yours, Phaedrus, Love, the overseer of beautiful boys." He comments on the speech a few lines further on as "actually done playfully in fun" (265b8–c9).

The underlying subject of the dialogue, established right at the beginning, is about the nature of language (in this case expressed in speeches) as a medium capable of leading the participants toward a realization of the truth. Already in the introductory sections of the dialogue, Socrates' strange and uncharacteristic enthusiasm for the performance of speeches (a genre that elsewhere in Plato's dialogues he regularly deprecates in favor of dialectical exchange[21]) is designed as an initial stimulus to lead Phaedrus from his devotion to the superficial works of contem-

---

[21] For example, *Protagoras* 320c–29bff.

porary[22] speechwriters toward an appreciation of real dialectic later on. What was not done "playfully" in his second speech, as Socrates immediately makes clear (265c9ff.), was the definition of love as a form of madness right at the beginning of his speech by means of Collection and Division in order to establish what is true from what is false. In immediately following this with the tightly constructed definition of the nature of soul, reminiscent of the pre-Socratics in language and content (245c1–46a2), Socrates lays down the twin philosophical pillars upon which the remainder of his *muthos* is based. In composing his myth of the journey of the winged soul, Socrates' dramatic and colorful exposition has a number of aims that he expresses on different levels, which are specifically tailored to Phaedrus' likely comprehension. The probability that this is the case is strengthened by Socrates' comment at the end of the speech that it is actually Phaedrus who is forcing him to "to speak in poetic language" (257a5–6).

So the underlying trajectory of the whole dialogue lies in the need to reach and interact with Phaedrus' soul, in order to convert him from the sterile competitive speech-making of Lysias. The key concept linking the different parts together is the "guiding of the soul" (*psychagōgia*), which is, as Socrates says (271c10), the function of speech, where words spoken with knowledge are written in the soul of the recipient. So the relationship of the lover of the *palinode* with the soul of his beloved is both erotic and educational and has a parallel in that of the teacher of true dialectic, who, in order to have an interactive relationship

---

[22] "Contemporary," whether in the dramatic context (late 5th century) or that of the actual date of composition, Plato's own maturity (mid-4th century; see Appendix).

with his pupil, must have an intimate knowledge of his soul, just as the winged soul of the lover in the myth needs to lead and teach the soul of his beloved (253b–c).

By the end of the dialogue, Socrates has instructed Phaedrus that speaking to the listener's soul is the basis of true *erōs* and expresses the hope that they may both become converted to this view, a wish that Phaedrus fervently echoes (see 278b5–6). So at the end Phaedrus' conversion is presumed to have been successful. But, judging by his interaction with Socrates throughout the dialogue, how far Plato intends us to believe that Socrates has actually won Phaedrus over permanently is surely open to doubt.[23]

APPENDIX: DRAMATIC AND COMPOSTIONAL DATES OF PHAEDRUS

As to the likely dramatic date of the dialogue, the obvious necessity of placing it before Socrates' trial and execution in 399 suggests the early part of Lysias' career (born probably in the 440s), which also fits the picture of Isocrates (b. 436) "still young" (278e10). Phaedrus (b. ca. 445), a major character also in *Symposium*, fled into exile to avoid trial following his participation in the religious sacrilege involving desecration of images of the god Hermes and profanation of the Mysteries, which was committed im-

---

[23] On either side of the argument, see, e.g., Yunis, 17 ("No wonder [Phaedrus] converts so readily once S. introduces him to divine *erōs* in the palinode"), and Rowe, 12 ("some commentators claim that by the end of the dialogue Socrates' arguments have cured [Phaedrus], but in my view the signs are distinctly ambigu-

mediately prior to the Sicilian expedition during the Peloponnesian War in 415 (Thucydides 6.27–9); see Introduction to the *Symposium*, §5. This puts a possible date either before the sacrilege or after Phaedrus' return, but before 404, which is when Lysias' brother Polemarchus (at 257b4 spoken of as still alive) was executed, and Sophocles and Euripides (268c5) are also spoken of as still alive (i.e., before 406, when Euripides died). Sometime during last decade of the fifth century might be presumed, but as so often with Platonic dialogues, no precise dramatic date consistent with known events can be determined or perhaps even intended.

For the date of composition there is no direct evidence. The extensive references to orators and rhetoricians in the second part of the dialogue could cover any period of the late fifth and first half of the fourth centuries. However, the detailed description of the soul, its tripartite nature, the Theory of Recollection of the Forms, and the soul's progress through reincarnated lives (*Phaedrus* 245–249) strongly suggests familiarity with *Meno*, *Phaedo*, and *Republic*, the last of which almost definitely postdates *Symposium*. In addition, the introduction of Collection and Division (237d, 244–45, 265dff.), a key element in later dialogues, such as *Statesman*, is first introduced in *Phaedrus*—all of which suggests a date in the late Middle Period, that is, the 370s (see Chronology of Plato's Life and Works).

---

ous, and meant to be so"). One might argue further that if there is ambiguity in the ending, this may be intended by Plato to indicate the provisional nature of the written words of the dialogue; further spoken interaction is needed between Socrates and Phaedrus to reach the latter's soul.

ΦΑΙΔΡΟΣ

ΣΩΚΡΑΤΗΣ   ΦΑΙΔΡΟΣ

227 ΣΩΚΡΑΤΗΣ ῏Ω φίλε Φαῖδρε, ποῖ δὴ καὶ πόθεν;

ΦΑΙΔΡΟΣ Παρὰ Λυσίου, ὦ Σώκρατες, τοῦ Κεφάλου, πορεύομαι δὲ πρὸς περίπατον ἔξω τείχους· συχνὸν γὰρ ἐκεῖ διέτριψα χρόνον καθήμενος ἐξ ἑωθινοῦ. τῷ δὲ σῷ καὶ | ἐμῷ ἑταίρῳ πειθόμενος Ἀκουμενῷ κατὰ τὰς ὁδοὺς ποιοῦμαι τοὺς περιπάτους· φησὶ γὰρ ἀκοπωτέρους εἶναι τῶν ἐν τοῖς δρόμοις.

b ΣΩ. Καλῶς γάρ, ὦ ἑταῖρε, λέγει. ἀτὰρ Λυσίας ἦν, ὡς ἔοικεν, ἐν ἄστει.

ΦΑΙ. Ναί, παρ᾽ Ἐπικράτει, ἐν τῇδε τῇ πλησίον τοῦ | Ὀλυμπίου οἰκίᾳ τῇ Μορυχίᾳ.

ΣΩ. Τίς οὖν δὴ ἦν ἡ διατριβή; ἢ δῆλον ὅτι τῶν λόγων ὑμᾶς Λυσίας εἱστία;

ΦΑΙ. Πεύσῃ, εἴ σοι σχολὴ προϊόντι ἀκούειν.

---

1 Phaedrus is well-known to Plato's Socrates, figuring prominently in the *Symposium*.

2 Acumenus was the father of Eryximachus, who figures prominently in the *Symposium*.

3 His actual residence was in the Piraeus with his brother

344

PHAEDRUS

SOCRATES   PHAEDRUS

SOCRATES My dear friend Phaedrus![1] Where is it 227
you're going and where have you come from?

PHAEDRUS From Lysias, Socrates, Cephalus' son,
and I'm on my way for a walk outside the wall. That's because I've spent a long time sitting there since daybreak.
Persuaded by your friend and mine Acumenus,[2] I'm taking my walks along the open roads: for he says that they're
more refreshing than those in the colonnades.

S. Yes, and he's right, my friend. But Lysias was in town,   b
it seems.[3]

P. Yes, with Epicrates, in the house which used to belong to Morichus[4] near the temple of Olympian Zeus.

S. So what did you do to pass the time? Or does it
go without saying that Lysias gave you all a feast of his
speeches?

P. You'll find out, if you have time to listen while you
walk.

Polemarchus in or near the house of their father, Cephalus (*Republic* 1.328b).

[4] Morichus, briefly mentioned in comedy for a luxurious life-
style (see Nails, 208). Epicrates (b4) is a democratic politician
who was prominent in the restoration of the democracy in 403.

ΣΩ. Τί δέ; οὐκ ἂν οἴει με κατὰ Πίνδαρον "καὶ ἀσχολίας | ὑπέρτερον" πρᾶγμα ποιήσασθαι τὸ τεήν τε καὶ Λυσίου διατριβὴν ἀκοῦσαι;

c   ΦΑΙ. Πρόαγε δή.

ΣΩ. Λέγοις ἄν.

ΦΑΙ. Καὶ μήν, ὦ Σώκρατες, προσήκουσα γέ σοι ἡ ἀκοή· ὁ γάρ τοι λόγος ἦν, περὶ ὃν διετρίβομεν, οὐκ οἶδ᾽ ὅντινα | τρόπον ἐρωτικός. γέγραφε γὰρ δὴ ὁ Λυσίας πειρώμενόν τινα τῶν καλῶν, οὐχ ὑπ᾽ ἐραστοῦ δέ, ἀλλ᾽ αὐτὸ δὴ τοῦτο καὶ κεκόμψευται· λέγει γὰρ ὡς χαριστέον μὴ ἐρῶντι μᾶλλον ἢ ἐρῶντι.

ΣΩ. Ὦ γενναῖος. εἴθε γράψειεν ὡς χρὴ πένητι μᾶλλον ἢ πλουσίῳ, καὶ πρεσβυτέρῳ ἢ νεωτέρῳ, καὶ

d ὅσα ἄλλα ἐμοί τε πρόσεστι καὶ τοῖς πολλοῖς ἡμῶν· ἦ γὰρ ἂν ἀστεῖοι καὶ δημωφελεῖς εἶεν οἱ λόγοι. ἔγωγ᾽ οὖν οὕτως ἐπιτεθύμηκα ἀκοῦσαι, ὥστ᾽ ἐὰν βαδίζων ποιῇ τὸν περίπατον Μέγαράδε καὶ κατὰ Ἡρόδικον προσβὰς τῷ τείχει πάλιν ἀπίῃς, | οὐ μή σου ἀπολειφθῶ.

228   ΦΑΙ. Πῶς λέγεις, ὦ βέλτιστε Σώκρατες; οἴει με, ἃ Λυσίας ἐν πολλῷ χρόνῳ κατὰ σχολὴν συνέθηκε, δεινότατος ὢν τῶν νῦν γράφειν, ταῦτα ἰδιώτην ὄντα ἀπομνημονεύσειν ἀξίως ἐκείνου; πολλοῦ γε δέω· καίτοι ἐβουλόμην γ᾽ ἂν μᾶλλον ἤ μοι πολὺ χρυσίον γενέσθαι. |

---

5 *Isthmian* 1.1–3.

6 For Herodicus, see Nails, 164. Socrates makes a joke: a stroll

S. What? Do you think I wouldn't value hearing how you and Lysias' spent your time "even above the absence of leisure," as Pindar puts it?[5]

P. Lead the way then.   c

S. Perhaps you'd like to tell me about it.

P. Very well, Socrates, you're just the person to hear it. You see the speech we were discussing was in a certain kind of way about love. You see, Lysias has actually depicted someone good-looking being propositioned, but not by a lover—but that's the very point he's really being clever about: for he says that one should gratify one who isn't a lover rather than one who is.

S. What a magnificent fellow! If only he'd written that it should be to a poor man rather than a rich one, an older rather than a younger one and whatever else is appropriate to myself and the majority of us. For that would make the   d
speeches stylish and useful to people. Anyway for my part I've become so keen to listen that even if you take your walk as far as Megara and, as Herodicus says, you get to the wall and come back again, you can be sure I won't get left behind.[6]

P. What do you mean, my dearest Socrates? Do you   228
think that an ordinary fellow like me could recall what Lysias, the most accomplished of today's writers, has put together at leisure over a long period of time in a manner worthy of him? I'm far from good enough. And yet I wish I could, rather than acquire a lot of money.

to Megara would involve nearly twenty-six miles walking in the opposite direction from their present route. The reference to the wall is uncertain but probably pokes fun at Herodicus, of whose expertise Plato had no high opinion (cf. *Republic* 406a–b).

PLATO

ΣΩ. Ὦ Φαῖδρε, εἰ ἐγὼ Φαῖδρον ἀγνοῶ, καὶ ἐμαυτοῦ
ἐπιλέλησμαι. ἀλλὰ γὰρ οὐδέτερά ἐστι τούτων· εὖ οἶδα
ὅτι Λυσίου λόγον ἀκούων ἐκεῖνος οὐ μόνον ἅπαξ
ἤκουσεν, ἀλλὰ πολλάκις ἐπαναλαμβάνων ἐκέλευέν οἱ
b λέγειν, ὁ δὲ ἐπείθετο προθύμως. τῷ δὲ οὐδὲ ταῦτα ἦν
ἱκανά, ἀλλὰ τελευτῶν παραλαβὼν τὸ βιβλίον ἃ μάλιστα ἐπεθύμει ἐπεσκόπει, καὶ τοῦτο δρῶν ἐξ ἑωθινοῦ
καθήμενος ἀπειπὼν εἰς περίπατον ᾔει, ὡς μὲν ἐγὼ
οἶμαι, νὴ τὸν κύνα, ἐξεπιστάμενος τὸν | λόγον, εἰ μὴ
πάνυ τι ἦν μακρός. ἐπορεύετο δ᾽ ἐκτὸς τείχους ἵνα
μελετῴη. ἀπαντήσας δὲ τῷ νοσοῦντι περὶ λόγων
ἀκοήν, ἰδὼν μέν, ἰδών, ἥσθη ὅτι ἕξοι τὸν συγκορυβαν-
c τιῶντα, καὶ προάγειν ἐκέλευε. δεομένου δὲ λέγειν τοῦ
τῶν λόγων ἐραστοῦ, ἐθρύπτετο ὡς δὴ οὐκ ἐπιθυμῶν
λέγειν· τελευτῶν δὲ ἔμελλε καὶ εἰ μή τις ἑκὼν ἀκούοι
βίᾳ ἐρεῖν. σὺ οὖν, ὦ Φαῖδρε, αὐτοῦ δεήθητι ὅπερ
τάχα πάντως ποιήσει νῦν ἤδη | ποιεῖν.

ΦΑΙ. Ἐμοὶ ὡς ἀληθῶς πολὺ κράτιστόν ἐστιν οὕτως
ὅπως δύναμαι λέγειν, ὥς μοι δοκεῖς σὺ οὐδαμῶς με
ἀφήσειν πρὶν ἂν εἴπω ἁμῶς γέ πως.

ΣΩ. Πάνυ γάρ σοι ἀληθῆ δοκῶ.

d ΦΑΙ. Οὑτωσὶ τοίνυν ποιήσω. τῷ ὄντι γάρ, ὦ Σώκρατες, παντὸς μᾶλλον τά γε ῥήματα οὐκ ἐξέμαθον·
τὴν μέντοι διάνοιαν σχεδὸν ἁπάντων, οἷς ἔφη διαφέ-

---

7 An oath characteristic of Socrates, though not exclusive to
him (see Aristophanes, Wasps 83), refers to the Egyptian jackal-
headed god Anubis (see Apology 21e; Gorgias 482b).

S. Oh Phaedrus! If I don't know Phaedrus, I've forgotten who I am too. But the fact is that it's neither of these things. I know perfectly well that in hearing Lysias' speech, that man not only listened to it once, but he asked him to repeat it to him again and again and Lysias was eager to oblige. Yet not even this was enough, but he ended up   b
borrowing the book and scrutinizing the parts he liked the most and, exhausted from sitting doing this from early in the morning, he went off for a walk and, as I think, by the Dog,[7] he knew the speech off by heart, unless it was really quite long. He was walking outside the wall in order to practice it. On meeting a man who was sick with desire for listening to speeches, and when he saw him, well, when he saw him, he was delighted that he'd have someone to share his Corybantic passion and told him to lead on.[8] But   c
when the lover of speeches asked him to declaim, he pretended to be coy as if he wasn't really keen to speak. But he was going to deliver the speech by force in the end, even if no one was willing to listen. So, Phaedrus, ask him yourself to do right now what he'll soon do anyway.

P. To tell the truth, it's much the best thing for me to speak as best I can, since I don't think there's any way you'll let me go until I speak, somehow or other.

S. Yes, you've got quite the right idea about me.

P. Then that is what I shall do. You see, Socrates, in   d
truth the last thing you should think is that I have learned the words off by heart. However, I'll go through the general sense of almost all the things by which he said he

[8] The Corybantes were priests of the Phrygian goddess Cybele, who performed frenzied dancing to the accompaniment of flutes and drums.

ρειν τὰ τοῦ ἐρῶντος ἢ τὰ τοῦ μή, ἐν κεφαλαίοις ἕκα-
στον ἐφεξῆς δίειμι, | ἀρξάμενος ἀπὸ τοῦ πρώτου.

ΣΩ. Δείξας γε πρῶτον, ὦ φιλότης, τί ἄρα ἐν τῇ
ἀριστερᾷ ἔχεις ὑπὸ τῷ ἱματίῳ· τοπάζω γάρ σε ἔχειν
τὸν λόγον αὐτόν. εἰ δὲ τοῦτό ἐστιν, οὑτωσὶ διανοοῦ
περὶ ἐμοῦ, ὡς ἐγώ σε πάνυ μὲν φιλῶ, παρόντος δὲ καὶ
Λυσίου, ἐμαυτόν σοι ἐμμελετᾶν παρέχειν οὐ πάνυ δέ-
e δοκται. ἀλλ᾽ ἴθι, δείκνυε.

ΦΑΙ. Παῦε. ἐκκέκρουκάς με ἐλπίδος, ὦ Σώκρατες,
ἣν εἶχον ἐν σοὶ ὡς ἐγγυμνασόμενος. ἀλλὰ ποῦ δὴ
βούλει | καθιζόμενοι ἀναγνῶμεν;

229 ΣΩ. Δεῦρ᾽ ἐκτραπόμενοι κατὰ τὸν Ἰλισὸν ἴωμεν,
εἶτα ὅπου ἂν δόξῃ ἐν ἡσυχίᾳ καθιζησόμεθα.

ΦΑΙ. Εἰς καιρόν, ὡς ἔοικεν, ἀνυπόδητος ὢν ἔτυχον·
σὺ μὲν γὰρ δὴ ἀεί. ῥᾷστον οὖν ἡμῖν κατὰ τὸ ὑδάτιον
βρέχουσι | τοὺς πόδας ἰέναι, καὶ οὐκ ἀηδές, ἄλλως τε
καὶ τήνδε τὴν ὥραν τοῦ ἔτους τε καὶ τῆς ἡμέρας.

ΣΩ. Πρόαγε δή, καὶ σκόπει ἅμα ὅπου καθιζησόμεθα.

ΦΑΙ. Ὁρᾷς οὖν ἐκείνην τὴν ὑψηλοτάτην πλάτανον;
ΣΩ. Τί μήν;

b ΦΑΙ. Ἐκεῖ σκιά τ᾽ ἐστὶν καὶ πνεῦμα μέτριον, καὶ
πόα καθίζεσθαι ἢ ἂν βουλώμεθα κατακλιθῆναι.

ΣΩ. Προάγοις ἄν.

distinguished the characteristics of the lover and the non-lover in turn, under separate headings beginning from the first.

S. Yes, but only after you've first shown me, my good friend, what you've got in your left hand under your cloak. My guess is that you've got the actual speech. If this is so, consider my position: that while I'm very fond of you, as we've got Lysias here too I'm not altogether inclined to offer myself for you to practice on. But go on, show me.　　e

P. Stop! You've shattered my hope, Socrates, which I had, that I'd practice on you. But where do you actually want us to sit down and read?

S. Let's turn off this way and walk along the Ilissus,　229 then we can sit down in a quiet spot wherever you think best.[9]

P. Lucky then, it seems, that I happen to have no shoes on: you of course never do.[10] So it will be easiest for us to go along the stream getting our feet wet, and not unpleasant either, especially at this time of year and this time of day.

S. Right, lead on and keep an eye open for a place for us to sit down.

P. So do you see that very tall plane tree?

S. Yes indeed.

P. There's shade there and a bit of a light breeze, and　b grass to sit on, or, if we want, lie down on.

S. So please lead the way.

[9] For the probable route, see Wycherley, "The Scene of Plato's *Phaidros*."

[10] Note Socrates' exceptionally smart appearance, wearing sandals to Agathon's party at *Symposium* 174a3–4.

ΦΑΙ. Εἰπέ μοι, ὦ Σώκρατες, οὐκ ἐνθένδε μέντοι ποθὲν | ἀπὸ τοῦ Ἰλισοῦ λέγεται ὁ Βορέας τὴν Ὠρείθυιαν ἁρπάσαι;

ΣΩ. Λέγεται γάρ.

ΦΑΙ. Ἆρ᾽ οὖν ἐνθένδε; χαρίεντα γοῦν καὶ καθαρὰ καὶ διαφανῆ τὰ ὑδάτια φαίνεται, καὶ ἐπιτήδεια κόραις παίζειν παρ᾽ αὐτά.

c ΣΩ. Οὔκ, ἀλλὰ κάτωθεν ὅσον δύ᾽ ἢ τρία στάδια, ᾗ πρὸς τὸ ἐν Ἄγρας διαβαίνομεν· καί πού τίς ἐστι βωμὸς αὐτόθι Βορέου.

ΦΑΙ. Οὐ πάνυ νενόηκα· ἀλλ᾽ εἰπὲ πρὸς Διός, ὦ Σώκρατες, | σὺ τοῦτο τὸ μυθολόγημα πείθῃ ἀληθὲς εἶναι;

ΣΩ. Ἀλλ᾽ εἰ ἀπιστοίην, ὥσπερ οἱ σοφοί, οὐκ ἂν ἄτοπος εἴην, εἶτα σοφιζόμενος φαίην αὐτὴν πνεῦμα Βορέου κατὰ τῶν πλησίον πετρῶν σὺν Φαρμακείᾳ παίζουσαν ὦσαι, καὶ οὕτω δὴ τελευτήσασαν λεχθῆναι ὑπὸ τοῦ Βορέου ἀνάρπαστον γεγονέναι—ἢ ἐξ

d Ἀρείου πάγου· λέγεται γὰρ αὖ καὶ οὗτος ὁ λόγος, ὡς ἐκεῖθεν ἀλλ᾽ οὐκ ἐνθένδε ἡρπάσθη.[1] ἐγὼ δέ, ὦ Φαῖδρε, ἄλλως μὲν τὰ τοιαῦτα χαρίεντα ἡγοῦμαι, λίαν δὲ δεινοῦ καὶ ἐπιπόνου καὶ οὐ πάνυ εὐτυχοῦς ἀνδρός, κατ᾽ ἄλλο | μὲν οὐδέν, ὅτι δ᾽ αὐτῷ ἀνάγκη μετὰ τοῦτο τὸ τῶν Ἱπποκενταύρων εἶδος ἐπανορθοῦσθαι, καὶ αὖθις τὸ τῆς Χιμαίρας, καὶ ἐπιρρεῖ δὲ ὄχλος τοιούτων Γορ-

[1] ἢ ἐξ . . . ἡρπάσθη secl. Bast

P. Tell me, Socrates, wasn't it in fact from somewhere around here where Boreas is said to have abducted Oreithyia from the Ilissus?[11]

S. Yes, that's what they say.

P. From this actual spot then? At any rate the water looks nice and pure and clear, and just right for girls to play beside.

S. No, actually it's from about two or three stades[12] downstream where we cross to the shrine in Agra—and I think there's an altar to Boreas somewhere about there.

P. I've not really noticed. But tell me, by Zeus, Socrates, do you believe this myth is true?

S. Well if I didn't believe it, like the wise men,[13] I wouldn't be the odd man out. Trying to rationalize it I'd then say that the breath of Boreas pushed her down from the nearby rocks as she played with Pharmaceia, and dying in that way was said to have been snatched up by Boreas— or it was from Ares' Hill: for this version of the story is also told that she was abducted from there and not from here.[14] But I, Phaedrus, think that while stories like these are pleasing for other reasons, they are typical of a man who is too clever and painstaking, but not very successful, if only because that after this he has to put to rights the form of the Centaurs and again that of the Chimera, and there pours in an inundation of such things as Gorgons and

c

d

---

[11] See Herodotus 7.189. Boreas is the North Wind.

[12] About a quarter of a mile.

[13] "The intellectuals," "the experts."   [14] The Areopagus, west-northwest of the Acropolis. Some editors have suggested bracketing "or it was from Ares' Hill [the Areopagus] . . . not from here" as a later learned comment (see textual note).

PLATO

γόνων καὶ Πηγάσων καὶ ἄλλων ἀμηχάνων πλήθη τε
e καὶ ἀτοπίαι τερατολόγων τινῶν φύσεων· αἷς εἴ τις
ἀπιστῶν προσβιβᾷ κατὰ τὸ εἰκὸς ἕκαστον, ἅτε
ἀγροίκῳ τινὶ σοφίᾳ χρώμενος, πολλῆς αὐτῷ σχολῆς
δεήσει. ἐμοὶ δὲ πρὸς αὐτὰ οὐδαμῶς ἐστι σχολή· τὸ δὲ
| αἴτιον, ὦ φίλε, τούτου τόδε. οὐ δύναμαί πω κατὰ τὸ
Δελφικὸν γράμμα γνῶναι ἐμαυτόν· γελοῖον δή μοι
φαίνεται τοῦτο ἔτι ἀγνοοῦντα τὰ ἀλλότρια σκοπεῖν.
230 ὅθεν δὴ χαίρειν ἐάσας ταῦτα, πειθόμενος δὲ τῷ νο-
μιζομένῳ περὶ αὐτῶν, ὃ νυνδὴ ἔλεγον, σκοπῶ οὐ
ταῦτα ἀλλ' ἐμαυτόν, εἴτε τι θηρίον ὂν τυγχάνω Τυφῶ-
νος πολυπλοκώτερον καὶ μᾶλλον ἐπιτεθυμμένον, | εἴτε
ἡμερώτερόν τε καὶ ἁπλούστερον ζῷον, θείας τινὸς καὶ
ἀτύφου μοίρας φύσει μετέχον. ἀτάρ, ὦ ἑταῖρε, μεταξὺ
τῶν λόγων, ἆρ' οὐ τόδε ἦν τὸ δένδρον ἐφ' ὅπερ ἦγες
ἡμᾶς;
b   ΦΑΙ. Τοῦτο μὲν οὖν αὐτό.
   ΣΩ. Νὴ τὴν Ἥραν, καλή γε ἡ καταγωγή. ἥ τε γὰρ
πλάτανος αὕτη μάλ' ἀμφιλαφής τε καὶ ὑψηλή, τοῦ
τε ἄγνου τὸ ὕψος καὶ τὸ σύσκιον πάγκαλον, καὶ ὡς
ἀκμὴν ἔχει τῆς | ἄνθης, ὡς ἂν εὐωδέστατον παρέχοι
τὸν τόπον· ἥ τε αὖ πηγὴ χαριεστάτη ὑπὸ τῆς πλατά-
νου ῥεῖ μάλα ψυχροῦ ὕδατος, ὥστε γε τῷ ποδὶ τεκμή-
ρασθαι. Νυμφῶν τέ τινων καὶ Ἀχελῴου ἱερὸν ἀπὸ τῶν
c κορῶν τε καὶ ἀγαλμάτων ἔοικεν εἶναι. εἰ δ' αὖ βούλει,

354

Pegasuses and a horde of other impossibilities and absurdities consisting of fantastic beings of one kind or another. If anyone doesn't believe in these and will try to reduce e each into accordance with probability, as if applying some kind of everyday wisdom, he'll need a lot of time for it. I myself have no time at all for this, and the reason, my friend, is as follows: I'm unable as yet to know myself, as the inscription at Delphi says.[15] Indeed it seems ridiculous that I should examine things outside my sphere while I still don't know this. So then, saying goodbye to this and trust- 230 ing in the conventional belief in them, as I was saying just now, I shall examine not them but myself, to see if I really am either some monster more tangled up and more raging than Typhon, or a tamer and simpler animal with some natural share of the divine and calm. But, my friend, to interrupt what we've been saying, wasn't this the tree you were bringing us to?

P. Yes indeed, this is the very one. b

S. By Hera; what a fine place to stop! For this plane tree is widespreading and tall, and the height and the shadiness of the agnus tree are very lovely, and now that it's in full bloom it will make the place particularly fragrant. And again, the stream beneath the plane tree flows most delightfully with very cold water, as I can tell by dipping my foot in it. It seems to be a sanctuary of some nymphs and Achelous[16] judging by the votive figurines and statuettes. And again, if you like, how delightful and c

[15] The inscription in the forecourt of the temple of Apollo at Delphi allegedly read "know yourself" (Pausanias 10.24.1).

[16] God of freshwater streams, father of nymphs, named after the great river in Acarnania (N.W. Greece).

τὸ εὔπνουν τοῦ τόπου ὡς ἀγαπητὸν καὶ σφόδρα ἡδύ·
θερινόν τε καὶ λιγυρὸν ὑπηχεῖ τῷ τῶν τεττίγων χορῷ.
πάντων δὲ κομψότατον τὸ τῆς πόας, ὅτι ἐν ἠρέμα
προσάντει ἱκανὴ πέφυκε κατακλινέντι τὴν κεφαλὴν
παγκάλως ἔχειν. | ὥστε ἄριστά σοι ἐξενάγηται, ὦ
φίλε Φαῖδρε.

ΦΑΙ. Σὺ δέ γε, ὦ θαυμάσιε, ἀτοπώτατός τις φαίνῃ.
ἀτεχνῶς γάρ, ὃ λέγεις, ξεναγουμένῳ τινὶ καὶ οὐκ ἐπι-
d χωρίῳ ἔοικας· οὕτως ἐκ τοῦ ἄστεος οὔτ᾽ εἰς τὴν ὑπερ-
ορίαν ἀποδημεῖς, οὔτ᾽ ἔξω τείχους ἔμοιγε δοκεῖς τὸ
παράπαν ἐξιέναι.

ΣΩ. Συγγίγνωσκέ μοι, ὦ ἄριστε. φιλομαθὴς γάρ
εἰμι· τὰ μὲν οὖν χωρία καὶ τὰ δένδρα οὐδέν μ᾽ ἐθέλει
διδάσκειν, | οἱ δ᾽ ἐν τῷ ἄστει ἄνθρωποι. σὺ μέντοι
δοκεῖς μοι τῆς ἐμῆς ἐξόδου τὸ φάρμακον ηὑρηκέναι.
ὥσπερ γὰρ οἱ τὰ πεινῶντα θρέμματα θαλλὸν ἤ τινα
καρπὸν προσείοντες ἄγουσιν, σὺ ἐμοὶ λόγους οὕτω
προτείνων ἐν βιβλίοις τήν τε Ἀττικὴν φαίνῃ περι-
e άξειν ἅπασαν καὶ ὅποι ἂν ἄλλοσε βούλῃ. νῦν δ᾽ οὖν
ἐν τῷ παρόντι δεῦρ᾽ ἀφικόμενος ἐγὼ μέν μοι δοκῶ
κατακείσεσθαι, σὺ δ᾽ ἐν ὁποίῳ σχήματι οἴει ῥᾷστα
ἀναγνώσεσθαι, τοῦθ᾽ ἑλόμενος ἀναγίγνωσκε. |

ΦΑΙ. Ἄκουε δή.

---

17 Socrates' excursus (b2–c5), in the style of a formal *ekphrasis* (description) is uncharacteristic of him and may reflect, as
Phaedrus suggests (c6–d2), the influence of his unaccustomed
countryside surroundings.

very sweet the fresh smell of the place is. It echoes summer-like and shrill to the chorus of cicadas. Most delightful of all is the effect of the grass, because it's thick enough on its gentle upward slope to make it perfect to rest one's head upon when you lie down. You've done your job as guide very well, Phaedrus.[17]

P. But you, you strange fellow, seem to be very much out of place. For as you say you seem simply like someone being guided round as a stranger and not someone who belongs here. This comes from your not going out of the city either to the border nor, I think, outside the wall at all.[18]

S. Forgive me, my friend. You see I'm a lover of learning: the countryside and trees don't want to teach me anything, but people in town do. However you seem to me to have discovered the charm to get me out here. For just as men lead their hungry animals by shaking a branch or some vegetable in front of them, so you, by holding speeches in books in front of me, appear to be about to lead me around the whole of Attica and wherever else you wish. But now for the present, having got here, I think I'm going to lie down, but you choose whatever position in which you think you are most comfortable for reading, and read.

P. Right, listen.

[18] For Socrates' reputation for hardly ever going outside the boundary walls of Athens, see also *Crito*, 52b.

Περὶ μὲν τῶν ἐμῶν πραγμάτων ἐπίστασαι, καὶ ὡς
νομίζω συμφέρειν ἡμῖν γενομένων τούτων ἀκήκοας·
ἀξιῶ δὲ μὴ διὰ τοῦτο ἀτυχῆσαι ὧν δέομαι, ὅτι οὐκ
231 ἐραστὴς ὤν σου τυγχάνω. ὡς ἐκείνοις μὲν τότε μεταμέλει ὧν ἂν εὖ ποιήσωσιν, ἐπειδὰν τῆς ἐπιθυμίας
παύσωνται· τοῖς δὲ οὐκ ἔστι χρόνος ἐν ᾧ μεταγνῶναι
προσήκει. οὐ γὰρ ὑπ᾽ ἀνάγκης ἀλλ᾽ | ἑκόντες, ὡς ἂν
ἄριστα περὶ τῶν οἰκείων βουλεύσαιντο, πρὸς τὴν δύναμιν τὴν αὑτῶν εὖ ποιοῦσιν. ἔτι δὲ οἱ μὲν ἐρῶντες
σκοποῦσιν ἅ τε κακῶς διέθεντο τῶν αὑτῶν διὰ τὸν
ἔρωτα καὶ ἃ πεποιήκασιν εὖ, καὶ ὃν εἶχον πόνον
προστιθέντες ἡγοῦνται πάλαι τὴν ἀξίαν ἀποδεδωκέ-
b ναι χάριν τοῖς ἐρωμένοις· τοῖς δὲ μὴ ἐρῶσιν οὔτε τὴν
τῶν οἰκείων ἀμέλειαν διὰ τοῦτο ἔστιν προφασίζεσθαι,
οὔτε τοὺς παρεληλυθότας πόνους ὑπολογίζεσθαι, οὔτε
τὰς πρὸς τοὺς προσήκοντας | διαφορὰς αἰτιάσασθαι·
ὥστε περιῃρημένων τοσούτων κακῶν οὐδὲν ὑπολείπε-
ται ἀλλ᾽ ἢ ποιεῖν προθύμως ὅτι ἂν αὑτοῖς οἴωνται
πράξαντες χαριεῖσθαι. ἔτι δὲ εἰ διὰ τοῦτο ἄξιον τοὺς
c ἐρῶντας περὶ πολλοῦ ποιεῖσθαι, ὅτι τούτους μάλιστά
φασιν φιλεῖν ὧν ἂν ἐρῶσιν, καὶ ἕτοιμοί εἰσι καὶ ἐκ
τῶν λόγων καὶ ἐκ τῶν ἔργων τοῖς ἄλλοις ἀπεχθανό-

---

19 "My situation," "if this were to happen" are the first of a
string of euphemisms throughout the speech, which were standard in discussions of sex in Athenian oratory (see Dover, *GPM*,
206ff.). Whether this is a genuine speech by Lysias or a Platonic
parody is uncertain (see Introduction, §3(ii) and n. 6).

You know about my situation and you have heard that I think that it is of benefit to us if this were to happen.[19] I claim I should not fail to achieve what I ask for this reason: that I am not actually in love with you. Those who are in 231 love regret whatever favors they do at the point when their passions cease. But for the others there is no time that is appropriate for regret. For not from constraint but of their own free will, having due regard to their own best interests, they do favors in proportion to their own resources. Again,[20] lovers take into consideration what damage they have done to their own interests on account of their love and what favors they have performed, and by adding on the trouble they have had they consider they have long since paid back an appropriate favor to their loved ones. On the other hand, those who are not in love cannot use b being in love as an excuse for the neglect of their own interests, nor are the troubles they have been through in the past to be taken into account, nor can they lay the blame on their disagreements with their relatives. Consequently when such major problems have been stripped away, nothing is left except to do eagerly whatever they think will give their loved ones pleasure when done. And again if for this reason it is right to value lovers highly—namely because they say that they have particular c affection for the ones they love and are ready to gratify them, even if they are hateful to others as a result of what

[20] This connective "again" (*eti de*), which occurs at intervals throughout the speech (231b7, 232a6, 233d5) emphasizes the arbitrary order of the points made and the absence of logical connection, "thrown together wholesale" (Socrates at 264b3–4).

μενοι τοῖς ἐρωμένοις χαρίζεσθαι, ῥᾴδιον γνῶναι, εἰ
ἀληθῆ λέγουσιν, ὅτι ὅσων ἂν | ὕστερον ἐρασθῶσιν,
ἐκείνους αὑτῶν περὶ πλείονος ποιήσονται, καὶ δῆλον
ὅτι, ἐὰν ἐκείνοις δοκῇ, καὶ τούτους κακῶς ποιήσουσιν.

d καίτοι πῶς εἰκός ἐστι τοιοῦτον πρᾶγμα προέσθαι τοιαύτην ἔχοντι συμφοράν, ἣν οὐδ' ἂν ἐπιχειρήσειεν
οὐδεὶς ἔμπειρος ὢν ἀποτρέπειν; καὶ γὰρ αὐτοὶ ὁμολο-
γοῦσι νοσεῖν μᾶλλον ἢ σωφρονεῖν, καὶ εἰδέναι ὅτι
κακῶς φρονοῦσιν, ἀλλ' οὐ δύνασθαι αὑτῶν κρατεῖν·
ὥστε πῶς ἂν εὖ φρονήσαντες | ταῦτα καλῶς ἔχειν
ἡγήσαιντο περὶ ὧν οὕτω διακείμενοι βουλεύονται; καὶ
μὲν δὴ εἰ μὲν ἐκ τῶν ἐρώντων τὸν βέλτιστον αἱροῖο,
ἐξ ὀλίγων ἄν σοι ἡ ἔκλεξις εἴη· εἰ δ' ἐκ τῶν ἄλλων
τὸν σαυτῷ ἐπιτηδειότατον, ἐκ πολλῶν· ὥστε πολὺ
πλείων ἐλπὶς ἐν τοῖς πολλοῖς ὄντα τυχεῖν τὸν ἄξιον
τῆς σῆς φιλίας.

e Εἰ τοίνυν τὸν νόμον τὸν καθεστηκότα δέδοικας, μὴ
πυθομένων τῶν ἀνθρώπων ὄνειδός σοι γένηται, εἰκός
232 ἐστι τοὺς μὲν ἐρῶντας, οὕτως ἂν οἰομένους καὶ ὑπὸ
τῶν ἄλλων ζηλοῦσθαι ὥσπερ αὐτοὺς ὑφ' αὑτῶν,
ἐπαρθῆναι τῷ λέγειν καὶ φιλοτιμουμένους ἐπιδείκνυ-
σθαι πρὸς ἅπαντας ὅτι οὐκ ἄλλως αὐτοῖς πεπόνηται·
τοὺς δὲ μὴ ἐρῶντας, κρείττους | αὑτῶν ὄντας, τὸ βέλ-
τιστον ἀντὶ τῆς δόξης τῆς παρὰ τῶν ἀνθρώπων αἱρεῖ-

---

21 "And another point" (*kai men dē*): this connective, like "and
again" (see previous note) serves as a connective for unrelated

they say and do, it is easy to recognize, if they are telling the truth, that they will value any later individuals they love more highly than the earlier ones, and it's clear that, if the later loves want it, they will treat the earlier ones badly in their turn. And indeed, how is it reasonable to d
give up such a thing [i.e. your virtue] to someone with an affliction of such a kind, which no one at all with any experience of it would even try to avert? For even they themselves admit they are sick rather than sound in mind, and know they are out of their mind, but are unable to control themselves. Consequently how could they, when they attain their right mind, believe that the decisions which they made when in that condition were right? And another point:[21] if you were to choose the best of your lovers, your choice would be from the few, but if it were the one most suited to yourself out of the rest, it would be from many. Accordingly there is a much greater hope that you will come across someone worthy of your affection among the many.

Now if you are afraid of the established convention, lest e
you become an object of reproach when people find out, it is likely that lovers, thinking that they would be admired 232
by others in the same way as they are by themselves, would be carried away in talking about it and being eager to show to all that they had not toiled in vain; while those who are not in love, who have control over themselves, choose what is the best instead of what comes from their popular

points (232b5, e1; 233a4, d8). It is significant that this connective is notably common in genuine Lysias (twenty-one times, see Denniston, 395–96), which could point to a genuine speech by Lysias, or, of course, a skilled Platonic parody.

σθαι. ἔτι δὲ τοὺς μὲν ἐρῶντας πολλοὺς ἀνάγκη πυθέ-
σθαι καὶ ἰδεῖν ἀκολουθοῦντας τοῖς ἐρωμένοις καὶ
ἔργον τοῦτο ποιουμένους, ὥστε ὅταν ὀφθῶσι διαλεγόμενοι ἀλλήλοις, τότε αὐτοὺς οἴονται ἢ γεγενημένης ἢ
b μελλούσης ἔσεσθαι τῆς ἐπιθυμίας συνεῖναι· τοὺς δὲ
μὴ ἐρῶντας οὐδ᾽ αἰτιᾶσθαι διὰ τὴν συνουσίαν ἐπιχει-
ροῦσιν, εἰδότες ὅτι ἀναγκαῖόν ἐστιν ἢ διὰ φιλίαν τῳ
διαλέγεσθαι ἢ δι᾽ ἄλλην | τινὰ ἡδονήν. καὶ μὲν δὴ εἴ
σοι δέος παρέστηκεν ἡγουμένῳ χαλεπὸν εἶναι φιλίαν
συμμένειν, καὶ ἄλλῳ μὲν τρόπῳ διαφορᾶς γενομένης
κοινὴν ‹ἂν› ἀμφοτέροις καταστῆναι τὴν συμφοράν,
προεμένου δέ σου ἃ περὶ πλείστου ποιῇ μεγάλην ἂν
c σοι βλάβην ἂν γενέσθαι, εἰκότως ἂν τοὺς ἐρῶντας
μᾶλλον ἂν φοβοῖο· πολλὰ γὰρ αὐτούς ἐστι τὰ λυ-
ποῦντα, καὶ πάντ᾽ ἐπὶ τῇ αὑτῶν βλάβῃ νομίζουσι γί-
γνεσθαι. διόπερ | καὶ τὰς πρὸς τοὺς ἄλλους τῶν ἐρω-
μένων συνουσίας ἀποτρέπουσιν, φοβούμενοι τοὺς μὲν
οὐσίαν κεκτημένους μὴ χρήμασιν αὐτοὺς ὑπερβάλων-
ται, τοὺς δὲ πεπαιδευμένους μὴ συνέσει κρείττους
γένωνται· τῶν δὲ ἄλλο τι κεκτημένων ἀγαθὸν τὴν
d δύναμιν ἑκάστου φυλάττονται. πείσαντες μὲν οὖν ἀπ-
εχθέσθαι σε τούτοις εἰς ἐρημίαν φίλων καθιστᾶσιν,

---

22 In this situation the *erastēs* (lover) would gain admiration
for his achievement if the affair became public, whereas the *erōmenos* (loved one) would attract public censure if it became
known that he had submitted. The nonlover would, however, be
discreet in avoiding both admiration directed toward himself and

reputation.[22] Again many people are bound to be aware of
lovers and see them following the ones they love and making this their business, so that when they are seen talking
to each other then many think they are together either
having just satisfied their desire or are about to. On the   b
other hand people don't so much as even try to censure
those not in love on account of their being together, knowing that it is necessary to talk to someone either through
friendship, or some other pleasure. And another point: if
you are frightened when you think that it is difficult for
affection to hold together, and that in other circumstances
if some disagreement over some matter has arisen, the
misfortune would affect both parties, but that, on the
other hand it would cause *you* great harm if you let go of
what you value most highly: in that case, it would be rea-   c
sonable for you to be more afraid of those who are lovers,
because there are many things which hurt them, and they
think that everything that happens is done to cause harm
to themselves. For just this reason they steer their loved
ones away from associating with others, as they are afraid
that those with the wherewithal will outbid them with
their money, and those who are educated will prove to be
superior in terms of their intellect. And they are wary of
the influence of each of those who have acquired some
other advantage. Indeed by persuading you to become   d
hateful to these people, they put you in a position of being
abandoned by your friends, but if you look at your own

reproach aimed at the loved one. This argument is based on an
acknowledgment of Athenian "double standards"; see General
Introduction, §2; and Dover, *GPM*, 215.

ἐὰν δὲ τὸ σεαυτοῦ σκοπῶν ἄμεινον ἐκείνων φρονῇς,
ἥξεις αὐτοῖς εἰς διαφοράν· ὅσοι δὲ μὴ ἐρῶντες ἔτυχον,
ἀλλὰ δι᾽ | ἀρετὴν ἔπραξαν ὧν ἐδέοντο, οὐκ ἂν τοῖς
συνοῦσι φθονοῖεν, ἀλλὰ τοὺς μὴ ἐθέλοντας μισοῖεν,
ἡγούμενοι ὑπ᾽ ἐκείνων μὲν ὑπερορᾶσθαι, ὑπὸ τῶν
συνόντων δὲ ὠφελεῖσθαι, ὥστε πολὺ πλείων ἐλπὶς φιλίαν αὐτοῖς ἐκ τοῦ πράγματος ἢ ἔχθραν γενέσθαι.

e   Καὶ μὲν δὴ τῶν μὲν ἐρώντων πολλοὶ πρότερον τοῦ
σώματος ἐπεθύμησαν ἢ τὸν τρόπον ἔγνωσαν καὶ τῶν
ἄλλων | οἰκείων ἔμπειροι ἐγένοντο, ὥστε ἄδηλον αὐ-
τοῖς εἰ ἔτι τότε βουλήσονται φίλοι εἶναι, ἐπειδὰν τῆς
233   ἐπιθυμίας παύσωνται· τοῖς δὲ μὴ ἐρῶσιν, οἳ καὶ πρότερον ἀλλήλοις φίλοι ὄντες ταῦτα ἔπραξαν, οὐκ ἐξ ὧν
ἂν εὖ πάθωσι ταῦτα εἰκὸς ἐλάττω τὴν φιλίαν αὐτοῖς
ποιῆσαι, ἀλλὰ ταῦτα μνημεῖα καταλειφθῆναι τῶν
μελλόντων ἔσεσθαι. καὶ μὲν δὴ βελτίονί σοι | προσή-
κει γενέσθαι ἐμοὶ πειθομένῳ ἢ ἐραστῇ. ἐκεῖνοι μὲν
γὰρ καὶ παρὰ τὸ βέλτιστον τά τε λεγόμενα καὶ τὰ
πραττόμενα ἐπαινοῦσιν, τὰ μὲν δεδιότες μὴ ἀπέχθων-
ται, τὰ δὲ καὶ αὐτοὶ χεῖρον διὰ τὴν ἐπιθυμίαν γιγνώ-
b   σκοντες. τοιαῦτα γὰρ ὁ ἔρως ἐπιδείκνυται· δυστυχοῦν-
τας μέν, ἃ μὴ λύπην τοῖς ἄλλοις παρέχει, ἀνιαρὰ
ποιεῖ νομίζειν· εὐτυχοῦντας δὲ καὶ τὰ μὴ ἡδονῆς ἄξια
παρ᾽ ἐκείνων ἐπαίνου ἀναγκάζει | τυγχάνειν· ὥστε

---

23 Another of the many euphemisms for sex.
24 The repeated use of the particles *men . . . de* (on the one

position and have better sense than they do, you will end up in dispute with them. But such people as were not actually lovers, but achieved what they asked for through their merit, would not begrudge those who associated with you, but would dislike those who were unwilling, thinking that they were being looked down on by the latter, but helped by those who associated with you, so that there is a much greater expectation that friendship would result for them from the affair rather than enmity.

And there again many of the lovers have a physical   e
desire before they discover the beloved's character and gain experience of his other personal circumstances, so that it is unclear to them if they still want to be friends when they lose their desire. But for those not in love, since   233
they were friends with each other before they engaged in their activity,[23] their friendship would not be likely to become less as a result of whatever good experience they have, but would remain as reminders of things yet to come. And another point: it is in your interest to become better by following *my* advice rather than a lover's. You see they approve what is said and done contrary to what is best, on the one hand because they are afraid of arousing hostility and on the other because they are showing inferior judgment through their desire. For such are the ways   b
in which love manifests itself. On the one hand it makes those who are unsuccessful consider things distressing which do not cause pain for any others, and on the other,[24] for those who are successful, through its compulsion even things which ought not to give pleasure are objects of

hand . . . on the other) highlight the straitjacketed formality of Lysias' (Plato's) speech.

πολὺ μᾶλλον ἐλεεῖν τοῖς ἐρωμένοις ἢ ζηλοῦν αὐτοὺς
προσήκει. ἐὰν δέ μοι πείθῃ, πρῶτον μὲν οὐ τὴν πα-
ροῦσαν ἡδονὴν θεραπεύων συνέσομαί σοι, ἀλλὰ καὶ
c τὴν μέλλουσαν ὠφελίαν ἔσεσθαι, οὐχ ὑπ᾽ ἔρωτος ἡτ-
τώμενος ἀλλ᾽ ἐμαυτοῦ κρατῶν, οὐδὲ διὰ σμικρὰ ἰσχυρὰν ἔχθραν ἀναιρούμενος ἀλλὰ διὰ μεγάλα βραδέως
ὀλίγην ὀργὴν ποιούμενος, τῶν μὲν ἀκουσίων συγγνώ-
μην ἔχων, τὰ δὲ ἑκούσια | πειρώμενος ἀποτρέπειν·
ταῦτα γάρ ἐστι φιλίας πολὺν χρόνον ἐσομένης τεκμήρια. εἰ δ᾽ ἄρα σοι τοῦτο παρέστηκεν, ὡς οὐχ οἷόν τε
ἰσχυρὰν φιλίαν γενέσθαι ἐὰν μή τις ἐρῶν τυγχάνῃ,
d ἐνθυμεῖσθαι χρὴ ὅτι οὔτ᾽ ἂν τοὺς ὑεῖς περὶ πολλοῦ
ἐποιούμεθα οὔτ᾽ ἂν τοὺς πατέρας καὶ τὰς μητέρας,
οὔτ᾽ ἂν πιστοὺς φίλους ἐκεκτήμεθα, οἳ οὐκ ἐξ ἐπι-
θυμίας τοιαύτης γεγόνασιν | ἀλλ᾽ ἐξ ἑτέρων ἐπιτηδευ-
μάτων. |

Ἔτι δὲ εἰ χρὴ τοῖς δεομένοις μάλιστα χαρίζεσθαι,
προσήκει καὶ τοῖς ἄλλοις μὴ τοὺς βελτίστους ἀλλὰ
τοὺς ἀπορωτάτους εὖ ποιεῖν· μεγίστων γὰρ ἀπαλλα-
γέντες κακῶν πλείστην χάριν αὐτοῖς εἴσονται. καὶ
μὲν δὴ καὶ ἐν ταῖς ἰδίαις δαπάναις οὐ τοὺς φίλους
ἄξιον παρακαλεῖν, ἀλλὰ τοὺς προσαιτοῦντας καὶ τοὺς
e δεομένους πλησμονῆς· ἐκεῖνοι γὰρ καὶ ἀγαπήσουσιν
καὶ ἀκολουθήσουσιν καὶ ἐπὶ τὰς θύρας ἥξουσι καὶ
μάλιστα ἡσθήσονται καὶ οὐκ ἐλαχίστην χάριν |
εἴσονται καὶ πολλὰ ἀγαθὰ αὐτοῖς εὔξονται. ἀλλ᾽ ἴσως

praise: so it is much more fitting for loved ones to feel pity rather than to emulate them. But if you accept what I'm saying, firstly I shall associate with you in nurturing not your present pleasure, but what will also be to your benefit in the future, not because I am overcome by love, but   c because I am in control of myself, and not taking up some virulent hostility for petty reasons, but slowly feeling a little anger for important reasons, by pardoning what is unintentional and by attempting to avert what is intentional. For these are the signs of a friendship which will last a long time. If this has nevertheless occurred to you, that a strong relationship is impossible unless one is actually in love, you must bear in mind that in that case   d we would not place much value on our sons, nor our fathers and mothers, nor would we have gained trustworthy friends who have become so as a result not of desire of that sort, but from other practices.

Again, if we ought to oblige those who especially need it, it is also fitting in other respects too to benefit not the best, but those who need the most help. For since they have been relieved of the greatest troubles they will be most grateful to their benefactors. And there again in the case of private functions too one ought to invite not friends, but those who plead with us, and those who need a good square meal. For they are the ones who will greet   e us with a show of affection, will attend on us, visit us at home, and will enjoy it the most and be by no means the least grateful to us and pray for many good things for us.[25]

[25] d5–e5 represent not genuinely held views but the speaker playing devil's advocate. "Yet, perhaps" (e5) represents the resumption of the speaker's actual view.

προσήκει οὐ τοῖς σφόδρα δεομένοις χαρίζεσθαι, ἀλλὰ
τοῖς μάλιστα ἀποδοῦναι χάριν δυναμένοις· οὐδὲ τοῖς
προσαιτοῦσι[2] μόνον, ἀλλὰ τοῖς τοῦ πράγματος ἀξί-
234 οις· οὐδὲ ὅσοι τῆς σῆς ὥρας ἀπολαύσονται, ἀλλ' οἵτινες πρεσβυτέρῳ γενομένῳ τῶν σφετέρων ἀγαθῶν
μεταδώσουσιν· οὐδὲ οἱ διαπραξάμενοι πρὸς τοὺς
ἄλλους φιλοτιμήσονται, ἀλλ' οἵτινες αἰσχυνόμενοι |
πρὸς ἅπαντας σιωπήσονται· οὐδὲ τοῖς ὀλίγον χρόνον
σπουδάζουσιν, ἀλλὰ τοῖς ὁμοίως διὰ παντὸς τοῦ βίου
φίλοις ἐσομένοις· οὐδὲ οἵτινες παυόμενοι τῆς ἐπιθυμίας ἔχθρας πρόφασιν ζητήσουσιν, ἀλλ' οἱ παυσαμένου τῆς ὥρας τότε τὴν αὑτῶν ἀρετὴν ἐπιδείξονται.
b σὺ οὖν τῶν τε εἰρημένων μέμνησο καὶ ἐκεῖνο ἐνθυμοῦ,
ὅτι τοὺς μὲν ἐρῶντας οἱ φίλοι νουθετοῦσιν ὡς ὄντος
κακοῦ τοῦ ἐπιτηδεύματος, τοῖς δὲ μὴ ἐρῶσιν οὐδεὶς
πώποτε τῶν οἰκείων ἐμέμψατο ὡς διὰ τοῦτο | κακῶς
βουλευομένοις περὶ ἑαυτῶν.

Ἴσως ἂν οὖν ἔροιό με εἰ ἅπασίν σοι παραινῶ τοῖς
μὴ ἐρῶσι χαρίζεσθαι. ἐγὼ μὲν οἶμαι οὐδ' ἂν τὸν
ἐρῶντα πρὸς ἅπαντάς σε κελεύειν τοὺς ἐρῶντας ταύ-
c την ἔχειν τὴν διάνοιαν. οὔτε γὰρ τῷ λαμβάνοντι χάριτος ἴσης ἄξιον, οὔτε σοὶ βουλομένῳ τοὺς ἄλλους
λανθάνειν ὁμοίως δυνατόν· δεῖ δὲ βλάβην μὲν ἀπ'
αὐτοῦ μηδεμίαν, ὠφελίαν δὲ ἀμφοῖν γίγνεσθαι. ἐγὼ
μὲν οὖν ἱκανά μοι νομίζω τὰ εἰρημένα· | εἰ δ' ἔτι ⟨τι⟩
σὺ ποθεῖς, ἡγούμενος παραλελεῖφθαι, ἐρώτα.

[2] προσαιτοῦσι Ast, Burnet: ἐρῶσι TW

Yet, perhaps one ought not to bestow favors on those in dire need, but rather on those who are best able to return the favor: and not only those who beg from you,[26] but those worthy of what you are doing; and not such people as gain pleasure from your youthfulness, but those who will share their good things with you when you have grown older; and not those who, having achieved their aim, look for recognition among everyone else, but those who out of modesty will keep silent in everyone's presence; and not those whose enthusiasm for you lasts only a short time, but who will remain friends consistently for the whole of their life; and not those who will look for an excuse to make you their enemy when their passion ceases, but who will display their own good qualities when your youthful charms have passed. You, therefore, remember what I have said and think about the fact that their friends tell off those in love on the grounds that what they are doing is bad, but none of those close to them has ever yet reproached those who are not in love on the grounds that they have made bad judgments on that score about their own interests.

Perhaps then you may ask me if I'm advising you to bestow your favors on all who are not in love with you. I myself think that not even the man in love with you would tell you take this attitude toward all those who are in love. For it would not merit the same degree of gratitude from the one who receives the favor, nor could you conceal it from everyone else in the same way if you wished to; but no harm should come from the relationship, but benefit for both sides. Well then, I think enough has been said. But if you are still expecting something you think has been left out, ask me.

234

b

c

[26] Or, "those in love with you" (see textual note).

PLATO

ΦΑΙ. Τί σοι φαίνεται, ὦ Σώκρατες, ὁ λόγος; οὐχ ὑπερφυῶς τά τε ἄλλα καὶ τοῖς ὀνόμασιν εἰρῆσθαι;

d ΣΩ. Δαιμονίως μὲν οὖν, ὦ ἑταῖρε, ὥστε με ἐκπλαγῆναι. καὶ τοῦτο ἐγὼ ἔπαθον διὰ σέ, ὦ Φαῖδρε, πρὸς σὲ ἀποβλέπων, ὅτι ἐμοὶ ἐδόκεις γάννυσθαι ὑπὸ τοῦ λόγου μεταξὺ ἀναγιγνώσκων· ἡγούμενος γὰρ σὲ μᾶλλον ἢ ἐμὲ ἐπαΐειν | περὶ τῶν τοιούτων σοὶ εἱπόμην, καὶ ἑπόμενος συνεβάκχευσα μετὰ σοῦ τῆς θείας κεφαλῆς.

ΦΑΙ. Εἶεν· οὕτω δὴ δοκεῖ παίζειν;

ΣΩ. Δοκῶ γάρ σοι παίζειν καὶ οὐχὶ ἐσπουδακέναι;

e ΦΑΙ. Μηδαμῶς, ὦ Σώκρατες, ἀλλ᾽ ὡς ἀληθῶς εἰπὲ πρὸς Διὸς φιλίου, οἴει ἄν τινα ἔχειν εἰπεῖν ἄλλον τῶν Ἑλλήνων ἕτερα τούτων μείζω καὶ πλείω περὶ τοῦ αὐτοῦ πράγματος; |

ΣΩ. Τί δέ; καὶ ταύτῃ δεῖ ὑπ᾽ ἐμοῦ τε καὶ σοῦ τὸν λόγον ἐπαινεθῆναι, ὡς τὰ δέοντα εἰρηκότος τοῦ ποιητοῦ, ἀλλ᾽ οὐκ ἐκείνῃ μόνον, ὅτι σαφῆ καὶ στρογγύλα, καὶ ἀκριβῶς ἕκαστα τῶν ὀνομάτων ἀποτετόρνευται; εἰ γὰρ δεῖ, συγχωρητέον χάριν σήν, ἐπεὶ ἐμέ γε ἔλαθεν
235 ὑπὸ τῆς ἐμῆς οὐδενίας· τῷ γὰρ ῥητορικῷ αὐτοῦ μόνῳ τὸν νοῦν προσεῖχον, τοῦτο δὲ οὐδ᾽ ⟨ἀν⟩αὐτὸν ᾤμην Λυσίαν οἴεσθαι ἱκανὸν εἶναι. καὶ οὖν μοι ἔδοξεν, ὦ Φαῖδρε, εἰ μή τι σὺ ἄλλο λέγεις, δὶς καὶ τρὶς τὰ αὐτὰ εἰρηκέναι, ὡς οὐ πάνυ εὐπορῶν | τοῦ πολλὰ λέγειν περὶ τοῦ αὐτοῦ, ἢ ἴσως οὐδὲν αὐτῷ μέλον τοῦ τοιού-

P. What do you think of the speech, Socrates? Isn't it magnificently expressed, especially in its choice of words?

S. No, rather spoken divinely, my friend, with the result   d
I was astounded.[27] And gazing at you I felt this because of you, Phaedrus, because as you were reading the speech, you seemed to me to be glowing with delight. For thinking that you had a greater understanding of such matters than I, I followed you, and in following your lead I joined in the ecstasy with you as a man of divine inspiration.

P. I see, so you think it's something to joke about then?

S. Do I really look as if I'm joking and didn't take it seriously?

P. Don't, Socrates, but tell me truly, by Zeus the god of   e
friendship, do you think any other Greek would be able to find different things to say about the same subject greater in weight and number than these?

S. What? Must the speech be praised both by me and you for this reason, that the writer said what was necessary, and not just on the grounds that it was clear and well rounded, and each of the phrases was precisely formed? For if I must, I have to agree for your sake, since I at least failed to see it thanks to my worthlessness. You see I was   235
concentrating only on its rhetorical aspect, but in this other respect I didn't think that even Lysias himself would think it adequate. And in fact it seemed to me, Phaedrus, unless you say otherwise, he said the same things two or three times as if he wasn't finding it easy to say many things about the same subject, or perhaps he has no interest in such matters. Indeed he seemed to me to be behaving like

[27] Note the same ironic reaction by Socrates to Agathon's speech at *Symposium* 198b.

του· καὶ ἐφαίνετο δή μοι νεανιεύεσθαι ἐπιδεικνύμενος
ὡς οἷός τε ὢν ταὐτὰ ἑτέρως τε καὶ ἑτέρως λέγων ἀμ-
φοτέρως εἰπεῖν ἄριστα.

b   ΦΑΙ. Οὐδὲν λέγεις, ὦ Σώκρατες· αὐτὸ γὰρ τοῦτο
καὶ μάλιστα ὁ λόγος ἔχει. τῶν γὰρ ἐνόντων ἀξίως
ῥηθῆναι ἐν τῷ πράγματι οὐδὲν παραλέλοιπεν, ὥστε
παρὰ τὰ ἐκείνῳ εἰρημένα μηδέν‹ ἄν ›ποτε δύνασθαι
εἰπεῖν ἄλλα πλείω καὶ | πλείονος ἄξια.

    ΣΩ. Τοῦτο ἐγώ σοι οὐκέτι οἷός τ᾿ ἔσομαι πιθέσθαι·
παλαιοὶ γὰρ καὶ σοφοὶ ἄνδρες τε καὶ γυναῖκες περὶ
αὐτῶν εἰρηκότες καὶ γεγραφότες ἐξελέγξουσί με, ἐάν
σοι χαριζόμενος συγχωρῶ.

c   ΦΑΙ. Τίνες οὗτοι; καὶ ποῦ σὺ βελτίω τούτων ἀκήκοας;

    ΣΩ. Νῦν μὲν οὕτως οὐκ ἔχω εἰπεῖν· δῆλον δὲ ὅτι
τινῶν ἀκήκοα, ἤ που Σαπφοῦς τῆς καλῆς ἢ Ἀνακρέ-
οντος τοῦ σοφοῦ ἢ καὶ συγγραφέων τινῶν. πόθεν δὴ
τεκμαιρόμενος | λέγω; πλῆρές πως, ὦ δαιμόνιε, τὸ
στῆθος ἔχων αἰσθάνομαι παρὰ ταῦτα ἂν ἔχειν εἰπεῖν
ἕτερα μὴ χείρω. ὅτι μὲν οὖν παρά γε ἐμαυτοῦ οὐδὲν
αὐτῶν ἐννενόηκα, εὖ οἶδα, συνειδὼς ἐμαυτῷ ἀμαθίαν·
λείπεται δὴ οἶμαι ἐξ ἀλλοτρίων ποθὲν ναμάτων διὰ
d τῆς ἀκοῆς πεπληρῶσθαί με δίκην ἀγγείου. ὑπὸ δὲ
νωθείας αὖ καὶ αὐτὸ τοῦτο ἐπιλέλησμαι, ὅπως τε καὶ
ὧντινων ἤκουσα.

---

28 Socrates "fails to see" that Lysias has dealt adequately with
"what was necessary" (*ta deonta*), that is, the content in his

some swaggering youth, showing off the fact that he can say the same thing in this way and in that, and say it very well in both ways.[28]

P. That's a load of nonsense, Socrates. You see that is the very thing the speech does so very well. For none of the things that can be fitly said on the subject have been left out, so that no one could ever say anything else more fully and of more value apart from what he's said. b

S. On this I shall no longer be able to agree with you, for wise men and women in the past, who have written and spoken about these things will prove me wrong if I go along with you just to please you.

P. Who are these people? And where have you heard c
anything better than this?

S. I can't exactly say offhand right now; but obviously I've heard something, from the beautiful Sappho, perhaps, or the wise Anacreon or maybe some of the prose writers.[29] What evidence do I have for this? With my heart full, as it were, my fine fellow, I feel I would have other things to say no worse in comparison with these of Lysias. Now I know well that I have invented none of these things from my own mind, being aware of my ignorance. All that's left, I think, is to say that I am filled through my hearing from someone else's springs, like a vessel. And as a result of my d
indolence I have even forgotten this too: how and from whom I heard it.

speech, though appearing (ironically) to concede its stylistic qualities.

[29] Both Sappho and Anacreon were famous for erotic poetry. "Prose writers" may be an allusion to prose discourses on love, which were not uncommon in the fourth century, possibly including Lysias' (or Plato's) own.

PLATO

ΦΑΙ. Ἀλλ᾽, ὦ γενναιότατε, κάλλιστα εἴρηκας. σὺ γὰρ | ἐμοὶ ὧντινων μὲν καὶ ὅπως ἤκουσας μηδ᾽ ἂν κελεύω εἴπῃς, τοῦτο δὲ αὐτὸ ὃ λέγεις ποίησον· τῶν ἐν τῷ βιβλίῳ βελτίω τε καὶ μὴ ἐλάττω ἕτερα ὑπέσχησαι εἰπεῖν τούτων ἀπεχόμενος, καί σοι ἐγώ, ὥσπερ οἱ ἐννέα ἄρχοντες, ὑπισχνοῦμαι χρυσῆν εἰκόνα ἰσομέτρητον εἰς Δελφοὺς ἀναθήσειν, οὐ μόνον ἐμαυτοῦ ἀλλὰ καὶ σήν.

e   ΣΩ. Φίλτατος εἶ καὶ ὡς ἀληθῶς χρυσοῦς, ὦ Φαῖδρε, εἴ με οἴει λέγειν ὡς Λυσίας τοῦ παντὸς ἡμάρτηκεν, καὶ οἷόν τε δὴ παρὰ πάντα ταῦτα ἄλλα εἰπεῖν· τοῦτο δὲ οἶμαι οὐδ᾽ | ἂν τὸν φαυλότατον παθεῖν συγγραφέα. αὐτίκα περὶ οὗ ὁ λόγος, τίνα οἴει λέγοντα ὡς χρὴ μὴ ἐρῶντι μᾶλλον ἢ ἐρῶντι χαρίζεσθαι, παρέντα τοῦ μὲν τὸ φρόνιμον ἐγκωμιάζειν, τοῦ δὲ τὸ ἄφρον ψέγειν, ἀναγκαῖα γοῦν ὄντα, εἶτ᾽ ἄλλ᾽ ἄττα ἕξειν λέ-
236 γειν; ἀλλ᾽ οἶμαι τὰ μὲν τοιαῦτα ἐατέα καὶ συγγνωστέα λέγοντι· καὶ τῶν μὲν τοιούτων οὐ τὴν εὕρεσιν ἀλλὰ τὴν διάθεσιν ἐπαινετέον, τῶν δὲ μὴ ἀναγκαίων | τε καὶ χαλεπῶν εὑρεῖν πρὸς τῇ διαθέσει καὶ τὴν εὕρεσιν.

ΦΑΙ. Συγχωρῶ ὃ λέγεις· μετρίως γάρ μοι δοκεῖς εἰρηκέναι. ποιήσω οὖν καὶ ἐγὼ οὕτως· τὸ μὲν τὸν ἐρῶντα τοῦ μὴ ἐρῶντος μᾶλλον νοσεῖν δώσω σοι ὑπο-

---

30 The nine Archons, chief magistrates of Athens, swore an oath not to take bribes, the penalty being the dedication of a golden statue ([Aristotle], *Athenaiōn Politeia* 7.1.55.5).

P. Oh, that's very well said, my most noble friend! Look, don't tell me from whom and how you heard it, even if I urge you to, but do exactly what you say. You have promised that you can tell me what other things are better and no fewer in quantity, while steering clear of what's in the book; and I promise you, like the nine Archons, I'll set up in Delphi a golden statue of equal weight not only of myself but of you too.[30]

S. You are a darling and truly made of gold, Phaedrus,   e if you think I'm saying that Lysias got it all wrong and that it's possible to say things which are entirely different from all those which he says. I don't think this could happen even to the weakest writer. To start with, what the speech is about: who do you think, in asserting that you should bestow your favors on someone who is not in love rather than one who is, can neglect praising the one for his good sense and reproaching the other for his lack of sense, these certainly being essential points, and then still have something else to say? Well I think one must be allowed to make   236 such points and be forgiven for doing so, and it's not the invention of such things that should be praised, but the arrangement, whereas with the inessentials and things hard to invent, the invention should be praised in addition to the arrangement.[31]

P. I agree with what you say. For I think what you said is fair. So I too shall do as follows. On the one hand I shall allow you to assume that the lover will be sicker than he

---

[31] That is, the argumentative points ("invention," *heuresis*) are in this case obvious (235e6–7); so what is to be commended would be the skillful arrangement of arguments to have maximum persuasive effect (where Lysias is subsequently found lacking).

b τίθεσθαι, τῶν δὲ λοιπῶν ἕτερα πλείω καὶ πλείονος
ἄξια εἰπὼν τῶνδε [Λυσίου] παρὰ τὸ Κυψελιδῶν ἀνά-
θημα σφυρήλατος ἐν Ὀλυμπίᾳ στάθητι. |

ΣΩ. Ἐσπούδακας, ὦ Φαῖδρε, ὅτι σου τῶν παιδικῶν
ἐπελαβόμην ἐρεσχηλῶν σε, καὶ οἴει δή με ὡς ἀληθῶς
ἐπιχειρήσειν εἰπεῖν παρὰ τὴν ἐκείνου σοφίαν ἕτερόν
τι ποικιλώτερον;

ΦΑΙ. Περὶ μὲν τούτου, ὦ φίλε, εἰς τὰς ὁμοίας λα-
c βὰς ἐλήλυθας. ῥητέον μὲν γάρ σοι παντὸς μᾶλλον
οὕτως ὅπως οἷός τε εἶ, ἵνα μὴ τὸ τῶν κωμῳδῶν φορ-
τικὸν πρᾶγμα ἀναγκαζώμεθα ποιεῖν ἀνταποδιδόντες
ἀλλήλοις [εὐλαβήθητι], καὶ μὴ βούλου με ἀναγκάσαι
λέγειν ἐκεῖνο τὸ "εἰ ἐγώ, ὦ | Σώκρατες, Σωκράτην
ἀγνοῶ, καὶ ἐμαυτοῦ ἐπιλέλησμαι," καὶ ὅτι "ἐπεθύμε
μὲν λέγειν, ἐθρύπτετο δέ·" ἀλλὰ διανοήθητι ὅτι
ἐντεῦθεν οὐκ ἄπιμεν πρὶν ἂν σὺ εἴπῃς ἃ ἔφησθα ἐν
τῷ στήθει ἔχειν. ἐσμὲν δὲ μόνω ἐν ἐρημίᾳ, ἰσχυρότε-
d ρος δ' ἐγὼ καὶ νεώτερος, ἐκ δὲ ἀπάντων τούτων "σύνες
ὅ τοι λέγω," καὶ μηδαμῶς πρὸς βίαν βουληθῇς μᾶλλον ἢ ἑκὼν λέγειν.

ΣΩ. Ἀλλ', ὦ μακάριε Φαῖδρε, γελοῖος ἔσομαι παρ'
| ἀγαθὸν ποιητὴν ἰδιώτης αὐτοσχεδιάζων περὶ τῶν
αὐτῶν.

---

32 That is, caught with the same trick as used by Socrates at
227d2ff., when he compelled Phaedrus to read Lysias' speech.
The metaphor is from wrestling (see *Republic* 544b5). Phaedrus
goes on to parody Socrates' teasing comments at 228a5ff.

who is not in love, but as far as the remaining points are   b
concerned, when you have said more of a different kind
and of greater value than these here, may you be set up as
a statue in wrought metal alongside the offering of the
Cypselidae in Olympia.

S. Have you been seriously upset, Phaedrus, because
in teasing you I attacked your beloved, and do you think I
would really try to say something else more elaborate to
set against that fellow's expertise?

P. As for that, my friend, you've got yourself into the
same hold.[32] You see, you absolutely must speak as best   c
you can in order for us not to be forced to commit the
vulgar practice of the comic playwrights, exchanging in-
sults with each other. And don't deliberately force me to
roll out that "If I, Socrates, don't know Socrates, I've forgotten who I am too," and that "He was keen to speak, but
pretended to be coy," but bear in mind that we're not
leaving here before you tell me what you said was in your
heart. We are alone in a deserted place; I'm stronger and
younger than you and as a result of all this "mark what I'm   d
saying,"[33] and don't elect to speak under duress rather
than of your own free will.

S. Well, Phaedrus, you lucky man, I shall be a laughing
stock if I, a layman, improvise against a good writer[34] on
the same subjects.

[33] A quotation from Pindar, fr.105 Snell.

[34] "Writer" = *poiētēs*, usually meaning "poet" as opposed to
"speechwriter," but here ironically emphasizing "expert" Phae-
drus/Lysias as against layman (*idiōtēs*) Socrates.

ΦΑΙ. Οἶσθ᾽ ὡς ἔχει; παῦσαι πρός με καλλωπιζό-
μενος· σχεδὸν γὰρ ἔχω ὃ εἰπὼν ἀναγκάσω σε λέγειν.

ΣΩ. Μηδαμῶς τοίνυν εἴπῃς.

ΦΑΙ. Οὔκ, ἀλλὰ καὶ δὴ λέγω· ὁ δέ μοι λόγος ὅρκος
| ἔσται. ὄμνυμι γάρ σοι—τίνα μέντοι, τίνα θεῶν; ἢ
e βούλει τὴν πλάτανον ταυτηνί;—ἦ μήν, ἐάν μοι μὴ
εἴπῃς τὸν λόγον ἐναντίον αὐτῆς ταύτης, μηδέποτέ σοι
ἕτερον λόγον μηδένα μηδενὸς μήτε ἐπιδείξειν μήτε
ἐξαγγελεῖν.

ΣΩ. Βαβαῖ, ὦ μιαρέ, ὡς εὖ ἀνηῦρες τὴν ἀνάγκην
ἀνδρὶ | φιλολόγῳ ποιεῖν ὃ ἂν κελεύῃς.

ΦΑΙ. Τί δῆτα ἔχων στρέφῃ;

ΣΩ. Οὐδὲν ἔτι, ἐπειδὴ σύ γε ταῦτα ὀμώμοκας. πῶς
γὰρ ἂν οἷός τ᾽ εἴην τοιαύτης θοίνης ἀπέχεσθαι;

237   ΦΑΙ. Λέγε δή.

ΣΩ. Οἶσθ᾽ οὖν ὡς ποιήσω;

ΦΑΙ. Τοῦ πέρι;

ΣΩ. Ἐγκαλυψάμενος ἐρῶ, ἵν᾽ ὅτι τάχιστα δια-
δράμω | τὸν λόγον καὶ μὴ βλέπων πρὸς σὲ ὑπ᾽ αἰσχύ-
νης διαπορῶμαι.

ΦΑΙ. Λέγε μόνον, τὰ δ᾽ ἄλλα ὅπως βούλει ποίει.

ΣΩ. Ἄγετε δή, ὦ Μοῦσαι, εἴτε δι᾽ ᾠδῆς εἶδος λί-
γειαι, εἴτε διὰ γένος μουσικὸν τὸ Λιγύων ταύτην
ἔσχετ᾽ ἐπωνυμίαν, "ξύμ μοι λάβεσθε" τοῦ μύθου, ὅν
με ἀναγκάζει | ὁ βέλτιστος οὑτοσὶ λέγειν, ἵν᾽ ὁ ἑταῖρος

P. Do you realize how things stand? Stop being coy with me. I daresay I've got something to say which will force you to speak.

S. Then don't say it on any account.

P. No, I shall speak anyway. And my speech will be an oath. For I swear to you—but by whom, which of the gods? Or do you want it by this plane tree here? Now look, e unless you give your speech in the presence of this very tree, I shall never show or report to you any other speech by anyone ever again.

S. My word, you devil! How well you've found the way to force a man who loves speeches to do what you tell him.

P. Then why do you keep twisting and turning?

S. I don't any longer, since you have sworn an oath. For how would I be able to keep away from such a feast as that?

P. Speak then. 237

S. Do you know then what I shall do?

P. About what?

S. I shall speak with my head covered in order to get through my speech as quickly as possible and not get myself confused through shame whenever I look at you.[35]

P. Just speak, and do the rest as you want.

S. Come then, you Muses, whether you are called "clear-voiced" on account of the nature of your song, or whether you have this name from the musical race of the Ligurians, "with me partake" in the story which this excellent fellow here compels me to tell in order that his com-

[35] For significance of Socrates' head being covered, see his introduction to the "palinode" at 243a3–b7.

379

αὐτοῦ, καὶ πρότερον δοκῶν τούτῳ σοφὸς εἶναι, νῦν ἔτι μᾶλλον δόξῃ.

b   Ἦν οὕτω δὴ παῖς, μᾶλλον δὲ μειρακίσκος, μάλα καλός· τούτῳ δὲ ἦσαν ἐρασταὶ πάνυ πολλοί. εἷς δέ τις αὐτῶν αἱμύλος ἦν, ὃς οὐδενὸς ἧττον ἐρῶν ἐπεπείκει τὸν παῖδα ὡς | οὐκ ἐρῴη. καί ποτε αὐτὸν αἰτῶν ἔπειθεν τοῦτ' αὐτό, ὡς μὴ ἐρῶντι πρὸ τοῦ ἐρῶντος δέοι χαρίζεσθαι, ἔλεγέν τε ὧδε—

    Περὶ παντός, ὦ παῖ, μία ἀρχὴ τοῖς μέλλουσι καλῶς
c βουλεύσεσθαι· εἰδέναι δεῖ περὶ οὗ ἂν ᾖ ἡ βουλή, ἢ παντὸς ἁμαρτάνειν ἀνάγκη. τοὺς δὲ πολλοὺς λέληθεν ὅτι οὐκ ἴσασι τὴν οὐσίαν ἑκάστου. ὡς οὖν εἰδότες οὐ διομολογοῦνται ἐν ἀρχῇ τῆς σκέψεως, προελθόντες δὲ τὸ εἰκὸς ἀποδιδόασιν· | οὔτε γὰρ ἑαυτοῖς οὔτε ἀλλήλοις ὁμολογοῦσιν. ἐγὼ οὖν καὶ σὺ μὴ πάθωμεν ὃ ἄλλοις ἐπιτιμῶμεν, ἀλλ' ἐπειδὴ σοὶ καὶ ἐμοὶ ὁ λόγος πρόκειται πότερα ἐρῶντι ἢ μὴ μᾶλλον εἰς φιλίαν ἰτέον, περὶ ἔρωτος οἷόν τ' ἔστι καὶ ἣν ἔχει δύναμιν, ὁμολογίᾳ θέμενοι ὅρον, εἰς τοῦτο ἀποβλέποντες καὶ
d ἀναφέροντες τὴν σκέψιν ποιώμεθα εἴτε ὠφελίαν εἴτε βλάβην παρέχει. ὅτι μὲν οὖν δὴ ἐπιθυμία τις ὁ ἔρως,

36 ". . . with me partake": the language, Greek ξύμ μοι λάβεσθε, with initial xi for sigma (xum) and euphonic mu for nu before moi, clearly imitates the poetic style of an invocation. This traditional invocation of epic poets to the Muses for inspiration (Homer, Hesiod), and the fanciful etymological connection be-

panion, who seemed to him to be wise even before, shall now seem still more so.[36]

So, there was once a boy, or rather a lad, who was very b good-looking. And this boy had very many lovers. One of these was crafty, who, while loving him no less than anyone else, had persuaded him he was not in love. And one day in urging his claim he set about persuading him of this very point: that he should grant his favors to a nonlover in preference to a lover. And this is what he said:

In all things, my boy, there is one place to start from for those who intend to deliberate successfully. It is es- c sential to know what you are deliberating about, or you are bound to fail completely. But most people have failed to see that they don't know the essential nature of each thing. So, assuming that they actually do know, they do not agree at the beginning of their search, and proceeding further they pay the expected penalty; you see they don't agree with themselves or each other. Therefore let neither I nor you suffer what we blame others for, but since the question lies in front of both you and me, whether one should enter into a friendship with a lover or a nonlover, having agreed on a definition about what kind of thing love is and what power it has, let's look at this and referring to it, let d us make an inquiry whether it brings advantage or harm. Well then, the fact that love is some kind of desire is clear

tween the "clear-voiced" (*ligeiai*) Muses and the Ligurians (a race from the west without, as far as we know, vocal pretensions), together with Socrates' self-deprecating praise of Phaedrus' "companion," Lysias (a10–b1), clearly marks the passage as parody.

ἅπαντι δῆλον· ὅτι δ᾽ αὖ καὶ μὴ ἐρῶντες ἐπιθυμοῦσι
τῶν | καλῶν, ἴσμεν. τῷ δὴ τὸν ἐρῶντά τε καὶ μὴ κρι-
νοῦμεν; δεῖ αὖ νοῆσαι ὅτι ἡμῶν ἐν ἑκάστῳ δύο τινέ
ἐστον ἰδέα ἄρχοντε καὶ ἄγοντε, οἷν ἑπόμεθα ᾗ ἂν
ἄγητον, ἡ μὲν ἔμφυτος οὖσα ἐπιθυμία ἡδονῶν, ἄλλη
δὲ ἐπίκτητος δόξα, ἐφιεμένη τοῦ ἀρίστου. τούτω δὲ ἐν
ἡμῖν τοτὲ μὲν ὁμονοεῖτον, ἔστι δὲ ὅτε στασιάζετον·
e καὶ τοτὲ μὲν ἡ ἑτέρα, ἄλλοτε δὲ ἡ ἑτέρα κρατεῖ. δόξης
μὲν οὖν ἐπὶ τὸ ἄριστον λόγῳ ἀγούσης καὶ κρατούσης
τῷ κράτει σωφροσύνη ὄνομα· ἐπιθυμίας δὲ ἀλόγως
ἑλκούσης ἐπὶ ἡδονὰς καὶ ἀρξάσης ἐν ἡμῖν τῇ ἀρχῇ
238 ὕβρις ἐπωνομάσθη. ὕβρις δὲ δὴ πολυώνυμον—πολυ-
μελὲς γὰρ καὶ πολυμερές—καὶ τούτων τῶν ἰδεῶν ἐκ-
πρεπὴς ἣ ἂν τύχῃ γενομένη, τὴν αὑτῆς ἐπωνυμίαν
ὀνομαζόμενον | τὸν ἔχοντα παρέχεται, οὔτε τινὰ κα-
λὴν οὔτ᾽ ἐπαξίαν κεκτῆσθαι. περὶ μὲν γὰρ ἐδωδὴν
κρατοῦσα τοῦ λόγου τε τοῦ ἀρίστου καὶ τῶν ἄλλων
ἐπιθυμιῶν ἐπιθυμία γαστριμαργία τε καὶ τὸν ἔχοντα
b ταὐτὸν τοῦτο κεκλημένον παρέξεται· περὶ δ᾽ αὖ μέθας
τυραννεύσασα, τὸν κεκτημένον ταύτῃ ἄγουσα, δῆλον
οὗ τεύξεται προσρήματος· καὶ τἆλλα δὴ τὰ τούτων
ἀδελφὰ καὶ ἀδελφῶν ἐπιθυμιῶν ὀνόματα τῆς | ἀεὶ δυ-
ναστευούσης ᾗ προσήκει καλεῖσθαι πρόδηλον. ἧς δ᾽

to everyone. But there again we know that those who are not in love also have desires for the beautiful. In what way then do we distinguish between the one who loves and the one who doesn't? Again we must bear in mind that in each of us there are two principles ruling and leading us which we follow wherever the two of them lead, the one an innate desire for pleasures, the other an acquired judgment which aims for the best. At times these two exist in agreement within us, but there are times when they conflict, and sometimes the one, sometimes the other prevails. So   e
then, when judgment leads to the best by reason and prevails by its strength, it has the name of moderation, while the desire that drags us without reason toward pleasures and rules over us by its power is called excess.[37] Now ex-   238
cess has many names—indeed it has many limbs and many forms—and of these forms whichever happens to stand out gives its own name to him who possesses it, and it is neither a good nor worthwhile name to acquire. For example when the desire for food prevails over both reasoning for the best and the other desires it is called gluttony and will cause the man who possesses it to have this same name. And again with regard to strong drink, when it has   b
gained total control and leads the man who has acquired it in this direction, it's clear what nomenclature he'll get. And in the case of the other names that are related to these and kindred desires it's quite clear that the man having them will be given the name of the one which is constantly in control at any given time, as is appropriate. As for the

[37] "Moderation" = *sōphrosyne*; "Excess" = *hybris* (in common Greek, "violent or insolent treatment of another"; see Dover, *GPM*, 54ff.).

ἕνεκα πάντα τὰ πρόσθεν εἴρηται, σχεδὸν μὲν ἤδη φα-
νερόν, λεχθὲν δὲ ἢ μὴ λεχθὲν πάντως σαφέστερον· ἡ
γὰρ ἄνευ λόγου δόξης ἐπὶ τὸ ὀρθὸν ὁρμώσης κρατή-
c σασα ἐπιθυμία πρὸς ἡδονὴν ἀχθεῖσα κάλλους, καὶ
ὑπὸ αὖ τῶν ἑαυτῆς συγγενῶν ἐπιθυμιῶν ἐπὶ σωμάτων
κάλλος ἐρρωμένως ῥωσθεῖσα νικήσασα ἀγωγῇ, ἀπ'
αὐτῆς τῆς ῥώμης ἐπωνυμίαν λαβοῦσα, ἔρως ἐκλήθη. |

Ἀτάρ, ὦ φίλε Φαῖδρε, δοκῶ τι σοί, ὥσπερ ἐμαυτῷ,
θεῖον πάθος πεπονθέναι;

ΦΑΙ. Πάνυ μὲν οὖν, ὦ Σώκρατες, παρὰ τὸ εἰωθὸς
εὔροιά τίς σε εἴληφεν.

d ΣΩ. Σιγῇ τοίνυν μου ἄκουε. τῷ ὄντι γὰρ θεῖος
ἔοικεν ὁ τόπος εἶναι, ὥστε ἐὰν ἄρα πολλάκις νυμφό-
ληπτος προϊόντος τοῦ λόγου γένωμαι, μὴ θαυμάσῃς·
τὰ νῦν γὰρ οὐκέτι πόρρω διθυράμβων φθέγγομαι.

ΦΑΙ. Ἀληθέστατα λέγεις. |

ΣΩ. Τούτων μέντοι σὺ αἴτιος. ἀλλὰ τὰ λοιπὰ ἄκουε·
ἴσως γὰρ κἂν ἀποτράποιτο τὸ ἐπιόν. ταῦτα μὲν οὖν
θεῷ μελήσει, ἡμῖν δὲ πρὸς τὸν παῖδα πάλιν τῷ λόγῳ
ἰτέον.

Εἶεν, ὦ φέριστε· ὃ μὲν δὴ τυγχάνει ὂν περὶ οὗ
βουλευτέον, εἴρηταί τε καὶ ὥρισται, βλέποντες δὲ δὴ
e πρὸς αὐτὸ τὰ λοιπὰ λέγωμεν τίς ὠφελία ἢ βλάβη
ἀπό τε ἐρῶντος καὶ μὴ τῷ χαριζομένῳ ἐξ εἰκότος συμ-

desire for the sake of which all the foregoing has been said,
it is already fairly clear, but it's altogether clearer when
said rather than not said. You see a desire without reason
which has taken control of a judgment which is urging
toward what is right, led toward pleasure in beauty, and   c
forcibly strengthened further by its own kindred desires
toward physical beauty, prevailing by its impulse and having gained its name its own strength, is called love.[38]

Well then, my dear Phaedrus, do you think, as I do
myself, that I have experienced something divine?

P. Very much so, Socrates; an unusual fluency has taken
hold of you.

S. Then be quiet and listen to me. For the place seems   d
truly inspired by a god, so don't be surprised if I perhaps
become possessed by the nymphs as the speech progresses. You see at the moment I'm almost on the point of
breaking out into dithyrambs.

P. That's very true.

S. Well, you're the one to blame for this. But listen to
the rest. For perhaps the onset may be averted. Anyway
that will be a god's concern; we must go back to the boy in
our speech.

Well then, my noble friend, what it actually is that we
must deliberate upon has been discussed and defined; so
then, keeping that in sight, let's discuss in what follows   e
what advantage and what disadvantage will likely turn out
for the one granting the favors, both from lover and non-

[38] Strength (*rhōmē*) is here being etymologically related, not
entirely seriously, to "love," *erōs* (and associated words, "forcibly
strengthened," *errōmenōs*, *rhōstheisa*, c2) .

βήσεται. τῷ δὴ ὑπὸ ἐπιθυμίας ἀρχομένῳ δουλεύοντί
τε ἡδονῇ ἀνάγκη που τὸν ἐρώμενον ὡς ἥδιστον ἑαυτῷ
παρασκευάζειν· νοσοῦντι | δὲ πᾶν ἡδὺ τὸ μὴ ἀντιτεῖ-
239   νον, κρεῖττον δὲ καὶ ἴσον ἐχθρόν. οὔτε δὴ κρείττω
οὔτε ἰσούμενον ἑκὼν ἐραστὴς παιδικὰ ἀνέξεται, ἥττω
δὲ καὶ ὑποδεέστερον ἀεὶ ἀπεργάζεται· ἥττων δὲ ἀμα-
θὴς σοφοῦ, δειλὸς ἀνδρείου, ἀδύνατος εἰπεῖν ῥητορικοῦ, βραδὺς ἀγχίνου. τοσούτων κακῶν καὶ ἔτι πλειό-
νων | κατὰ τὴν διάνοιαν ἐραστὴν ἐρωμένῳ ἀνάγκη
γιγνομένων τε καὶ φύσει ἐνόντων [τῶν] μὲν ἥδεσθαι,
τὰ δὲ παρασκευάζειν, ἢ στέρεσθαι τοῦ παραυτίκα
b   ἡδέος. φθονερὸν δὴ ἀνάγκη εἶναι, καὶ πολλῶν μὲν
ἄλλων συνουσιῶν ἀπείργοντα καὶ ὠφελίμων ὅθεν ἂν
μάλιστ᾽ ἀνὴρ γίγνοιτο, μεγάλης αἴτιον εἶναι βλάβης,
μεγίστης δὲ τῆς ὅθεν ἂν φρονιμώτατος εἴη. τοῦτο δὲ
ἡ θεία φιλοσοφία τυγχάνει ὄν, ἧς ἐραστὴν παιδικὰ |
ἀνάγκη πόρρωθεν εἴργειν, περίφοβον ὄντα τοῦ κατα-
φρονηθῆναι· τά τε ἄλλα μηχανᾶσθαι ὅπως ἂν ᾖ
πάντα ἀγνοῶν καὶ πάντα ἀποβλέπων εἰς τὸν ἐραστήν, οἷος ὢν τῷ μὲν ἥδιστος, ἑαυτῷ δὲ βλαβερώτα-
τος ἂν εἴη. τὰ μὲν οὖν κατὰ διάνοιαν ἐπίτροπός τε καὶ
κοινωνὸς οὐδαμῇ λυσιτελὴς ἀνὴρ ἔχων ἔρωτα.

c   Τὴν δὲ τοῦ σώματος ἕξιν τε καὶ θεραπείαν οἵαν τε
καὶ ὡς θεραπεύσει οὗ ἂν γένηται κύριος, ὃς ἡδὺ πρὸ
ἀγαθοῦ | ἠνάγκασται διώκειν, δεῖ μετὰ ταῦτα ἰδεῖν.

lover. Now he who is ruled by desire, in fact a slave to pleasure, must necessarily, I suppose, make his loved one as pleasing as possible to himself. To a sick man everything that does not go against him is pleasant, but anything stronger or equal is his enemy. No lover will willingly tolerate a loved one who is the stronger or the equal, but always works toward making him weaker and inferior. The ignorant man is weaker than the wise, the coward than the brave, he who cannot speak than the articulate, he who is slow than a quick-thinker. Given such great weaknesses in the mind of the beloved and even more besides, the lover must either enjoy them if they develop or are naturally within him, and procure others, or deprive himself of immediate pleasure. Necessarily, then, he must be jealous and by keeping his beloved away from many other associates, even beneficial ones who would be most likely to make a man of him, the lover will be the cause of great harm; but the greatest harm is keeping him from that from which he would gain the most understanding. This is actually that thing inspired by the gods, philosophy, from which the lover must keep his loved one well away, out of the great fear of being despised. He must contrive in everything else to make the loved one ignorant of everything and look to his lover in all matters, in which position he would afford the latter most pleasure, but be most harmful to himself. Therefore in respect of the intellect a man who is in love is in no way of any use as a guardian and companion.

But following this, we must look at both the condition and care of the body, of what kind it is and how the man who has been compelled to pursue what is pleasing rather than what is good will treat him whose master he would

239

b

c

ὀφθήσεται δὴ μαλθακόν τινα καὶ οὐ στερεὸν διώκων,
οὐδ᾽ ἐν ἡλίῳ καθαρῷ τεθραμμένον ἀλλὰ ὑπὸ συμμιγεῖ
σκιᾷ, πόνων μὲν ἀνδρείων καὶ ἱδρώτων ξηρῶν ἄπει-
d ρον, ἔμπειρον δὲ ἁπαλῆς καὶ ἀνάνδρου διαίτης, ἀλλο-
τρίοις χρώμασι καὶ κόσμοις χήτει οἰκείων κοσμούμε-
νον, ὅσα τε ἄλλα τούτοις ἕπεται πάντα ἐπιτηδεύοντα,
ἃ δῆλα καὶ οὐκ ἄξιον περαιτέρω προβαίνειν, ἀλλὰ ἓν
κεφάλαιον ὁρισαμένους ἐπ᾽ ἄλλο ἰέναι· τὸ γὰρ τοιοῦ-
τον | σῶμα ἐν πολέμῳ τε καὶ ἄλλαις χρείαις ὅσαι
μεγάλαι οἱ μὲν ἐχθροὶ θαρροῦσιν, οἱ δὲ φίλοι καὶ
αὐτοὶ οἱ ἐρασταὶ φοβοῦνται.

Τοῦτο μὲν οὖν ὡς δῆλον ἐατέον, τὸ δ᾽ ἐφεξῆς ῥη-
e τέον, τίνα ἡμῖν ὠφελίαν ἢ τίνα βλάβην περὶ τὴν κτῆσιν ἡ τοῦ ἐρῶντος ὁμιλία τε καὶ ἐπιτροπεία παρέξεται. σαφὲς δὴ τοῦτό γε παντὶ μέν, μάλιστα δὲ τῷ
ἐραστῇ, ὅτι τῶν φιλτάτων τε καὶ εὐνουστάτων καὶ
θειοτάτων κτημάτων ὀρφανὸν | πρὸ παντὸς εὔξαιτ᾽ ἂν
εἶναι τὸν ἐρώμενον· πατρὸς γὰρ καὶ μητρὸς καὶ συγ-
240 γενῶν καὶ φίλων στέρεσθαι ἂν αὐτὸν δέξαιτο, δια-
κωλυτὰς καὶ ἐπιτιμητὰς ἡγούμενος τῆς ἡδίστης
πρὸς αὐτὸν ὁμιλίας. ἀλλὰ μὴν οὐσίαν γ᾽ ἔχοντα χρυσοῦ ἤ τινος ἄλλης κτήσεως οὔτε εὐάλωτον ὁμοίως
οὔτε ἁλόντα εὐμεταχείριστον ἡγήσεται· ἐξ ὧν πᾶσα
ἀνάγκη ἐραστὴν παιδικοῖς | φθονεῖν μὲν οὐσίαν
κεκτημένοις, ἀπολλυμένης δὲ χαίρειν. ἔτι τοίνυν ἄγα-
μον, ἄπαιδα, ἄοικον ὅτι πλεῖστον χρόνον παιδικὰ
ἐραστὴς εὔξαιτ᾽ ἂν γενέσθαι, τὸ αὑτοῦ γλυκὺ ὡς
πλεῖστον χρόνον καρποῦσθαι ἐπιθυμῶν.

become. He will be seen of course as pursuing someone feeble, not robust, and not brought up in direct sunlight, but in mottled shade with no experience of harsh sweated manly labor, but experienced in a fastidious unmanly way of life, adorning himself with alien colors and ornaments   d
through lack of his own, and involving himself in all other such practices as follow on from these, which are obvious and it's not worth going any further with them, but will enable us to go on to something else once we've established one key point: you see, such a physique in war and other great crises emboldens our enemies, but strikes fear into our friends and into our lovers themselves.

Therefore let's leave this topic as self-evident and let's discuss this next: what benefit or what harm with regard   e
to our possessions the comradeship and guardianship of a lover will bring. This at least is clear to everyone, but especially to the lover: that before all else he would pray that one he loves is bereft of the dearest, kindest and most divine possessions. You see he would gladly see his beloved deprived of his father and mother and relatives and friends, thinking that these are hindrances and discour-   240
agements to his most enjoyable intercourse with his beloved. Then again he'll think that if his beloved has property in the form of gold or some other possession he is neither as easy to get, nor once gained equally easy to handle. From this it is absolutely necessary for a lover to begrudge a loved one his possession of property and be delighted when he has lost it. Further still, a lover should pray that his loved one be unmarried, childless, homeless for as long as possible, being eager to pluck the sweet fruit of his own enjoyment for as long as possible.

b   Ἔστι μὲν δὴ καὶ ἄλλα κακά, ἀλλά τις δαίμων
ἔμειξε τοῖς πλείστοις ἐν τῷ παραυτίκα ἡδονήν, οἷον
κόλακι, δεινῷ θηρίῳ καὶ βλάβῃ μεγάλῃ, ὅμως ἐπέμει-
ξεν ἡ φύσις ἡδονήν τινα οὐκ ἄμουσον, καί τις ἑταί-
ραν ὡς βλαβερὸν ψέξειεν ἄν, καὶ ἄλλα πολλὰ τῶν
τοιουτοτρόπων θρεμμάτων τε καὶ ἐπιτηδευμάτων, | οἷς
τό γε καθ᾽ ἡμέραν ἡδίστοισιν εἶναι ὑπάρχει· παιδικοῖς
δὲ ἐραστὴς πρὸς τῷ βλαβερῷ καὶ εἰς τὸ συνημερεύειν
c πάντων ἀηδέστατον. ἥλικα γὰρ δὴ καὶ ὁ παλαιὸς λόγος τέρπειν τὸν ἥλικα—ἡ γὰρ οἶμαι χρόνου ἰσότης
ἐπ᾽ ἴσας ἡδονὰς ἄγουσα δι᾽ ὁμοιότητα φιλίαν παρέχεται—ἀλλ᾽ ὅμως κόρον γε καὶ ἡ τούτων συνουσία
ἔχει. καὶ μὴν τό γε ἀναγκαῖον αὖ βαρὺ | παντὶ περὶ
πᾶν λέγεται· ὃ δὴ πρὸς τῇ ἀνομοιότητι μάλιστα ἐραστὴς πρὸς παιδικὰ ἔχει. νεωτέρῳ γὰρ πρεσβύτερος
συνὼν οὔθ᾽ ἡμέρας οὔτε νυκτὸς ἑκὼν ἀπολείπεται,
d ἀλλ᾽ ὑπ᾽ ἀνάγκης τε καὶ οἴστρου ἐλαύνεται, ὃς ἐκείνῳ
μὲν ἡδονὰς ἀεὶ διδοὺς ἄγει, ὁρῶντι, ἀκούοντι, ἁπτο-
μένῳ, καὶ πᾶσαν αἴσθησιν αἰσθανομένῳ τοῦ ἐρωμένου, ὥστε μεθ᾽ ἡδονῆς ἀραρότως αὐτῷ ὑπηρετεῖν· τῷ
δὲ δὴ ἐρωμένῳ ποῖον παραμύθιον ἢ τίνας | ἡδονὰς
διδοὺς ποιήσει τὸν ἴσον χρόνον συνόντα μὴ οὐχὶ ἐπ᾽
ἔσχατον ἐλθεῖν ἀηδίας—ὁρῶντι μὲν ὄψιν πρεσβυτέ-
ραν καὶ οὐκ ἐν ὥρᾳ, ἑπομένων δὲ τῶν ἄλλων ταύτῃ,
e ἃ καὶ λόγῳ ἐστὶν ἀκούειν οὐκ ἐπιτερπές, μὴ ὅτι δὴ
ἔργῳ ἀνάγκης ἀεὶ προσκειμένης μεταχειρίζεσθαι, φυ-
λακάς τε δὴ καχυποτόπους φυλαττομένῳ διὰ παντὸς
καὶ πρὸς ἅπαντας, ἀκαίρους τε ἐπαίνους καὶ ὑπερ-

There are indeed other bad aspects too, but with most   b
of them some divine being has mingled a momentary pleasure, such as in a flatterer, a terrible beast and very harmful, where nature has nevertheless combined a degree of
not unrefined pleasure; indeed one might find fault with
a prostitute as being harmful, and many other of the creatures of similar type and habits which can be very pleasant,
at any rate on an everyday basis. But for the loved one the
lover, in addition to being harmful, is most unpleasant to
spend the day with. For, as the old saying goes, the young   c
delight the young—for I think the similarity of age leads
to shared pleasures and offers friendship because of their
similarity—but nevertheless even the companionship of
these can be too much. Moreover it's said again that in
every circumstance compulsion is a real burden for everyone, which indeed applies very much to the lover and his
beloved, in addition to their differences. For the older
man does not willingly let the younger leave his company
by day or night, but is driven by the sting of necessity
which leads him on by constantly giving him pleasures   d
when he sees, hears, touches and feels the loved one
through all his senses, so that he attentively serves him
with pleasure. But as for the loved one, what comfort or
what pleasures will the lover give him and prevent him,
when spending an equal period of time with him, from
reaching the extreme of disgust when he sees the aging
face no longer in its prime, along with other things which
accompany that state, which are not pleasant even to hear
talked about, much less to be under continuous compul-   e
sion to engage with in practice, while being suspiciously
guarded constantly and in all situations, hearing untimely
and excessive praise, and in just the same way intolerable

391

βάλλοντας ἀκούοντι, ὡς δ' αὕτως ψόγους | νήφοντος
μὲν οὐκ ἀνεκτούς, εἰς δὲ μέθην ἰόντος πρὸς τῷ μὴ
ἀνεκτῷ ἐπαισχεῖς, παρρησίᾳ κατακορεῖ καὶ ἀναπεπτα-
μένῃ χρωμένου;

Καὶ ἐρῶν μὲν βλαβερός τε καὶ ἀηδής, λήξας δὲ
τοῦ ἔρωτος εἰς τὸν ἔπειτα χρόνον ἄπιστος, εἰς ὃν
πολλὰ καὶ | μετὰ πολλῶν ὅρκων τε καὶ δεήσεων ὑπ-
ισχνούμενος μόγις κατεῖχε τήν γ' ἐν τῷ τότε συνου-
241   σίαν ἐπίπονον οὖσαν φέρειν δι' ἐλπίδα ἀγαθῶν. τότε
δὴ δέον ἐκτίνειν, μεταβαλὼν ἄλλον ἄρχοντα ἐν αὑτῷ
καὶ προστάτην, νοῦν καὶ σωφροσύνην ἀντ' ἔρωτος
καὶ μανίας, ἄλλος γεγονὼς λέληθεν τὰ παιδικά. καὶ |
ὁ μὲν αὐτὸν χάριν ἀπαιτεῖ τῶν τότε, ὑπομιμνήσκων
τὰ πραχθέντα καὶ λεχθέντα, ὡς τῷ αὐτῷ διαλεγόμε-
νος· ὁ δὲ ὑπ' αἰσχύνης οὔτε εἰπεῖν τολμᾷ ὅτι ἄλλος
γέγονεν, οὔθ' ὅπως τὰ τῆς προτέρας ἀνοήτου ἀρχῆς
ὁρκωμόσιά τε καὶ ὑποσχέσεις ἐμπεδώσῃ ἔχει, νοῦν
b   ἤδη ἐσχηκὼς καὶ σεσωφρονηκώς, ἵνα μὴ πράττων
ταὐτὰ τῷ πρόσθεν ὅμοιός τε ἐκείνῳ καὶ ὁ αὐτὸς πάλιν
γένηται. φυγὰς δὴ γίγνεται ἐκ τούτων, καὶ ἀπεστερηκὼς ὑπ' ἀνάγκης ὁ πρὶν ἐραστής, ὀστράκου μεταπε-
σόντος, | ἵεται φυγῇ μεταβαλών· ὁ δὲ ἀναγκάζεται
διώκειν ἀγανακτῶν καὶ ἐπιθεάζων, ἠγνοηκὼς τὸ ἅπαν
ἐξ ἀρχῆς, ὅτι οὐκ ἄρα ἔδει ποτὲ ἐρῶντι καὶ ὑπ' ἀνάγ-

---

39 An allusion to a children's game (scholiast Hermias 59–60
ad loc.) where the fall of a potsherd determined which group

reproaches, not to be borne when his lover is sober, but shaming on top of what is intolerable when he's been drinking, and resorts in his speech to excessive and unrestrained license?

And while he's in love he is both harmful and unpleasant, but when he has ceased loving he is untrustworthy regarding the future, for which he made many promises with oaths and entreaties, and with difficulty prevailed on the beloved to put up with their relationship, then irksome enough, through the expectation of good things to come. Then indeed, when it ought to be payback time, he assumes a new leader and ruler within himself, and adopts sense and self-control in place of love and madness, having become another person without his beloved noticing. The latter demands a favor from him in return for those of the past, reminding him of what was done and said, as if talking to the same person. But the other out of shame has neither the courage to say he's become different, nor, now that he has regained his right mind and self-control, does he know how he is to make good the oaths and promises of his former mindless regime, in order to avoid doing the same things as that person he was before and so becoming again his former self. So the former lover becomes a fugitive as a result of all this and, compelled to default when the shard has fallen the other way up, he changes sides and launches himself into flight instead.[39] But the other is compelled to pursue him out of anger and call down the gods against him, completely ignorant that from the beginning he should actually never have bestowed his favor

241

b

pursued and which fled. In this case, the traditional pursuer (*erastēs*) and the beloved (*erōmenos*) switch roles.

κης ἀνοήτῳ χαρίζεσθαι, ἀλλὰ πολὺ μᾶλλον μὴ ἐρῶντι
c καὶ νοῦν ἔχοντι· εἰ δὲ μή, ἀναγκαῖον εἴη ἐνδοῦναι
αὑτὸν ἀπίστῳ, δυσκόλῳ, φθονερῷ, ἀηδεῖ, βλαβερῷ
μὲν πρὸς οὐσίαν, βλαβερῷ δὲ πρὸς τὴν τοῦ σώματος
ἕξιν, πολὺ δὲ βλαβερωτάτῳ πρὸς τὴν τῆς | ψυχῆς
παίδευσιν, ἧς οὔτε ἀνθρώποις οὔτε θεοῖς τῇ ἀληθείᾳ
τιμιώτερον οὔτε ἔστιν οὔτε ποτὲ ἔσται. ταῦτά τε οὖν
χρή, ὦ παῖ, συννοεῖν, καὶ εἰδέναι τὴν ἐραστοῦ φιλίαν
ὅτι οὐ μετ᾽ εὐνοίας γίγνεται, ἀλλὰ σιτίου τρόπον, χά-
d ριν πλησμονῆς, ὡς λύκοι ἄρνας ἀγαπῶσιν, ὡς παῖδα
φιλοῦσιν ἐρασταί.

Τοῦτ᾽ ἐκεῖνο, ὦ Φαῖδρε. οὐκέτ᾽ ἂν τὸ πέρα ἀκούσαις
ἐμοῦ λέγοντος, ἀλλ᾽ ἤδη σοι τέλος ἐχέτω ὁ λόγος.

ΦΑΙ. Καίτοι ᾤμην γε μεσοῦν αὐτόν, καὶ ἐρεῖν τὰ
ἴσα | περὶ τοῦ μὴ ἐρῶντος, ὡς δεῖ ἐκείνῳ χαρίζεσθαι
μᾶλλον, λέγων ὅσα αὖ ἔχει ἀγαθά· νῦν δὲ δή, ὦ Σώκρατες, τί ἀποπαύῃ;

e ΣΩ. Οὐκ ᾔσθου, ὦ μακάριε, ὅτι ἤδη ἔπη φθέγγομαι
ἀλλ᾽ οὐκέτι διθυράμβους, καὶ ταῦτα ψέγων; ἐὰν δ᾽
ἐπαινεῖν τὸν ἕτερον ἄρξωμαι, τί με οἴει ποιήσειν; ἆρ᾽
οἶσθ᾽ ὅτι ὑπὸ τῶν Νυμφῶν, αἷς με σὺ προύβαλες ἐκ
προνοίας, σαφῶς | ἐνθουσιάσω; λέγω οὖν ἑνὶ λόγῳ ὅτι
ὅσα τὸν ἕτερον λελοιδορήκαμεν, τῷ ἑτέρῳ τἀναντία
τούτων ἀγαθὰ πρόσεστιν. καὶ τί δεῖ μακροῦ λόγου;
περὶ γὰρ ἀμφοῖν ἱκανῶς εἴρηται. καὶ οὕτω δὴ ὁ μῦθος

---

40 Cited in the scholia to Homer, *Iliad* 22.263, and almost in
epic (i.e., hexameter) meter (see Socrates at e1 below).

on a man in love and necessarily out of his mind, but much rather on one who is not in love and is sane. Failing this, c he is bound to give himself up to an untrustworthy, difficult, jealous, unpleasant fellow, detrimental to his property, detrimental to his physical state, but by far the most detrimental to the education of his soul, than which nothing in truth either is or ever will be more valuable in the eyes of men or gods. Therefore these are the things, my boy, you must bear in mind, and know that the friendship of a lover does not come about with goodwill, but like food, for the sake of reaching satiety: as wolves delight in lambs, d so is lovers' affection for a boy.[40]

That's it, Phaedrus, You're not going to hear me talking any further, but if you please, let my speech end right there.

P. And yet I really thought it was only half way through and you would go on to talk in equal measure about the one who isn't in love, to show that you have rather to grant a favor to him by telling all the good points he has too. Come on then, Socrates, why are you stopping?

S. Haven't you realized, my dear friend, that I'm now e uttering epic lines, but not dithyrambs any more, even though I'm speaking critically?[41] But if I start to praise the other man, what do you think I shall do? Do you actually realize that I'll be clearly possessed by the Nymphs to whom you have deliberately exposed me? In a word then, I say that for whatever we reviled the one, the other has the opposite of these as good points. And what need is there of a long speech? Enough has been said about both.

[41] Epic meter was traditionally the verse form of praise, inappropriate for Socrates' critical stance against the *erastēs*.

242　ὅτι πάσχειν προσήκει αὐτῷ, τοῦτο πείσεται· κἀγὼ τὸν
ποταμὸν τοῦτον διαβὰς ἀπέρχομαι πρὶν ὑπὸ σοῦ τι
μεῖζον ἀναγκασθῆναι.

ΦΑΙ. Μήπω γε, ὦ Σώκρατες, πρὶν ἂν τὸ καῦμα
παρέλθῃ. ἢ οὐχ ὁρᾷς ὡς σχεδὸν ἤδη μεσημβρία
ἵσταται ἡ δὴ καλουμένη σταθερά; | ἀλλὰ περιμείναν-
τες καὶ ἅμα περὶ τῶν εἰρημένων διαλεχθέντες, τάχα
ἐπειδὰν ἀποψυχῇ ἴμεν.

ΣΩ. Θεῖός γ᾽ εἶ περὶ τοὺς λόγους, ὦ Φαῖδρε, καὶ
ἀτεχνῶς θαυμάσιος. οἶμαι γὰρ ἐγὼ τῶν ἐπὶ τοῦ σοῦ
βίου γεγονότων λόγων μηδένα πλείους ἢ σὲ πεποιη-
b κέναι γεγενῆσθαι ἤτοι αὐτὸν λέγοντα ἢ ἄλλους ἑνί
γέ τῳ τρόπῳ προσαναγκάζοντα—Σιμμίαν Θηβαῖον
ἐξαιρῶ λόγου· τῶν δὲ ἄλλων πάμπολυ κρατεῖς—καὶ
νῦν αὖ δοκεῖς αἴτιός μοι γεγενῆσθαι λόγῳ τινὶ | ῥη-
θῆναι.

ΦΑΙ. Οὐ πόλεμόν γε ἀγγέλλεις. ἀλλὰ πῶς δὴ καὶ
τίνι τούτῳ;

ΣΩ. Ἡνίκ᾽ ἔμελλον, ὠγαθέ, τὸν ποταμὸν διαβαί-
νειν, τὸ δαιμόνιόν τε καὶ τὸ εἰωθὸς σημεῖόν μοι γίγνε-
c σθαι ἐγένετο—ἀεὶ δέ με ἐπίσχει ὃ ἂν μέλλω πράττειν—καί τινα φωνὴν ἔδοξα αὐτόθεν ἀκοῦσαι, ἥ με
οὐκ ἐᾷ ἀπιέναι πρὶν ἂν ἀφοσιώσωμαι, ὡς δή τι ἡμαρ-
τηκότα εἰς τὸ θεῖον. εἰμὶ δὴ οὖν μάντις μέν, οὐ πάνυ

---

42 Simmias, a Pythagorean friend of Socrates, is one of the two
main speakers in *Phaedo*, a dialogue set in prison on Socrates' last
day of life.

And that being so, my story will meet an appropriate fate. As for me I'm away across this river before I'm forced by 242 you into something worse.

P. Not yet, Socrates, not until the heat of the day has passed. Or don't you see that it's just about midday, the so-called high noon? But if we wait around and at the same time discuss what's been said, we'll go presently when it's cooled off.

S. You really are godlike when it comes to speeches, Phaedrus, and simply astonishing. You see I myself think that of the speeches that have been produced in your life-time, no one has caused more to be written than you, either delivering them yourself, or prevailing on others to b do so in one way or another—I leave Simmias the Theban out of the count.[42] You beat the rest hands down—and now once more you seem to have become responsible for me making a speech.

P. That's good news.[43] But how come, and what sort of speech is this?

S. When I was about to cross the river, my good friend, the supernatural, that is my accustomed sign, came to me—it always holds me back from whatever I'm about to c do[44]—and I seemed to hear a voice from the very spot, which does not allow me to go away before I have made atonement for having offended against the divine. Now, I

[43] A colloquial expression, literally, "at least you're not declaring war."

[44] The most famous reference to Socrates' supernatural sign (*to daimonion*), which held him back from actions, is *Apology* 31c–d, where he explains why he has not entered Athenian politics.

δὲ σπουδαῖος, ἀλλ' ὥσπερ οἱ τὰ | γράμματα φαῦλοι,
ὅσον μὲν ἐμαυτῷ μόνον ἱκανός· σαφῶς οὖν ἤδη μανθάνω τὸ ἁμάρτημα. ὡς δή τοι, ὦ ἑταῖρε, μαντικόν γέ
τι καὶ ἡ ψυχή· ἐμὲ γὰρ ἔθραξε μέν τι καὶ πάλαι λέγοντα τὸν λόγον, καί πως ἐδυσωπούμην κατ' Ἴβυκον,
μή τι παρὰ θεοῖς

d   ἀμβλακὼν τιμὰν πρὸς ἀνθρώπων ἀμείψω·

νῦν δ' ᾔσθημαι τὸ ἁμάρτημα.

ΦΑΙ. Λέγεις δὲ δὴ τί;

ΣΩ. Δεινόν, ὦ Φαῖδρε, δεινὸν λόγον αὐτός τε ἐκό-
μισας | ἐμέ τε ἠνάγκασας εἰπεῖν.

ΦΑΙ. Πῶς δή;

ΣΩ. Εὐήθη καὶ ὑπό τι ἀσεβῆ· οὗ τίς ἂν εἴη δεινό-
τερος;

ΦΑΙ. Οὐδείς, εἴ γε σὺ ἀληθῆ λέγεις.

ΣΩ. Τί οὖν; τὸν Ἔρωτα οὐκ Ἀφροδίτης καὶ θεόν
τινα ἡγῇ; |

ΦΑΙ. Λέγεταί γε δή.

ΣΩ. Οὔ τι ὑπό γε Λυσίου, οὐδὲ ὑπὸ τοῦ σοῦ λόγου,
ὃς διὰ τοῦ ἐμοῦ στόματος καταφαρμακευθέντος ὑπὸ
e σοῦ ἐλέχθη. εἰ δ' ἔστιν, ὥσπερ οὖν ἔστι, θεὸς ἤ τι
θεῖον ὁ Ἔρως, οὐδὲν ἂν κακὸν εἴη, τὼ δὲ λόγω τὼ
νυνδὴ περὶ αὐτοῦ εἰπέτην ὡς τοιούτου ὄντος· ταύτῃ τε
οὖν ἡμαρτανέτην περὶ τὸν Ἔρωτα, | ἔτι τε ἡ εὐήθεια
αὐτοῖν πάνυ ἀστεία, τὸ μηδὲν ὑγιὲς λέγοντε μηδὲ

---

45 Ibycus, fr. 25 Edmonds (*Lyra Graeca*).

am a prophet, not a very serious one, but like those who are weak at letters, just competent enough for my own needs. Therefore I already clearly understand what I've done wrong. For the fact is, my friend, the soul too is prophetic in a way. For something bothered me a while ago while I was making my speech and I was somehow made to feel uncomfortable lest, in the words of Ibycus, before the gods:

> Having sinned, in exchange I shall gain the respect of   d
> men[45]

But now I recognize my error.

P. But what do you mean?

S. A terrible speech it was, Phaedrus, terrible: the one you yourself brought with you and the one you forced me to make.

P. How come?

S. A silly one and verging on the impious. What speech could be more terrible than that?

P. None, at least if you're telling the truth.

S. What? Do you not think that Eros is the son of Aphrodite and a god?

P. Well, that's what he's said to be.

S. Not at all by Lysias, and not according to your speech which was delivered through my mouth bewitched by you. But if Eros is a god, as indeed he is, or some divine being,   e he could not be anything evil, but the two speeches were speaking of him just now as if he were so. Now both were wrong about Eros in this respect, and furthermore the silliness of both was quite elegant—putting on airs as if they were worth something while actually saying what is

399

ἀληθὲς σεμνύνεσθαι ὡς τὶ ὄντε, εἰ ἄρα ἀνθρωπίσκους
243 τινὰς ἐξαπατήσαντε εὐδοκιμήσετον ἐν αὐτοῖς. ἐμοὶ
μὲν οὖν, ὦ φίλε, καθήρασθαι ἀνάγκη· ἔστιν δὲ τοῖς
ἁμαρτάνουσι περὶ μυθολογίαν καθαρμὸς ἀρχαῖος, ὃν
Ὅμηρος μὲν οὐκ ᾔσθετο, | Στησίχορος δέ. τῶν γὰρ
ὀμμάτων στερηθεὶς διὰ τὴν Ἑλένης κακηγορίαν οὐκ
ἠγνόησεν ὥσπερ Ὅμηρος, ἀλλ' ἅτε μουσικὸς ὢν
ἔγνω τὴν αἰτίαν, καὶ ποιεῖ εὐθύς—

    Οὐκ ἔστ' ἔτυμος λόγος οὗτος,
    οὐδ' ἔβας ἐν νηυσὶν εὐσέλμοις,
b   οὐδ' ἵκεο Πέργαμα Τροίας·

καὶ ποιήσας δὴ πᾶσαν τὴν καλουμένην Παλινῳδίαν
παραχρῆμα ἀνέβλεψεν. ἐγὼ οὖν σοφώτερος ἐκείνων
γενήσομαι κατ' αὐτό γε τοῦτο· πρὶν γάρ τι παθεῖν διὰ
τὴν τοῦ Ἔρωτος | κακηγορίαν πειράσομαι αὐτῷ ἀπο-
δοῦναι τὴν παλινῳδίαν, γυμνῇ τῇ κεφαλῇ καὶ οὐχ
ὥσπερ τότε ὑπ' αἰσχύνης ἐγκεκαλυμμένος.

    ΦΑΙ. Τουτωνί, ὦ Σώκρατες, οὐκ ἔστιν ἅττ' ἂν ἐμοὶ
εἶπες ἡδίω.

c   ΣΩ. Καὶ γάρ, ὠγαθὲ Φαῖδρε, ἐννοεῖς ὡς ἀναιδῶς
εἴρησθον τὼ λόγω, οὗτός τε καὶ ὁ ἐκ τοῦ βιβλίου
ῥηθείς. εἰ γὰρ ἀκούων τις τύχοι ἡμῶν γεννάδας καὶ
πρᾷος τὸ ἦθος, ἑτέρου δὲ τοιούτου ἐρῶν ἢ καὶ πρότε-
ρόν ποτε ἐρασθείς, λεγόντων | ὡς διὰ σμικρὰ μεγά-

in no way beneficial or true, in case having deceived some worthless people, they would have some repute among them. I must therefore purify myself, my friend. There is 243 an ancient purification for those who have erred in their storytelling, of which Homer had no understanding, but Stesichorus did. For having been deprived of his sight through his libel against Helen, he was not ignorant, like Homer, but because he was in touch with the Muse he knew the reason and immediately wrote:

> This is not a true story,
> You did not embark on the fine-benched ships,
> You did not reach the stronghold of Troy.[46]   b

And after composing the whole of his so-called *Palinode* he immediately got his sight back. Therefore, I shall become wiser than those poets in just this respect. You see before I suffer anything because of my libel of Eros, I shall try to offer my Palinode to him with my head bare and not covered up, as before, through shame.

P. There's nothing you could have said to me, Socrates, more pleasing than these words.

S. Indeed, my good Phaedrus, for you understand how   c shamelessly the two speeches were phrased, both the latter and the one read out of the book. You see, if anyone with a generous and gentle character, who was in love with another of such a nature or who perhaps had been in love

---

[46] Stesichorus, *Helen* fr. 192–93 Davies. The "libel against Helen" (a5–6) committed by Homer and Stesichorus was that they made her the cause of the Trojan War (*Iliad* 3). Stesichorus recanted in his Palinode, saying that it was a phantom of Helen that went to Troy.

PLATO

λας ἔχθρας οἱ ἐρασταὶ ἀναιροῦνται καὶ ἔχουσι πρὸς
τὰ παιδικὰ φθονερῶς τε καὶ βλαβερῶς, πῶς οὐκ ἂν
οἴει αὐτὸν ἡγεῖσθαι ἀκούειν ἐν ναύταις που τεθραμ-
μένων καὶ οὐδένα ἐλεύθερον ἔρωτα ἑωρακότων, πολλοῦ δ' ἂν δεῖν ἡμῖν ὁμολογεῖν ἃ ψέγομεν τὸν Ἔρωτα;

d   ΦΑΙ. Ἴσως νὴ Δί᾽, ὦ Σώκρατες.

ΣΩ. Τοῦτόν γε τοίνυν ἔγωγε αἰσχυνόμενος, καὶ
αὐτὸν τὸν Ἔρωτα δεδιώς, ἐπιθυμῶ ποτίμῳ λόγῳ οἷον
ἁλμυρὰν | ἀκοὴν ἀποκλύσασθαι· συμβουλεύω δὲ καὶ
Λυσίᾳ ὅτι τάχιστα γράψαι ὡς χρὴ ἐραστῇ μᾶλλον ἢ
μὴ ἐρῶντι ἐκ τῶν ὁμοίων χαρίζεσθαι.

ΦΑΙ. Ἀλλ' εὖ ἴσθι ὅτι ἕξει τοῦθ' οὕτω· σοῦ γὰρ
εἰπόντος τὸν τοῦ ἐραστοῦ ἔπαινον, πᾶσα ἀνάγκη Λυσίαν ὑπ' ἐμοῦ ἀναγκασθῆναι γράψαι αὖ περὶ τοῦ
αὐτοῦ λόγον.

e   ΣΩ. Τοῦτο μὲν πιστεύω, ἕωσπερ ἂν ᾖς ὃς εἶ.

ΦΑΙ. Λέγε τοίνυν θαρρῶν.

ΣΩ. Ποῦ δή μοι ὁ παῖς πρὸς ὃν ἔλεγον; ἵνα καὶ
τοῦτο | ἀκούσῃ, καὶ μὴ ἀνήκοος ὢν φθάσῃ χαρισάμε-
νος τῷ μὴ ἐρῶντι.

ΦΑΙ. Οὗτος παρά σοι μάλα πλησίον ἀεὶ πάρεστιν,
ὅταν σὺ βούλῃ.

244   ΣΩ. Οὑτωσὶ τοίνυν, ὦ παῖ καλέ, ἐννόησον, ὡς ὁ
μὲν πρότερος ἦν λόγος Φαίδρου τοῦ Πυθοκλέους,

---

47 In his reply, Phaedrus clearly demonstrates that he has
missed the point of Socrates' previous confession; "For Phaedrus,
and so by implication for Lysias, speech-making and speech writ-

sometime before, were to happen to hear us saying that lovers conceive great enmity for petty reasons, and who are resentful and harmful toward their beloved, how can you fail to think that he imagines he's listening to those who have been brought up perhaps among sailors and have not seen the love of free men, and that he would be far from agreeing on the things for which we reproach Eros?

P. Perhaps, Socrates, by Zeus.   d

S. Well then, feeling a sense of shame before this man and in fear of Eros himself I myself am eager to wash the salt water out of my ears, as it were, with a fresh speech. And I advise Lysias to write as soon as possible that one should act impartially by bestowing one's favors on a lover rather than one who is not in love.

P. Well, be assured that that this will be the case. For when you have spoken in praise of the lover, there will be every necessity for Lysias to be forced by me to write a speech in turn on the same subject.[47]

S. This I believe, as long as you are the man you are.   e

P. Right, come on then and speak with confidence.

S. But where is the boy I was talking to? I want him to hear this too, since, if he does not hear it he may anticipate us and grant his favors to the one who is not in love

P. Here he is, right beside you as always, whenever you want.

S. Well then understand this, you handsome boy,[48] that   244 the previous speech came from Phaedrus, son of Pytho-

ing are not about truth, but about competition," Rowe, note on 243 d8–e1.   [48] That is, the fictitious *erōmenos* being addressed in the speech.

Μυρρινουσίου ἀνδρός· ὃν δὲ μέλλω λέγειν, Στησιχό-
ρου τοῦ Εὐφήμου, Ἱμεραίου. λεκτέος δὲ ὧδε, ὅτι Οὐκ
ἔστ᾽ ἔτυμος λόγος ὃς ἂν παρόντος ἐραστοῦ τῷ μὴ
ἐρῶντι μᾶλλον φῇ δεῖν χαρίζεσθαι, | διότι δὴ ὁ μὲν
μαίνεται, ὁ δὲ σωφρονεῖ. εἰ μὲν γὰρ ἦν ἁπλοῦν τὸ
μανίαν κακὸν εἶναι, καλῶς ἂν ἐλέγετο· νῦν δὲ τὰ μέγιστα τῶν ἀγαθῶν ἡμῖν γίγνεται διὰ μανίας, θείᾳ
b   μέντοι δόσει διδομένης. ἥ τε γὰρ δὴ ἐν Δελφοῖς προ-
φῆτις αἵ τ᾽ ἐν Δωδώνῃ ἱέρειαι μανεῖσαι μὲν πολλὰ δὴ
καὶ καλὰ ἰδίᾳ τε καὶ δημοσίᾳ τὴν Ἑλλάδα ἠργά-
σαντο, σωφρονοῦσαι δὲ βραχέα ἢ οὐδέν· καὶ ἐὰν δὴ
λέγωμεν Σίβυλλάν τε καὶ ἄλλους, ὅσοι μαντικῇ χρώ-
μενοι ἐνθέῳ πολλὰ δὴ πολλοῖς προλέγοντες | εἰς τὸ
μέλλον ὤρθωσαν, μηκύνοιμεν ἂν δῆλα παντὶ λέγοντες. τόδε μὴν ἄξιον ἐπιμαρτύρασθαι, ὅτι καὶ τῶν παλαιῶν οἱ τὰ ὀνόματα τιθέμενοι οὐκ αἰσχρὸν ἡγοῦντο
c   οὐδὲ ὄνειδος μανίαν· οὐ γὰρ ἂν τῇ καλλίστῃ τέχνῃ, ᾗ
τὸ μέλλον κρίνεται, αὐτὸ τοῦτο τοὔνομα ἐμπλέκοντες
μανικὴν ἐκάλεσαν. ἀλλ᾽ ὡς καλοῦ ὄντος, ὅταν θείᾳ
μοίρᾳ γίγνηται, οὕτω νομίσαντες ἔθεντο, οἱ δὲ νῦν
ἀπειροκάλως τὸ ταῦ ἐπεμβάλλοντες | μαντικὴν ἐκάλε-

---

49 Phaedrus is given his "official" identification, name of father and Athenian deme, in order to introduce Stesichorus' (dis-
puted) parentage and place of origin, which are significant: Euphemus = "fair, auspicious speech"; Himera suggests (*himeros*)
"desire."

50 See Stesichorus at 243a8.

51 At both Delphi and Dodona, the principal prophetic cen-

cles, citizen of Myrrhinous. But the one I intend to make comes from Stesichorus son of Euphemus of Himera.[49] The speech must go as follows: that "The story is not true"[50] which says that when a lover is around you should bestow your favors rather on the one who is not in love just because the one is mad and the other sound in mind. For if it was simply that madness is an evil thing, it would be right to say so. But as it is, the greatest of good things come to us through madness, the sort, mind you, which is given as a divine gift. For both the prophetess in Delphi and the priestesses at Dodona when in a mad frenzy have performed many good services for Greece, both in private and in public matters, but have done little or nothing when they're in their right senses. And if we say that the Sybil and others who, by practicing god-inspired prophecy and foretelling many things to many people, have set them straight regarding the future, we would protract matters by saying things which are obvious to everyone.[51] However the following is worth citing as evidence that of the ancients too those who assigned names to things did not consider madness (*mania*) shameful, or a reproach; for otherwise they would not have connected this very name to the finest art, that by which the future is judged, and called it "manic" (*manikē*). Rather they named it so on the grounds that it is a fine thing when it comes about by divine dispensation, but these days people in vulgar fashion

ters of Greece, the priestesses pronounced true oracular predictions while in a trance, delivered both to private individuals and to cities (*idiai kai dēmosiai*, b1–2). Likewise, the Sibyl, attributed to many places, the most famous being at Cumae in Campania (Italy), who while in a frenzy of madness predicted the future of Rome to the Trojan hero Aeneas (Virgil, *Aeneid* 6).

σαν. ἐπεὶ καὶ τήν γε τῶν ἐμφρόνων, ζήτησιν τοῦ μέλλοντος διά τε ὀρνίθων ποιουμένων καὶ τῶν ἄλλων
σημείων, ἅτ᾽ ἐκ διανοίας ποριζομένων ἀνθρωπίνῃ οἰή-
σει νοῦν τε καὶ ἱστορίαν, οἰονοϊστικὴν ἐπωνόμασαν,
ἣν νῦν οἰωνιστικὴν τῷ ⟨ω⟩ σεμνύνοντες οἱ νέοι κα-
d λοῦσιν· ὅσῳ δὴ οὖν τελεώτερον καὶ ἐντιμότερον μαντικὴ οἰωνιστικῆς, τό τε ὄνομα τοῦ ὀνόματος ἔργον τ᾽
ἔργου, τόσῳ κάλλιον μαρτυροῦσιν οἱ παλαιοὶ μανίαν
σωφροσύνης τὴν ἐκ θεοῦ τῆς | παρ᾽ ἀνθρώπων γιγνο-
μένης. ἀλλὰ μὴν νόσων γε καὶ πόνων τῶν μεγίστων,
ἃ δὴ παλαιῶν ἐκ μηνιμάτων ποθὲν ἔν τισι τῶν γενῶν
ἡ μανία ἐγγενομένη καὶ προφητεύσασα, οἷς ἔδει
ἀπαλλαγὴν ηὕρετο, καταφυγοῦσα πρὸς θεῶν εὐχάς
e τε καὶ λατρείας, ὅθεν δὴ καθαρμῶν τε καὶ τελετῶν
τυχοῦσα ἐξάντη ἐποίησε τὸν [ἑαυτῆς] ἔχοντα πρός τε
τὸν παρόντα καὶ τὸν ἔπειτα χρόνον, λύσιν τῷ ὀρθῶς
μανέντι τε καὶ κατασχομένῳ τῶν παρόντων κακῶν
245 εὑρομένη. τρίτη δὲ ἀπὸ Μουσῶν κατοκωχή τε καὶ μανία, λαβοῦσα ἁπαλὴν καὶ ἄβατον ψυχήν, ἐγείρουσα
καὶ ἐκβακχεύουσα κατά τε ᾠδὰς καὶ κατὰ τὴν ἄλλην
ποίησιν, μυρία τῶν παλαιῶν ἔργα κοσμοῦσα τοὺς |

---

52 "Vulgar," because obscuring the link that *mania* demonstrates between madness and prediction of the future.

53 *Oiōnistics* = "divination from birds" (*oiōnoi*).

54 According to Plato, the rational nature of "oiōnoistics," inferior to *mantikē*, derives from an etymology combining "insight"
(*nous*), "information" (*historia*), and "[human] thought" (*oiēsis*).
The addition of *omega* has the same effect as with *mantikē*.

throw in a *tau* and call it "mantic."[52] So too in the case of
the investigation made by people when in their right mind,
involving the investigation of the future by means of birds
and other signs, in as much as they provide insight and
information in a rational way through human thought,
they give it the name "oionoistics," which these days
the youngsters, putting on airs, call "oiōnistics" with an   d
omega;[53] so indeed, to the extent that the mantic art is
more perfect and more respected than the oiōnistic, both
in the comparison of their names and their functions, to
that extent the ancients testify that the madness that
comes from god is to be preferred to the sanity that comes
from human beings.[54] And further, in the case of the greatest ills and sufferings which come about among certain
families as a result of some long-standing divine anger, the
madness, when it arises in them and provides interpretation, finds a remedy for those in need by resorting to
prayers and worship of the gods; from which it chances   e
upon purifications and rituals and brings the afflicted one
out of danger both for the present and the future, discovering for the one who is truly mad and possessed a release
from his existing troubles.[55] The third kind of possession   245
and madness comes from the Muses, seizing a delicate,
virginal soul, rousing and exciting it to Bacchic frenzy in
lyric and other forms of poetry, and by embellishing
countless deeds of men of old it educates their successors.

[55] This second kind of madness appears to have no straight-
forward parallel in extant Greek literature, though Plato may be
alluding to a lost source or generally to a variant on the "inherited
curse" theme, e.g., the House of Atreus in Aeschylus' *Oresteia*.

ἐπιγιγνομένους παιδεύει· ὃς δ᾽ ἂν ἄνευ μανίας Μουσῶν ἐπὶ ποιητικὰς θύρας ἀφίκηται, πεισθεὶς ὡς ἄρα
ἐκ τέχνης ἱκανὸς ποιητὴς ἐσόμενος, ἀτελὴς αὐτός τε
καὶ ἡ ποίησις ὑπὸ τῆς τῶν μαινομένων ἡ τοῦ σωφρο-
νοῦντος ἠφανίσθη.

b   Τοσαῦτα μέν σοι καὶ ἔτι πλείω ἔχω μανίας γιγνο-
μένης ἀπὸ θεῶν λέγειν καλὰ ἔργα. ὥστε τοῦτό γε
αὐτὸ μὴ φοβώμεθα, μηδέ τις ἡμᾶς λόγος θορυβείτω
δεδιττόμενος ὡς πρὸ τοῦ κεκινημένου τὸν σώφρονα
δεῖ προαιρεῖσθαι φίλον· ἀλλὰ | τόδε πρὸς ἐκείνῳ δεί-
ξας φερέσθω τὰ νικητήρια, ὡς οὐκ ἐπ᾽ ὠφελίᾳ ὁ ἔρως
τῷ ἐρῶντι καὶ τῷ ἐρωμένῳ ἐκ θεῶν ἐπιπέμπεται. ἡμῖν
δὲ ἀποδεικτέον αὖ τοὐναντίον, ὡς ἐπ᾽ εὐτυχίᾳ τῇ με-
c   γίστῃ παρὰ θεῶν ἡ τοιαύτη μανία δίδοται· ἡ δὲ δὴ
ἀπόδειξις ἔσται δεινοῖς μὲν ἄπιστος, σοφοῖς δὲ πι-
στή. δεῖ οὖν πρῶτον ψυχῆς φύσεως πέρι θείας τε καὶ
ἀνθρωπίνης ἰδόντα πάθη τε καὶ ἔργα τἀληθὲς νοῆσαι·
ἀρχὴ δὲ ἀποδείξεως ἥδε. |

Ψυχὴ πᾶσα ἀθάνατος. τὸ γὰρ ἀεικίνητον[3] ἀθάνα-

---

3 ἀεικίνητον BTW: αὐτοκίνητον P.Oxy.

---

56 Or "Every soul": though here Plato's emphasis is largely on
"soul" as an undifferentiated entity, rather than as a proof of
personal immortality; see also, below, 246b6, but see too 247d2,
where the capacity of every [individual] soul to receive nourishment from contemplation of the Forms appears to be asserted.
Plato's proof of the immortality of the soul based on demonstrating that it is a self-moving first principle reflects that of the Py-

But whoever has approached the gates of poetry without the madness of the Muses, being convinced he'll actually be a competent poet as a result of his art, he himself, uninitiated, together with his poetry, that of a man of sound mind, are eclipsed in the face of that of those who are mad.

So many and still more are the examples of fine achieve-   b
ments I can relate to you which come from madness inspired by the gods. And so let us not be afraid at least on that point, and don't let any argument throw us into confusion and frighten us into thinking we must prefer the sane man as a friend to the one who is disturbed. But when it demonstrates this in addition to that last point: that love is not sent from the gods for the benefit of the lover and his beloved, let it carry off the prizes of victory. It's up to us to demonstrate on the contrary, that such madness is bestowed by the gods for our greatest good fortune. Now the   c
demonstration will not be believed by the clever, but it will be by the wise. Therefore we must firstly understand the truth with regard to the nature of the soul, both divine and human, looking at what it experiences and what it does. And the beginning of our demonstration goes as follows:

All soul[56] is immortal. For what is in perpetual motion[57]

thagorean Alcmaeon of Croton (DK 24A12, trans. in Kirk–Raven, 347). The oracular quality of the utterance suggests stylistically Ionian philosophical prose, e.g., the pre-Socratic Anaxagoras, DK 59B12 (Waterfield, 125).

[57] For the alternative reading, see an ancient variant *autokinēton* (self-moving). The reading adopted by OCT (Burnet) and most editors, "in perpetual motion" (*aeikinēton*), makes logical sense of c7–9, "only that which moves itself . . . never ceases to move" (see textual note).

τον· τὸ δ᾽ ἄλλο κινοῦν καὶ ὑπ᾽ ἄλλου κινούμενον,
παῦλαν ἔχον κινήσεως, παῦλαν ἔχει ζωῆς. μόνον δὴ
τὸ αὐτὸ κινοῦν, ἅτε οὐκ ἀπολεῖπον ἑαυτό, οὔποτε λήγει κινούμενον, ἀλλὰ καὶ τοῖς ἄλλοις ὅσα κινεῖται
d τοῦτο πηγὴ καὶ ἀρχὴ κινήσεως. ἀρχὴ δὲ ἀγένητον. ἐξ
ἀρχῆς γὰρ ἀνάγκη πᾶν τὸ γιγνόμενον γίγνεσθαι,
αὐτὴν δὲ μηδ᾽ ἐξ ἑνός· εἰ γὰρ ἔκ του ἀρχὴ γίγνοιτο,
οὐκ ἂν ἔτι ἀρχὴ γίγνοιτο. ἐπειδὴ δὲ ἀγένητόν ἐστιν,
καὶ ἀδιάφθορον αὐτὸ ἀνάγκη εἶναι. ἀρχῆς γὰρ δὴ |
ἀπολομένης οὔτε αὐτή ποτε ἔκ του οὔτε ἄλλο ἐξ ἐκείνης γενήσεται, εἴπερ ἐξ ἀρχῆς δεῖ τὰ πάντα γίγνεσθαι. οὕτω δὴ κινήσεως μὲν ἀρχὴ τὸ αὐτὸ αὑτὸ
κινοῦν. τοῦτο δὲ οὔτ᾽ ἀπόλλυσθαι οὔτε γίγνεσθαι δυνατόν, ἢ πάντα τε οὐρανὸν πᾶσάν τε γῆν εἰς ἓν[4] συμ-
πεσοῦσαν στῆναι καὶ μήποτε αὖθις ἔχειν ὅθεν κινη-
e θέντα γενήσεται. ἀθανάτου δὲ πεφασμένου τοῦ ὑφ᾽
ἑαυτοῦ κινουμένου, ψυχῆς οὐσίαν τε καὶ λόγον τοῦτον
αὐτόν τις λέγων οὐκ αἰσχυνεῖται. πᾶν γὰρ σῶμα, | ᾧ
μὲν ἔξωθεν τὸ κινεῖσθαι, ἄψυχον, ᾧ δὲ ἔνδοθεν αὐτῷ
ἐξ αὑτοῦ, ἔμψυχον, ὡς ταύτης οὔσης φύσεως ψυχῆς·
εἰ δ᾽ ἔστιν τοῦτο οὕτως ἔχον, μὴ ἄλλο τι εἶναι τὸ αὐτὸ

---

[4] γῆν εἰς ἕν Philoponus, Burnet: γένεσιν BT Hermias,
Stobaeus

---

[58] That is, it does not abandon its essential nature as First
Mover.

is immortal, but what moves something else and is moved by something else, when it has a cessation of movement has a cessation of life. In fact only that which moves itself, in as much as it doesn't abandon itself,[58] never ceases to move, but also, for the other things which move, this is the source and first principle of motion. And the first principle is something which does not come into being. For every-   d
thing that comes into being must do so from a first prin-
ciple, but the principle itself cannot come from anything whatever. For if a first principle came into being from something it would no longer be a first principle. Since it does not come into being, it must also be indestructible. For if a first principle is destroyed, neither will it ever be brought into being from anything, nor anything else from it, given that all things must come into being from a first principle. This is the way, then, that that which moves itself is a first principle of motion, and this means it can neither be destroyed nor come into being, otherwise the whole of heaven and earth, having collapsed into one,[59] might come to a stop and never ever again have the means by which they will come to be moved. And since it has   e
been shown that that which is moved by itself is immortal, no one will be ashamed to say that this is actually the es-
sence and definition of soul. For every body which gets its motion from outside is without soul, and that which gets it from within and from itself has soul on the grounds that this is the nature of soul. And if this is the case, that that which sets itself in motion is nothing other than soul, of

---

[59] Most editors prefer the MS reading here ($\gamma\acute{\epsilon}\nu\epsilon\sigma\iota\nu$, see textual note): "or all the heavens and all generation falling in ruin might come to a stop."

PLATO

ἑαυτὸ κινοῦν ἢ ψυχήν, ἐξ ἀνάγκης ἀγένητόν τε καὶ
ἀθάνατον ψυχὴ ἂν εἴη.

246   Περὶ μὲν οὖν ἀθανασίας αὐτῆς ἱκανῶς· περὶ δὲ τῆς
ἰδέας αὐτῆς ὧδε λεκτέον. οἷον μέν ἐστι, πάντῃ πάντως
θείας | εἶναι καὶ μακρᾶς διηγήσεως, ᾧ δὲ ἔοικεν, ἀν-
θρωπίνης τε καὶ ἐλάττονος· ταύτῃ οὖν λέγωμεν. ἐοι-
κέτω δὴ συμφύτῳ δυνάμει ὑποπτέρου ζεύγους τε καὶ
ἡνιόχου. θεῶν μὲν οὖν ἵπποι τε καὶ ἡνίοχοι πάντες
αὐτοί τε ἀγαθοὶ καὶ ἐξ ἀγαθῶν, τὸ δὲ τῶν ἄλλων
b   μέμεικται. καὶ πρῶτον μὲν ἡμῶν ὁ ἄρχων συνωρίδος
ἡνιοχεῖ, εἶτα τῶν ἵππων ὁ μὲν αὐτῷ καλός τε καὶ ἀγαθὸς καὶ ἐκ τοιούτων, ὁ δ᾽ ἐξ ἐναντίων τε καὶ ἐναντίος·
χαλεπὴ δὴ καὶ δύσκολος ἐξ ἀνάγκης ἡ περὶ ἡμᾶς
ἡνιόχησις. | πῇ δὴ οὖν θνητόν τε καὶ ἀθάνατον ζῷον
ἐκλήθη πειρατέον εἰπεῖν. ψυχὴ πᾶσα παντὸς ἐπιμε-
λεῖται τοῦ ἀψύχου, πάντα δὲ οὐρανὸν περιπολεῖ, ἄλ-
λοτ᾽ ἐν ἄλλοις εἴδεσι γιγνομένη. τελέα μὲν οὖν οὖσα
καὶ ἐπτερωμένη μετεωροπορεῖ τε καὶ πάντα τὸν κό-
c   σμον διοικεῖ, ἡ δὲ πτερορρυήσασα φέρεται ἕως ἂν
στερεοῦ τινος ἀντιλάβηται, οὗ κατοικισθεῖσα, σῶμα
γήϊνον λαβοῦσα, αὐτὸ αὑτὸ δοκοῦν κινεῖν διὰ τὴν
ἐκείνης δύναμιν, | ζῷον τὸ σύμπαν ἐκλήθη, ψυχὴ καὶ
σῶμα παγέν, θνητόν τ᾽ ἔσχεν ἐπωνυμίαν· ἀθάνατον δὲ
οὐδ᾽ ἐξ ἑνὸς λόγου λελογισμένου, ἀλλὰ πλάττομεν
οὔτε ἰδόντες οὔτε ἱκανῶς νοήσαντες θεόν, ἀθάνατόν τι
ζῷον, ἔχον μὲν ψυχήν, ἔχον δὲ σῶμα, τὸν ἀεὶ δὲ χρό-
d   νον ταῦτα συμπεφυκότα. ἀλλὰ ταῦτα μὲν δή, ὅπῃ τῷ
θεῷ φίλον, ταύτῃ ἐχέτω τε καὶ λεγέσθω· τὴν δὲ αἰτίαν

412

necessity soul would be something that does not come into being and is immortal.

Well then, that's enough about its immortality, but as for its form we have to put it as follows. To explain what kind of thing it is would require an entirely superhuman and lengthy explanation, but what it is like, needs a shorter one, and within the bounds of human ability. So let's put it like that. Let it be like the combined power of a winged yoke of horses and their charioteer. Now the horses and charioteers of the gods are all themselves good and of good lineage. But what the rest have is a mixture. Firstly, our horseman drives a pair of horses, secondly, one of his horses is good and noble and is from stock of this kind, while the other is from the opposite kind and is the opposite. Consequently driving a chariot in our case has to be difficult and troublesome. So how a living being is called immortal and mortal we must now try to explain. All soul has the care of everything soulless, and travels around all the heavens appearing in different forms at different times. Now when it's perfectly winged it travels through the heavens and governs the whole universe, but the one that is stripped of its wings is carried along until it gets hold of something solid where, once settled and taking on an earthly body, it appears to move itself by itself because of the power of the soul, and the whole thing is called a living creature, soul and body joined together, and it gets the name "mortal"; it is immortal on the basis of no single reasoned argument, yet, because we have neither seen nor thought adequately about divinity, we construct a kind of immortal being with a soul and a body united thus for the whole of time. Well, let this and how we express it be as it pleases the god. Let's take up the reason

246

b

c

d

413

τῆς τῶν πτερῶν ἀποβολῆς, δι᾽ ἣν ψυχῆς ἀπορρεῖ, |
λάβωμεν. ἔστι δέ τις τοιάδε.

Πέφυκεν ἡ πτεροῦ δύναμις τὸ ἐμβριθὲς ἄγειν ἄνω
μετεωρίζουσα ᾗ τὸ τῶν θεῶν γένος οἰκεῖ, κεκοινώνηκε
δέ πῃ μάλιστα τῶν περὶ τὸ σῶμα τοῦ θείου [ψυχή], τὸ
δὲ θεῖον καλόν, σοφόν, ἀγαθόν, καὶ πᾶν ὅτι τοιοῦτον·
e τούτοις δὴ τρέφεταί τε καὶ αὔξεται μάλιστά γε τὸ τῆς
ψυχῆς πτέρωμα, αἰσχρῷ δὲ καὶ κακῷ καὶ τοῖς ἐναντίοις φθίνει τε καὶ διόλλυται. ὁ μὲν δὴ μέγας ἡγε-
μὼν ἐν οὐρανῷ Ζεύς, ἐλαύνων | πτηνὸν ἅρμα, πρῶτος
πορεύεται, διακοσμῶν πάντα καὶ ἐπιμελούμενος· τῷ δ᾽
ἕπεται στρατιὰ θεῶν τε καὶ δαιμόνων, κατὰ ἕνδεκα
247 μέρη κεκοσμημένη. μένει γὰρ Ἑστία ἐν θεῶν οἴκῳ
μόνη· τῶν δὲ ἄλλων ὅσοι ἐν τῷ τῶν δώδεκα ἀριθμῷ
τεταγμένοι θεοὶ ἄρχοντες ἡγοῦνται κατὰ τάξιν ἣν
ἕκαστος ἐτάχθη. πολλαὶ μὲν οὖν καὶ μακάριαι θέαι τε
καὶ διέξοδοι | ἐντὸς οὐρανοῦ, ἃς θεῶν γένος εὐδαιμό-
νων ἐπιστρέφεται πράττων ἕκαστος αὐτῶν τὸ αὑτοῦ,
ἕπεται δὲ ὁ ἀεὶ ἐθέλων τε καὶ δυνάμενος· φθόνος γὰρ
ἔξω θείου χοροῦ ἵσταται. ὅταν δὲ δὴ πρὸς δαῖτα καὶ
ἐπὶ θοίνην ἴωσιν, ἄκραν ἐπὶ τὴν ὑπουράνιον ἁψῖδα
b πορεύονται πρὸς ἄναντες, ᾗ δὴ τὰ μὲν θεῶν ὀχήματα
ἰσορρόπως εὐήνια ὄντα ῥᾳδίως πορεύεται, τὰ δὲ ἄλλα
μόγις· βρίθει γὰρ ὁ τῆς κάκης ἵππος μετέχων, ἐπὶ τὴν
γῆν ῥέπων τε καὶ βαρύνων ᾧ μὴ καλῶς ἦν τεθραμμέ-

---

60 Eleven, because Hestia, the twelfth of the Olympian gods,

for the loss of wings, why they fall away from soul. It goes something like this.

The natural function of a wing is to take something heavy, raising it upward to where the race of gods lives, and, somehow more than any other thing in what makes up the physical side, it has the greatest share in the divine; the divine being beautiful, wise, good and everything that is of this kind. By these qualities then the plumage of the   e
soul is especially nurtured and increased; but by what is shameful and bad and what is opposed it is reduced and destroyed. Now the great leader in heaven, Zeus, driving his winged chariot, goes first, organizing and taking care of everything, and the army of gods and divine beings follow him, drawn up in eleven groups. For Hestia stays in   247
the house of the gods alone;[60] but of the rest, those gods in the number of the twelve who have been appointed as leaders, lead according to the rank to which each has been assigned. Now there are many blessed sights and pathways inside the heaven through which the race of happy gods wind their way, each one carrying out his own function, and he who is always willing and able follows, for jealousy is excluded from the divine chorus. Then whenever they go to a feast and a banquet, they make their way steeply uphill to the apex of the arch under the heaven, where the   b
carriages of the gods, well-balanced and obedient to the rein, easily make their way, but others with difficulty. For the horse with some bad qualities weighs them down, inclining them toward the ground and burdensome for any

remains centered as the goddess of the hearth and home and does not feature in mythological stories (see *Homeric Hymn* 29, *To Hestia*).

νος | τῶν ἡνιόχων. ἔνθα δὴ πόνος τε καὶ ἀγὼν ἔσχα-
τος ψυχῇ πρόκειται. αἱ μὲν γὰρ ἀθάνατοι καλούμεναι,
ἡνίκ᾽ ἂν πρὸς ἄκρῳ γένωνται, ἔξω πορευθεῖσαι ἔστη-
σαν ἐπὶ τῷ τοῦ οὐρανοῦ νώτῳ, στάσας δὲ αὐτὰς περι-
άγει ἡ περιφορά, αἱ δὲ θεωροῦσι τὰ ἔξω τοῦ οὐρανοῦ.

c   Τὸν δὲ ὑπερουράνιον τόπον οὔτε τις ὕμνησέ πω τῶν
τῇδε ποιητὴς οὔτε ποτὲ ὑμνήσει κατ᾽ ἀξίαν. ἔχει δὲ
ὧδε—τολμητέον | γὰρ οὖν τό γε ἀληθὲς εἰπεῖν, ἄλλως
τε καὶ περὶ ἀληθείας λέγοντα—ἡ γὰρ ἀχρώματός τε
καὶ ἀσχημάτιστος καὶ ἀναφὴς οὐσία ὄντως οὖσα, ψυχῆς κυβερνήτῃ μόνῳ θεατὴ νῷ, περὶ ἣν τὸ τῆς ἀλη-
d   θοῦς ἐπιστήμης γένος, τοῦτον ἔχει τὸν τόπον. ἅτ᾽ οὖν
θεοῦ διάνοια νῷ τε καὶ ἐπιστήμῃ ἀκηράτῳ τρεφομένη,
καὶ ἁπάσης ψυχῆς ὅσῃ ἂν μέλῃ τὸ προσῆκον δέξασθαι, ἰδοῦσα διὰ χρόνου τὸ ὂν ἀγαπᾷ τε καὶ θεω-
ροῦσα τἀληθῆ τρέφεται καὶ εὐπαθεῖ, ἕως ἂν κύκλῳ ἡ
| περιφορὰ εἰς ταὐτὸν περιενέγκῃ. ἐν δὲ τῇ περιόδῳ
καθορᾷ μὲν αὐτὴν δικαιοσύνην, καθορᾷ δὲ σωφροσύνην, καθορᾷ δὲ ἐπιστήμην, οὐχ ᾗ γένεσις πρόσεστιν,
οὐδ᾽ ἥ ἐστίν που ἑτέρα ἐν ἑτέρῳ οὖσα ὧν ἡμεῖς νῦν
e   ὄντων καλοῦμεν, ἀλλὰ τὴν ἐν τῷ ὅ ἐστιν ὂν ὄντως
ἐπιστήμην οὖσαν· καὶ τἆλλα ὡσαύτως τὰ ὄντα ὄντως
θεασαμένη καὶ ἑστιαθεῖσα, δῦσα πάλιν εἰς τὸ εἴσω

───────────────

61 The heavens are conceived as a revolving sphere, on the
inside of which the chariots of the gods and mortals are carried
around. The gods ("the souls called immortal," b6) and, partially,

of the charioteers whose horse has not been well trained.
Here the utmost toil and struggle is in store for the soul.
Now the souls called immortal, when they reach the top,
make their way outside and stand on the outer back of
heaven, and thus stationed the revolution carries them
round, and they gaze on what is outside the heavens.[61]

No poet of those here on earth has ever yet sung of the   c
place above the heavens as it deserves, nor will any ever
do so. The situation is as follows—for one really must dare
to tell what is true, especially when talking about truth—
for the colorless, formless and intangible essence, that
which truly exists, with which the class of true knowledge
is concerned, holds this region, being visible only to the
mind, the governor of soul. So in as much as a god's intel-   d
ligence is nurtured both by pure mind and intellect, and
that of every soul to the extent that it is concerned to receive its proper nourishment, in the course of time it sees
reality and is both well content and in contemplating the
truth it is fed and made happy until the circuit carries it
round in a circle and brings it back to the same place. And
in the course of revolution it sees actual justice, it sees
temperance, it sees knowledge, not that to which coming
into being belongs, nor even that which is somehow different in different circumstances—knowledge of what we
now call realities, but that in which there is real knowledge   e
of real being. And similarly having observed and feasted
on the rest of what really exists, and having sunk back into

mortal souls when they reach the apex of the sphere, are able to
pass from the topmost point of the sphere and, from a position on
the outer surface, see what lies beyond (c3ff).

τοῦ οὐρανοῦ, οἴκαδε ἦλθεν. ἐλθούσης δὲ αὐτῆς ὁ | ἡνί-
οχος πρὸς τὴν φάτνην τοὺς ἵππους στήσας παρέβα-
λεν ἀμβροσίαν τε καὶ ἐπ᾽ αὐτῇ νέκταρ ἐπότισεν.

248 Καὶ οὗτος μὲν θεῶν βίος· αἱ δὲ ἄλλαι ψυχαί, ἡ μὲν
ἄριστα θεῷ ἑπομένη καὶ εἰκασμένη ὑπερῆρεν εἰς τὸν
ἔξω τόπον τὴν τοῦ ἡνιόχου κεφαλήν, καὶ συμπερι-
ηνέχθη τὴν περιφοράν, θορυβουμένη ὑπὸ τῶν ἵππων
καὶ μόγις καθορῶσα | τὰ ὄντα· ἡ δὲ τοτὲ μὲν ἦρεν,
τοτὲ δ᾽ ἔδυ, βιαζομένων δὲ τῶν ἵππων τὰ μὲν εἶδεν, τὰ
δ᾽ οὔ. αἱ δὲ δὴ ἄλλαι γλιχόμεναι μὲν ἅπασαι τοῦ ἄνω
ἕπονται, ἀδυνατοῦσαι δέ, ὑποβρύχιαι συμπεριφέρον-
ται, πατοῦσαι ἀλλήλας καὶ ἐπιβάλλουσαι, ἑτέρα πρὸ
b τῆς ἑτέρας πειρωμένη γενέσθαι. θόρυβος οὖν καὶ
ἅμιλλα καὶ ἱδρὼς ἔσχατος γίγνεται, οὗ δὴ κακίᾳ
ἡνιόχων πολλαὶ μὲν χωλεύονται, πολλαὶ δὲ πολλὰ
πτερὰ θραύονται· πᾶσαι δὲ πολὺν ἔχουσαι πόνον ἀτε-
λεῖς τῆς τοῦ ὄντος θέας | ἀπέρχονται, καὶ ἀπελθοῦσαι
τροφῇ δοξαστῇ χρῶνται. οὗ δ᾽ ἕνεχ᾽ ἡ πολλὴ σπουδὴ
τὸ ἀληθείας ἰδεῖν πεδίον οὗ ἐστιν, ἥ τε δὴ προσή-
κουσα ψυχῆς τῷ ἀρίστῳ νομὴ ἐκ τοῦ ἐκεῖ λειμῶνος
c τυγχάνει οὖσα, ἥ τε τοῦ πτεροῦ φύσις, ᾧ ψυχὴ κου-
φίζεται, τούτῳ τρέφεται. θεσμός τε Ἀδραστείας ὅδε.
ἥτις ἂν ψυχὴ θεῷ συνοπαδὸς γενομένη κατίδῃ τι τῶν
ἀληθῶν, μέχρι τε τῆς ἑτέρας περιόδου εἶναι ἀπήμονα,

---

62 See *Iliad* 5.368–69   63 That is, the Forms.
64 "Necessity" ("that from which one cannot run away"), i.e.,
Plato's doctrine of metempsychosis (the reincarnation of souls),

what is inside the universe, it comes home. And when it has returned, the charioteer stands his horses at the manger, throws them ambrosia and in addition gives them nectar to drink.[62]

And this is the life of gods, but of the rest of the souls, 248 the one which follows a god best and resembles him most, raises up the charioteer's head into the region outside and is carried around the circuit, but he is thrown into confusion by his horses and with difficulty catches sight of what really exists[63] and at one moment rises up and at another sinks back and, because the horses constrain him, sees some things, but not others. But the rest all follow after in their longing to ascend, but lacking the strength are carried around together below the surface trampling and jostling each other in their attempts to get ahead of the next one. Consequently there is confusion and rivalry and b the utmost sweat, and by the incompetent driving of the charioteers many become maimed and many have their wings all broken, and all with much toil end up without managing to get a view of reality, and away they go and feed on what they imagine nourishes them. The reason why there is so much eagerness to see the whereabouts of the plain of truth is this: that the pasturage which is fit for the best part of the soul actually comes from the meadow there, and the nature of the wing by which a soul is made c light is fed by this. And the law of Adrasteia[64] is as follows: whichever soul has become a follower of a god and perceives something of what is true, remains without sorrow

in a tradition that goes back to the Orphics (DK1 B13) and Pythagoreans (see Empedocles, DK 31B115, Waterfield, 153–54). See also *Republic* 10.614bff.

κἂν ἀεὶ | τοῦτο δύνηται ποιεῖν, ἀεὶ ἀβλαβῆ εἶναι· ὅταν
δὲ ἀδυνατήσασα ἐπισπέσθαι μὴ ἴδῃ, καί τινι συν-
τυχίᾳ χρησαμένη λήθης τε καὶ κακίας πλησθεῖσα
βαρυνθῇ, βαρυνθεῖσα δὲ πτερορρυήσῃ τε καὶ ἐπὶ τὴν
d γῆν πέσῃ, τότε νόμος ταύτην μὴ φυτεῦσαι εἰς μηδεμίαν θήρειον φύσιν ἐν τῇ πρώτῃ γενέσει, ἀλλὰ τὴν
μὲν πλεῖστα ἰδοῦσαν εἰς γονὴν ἀνδρὸς γενησομένου
φιλοσόφου ἢ φιλοκάλου ἢ μουσικοῦ τινος καὶ ἐρωτικοῦ, τὴν δὲ δευτέραν εἰς βασιλέως ἐννόμου ἢ πολεμι-
κοῦ | καὶ ἀρχικοῦ, τρίτην εἰς πολιτικοῦ ἤ τινος οἰκο-
νομικοῦ ἢ χρηματιστικοῦ, τετάρτην εἰς φιλοπόνου
⟨ἢ⟩[5] γυμναστικοῦ ἢ περὶ σώματος ἴασίν τινος ἐσομέ-
νου, πέμπτην μαντικὸν βίον ἤ τινα τελεστικὸν ἕξου-
e σαν· ἕκτῃ ποιητικὸς ἢ τῶν περὶ μίμησίν τις ἄλλος
ἁρμόσει, ἑβδόμῃ δημιουργικὸς ἢ γεωργικός, ὀγδόῃ
σοφιστικὸς ἢ δημοκοπικός, ἐνάτῃ τυραννικός. ἐν δὴ
τούτοις ἅπασιν ὃς μὲν ἂν δικαίως διαγάγῃ ἀμείνονος
μοίρας | μεταλαμβάνει, ὃς δ' ἂν ἀδίκως, χείρονος·
εἰς μὲν γὰρ τὸ αὐτὸ ὅθεν ἥκει ἡ ψυχὴ ἑκάστη οὐκ
ἀφικνεῖται ἐτῶν μυρίων—οὐ γὰρ πτεροῦται πρὸ τοσ-
249 ούτου χρόνου—πλὴν ἡ τοῦ φιλοσοφήσαντος ἀδόλως
ἢ παιδεραστήσαντος μετὰ φιλοσοφίας, αὗται δὲ
τρίτῃ περιόδῳ τῇ χιλιετεῖ, ἐὰν ἕλωνται τρὶς ἐφεξῆς
τὸν βίον τοῦτον, οὕτω πτερωθεῖσαι τρισχιλιοστῷ ἔτει

5 add. Burnet

until the next circuit, and if it is always able to do this, is to remain unharmed always; but whenever it cannot see because it is unable to keep up, and experiencing some misfortune it is weighed down, filled with forgetfulness and incapacity, and in being weighed down it sheds its wings and falls to the ground: then the law is that this soul   d shall not be implanted in any wild creature in its first incarnation, but the one that has seen most shall be implanted in the seed which will become a man who loves wisdom, who loves beauty, some aspect of the Muses, or love; and the second in that of a law-abiding king, or one skilled in warfare, or government; the third in that of one engaged in state or domestic life, or in commerce; and the fourth in one who will become engaged in the hard work of physical training,[65] or someone concerned with healing the body; the fifth will have the life of the seer, or someone concerned with mystic rites; fitting for the sixth will be the   e life of someone who is a poet, or some other of those engaged in imitation; the seventh a craftsman or a farmer; the eighth a sophist or a demagogue, the ninth a tyrant. Among all of these then, he who lives justly gains a better share, he who lives unjustly gains a worse one. For each soul does not return to the place from which it came before ten thousand years are up—for it doesn't get its wings back until such a length of time has passed—except the   249 soul of the person who has honestly pursued wisdom, or one who has combined love of a boy with philosophy. And these souls, on the third circuit of a thousand years, if they choose this life three times in a row, in the three-thousandth

---

[65] We translate assuming the omission of ⟨ἤ⟩ (d6) proposed by Badham and included by Burnet in OCT (see textual note).

PLATO

ἀπέρχονται. | αἱ δὲ ἄλλαι, ὅταν τὸν πρῶτον βίον τε-
λευτήσωσιν, κρίσεως ἔτυχον, κριθεῖσαι δὲ αἱ μὲν εἰς
τὰ ὑπὸ γῆς δικαιωτήρια ἐλθοῦσαι δίκην ἐκτίνουσιν,
αἱ δ' εἰς τοὐρανοῦ τινα τόπον ὑπὸ τῆς Δίκης κουφι-
σθεῖσαι διάγουσιν ἀξίως οὗ ἐν ἀνθρώπου εἴδει ἐβίω-
b σαν βίου. τῷ δὲ χιλιοστῷ ἀμφότεραι ἀφικνούμεναι
ἐπὶ κλήρωσίν τε καὶ αἵρεσιν τοῦ δευτέρου βίου αἱ-
ροῦνται ὃν ἂν θέλῃ ἑκάστη· ἔνθα καὶ εἰς θηρίου βίον
ἀνθρωπίνη ψυχὴ ἀφικνεῖται, καὶ ἐκ θηρίου ὅς ποτε |
ἄνθρωπος ἦν πάλιν εἰς ἄνθρωπον. οὐ γὰρ ἥ γε μήποτε ἰδοῦσα τὴν ἀλήθειαν εἰς τόδε ἥξει τὸ σχῆμα. δεῖ
γὰρ ἄνθρωπον συνιέναι κατ' εἶδος λεγόμενον, ἐκ πολλῶν ἰὸν αἰσθήσεων εἰς ἓν λογισμῷ συναιρούμενον·
c τοῦτο δ' ἐστὶν ἀνάμνησις ἐκείνων ἅ ποτ' εἶδεν ἡμῶν
ἡ ψυχὴ συμπορευθεῖσα θεῷ καὶ ὑπεριδοῦσα ἃ νῦν
εἶναί φαμεν, καὶ ἀνακύψασα εἰς τὸ ὂν ὄντως. διὸ δὴ
δικαίως μόνη πτεροῦται ἡ τοῦ φιλοσόφου | διάνοια·
πρὸς γὰρ ἐκείνοις ἀεί ἐστιν μνήμῃ κατὰ δύναμιν,
πρὸς οἷσπερ θεὸς ὢν θεῖός ἐστιν. τοῖς δὲ δὴ τοιούτοις
ἀνὴρ ὑπομνήμασιν ὀρθῶς χρώμενος, τελέους ἀεὶ
τελετὰς τελούμενος, τέλεος ὄντως μόνος γίγνεται·
d ἐξιστάμενος δὲ τῶν ἀνθρωπίνων σπουδασμάτων καὶ

---

66 For the three-thousand-year circuits of those who pursue
philosophy (249a3–5), see Pindar, *Olympians* 2.68ff. Versions of
the theme of the Judgment of the Dead (a5ff.) are also to be found
in *Republic* 10.614b–21b, *Gorgias* 523a1–27e7, and *Phaedo*
107d–8c, 113d–14c.

year get their wings back and leave. But the rest when they have completed their first life are put on trial, and some, after being tried, go to places of punishment below ground and pay their penalty, but others are raised up by Justice to some place in heaven and spend their time in a fashion worthy of the life they led in the form of a human being. But in the thousandth year both groups come to the alloca- b tion and selection of their second life and pick whichever one each wishes. At this point then a human soul can enter the life of a wild animal and what was once a man back to a man again from a wild animal.[66] For the one that has never seen the truth will never come to enter this form.[67] For a man must understand what is said with respect to form, as it is gathered from many perceptions into a unity, being assembled by reasoning. This is recollection of those c things which our soul once saw when traveling with a god and, looking down on what we now say is real here, raised its head to what really exists.[68] This then is why only the mind of a philosopher justly becomes winged. For through his memory as far as he can, he is always close to those things[69] a god's closeness to which makes him divine. The man then who makes proper use of such reminders, and being continually initiated into perfect mysteries, alone becomes truly perfect. But in standing aside from human d

[67] "this form," i.e., human form. All humans, as opposed to animals, have seen true reality to some extent.

[68] Plato's Theory of Anamnesis (Recollection) is elaborated in *Meno* 80d–86c and *Phaedo* 72e–76e.

[69] That is, the Forms.

πρὸς τῷ θείῳ γιγνόμενος, νουθετεῖται μὲν ὑπὸ τῶν
πολλῶν ὡς παρακινῶν, ἐνθουσιάζων δὲ λέληθεν τοὺς
πολλούς.

Ἔστι δὴ οὖν δεῦρο ὁ πᾶς ἥκων λόγος περὶ τῆς
τετάρτης | μανίας—ἣν ὅταν τὸ τῇδέ τις ὁρῶν κάλλος,
τοῦ ἀληθοῦς ἀναμιμνησκόμενος, πτερῶταί τε καὶ ἀνα-
πτερούμενος προθυμούμενος ἀναπτέσθαι, ἀδυνατῶν
δέ, ὄρνιθος δίκην βλέπων ἄνω, τῶν κάτω δὲ ἀμελῶν,
e αἰτίαν ἔχει ὡς μανικῶς διακείμενος—ὡς ἄρα αὕτη
πασῶν τῶν ἐνθουσιάσεων ἀρίστη τε καὶ ἐξ ἀρίστων
τῷ τε ἔχοντι καὶ τῷ κοινωνοῦντι αὐτῆς γίγνεται, καὶ
ὅτι ταύτης μετέχων τῆς μανίας ὁ ἐρῶν τῶν καλῶν
ἐραστὴς καλεῖται. καθάπερ γὰρ εἴρηται, πᾶσα μὲν |
ἀνθρώπου ψυχὴ φύσει τεθέαται τὰ ὄντα, ἢ οὐκ ἂν
250 ἦλθεν εἰς τόδε τὸ ζῷον· ἀναμιμνήσκεσθαι δὲ ἐκ τῶνδε
ἐκεῖνα οὐ ῥᾴδιον ἁπάσῃ, οὔτε ὅσαι βραχέως εἶδον
τότε τἀκεῖ, οὔθ᾽ αἱ δεῦρο πεσοῦσαι ἐδυστύχησαν,
ὥστε ὑπό τινων ὁμιλιῶν ἐπὶ τὸ ἄδικον τραπόμεναι
λήθην ὧν τότε εἶδον ἱερῶν ἔχειν. | ὀλίγαι δὴ λείπονται
αἷς τὸ τῆς μνήμης ἱκανῶς πάρεστιν· αὗται δέ, ὅταν τι
τῶν ἐκεῖ ὁμοίωμα ἴδωσιν, ἐκπλήττονται καὶ οὐκέτ᾽
⟨ἐν⟩ αὑτῶν γίγνονται, ὃ δ᾽ ἔστι τὸ πάθος ἀγνοοῦσι
b διὰ τὸ μὴ ἱκανῶς διαισθάνεσθαι. δικαιοσύνης μὲν οὖν

---

70 "which" (*hēn*) is left hanging in the grammar of the sentence, conveying the excitement of Socrates as he nears the climax of his depiction of *erōs*; the "argument" (*logos*, d4) is re-

pursuits and getting close to the divine he is reproached by most people for being out of his mind, whereas the majority fail to realize he is inspired by a god.

Now it is to this point that the whole of my argument about the fourth kind of madness has been coming—which,[70] when the possessor sees beauty here, and recalling the true beauty, starts to grow wings and getting his feathers back is eager to fly up, but being unable to, looking upward like a bird, and with no regard for what is below, is accused of being in a state of madness—I conclude that this actually turns out to be both the best of all the kinds of divine possession, and comes from the best source for him who has it and shares it, and that in sharing in this madness the lover of things beautiful is called a lover. For according to what has been said, every human soul has in the nature of things seen what is real, or it would not have come into this living being. But it isn't easy for every soul to recall things that are up there from what is down here, neither those who have seen what is there briefly at an earlier time, nor those who, having fallen back to earth here, have had the bad luck to be turned to wrongdoing because of certain associates, and to be forgetful of the sacred things they saw at that time. There are in fact few souls remaining for whom there is an adequate recollection, but when these see something which has a resemblance to what is up there they become astounded and are no longer in control of themselves, though they are ignorant of what has happened to them because they do not distinguish things clearly enough. Now in the resem-   b

e

250

sumed at e1: "I conclude that this . . ." (*hōs . . . hautē*) (i.e., the fourth kind of madness).

καὶ σωφροσύνης καὶ ὅσα ἄλλα τίμια ψυχαῖς οὐκ ἔν-
εστι φέγγος οὐδὲν ἐν τοῖς τῇδε ὁμοιώμασιν, ἀλλὰ δι᾽
ἀμυδρῶν ὀργάνων μόγις αὐτῶν καὶ ὀλίγοι ἐπὶ τὰς
εἰκόνας ἰόντες | θεῶνται τὸ τοῦ εἰκασθέντος γένος·
κάλλος δὲ τότ᾽ ἦν ἰδεῖν λαμπρόν, ὅτε σὺν εὐδαίμονι
χορῷ μακαρίαν ὄψιν τε καὶ θέαν, ἑπόμενοι μετὰ μὲν
Διὸς ἡμεῖς, ἄλλοι δὲ μετ᾽ ἄλλου θεῶν, εἶδόν τε καὶ
ἐτελοῦντο τῶν τελετῶν ἣν θέμις λέγειν μακαριωτάτην,
c ἣν ὠργιάζομεν ὁλόκληροι μὲν αὐτοὶ ὄντες καὶ ἀπα-
θεῖς κακῶν ὅσα ἡμᾶς ἐν ὑστέρῳ χρόνῳ ὑπέμενεν,
ὁλόκληρα δὲ καὶ ἁπλᾶ καὶ ἀτρεμῆ καὶ εὐδαίμονα
φάσματα μυούμενοί τε καὶ ἐποπτεύοντες ἐν αὐγῇ
καθαρᾷ, καθαροὶ | ὄντες καὶ ἀσήμαντοι τούτου ὃ νῦν
δὴ σῶμα περιφέροντες ὀνομάζομεν, ὀστρέου τρόπον
δεδεσμευμένοι.

Ταῦτα μὲν οὖν μνήμῃ κεχαρίσθω, δι᾽ ἣν πόθῳ τῶν
τότε νῦν μακρότερα εἴρηται· περὶ δὲ κάλλους, ὥσπερ
d εἴπομεν, μετ᾽ ἐκείνων τε ἔλαμπεν ὄν, δεῦρό τ᾽ ἐλθόντες
κατειλήφαμεν αὐτὸ διὰ τῆς ἐναργεστάτης αἰσθήσεως
τῶν ἡμετέρων στίλβον ἐναργέστατα. ὄψις γὰρ ἡμῖν
ὀξυτάτη τῶν διὰ τοῦ σώματος ἔρχεται αἰσθήσεων, ᾗ
φρόνησις οὐχ ὁρᾶται—δεινοὺς γὰρ ἂν | παρεῖχεν ἔρω-
τας, εἴ τι τοιοῦτον ἑαυτῆς ἐναργὲς εἴδωλον παρείχετο
εἰς ὄψιν ἰόν—καὶ τἆλλα ὅσα ἐραστά· νῦν δὲ κάλλος

---

71 Note the Orphic teaching of the body as a tomb (sōma/
sēma); cf. Gorgias 493a, Phaedo 81a. The whole of this paragraph

blances here on earth of justice and temperance and other such things of value to souls there is no brightness, but by means of dimmed faculties just a few approach the images of them with difficulty, and gaze on the nature of what is represented. But formerly it was possible to see beauty gleaming brightly, when we, with the happy band following Zeus, and others with other gods, saw the blessed sight and vision and were initiated into the mysteries which it is right to call the most blessed, which we celebrated being   c perfect in ourselves, and untouched by the troubles that were awaiting us in time hereafter, but as initiates and members of the highest rank we welcomed the whole, simple, unchanging, blessed visions, seen in pure light, being pure in ourselves and not entombed in this thing, which we now carry around and call the body, imprisoned like an oyster.[71]

So then let this be our tribute to memory on account of which, in longing for things of the past, there has now been discussion at some length. But with regard to beauty, as we have said, it shone out when it was among those visions up there, and now we have come down here we have   d apprehended it gleaming most clearly through the clearest of our senses. You see of the perceptions that come to us through the body, sight is the keenest—though wisdom is not seen by it—for the feelings of love it would cause in us would be terrible, if it produced some kind of bright image of itself on coming into our vision—and so with the rest of the objects of love. But as it is, only beauty has this

is full of terminology appropriate for initiates into the Eleusinian Mysteries.

μόνον ταύτην ἔσχε μοῖραν, ὥστ᾽ ἐκφανέστατον εἶναι
e καὶ ἐρασμιώτατον. ὁ μὲν οὖν μὴ νεοτελὴς ἢ διεφθαρ-
μένος οὐκ ὀξέως ἐνθένδε ἐκεῖσε φέρεται πρὸς αὐτὸ τὸ
κάλλος, θεώμενος αὐτοῦ τὴν τῇδε ἐπωνυμίαν, ὥστ᾽ οὐ
σέβεται προσορῶν, ἀλλ᾽ ἡδονῇ παραδοὺς τετράποδος
νόμον βαίνειν | ἐπιχειρεῖ καὶ παιδοσπορεῖν, καὶ ὕβρει
προσομιλῶν οὐ δέδοικεν οὐδ᾽ αἰσχύνεται παρὰ φύσιν
251 ἡδονὴν διώκων· ὁ δὲ ἀρτιτελής, ὁ τῶν τότε πολυθεά-
μων, ὅταν θεοειδὲς πρόσωπον ἴδῃ κάλλος εὖ μεμιμη-
μένον ἤ τινα σώματος ἰδέαν, πρῶτον μὲν ἔφριξε καί
τι τῶν τότε ὑπῆλθεν αὐτὸν δειμάτων, εἶτα | προσορῶν
ὡς θεὸν σέβεται, καὶ εἰ μὴ ἐδεδίει τὴν τῆς σφόδρα
μανίας δόξαν, θύοι ἂν ὡς ἀγάλματι καὶ θεῷ τοῖς παιδικοῖς. ἰδόντα δ᾽ αὐτὸν οἷον ἐκ τῆς φρίκης μεταβολή
b τε καὶ ἱδρὼς καὶ θερμότης ἀήθης λαμβάνει· δεξάμε-
νος γὰρ τοῦ κάλλους τὴν ἀπορροὴν διὰ τῶν ὀμμάτων
ἐθερμάνθη ᾗ ἡ τοῦ πτεροῦ φύσις ἄρδεται, θερμανθέν-
τος δὲ ἐτάκη τὰ περὶ τὴν ἔκφυσιν, ἃ πάλαι ὑπὸ σκλη-
ρότητος συμμεμυκότα εἶργε | μὴ βλαστάνειν, ἐπιρρυ-
είσης δὲ τῆς τροφῆς ᾤδησέ τε καὶ ὥρμησε φύεσθαι
ἀπὸ τῆς ῥίζης ὁ τοῦ πτεροῦ καυλὸς ὑπὸ πᾶν τὸ τῆς
c ψυχῆς εἶδος· πᾶσα γὰρ ἦν τὸ πάλαι πτερωτή. ζεῖ οὖν
ἐν τούτῳ ὅλη καὶ ἀνακηκίει, καὶ ὅπερ τὸ τῶν ὀδοντο-
φυούντων πάθος περὶ τοὺς ὀδόντας γίγνεται ὅταν

distinction, that it is the most visible and beloved. Now the   e
one who is not newly initiated, or has been contaminated,
does not move swiftly from here to there, toward actual
beauty, while contemplating the name derived from it
down here on earth, so that he does not revere it when he's
looking at it, but having surrendered to pleasure tries to
copulate in the manner of four-footed animals and father
children, and being familiar with excess is neither afraid
nor ashamed when pursuing pleasure unnaturally. But the   251
newly initiated, who observes much of what he saw before,
whenever he sees a godlike face or some image of the body
that has imitated beauty well, first shudders and something of the fears he had before comes over him; then,
looking at it, reveres it like a god, and if he weren't afraid
of being thought excessively mad, he would make sacrifice
to his loved one as if to a statue, even one of a god. And
on seeing him, a change, a sweating and an unaccustomed
fever seizes him as you would expect after the shivering:
for on receiving the emanation of beauty through his   b
eyes[72] he grows warm at the point at which the wing is
naturally moistened, and on heating up it melts around its
growth point, which, being long since closed up by hard-
ening, prevented it from growing. But with nourishment
flowing in, the quills of the feathers swell and start to grow
from their root under the whole shape of the soul; for   c
originally in the past the whole soul had wings. So meanwhile the whole palpitates and throbs violently, and like
the sensation that arises around the teeth when they

---

[72] The theory that perception results from effluences from the
perceived object, received by the eyes of the beholder, goes back
to the pre-Socratic Empedocles, DK 31A86 (Waterfield, 156–57).

ἄρτι φύωσιν, κνῆσίς τε καὶ ἀγανάκτησις περὶ τὰ
οὖλα, ταὐτὸν δὴ πέπονθεν ἡ τοῦ πτεροφυεῖν ἀρχομέ-
νου ψυχή· ζεῖ τε καὶ | ἀγανακτεῖ καὶ γαργαλίζεται
φύουσα τὰ πτερά. ὅταν μὲν οὖν βλέπουσα πρὸς τὸ
τοῦ παιδὸς κάλλος, ἐκεῖθεν μέρη ἐπιόντα καὶ ῥέ-
οντ'—ἃ δὴ διὰ ταῦτα ἵμερος καλεῖται—δεχομένη [τὸν
ἵμερον] ἄρδηταί τε καὶ θερμαίνηται, λωφᾷ τε τῆς ὀδύ-
d νης καὶ γέγηθεν· ὅταν δὲ χωρὶς γένηται καὶ αὐχμήσῃ,
τὰ τῶν διεξόδων στόματα ᾗ τὸ πτερὸν ὁρμᾷ, συναυ-
αινόμενα μύσαντα ἀποκλῄει τὴν βλάστην τοῦ πτεροῦ, ἡ δ' ἐντὸς μετὰ τοῦ ἱμέρου ἀποκεκλῃμένη, πη-
δῶσα οἷον τὰ σφύζοντα, τῇ διεξόδῳ | ἐγχρίει ἑκάστη
τῇ καθ' αὑτήν, ὥστε πᾶσα κεντουμένη κύκλῳ ἡ ψυχὴ
οἰστρᾷ καὶ ὀδυνᾶται, μνήμην δ' αὖ ἔχουσα τοῦ καλοῦ
γέγηθεν. ἐκ δὲ ἀμφοτέρων μεμειγμένων ἀδημονεῖ τε
e τῇ ἀτοπίᾳ τοῦ πάθους καὶ ἀποροῦσα λυττᾷ, καὶ ἐμ-
μανὴς οὖσα οὔτε νυκτὸς δύναται καθεύδειν οὔτε μεθ'
ἡμέραν οὗ ἂν ᾖ μένειν, θεῖ δὲ ποθοῦσα ὅπου ἂν οἴηται
ὄψεσθαι τὸν ἔχοντα τὸ κάλλος· ἰδοῦσα δὲ καὶ ἐποχε-
τευσαμένη ἵμερον ἔλυσε μὲν τὰ τότε συμπεφραγμένα,
ἀναπνοὴν δὲ λαβοῦσα κέντρων τε | καὶ ὠδίνων ἔλη-
ξεν, ἡδονὴν δ' αὖ ταύτην γλυκυτάτην ἐν τῷ παρόντι
καρποῦται.

252 Ὅθεν δὴ ἑκοῦσα εἶναι οὐκ ἀπολείπεται, οὐδέ τινα
τοῦ καλοῦ περὶ πλείονος ποιεῖται, ἀλλὰ μητέρων τε
καὶ ἀδελφῶν καὶ ἑταίρων πάντων λέλησται, καὶ οὐ-

are cutting and are newly grown, the irritation and pain around the gums is exactly the same as with the soul of the man beginning to grow wings: as it grows feathers, the soul throbs, feels pain and tickles. And when looking at the beauty of a boy and receiving particles from there coming in a rush—which indeed for this reason are called desire[73]—it is nourished and warmed, and it is relieved of its pain and rejoices. But whenever the soul becomes separated and parched, the mouths of the outlets from which the feathers grow, being completely dried up and closed, shut in the shoot of the wing which, being shut away inside with the desire, throbbing like pulsating arteries, stings, each of them at its own particular outlet, so that being pricked all over the soul goes mad and feels pain, but having the memory of the beautiful boy again it feels joy. But as a result of both feelings being mixed together it is much troubled at the strangeness of the experience and rages helplessly, and being frantic is unable to get to sleep at night, or remain wherever it is by day, but runs in yearning wherever it thinks it will see the possessor of beauty. And when it has seen him and channeled into itself the water of desire, it opens up the former blockages and, gaining a breathing space, it ceases from the stinging birth pains, and again for the present moment enjoys this as the sweetest pleasure.

    As a result it is not willing to give this up, and doesn't regard anyone of greater value than the beautiful one, but forgets mothers and brothers and all companions and

d

e

252

---

[73] More fanciful (and obscure) etymological "derivations": "particles" (*merē*, c6), "coming" (*epionta*, c6) "in a rush" (*rheonta*, c7) = "desire" (*himeros*, c7).

σίας δι᾽ ἀμέλειαν ἀπολλυμένης παρ᾽ οὐδὲν τίθεται,
νομίμων δὲ | καὶ εὐσχημόνων, οἷς πρὸ τοῦ ἐκαλλωπί-
ζετο, πάντων καταφρονήσασα δουλεύειν ἑτοίμη καὶ
κοιμᾶσθαι ὅπου ἂν ἐᾷ τις ἐγγυτάτω τοῦ πόθου· πρὸς
γὰρ τῷ σέβεσθαι τὸν τὸ κάλλος ἔχοντα ἰατρὸν ηὕ-
b ρηκε μόνον τῶν μεγίστων πόνων. τοῦτο δὲ τὸ πάθος,
ὦ παῖ καλέ, πρὸς ὃν δή μοι ὁ λόγος, ἄνθρωποι μὲν
ἔρωτα ὀνομάζουσιν, θεοὶ δὲ ὃ καλοῦσιν ἀκούσας εἰκότως διὰ νεότητα γελάσῃ. λέγουσι δὲ οἶμαί τινες Ὁμη-
ριδῶν ἐκ | τῶν ἀποθέτων ἐπῶν δύο ἔπη εἰς τὸν Ἔρωτα,
ὧν τὸ ἕτερον ὑβριστικὸν πάνυ καὶ οὐ σφόδρα τι ἔμ-
μετρον· ὑμνοῦσι δὲ ὧδε—

> τὸν δ᾽ ἤτοι θνητοὶ μὲν Ἔρωτα καλοῦσι ποτηνόν,
> ἀθάνατοι δὲ Πτέρωτα, διὰ πτεροφύτορ᾽ ἀνάγκην.

c τούτοις δὴ ἔξεστι μὲν πείθεσθαι, ἔξεστιν δὲ μή· ὅμως
δὲ ἥ γε αἰτία καὶ τὸ πάθος τῶν ἐρώντων τοῦτο ἐκεῖνο
τυγχάνει ὄν.

Τῶν μὲν οὖν Διὸς ὀπαδῶν ὁ ληφθεὶς ἐμβριθέστε-
ρον δύναται φέρειν τὸ τοῦ πτερωνύμου ἄχθος· ὅσοι δὲ
Ἄρεώς | τε θεραπευταὶ καὶ μετ᾽ ἐκείνου περιεπόλουν,
ὅταν ὑπ᾽ Ἔρωτος ἁλῶσι καί τι οἰηθῶσιν ἀδικεῖσθαι
ὑπὸ τοῦ ἐρωμένου, φονικοὶ καὶ ἕτοιμοι καθιερεύειν

---

74 A group of poetic singers from Chios devoted to reciting
the works of Homer.

75 An obscure joke. "Pteros" combines *pteron* (winged) and
erōs (love). The second line (b9) is called "outrageous" because

thinks nothing of it if its substance is wasted through neglect; as for its usual habits and respectable practices on
which it formerly prided itself, despising all of them, it is
ready to be a slave and sleep where anyone allows it nearest to the object of its longing. For in addition to its reverence for the one in possession of beauty, it has found the
only healer of its greatest sufferings. And this suffering,   b
my handsome boy, to which my argument is directed, men
call love, but when you've heard what the gods call it,
you'll probably laugh on account of your youth. But I believe some of the Homeridae[74] quote two verses to Eros
from the less familiar poems, of which the second line is
quite outrageous and not particularly metrical. They go as
follows:

> Indeed mortals call him Eros the winged one,
> But the immortals call him Pteros because of his
>   need to grow wings.[75]

You can believe this or not. Nevertheless the cause and   c
what the lovers experience is at any rate just what I described above.

Now if he who is captivated by love is one of those who
were attendants of Zeus he is able to bear the burden of
the one named from his feathers[76] with greater steadfastness, but those who serve Ares and used to roam around
with that god, whenever they are seized by Eros and think
they are being wronged by their loved one in any way, they
become murderous and are ready to sacrifice themselves

unmetrical. Homer's "less familiar" work is clearly Plato's rather
labored invention/joke (note his following words at c1).

[76] That is, Eros (see previous note).

d αὐτούς τε καὶ τὰ παιδικά. καὶ οὕτω καθ᾽ ἕκαστον
θεόν, οὗ ἕκαστος ἦν χορευτής, ἐκεῖνον τιμῶν τε καὶ
μιμούμενος εἰς τὸ δυνατὸν ζῇ, ἕως ἂν ᾖ ἀδιάφθορος
καὶ τὴν τῇδε πρώτην γένεσιν βιοτεύῃ, καὶ τούτῳ τῷ
τρόπῳ πρός τε τοὺς ἐρωμένους καὶ τοὺς ἄλλους | ὁμι-
λεῖ τε καὶ προσφέρεται. τόν τε οὖν Ἔρωτα τῶν καλῶν
πρὸς τρόπου ἐκλέγεται ἕκαστος, καὶ ὡς θεὸν αὐτὸν
ἐκεῖνον ὄντα ἑαυτῷ οἷον ἄγαλμα τεκταίνεταί τε καὶ
e κατακοσμεῖ, ὡς τιμήσων τε καὶ ὀργιάσων. οἱ μὲν δὴ
οὖν Διὸς δῖόν τινα εἶναι ζητοῦσι τὴν ψυχὴν τὸν
ὑφ᾽ αὑτῶν ἐρώμενον· σκοποῦσιν οὖν εἰ φιλόσοφός τε
καὶ ἡγεμονικὸς τὴν φύσιν, καὶ ὅταν αὐτὸν εὑρόντες
ἐρασθῶσι, πᾶν ποιοῦσιν ὅπως τοιοῦτος | ἔσται. ἐὰν
οὖν μὴ πρότερον ἐμβεβῶσι τῷ ἐπιτηδεύματι, τότε ἐπι-
χειρήσαντες μανθάνουσί τε ὅθεν ἄν τι δύνωνται καὶ
253 αὐτοὶ μετέρχονται, ἰχνεύοντες δὲ παρ᾽ ἑαυτῶν ἀνευρί-
σκειν τὴν τοῦ σφετέρου θεοῦ φύσιν εὐποροῦσι διὰ τὸ
συντόνως ἠναγκάσθαι πρὸς τὸν θεὸν βλέπειν, καὶ
ἐφαπτόμενοι αὐτοῦ τῇ μνήμῃ ἐνθουσιῶντες ἐξ ἐκείνου
λαμβάνουσι τὰ ἔθη καὶ τὰ ἐπιτηδεύματα, καθ᾽ ὅσον
δυνατὸν θεοῦ ἀνθρώπῳ μετασχεῖν· | καὶ τούτων δὴ τὸν
ἐρώμενον αἰτιώμενοι ἔτι τε μᾶλλον ἀγαπῶσι, κἂν ἐκ
Διὸς ἀρύτωσιν ὥσπερ αἱ βάκχαι, ἐπὶ τὴν τοῦ ἐρωμένου ψυχὴν ἐπαντλοῦντες ποιοῦσιν ὡς δυνατὸν ὁμοιό-
b τατον τῷ σφετέρῳ θεῷ. ὅσοι δ᾽ αὖ μεθ᾽ Ἥρας εἵποντο,

77 That is, as in the case of the divinely inspired followers of

and their beloved. And so, after the manner of each god   d
in whose chorus each danced attendance, he lives, honoring and imitating him as far as he can, as long as he is
uncorrupted and is living his first life here on earth; and in
this way he mixes with and is drawn toward both his loved
ones and everybody else. Therefore each one chooses his
Love from the beautiful ones according to disposition, and
as if that very one were himself a god in his eyes, he shapes
and adorns him like a statue with the intention of honoring
and celebrating him with mystic rites. So indeed those   e
who are followers of Zeus are seeking that the one who is
loved by them should be like Zeus in his soul. And so then
they look to see if he is naturally a philosopher and leader,
and when they find him and fall in love with him, they do
everything to make him so. If then they haven't embarked
upon this path before, they take the matter up now and
learn from any source they can and pursue it themselves;
and in tracing it from within themselves they succeed in   253
discovering the nature of their own god through being
forced to look intensely in the direction of the god, and
grasping him through their memory they are possessed
and take from him their character and habits as far as it's
possible for a human being to share in a god. Indeed,
because they hold their loved one responsible for these
things they love him even more, and if it is from Zeus that
they draw inspiration, like the followers of Bacchus[77] they
pour it out over their loved one's soul and make him as
much like their own god as possible. Those in turn who   b

Bacchus, who draw milk and honey from rivers, so lovers acquire
their characteristics from specific deities and pour them out on
the beloved.

βασιλικὸν ζητοῦσι, καὶ εὑρόντες περὶ τοῦτον πάντα
δρῶσιν τὰ αὐτά. οἱ δὲ Ἀπόλλωνός τε καὶ ἑκάστου τῶν
θεῶν οὕτω κατὰ τὸν θεὸν ἰόντες ζητοῦσι τὸν σφέτερον
παῖδα πεφυκέναι, | καὶ ὅταν κτήσωνται, μιμούμενοι
αὐτοί τε καὶ τὰ παιδικὰ πείθοντες καὶ ῥυθμίζοντες εἰς
τὸ ἐκείνου ἐπιτήδευμα καὶ ἰδέαν ἄγουσιν, ὅση ἑκάστῳ
δύναμις, οὐ φθόνῳ οὐδ' ἀνελευθέρῳ δυσμενείᾳ χρώμενοι πρὸς τὰ παιδικά, ἀλλ' εἰς ὁμοιότητα αὑτοῖς καὶ
τῷ θεῷ ὃν ἂν τιμῶσι πᾶσαν πάντως ὅτι μάλιστα πει-
c ρώμενοι ἄγειν οὕτω ποιοῦσι. προθυμία μὲν οὖν τῶν
ὡς ἀληθῶς ἐρώντων καὶ τελετή,[6] ἐάν γε διαπράξωνται
ὃ προθυμοῦνται ᾗ λέγω, οὕτω καλή τε καὶ εὐδαιμο-
νικὴ ὑπὸ τοῦ | δι' ἔρωτα μανέντος φίλου τῷ φιληθέντι
γίγνεται, ἐὰν αἱρεθῇ· ἁλίσκεται δὲ δὴ ὁ αἱρεθεὶς τοιῷδε τρόπῳ.

Καθάπερ ἐν ἀρχῇ τοῦδε τοῦ μύθου τριχῇ διείλομεν
ψυχὴν ἑκάστην, ἱππομόρφω μὲν δύο τινὲ εἴδη, ἡνιο-
χικὸν δὲ εἶδος τρίτον, καὶ νῦν ἔτι ἡμῖν ταῦτα μενέτω.
d τῶν δὲ δὴ ἵππων ὁ μέν, φαμέν, ἀγαθός, ὁ δ' οὔ· ἀρετὴ
δὲ τίς τοῦ ἀγαθοῦ ἢ κακοῦ κακία, οὐ διείπομεν, νῦν
δὲ λεκτέον. ὁ μὲν τοίνυν αὐτοῖν ἐν τῇ καλλίονι στάσει
ὢν τό τε εἶδος ὀρθὸς καὶ | διηρθρωμένος, ὑψαύχην,
ἐπίγρυπος, λευκὸς ἰδεῖν, μελανόμματος, τιμῆς ἐραστὴς μετὰ σωφροσύνης τε καὶ αἰδοῦς, καὶ ἀληθινῆς

6 τελετή corr. Par. 1808, Burnet: τελευτή BTW

followed in company with Hera seek one of royal stature and when they have found him they do all the same things with him. The followers of Apollo and of each of the gods, proceeding thus according to their god, seek that their boy should be of that nature, and when they get him, themselves by way of imitation persuade and train their loved one and lead him to the ways and image of that god, in as far as each one is able, without resorting to resentment or niggardly ill will toward the loved one; but they act as they do because they are trying to the very utmost to bring him to a complete likeness of themselves in every way, and whichever god they revere. The enthusiasm therefore of those who are truly in love and the initiation,[78] if in fact they accomplish what they desire in the way I say, thus becomes beautiful and brings happiness from the friend maddened by love to the loved one, if he is won over; and the one who is caught is captured in the following way:

Just as at the beginning of this tale we divided each soul three ways, two in the shape of horses, and the third in that of a charioteer, so for our purposes let this still remain as it is. As to the horses, one we say is good, the other not, but we did not define what the excellence of the good one is, or the badness of the bad one, but now we must discuss it. Well then, one of them, being on the nobler side, upright in form, with good joints, the neck held high, somewhat hook-nosed, white in color with black eyes, a lover of honor along with temperance and a sense of shame, a

c

d

---

[78] *teletē* (initiation) is the reading of OCT (for a defense, see Yunis, n. ad loc.) The reading *teleutē* (consummation, issue) is accepted by many editors (see Rowe, n. ad loc.). See also textual note.

δόξης ἑταῖρος, ἄπληκτος, κελεύσματι μόνον καὶ λόγῳ
e ἡνιοχεῖται· ὁ δ' αὖ σκολιός, πολύς, εἰκῇ συμπεφορη-
μένος, κρατεραύχην, βραχυτράχηλος, σιμοπρόσω-
πος, μελάγχρως, γλαυκόμματος, ὕφαιμος, ὕβρεως καὶ
ἀλαζονείας ἑταῖρος, περὶ ὦτα λάσιος, κωφός, μάστιγι
μετὰ κέντρων μόγις ὑπείκων. | ὅταν δ' οὖν ὁ ἡνίοχος
ἰδὼν τὸ ἐρωτικὸν ὄμμα, πᾶσαν αἰσθήσει διαθερμήνας
τὴν ψυχήν, γαργαλισμοῦ τε καὶ πόθου κέντρων ὑπο-
254 πλησθῇ, ὁ μὲν εὐπειθὴς τῷ ἡνιόχῳ τῶν ἵππων, ἀεί τε
καὶ τότε αἰδοῖ βιαζόμενος, ἑαυτὸν κατέχει μὴ ἐπιπη-
δᾶν τῷ ἐρωμένῳ· ὁ δὲ οὔτε κέντρων ἡνιοχικῶν οὔτε
μάστιγος ἔτι ἐντρέπεται, σκιρτῶν δὲ βίᾳ φέρεται, καὶ
πάντα | πράγματα παρέχων τῷ σύζυγί τε καὶ ἡνιόχῳ
ἀναγκάζει ἰέναι τε πρὸς τὰ παιδικὰ καὶ μνείαν ποιεῖσθαι τῆς τῶν ἀφροδισίων χάριτος. τὼ δὲ κατ' ἀρχὰς
μὲν ἀντιτείνετον ἀγανακτοῦντε, ὡς δεινὰ καὶ παρά-
b νομα ἀναγκαζομένω· τελευτῶντε δέ, ὅταν μηδὲν ᾖ
πέρας κακοῦ, πορεύεσθον ἀγομένω, εἴξαντε καὶ ὁμο-
λογήσαντε ποιήσειν τὸ κελευόμενον. καὶ πρὸς αὐτῷ
τ' ἐγένοντο καὶ εἶδον τὴν ὄψιν τὴν τῶν παιδικῶν |
ἀστράπτουσαν. ἰδόντος δὲ τοῦ ἡνιόχου ἡ μνήμη πρὸς
τὴν τοῦ κάλλους φύσιν ἠνέχθη, καὶ πάλιν εἶδεν αὐτὴν
μετὰ σωφροσύνης ἐν ἁγνῷ βάθρῳ βεβῶσαν· ἰδοῦσα
δὲ ἔδεισέ τε καὶ σεφθεῖσα ἀνέπεσεν ὑπτία, καὶ ἅμα
ἠναγκάσθη εἰς τοὐπίσω ἑλκύσαι τὰς ἡνίας οὕτω σφό-
c δρα, ὥστ' ἐπὶ τὰ ἰσχία ἄμφω καθίσαι τὼ ἵππω, τὸν
μὲν ἑκόντα διὰ τὸ μὴ ἀντιτείνειν, τὸν δὲ ὑβριστὴν
μάλ' ἄκοντα. ἀπελθόντε δὲ ἀπωτέρω, ὁ μὲν ὑπ' αἰσχύ-

companion of true glory, needing no whip, is guided by
the word of command alone. But the other is crooked,   e
massive, put together in a ramshackle way, with a short,
strong neck, snub-nosed, black-skinned, gray-eyed, blood-
shot, a companion of excess and imposture, shaggy round
the ears, deaf, barely yielding to the whip and goad together. Now whenever the charioteer, seeing the light
of his love, having sent warmth through his whole soul
through his perception, is filled with a tickling and the
goads of longing, one of the horses, obedient to the char-   254
ioteer because constrained then as ever by its sense of
respect, holds itself in check from leaping on the loved
one, but the other is no longer compliant with the charioteer's goads or whip, but leaping, it surges violently
ahead, and giving its yoke fellow and charioteer every kind
of difficulty, forces them to go toward his loved one and
give a reminder of the pleasure of sex. At the beginning
the two of them resist, irritated because they are being
forced to make terrible and improper moves. But finally,   b
as there is no end to their trouble, they move forward
under its lead, yield and agree to do what it orders. And
they get close to the beloved and see his face gleaming.
When he sees it, the memory of the charioteer is carried
back to the nature of beauty and he sees it again standing
with temperance on a sacred pedestal. On seeing it he is
afraid and falls on his back in awe, and at the same time
he is forced to draw the reins back so hard that the two
horses sit back on their haunches, one willingly because it   c
offers no resistance, the insolent one very reluctantly.
Both having moved further away the one drenches its

νης τε καὶ θάμβους ἱδρῶτι πᾶσαν | ἔβρεξε τὴν ψυχήν,
ὁ δὲ λήξας τῆς ὀδύνης, ἣν ὑπὸ τοῦ χαλινοῦ τε ἔσχεν
καὶ τοῦ πτώματος, μόγις ἐξαναπνεύσας ἐλοιδόρησεν
ὀργῇ, πολλὰ κακίζων τόν τε ἡνίοχον καὶ τὸν ὁμόζυγα
ὡς δειλίᾳ τε καὶ ἀνανδρίᾳ λιπόντε τὴν τάξιν καὶ ὁμο-
d λογίαν· καὶ πάλιν οὐκ ἐθέλοντας προσιέναι ἀναγκάζων μόγις συνεχώρησεν δεομένων εἰς αὖθις ὑπερ-
βαλέσθαι. ἐλθόντος δὲ τοῦ συντεθέντος χρόνου [οὗ]
ἀμνημονεῖν προσποιουμένω ἀναμιμνήσκων, βιαζόμε-
νος, χρεμετίζων, ἕλκων | ἠνάγκασεν αὖ προσελθεῖν
τοῖς παιδικοῖς ἐπὶ τοὺς αὐτοὺς λόγους, καὶ ἐπειδὴ
ἐγγὺς ἦσαν, ἐγκύψας καὶ ἐκτείνας τὴν κέρκον, ἐνδα-
e κὼν τὸν χαλινόν, μετ᾿ ἀναιδείας ἕλκει· ὁ δ᾿ ἡνίοχος ἔτι
μᾶλλον ταὐτὸν πάθος παθών, ὥσπερ ἀπὸ ὕσπληγος
ἀναπεσών, ἔτι μᾶλλον τοῦ ὑβριστοῦ ἵππου ἐκ τῶν
ὀδόντων βίᾳ ὀπίσω σπάσας τὸν χαλινόν, τήν τε κα-
κηγόρον γλῶτταν καὶ τὰς γνάθους καθήμαξεν καὶ τὰ
σκέλη τε καὶ | τὰ ἰσχία πρὸς τὴν γῆν ἐρείσας ὀδύναις
ἔδωκεν. ὅταν δὲ ταὐτὸν πολλάκις πάσχων ὁ πονηρὸς
τῆς ὕβρεως λήξῃ, ταπεινωθεὶς ἕπεται ἤδη τῇ τοῦ
ἡνιόχου προνοίᾳ, καὶ ὅταν ἴδῃ τὸν καλόν, φόβῳ διόλ-
255 λυται· ὥστε συμβαίνει τότ᾿ ἤδη τὴν τοῦ ἐραστοῦ
ψυχὴν τοῖς παιδικοῖς αἰδουμένην τε καὶ δεδιυῖαν
ἕπεσθαι. ἅτε οὖν πᾶσαν θεραπείαν ὡς ἰσόθεος θερα-

---

79 *Husplēx*. LSJ has as its meaning "snare" (starting back from
stepping unawares into a trap or snare) or "starting-barrier" (in a

whole soul in sweat through shame and amazement, but
the other, as soon as he has recovered from the pain of the
bit and the fall, and having barely got its breath back, rages
in anger and continually abuses both charioteer and its
yoke fellow for deserting their place and abandoning their
cooperation out of cowardice and unmanliness. And again   d
in trying to force them to go forward against their will he
concedes grudgingly when they beg him to hold back until later. When the agreed time comes and the two pretend
to have forgotten, by reminding them, coercing them,
neighing and dragging them it forces them to approach
the loved one again with the same proposition, and when
they are near, hunched down, and stretching out its tail
and gnawing at the bit, it drags them shamelessly. But the   e
charioteer experiencing the same feelings even more, falling back as if from a turning post,[79] pulling the bit back
even more forcibly from the teeth of the violent horse,
covers its abusive tongue and jaws with blood and by push-
ing both its legs and haunches to the ground, gives it over
to pain. And when it undergoes the same experience again
and again, the bad horse stops being violent and now hum-
bly follows the foresight of the charioteer, and when it sees
the beautiful boy, it is frightened to death. Consequently
then finally the soul of the lover follows the loved one with
respect and fear. So, in as much as he is receiving every   255
attention as one equal to the gods, not from a contriving

race, possibly pulling the horse up for an initial surge forward at
the start). We have accepted here an alternative editorial suggestion of "turning post" as more plausible: "the charioteer leans
back . . . and reins in the horses as if to avoid crashing into the
turning-post in a race" (Yunis, n. ad loc.).

πευόμενος οὐχ ὑπὸ σχηματιζομένου τοῦ ἐρῶντος ἀλλ'
ἀληθῶς τοῦτο πεπονθότος, καὶ αὐτὸς ὢν φύσει φίλος
τῷ θεραπεύοντι, ἐὰν ἄρα καὶ ἐν τῷ πρόσθεν ὑπὸ συμ-
φοιτητῶν ἤ | τινων ἄλλων διαβεβλημένος ᾖ, λεγόντων
ὡς αἰσχρὸν ἐρῶντι πλησιάζειν, καὶ διὰ τοῦτο ἀπωθῇ
τὸν ἐρῶντα, προϊόντος δὲ ἤδη τοῦ χρόνου ἥ τε ἡλικία
καὶ τὸ χρεὼν ἤγαγεν εἰς τὸ προσέσθαι αὐτὸν εἰς ὁμι-
b λίαν· οὐ γὰρ δήποτε εἵμαρται κακὸν κακῷ φίλον οὐδ'
ἀγαθὸν μὴ φίλον ἀγαθῷ εἶναι. προσεμένου δὲ καὶ
λόγον καὶ ὁμιλίαν δεξαμένου, ἐγγύθεν ἡ εὔνοια γι-
γνομένη τοῦ ἐρῶντος ἐκπλήττει τὸν ἐρώμενον | διαι-
σθανόμενον ὅτι οὐδ' οἱ σύμπαντες ἄλλοι φίλοι τε καὶ
οἰκεῖοι μοῖραν φιλίας οὐδεμίαν παρέχονται πρὸς τὸν
ἔνθεον φίλον. ὅταν δὲ χρονίζῃ τοῦτο δρῶν καὶ πλησι-
άζῃ μετὰ τοῦ ἅπτεσθαι ἔν τε γυμνασίοις καὶ ἐν ταῖς
ἄλλαις ὁμιλίαις, τότ' ἤδη ἡ τοῦ ῥεύματος ἐκείνου
πηγή, ὃν ἵμερον Ζεὺς Γανυμήδους ἐρῶν ὠνόμασε,
c πολλὴ φερομένη πρὸς τὸν ἐραστήν, ἡ μὲν εἰς αὐτὸν
ἔδυ, ἡ δ' ἀπομεστουμένου ἔξω ἀπορρεῖ· καὶ οἷον
πνεῦμα ἤ τις ἠχὼ ἀπὸ λείων τε καὶ | στερεῶν ἀλλο-
μένη πάλιν ὅθεν ὡρμήθη φέρεται, οὕτω τὸ τοῦ κάλλους ῥεῦμα πάλιν εἰς τὸν καλὸν διὰ τῶν ὀμμάτων ἰόν,
ᾗ πέφυκεν ἐπὶ τὴν ψυχὴν ἰέναι ἀφικόμενον καὶ ἀνα-
d πτερῶσαν, τὰς διόδους τῶν πτερῶν ἄρδει τε καὶ ὥρμησε πτεροφυεῖν τε καὶ τὴν τοῦ ἐρωμένου αὖ ψυχὴν
ἔρωτος ἐνέπλησεν. ἐρᾷ μὲν οὖν, ὅτου δὲ ἀπορεῖ· καὶ

lover, but one who is genuine in his feelings, and being naturally friendly to his attendant, even if in the past he has been maybe misled by his schoolmates or anyone else who say it's a disgrace to associate with a lover, and for this reason he rebuffs the lover, with the passage of time both his age and need lead the loved one to admit him into his company. For surely it is never fated that a bad person b must be a friend to a bad one, nor that a good person is not to be a friend of a good one.[80] But when he has admitted and accepted him into his conversation and company, the goodwill that arises from being near his lover astounds the loved one when he perceives clearly that not even all his other friends and relatives can provide him with any share of friendship in comparison with the friend inspired by a god. When he perseveres in doing this and draws close to him with physical contact in the gymnasia and other meeting places, at that point the source of that stream which Zeus, in love with Ganymede, called desire[81] is carried along in floods toward the lover, some sinking c into him, some flowing away outside as he brims over; and like a breath of wind or an echo rebounding off smooth and hard surfaces is carried back to where it started from, so the stream of beauty passes back to the beautiful one through his eyes, and having arrived at the natural inlet to the soul and arousing him, it waters the pathways of the d feathers and both stimulates the growth of the wings and fills the soul of the loved one in his turn with love. So he's in love, but cannot tell with what; and he neither knows

[80] This has the feel of a proverbial sentiment (see Homer, *Odyssey* 17.218).   [81] For Zeus and Ganymede, see *Homeric Hymn to Aphrodite* 202–17.

οὔθ᾽ ὅτι πέπονθεν οἶδεν οὐδ᾽ ἔχει φράσαι, ἀλλ᾽ οἷον
ἀπ᾽ ἄλλου | ὀφθαλμίας ἀπολελαυκὼς πρόφασιν εἰπεῖν
οὐκ ἔχει, ὥσπερ δὲ ἐν κατόπτρῳ ἐν τῷ ἐρῶντι ἑαυτὸν
ὁρῶν λέληθεν. καὶ ὅταν μὲν ἐκεῖνος παρῇ, λήγει κατὰ
ταὐτὰ ἐκείνῳ τῆς ὀδύνης, ὅταν δὲ ἀπῇ, κατὰ ταὐτὰ αὖ
ποθεῖ καὶ ποθεῖται, εἴδωλον ἔρωτος ἀντέρωτα ἔχων·
e καλεῖ δὲ αὐτὸν καὶ οἴεται οὐκ ἔρωτα ἀλλὰ φιλίαν εἶναι. ἐπιθυμεῖ δὲ ἐκείνῳ παραπλησίως μέν, ἀσθενεστέ-
ρως δέ, ὁρᾶν, ἅπτεσθαι, φιλεῖν, συγκατακεῖσθαι· καὶ
δή, οἷον εἰκός, ποιεῖ τὸ μετὰ τοῦτο ταχὺ ταῦτα. ἐν οὖν
| τῇ συγκοιμήσει τοῦ μὲν ἐραστοῦ ὁ ἀκόλαστος ἵππος
ἔχει ὅτι λέγῃ πρὸς τὸν ἡνίοχον, καὶ ἀξιοῖ ἀντὶ πολ-
256 λῶν πόνων σμικρὰ ἀπολαῦσαι· ὁ δὲ τῶν παιδικῶν ἔχει
μὲν οὐδὲν εἰπεῖν, σπαργῶν δὲ καὶ ἀπορῶν περιβάλλει
τὸν ἐραστὴν καὶ φιλεῖ, ὡς σφόδρ᾽ εὔνουν ἀσπαζόμενος, ὅταν τε συγκατακέωνται, οἷός ἐστι μὴ ἂν ἀπαρ-
νηθῆναι τὸ αὑτοῦ μέρος χαρίσασθαι | τῷ ἐρῶντι, εἰ
δεηθείη τυχεῖν· ὁ δὲ ὁμόζυξ αὖ μετὰ τοῦ ἡνιόχου πρὸς
ταῦτα μετ᾽ αἰδοῦς καὶ λόγου ἀντιτείνει. ἐὰν μὲν δὴ
οὖν εἰς τεταγμένην τε δίαιταν καὶ φιλοσοφίαν νικήσῃ
τὰ βελτίω τῆς διανοίας ἀγαγόντα, μακάριον μὲν καὶ
b ὁμονοητικὸν τὸν ἐνθάδε βίον διάγουσιν, ἐγκρατεῖς
αὑτῶν καὶ κόσμιοι ὄντες, δουλωσάμενοι μὲν ᾧ κακία
ψυχῆς ἐνεγίγνετο, ἐλευθερώσαντες δὲ ᾧ ἀρετή· τελευτήσαντες δὲ δὴ ὑπόπτεροι καὶ ἐλαφροὶ γεγονότες τῶν
τριῶν παλαισμάτων | τῶν ὡς ἀληθῶς Ὀλυμπιακῶν ἐν

---

[82] That is, the first of the three lives through which the philo-

what he has experienced, nor does he have any way of explaining it; but just as one who has caught someone else's ophthalmia, he cannot say what the cause is, but he is unaware he is seeing himself in his lover as if in a mirror. And when his lover is present, like him his pain stops, and when he's away, again, as with him, he misses him and is missed, having a reflection of love in exchange for love. But he calls it, and thinks it to be not love, but friendship. **e** Like the lover, but less strongly, he desires to see, touch and kiss and lie down with him. And indeed, as you'd expect, he soon does just that shortly afterward. Now while they are sleeping together the undisciplined horse of the lover has something to suggest to the charioteer and thinks it worth a little pleasure in return for many labors. But the **256** horse of the loved one has nothing to say, but swelling with passion and unsure what to do, he throws his arms around his lover and kisses him, embracing him as someone particularly well-intentioned; and whenever they do lie with each other, he is inclined never to deny doing his part in giving pleasure to his lover if he should beg for it. But his yoke fellow on his side strains against this with the charioteer out of a sense of shame and reason. So then, if the better side of their minds wins the day by leading them to an ordered way of life and philosophy, they lead a blessed and harmonious life here on earth, in control of them- **b** selves and well-behaved, having enslaved the part where evil was entering the soul, but setting free the part where virtue was entering. And when they die having become winged and nimble they have won one of the three truly Olympian wrestling bouts,[82] than which neither human

sophical followers of Zeus must travel successfully to regain their wings and rejoin the heavenly procession.

νενικήκασιν, οὗ μεῖζον ἀγαθὸν οὔτε σωφροσύνη ἀν-
θρωπίνη οὔτε θεία μανία δυνατὴ πορίσαι ἀνθρώπῳ.
c ἐὰν δὲ δὴ διαίτῃ φορτικωτέρᾳ τε καὶ ἀφιλοσόφῳ, φι-
λοτίμῳ δὲ χρήσωνται, τάχ᾽ ἄν που ἐν μέθαις ἤ τινι
ἄλλῃ ἀμελείᾳ τὼ ἀκολάστω αὐτοῖν ὑποζυγίω λαβόντε
τὰς ψυχὰς ἀφρούρους, συναγαγόντε εἰς ταὐτόν, τὴν
ὑπὸ τῶν πολλῶν μακαριστὴν αἵρεσιν εἱλέσθην τε καὶ
διεπραξάσθην· | καὶ διαπραξαμένω τὸ λοιπὸν ἤδη
χρῶνται μὲν αὐτῇ, σπανίᾳ δέ, ἅτε οὐ πάσῃ δεδογμένα
d τῇ διανοίᾳ πράττοντες. φίλω μὲν οὖν καὶ τούτω, ἧττον
δὲ ἐκείνων, ἀλλήλοιν διά τε τοῦ ἔρωτος καὶ ἔξω γενο-
μένω διάγουσι, πίστεις τὰς μεγίστας ἡγουμένω ἀλλήλοιν δεδωκέναι τε καὶ δεδέχθαι, ἃς οὐ θεμιτὸν εἶναι
λύσαντας εἰς ἔχθραν ποτὲ ἐλθεῖν. ἐν δὲ τῇ τελευτῇ
ἄπτεροι μέν, ὡρμηκότες δὲ πτεροῦσθαι ἐκβαίνουσι |
τοῦ σώματος, ὥστε οὐ σμικρὸν ἆθλον τῆς ἐρωτικῆς
μανίας φέρονται· εἰς γὰρ σκότον καὶ τὴν ὑπὸ γῆς
πορείαν οὐ νόμος ἐστὶν ἔτι ἐλθεῖν τοῖς κατηργμένοις
ἤδη τῆς ὑπουρανίου πορείας, ἀλλὰ φανὸν βίον διά-
γοντας εὐδαιμονεῖν μετ᾽ ἀλλήλων πορευομένους, καὶ
ὁμοπτέρους ἔρωτος χάριν, ὅταν γένωνται, γενέσθαι.

e Ταῦτα τοσαῦτα, ὦ παῖ, καὶ θεῖα οὕτω σοι δωρήσε-
ται ἡ παρ᾽ ἐραστοῦ φιλία· ἡ δὲ ἀπὸ τοῦ μὴ ἐρῶντος
οἰκειότης, | σωφροσύνῃ θνητῇ κεκραμένη, θνητά τε
καὶ φειδωλὰ οἰκονομοῦσα, ἀνελευθερίαν ὑπὸ πλήθους
ἐπαινουμένην ὡς ἀρετὴν τῇ φίλῃ ψυχῇ ἐντεκοῦσα, ἐν-

temperance nor divine madness is capable of providing greater good for a man. But if, in a more common way of life without philosophy, they pursue honor, perhaps, I suppose, when they are drinking or in some other careless pursuit, the uncontrolled horses in the two of them, catching their souls in an unguarded moment, bring them together and carry through a choice which is called blissful in the eyes of most people. And having accomplished it, from now on they continue with it, but rarely, in that their doing it does not seem right to the whole of their way of thinking. These two also live as friends with each other, but less than the former pair, both while they are in love with each other and afterward, thinking they have given and received the most serious pledges from each other which it is not lawful for them to break or ever become enemies. But when they die, they leave the body without wings but with eagerness to regain them, so that they actually win no small prize for their erotic madness. For it is not the law that those who have already embarked on the journey beneath heavens should go any more into darkness and make the journey under the earth, but that they should lead a joyous life and be happy as they make their way with each other and acquire the same plumage as each other when it grows, because of their love.

Such great and godlike gifts as these, my boy, the friendship of a lover will give you in this way. But the relationship which originates from one who does not love, mixed with worldly temperance, dispensing gifts of a mortal and sparing kind, producing in his friend's soul a lack of freedom which is lauded by the masses as a virtue, will

c

d

e

447

νέα χιλιάδας ἐτῶν περὶ γῆν κυλινδουμένην αὐτὴν καὶ
ὑπὸ γῆς ἄνουν παρέξει.

257   Αὕτη σοι, ὦ φίλε Ἔρως, εἰς ἡμετέραν δύναμιν ὅτι
καλλίστη καὶ ἀρίστη δέδοταί τε καὶ ἐκτέτεισται πα-
λινῳδία, τά I τε ἄλλα καὶ τοῖς ὀνόμασιν ἠναγκασμένη
ποιητικοῖς τισιν διὰ Φαῖδρον εἰρῆσθαι. ἀλλὰ τῶν
προτέρων τε συγγνώμην καὶ τῶνδε χάριν ἔχων, εὐ-
μενὴς καὶ ἵλεως τὴν ἐρωτικήν μοι τέχνην ἣν ἔδωκας
μήτε ἀφέλῃ μήτε πηρώσῃς δι' ὀργήν, δίδου τ' ἔτι
μᾶλλον ἢ νῦν παρὰ τοῖς καλοῖς τίμιον εἶναι. ἐν τῷ
πρόσθεν δ' εἴ τι λόγῳ σοι ἀπηχὲς εἴπομεν Φαῖδρός
b   τε καὶ ἐγώ, Λυσίαν τὸν τοῦ λόγου πατέρα αἰτιώμενος
παῦε τῶν τοιούτων λόγων, ἐπὶ φιλοσοφίαν δέ, ὥσπερ
ἀδελφὸς αὐτοῦ Πολέμαρχος τέτραπται, τρέψον, ἵνα
καὶ ὁ ἐραστὴς I ὅδε αὐτοῦ μηκέτι ἐπαμφοτερίζῃ καθάπερ νῦν, ἀλλ' ἁπλῶς πρὸς Ἔρωτα μετὰ φιλοσόφων
λόγων τὸν βίον ποιῆται.

ΦΑΙ. Συνεύχομαί σοι, ὦ Σώκρατες, εἴπερ ἄμεινον
c   ταῦθ' ἡμῖν εἶναι, ταῦτα γίγνεσθαι. τὸν λόγον δέ σου
πάλαι θαυμάσας ἔχω, ὅσῳ καλλίω τοῦ προτέρου
ἀπηργάσω· ὥστε ὀκνῶ μή μοι ὁ Λυσίας ταπεινὸς
φανῇ, ἐὰν ἄρα καὶ ἐθελήσῃ πρὸς αὐτὸν ἄλλον ἀντι-
παρατεῖναι. καὶ γάρ τις αὐτόν, ὦ I θαυμάσιε, ἔναγχος
τῶν πολιτικῶν τοῦτ' αὐτὸ λοιδορῶν ὠνείδιζε, καὶ διὰ

---

83 On the human cycles, see 248e4ff. "Nine thousand years"
represents nine periods of existence in mortal form that the soul

cause it to trundle mindlessly about and under the earth for nine thousand years.[83]

This, dear Eros, is given and paid out to you as the fin- 257 est and best possible palinode up to the limits of my pow-ers, especially since it was forced to speak in poetic lan-guage because of Phaedrus. But forgive what went before and be favorable toward these words; be kind and gra-cious, and do not take away the erotic art you gave me and do not harm it out of anger. And allow me to be honored even more than now by those who are beautiful. And if in the previous speeches Phaedrus and I said anything dis-cordant against you, blame Lysias the father of the speech b and stop him making such speeches and turn him to phi-losophy, as his brother Polemarchus has been turned,[84] so that his lover here may no longer waver from one side to the other, as he does now, but may make a life simply in accordance with Eros aided by philosophical discussion.

P. I pray with you, Socrates, that this happens, if this is in fact better for us. For some time I've marveled at how c much finer you made your speech than the previous one. Consequently I hesitate to say whether Lysias may not appear to me to be humbled, if he should actually be will-ing to put up another speech alongside it in competition. For indeed, only recently, my good fellow, one of the politicians was abusing and reviling him on this very point, and throughout the whole of his tirade kept calling him a

of the loved one who associates with a nonlover will have to en-dure, including punishment under the earth after death.

[84] Polemarchus' interest in philosophy is clearly demonstrated in exchanges with Socrates in *Republic* 1.331d–36a.

πάσης τῆς λοιδορίας ἐκάλει λογογράφον· τάχ᾽ οὖν ἂν
ὑπὸ φιλοτιμίας ἐπίσχοι ἡμῖν ἂν τοῦ γράφειν.

ΣΩ. Γελοῖόν γ᾽, ὦ νεανία, τὸ δόγμα λέγεις, καὶ τοῦ
d ἑταίρου συχνὸν διαμαρτάνεις, εἰ αὐτὸν οὕτως ἡγῇ
τινα ψοφοδεᾶ. ἴσως δὲ καὶ τὸν λοιδορούμενον αὐτῷ
οἴει ὀνειδίζοντα λέγειν ἃ ἔλεγεν.

ΦΑΙ. Ἐφαίνετο γάρ, ὦ Σώκρατες· καὶ σύνοισθά
που | καὶ αὐτὸς ὅτι οἱ μέγιστον δυνάμενοί τε καὶ σε-
μνότατοι ἐν ταῖς πόλεσιν αἰσχύνονται λόγους τε γράφειν καὶ καταλείπειν συγγράμματα ἑαυτῶν, δόξαν
φοβούμενοι τοῦ ἔπειτα χρόνου, μὴ σοφισταὶ καλῶν-
ται.

ΣΩ. Γλυκὺς ἀγκών, ὦ Φαῖδρε, λέληθέν σε ὅτι ἀπὸ
e τοῦ μακροῦ ἀγκῶνος τοῦ κατὰ Νεῖλον ἐκλήθη·[7] καὶ
πρὸς τῷ ἀγκῶνι λανθάνει σε ὅτι οἱ μέγιστον φρονοῦν-
τες τῶν πολιτικῶν μάλιστα ἐρῶσι λογογραφίας τε
καὶ καταλείψεως συγγραμμάτων, οἵ γε καὶ ἐπειδάν
τινα γράφωσι λόγον, | οὕτως ἀγαπῶσι τοὺς ἐπαινέ-
τας, ὥστε προσπαραγράφουσι πρώτους οἳ ἂν ἑκα-
σταχοῦ ἐπαινῶσιν αὐτούς.

ΦΑΙ. Πῶς λέγεις τοῦτο; οὐ γὰρ μανθάνω.

---

[7] ὅτι . . . ἐκλήθη secl. Heindorf

---

[85] "Speechwriter" (logographos): As a metic (metoikos = non-
Athenian settler without citizen rights), Lysias could not plead in
person in court, and so his activity as a speechwriter was confined
to composing speeches for display or for litigants to deliver; he

speechwriter: so perhaps then we may find him refraining from writing through concern for his reputation.[85]

S. A ridiculous opinion you're expressing, young man, and you are very much mistaken about your companion if   d
you think he's someone who's so easily frightened at a bit of noise. But perhaps you think the man abusing him meant what he was saying as a reproach.

P. Yes, he appeared to, Socrates, and I think you know too yourself that those most powerful and respected in our cities are ashamed both of writing speeches and leaving their own writings behind, fearing for their reputation in time to come: that they'll be called sophists.

S. You've forgotten "Sweet Bend," Phaedrus, which is so-called from the long bend in the Nile.[86] And in addition   e
to the bend you're failing to see that those politicians who have very high opinions of themselves are the ones most in love both with speechwriting and with leaving behind writings, since indeed it is they who, whenever they write a speech, are so well-disposed to those who praise it that at the beginning they add in the names of those who praise them on each occasion.

P. What do you mean by that? I don't understand.

was also, of course as a noncitizen, debarred from attending the Athenian Assembly and so making political speeches.

[86] Proverbial, referring to what was apparently a dangerous bend in the River Nile, and called "sweet" (the phrase indicating words used in one sense but meaning their opposite); hence, Phaedrus should not take politicians at their word. Some editors bracket the explanatory words "which is so-called . . . Nile" as a later didactic gloss (see textual note).

258   ΣΩ. Οὐ μανθάνεις ὅτι ἐν ἀρχῇ ἀνδρὸς πολιτικοῦ
[συγγράμματι] πρῶτος ὁ ἐπαινέτης γέγραπται.

ΦΑΙ. Πῶς;

ΣΩ. Ἔδοξέ πού φησιν τῇ βουλῇ ἢ τῷ δήμῳ |
ἢ ἀμφοτέροις, καὶ ὃς ‹καὶ ὃς›εἶπεν—τὸν αὐτὸν δὴ
λέγων μάλα σεμνῶς καὶ ἐγκωμιάζων ὁ συγγραφεύς—
ἔπειτα λέγει δὴ μετὰ τοῦτο, ἐπιδεικνύμενος τοῖς ἐπαι-
νέταις τὴν ἑαυτοῦ σοφίαν, ἐνίοτε πάνυ μακρὸν ποιη-
σάμενος σύγγραμμα· ἤ σοι ἄλλο τι φαίνεται τὸ
τοιοῦτον ἢ λόγος συγγεγραμμένος;

b   ΦΑΙ. Οὐκ ἔμοιγε.

ΣΩ. Οὐκοῦν ἐὰν μὲν οὗτος ἐμμένῃ, γεγηθὼς ἀπέρχεται ἐκ τοῦ θεάτρου ὁ ποιητής· ἐὰν δὲ ἐξαλειφθῇ καὶ
ἄμοιρος γένηται λογογραφίας τε καὶ τοῦ ἄξιος εἶναι
συγγράφειν, | πενθεῖ αὐτός τε καὶ οἱ ἑταῖροι.

ΦΑΙ. Καὶ μάλα.

ΣΩ. Δῆλόν γε ὅτι οὐχ ὡς ὑπερφρονοῦντες τοῦ
ἐπιτηδεύματος, ἀλλ' ὡς τεθαυμακότες.

ΦΑΙ. Πάνυ μὲν οὖν. |

ΣΩ. Τί δέ; ὅταν ἱκανὸς γένηται ῥήτωρ ἢ βασιλεύς,
ὥστε λαβὼν τὴν Λυκούργου ἢ Σόλωνος ἢ Δαρείου
c   δύναμιν ἀθάνατος γενέσθαι λογογράφος ἐν πόλει, ἆρ'
οὐκ ἰσόθεον ἡγεῖται αὐτός τε αὑτὸν ἔτι ζῶν, καὶ οἱ
ἔπειτα γιγνόμενοι ταὐτὰ ταῦτα περὶ αὐτοῦ νομίζουσι,
θεώμενοι αὐτοῦ τὰ συγγράμματα; |

---

87 Lycurgus was traditionally regarded as the founder of the

S. Don't you understand that at the beginning of a   258
politician's work the name of his supporter is the first thing
written down?

P. How do you mean?

S. The writer says, I suppose: "It was decided by the
council," or "by the people," or both, and "so-and-so
spoke"—actually mentioning and lauding his own self with
great solemnity—then after that he delivers his speech,
displaying his own wisdom to his admirers, sometimes
making a very long composition; or does such a thing seem
to you to be at all different from a written speech?

P. Not to me.   b

S. Therefore if this becomes permanent, the author
leaves the theater a happy man, but if it's erased and he
loses the chance of being recognized as a speechwriter and
worthy of permanent record, he and his companions go
into mourning.

P. Indeed they do.

S. And clearly not as those who look down on the activity, but as admirers.

P. Very much so.

S. Well then: whenever he becomes an orator or king
competent to take on the power of a Lycurgus, a Solon or
a Darius,[87] and becomes an immortal speechwriter in his
city, does he not think himself equal to a god even while   c
still alive, and those who come after think the very same
thing about him when they gaze on his writings?

Spartan constitution, Solon was regarded as the founder of Athenian democracy, and Darius, king of Persia, represents monarchi-
cal authority. All three are associated with codes of law, presumably written down, and so permanent in memory.

ΦΑΙ. Καὶ μάλα.

ΣΩ. Οἴει τινὰ οὖν τῶν τοιούτων, ὅστις καὶ ὁπω-
στιοῦν δύσνους Λυσίᾳ, ὀνειδίζειν αὐτὸ τοῦτο ὅτι συγ-
γράφει;

ΦΑΙ. Οὔκουν εἰκός γε ἐξ ὧν σὺ λέγεις· καὶ γὰρ ἂν
τῇ ‖ ἑαυτοῦ ἐπιθυμίᾳ, ὡς ἔοικεν, ὀνειδίζοι.

d   ΣΩ. Τοῦτο μὲν ἄρα παντὶ δῆλον, ὅτι οὐκ αἰσχρὸν
αὐτό γε τὸ γράφειν λόγους.

ΦΑΙ. Τί γάρ;

ΣΩ. Ἀλλ᾽ ἐκεῖνο οἶμαι αἰσχρὸν ἤδη, τὸ μὴ καλῶς
λέγειν ‖ τε καὶ γράφειν ἀλλ᾽ αἰσχρῶς τε καὶ κακῶς.

ΦΑΙ. Δῆλον δή.

ΣΩ. Τίς οὖν ὁ τρόπος τοῦ καλῶς τε καὶ μὴ γράφειν;
δεόμεθά τι, ὦ Φαῖδρε, Λυσίαν τε περὶ τούτων ἐξετά-
σαι καὶ ἄλλον ὅστις πώποτέ τι γέγραφεν ἢ γράψει,
εἴτε πολιτικὸν ‖ σύγγραμμα εἴτε ἰδιωτικόν, ἐν μέτρῳ
ὡς ποιητὴς ἢ ἄνευ μέτρου ὡς ἰδιώτης;

e   ΦΑΙ. Ἐρωτᾷς εἰ δεόμεθα; τίνος μὲν οὖν ἕνεκα κἄν
τις ὡς εἰπεῖν ζῴη, ἀλλ᾽ ἢ τῶν τοιούτων ἡδονῶν ἕνεκα;
οὐ γάρ που ἐκείνων γε ὧν προλυπηθῆναι δεῖ ἢ μηδὲ
ἡσθῆναι, ὃ δὴ ὀλίγου πᾶσαι αἱ περὶ τὸ σῶμα ἡδοναὶ
ἔχουσι· διὸ καὶ ‖ δικαίως ἀνδραποδώδεις κέκληνται.

ΣΩ. Σχολὴ μὲν δή, ὡς ἔοικε· καὶ ἅμα μοι δοκοῦσιν
ὡς ἐν τῷ πνίγει ὑπὲρ κεφαλῆς ἡμῶν οἱ τέττιγες ᾄδοντες καὶ ἀλλήλοις διαλεγόμενοι καθορᾶν καὶ ἡμᾶς.

---

88 The idea that physical pleasures necessarily involve previ-

P. Yes indeed.

S. Do you think that one of this sort, whoever he is and however disaffected toward Lysias, makes his reproach on just this count, that he is a writer?

P. It's certainly not likely, at any rate, from what you're saying: for in that case he would be reproaching him for his own passion, it seems.

S. This much then is clear to everyone, that writing   d speeches is, in itself at least, no disgrace.

P. No, why should it be?

S. Yet what I *do* think is a disgrace is not to speak and write well, but disgracefully and badly.

P. Obviously.

S. So what then is the way to write well and not well? Do we need, Phaedrus, to question Lysias about these things and anybody else who has ever written or will write anything, whether it's a treatise on matters concerning the city, or a personal one, in verse as a poet does, or without meter by someone writing in prose?

P. Are you asking me if we need to? On the contrary   e for what reason would anyone live, so to speak, except for the sake of such pleasures? For I can't imagine it's for the sake of those pleasures in which one must suffer pain beforehand or otherwise not have any pleasure at all, which is what nearly all physical pleasures entail: indeed that's why they are rightly called servile.[88]

S. We have the leisure, it seems, to do it. And at the same time I think the cicadas, singing above our heads in the stifling heat, and talking among themselves, are look-

ous pain is developed at *Gorgias* 496c–97a, *Phaedo* 60b, *Republic* 583c–d, *Philebus* 51aff.

259 εἰ οὖν ἴδοιεν καὶ νὼ καθάπερ τοὺς πολλοὺς ἐν μεσημ-
βρίᾳ μὴ διαλεγομένους ἀλλὰ νυστάζοντας καὶ κηλου-
μένους ὑφ᾽ αὑτῶν δι᾽ ἀργίαν τῆς διανοίας, δικαίως ἂν
καταγελῷεν, ἡγούμενοι ἀνδράποδ᾽ | ἄττα σφίσιν ἐλ-
θόντα εἰς τὸ καταγώγιον ὥσπερ προβάτια μεσημβρι-
άζοντα περὶ τὴν κρήνην εὕδειν· ἐὰν δὲ ὁρῶσι διαλεγομένους καὶ παραπλέοντάς σφας ὥσπερ Σειρῆνας
b ἀκηλήτους, ὃ γέρας παρὰ θεῶν ἔχουσιν ἀνθρώποις
διδόναι, τάχ᾽ ἂν δοῖεν ἀγασθέντες.

ΦΑΙ. Ἔχουσι δὲ δὴ τί τοῦτο; ἀνήκοος γάρ, ὡς
ἔοικε, τυγχάνω ὤν. |

ΣΩ. Οὐ μὲν δὴ πρέπει γε φιλόμουσον ἄνδρα τῶν
τοιούτων ἀνήκοον εἶναι. λέγεται δ᾽ ὥς ποτ᾽ ἦσαν οὗτοι
ἄνθρωποι τῶν πρὶν Μούσας γεγονέναι, γενομένων δὲ
Μουσῶν καὶ φανείσης ᾠδῆς οὕτως ἄρα τινὲς τῶν τότε
ἐξεπλάγησαν ὑφ᾽ ἡδονῆς, ὥστε ᾄδοντες ἠμέλησαν
c σίτων τε καὶ ποτῶν, καὶ ἔλαθον τελευτήσαντες αὑτούς·
ἐξ ὧν τὸ τεττίγων γένος μετ᾽ ἐκεῖνο φύεται, γέρας
τοῦτο παρὰ Μουσῶν λαβόν, μηδὲν τροφῆς δεῖσθαι
γενόμενον, ἀλλ᾽ ἄσιτόν τε καὶ ἄποτον εὐθὺς ᾄδειν, |
ἕως ἂν τελευτήσῃ, καὶ μετὰ ταῦτα ἐλθὸν παρὰ Μούσας ἀπαγγέλλειν τίς τίνα αὐτῶν τιμᾷ τῶν ἐνθάδε.
Τερψιχόρᾳ μὲν οὖν τοὺς ἐν τοῖς χοροῖς τετιμηκότας
d αὐτὴν ἀπαγγέλλοντες ποιοῦσι προσφιλεστέρους, τῇ
δὲ Ἐρατοῖ τοὺς ἐν τοῖς ἐρωτικοῖς, καὶ ταῖς ἄλλαις
οὕτως, κατὰ τὸ εἶδος ἑκάστης τιμῆς· τῇ δὲ πρεσβυ-
τάτῃ Καλλιόπῃ καὶ τῇ μετ᾽ αὐτὴν Οὐρανίᾳ τοὺς ἐν
φιλοσοφίᾳ διάγοντάς τε καὶ τιμῶντας τὴν | ἐκείνων

ing down on us too. So if they were to see us two as well,   259
just like most people in the middle of the day, not talking
to each other, but snoozing and beguiled by them through
the idleness of our minds, they would rightly laugh at us,
thinking that some slaves had come to their resting place,
sleeping at noon around the spring like sheep. But if they
see us talking and sailing past them as if immune to the
Sirens' spell, perhaps in wonderment they would give us   b
the gift which they have from the gods to give to men.

P. What's this they have then? For I don't actually seem
to have heard of it.

S. But really, it's not fitting for a man who is a lover of
the Muses not to have heard of such things. It's said that
these cicadas were once humans before the Muses were
born, but after the Muses were born and song came on the
scene, some of those who were living at the time were
actually so astounded with pleasure that while singing they
neglected their food and drink and died without realizing   c
it. From them afterward the race of cicadas was born, having accepted this gift from the Muses: that after their birth
they have no need of sustenance, but sing immediately,
without food and drink, until they die, and after this they
go and inform the Muses which of those down here honors
which of them. To Terpsichore they report those who have
honored her by dancing in choruses, and they make them
dearer to her; to Erato those who have honored her in the   d
affairs of love, and so on with the rest according to the
form of honor related to each. But to the eldest, Calliope,
and after her Urania, they announce those who spend
their time on philosophy and honor their kind of music,

457

PLATO

μουσικὴν ἀγγέλλουσιν, αἳ δὴ μάλιστα τῶν Μουσῶν
περί τε οὐρανὸν καὶ λόγους οὖσαι θείους τε καὶ ἀνθρωπίνους ἱᾶσιν καλλίστην φωνήν. πολλῶν δὴ οὖν
ἕνεκα λεκτέον τι καὶ οὐ καθευδητέον ἐν τῇ μεσημ-
βρίᾳ.

ΦΑΙ. Λεκτέον γὰρ οὖν.

e ΣΩ. Οὐκοῦν, ὅπερ νῦν προυθέμεθα σκέψασθαι, τὸν
λόγον ὅπῃ καλῶς ἔχει λέγειν τε καὶ γράφειν καὶ ὅπῃ
μή, σκεπτέον.

ΦΑΙ. Δῆλον.

ΣΩ. Ἆρ' οὖν οὐχ ὑπάρχειν δεῖ τοῖς εὖ γε καὶ καλῶς
| ῥηθησομένοις τὴν τοῦ λέγοντος διάνοιαν εἰδυῖαν τὸ
ἀληθὲς ὧν ἂν ἐρεῖν πέρι μέλλῃ;

ΦΑΙ. Οὑτωσὶ περὶ τούτου ἀκήκοα, ὦ φίλε Σώκρατες, οὐκ εἶναι ἀνάγκην τῷ μέλλοντι ῥήτορι ἔσεσθαι
260 τὰ τῷ ὄντι δίκαια μανθάνειν ἀλλὰ τὰ δόξαντ' ἂν πλήθει οἵπερ δικάσουσιν, οὐδὲ τὰ ὄντως ἀγαθὰ ἢ καλὰ
ἀλλ' ὅσα δόξει· ἐκ γὰρ τούτων εἶναι τὸ πείθειν ἀλλ'
οὐκ ἐκ τῆς ἀληθείας. |

ΣΩ. "Οὔτοι ἀπόβλητον ἔπος" εἶναι δεῖ, ὦ Φαῖδρε,
ὃ ἂν εἴπωσι σοφοί, ἀλλὰ σκοπεῖν μή τι λέγωσι· καὶ
δὴ καὶ τὸ νῦν λεχθὲν οὐκ ἀφετέον.

ΦΑΙ. Ὀρθῶς λέγεις.

ΣΩ. Ὧδε δὴ σκοπῶμεν αὐτό. |

---

89 Calliope "of the beautiful voice" and Urania "of the heavens" indicate that philosophical discourse is the most beautiful
and is concerned with the heavens and what is divine.

they being the ones who most of all among the Muses are concerned with the heavens and divine and human discourse, and give forth the most beautiful utterance. For many reasons therefore, we must say something and not sleep in the midday sun.[89]

P. Yes, indeed we must.

S. Therefore we must consider, given what we have just proposed to examine, in what way the speaking and writing of a speech is good, and in what way it isn't.

P. Clearly.

S. So for what is to be uttered well and beautifully at least, must not there be knowledge of the truth in the mind of the speaker about whatever he proposes to speak about?

P. Well, my dear Socrates, on this matter I have heard as follows: that it is not necessary for someone who is intending to be an orator to understand what things are actually just, but what would seem to be just to the crowd who are going to pass judgment, and not what is really good or fine, but such as will seem so; for persuasion comes from that, but not from the truth.[90]

S. "The word is not to be set aside,"[91] Phaedrus, must apply to whatever wise men say—and we must look at it in case they are correct. And in particular we must not dismiss what has just been said.

P. You're right.

S. Then let's look at it as follows.

[90] A claim made, according to Plato, by the sophist and rhetorician Gorgias (*Gorgias* 452ff.).

[91] Homer, *Iliad* 2.361.

ΦΑΙ. Πῶς;

b   ΣΩ. Εἴ σε πείθοιμι ἐγὼ πολεμίους ἀμύνειν κτησάμενον ἵππον, ἄμφω δὲ ἵππον ἀγνοοῖμεν, τοσόνδε μέντοι τυγχάνοιμι εἰδὼς περὶ σοῦ, ὅτι Φαῖδρος ἵππον
ἡγεῖται τὸ τῶν ἡμέρων ζῴων μέγιστα ἔχον ὦτα—|

ΦΑΙ. Γελοῖόν γ᾿ ἄν, ὦ Σώκρατες, εἴη.

ΣΩ. Οὔπω γε· ἀλλ᾿ ὅτε δὴ σπουδῇ σε πείθοιμι,
συντιθεὶς λόγον ἔπαινον κατὰ τοῦ ὄνου, ἵππον ἐπονο-
μάζων καὶ λέγων ὡς παντὸς ἄξιον τὸ θρέμμα οἴκοι τε
κεκτῆσθαι καὶ ἐπὶ στρατιᾶς, ἀποπολεμεῖν τε χρήσιμον καὶ πρός γ᾿ ἐνεγκεῖν δυνατὸν σκεύη καὶ ἄλλα
πολλὰ ὠφέλιμον.

c   ΦΑΙ. Παγγέλοιόν γ᾿ ἂν ἤδη εἴη.

ΣΩ. Ἆρ᾿ οὖν οὐ κρεῖττον γελοῖον καὶ φίλον ἢ δει-
νόν τε καὶ ἐχθρὸν [εἶναι ἢ φίλον]; |

ΦΑΙ. Φαίνεται.

ΣΩ. Ὅταν οὖν ὁ ῥητορικὸς ἀγνοῶν ἀγαθὸν καὶ
κακόν, λαβὼν πόλιν ὡσαύτως ἔχουσαν πείθῃ, μὴ
περὶ ὄνου σκιᾶς ὡς ἵππου τὸν ἔπαινον ποιούμενος,
ἀλλὰ περὶ κακοῦ ὡς ἀγαθοῦ, δόξας δὲ πλήθους μεμε-
λετηκὼς πείσῃ κακὰ πράττειν | ἀντ᾿ ἀγαθῶν, ποῖόν
τιν᾿ ἂ<ν>οἴει μετὰ ταῦτα τὴν ῥητορικὴν καρπὸν ὧν
ἔσπειρε θερίζειν;

d   ΦΑΙ. Οὐ πάνυ γε ἐπιεική.

ΣΩ. Ἆρ᾿ οὖν, ὦ ἀγαθέ, ἀγροικότερον τοῦ δέοντος
λελοιδορήκαμεν τὴν τῶν λόγων τέχνην; ἡ δ᾿ ἴσως ἂν
εἴποι· Τί | ποτ᾿, ὦ θαυμάσιοι, ληρεῖτε; ἐγὼ γὰρ οὐδέν᾿

460

P. How?

S. If I were to persuade you to get a horse and fight off   b
the enemy and neither of us knew what a horse was, and
yet I actually knew just this much about you that Phaedrus
thinks a horse is one of the tame animals that has very big
ears –

P. That would be ridiculous, Socrates.

S. Not quite yet. But it would be when I seriously tried
to persuade you by putting together a speech in praise of
a donkey, naming it a horse and saying that the creature
was supremely worth acquiring both for domestic purposes and on a military campaign, both useful for fighting
from and in addition capable of carrying baggage and useful in many other ways.

P. Now that would be utterly ridiculous.   c

S. So would it not be better to be ridiculous and well-
disposed rather than clever and hostile?

P. It seems so.

S. Therefore whenever an orator, ignorant of good and
evil, comes upon a city in the same sort of situation and,
not by making a eulogy about a wretched donkey[92] as if it
were a horse, but about evil as if it were good, and having
studied the opinion of the crowd, persuades them to do
bad things instead of good, what kind of harvest would you
think rhetoric would reap after that from what it sowed?

P. Not a very good one.   d

S. Have we then, my good man, abused the art of
speaking more crudely than necessary? Perhaps she might
say: "Why on earth are you talking such nonsense, you
extraordinary people? For I am not insisting that anyone

[92] Literally, a "shadow of a donkey."

PLATO

ἀγνοοῦντα τἀληθὲς ἀναγκάζω μανθάνειν λέγειν, ἀλλ᾽,
εἴ τι ἐμὴ συμβουλή, κτησάμενον ἐκεῖνο οὕτως ἐμὲ
λαμβάνειν· τόδε δ᾽ οὖν μέγα λέγω, ὡς ἄνευ ἐμοῦ τῷ
τὰ ὄντα εἰδότι οὐδέν τι μᾶλλον ἔσται πείθειν τέχνῃ.

e ΦΑΙ. Οὐκοῦν δίκαια ἐρεῖ, λέγουσα ταῦτα;

ΣΩ. Φημί, ἐὰν οἵ γ᾽ ἐπιόντες αὐτῇ λόγοι μαρτυ-
ρῶσιν εἶναι τέχνη. ὥσπερ γὰρ ἀκούειν δοκῶ τινων
προσιόντων καὶ διαμαρτυρομένων λόγων, ὅτι ψεύδε-
ται καὶ οὐκ ἔστι τέχνη | ἀλλ᾽ ἄτεχνος τριβή· τοῦ δὲ
λέγειν, φησὶν ὁ Λάκων, ἔτυμος τέχνη ἄνευ τοῦ ἀληθείας ἧφθαι οὔτ᾽ ἔστιν οὔτε μή ποτε ὕστερον γένηται.

261 ΦΑΙ. Τούτων δεῖ τῶν λόγων, ὦ Σώκρατες· ἀλλὰ
δεῦρο αὐτοὺς παράγων ἐξέταζε τί καὶ πῶς λέγουσιν.

ΣΩ. Πάριτε δή, θρέμματα γενναῖα, καλλίπαιδά τε
Φαῖδρον πείθετε ὡς ἐὰν μὴ ἱκανῶς φιλοσοφήσῃ, οὐδὲ
ἱκανός | ποτε λέγειν ἔσται περὶ οὐδενός. ἀποκρινέσθω
δὴ ὁ Φαῖδρος.

ΦΑΙ. Ἐρωτᾶτε.

ΣΩ. Ἆρ᾽ οὖν οὐ τὸ μὲν ὅλον ἡ ῥητορικὴ ἂν εἴη
τέχνη ψυχαγωγία τις διὰ λόγων, οὐ μόνον ἐν δικαστηρίοις καὶ ὅσοι ἄλλοι δημόσιοι σύλλογοι, ἀλλὰ
b καὶ ἐν ἰδίοις, ἡ αὐτὴ σμικρῶν τε καὶ μεγάλων πέρι,

---

93 Throughout this section of the dialogue, we have chosen
"art" to translate *technē*, also often rendered "craft," "skill," or
"science," which may convey more of the idea of a rational procedure that Plato wishes to give the word; however, the modern
connotations of these words tend to be much narrower than the
Greek, and rather misleading in the context.

learning to speak should be ignorant of the truth, but if my advice means anything, it is that he should acquire it and on that condition take me on. This in any case I say loud and clear: that without me in no way at all will it be possible for him who knows the truth to persuade by his art."[93]

P. So will she be right in saying this?　　　　　　　　　e

S. I say yes, if, that is, the arguments advancing on her testify that she is an art. For it's as if I seem to hear some of the arguments approaching and bearing witness in a preliminary hearing that she is lying and is not an art, but artless routine:[94] but a true art of speaking, says the Laconian,[95] that has been grasped without the truth, neither exists, nor will it ever come into being in the future.

P. We need these arguments, Socrates. Well, bring 261 them forward and examine them as to what they are saying and how they are expressing it.

S. Step forward then, noble creatures, persuade Phaedrus blessed with fair children[96] that if he does not engage adequately with philosophy, he will also never be competent enough to speak about anything. Let Phaedrus answer!

P. Put your questions.

S. Well then, wouldn't rhetoric taken as a whole be a kind of art of leading the soul by means of words, not only in the law courts and other such public assemblies, but also in private situations—the same when dealing with　b

94 "artless routine" (*atechnos tribē*) is a close reminiscence of *Gorgias* 463b.

95 That is, a source of concise wisdom; Spartans were renowned for blunt speech. See Plutarch, *Moralia* 233b.

96 That is, Phaedrus' speeches.

PLATO

καὶ οὐδὲν ἐντιμότερον τό γε ὀρθὸν περὶ σπουδαῖα ἢ
περὶ φαῦλα γιγνόμενον; ἢ πῶς σὺ ταῦτ᾽ ἀκήκοας;

ΦΑΙ. Οὐ μὰ τὸν Δί᾽ οὐ παντάπασιν οὕτως, ἀλλὰ
μάλιστα μέν πως περὶ τὰς δίκας | λέγεταί τε καὶ γρά-
φεται τέχνῃ, λέγεται δὲ καὶ περὶ δημηγορίας· ἐπὶ
πλέον δὲ οὐκ ἀκήκοα.

ΣΩ. Ἀλλ᾽ ἦ τὰς Νέστορος καὶ Ὀδυσσέως τέχνας
μόνον περὶ λόγων ἀκήκοας, ἃς ἐν Ἰλίῳ σχολάζοντες
συνεγραψάτην, τῶν δὲ Παλαμήδους ἀνήκοος γέγονας;

c   ΦΑΙ. Καὶ ναὶ μὰ Δί᾽ ἔγωγε τῶν Νέστορος, εἰ μὴ
Γοργίαν Νέστορά τινα κατασκευάζεις, ἤ τινα Θρασύ-
μαχόν τε καὶ Θεόδωρον Ὀδυσσέα.

ΣΩ. Ἴσως. ἀλλὰ γὰρ τούτους ἐῶμεν· σὺ δ᾽ εἰπέ, ἐν
| δικαστηρίοις οἱ ἀντίδικοι τί δρῶσιν; οὐκ ἀντιλέγου-
σιν μέντοι; ἢ τί φήσομεν;

ΦΑΙ. Τοῦτ᾽ αὐτό.

ΣΩ. Περὶ τοῦ δικαίου τε καὶ ἀδίκου;

ΦΑΙ. Ναί. |

d   ΣΩ. Οὐκοῦν ὁ τέχνῃ τοῦτο δρῶν ποιήσει φανῆναι
τὸ αὐτὸ τοῖς αὐτοῖς τοτὲ μὲν δίκαιον, ὅταν δὲ βούληται, ἄδικον;

ΦΑΙ. Τί μήν;

---

97 The epic heroes Nestor and Odysseus were famous for their
skill at speaking (Homer, *Iliad* 1.249, 3.223). Palamedes was an
epic hero (not mentioned in Homer) proverbial for his cleverness,
in particular for tricking Odysseus into serving in the Trojan War,

small and great matters, and at any rate as far as its proper use is concerned, having no more value when you are dealing with serious than with trivial matters? Or how have you heard this expressed?

P. No, by Zeus, not altogether like that, but speaking and writing with art is perhaps particularly relevant to lawsuits; also speaking in public debate. Beyond that I've not heard of anything.

S. But have you only heard the treatises on oratory of Nestor and Odysseus which the two wrote in Troy when they had nothing to do, and you've not heard of those by Palamedes?

P. No indeed, by Zeus, I've not heard of Nestor's, unless   c you're passing off Gorgias as a Nestor, or perhaps Thrasymachus and Theodorus as Odysseus.[97]

S. Perhaps I am. But let's pass over them. *You* tell me: what do the opposing sides in the law courts do? Does each not just argue against the other, or what shall we say?

P. Just that.

S. About the just and the unjust?

P. Yes.

S. Then will he who does this using his art make the   d same thing seem just to the same people at one moment, and when he wishes unjust?

P. Yes.

Cypria, (Proclus, *Chrestomathy* 1), and also a great inventor (Plato, *Laws* 677d). Thrasymachus of Chalcedon and Theodorus of Byzantium were prominent fifth-century sophists and teachers of rhetoric (the former well-known to us from his prominent role in Plato, *Republic* 1).

ΣΩ. Καὶ ἐν δημηγορίᾳ δὴ τῇ πόλει δοκεῖν τὰ αὐτὰ τοτὲ μὲν ἀγαθά, τοτὲ δ᾽ αὖ τἀναντία; |

ΦΑΙ. Οὕτως.

ΣΩ. Τὸν οὖν Ἐλεατικὸν Παλαμήδην λέγοντα οὐκ ἴσμεν τέχνῃ, ὥστε φαίνεσθαι τοῖς ἀκούουσι τὰ αὐτὰ ὅμοια καὶ ἀνόμοια, καὶ ἓν καὶ πολλά, μένοντά τε αὖ καὶ φερόμενα;

ΦΑΙ. Μάλα γε. |

e ΣΩ. Οὐκ ἄρα μόνον περὶ δικαστήριά τέ ἐστιν ἡ ἀντιλογικὴ καὶ περὶ δημηγορίαν, ἀλλ᾽, ὡς ἔοικε, περὶ πάντα τὰ λεγόμενα μία τις τέχνη, εἴπερ ἔστιν, αὕτη ἂν εἴη, ᾗ τις οἷός τ᾽ ἔσται πᾶν παντὶ ὁμοιοῦν τῶν δυνατῶν καὶ οἷς δυνατόν, καὶ ἄλλου ὁμοιοῦντος καὶ ἀποκρυπτομένου εἰς φῶς ἄγειν. |

ΦΑΙ. Πῶς δὴ τὸ τοιοῦτον λέγεις;

ΣΩ. Τῇδε δοκῶ ζητοῦσιν φανεῖσθαι. ἀπάτη πότερον ἐν πολὺ διαφέρουσι γίγνεται μᾶλλον ἢ ὀλίγον;

262 ΦΑΙ. Ἐν τοῖς ὀλίγον.

ΣΩ. Ἀλλά γε δὴ κατὰ σμικρὸν μεταβαίνων μᾶλλον λήσεις ἐλθὼν ἐπὶ τὸ ἐναντίον ἢ κατὰ μέγα.

ΦΑΙ. Πῶς δ᾽ οὔ; |

ΣΩ. Δεῖ ἄρα τὸν μέλλοντα ἀπατήσειν μὲν ἄλλον, αὐτὸν δὲ μὴ ἀπατήσεσθαι, τὴν ὁμοιότητα τῶν ὄντων καὶ ἀνομοιότητα ἀκριβῶς διειδέναι.

---

98 "The Eleatic Palamedes" is a reference to the paradoxical arguments of Zeno of Elea (early 5th century) allegedly matching the hero Palamedes' skill in argument. "The art of disputation"

S. And in a speech in a public assembly, will he make the same things good for the city at one time and the opposite at another?

P. Yes.

S. Then do we not know that the Eleatic Palamedes speaks with art so that to his audience the same things appear to be similar and dissimilar, and one and many, and stationary and moving?[98]

P. Certainly.

S. So the art of disputation is not only about the law courts and public discourse, but, it seems, in relation to   e
everything that is said there would be a single art, if indeed it is one, by which one will be able to make every one of those things that can be made to resemble something else resemble everything which it can possibly resemble, and when someone else makes a resemblance and conceals it, to bring it to light.

P. What sort of thing do you actually mean?

S. I think if we look at it, it will appear as follows: does deception occur more among things which differ greatly, or in some small way?

P. Among those differing in a small way.   262

S. Moreover by moving across a little bit at a time you're more likely to reach the opposite without being noticed than by taking great strides.

P. Of course.

S. Then he who intends to mislead another, but not be misled himself must have the knowledge to distinguish the similarity and dissimilarity of real objects precisely.

(*antilogikē*, d10) is the state of argument where contrary predicates are made to seem true to the same people at different times.

ΦΑΙ. Ἀνάγκη μὲν οὖν.

ΣΩ. Ἦ οὖν οἷός τε ἔσται, ἀλήθειαν ἀγνοῶν ἑκά-
στου, τὴν | τοῦ ἀγνοουμένου ὁμοιότητα σμικράν τε
καὶ μεγάλην ἐν τοῖς ἄλλοις διαγιγνώσκειν;

b   ΦΑΙ. Ἀδύνατον.

ΣΩ. Οὐκοῦν τοῖς παρὰ τὰ ὄντα δοξάζουσι καὶ
ἀπατωμένοις δῆλον ὡς τὸ πάθος τοῦτο δι᾽ ὁμοιοτήτων
τινῶν εἰσερρύη.

ΦΑΙ. Γίγνεται γοῦν οὕτως. |

ΣΩ. Ἔστιν οὖν ὅπως τεχνικὸς ἔσται μεταβιβάζειν
κατὰ σμικρὸν διὰ τῶν ὁμοιοτήτων ἀπὸ τοῦ ὄντος ἑκά-
στοτε ἐπὶ τοὐναντίον ἀπάγων, ἢ αὐτὸς τοῦτο διαφεύγειν, ὁ μὴ ἐγνωρικὼς ὃ ἔστιν ἕκαστον τῶν ὄντων;

ΦΑΙ. Οὐ μή ποτε.

c   ΣΩ. Λόγων ἄρα τέχνην, ὦ ἑταῖρε, ὁ τὴν ἀλήθειαν
μὴ εἰδώς, δόξας δὲ τεθηρευκώς, γελοίαν τινά, ὡς
ἔοικε, καὶ ἄτεχνον παρέξεται.

ΦΑΙ. Κινδυνεύει. |

ΣΩ. Βούλει οὖν ἐν τῷ Λυσίου λόγῳ ὃν φέρεις, καὶ
ἐν οἷς ἡμεῖς εἴπομεν ἰδεῖν τι ὧν φαμεν ἀτέχνων τε καὶ
ἐντέχνων εἶναι;

ΦΑΙ. Πάντων γέ που μάλιστα, ὡς νῦν γε ψιλῶς
πως λέγομεν, οὐκ ἔχοντες ἱκανὰ παραδείγματα. |

ΣΩ. Καὶ μὴν κατὰ τύχην γέ τινα, ὡς ἔοικε, ἐρρη-
θήτην τὼ λόγω ἔχοντέ τι παράδειγμα, ὡς ἂν ὁ εἰδὼς

---

99 It is uncertain which two speeches Socrates is referring to
here: whether Lysias' and his (Socrates') first (Rowe, ad loc.) or

468

P. Indeed he must.

S. If he doesn't know the true nature of each thing, will he be able therefore to distinguish in other things the resemblance, small or great, to what he does not know?

P. Impossible.   b

S. Therefore for those who hold opinions contrary to what is true and are misled it's clear that this experience has crept in through certain similarities.

P. Yes, this *is* how it happens.

S. Is there any way someone will be expert at making someone change position bit by bit by resemblances, leading them away from the reality each time toward the opposite, or escape this himself, if he hasn't discovered what each of the realities actually is?

P. No, never.

S. Then, my friend, he who does not know the truth,   c
but has hunted down appearances, will produce an art of speaking that is ridiculous, it seems, and without art.

P. There is that possibility.

S. Do you wish to see in Lysias' speech which you are holding and in those we delivered something of elements we say are artless and those that demonstrate art?

P. That is especially needed, I think, as right now what we're saying is somehow a bit thin as we don't have sufficient examples.

S. And by some chance furthermore it seems the two speeches[99] were made with an example of how one know-

Socrates' two speeches, as also in c6 (since Lysias, as has been demonstrated, cannot be described as one who knows the truth; see Yunis, n. ad loc.), or all three, i.e., Lysias' and Socrates' two speeches taken as one (Hackforth, De Vries).

τὸ ἀληθὲς προσπαίζων ἐν λόγοις παράγοι τοὺς ἀκού-
d οντας. καὶ ἔγωγε, ὦ Φαῖδρε, αἰτιῶμαι τοὺς ἐντοπίους
θεούς· ἴσως δὲ καὶ οἱ τῶν Μουσῶν προφῆται οἱ ὑπὲρ
κεφαλῆς ᾠδοὶ ἐπιπεπνευκότες ἂν ἡμῖν εἶεν τοῦτο τὸ
γέρας· οὐ γάρ που ἔγωγε τέχνης τινὸς τοῦ λέγειν
μέτοχος.

ΦΑΙ. Ἔστω ὡς λέγεις· μόνον δήλωσον ὃ φής.

ΣΩ. Ἴθι δή μοι ἀνάγνωθι τὴν τοῦ Λυσίου λόγου
ἀρχήν.

e ΦΑΙ. Περὶ μὲν τῶν ἐμῶν πραγμάτων ἐπίστασαι,
καὶ ὡς νομίζω συμφέρειν ἡμῖν τούτων γενομένων,
ἀκήκοας. ἀξιῶ δὲ μὴ διὰ τοῦτο ἀτυχῆσαι ὧν δέομαι,
ὅτι οὐκ ἐραστὴς ὢν σοῦ τυγχάνω. ὡς ἐκείνοις μὲν
τότε μεταμέλει—|

ΣΩ. Παῦσαι. τί δὴ οὖν οὗτος ἁμαρτάνει καὶ ἄτεχνον
ποιεῖ λεκτέον· ἢ γάρ;

263 ΦΑΙ. Ναί.

ΣΩ. Ἆρ᾽ οὖν οὐ παντὶ δῆλον τό γε τοιόνδε, ὡς περὶ
μὲν ἔνια τῶν τοιούτων ὁμονοητικῶς ἔχομεν, περὶ δ᾽
ἔνια στασιωτικῶς; |

ΦΑΙ. Δοκῶ μὲν ὃ λέγεις μανθάνειν, ἔτι δ᾽ εἰπὲ
σαφέστερον.

ΣΩ. Ὅταν τις ὄνομα εἴπῃ σιδήρου ἢ ἀργύρου, ἆρ᾽
οὐ τὸ αὐτὸ πάντες διενοήθημεν;

ΦΑΙ. Καὶ μάλα.

ΣΩ. Τί δ᾽ ὅταν δικαίου ἢ ἀγαθοῦ; οὐκ ἄλλος ἄλλῃ
| φέρεται, καὶ ἀμφισβητοῦμεν ἀλλήλοις τε καὶ ἡμῖν
αὐτοῖς;

ing the truth can mislead his audience by playing games in his words. I myself, Phaedrus, blame the local gods; and perhaps also the interpreters of the Muses who sing above our heads[100] may have inspired us with this gift. For I am pretty sure I do not share in any art of speaking.

P. Let it be as you say. Just make it clear to me what you are saying.

S. Come on then, read me the beginning of Lysias' speech.

P. "You know about my situation and you have heard that I think that it is of benefit to us if this were to happen. But I claim that I should not fail to achieve what I ask for this reason: that I am not actually in love with you. Those who are in love regret—"

S. Stop. We have to say where he is wrong and writing without art; isn't that so?

P. Yes.

S. Therefore isn't the following at least clear to everyone, that we are of one mind about some things of this kind and at variance about others?

P. I think I understand what you are saying, but say it again more clearly.

S. Whenever someone says the word "iron" or "silver" we all have the same thing in mind, don't we?

P. Yes, certainly.

S. What about when we say the word "just" or "good": isn't one person carried one way and another another, and we dispute both with each other and ourselves?

---

[100] The cicadas.

ΦΑΙ. Πάνυ μὲν οὖν.

b   ΣΩ. Ἐν μὲν ἄρα τοῖς συμφωνοῦμεν, ἐν δὲ τοῖς οὔ.

ΦΑΙ. Οὕτω.

ΣΩ. Ποτέρωθι οὖν εὐαπατητότεροί ἐσμεν, καὶ ἡ ῥητορικὴ ἐν ποτέροις μεῖζον δύναται; |

ΦΑΙ. Δῆλον ὅτι ἐν οἷς πλανώμεθα.

ΣΩ. Οὐκοῦν τὸν μέλλοντα τέχνην ῥητορικὴν μετιέναι πρῶτον μὲν δεῖ ταῦτα ὁδῷ διῃρῆσθαι, καὶ εἰληφέναι τινὰ χαρακτῆρα ἑκατέρου τοῦ εἴδους, ἐν ᾧ τε ἀνάγκη τὸ πλῆθος πλανᾶσθαι καὶ ἐν ᾧ μή.

c   ΦΑΙ. Καλὸν γοῦν ἄν, ὦ Σώκρατες, εἶδος[8] εἴη κατανενοηκὼς ὁ τοῦτο λαβών.

ΣΩ. Ἔπειτά γε οἶμαι πρὸς ἑκάστῳ γιγνόμενον μὴ λανθάνειν ἀλλ᾽ ὀξέως αἰσθάνεσθαι περὶ οὗ ἂν μέλλῃ ἐρεῖν | ποτέρου ὂν τυγχάνει τοῦ γένους.

ΦΑΙ. Τί μήν;

ΣΩ. Τί οὖν; τὸν ἔρωτα πότερον φῶμεν εἶναι τῶν ἀμφισβητησίμων ἢ τῶν μή;

ΦΑΙ. Τῶν ἀμφισβητησίμων δήπου· ἢ οἴει ἄν σοι ἐγχωρῆσαι | εἰπεῖν ἃ νυνδὴ εἶπες περὶ αὐτοῦ, ὡς βλάβη τέ ἐστι τῷ ἐρωμένῳ καὶ ἐρῶντι, καὶ αὖθις ὡς μέγιστον ⟨ὂν⟩τῶν ἀγαθῶν τυγχάνει;

d   ΣΩ. Ἄριστα λέγεις· ἀλλ᾽ εἰπὲ καὶ τόδε—ἐγὼ γάρ τοι διὰ τὸ ἐνθουσιαστικὸν οὐ πάνυ μέμνημαι—εἰ ὡρισάμην ἔρωτα ἀρχόμενος τοῦ λόγου.

ΦΑΙ. Νὴ Δία ἀμηχάνως γε ὡς σφόδρα. |

8 εἶδος secl. Richards

472

P. Very much so.

S. Then we agree on some things, but not on others.   b

P. Just so.

S. So on which of the two are we more easily misled, and in which does rhetoric have greater force?

P. Clearly where we waver to and fro.

S. Therefore he who intends to go for rhetorical art must firstly have distinguished these things systematically and have grasped some feature of each of the two types: those in which the majority necessarily waver, and those in which they do not.

P. He who grasps this,[101] Socrates, would at any rate   c have understood something fine.

S. And then, I think, when he gets to each thing, he must not be unaware, but sharply perceive to which of the two kinds the thing he is going to speak about actually belongs.

P. Of course.

S. So what do you think? Are we to say that love is one of those things we argue about or not?

P. One of the things we argue about, surely. Otherwise do you think it would have been possible for you to say what you just said about it, that it is harmful both to the loved one and the lover, and again that it is actually the greatest of good things?

S. That's very well put. But tell me this too—you see   d it's because of my inspired state I don't entirely recall— whether I defined love when I began my speech.

P. Yes, by Zeus you most certainly did!

---

[101] Omitting εἶδος (OCT) with Richards (see textual note).

ΣΩ. Φεῦ, ὅσῳ λέγεις τεχνικωτέρας Νύμφας τὰς
Ἀχελῴου καὶ Πᾶνα τὸν Ἑρμοῦ Λυσίου τοῦ Κεφάλου
πρὸς λόγους εἶναι. οὐδὲν λέγω, ἀλλὰ καὶ ὁ Λυσίας
ἀρχόμενος τοῦ ἐρωτικοῦ ἠνάγκασεν ἡμᾶς ὑπολαβεῖν
τὸν Ἔρωτα ἕν τι τῶν ὄντων ὃ αὐτὸς ἐβουλήθη, καὶ
πρὸς τοῦτο ἤδη συνταξάμενος πάντα τὸν ὕστερον λό-
e γον διεπεράνατο; βούλει πάλιν ἀναγνῶμεν τὴν ἀρχὴν
αὐτοῦ;

ΦΑΙ. Εἰ σοί γε δοκεῖ· ὃ μέντοι ζητεῖς οὐκ ἔστ᾿
αὐτόθι. |

ΣΩ. Λέγε, ἵνα ἀκούσω αὐτοῦ ἐκείνου.

ΦΑΙ. Περὶ μὲν τῶν ἐμῶν πραγμάτων ἐπίστασαι,
καὶ ὡς νομίζω συμφέρειν ἡμῖν τούτων γενομένων,
ἀκήκοας. ἀξιῶ δὲ μὴ διὰ τοῦτο ἀτυχῆσαι ὧν δέομαι,
264 ὅτι οὐκ ἐραστὴς ὢν σοῦ τυγχάνω. ὡς ἐκείνοις μὲν
τότε μεταμέλει ὧν ἂν εὖ ποιήσωσιν, ἐπειδὰν τῆς ἐπιθυμίας παύσωνται—

ΣΩ. Ἦ πολλοῦ δεῖν ἔοικε ποιεῖν ὅδε γε ὃ ζητοῦμεν,
ὃς | οὐδὲ ἀπ᾿ ἀρχῆς ἀλλ᾿ ἀπὸ τελευτῆς ἐξ ὑπτίας ἀνά-
παλιν διανεῖν ἐπιχειρεῖ τὸν λόγον, καὶ ἄρχεται ἀφ᾿ ὧν
πεπαυμένος ἂν ἤδη ὁ ἐραστὴς λέγοι πρὸς τὰ παιδικά.
ἢ οὐδὲν εἶπον, Φαῖδρε, φίλη κεφαλή;

b ΦΑΙ. Ἔστιν γέ τοι δή, ὦ Σώκρατες, τελευτή, περὶ
οὗ τὸν λόγον ποιεῖται.

ΣΩ. Τί δὲ τἆλλα; οὐ χύδην δοκεῖ βεβλῆσθαι τὰ
τοῦ λόγου; ἢ φαίνεται τὸ δεύτερον εἰρημένον ἔκ τινος
ἀνάγκης | δεύτερον δεῖν τεθῆναι, ἤ τι ἄλλο τῶν ῥηθέν-
των; ἐμοὶ μὲν γὰρ ἔδοξεν, ὡς μηδὲν εἰδότι, οὐκ ἀγεν-

S. Oh dear! You're saying how much greater in artistic skill are the Nymphs, daughters of Achelous, and Pan, son of Hermes, when it comes to speeches, than Lysias, son of Cephalus. Or am I talking nonsense? At the beginning of his speech about love did Lysias also force us to suppose that Eros is one particular existing thing which he himself chose, and did he bring the whole of the speech that followed after to a conclusion having arranged it for this purpose? Do you want us to read the beginning of it again? e

P. If you think it's a good idea. However what you're looking for isn't there.

S. Read it, so that I may hear the man himself.

P. "You know about my situation and you have heard that I think that it is of benefit to us if this were to happen. I claim that I should not fail to achieve what I ask for this reason: that I'm not actually in love with you. Those who 264 are in love regret what services they do at the point when their passions cease."—

S. Indeed he seems to fall far short of doing what we're looking for, since he's trying to swim downstream on his back through his speech, not even from the beginning, but from the end, and begins from what the lover would say to his loved one when he's already left off. Or am I wrong, my dear Phaedrus?

P. It certainly is an ending, Socrates, that he's making b his speech about.

S. But what about the rest? Don't the parts of the speech appear to have been thrown together wholesale? Or does it look as if what is said second has to be put second for some cogent reason, or with any of the other things that have been said? For it seemed to me, given that I

νῶς τὸ ἐπιὸν εἰρῆσθαι τῷ γράφοντι· σὺ δ' ἔχεις τινὰ
ἀνάγκην λογογραφικὴν ᾗ ταῦτα ἐκεῖνος οὕτως ἐφεξῆς
παρ' ἄλληλα ἔθηκεν;

ΦΑΙ. Χρηστὸς εἶ, ὅτι με ἡγῇ ἱκανὸν εἶναι τὰ ἐκείνου οὕτως ἀκριβῶς διιδεῖν.

c   ΣΩ. Ἀλλὰ τόδε γε οἶμαί σε φάναι ἄν, δεῖν πάντα
λόγον ὥσπερ ζῷον συνεστάναι σῶμά τι ἔχοντα αὐτὸν
αὑτοῦ, ὥστε μήτε ἀκέφαλον εἶναι μήτε ἄπουν, ἀλλὰ
μέσα τε ἔχειν | καὶ ἄκρα, πρέποντα ἀλλήλοις καὶ τῷ
ὅλῳ γεγραμμένα.

ΦΑΙ. Πῶς γὰρ οὔ;

ΣΩ. Σκέψαι τοίνυν τὸν τοῦ ἑταίρου σου λόγον εἴτε
οὕτως εἴτε ἄλλως ἔχει, καὶ εὑρήσεις τοῦ ἐπιγράμμα-
τος οὐδὲν διαφέροντα, ὃ Μίδᾳ τῷ Φρυγί φασίν τινες
ἐπιγεγράφθαι.

d   ΦΑΙ. Ποῖον τοῦτο, καὶ τί πεπονθός;

ΣΩ. Ἔστι μὲν τοῦτο τόδε—

Χαλκῆ παρθένος εἰμί, Μίδα δ' ἐπὶ σήματι κεῖμαι.
ὄφρ' ἂν ὕδωρ τε νάῃ καὶ δένδρεα μακρὰ τεθήλῃ, |
αὐτοῦ τῇδε μένουσα πολυκλαύτου ἐπὶ τύμβου,
ἀγγελέω παριοῦσι Μίδας ὅτι τῇδε τέθαπται.

e   ὅτι δ' οὐδὲν διαφέρει αὐτοῦ πρῶτον ἢ ὕστατόν τι λέγεσθαι, ἐννοεῖς που, ὡς ἔγωμαι.

ΦΑΙ. Σκώπτεις τὸν λόγον ἡμῶν, ὦ Σώκρατες.

know nothing, that what was said, not ignobly, was what just happened to come into the writer's head. But have you any necessary rule of composition to suggest, by which he wrote down these ideas as he did next to each other in order?

P. It's kind of you to think that I'm capable of distinguishing what he has done so precisely.

S. But I think you would say this at least: that every   c
speech must be put together like a living creature as it were, with a body of its own so that it is neither headless nor without feet, but with a middle and extremities, written so as to fit with one another and with the whole.

P. Of course.

S. Consider therefore whether your friend's speech is of this kind or otherwise, and you will find it no different from the epigram which some say was written for Midas the Phrygian.

P. What epigram is that, and what is the matter with it?   d

S. It goes like this:

"I am a bronze maiden and I am placed on Midas'
    tomb
As long as water flows and trees grow tall
Remaining here upon the tear-drenched tomb
I tell the passersby that here Midas is buried"[102]

I think you surely notice that it makes no difference which   e
part of it is quoted first or last.

P. You're mocking our speech, Socrates.

[102] Ascribed by Diogenes Laertius (1.89–90) to Cleobulus of Lindos, one of the Seven Sages (fl. ?6th century), but possibly composed by Plato himself.

ΣΩ. Τοῦτον μὲν τοίνυν, ἵνα μὴ σὺ ἄχθῃ, ἐάσω-
μεν—| καίτοι συχνά γε ἔχειν μοι δοκεῖ παραδείγματα
πρὸς ἅ τις βλέπων ὀνίναιτ᾽ ἄν, μιμεῖσθαι αὐτὰ ἐπιχειρῶν μὴ πάνυ τι—εἰς δὲ τοὺς ἑτέρους λόγους ἴωμεν.
ἦν γάρ τι ἐν αὐτοῖς, ὡς δοκῶ, προσῆκον ἰδεῖν τοῖς
βουλομένοις περὶ λόγων σκοπεῖν.

265   ΦΑΙ. Τὸ ποῖον δὴ λέγεις;

ΣΩ. Ἐναντίω που ἤστην· ὁ μὲν γὰρ ὡς τῷ ἐρῶντι,
ὁ δ᾽ ὡς τῷ μὴ δεῖ χαρίζεσθαι, ἐλεγέτην.

ΦΑΙ. Καὶ μάλ᾽ ἀνδρικῶς. |

ΣΩ. Ὤιμην σε τἀληθὲς ἐρεῖν, ὅτι μανικῶς· ὃ μέντοι
ἐζήτουν ἐστὶν αὐτὸ τοῦτο. μανίαν γάρ τινα ἐφήσαμεν
εἶναι τὸν ἔρωτα. ἦ γάρ;

ΦΑΙ. Ναί.

ΣΩ. Μανίας δέ γε εἴδη δύο, τὴν μὲν ὑπὸ νοσημά-
των | ἀνθρωπίνων, τὴν δὲ ὑπὸ θείας ἐξαλλαγῆς τῶν
εἰωθότων νομίμων γιγνομένην.

b   ΦΑΙ. Πάνυ γε.

ΣΩ. Τῆς δὲ θείας τεττάρων θεῶν τέτταρα μέρη
διελόμενοι, μαντικὴν μὲν ἐπίπνοιαν Ἀπόλλωνος θέν-
τες, Διονύσου δὲ τελεστικήν, Μουσῶν δ᾽ αὖ ποιητι-
κήν, τετάρτην δὲ Ἀφροδίτης | καὶ Ἔρωτος, ἐρωτικὴν
μανίαν ἐφήσαμέν τε ἀρίστην εἶναι, καὶ οὐκ οἶδ᾽ ὅπῃ
τὸ ἐρωτικὸν πάθος ἀπεικάζοντες, ἴσως μὲν ἀληθοῦς
τινος ἐφαπτόμενοι, τάχα δ᾽ ἂν καὶ ἄλλοσε παραφερό-

S. Then let's leave this one aside, so that you don't get annoyed—and yet it seems to me to have plenty of examples from which a person would derive benefit from looking at them, so long as he doesn't try to imitate them at all—and let's move on to the other speeches. For there was something in them worth noticing, in my opinion, for those who want to look at speeches.

P. So what sort of thing are you talking about?   265

S. They were two the opposite of each other, I think, the one was saying that you should grant favors to the lover, and the other to the one who isn't.[103]

P. And they did so very manfully.

S. I thought you were going to tell the truth and say "madly";[104] and that certainly is the very point I was looking for. For we said that love is a kind of madness. Isn't that so?

P. Yes.

S. And that there are two forms of madness: one resulting from human illnesses, the other arising from a divinely-inspired change in our normal behavior.

P. Very much so.   b

S. Of the divine madness, when we distinguished four parts belonging to four gods, proposing the prophetic part to be the inspiration of Apollo, mystic rites to be associated with Dionysus, again poetic madness associated with the Muses, and the fourth belonging to Aphrodite and Eros, we said that the madness of love is the best, expressing the experience of love in some kind of image, maybe perhaps grasping some truth, but perhaps also being carried away

---

[103] That is, Socrates' two speeches.
[104] *Andrikōs* (manfully) contrasted with *manikōs* (madly).

μενοι, κεράσαντες οὐ παντάπασιν ἀπίθανον λόγον,
μυθικόν τινα ὕμνον προσεπαίσαμεν μετρίως τε καὶ
εὐφήμως τὸν ἐμόν τε καὶ σὸν δεσπότην Ἔρωτα, ὦ
c Φαῖδρε, καλῶν παίδων ἔφορον.

ΦΑΙ. Καὶ μάλα ἔμοιγε οὐκ ἀηδῶς ἀκοῦσαι. |

ΣΩ. Τόδε τοίνυν αὐτόθεν λάβωμεν, ὡς ἀπὸ τοῦ
ψέγειν πρὸς τὸ ἐπαινεῖν ἔσχεν ὁ λόγος μεταβῆναι.

ΦΑΙ. Πῶς δὴ οὖν αὐτὸ λέγεις;

ΣΩ. Ἐμοὶ μὲν φαίνεται τὰ μὲν ἄλλα τῷ ὄντι παιδιᾷ
πεπαῖσθαι· τούτων δέ τινων ἐκ τύχης ῥηθέντων δυοῖν
d εἰδοῖν, εἰ αὐτοῖν τὴν δύναμιν τέχνῃ λαβεῖν δύναιτό
τις, οὐκ ἄχαρι.

ΦΑΙ. Τίνων δή;

ΣΩ. Εἰς μίαν τε ἰδέαν συνορῶντα ἄγειν τὰ πολλαχῇ διεσπαρμένα, ἵνα ἕκαστον ὁριζόμενος δῆλον
ποιῇ περὶ οὗ ἂν | ἀεὶ διδάσκειν ἐθέλῃ. ὥσπερ τὰ
νυνδὴ περὶ Ἔρωτος—ὃ ἔστιν ὁρισθέν—εἴτ᾽ εὖ εἴτε
κακῶς ἐλέχθη, τὸ γοῦν σαφὲς καὶ τὸ αὐτὸ αὑτῷ ὁμο-
λογούμενον διὰ ταῦτα ἔσχεν εἰπεῖν ὁ λόγος.

ΦΑΙ. Τὸ δ᾽ ἕτερον δὴ εἶδος τί λέγεις, ὦ Σώκρατες;

e ΣΩ. Τὸ πάλιν κατ᾽ εἴδη δύνασθαι διατέμνειν κατ᾽
ἄρθρα ᾗ πέφυκεν, καὶ μὴ ἐπιχειρεῖν καταγνύναι μέρος μηδέν, κακοῦ μαγείρου τρόπῳ χρώμενον· ἀλλ᾽
ὥσπερ ἄρτι τὼ λόγω τὸ μὲν ἄφρον τῆς διανοίας ἕν τι
κοινῇ εἶδος ἐλαβέτην, ὥσπερ δὲ σώματος ἐξ ἑνὸς δι-
πλᾶ καὶ ὁμώνυμα πέφυκε, σκαιά, τὰ δὲ δεξιὰ κλη-
266 θέντα, οὕτω καὶ τὸ τῆς παρανοίας ὡς ⟨ἐν⟩ ἐν ἡμῖν

480

in another direction; mixing together a not altogether unpersuasive speech, we playfully sang a hymn in the form
of a story in appropriate and pious fashion to my master
and yours, Phaedrus, Love, the overseer of beautiful boys. c

P. And it was really very pleasant for me to listen to.

S. Then let's pick up this next point from it, how the
speech had the ability to cross from censure to praise.[105]

P. What do you actually mean by that?

S. It seems to me that the rest was actually done playfully in fun, but since these two forms came up by chance
from what was said, it would not be unrewarding if one d
were to use art to be able to grasp their power.

P. Indeed what were those?

S. Seeing together and bringing into a single form
things that are scattered about in many directions in order
to define each one and make it clear whatever one wants
to teach at any given time. Just as a moment ago with matters concerning love—what it is when it has been defined—whether it was rightly or wrongly expressed, at
least because of that the speech was able to express what
was at any rate clear and consistent with itself.

P. And what is the other form you're talking about,
Socrates?

S. The ability to dissect it again, form by form, accord- e
ing to its natural joints and not try to smash any part, acting like a bad butcher. But as just now my two speeches
took the irrational part of the mind as a single general
form, and just as from a single body there are naturally
twofold parts with the same name called respectively left
and right, so too the two speeches regarded the form of 266

[105] That is, in Socrates' two speeches taken together.

πεφυκὸς εἶδος ἡγησαμένω τὼ λόγω, ὁ μὲν τὸ ἐπ᾿ ἀρι-
στερὰ τεμνόμενος μέρος, πάλιν τοῦτο τέμνων οὐκ
ἐπανῆκεν πρὶν ἐν | αὐτοῖς ἐφευρὼν ὀνομαζόμενον
σκαιόν τινα ἔρωτα ἐλοιδόρησεν μάλ᾿ ἐν δίκῃ, ὁ δ᾿ εἰς
τὰ ἐν δεξιᾷ τῆς μανίας ἀγαγὼν ἡμᾶς, ὁμώνυμον μὲν
b ἐκείνῳ, θεῖον δ᾿ αὖ τινα ἔρωτα ἐφευρὼν καὶ προτεινά-
μενος ἐπῄνεσεν ὡς μεγίστων αἴτιον ἡμῖν ἀγαθῶν.

ΦΑΙ. Ἀληθέστατα λέγεις.

ΣΩ. Τούτων δὴ ἔγωγε αὐτός τε ἐραστής, ὦ Φαῖδρε,
τῶν διαιρέσεων καὶ συναγωγῶν, ἵνα οἷός τε ὦ λέγειν
τε καὶ | φρονεῖν· ἐάν τέ τιν᾿ ἄλλον ἡγήσωμαι δυνατὸν
εἰς ἓν καὶ ἐπὶ πολλὰ πεφυκόθ᾿ ὁρᾶν, τοῦτον διώκω
"κατόπισθε μετ᾿ ἴχνιον ὥστε θεοῖο." καὶ μέντοι καὶ τοὺς
δυναμένους αὐτὸ δρᾶν εἰ μὲν ὀρθῶς ἢ μὴ προσαγο-
ρεύω, θεὸς οἶδε, καλῶ δὲ οὖν μέχρι τοῦδε διαλεκτι-
c κούς. τὰ δὲ νῦν παρὰ σοῦ τε καὶ Λυσίου μαθόντας
εἰπὲ τί χρὴ καλεῖν· ἢ τοῦτο ἐκεῖνό ἐστιν ἡ λόγων τέχνη, ᾗ Θρασύμαχός τε καὶ οἱ ἄλλοι χρώμενοι σοφοὶ
μὲν αὐτοὶ λέγειν γεγόνασιν, ἄλλους τε ποιοῦσιν, οἳ
ἂν | δωροφορεῖν αὐτοῖς ὡς βασιλεῦσιν ἐθέλωσιν;

ΦΑΙ. Βασιλικοὶ μὲν ἄνδρες, οὐ μὲν δὴ ἐπιστήμονές
γε ὧν ἐρωτᾷς. ἀλλὰ τοῦτο μὲν τὸ εἶδος ὀρθῶς ἔμοιγε

---

106 *erastēs*: in his unusual use of this term, normally reserved
for intense and erotic feelings, Socrates reveals the link between
the passionate lover of his *palinode* and his dialectical search for
the truth.   107 Adaptation of a common Homeric formula:
see Homer, *Odyssey* 2.406, etc.

madness to be naturally a single form within us: the one speech, separating the part on the left and, dividing it again, did not stop before discovering in the parts a love called left-handed and very rightly disparaged it; but the other speech, leading us to the parts of madness which are on the right hand side, and discovering and proposing a kind of love sharing the same name as the other, but divine, praised it for being the source of the greatest good in us.

P. What you say is very true.

S. Now, Phaedrus, I am myself a lover[106] of these divisions and collections which enable me both to speak and think. And if I think anyone else is naturally capable of seeing one and many, that person I pursue "from behind in his footsteps as if in those of a god."[107] And furthermore those able to do it, whether I address them correctly or not, god knows—these at any rate up to now I have been calling dialecticians.[108] But as things stand now, tell me what we must call them if we learned from you and Lysias: or is this that very thing—namely the art of making speeches—which Thrasymachus and others employ, in using which they become expert at speaking themselves, and pass this on to others, if they are willing to bring them presents as if they were kings?

P. Men with kingly aspect, yet they certainly have no understanding of what you're asking about, but in calling

---

[108] From the Greek *dialegesthai* (to have a conversation), the typical Platonic philosophical method, particularly in the early "Socratic" dialogues; it means here those expert in philosophical reasoning, for whom Collection and Division were the essential skills.

δοκεῖς καλεῖν, διαλεκτικὸν καλῶν· τὸ δὲ ῥητορικὸν
δοκεῖ μοι διαφεύγειν ἔθ᾽ ἡμᾶς.

d   ΣΩ. Πῶς φῄς; καλόν πού τι ἂν εἴη, ὃ τούτων ἀπο-
λειφθὲν ὅμως τέχνῃ λαμβάνεται; πάντως δ᾽ οὐκ ἀτι-
μαστέον αὐτὸ σοί τε καὶ ἐμοί, λεκτέον δὲ τί μέντοι καὶ
ἔστι τὸ λειπόμενον τῆς ῥητορικῆς. |

   ΦΑΙ. Καὶ μάλα που συχνά, ὦ Σώκρατες, τά γ᾽ ἐν
τοῖς βιβλίοις τοῖς περὶ λόγων τέχνης γεγραμμένοις.

   ΣΩ. [Καὶ] καλῶς γε ὑπέμνησας. προοίμιον μὲν
οἶμαι πρῶτον ὡς δεῖ τοῦ λόγου λέγεσθαι ἐν ἀρχῇ·
ταῦτα λέγεις—ἦ γάρ;—τὰ κομψὰ τῆς τέχνης;

e   ΦΑΙ. Ναί.

   ΣΩ. Δεύτερον δὲ δὴ διήγησίν τινα μαρτυρίας τ᾽ ἐπ᾽
αὐτῇ, τρίτον τεκμήρια, τέταρτον εἰκότα· καὶ πίστωσιν
οἶμαι καὶ ἐπιπίστωσιν λέγειν τόν γε βέλτιστον λογο-
δαίδαλον Βυζάντιον ἄνδρα. |

   ΦΑΙ. Τὸν χρηστὸν λέγεις Θεόδωρον;

267   ΣΩ. Τί μήν; καὶ ἔλεγχόν γε καὶ ἐπεξέλεγχον ὡς
ποιητέον ἐν κατηγορίᾳ τε καὶ ἀπολογίᾳ. τὸν δὲ κάλλιστον Πάριον Εὐηνὸν ἐς μέσον οὐκ ἄγομεν, ὃς ὑπο-
δήλωσίν τε πρῶτος ηὗρεν καὶ παρεπαίνους—οἱ δ᾽

---

109 Socrates goes on to list the formal elements presumably
contained in contemporary rhetorical instruction manuals (now
all lost) and those rhetoricians supposedly responsible for their
invention; his assessment of their achievement is heavily ironic.
Thrasymachus (DK 85, Waterfield, 270), Gorgias (DK84, Water-

this form dialectical you seem to me to be giving it the right name; but it seems to me that rhetoric still eludes us.

S. What do you mean? Could there be anything fine d anywhere which without these things [collection and division] is nevertheless embraced by art? If so, it must not be treated with disrespect at all by you and me, but we must say just what the remaining part of rhetoric is.

P. A great deal, I would say, Socrates; the stuff that's written in the handbooks about the art of speaking.[109]

S. I'm glad you've reminded me. Firstly I think that a "preamble" should be given out at the beginning of the speech: this is what you mean—don't you—by the refinements of the art?

P. Yes. e

S. Then secondly some kind of "narration" and the "witness evidence" after it; thirdly "proofs," fourthly "arguments based on probabilities"; also I think "confirmation" and "further confirmation" which at least that excellent Byzantine wordsmith talks about.

P. You mean the worthy Theodorus?

S. Of course. Also that "refutation" and "further refutation" 267 are to be included in a prosecution and defense. But are we not to bring the excellent Parian Evenus onto center stage, who first discovered "insinuation" and "indirect praise"? They say that he also speaks his "indirect cen-

field, 222), Prodicus (DK84, Waterfield, 241), Hippias, (DK86, Waterfield, 251), and Protagoras (DK 80, Waterfield, 205) are also known from their writings (not primarily rhetorical speeches) and as characters in Plato's other dialogues. Evenos of Paros (below, 267a3) is mentioned in *Phaedo* 60d5 and *Apology* 20a–b, and Polus is a prominent character in *Gorgias*.

PLATO

αὐτὸν καὶ παραψόγους | φασὶν ἐν μέτρῳ λέγειν μνή-
μης χάριν—σοφὸς γὰρ ἀνήρ. Τεισίαν δὲ Γοργίαν τε
ἐάσομεν εὕδειν, οἳ πρὸ τῶν ἀληθῶν τὰ εἰκότα εἶδον
ὡς τιμητέα μᾶλλον, τά τε αὖ σμικρὰ μεγάλα καὶ τὰ
μεγάλα σμικρὰ φαίνεσθαι ποιοῦσιν διὰ ῥώμην λό-
b γου, καινά τε ἀρχαίως τά τ' ἐναντία καινῶς, συντο-
μίαν τε λόγων καὶ ἄπειρα μήκη περὶ πάντων ἀνηῦρον;
ταῦτα δὲ ἀκούων ποτέ μου Πρόδικος ἐγέλασεν, καὶ
μόνος αὐτὸς ηὑρηκέναι ἔφη ὧν δεῖ λόγων τέχνην· δεῖν
δὲ οὔτε μακρῶν οὔτε βραχέων | ἀλλὰ μετρίων.

ΦΑΙ. Σοφώτατά γε, ὦ Πρόδικε.

ΣΩ. Ἱππίαν δὲ οὐ λέγομεν; οἶμαι γὰρ ἂν σύμψηφον
αὐτῷ καὶ τὸν Ἠλεῖον ξένον γενέσθαι.

ΦΑΙ. Τί δ' οὔ; |

ΣΩ. Τὰ δὲ Πώλου πῶς φράσωμεν αὖ μουσεῖα λόγων—ὡς διπλασιολογίαν καὶ γνωμολογίαν καὶ εἰκο-
c νολογίαν—ὀνομάτων τε Λικυμνίων ἃ ἐκείνῳ ἐδωρή-
σατο πρὸς ποίησιν εὐεπείας;

ΦΑΙ. Πρωταγόρεια δέ, ὦ Σώκρατες, οὐκ ἦν μέντοι
| τοιαῦτ' ἄττα;

ΣΩ. Ὀρθοέπειά γέ τις, ὦ παῖ, καὶ ἄλλα πολλὰ καὶ
καλά. τῶν γε μὴν οἰκτρογόων ἐπὶ γῆρας καὶ πενίαν
ἑλκομένων λόγων κεκρατηκέναι τέχνῃ μοι φαίνεται τὸ
τοῦ Χαλκηδονίου σθένος, ὀργίσαι τε αὖ πολλοὺς ἅμα

486

sures" in verse as a way of remembering them: for he is a clever man. Shall we leave Tisias and Gorgias to sleep, who saw that probabilities are more to be respected than truths, and besides make small things seem great and great ones small through the power of their speech; and they express new things in an old way and their opposites in a new fashion, and on all subjects invented conciseness of speech and boundless length? When once hearing this, Prodicus laughed at me and said he himself alone had discovered the art for the kind of speeches that are necessary: we need not long or short speeches, but those of appropriate length.

P. Very clever, Prodicus!

S. And are we not to mention Hippias? For I think our friend from Elis would vote with Prodicus.

P. Certainly.

S. But how again shall we describe Polus' gallery of terms—such as "reduplication of words," "speaking with maxims," and "figurative speaking"—and Lycimnus' words which he presented to Polus for the creation of elegant language?

P. But weren't things of that kind Protagorean, Socrates?

S. Yes, some kind of "correctness of diction," my boy, and many other fine things. And furthermore, for piteous cries of woe dragged out at the prospect of old age and poverty—these, it appears to me, the might of the Chalcedonian[110] has mastered by his art, and the man has also become formidable at rousing many to anger and again

---

[110] Thrasymachus of Chalcedon (see previous note) features prominently in *Republic* 1.336bff.

487

δεινὸς ἀνὴρ γέγονεν, καὶ πάλιν ὠργισμένοις ἐπάδων

d κηλεῖν, ὡς ἔφη· διαβάλλειν τε καὶ ἀπολύσασθαι δια-
βολὰς ὁθενδὴ κράτιστος. τὸ δὲ δὴ τέλος τῶν λόγων
κοινῇ πᾶσιν ἔοικε συνδεδογμένον εἶναι, ᾧ τινες μὲν
ἐπάνοδον, ἄλλοι δ' ἄλλο τίθενται ὄνομα. |

ΦΑΙ. Τὸ ἐν κεφαλαίῳ ἕκαστα λέγεις ὑπομνῆσαι ἐπὶ
τελευτῆς τοὺς ἀκούοντας περὶ τῶν εἰρημένων;

ΣΩ. Ταῦτα λέγω, καὶ εἴ τι σὺ ἄλλο ἔχεις εἰπεῖν
λόγων τέχνης πέρι.

ΦΑΙ. Σμικρά γε καὶ οὐκ ἄξια λέγειν.

268 ΣΩ. Ἐῶμεν δὴ τά γε σμικρά· ταῦτα δὲ ὑπ' αὐγὰς
μᾶλλον ἴδωμεν, τίνα καὶ πότ' ἔχει τὴν τῆς τέχνης
δύναμιν.

ΦΑΙ. Καὶ μάλα ἐρρωμένην, ὦ Σώκρατες, ἔν γε δὴ
πλήθους συνόδοις. |

ΣΩ. Ἔχει γάρ. ἀλλ', ὦ δαιμόνιε, ἰδὲ καὶ σὺ εἰ ἄρα
καὶ σοὶ φαίνεται διεστηκὸς αὐτῶν τὸ ἤτριον ὥσπερ
ἐμοί.

ΦΑΙ. Δείκνυε μόνον.

ΣΩ. Εἰπὲ δή μοι· εἴ τις προσελθὼν τῷ ἑταίρῳ σου
Ἐρυξιμάχῳ ἢ τῷ πατρὶ αὐτοῦ Ἀκουμενῷ εἴποι ὅτι
Ἐγὼ | ἐπίσταμαι τοιαῦτ' ἄττα σώμασι προσφέρειν,

b ὥστε θερμαίνειν τ' ἐὰν βούλωμαι καὶ ψύχειν, καὶ ἐὰν
μὲν δόξῃ μοι, ἐμεῖν ποιεῖν, ἐὰν δ' αὖ, κάτω διαχωρεῖν,
καὶ ἄλλα πάμπολλα τοιαῦτα· καὶ ἐπιστάμενος αὐτὰ

charming those who are angry with his soothing songs, as
he put it. He is very powerful at both originating and refut-   d
ing calumnies no matter where they come from. And as
for the ending of speeches everyone seems to have generally agreed, some calling it the "recapitulation," but others
give it another name.

P. You mean by way of a summary, reminding the audience at the end about each of the things that have been
said?

S. That's what I mean, and anything else you have to
say about the art of speaking.

P. Some minor points, yes, but not worth mentioning.

S. Then let's leave the minor points. Let's hold these   268
things we have more closely up to the light and look at
them: what power does the art have and when?

P. It's very forceful, Socrates, at least in large assemblies.

S. Yes indeed so. But, good man, you look yourself and
see if after all it seems to you as it does to me, that their
warp has come apart.

P. Just show me.

S. Right, tell me: if one were to approach your friend
Eryximachus or his father Acumenus[111] and say that "I
understand what sort of things to apply to bodies to make
them warm, if I wish to, or cool them off, and if I think it   b
right, make them vomit, and again make their bowels
move: and all kinds of things like that; and knowing that I
claim to be an expert doctor and to be able to make an

[111] Eryximachus, a doctor like his father, is a major character
in *Symposium* (185e6–88e4).

ἀξιῶ ἰατρικὸς εἶναι καὶ ἄλλον ποιεῖν ᾧ ἂν τὴν τούτων
ἐπιστήμην παραδῶ, τί ἂν | οἴει ἀκούσαντας εἰπεῖν;

ΦΑΙ. Τί δ᾽ ἄλλο γε ἢ ἐρέσθαι εἰ προσεπίσταται
καὶ οὕστινας δεῖ καὶ ὁπότε ἕκαστα τούτων ποιεῖν, καὶ
μέχρι ὁπόσου;

ΣΩ. Εἰ οὖν εἴποι ὅτι Οὐδαμῶς· ἀλλ᾽ ἀξιῶ τὸν ταῦτα
παρ᾽ ἐμοῦ μαθόντα αὐτὸν οἷόν τ᾽ εἶναι [ποιεῖν] ἃ ἐρωτᾷς;

c   ΦΑΙ. Εἰπεῖν ἂν οἶμαι ὅτι μαίνεται ἄνθρωπος, καὶ
ἐκ βιβλίου ποθὲν ἀκούσας ἢ περιτυχὼν φαρμακίοις
ἰατρὸς οἴεται γεγονέναι, οὐδὲν ἐπαΐων τῆς τέχνης. |

ΣΩ. Τί δ᾽ εἰ Σοφοκλεῖ αὖ προσελθὼν καὶ Εὐριπίδῃ
τις λέγοι ὡς ἐπίσταται περὶ σμικροῦ πράγματος ῥή-
σεις παμμήκεις ποιεῖν καὶ περὶ μεγάλου πάνυ σμι-
κράς, ὅταν τε βούληται οἰκτράς, καὶ τοὐναντίον αὖ
φοβερὰς καὶ ἀπειλητικὰς ὅσα τ᾽ ἄλλα τοιαῦτα, καὶ
διδάσκων αὐτὰ τραγῳδίας ποίησιν οἴεται παραδιδό-
ναι;

d   ΦΑΙ. Καὶ οὗτοι ἄν, ὦ Σώκρατες, οἶμαι καταγελῷεν
εἴ τις οἴεται τραγῳδίαν ἄλλο τι εἶναι ἢ τὴν τούτων
σύστασιν | πρέπουσαν ἀλλήλοις τε καὶ τῷ ὅλῳ συν-
ισταμένην.

ΣΩ. Ἀλλ᾽ οὐκ ἂν ἀγροίκως γε οἶμαι λοιδορήσειαν,
ἀλλ᾽ ὥσπερ ἂν μουσικὸς ἐντυχὼν ἀνδρὶ οἰομένῳ ἁρ-
μονικῷ εἶναι, ὅτι δὴ τυγχάνει ἐπιστάμενος ὡς οἷόν τε
ὀξυτάτην καὶ βαρυτάτην χορδὴν ποιεῖν, οὐκ ἀγρίως
e   εἴποι ἄν· Ὦ μοχθηρέ, μελαγχολᾷς, ἀλλ᾽ ἅτε μουσικὸς
ὢν πρᾳότερον ὅτι Ὦ ἄριστε, ἀνάγκη μὲν καὶ ταῦτ᾽

490

expert of anyone else to whom I pass on my understanding of these things." What do you think they'd say when they heard this?

P. What else but ask him if he also knew to whom he should do all these things, and when, and to what extent?

S. If then he were to say "In no way: but I claim that he who has learned this from me is capable of doing what you ask for himself?"

P. I think they would say the fellow is mad, and having heard it from some book somewhere, or chancing upon some medicaments, he thinks he's become a doctor when he has no understanding of the art.

S. And what if someone were to approach Sophocles or Euripides and say that he has learned how to compose very lengthy speeches about small matters, and very short ones about something important, pitiful ones whenever he wishes, and again the opposite, frightening and threatening ones and other such things as that, and he thinks that by teaching them he's passing on the making of tragedy?

P. I think that they too, Socrates, would laugh if anyone thinks that tragedy is anything other than arranging the combination of these things in a way to fit in with each other and with the whole.

S. Well, I don't think they would abuse him in a boorish fashion, but like a musical expert who meets a man who thinks he knows about harmony just because he happens to understand how it's possible to make a string sound very high or very low, he would not say fiercely : "You wretch, you're insane" but in as much as he is musical he would do it more gently: "My good fellow, he who is going to be

PLATO

ἐπίστασθαι τὸν μέλλοντα ἁρμονικὸν ἔσεσθαι, οὐδὲν μὴν κωλύει μηδὲ σμικρὸν ἁρμονίας | ἐπαΐειν τὸν τὴν σὴν ἕξιν ἔχοντα· τὰ γὰρ πρὸ ἁρμονίας ἀναγκαῖα μαθήματα ἐπίστασαι ἀλλ' οὐ τὰ ἁρμονικά.

ΦΑΙ. Ὀρθότατά γε.

269   ΣΩ. Οὐκοῦν καὶ ὁ Σοφοκλῆς τόν σφισιν ἐπιδεικνύμενον τὰ πρὸ τραγῳδίας ἂν φαίη ἀλλ' οὐ τὰ τραγικά, καὶ ὁ Ἀκουμενὸς τὰ πρὸ ἰατρικῆς ἀλλ' οὐ τὰ ἰατρικά.

ΦΑΙ. Παντάπασι μὲν οὖν. |

ΣΩ. Τί δὲ τὸν μελίγηρυν Ἄδραστον οἰόμεθα ἢ καὶ Περικλέα, εἰ ἀκούσειαν ὧν νυνδὴ ἡμεῖς διῇμεν τῶν παγκάλων τεχνημάτων—βραχυλογιῶν τε καὶ εἰκονολογιῶν καὶ ὅσα ἄλλα διελθόντες ὑπ' αὐγὰς ἔφαμεν
b εἶναι σκεπτέα—πότερον χαλεπῶς ἂν αὐτούς, ὥσπερ ἐγώ τε καὶ σύ, ὑπ' ἀγροικίας ῥῆμά τι εἰπεῖν ἀπαίδευτον εἰς τοὺς ταῦτα γεγραφότας τε καὶ διδάσκοντας ὡς ῥητορικὴν τέχνην, ἢ ἅτε ἡμῶν ὄντας σοφωτέρους κἂν νῷν ἐπιπλῆξαι εἰπόντας· Ὦ Φαῖδρέ τε καὶ | Σώκρατες, οὐ χρὴ χαλεπαίνειν ἀλλὰ συγγιγνώσκειν, εἴ τινες μὴ ἐπιστάμενοι διαλέγεσθαι ἀδύνατοι ἐγένοντο ὁρίσασθαι τί ποτ' ἔστιν ῥητορική, ἐκ δὲ τούτου τοῦ πάθους τὰ πρὸ τῆς τέχνης ἀναγκαῖα μαθήματα ἔχοντες ῥη-
c τορικὴν ᾠήθησαν ηὑρηκέναι, καὶ ταῦτα δὴ διδάσκοντες ἄλλους ἡγοῦνταί σφισιν τελέως ῥητορικὴν δεδι-

---

112 Adrastus was a legendary king of Argos who led the expedition of the Seven against Thebes ("honey-voiced" from Tyrtaeus 12.8, Edmonds *Elegy and Iambus*).

skilled in harmony must certainly understand these things: however nothing at all prevents the man in your state from not having the slightest understanding of harmony. For you understand what has to be learned prior to harmony, not the elements of harmony itself."

P. Absolutely right.

S. Therefore Sophocles too would say that the man   269 presenting himself to them understands the preliminaries to tragedy, but not the essentials of tragedy, and Acumenus the same with the preliminaries of medicine, but not medicine proper.

P. Of course, absolutely.

S. What do we think of the "honey-voiced Adrastus,"[112] or even Pericles, if they heard of the splendid techniques that we were discussing just now—the "concise phraseology," "figurative speaking" and such other things we went through, and said we should hold them up to the light and examine them—would they, like me and you, be so boor-   b ish as to utter harshly some uneducated expression against those who have written these things and teach them as a rhetorical art, or, in as much as they are wiser than us, would they rebuke us both too and say: "Phaedrus and Socrates, you must not be upset, but pardon some people, if in not understanding how to engage in dialectic they turned out to be unable to define what rhetoric actually is, and as a result of this shortcoming they thought they had discovered rhetoric when they had only learned the necessary preliminaries to the art; and believe that by teaching   c these things to others, a complete course in rhetoric has

δάχθαι, τὸ δὲ ἕκαστα τούτων πιθανῶς λέγειν τε καὶ
τὸ ὅλον συνίστασθαι, οὐδὲν ἔργον ‹ὄν›, αὐτοὺς δεῖν
παρ' ἑαυτῶν τοὺς μαθητάς σφων πορίζεσθαι ἐν τοῖς |
λόγοις.

ΦΑΙ. Ἀλλὰ μήν, ὦ Σώκρατες, κινδυνεύει γε τοιοῦτόν
τι εἶναι τὸ τῆς τέχνης ἣν οὗτοι οἱ ἄνδρες ὡς ῥητορικὴν διδάσκουσίν τε καὶ γράφουσιν, καὶ ἔμοιγε δοκεῖς
ἀληθῆ εἰρηκέναι· ἀλλὰ δὴ τὴν τοῦ τῷ ὄντι ῥητορικοῦ
τε καὶ πιθανοῦ τέχνην πῶς καὶ πόθεν ἄν τις δύναιτο
πορίσασθαι;

d   ΣΩ. Τὸ μὲν δύνασθαι, ὦ Φαῖδρε, ὥστε ἀγωνιστὴν
τέλεον γενέσθαι, εἰκός—ἴσως δὲ καὶ ἀναγκαῖον—
ἔχειν ὥσπερ τἆλλα· εἰ μέν σοι ὑπάρχει φύσει ῥη-
τορικῷ εἶναι, ἔσῃ ῥήτωρ ἐλλόγιμος, | προσλαβὼν
ἐπιστήμην τε καὶ μελέτην, ὅτου δ' ἂν ἐλλείπῃς τούτων, ταύτῃ ἀτελὴς ἔσῃ. ὅσον δὲ αὐτοῦ τέχνη, οὐχ ᾗ
Λυσίας τε καὶ Θρασύμαχος πορεύεται δοκεῖ μοι φαίνεσθαι ἡ μέθοδος.

ΦΑΙ. Ἀλλὰ πῇ δή;

e   ΣΩ. Κινδυνεύει, ὦ ἄριστε, εἰκότως ὁ Περικλῆς πάντων τελεώτατος εἰς τὴν ῥητορικὴν γενέσθαι.

ΦΑΙ. Τί δή;

270   ΣΩ. Πᾶσαι ὅσαι μεγάλαι τῶν τεχνῶν προσδέονται
ἀδολεσχίας καὶ μετεωρολογίας φύσεως πέρι· τὸ γὰρ
ὑψηλόνουν τοῦτο καὶ πάντῃ τελεσιουργὸν ἔοικεν ἐν-
τεῦθέν ποθεν εἰσιέναι. ὃ καὶ Περικλῆς πρὸς τῷ εὐ-
φυὴς εἶναι ἐκτήσατο· προσπεσὼν γὰρ οἶμαι τοιούτῳ
ὄντι Ἀναξαγόρᾳ, μετεωρολογίας | ἐμπλησθεὶς καὶ ἐπὶ

been taught by them, and that as for the business of expressing each of these elements persuasively and putting the whole thing together, it being no big job, the students themselves would have to provide this for themselves in their speeches."

P. Well certainly, Socrates, it would seem that the basis of the art which these men teach and write about as rhetoric is something of that sort, and to me, at any rate, what you have said seems to be true, but on the other hand how and from where would one be able to provide oneself with the art of the true expert in rhetoric and the persuasive speaker?

S. The question of the ability to become a complete d debater, Phaedrus, is probably– perhaps even inevitably— like everything else. If it's in your nature to be an orator, you will be an orator of high repute when you have added in knowledge and application, and wherever you fall short on these, that's where you will be less complete. But as far as it involves art, I don't think it's the way by which Lysias and Thrasymachus seem to be proceeding.

P. Well which way is it then?

S. It is probably reasonable to suppose, my good man, e that Pericles became the supreme master of all in respect to rhetoric.

P. What do you mean?

S. All of the arts that are important have the additional 270 need of chattering and highbrow speculation about nature. For that elevated thought and overall effectiveness seem to come in from some such source as that. This is what Pericles also acquired in addition to his being naturally clever. For I think it was his having fallen in with Anaxagoras, who was such a man, which caused him to be

φύσιν νοῦ τε καὶ διανοίας⁹ ἀφικόμενος, ὧν δὴ πέρι
τὸν πολὺν λόγον ἐποιεῖτο Ἀναξαγόρας, ἐντεῦθεν εἵλ-
κυσεν ἐπὶ τὴν τῶν λόγων τέχνην τὸ πρόσφορον αὐτῇ.

ΦΑΙ. Πῶς τοῦτο λέγεις;

b   ΣΩ. Ὁ αὐτός που τρόπος τέχνης ἰατρικῆς ὅσπερ
καὶ ῥητορικῆς.

ΦΑΙ. Πῶς δή;

ΣΩ. Ἐν ἀμφοτέραις δεῖ διελέσθαι φύσιν, σώματος
μὲν | ἐν τῇ ἑτέρᾳ, ψυχῆς δὲ ἐν τῇ ἑτέρᾳ, εἰ μέλλεις, μὴ
τριβῇ μόνον καὶ ἐμπειρίᾳ ἀλλὰ τέχνῃ, τῷ μὲν φάρ-
μακα καὶ τροφὴν προσφέρων ὑγίειαν καὶ ῥώμην ἐμ-
ποιήσειν, τῇ δὲ λόγους τε καὶ ἐπιτηδεύσεις νομίμους
πειθὼ ἣν ἂν βούλῃ καὶ ἀρετὴν παραδώσειν. |

ΦΑΙ. Τὸ γοῦν εἰκός, ὦ Σώκρατες, οὕτως.

c   ΣΩ. Ψυχῆς οὖν φύσιν ἀξίως λόγου κατανοῆσαι
οἴει δυνατὸν εἶναι ἄνευ τῆς τοῦ ὅλου φύσεως;

ΦΑΙ. Εἰ μὲν Ἱπποκράτει γε τῷ τῶν Ἀσκληπιαδῶν
δεῖ τι πιθέσθαι, οὐδὲ περὶ σώματος ἄνευ τῆς μεθόδου
| ταύτης.

---

9 διανοίας V Aristides: ἀνοίας BT

---

113 "Thought" (dianoias) is the reading of OCT (Burnet). An
alternative MSS reading (anoias), preferred by most recent editors, gives: "of the nature of mind and absence of mind" (see
textual note).   114 The tone of this praise of Pericles is probably intended ironically, in view of Gorgias 515dff. (where he
signally fails to meet Socrates' criteria for a good statesman).
Likewise, see Socrates' negative verdict on Anaxagoras at Phaedo

filled with higher thoughts and to have arrived at the nature of mind and thought[113] which were exactly what Anaxagoras made much of in his talk, from which Pericles drew, for the art of speaking, whatever was relevant to it.[114]

P. How do you mean?

S. The procedure of the medical art is, I suppose, the   b
same as that of rhetorical art.

P. How come?

S. In both you have to distinguish their nature: that of the body in the one, and that of the soul in the other, if you're going to proceed not only by mere knack and experience, but by art, applying medicines and food to the one to instill health and strength, and words and cultivation of lawful habits to the other to bestow whatever persuasion and excellence you wish.[115]

P. Probably that is the case, Socrates.

S. Then do you think it's possible to understand the   c
nature of the soul in a way worth mentioning without understanding the nature of the whole?

P. If we are to place any reliance on Hippocrates of the Asclepiads, you certainly can't do it for the nature of body without this procedure.[116]

97b–99d, whose fragments are collected at DK 59 (see Waterfield, 116–32; Kirk–Raven, chap. 12).

[115] Criticism of proceeding in rhetoric by "knack and experience" (*tribē* and *empeiria*) closely resembles Socrates' criticism of Polus and Gorgias at *Gorgias* 463a–66a.   [116] By "the whole" in c2, the whole soul and its activities are meant (rather than a general reference to "the whole," meaning the Universe). The vagueness of the reference to Hippocrates in c3–5 appears to preclude citation of any particular Hippocratic treatise.

ΣΩ. Καλῶς γάρ, ὦ ἑταῖρε, λέγει· χρὴ μέντοι πρὸς τῷ Ἱπποκράτει τὸν λόγον ἐξετάζοντα σκοπεῖν εἰ συμφωνεῖ.

ΦΑΙ. Φημί.

ΣΩ. Τὸ τοίνυν περὶ φύσεως σκόπει τί ποτε λέγει Ἱπποκράτης | τε καὶ ὁ ἀληθὴς λόγος. ἆρ᾽ οὐχ ὧδε δεῖ

d διανοεῖσθαι περὶ ὁτουοῦν φύσεως· πρῶτον μέν, ἁπλοῦν ἢ πολυειδές ἐστιν οὗ πέρι βουλησόμεθα εἶναι αὐτοὶ τεχνικοὶ καὶ ἄλλον δυνατοὶ ποιεῖν, ἔπειτα δέ, ἂν μὲν ἁπλοῦν ᾖ, σκοπεῖν τὴν δύναμιν αὐτοῦ, τίνα πρὸς τί πέφυκεν εἰς τὸ δρᾶν ἔχον ἢ | τίνα εἰς τὸ παθεῖν ὑπὸ τοῦ, ἐὰν δὲ πλείω εἴδη ἔχῃ, ταῦτα ἀριθμησάμενον, ὅπερ ἐφ᾽ ἑνός, τοῦτ᾽ ἰδεῖν ἐφ᾽ ἑκάστου, τῷ τί ποιεῖν αὐτὸ πέφυκεν ἢ τῷ τί παθεῖν ὑπὸ τοῦ;

ΦΑΙ. Κινδυνεύει, ὦ Σώκρατες.

ΣΩ. Ἡ γοῦν ἄνευ τούτων μέθοδος ἐοίκοι ἂν ὥσπερ

e τυφλοῦ πορείᾳ. ἀλλ᾽ οὐ μὴν ἀπεικαστέον τόν γε τέχνῃ μετιόντα ὁτιοῦν τυφλῷ οὐδὲ κωφῷ, ἀλλὰ δῆλον ὡς, ἄν τῳ τις τέχνῃ λόγους διδῷ, τὴν οὐσίαν δείξει ἀκριβῶς τῆς φύσεως τούτου πρὸς ὃ τοὺς λόγους προσοίσει· ἔσται δέ που | ψυχὴ τοῦτο.

ΦΑΙ. Τί μήν;

271 ΣΩ. Οὐκοῦν ἡ ἅμιλλα αὐτῷ τέταται πρὸς τοῦτο πᾶσα· πειθὼ γὰρ ἐν τούτῳ ποιεῖν ἐπιχειρεῖ. ἢ γάρ;

ΦΑΙ. Ναί.

---

117 The reference to the "thing about which we will want to

S. Yes, and he's right, my friend; however, besides Hippocrates, we must look at our investigation and see if it tallies with him.

P. I agree.

S. So then, talking of nature, consider what it is Hippocrates and the true account says. Must we not think about the nature of anything whatever as follows: firstly, is d the thing about which we will want to be expert ourselves, and be able to make someone else so, simple, or has it many forms, and secondly, if it is simple, we must consider what its capacity is: what capacity it naturally has for acting and on what does it act, or what capacity for being acted upon and by what acted upon; or if it has many forms, after counting them, to observe for each as you do for one: with which of the forms it naturally does what, or with which form it suffers what at the hands of what?[117]

P. We probably must, Socrates.

S. At any rate procedure without these steps would seem like the progress of a blind man. But we should not e on any account liken a man in pursuit of an art to a blind or deaf person, but it's clear that if anyone teaches anyone speechmaking with art, he will show precisely the real nature of the thing toward which he (the pupil) will direct his words: and that will surely be the soul.

P. Yes indeed.

S. Therefore his whole effort is aimed toward that, for 271 it's there [i.e. in the soul] that he's attempting to produce conviction, isn't he?

P. Yes.

be expert ourselves," as e4–5 makes clear, is to the soul. Socrates is imagining himself instructing potential teachers of rhetoric.

ΣΩ. Δῆλον ἄρα ὅτι ὁ Θρασύμαχός τε καὶ ὃς ἂν ἄλλος | σπουδῇ τέχνην ῥητορικὴν διδῷ, πρῶτον πάσῃ ἀκριβείᾳ γράψει τε καὶ ποιήσει ψυχὴν ἰδεῖν, πότερον ἓν καὶ ὅμοιον πέφυκεν ἢ κατὰ σώματος μορφὴν πολυειδές· τοῦτο γάρ φαμεν φύσιν εἶναι δεικνύναι.

ΦΑΙ. Παντάπασι μὲν οὖν. |

ΣΩ. Δεύτερον δέ γε, ὅτῳ τί ποιεῖν ἢ παθεῖν ὑπὸ τοῦ πέφυκεν.

ΦΑΙ. Τί μήν;

b   ΣΩ. Τρίτον δὲ δὴ διαταξάμενος τὰ λόγων τε καὶ ψυχῆς γένη καὶ τὰ τούτων παθήματα δίεισι πάσας αἰτίας, προσαρμόττων ἕκαστον ἑκάστῳ καὶ διδάσκων οἷα οὖσα ὑφ᾽ οἵων λόγων δι᾽ ἣν αἰτίαν ἐξ ἀνάγκης ἡ μὲν πείθεται, ἡ δὲ | ἀπειθεῖ.

ΦΑΙ. Κάλλιστα γοῦν ἄν, ὡς ἔοικ᾽, ἔχοι οὕτως.

ΣΩ. Οὔτοι μὲν οὖν, ὦ φίλε, ἄλλως ἐνδεικνύμενον ἢ λεγόμενον τέχνῃ ποτὲ λεχθήσεται ἢ γραφήσεται οὔτε c τι ἄλλο οὔτε τοῦτο. ἀλλ᾽ οἱ νῦν γράφοντες, ὧν σὺ ἀκήκοας, τέχνας λόγων πανοῦργοί εἰσιν καὶ ἀποκρύπτονται, εἰδότες ψυχῆς πέρι παγκάλως· πρὶν ἂν οὖν τὸν τρόπον τοῦτον λέγωσί τε καὶ γράφωσι, μὴ πειθώμεθα αὐτοῖς τέχνῃ γράφειν. |

ΦΑΙ. Τίνα τοῦτον;

---

118 "The causes," which result in the different types of soul being affected by different kinds of speeches. As in 270d and 271d5ff, Socrates emphasizes the interactive nature of the rhetorical art.

S. Then it's clear that both Thrasymachus and whoever else is seriously teaching the rhetorical art will firstly write with total precision and will make us see whether soul is naturally a simple uniform entity, or complex, comparable to the form of a body: for this is what we mean by revealing the nature of something.

P. Yes, absolutely.

S. And secondly, he will clarify by virtue of what form the soul acts naturally upon what, or is acted upon by what.

P. Of course.

S. And thirdly, again after classifying the kinds of b speeches and soul and how these are affected, he will go through all the causes,[118] fitting each to each and teaching what kinds they are, and by what kind of speeches and for what reason one soul, being the kind it is, is of necessity persuaded and the other is not.

P. Certainly I think it would be best like this.

S. And what's more, my friend, in no other way [119] will there ever be spoken or written discourse in accord with art, whether put forward for display or spoken, not any other topic and not on this one.[120] But those who now c write the manuals of speechmaking, whom you have listened to, are rogues and keep hidden the fact that they know full well about the soul; so until they speak and write in this manner, let us not believe that they write with art.

P. What manner is this?

[119] That is, than the way that Socrates has outlined in 271a4–b5.

[120] That is, on the subject that they both have been practicing: love (*erōs*).

ΣΩ. Αὐτὰ μὲν τὰ ῥήματα εἰπεῖν οὐκ εὐπετές· ὡς δὲ
δεῖ γράφειν, εἰ μέλλει τεχνικῶς ἔχειν καθ᾽ ὅσον ἐν-
δέχεται, λέγειν ἐθέλω.

ΦΑΙ. Λέγε δή. |

ΣΩ. Ἐπειδὴ λόγου δύναμις τυγχάνει ψυχαγωγία
d οὖσα, τὸν μέλλοντα ῥητορικὸν ἔσεσθαι ἀνάγκη εἰδέναι ψυχὴ ὅσα εἴδη ἔχει. ἔστιν οὖν τόσα καὶ τόσα, καὶ
τοῖα καὶ τοῖα, ὅθεν οἱ μὲν τοιοίδε, οἱ δὲ τοιοίδε γίγνον-
ται· τούτων δὲ δὴ οὕτω διῃρημένων, λόγων αὖ τόσα
καὶ τόσα ἔστιν εἴδη, τοιόνδε | ἕκαστον. οἱ μὲν οὖν
τοιοίδε ὑπὸ τῶν τοιῶνδε λόγων διὰ τήνδε τὴν αἰτίαν
ἐς τὰ τοιάδε εὐπειθεῖς, οἱ δὲ τοιοίδε διὰ τάδε δυσπει-
θεῖς· δεῖ δὴ ταῦτα ἱκανῶς νοήσαντα, μετὰ ταῦτα θεώ-
μενον αὐτὰ ἐν ταῖς πράξεσιν ὄντα τε καὶ πραττόμενα,
e ὀξέως τῇ αἰσθήσει δύνασθαι ἐπακολουθεῖν, ἢ μηδὲν
εἶναί πω πλέον αὐτῷ ὧν τότε ἤκουεν λόγων συνών.
ὅταν δὲ εἰπεῖν τε ἱκανῶς ἔχῃ οἷος ὑφ᾽ οἵων πείθεται,
272 παραγιγνόμενόν τε δυνατὸς ᾖ διαισθανόμενος ἑαυτῷ
ἐνδείκνυσθαι ὅτι οὗτός ἐστι καὶ αὕτη ἡ φύσις περὶ ἧς
τότε ἦσαν οἱ λόγοι, νῦν ἔργῳ παροῦσά οἱ, ᾗ προσοι-
στέον τούσδε ὧδε τοὺς λόγους ἐπὶ τὴν τῶνδε πειθώ,
ταῦτα δ᾽ ἤδη πάντα ἔχοντι, προσλαβόντι καιροὺς τοῦ
πότε λεκτέον καὶ ἐπισχετέον, | βραχυλογίας τε αὖ καὶ
ἐλεινολογίας καὶ δεινώσεως ἑκάστων τε ὅσα ἂν εἴδη
μάθῃ λόγων, τούτων τὴν εὐκαιρίαν τε καὶ ἀκαιρίαν
διαγνόντι, καλῶς τε καὶ τελέως ἐστὶν ἡ τέχνη ἀπειρ-

121 See 261a7–8 above.

S. It's not easy to speak the actual words, but I want to talk about how one should write, if one is to be as much as possible in conformity with art.

P. Say on!

S. Since the function of speech is actually a guiding of the soul,[121] he who intends to be an orator must know how d many forms the soul has. There are so many of this and of that kind, and of such and such a kind, so that some people are like this, others like that. Then since they have been sorted out in this way, then again there are so many forms of speeches, and each of such and such a kind. Therefore people of a certain kind are easy to persuade for this reason by certain kinds of speech to certain kinds of opinion, but those of another kind are for these reasons not easy to persuade. Then when he has adequately understood these things, he must next look at them as they are in action and in practical situations and be able to follow them with acute perception, or else not get any advantage as yet from e the discussions he heard before when associating with his teacher. Whenever he is sufficiently able to say what sort of person is persuaded by what kind of things, and is capable of distinguishing the person there beside him, and 272 telling himself that this is the man and this the nature which the previous discussions were about, now present to him in reality, to which he must direct these kinds of speeches in this way to persuade him of these things; now at this point having possession of all of this and also grasping the right occasions for speaking and holding back, and again for speaking concisely and with tearful appeal and exaggeration and, for all the forms of speeches he may learn, distinguishing the right and wrong moment, his art has been well and fully brought to perfection, but not

b γασμένη, πρότερον δ' οὔ· ἀλλ' ὅτι ἂν αὐτῶν τις ἐλλείπῃ λέγων ἢ διδάσκων ἢ γράφων, φῇ δὲ τέχνῃ λέγειν, ὁ μὴ πειθόμενος κρατεῖ. Τί δὴ οὖν; φήσει ἴσως ὁ συγγραφεύς, ὦ Φαῖδρέ τε καὶ Σώκρατες, δοκεῖ οὕτως; μὴ[10] ἄλλως πως ἀποδεκτέον λεγομένης λόγων τέχνης; |

ΦΑΙ. Ἀδύνατόν που, ὦ Σώκρατες, ἄλλως· καίτοι οὐ σμικρόν γε φαίνεται ἔργον.

ΣΩ. Ἀληθῆ λέγεις. τούτου τοι ἕνεκα χρὴ πάντας τοὺς λόγους ἄνω καὶ κάτω μεταστρέφοντα ἐπισκοπεῖν εἴ τίς πῃ ῥάων καὶ βραχυτέρα φαίνεται ἐπ' αὐτὴν

c ὁδός, ἵνα μὴ μάτην πολλὴν ἀπίῃ καὶ τραχεῖαν, ἐξὸν ὀλίγην τε καὶ λείαν. ἀλλ' εἴ τινά πῃ βοήθειαν ἔχεις ἐπακηκοὼς Λυσίου ἤ τινος ἄλλου, πειρῶ λέγειν ἀναμιμνῃσκόμενος. |

ΦΑΙ. Ἕνεκα μὲν πείρας ἔχοιμ' ἄν, ἀλλ' οὔτι νῦν γ' οὕτως ἔχω.

ΣΩ. Βούλει οὖν ἐγώ τιν' εἴπω λόγον ὃν τῶν περὶ ταῦτά τινων ἀκήκοα;

ΦΑΙ. Τί μήν; |

ΣΩ. Λέγεται γοῦν, ὦ Φαῖδρε, δίκαιον εἶναι καὶ τὸ τοῦ λύκου εἰπεῖν.

d ΦΑΙ. Καὶ σύ γε οὕτω ποίει.

____

10 μὴ Burnet: ἢ ΒΤ

before. But in whichever of these someone falls short in   b
speaking, or teaching, or writing, and yet claims he speaks
with art, the person who is not convinced by him wins the
day. "What about it, then," perhaps the writer will say,
"Phaedrus and Socrates, "does this seem right to you?
Surely there is no other way of accepting a statement of
rhetorical art?"[122]

P. Impossible, in my view, Socrates, to accept any other
way. Yet it doesn't seem an easy task.

S. You're right. I tell you this is the reason we must turn
all our arguments upside down and consider if any easier
and shorter way to it appears anywhere, so that there's no   c
going off on a long rough path in vain, when it can be short
and smooth. Well, if you have any help anywhere you've
heard from Lysias or anyone else, try and remember it and
tell me.

P. If it depended on trying, I would tell you; but as
things are I'm just in no position to oblige.

S. So do you want me to tell you a saying which I've
heard from some of those who are interested in these
matters?

P. Yes, of course.

S. It's said, Phaedrus, that it's right at least to state the
wolf's point of view as well.[123]

P. You do that then.   d

[122] Translating OCT (Burnet). Most editors accept the MSS
reading (see textual note) and translate "Do you agree, or must it
be accepted if the art of speaking is stated in an alternative way?"

[123] That is, to play devil's advocate; see an Aesop fable (Plutarch, *Convivium Septem Sapientium* 156a). This is exactly what
Socrates does in d2ff.

ΣΩ. Φασὶ τοίνυν οὐδὲν οὕτω ταῦτα δεῖν σεμνύνειν
οὐδ' ἀνάγειν ἄνω μακρὰν περιβαλλομένους· παντάπασι γάρ, ὃ καὶ κατ' ἀρχὰς εἴπομεν τοῦδε τοῦ λόγου,
ὅτι οὐδὲν ἀληθείας | μετέχειν δέοι δικαίων ἢ ἀγαθῶν
πέρι πραγμάτων, ἢ καὶ ἀνθρώπων γε τοιούτων φύσει
ὄντων ἢ τροφῇ, τὸν μέλλοντα ἱκανῶς ῥητορικὸν ἔσεσθαι. τὸ παράπαν γὰρ οὐδὲν ἐν τοῖς δικαστηρίοις
τούτων ἀληθείας μέλειν οὐδενί, ἀλλὰ τοῦ πιθανοῦ·
e   τοῦτο δ' εἶναι τὸ εἰκός, ᾧ δεῖν προσέχειν τὸν μέλλοντα τέχνῃ ἐρεῖν. οὐδὲ γὰρ αὐτὰ ⟨τὰ⟩ πραχθέντα
δεῖν λέγειν ἐνίοτε, ἐὰν μὴ εἰκότως ᾖ πεπραγμένα,
ἀλλὰ τὰ εἰκότα, ἔν τε κατηγορίᾳ καὶ ἀπολογίᾳ, καὶ
πάντως λέγοντα τὸ δὴ εἰκὸς διωκτέον | εἶναι, πολλὰ
εἰπόντα χαίρειν τῷ ἀληθεῖ· τοῦτο γὰρ διὰ παντὸς τοῦ
λόγου γιγνόμενον τὴν ἅπασαν τέχνην πορίζειν.

273   ΦΑΙ. Αὐτά γε, ὦ Σώκρατες, διελήλυθας ἃ λέγουσιν
οἱ περὶ τοὺς λόγους τεχνικοὶ προσποιούμενοι εἶναι·
ἀνεμνήσθην γὰρ ὅτι ἐν τῷ πρόσθεν βραχέως τοῦ τοι-
ούτου ἐφηψάμεθα, | δοκεῖ δὲ τοῦτο πάμμεγα εἶναι τοῖς
περὶ ταῦτα.

ΣΩ. Ἀλλὰ μὴν τόν γε Τεισίαν αὐτὸν πεπάτηκας
ἀκριβῶς· εἰπέτω τοίνυν καὶ τόδε ἡμῖν ὁ Τεισίας, μή
τι ἄλλο λέγει τὸ εἰκὸς ἢ τὸ τῷ πλήθει δοκοῦν.

b   ΦΑΙ. Τί γὰρ ἄλλο;

ΣΩ. Τοῦτο δή, ὡς ἔοικε, σοφὸν εὑρὼν ἅμα καὶ
τεχνικὸν ἔγραψεν ὡς ἐάν τις ἀσθενὴς καὶ ἀνδρικὸς

S. They say that you should not make these things so grand, or even go with them back to first principles, taking the long route. For it's entirely as we said at the beginning of this discussion: the man who is going to be a competent orator has no need to have anything at all to do with the truth about just or good things, or even with such people who are of this type by nature or by nurture. For they say that no one in the law courts has the slightest interest whatever in the truth of these things, but in what is persuasive: and this is what is probable, which is what he who   e is going to speak with art must pay attention to. And they say that sometimes one should not even mention what was actually done, if what is done is improbable, but what is probable, both in the prosecution and the defense, and at all events when speaking, the probable is what one must pursue, and in much of one's discourse say goodbye to the truth. For when this occurs throughout the speech, it provides the entire art.

P. Socrates, you've gone through the very things that   273 those who lay claim to being proficient in speechmaking say. For I remember we briefly touched upon such a thing previously,[124] and it seems to be highly important to those interested in the subject.

S. But you have thumbed through the man Tisias himself in detail: so let Tisias tell us this too; is he saying that what is probable is just what the crowd think it is?

P. Yes, what else?   b

S. It seems, then, that it was on making just this clever and at the same time artistic discovery, that he wrote that

[124] At 267a6–7 "probabilities are more to be respected than truths" (attributed to Tisias and Gorgias).

ἰσχυρὸν καὶ | δειλὸν συγκόψας, ἱμάτιον ἤ τι ἄλλο
ἀφελόμενος, εἰς δικαστήριον ἄγηται, δεῖ δὴ τἀληθὲς
μηδέτερον λέγειν, ἀλλὰ τὸν μὲν δειλὸν μὴ ὑπὸ μόνου
φάναι τοῦ ἀνδρικοῦ συγκεκόφθαι, τὸν δὲ τοῦτο μὲν
ἐλέγχειν ὡς μόνω ἤστην, ἐκείνω δὲ καταχρήσασθαι
c τῷ Πῶς δ' ἂν ἐγὼ τοιόσδε τοιῷδε ἐπεχείρησα; ὁ δ'
οὐκ ἐρεῖ δὴ τὴν ἑαυτοῦ κάκην, ἀλλά τι ἄλλο ψεύδε-
σθαι ἐπιχειρῶν τάχ' ἂν ἔλεγχόν πη παραδοίη τῷ
ἀντιδίκω. καὶ περὶ τἆλλα δὴ τοιαῦτ' ἄττα ἐστὶ τὰ |
τέχνῃ λεγόμενα. οὐ γάρ, ὦ Φαῖδρε;

ΦΑΙ. Τί μήν;

ΣΩ. Φεῦ, δεινῶς γ' ἔοικεν ἀποκεκρυμμένην τέχνην
ἀνευρεῖν ὁ Τεισίας ἢ ἄλλος ὅστις δή ποτ' ὢν τυγχάνει καὶ ὁπόθεν χαίρει ὀνομαζόμενος. ἀτάρ, ὦ ἑταῖρε,
τούτω ἡμεῖς | πότερον λέγωμεν ἢ μὴ—

d ΦΑΙ. Τὸ ποῖον;

ΣΩ. Ὅτι, ὦ Τεισία, πάλαι ἡμεῖς, πρὶν καὶ σὲ παρελθεῖν, τυγχάνομεν λέγοντες ὡς ἄρα τοῦτο τὸ εἰκὸς
τοῖς πολλοῖς δι' ὁμοιότητα τοῦ ἀληθοῦς τυγχάνει ἐγ-
γιγνόμενον· τὰς δὲ | ὁμοιότητας ἄρτι διήλθομεν ὅτι
πανταχοῦ ὁ τὴν ἀλήθειαν εἰδὼς κάλλιστα ἐπίσταται
εὑρίσκειν. ὥστ' εἰ μὲν ἄλλο τι περὶ τέχνης λόγων
λέγεις, ἀκούοιμεν ἄν· εἰ δὲ μή, οἷς νυνδὴ διήλθομεν
πεισόμεθα, ὡς ἐὰν μή τις τῶν τε ἀκουσομένων τὰς
e φύσεις διαριθμήσηται, καὶ κατ' εἴδη τε διαιρεῖσθαι

---

125 Tisias' reputed teacher was Corax = "Crow."
126 At 261e–62b.

if a weak yet brave man beats up a strong yet cowardly
fellow and steals his cloak or something else and is taken
to court, neither of them should tell the truth, but the
coward should say he was not beaten up by the brave man
on his own, and the latter should establish that the two of
them were alone, and make use of that well-known argument: "How could the likes of me have tackled the likes   c
of him?" The other won't admit his cowardice, but in his
attempt to make up another lie may perhaps pass an opportunity for refutation onto his opponent. And in other
instances things spoken with art are something like this. Is
that not so, Phaedrus?

P. Of course.

S. Oh goodness! How cleverly hidden an art Tisias
seems to have discovered, or indeed someone else whoever it happens to be and wherever it is he is pleased to
be named from.[125] But anyway, my friend, are we to say to
him, or are we not . . .

P. What sort of thing?   d

S. . . . that before you came on the scene, Tisias, we
have as it happens long been saying that in fact this probability occurs to the majority of people owing to its resemblance to the truth. And we recently concluded that in all
cases it is he who knows the truth who understands best
how to find these resemblances.[126] Accordingly if there is
anything else you can say about the art of speaking, we
should like to hear it. But if not, we shall be convinced by
what we've just concluded, that unless someone counts up
the natures of those who will be listening to him and is
capable of classifying existing things according to type and   e
is able to embrace each one of them one after another in

τὰ ὄντα καὶ μιᾷ ἰδέᾳ δυνατὸς ᾖ καθ' ἓν ἕκαστον περι-
λαμβάνειν, οὔ ποτ' ἔσται τεχνικὸς λόγων πέρι καθ'
ὅσον δυνατὸν ἀνθρώπῳ. ταῦτα δὲ οὐ μή ποτε κτήση-
ται ἄνευ | πολλῆς πραγματείας· ἣν οὐχ ἕνεκα τοῦ λέ-
γειν καὶ πράττειν πρὸς ἀνθρώπους δεῖ διαπονεῖσθαι
τὸν σώφρονα, ἀλλὰ τοῦ θεοῖς κεχαρισμένα μὲν λέγειν
δύνασθαι, κεχαρισμένως δὲ πράττειν τὸ πᾶν εἰς δύναμιν. οὐ γὰρ δὴ ἄρα, ὦ Τεισία, φασὶν οἱ σοφώτεροι
ἡμῶν, ὁμοδούλοις δεῖ χαρίζεσθαι μελετᾶν τὸν νοῦν
ἔχοντα, ὅτι μὴ πάρεργον, ἀλλὰ δεσπόταις ἀγαθοῖς τε
274 καὶ ἐξ ἀγαθῶν. ὥστ' εἰ μακρὰ ἡ περίοδος, μὴ θαυμά-
σῃς· μεγάλων γὰρ ἕνεκα περιτέον, οὐχ ὡς σὺ δοκεῖς.
ἔσται μήν, ὡς ὁ λόγος φησίν, ἐάν τις ἐθέλῃ, καὶ
ταῦτα | κάλλιστα ἐξ ἐκείνων γιγνόμενα.

ΦΑΙ. Παγκάλως ἔμοιγε δοκεῖ λέγεσθαι, ὦ Σώκρατες, εἴπερ οἷός τέ τις εἴη.

ΣΩ. Ἀλλὰ καὶ ἐπιχειροῦντί τοι τοῖς καλοῖς καλὸν
καὶ πάσχειν ὅτι ἄν τῳ συμβῇ παθεῖν.

b   ΦΑΙ. Καὶ μάλα.

ΣΩ. Οὐκοῦν τὸ μὲν τέχνης τε καὶ ἀτεχνίας λόγων
πέρι ἱκανῶς ἐχέτω. |

ΦΑΙ. Τί μήν;

ΣΩ. Τὸ δ' εὐπρεπείας δὴ γραφῆς πέρι καὶ ἀπρε-
πείας, πῇ γιγνόμενον καλῶς ἂν ἔχοι καὶ ὅπῃ ἀπρε-
πῶς, λοιπόν. ἦ γάρ;

a single form, he will never be an expert as regards speaking to the extent a man is capable. And he will never acquire these skills without a great deal of careful study; this, a man of sound mind must work hard at, not for the sake of speaking and dealing with men, but to have the ability to speak in a way pleasing to the gods and to deal with everything in a way pleasing to them to the best of his ability. For I assure you, Tisias, those wiser than us say that the thinking man must not make a practice of gratifying his fellow slaves, except incidentally, but masters who are good and of noble lineage. So then, do not be surprised if 274 we have to go the long way round, for we must make the journey for important reasons, not for the reasons you think. Nevertheless these latter also, as our argument claims, will best come about from the others, if one is willing (to pursue the longer course).[127]

P. I think that's very well put, Socrates, if only one were capable of it.

S. But for someone who even attempts what is fine, it's fine also for him to undergo whatever is in store for him.

P. Yes, certainly.   b

S. In that case let that be enough about the art and the lack of it in rhetoric.

P. Yes, indeed.

S. What remains concerns writing that is acceptable and that which is not, and in what way it will be done acceptably and in what way unacceptably. Isn't that so?

[127] That is, Socrates' method for real dialectic ("the long way round") will also ultimately embrace "these latter" (a4), i.e., success in the law courts, etc.

ΦΑΙ. Ναί.

ΣΩ. Οἶσθ' οὖν ὅπῃ μάλιστα θεῷ χαριῇ λόγων πέρι
| πράττων ἢ λέγων;

ΦΑΙ. Οὐδαμῶς· σὺ δέ;

c   ΣΩ. Ἀκοήν γ' ἔχω λέγειν τῶν προτέρων, τὸ δ'
ἀληθὲς αὐτοὶ ἴσασιν. εἰ δὲ τοῦτο εὕροιμεν αὐτοί, ἆρά
γ' ἂν ἔθ' ἡμῖν μέλοι τι τῶν ἀνθρωπίνων δοξασμάτων;

ΦΑΙ. Γελοῖον ἤρου· ἀλλ' ἃ φῂς ἀκηκοέναι λέγε. |

ΣΩ. Ἤκουσα τοίνυν περὶ Ναύκρατιν τῆς Αἰγύπτου
γενέσθαι τῶν ἐκεῖ παλαιῶν τινα θεῶν, οὗ καὶ τὸ ὄρ-
νεον ἱερὸν ὃ δὴ καλοῦσιν Ἶβιν· αὐτῷ δὲ ὄνομα τῷ
d δαίμονι εἶναι Θεύθ. τοῦτον δὴ πρῶτον ἀριθμόν τε καὶ
λογισμὸν εὑρεῖν καὶ γεωμετρίαν καὶ ἀστρονομίαν, ἔτι
δὲ πεττείας τε καὶ κυβείας, καὶ δὴ καὶ γράμματα.
βασιλέως δ' αὖ τότε ὄντος Αἰγύπτου ὅλης Θαμοῦ
περὶ τὴν μεγάλην πόλιν τοῦ ἄνω τόπου ἣν οἱ Ἕλλη-
νες Αἰγυπτίας Θήβας καλοῦσι, καὶ τὸν θεὸν[11] Ἄμ-
μωνα, | παρὰ τοῦτον ἐλθὼν ὁ Θεὺθ τὰς τέχνας ἐπέδει-
ξεν, καὶ ἔφη δεῖν διαδοθῆναι τοῖς ἄλλοις Αἰγυπτίοις·
ὁ δὲ ἤρετο ἥντινα ἑκάστη ἔχοι ὠφελίαν, διεξιόντος δέ,
ὅτι καλῶς ἢ μὴ καλῶς δοκοῖ λέγειν, τὸ μὲν ἔψεγεν, τὸ

---

11 θεὸν BTW: Θαμοῦν Postgate

128 Or, on an alternative reading, favored by most editors:
"and they call Thamous Ammon" (see textual note). The style of
this fictional (see 275b3–4) historical narrative recalls Herodotus
Histories 2, and the apt choice of Egypt reflects that author's account of Egyptian preservation of the memory of the past (2.77).

P. Yes.

S. Do you know therefore how in relation to speaking, both practicing and speaking about it, you would especially please god?

P. Not at all; and you?

S. I can tell you, at least what I have heard from our   c
predecessors, but they themselves know the truth. If we were to discover this for ourselves, then would we have any concern any more for the mere opinions of mankind?

P. That's a ridiculous question; but tell me what you say you have heard.

S. Very well then, I heard that there was in the region of Naucratis in Egypt one of the ancient gods there, to whom the bird which they call the Ibis is sacred. The name of the divinity himself was Theuth. Now it is said he   d
was the first to discover number and arithmetic, geometry and astronomy, and also games involving drafts and dice, and in particular, writing. At the time the king of all of Egypt which surrounds the great city of the upper part of the country which the Greeks call Egyptian Thebes, was Thamous, and they call the god Ammon.[128] Theuth approached him and demonstrated his arts and said that they ought to be passed on to the rest of the Egyptians. But Thamous asked what would be the benefit of each of these, and as the other went through them, he criticized this and praised that wherever he thought that he, Theuth,

Theuth has the Greek Prometheus or Palamedes as a counterpart "first inventor" of arts and sciences and, in particular, writing. The Greeks had a trading station at Naucratis, probably from the late seventh century. Thamous-Ammon, the chief Egyptian god-king, was identified with Zeus.

e δ' ἐπῄνει. πολλὰ μὲν δὴ περὶ ἑκάστης τῆς τέχνης ἐπ'
ἀμφότερα Θαμοῦν τῷ Θευθ λέγεται ἀποφήνασθαι, ἃ
λόγος πολὺς ἂν εἴη διελθεῖν· ἐπειδὴ δὲ ἐπὶ τοῖς γράμ-
μασιν ἦν, Τοῦτο δέ, ὦ βασιλεῦ, τὸ | μάθημα, ἔφη ὁ
Θεύθ, σοφωτέρους Αἰγυπτίους καὶ μνημονικωτέρους
παρέξει· μνήμης τε γὰρ καὶ σοφίας φάρμακον ηὑρέθη.
ὁ δ' εἶπεν· Ὦ τεχνικώτατε Θεύθ, ἄλλος μὲν τεκεῖν δυνατὸς τὰ τέχνης, ἄλλος δὲ κρῖναι τίν' ἔχει μοῖραν
275 βλάβης τε καὶ ὠφελίας τοῖς μέλλουσι χρῆσθαι· καὶ
νῦν σύ, πατὴρ ὢν γραμμάτων, δι' εὔνοιαν τοὐναντίον
εἶπες ἢ δύναται. τοῦτο γὰρ τῶν μαθόντων λήθην μὲν
ἐν ψυχαῖς παρέξει μνήμης ἀμελετησίᾳ, ἅτε διὰ πίστιν
γραφῆς ἔξωθεν ὑπ' ἀλλοτρίων τύπων, οὐκ ἔνδοθεν
αὐτοὺς ὑφ' αὑτῶν ἀναμιμνησκομένους· | οὔκουν μνή-
μης ἀλλὰ ὑπομνήσεως φάρμακον ηὗρες. σοφίας δὲ
b τοῖς μαθηταῖς δόξαν, οὐκ ἀλήθειαν πορίζεις· πολυή-
κοοι γάρ σοι γενόμενοι ἄνευ διδαχῆς πολυγνώμονες
εἶναι δόξουσιν, ἀγνώμονες ὡς ἐπὶ τὸ πλῆθος ὄντες,
καὶ χαλεποὶ συνεῖναι, δοξόσοφοι γεγονότες ἀντὶ σο-
φῶν.

ΦΑΙ. Ὦ Σώκρατες, ῥᾳδίως σὺ Αἰγυπτίους καὶ ὁπο-
δαποὺς ἂν ἐθέλῃς λόγους ποιεῖς. |

ΣΩ. Οἱ δέ γ', ὦ φίλε, ἐν τῷ τοῦ Διὸς τοῦ Δωδωναίου
ἱερῷ δρυὸς λόγους ἔφησαν μαντικοὺς πρώτους γενέσθαι. τοῖς μὲν οὖν τότε, ἅτε οὐκ οὖσι σοφοῖς ὥσπερ
ὑμεῖς οἱ νέοι, ἀπέχρη δρυὸς καὶ πέτρας ἀκούειν ὑπ'

was right and wrong. It is said that Thamous expressed   e
himself at length about each art to Theuth on both sides,
which would take a long discussion to go through in detail.
But when it was on the subject of letters: "But this," said
Theuth, "my king, is the study that will make the Egyptians wiser and improve their memory: for what has been
discovered is a drug to enhance memory and wisdom."
But the other replied: "My most artful Theuth, one man
is able to give birth to the elements of an art, but it takes
another to judge what measure of harm and benefit it has
for those who are planning to use it. And now you, being   275
the father of letters, through your affection for them have
stated the opposite of their capabilities. For this invention
will bring about forgetfulness in the souls of its learners
from the lack of practice in use of their memory, inasmuch
as through their reliance on writing they are reminded of
things as a result of alien impressions which are from outside, and not from within, themselves by themselves. You
have found a drug not for memory but for reminding. You
are giving your students a semblance of wisdom, not the
real thing. You see, having become, through you, widely   b
read without teaching they will think they are very knowl-
edgeable, while for the most part they are ignorant and
will be difficult to associate with because they have acquired the appearance of wisdom instead of the reality."

P. Socrates, you easily make up stories about Egyptians
and any other people you like.

S. Well, my friend, those at the sanctuary of Zeus at
Dodona said that the words from an oak were the first
prophetic utterances. So for the people of that time, because of their simplemindedness in that they weren't wise
as you youngsters are, it was enough to listen to the oak

c εὐηθείας, εἰ μόνον ἀληθῆ λέγοιεν· σοὶ δ᾽ ἴσως διαφέρει τίς ὁ λέγων καὶ ποδαπός. οὐ γὰρ ἐκεῖνο μόνον
σκοπεῖς, εἴτε οὕτως εἴτε ἄλλως ἔχει;

ΦΑΙ. Ὀρθῶς ἐπέπληξας, καί μοι δοκεῖ περὶ γραμ-
μάτων ἔχειν ᾗπερ ὁ Θηβαῖος λέγει. |

ΣΩ. Οὐκοῦν ὁ τέχνην οἰόμενος ἐν γράμμασι κατα-
λιπεῖν, καὶ αὖ ὁ παραδεχόμενος ὥς τι σαφὲς καὶ βέβαιον ἐκ γραμμάτων ἐσόμενον, πολλῆς ἂν εὐηθείας
γέμοι καὶ τῷ ὄντι τὴν Ἄμμωνος μαντείαν ἀγνοοῖ,
πλέον τι οἰόμενος εἶναι λόγους γεγραμμένους τοῦ τὸν
εἰδότα ὑπομνῆσαι περὶ ὧν ἂν ᾖ τὰ γεγραμμένα.

d ΦΑΙ. Ὀρθότατα.

ΣΩ. Δεινὸν γάρ που, ὦ Φαῖδρε, τοῦτ᾽ ἔχει γραφή,
καὶ | ὡς ἀληθῶς ὅμοιον ζωγραφίᾳ. καὶ γὰρ τὰ ἐκείνης
ἔκγονα ἕστηκε μὲν ὡς ζῶντα, ἐὰν δ᾽ ἀνέρῃ τι, σεμνῶς
πάνυ σιγᾷ. ταὐτὸν δὲ καὶ οἱ λόγοι· δόξαις μὲν ἂν ὥς
τι φρονοῦντας αὐτοὺς λέγειν, ἐὰν δέ τι ἔρῃ τῶν λεγομένων βουλόμενος μαθεῖν, ἕν τι σημαίνει μόνον ταὐ-
e τὸν ἀεί. ὅταν δὲ ἅπαξ γραφῇ, κυλινδεῖται μὲν πανταχοῦ πᾶς λόγος ὁμοίως παρὰ τοῖς ἐπαΐουσιν, ὡς δ᾽
αὕτως παρ᾽ οἷς οὐδὲν προσήκει, καὶ οὐκ ἐπίσταται

---

129 The priestess would interpret the rustling of the leaves
from the sacred oak as conveying a prophetic message. "Oak and
the rock" (b8), a proverbial pairing implying "anything whatsoever" (see Homer, *Odyssey* 19.162–63; Hesiod, *Theogony* 35).

and the rock, provided only that they were telling the truth.[129] But for you perhaps it makes a difference who is speaking and where they come from. For whether it is the case or otherwise, that's not the only thing you consider, is it?[130]

P. You are right to tell me off, and I agree with what the Theban says about letters.

S. Therefore he who thinks that in writing he has left an art behind him and again he who accepts it believing that something clear and secure will emerge from the writing, would be totally simpleminded, and in reality ignorant of Ammon's prophecy, in thinking that words written down are anything more than a reminder for him who knows what the written words are about.

P. Absolutely right.

S. Yes, for I think, Phaedrus, writing has this strange thing about it and really it's like the art of painting. You see the offspring of painting stand as if they're alive, but if you ask them anything they preserve a quite grave silence. And it's the same with written words: you'd think they're saying something with intelligence, but if in your wish to learn you ask them a question about what they say, they only indicate the one same thing every time. And when once it's in writing, every discourse is circulated about in every direction in the same way among those who understand it and among those to whom it is of no concern at all, and it doesn't know how to speak to those whom it

---

[130] OCT (Burnet) inserts the question mark; as a statement (most editors), the line might also be translated as a reproof (which Phaedrus' reply in c3–4 suggests), "you don't just consider whether what he says is right or not" (trans. Rowe).

λέγειν οἷς δεῖ γε καὶ μή. πλημμελούμενος δὲ καὶ οὐκ
ἐν δίκῃ λοιδορηθεὶς τοῦ πατρὸς ἀεὶ δεῖται βοηθοῦ· |
αὐτὸς γὰρ οὔτ᾽ ἀμύνασθαι οὔτε βοηθῆσαι δυνατὸς
αὑτῷ.

ΦΑΙ. Καὶ ταῦτά σοι ὀρθότατα εἴρηται.

276   ΣΩ. Τί δ᾽; ἄλλον ὁρῶμεν λόγον τούτου ἀδελφὸν
γνήσιον, τῷ τρόπῳ τε γίγνεται, καὶ ὅσῳ ἀμείνων καὶ
δυνατώτερος τούτου φύεται;

ΦΑΙ. Τίνα τοῦτον καὶ πῶς λέγεις γιγνόμενον; |

ΣΩ. Ὃς μετ᾽ ἐπιστήμης γράφεται ἐν τῇ τοῦ μαν-
θάνοντος ψυχῇ, δυνατὸς μὲν ἀμῦναι ἑαυτῷ, ἐπιστή-
μων δὲ λέγειν τε καὶ σιγᾶν πρὸς οὓς δεῖ.

ΦΑΙ. Τὸν τοῦ εἰδότος λόγον λέγεις ζῶντα καὶ ἔμψυχον, οὗ ὁ γεγραμμένος εἴδωλον ἄν τι λέγοιτο δικαίως.

b   ΣΩ. Παντάπασι μὲν οὖν. τόδε δή μοι εἰπέ· ὁ νοῦν
ἔχων γεωργός, ὧν σπερμάτων κήδοιτο καὶ ἔγκαρπα
βούλοιτο γενέσθαι, πότερα σπουδῇ ἂν θέρους εἰς
Ἀδώνιδος κήπους ἀρῶν χαίροι θεωρῶν καλοὺς ἐν ἡμέ-
ραισιν ὀκτὼ γιγνομένους, | ἢ ταῦτα μὲν δὴ παιδιᾶς τε
καὶ ἑορτῆς χάριν δρῴη ἄν, ὅτε καὶ ποιοῖ· ἐφ᾽ οἷς δὲ
ἐσπούδακεν, τῇ γεωργικῇ χρώμενος ἂν τέχνῃ, σπεί-
ρας εἰς τὸ προσῆκον, ἀγαπῴη ἂν ἐν ὀγδόῳ μηνὶ ὅσα
ἔσπειρεν τέλος λαβόντα;

---

131 That is, the word is not just spoken and "living" (zōnta) but
is "animate" (empsuchon = "alive, ensouled"), "in the sense that
the speaker's purpose and intelligence are present and actively
guiding the discourse" (Yunis, n. ad loc.).

should speak to and those it shouldn't. When it is ill-treated and reviled unjustly it always needs the help of its father. You see, itself it has no power to defend or help itself.

P. You're absolutely right about that too.

S. So, can we look at another method of speaking, legitimate brother of this one, and see in what way it comes into being and how much it grows naturally better and more capable than the other one?

276

P. Which one is this, and what do you mean by "coming into being"?

S. The one which is written with knowledge in the soul of the learner, capable of defending itself, but knowing how to speak and how to keep silent before those it should.

P. You mean the living and animate speech of the man who understands, the written version of which would be rightly called a kind of reflected image.[131]

S. Yes, precisely. So tell me this: would a farmer with intelligence who had seeds he cared about and wanted to produce a fruitful harvest, seriously sow them during the summer in some gardens of Adonis and delight in watching them germinate beautifully within eight days,[132] or would he do this for fun and the occasion of a festival, when he would do it at all; but for those he took a serious interest in would he use his agricultural skill, sow them in suitable ground and would he be well pleased if all he had sowed came to fruition in the eighth month?

b

---

[132] That is, plants grown to mature within a very short time for the festival where women lamented the death of Adonis, who was a legendary beautiful youth and the lover of Aphrodite, and who died young.

c ΦΑΙ. Οὕτω που, ὦ Σώκρατες, τὰ μὲν σπουδῇ, τὰ
δὲ ὡς ἑτέρως ἂν ᾖ λέγεις ποιοῖ.

ΣΩ. Τὸν δὲ δικαίων τε καὶ καλῶν καὶ ἀγαθῶν
ἐπιστήμας ἔχοντα τοῦ γεωργοῦ φῶμεν ἧττον νοῦν
ἔχειν εἰς τὰ ἑαυτοῦ | σπέρματα;

ΦΑΙ. Ἥκιστά γε.

ΣΩ. Οὐκ ἄρα σπουδῇ αὐτὰ ἐν ὕδατι γράψει μέλανι
σπείρων διὰ καλάμου μετὰ λόγων ἀδυνάτων μὲν αὑτοῖς λόγῳ βοηθεῖν, ἀδυνάτων δὲ ἱκανῶς τἀληθῆ διδά-
ξαι. |

ΦΑΙ. Οὔκουν δὴ τό γ᾽ εἰκός.

d ΣΩ. Οὐ γάρ· ἀλλὰ τοὺς μὲν ἐν γράμμασι κήπους,
ὡς ἔοικε, παιδιᾶς χάριν σπερεῖ τε καὶ γράψει, ὅταν
[δὲ] γράφῃ, ἑαυτῷ τε ὑπομνήματα θησαυριζόμενος,
"εἰς τὸ λήθης γῆρας ἐὰν ἵκηται," καὶ παντὶ τῷ ταὐτὸν
ἴχνος μετιόντι, ἡσθήσεταί | τε αὐτοὺς θεωρῶν φυομέ-
νους ἁπαλούς· ὅταν ⟨δὲ⟩ ἄλλοι παιδιαῖς ἄλλαις χρῶνται, συμποσίοις τε ἄρδοντες αὑτοὺς ἑτέροις τε ὅσα
τούτων ἀδελφά, τότ᾽ ἐκεῖνος, ὡς ἔοικεν, ἀντὶ τούτων
οἷς λέγω παίζων διάξει.

e ΦΑΙ. Παγκάλην λέγεις παρὰ φαύλην παιδιάν, ὦ
Σώκρατες, τοῦ ἐν λόγοις δυναμένου παίζειν, δικαιοσύνης τε καὶ ἄλλων ὧν λέγεις πέρι μυθολογοῦντα.

---

133 The plural *epistēmas* = literally, "pieces of knowledge,"
might imply fragmentary areas of knowledge rather than complete understanding (see Rowe, n. ad loc.), but more likely simply
reflects the plural of "things just, beautiful and good," etc.

P. He'd do just that, I suppose, Socrates; he would deal c
with the one lot seriously, but the others differently, as you
say.

S. Are we to say that the man who has knowledge[133] of
things just, beautiful and good has less intelligence than
the farmer when it comes to his own seeds?

P. Far from it!

S. Then he won't be serious about writing them in black
water,[134] sowing them through his pen with words that are
unable to defend themselves in argument and are unable
to teach the truth competently.

P. Certainly that's not likely.

S. No indeed. But he will sow and write the gardens of d
letters it seems for fun, when he does write, storing up for
himself a treasure house of reminders, "when he attains
an old age of forgetfulness,"[135] and for everyone who is
pursuing the same path, he'll enjoy watching their tender
growth. But whenever others resort to other amusements,
irrigating themselves with drinking bouts and other things
that are related to these, then, it seems, instead of these
he will spend his time amusing himself with the things I'm
talking about.

P. You're talking about a very fine form of amusement, e
Socrates, compared with a base one—that of one who is
able to amuse himself with words, telling tales of justice
and other things you mention.[136]

[134] That is, ink. The phrase "to write in water" is proverbial
for a futile exercise.

[135] Possibly a quotation (unknown origin).

[136] "telling tales" (*muthologounta*) suggests Socrates' *palinode*
as an example.

ΣΩ. Ἔστι γάρ, ὦ φίλε Φαῖδρε, οὕτω· πολὺ δ' οἶμαι
| καλλίων σπουδὴ περὶ αὐτὰ γίγνεται, ὅταν τις τῇ
διαλεκτικῇ τέχνῃ χρώμενος, λαβὼν ψυχὴν προσήκου-
σαν, φυτεύῃ τε καὶ σπείρῃ μετ' ἐπιστήμης λόγους, οἳ
ἑαυτοῖς τῷ τε φυτεύσαντι βοηθεῖν ἱκανοὶ καὶ οὐχὶ
277 ἄκαρποι ἀλλὰ ἔχοντες σπέρμα, ὅθεν ἄλλοι ἐν ἄλλοις
ἤθεσι φυόμενοι τοῦτ' ἀεὶ ἀθάνατον παρέχειν ἱκανοί,
καὶ τὸν ἔχοντα εὐδαιμονεῖν ποιοῦντες εἰς ὅσον ἀν-
θρώπῳ δυνατὸν μάλιστα. |

ΦΑΙ. Πολὺ γὰρ τοῦτ' ἔτι κάλλιον λέγεις.

ΣΩ. Νῦν δὴ ἐκεῖνα ἤδη, ὦ Φαῖδρε, δυνάμεθα κρί-
νειν, τούτων ὡμολογημένων.

ΦΑΙ. Τὰ ποῖα;

ΣΩ. Ὧν δὴ πέρι βουληθέντες ἰδεῖν ἀφικόμεθα εἰς
τόδε, | ὅπως τὸ Λυσίου τε ὄνειδος ἐξετάσαιμεν τῆς
τῶν λόγων γραφῆς πέρι, καὶ αὐτοὺς τοὺς λόγους οἳ
b τέχνῃ καὶ ἄνευ τέχνης γράφοιντο. τὸ μὲν οὖν ἔν-
τεχνον καὶ μὴ δοκεῖ μοι δεδηλῶσθαι μετρίως.

ΦΑΙ. Ἔδοξέ γε δή· πάλιν δὲ ὑπόμνησόν με πῶς. |

ΣΩ. Πρὶν ἄν τις τό τε ἀληθὲς ἑκάστων εἰδῇ πέρι
ὧν λέγει ἢ γράφει, κατ' αὐτό τε πᾶν ὁρίζεσθαι δυνατὸς γένηται, ὁρισάμενός τε πάλιν κατ' εἴδη μέχρι τοῦ
ἀτμήτου τέμνειν ἐπιστηθῇ, περί τε ψυχῆς φύσεως δι-
ιδὼν κατὰ ταὐτά, τὸ προσαρμόττον ἑκάστῃ φύσει
c εἶδος ἀνευρίσκων, οὕτω τιθῇ καὶ διακοσμῇ τὸν λόγον,
ποικίλῃ μὲν ποικίλους ψυχῇ καὶ παναρμονίους διδοὺς

S. Yes, so it is, my dear Phaedrus; but I think it is much finer if one becomes serious about them, when one uses the art of dialectic, adopting a soul fit for purpose planting and sowing there words with knowledge which will be capable of helping themselves and him who planted them and are not fruitless, but bear a seed from which others   277 grow in other habitats, capable of making it for ever immortal, and making its possessor happy as far as that's possible for a human being.

P. This is still much finer, what you're talking about.

S. Then we are now in a position, Phaedrus, having agreed on these points, to be able to decide on those other issues.

P. Which ones?

S. Those which we wanted to look at, through which we have reached the following point: how we should investigate the reproach against Lysias about his writing of speeches and the speeches themselves, which ones were written with art and which without. Well, I think we have   b given a fair demonstration of what is done with art and what isn't.

P. It certainly did seem like that. Just remind me once again how.

S. Until a person knows the truth about each of the things he speaks or writes, and becomes capable of defining the whole by itself and, after he has defined it, knows how to go back and cut it up again form by form, up to the point where it is no longer divisible, and having discerned the nature of the soul on the same principles, discovering the form which agrees with each nature, and so orga-   c nizes and arranges his speech, offering elaborate speeches embracing all the modes to a complex soul and simple

λόγους, ἁπλοῦς δὲ ἁπλῇ, οὐ πρότερον δυνατὸν τέχνῃ
ἔσεσθαι καθ᾽ ὅσον πέφυκε μεταχειρισθῆναι | τὸ λό-
γων γένος, οὔτε τι πρὸς τὸ διδάξαι οὔτε τι πρὸς τὸ
πεῖσαι, ὡς ὁ ἔμπροσθεν πᾶς μεμήνυκεν ἡμῖν λόγος.

ΦΑΙ. Παντάπασι μὲν οὖν τοῦτό γε οὕτω πως ἐφάνη.

d ΣΩ. Τί δ᾽ αὖ περὶ τοῦ καλὸν ἢ αἰσχρὸν εἶναι τὸ
λόγους λέγειν τε καὶ γράφειν, καὶ ὅπῃ γιγνόμενον ἐν
δίκῃ λέγοιτ᾽ ἂν ὄνειδος ἢ μή, ἆρα οὐ δεδήλωκεν τὰ
λεχθέντα ὀλίγον ἔμπροσθεν—|

ΦΑΙ. Τὰ ποῖα;

ΣΩ. Ὡς εἴτε Λυσίας ἤ τις ἄλλος πώποτε ἔγραψεν
ἢ γράψει ἰδίᾳ ἢ δημοσίᾳ νόμους τιθείς, σύγγραμμα
πολιτικὸν γράφων καὶ μεγάλην τινὰ ἐν αὐτῷ βεβαι-
ότητα ἡγούμενος καὶ σαφήνειαν, οὕτω μὲν ὄνειδος τῷ
e γράφοντι, εἴτε τίς | φησιν εἴτε μή· τὸ γὰρ ἀγνοεῖν
ὕπαρ τε καὶ ὄναρ δικαίων καὶ ἀδίκων πέρι καὶ κακῶν
καὶ ἀγαθῶν οὐκ ἐκφεύγει τῇ ἀληθείᾳ μὴ οὐκ ἐπονείδιστον εἶναι, οὐδὲ ἂν ὁ πᾶς ὄχλος αὐτὸ ἐπαινέσῃ.

ΦΑΙ. Οὐ γὰρ οὖν. |

ΣΩ. Ὁ δέ γε ἐν μὲν τῷ γεγραμμένῳ λόγῳ περὶ
ἑκάστου παιδιάν τε ἡγούμενος πολλὴν ἀναγκαῖον εἶναι, καὶ οὐδένα πώποτε λόγον ἐν μέτρῳ οὐδ᾽ ἄνευ
μέτρου μεγάλης ἄξιον σπουδῆς γραφῆναι, οὐδὲ λεχθῆναι ὡς οἱ ῥαψῳδούμενοι ἄνευ ἀνακρίσεως καὶ διδαχῆς πειθοῦς ἕνεκα ἐλέχθησαν, ἀλλὰ τῷ ὄντι αὐτῶν

speeches to a simple one; not before this will he be capable
of handling the production of speeches with art as far as
their nature allows, whether in respect of teaching or persuading, as the whole of our previous discussion has revealed to us.[137]

P. Absolutely: this was just about how it appeared.

S. Again about it being fine or shameful to give and   d
write speeches, and where it would be right to say that it
has been a disgrace or not, hasn't what we said a little
earlier shown . . .

P. What sort of thing?

S. That whether Lysias or anyone else has ever written
or will write either for private consumption or public use
while proposing laws, and so writing a political pamphlet,
and thinks there is some great assurance and clarity in it,
then it is a disgrace for the writer, whether anyone says so
or not. For to be ignorant when awake or asleep about   e
what is just and unjust, bad and good, cannot in truth escape being a matter of disgrace, not even if the whole mass
of people praise it.

P. No, indeed not.

S. And the man who thinks that there must necessarily
be much for amusement in the written speech on any
topic, and that no speech in verse or in prose that is worthy
of much serious attention has ever yet been written or
even delivered, as the rhapsodes deliver theirs for the sake
of being convincing without questioning and instruction,
but that in reality the best of them have become a re-

[137] This speech of Socrates recalls his argument in 271dff.

278 τοὺς βελτίστους εἰδότων ὑπόμνησιν γεγονέναι, ἐν δὲ
τοῖς διδασκομένοις καὶ μαθήσεως χάριν λεγομένοις
καὶ τῷ ὄντι γραφομένοις ἐν ψυχῇ περὶ δικαίων τε καὶ
καλῶν καὶ ἀγαθῶν [ἐν] μόνοις ἡγούμενος τό τε ἐναρ-
γὲς εἶναι καὶ | τέλεον καὶ ἄξιον σπουδῆς· δεῖν δὲ τοὺς
τοιούτους λόγους αὐτοῦ λέγεσθαι οἷον ὑεῖς γνησίους
εἶναι, πρῶτον μὲν τὸν ἐν αὐτῷ, ἐὰν εὑρεθεὶς ἐνῇ,
b ἔπειτα εἴ τινες τούτου ἔκγονοί τε καὶ ἀδελφοὶ ἅμα ἐν
ἄλλαισιν ἄλλων ψυχαῖς κατ᾽ ἀξίαν ἐνέφυσαν· τοὺς δὲ
ἄλλους χαίρειν ἐῶν—οὗτος δὲ ὁ τοιοῦτος ἀνὴρ κινδυνεύει, ὦ Φαῖδρε, εἶναι οἷον ἐγώ τε καὶ σὺ εὐξαίμεθ᾽ ἂν
σέ τε καὶ ἐμὲ γενέσθαι. |

ΦΑΙ. Παντάπασι μὲν οὖν ἔγωγε βούλομαί τε καὶ
εὔχομαι ἃ λέγεις.

ΣΩ. Οὐκοῦν ἤδη πεπαίσθω μετρίως ἡμῖν τὰ περὶ
λόγων· καὶ σύ τε ἐλθὼν φράζε Λυσίᾳ ὅτι νὼ κατα-
βάντε ἐς τὸ Νυμφῶν νᾶμά τε καὶ μουσεῖον ἠκούσα-
c μεν λόγων, οἳ ἐπέστελλον λέγειν Λυσίᾳ τε καὶ εἴ τις
ἄλλος συντίθησι λόγους, καὶ Ὁμήρῳ καὶ εἴ τις ἄλλος
αὖ ποίησιν ψιλὴν ἢ ἐν ᾠδῇ συνέθηκε, τρίτον δὲ Σό-
λωνι καὶ ὅστις ἐν πολιτικοῖς λόγοις νόμους ὀνομάζων
συγγράμματα ἔγραψεν· εἰ μὲν εἰδὼς ᾗ τὸ | ἀληθὲς ἔχει
συνέθηκε ταῦτα, καὶ ἔχων βοηθεῖν, εἰς ἔλεγχον ἰὼν
περὶ ὧν ἔγραψε, καὶ λέγων αὐτὸς δυνατὸς τὰ γεγραμ-

---

138 Rhapsodes were professional reciters of poetry, in particular the works of Homer. On Plato's negative view of their pretensions to knowledge, see *Ion*.

minder for those who know:[138] who thinks that clarity and   278
completeness, and something worth serious attention, are
only to be found in those things that are being taught
about what is just, fine and good and delivered for the
purpose of learning, and are genuinely written in the soul:
that such speeches of his should be said to be as if they
were his legitimate sons, firstly the one inside him, if it is
to be found there, and then if any offspring and brothers   b
have grown at the same time in the souls of others as they
deserve—bidding farewell to the rest: such a man as this,
Phaedrus, is likely to be the sort of person that I and you
pray that you and I may become.[139]

P. I for my part wish and pray for what you say, above
all things.

S. So now let this be a moderate diversion we've enjoyed about speeches. And as for you, go and tell Lysias,
that the two of us came down to the spring and shrine of
the Nymphs and listened to speeches which commanded   c
us to say to Lysias, and if anyone else composes speeches,
and Homer and anyone else again who has composed
verse, without musical accompaniment or poetry set to
music, thirdly, Solon and whoever has written compositions in the form of political speeches, calling them laws:
if he has composed these knowing how the truth stands
and is able to support them, if he is put to the test over
what he has written and when speaking in person is able
to demonstrate that what he has written is paltry, then

---

[139] The whole of Socrates' speech at 277e5–78b4 is a single
long sentence, with a series of clauses hanging on "And the man
who thinks that," and concluding (278b3–4), "such a man as this,
Phaedrus. . . ."

PLATO

μένα φαῦλα ἀποδεῖξαι, οὔ τι τῶνδε ἐπωνυμίαν ἔχοντα
δεῖ λέγεσθαι τὸν τοιοῦτον, ἀλλ᾽ ἐφ᾽ οἷς ἐσπούδακεν
ἐκείνων.

d   ΦΑΙ. Τίνας οὖν τὰς ἐπωνυμίας αὐτῷ νέμεις;

ΣΩ. Τὸ μὲν σοφόν, ὦ Φαῖδρε, καλεῖν ἔμοιγε μέγα
εἶναι δοκεῖ καὶ θεῷ μόνῳ πρέπειν· τὸ δὲ ἢ φιλόσοφον
ἢ | τοιοῦτόν τι μᾶλλόν τε ἂν αὐτῷ καὶ ἁρμόττοι καὶ
ἐμμελεστέρως ἔχοι.

ΦΑΙ. Καὶ οὐδέν γε ἀπὸ τρόπου.

ΣΩ. Οὐκοῦν αὖ τὸν μὴ ἔχοντα τιμιώτερα ὧν συνέ-
θηκεν ἢ ἔγραψεν ἄνω κάτω στρέφων ἐν χρόνῳ, πρὸς
e ἄλληλα κολλῶν τε καὶ ἀφαιρῶν, ἐν δίκῃ που ποιητὴν
ἢ λόγων συγγραφέα ἢ νομογράφον προσερεῖς;

ΦΑΙ. Τί μήν;

ΣΩ. Ταῦτα τοίνυν τῷ ἑταίρῳ φράζε. |

ΦΑΙ. Τί δὲ σύ; πῶς ποιήσεις; οὐδὲ γὰρ οὐδὲ τὸν
σὸν ἑταῖρον δεῖ παρελθεῖν.

ΣΩ. Τίνα τοῦτον;

ΦΑΙ. Ἰσοκράτη τὸν καλόν· ᾧ τί ἀπαγγελεῖς, ὦ
Σώκρατες; τίνα αὐτὸν φήσομεν εἶναι; |

279   ΣΩ. Νέος ἔτι, ὦ Φαῖδρε, Ἰσοκράτης· ὃ μέντοι μαν-
τεύομαι κατ᾽ αὐτοῦ, λέγειν ἐθέλω.

ΦΑΙ. Τὸ ποῖον δή;

---

140 "these," i.e., written words (speeches), as opposed to spoken words, i.e., dialectic.

528

such a person should not be spoken of as if he had his name from such things as these, but from those about which he was serious.[140]

P. So which are the names you assign him?   d

S. To call him wise, Phaedrus, seems to me to be a big claim and fit only for a god: to call him a lover of wisdom or some such would be somewhat more fitting for him and more in keeping.

P. And not at all inappropriate.

S. On the other hand for a man who has nothing more to his credit than the things he has composed or written, twisting them this and that way in the course of time, pasting them together and taking them apart: would you   e rightly perhaps call him a poet, or speechwriter, or a drafter of laws?

P. Certainly.

S. Then tell that to your friend.

P. But what about you? What will you do? For we must not in any circumstances pass your friend by either.

S. Who's he?

P. The handsome Isocrates. What will you tell him, Socrates? What shall we call him?[141]

S. Isocrates is still young, Phaedrus. However I am   279 willing to say what I prophesy for him.

P. What's that then?

[141] That is, is Isocrates (436–338) speechwriter or philosopher? Isocrates, near-contemporary of Plato and young at the presumed dramatic date of *Phaedrus* (e10), became a renowned writer of speeches and, at around the presumed date of composition, Plato's great rival; see further Introduction, §4(iv) and Appendix.

ΣΩ. Δοκεῖ μοι ἀμείνων ἢ κατὰ τοὺς περὶ Λυσίαν
εἶναι λόγους τὰ τῆς φύσεως, ἔτι τε ἤθει γεννικωτέρῳ
κεκρᾶσθαι· | ὥστε οὐδὲν ἂν γένοιτο θαυμαστὸν προϊ-
ούσης τῆς ἡλικίας εἰ περὶ αὐτούς τε τοὺς λόγους, οἷς
νῦν ἐπιχειρεῖ, πλέον ἢ παίδων διενέγκοι τῶν πώποτε
ἁψαμένων λόγων, ἔτι τε εἰ αὐτῷ μὴ ἀποχρήσαι ταῦτα,
ἐπὶ μείζω δέ τις αὐτὸν ἄγοι ὁρμὴ θειοτέρα· φύσει γάρ,
ὦ φίλε, ἔνεστί τις φιλοσοφία τῇ τοῦ ἀνδρὸς διανοίᾳ.
b ταῦτα δὴ οὖν ἐγὼ μὲν παρὰ τῶνδε τῶν θεῶν ὡς ἐμοῖς
παιδικοῖς Ἰσοκράτει ἐξαγγέλλω, σὺ δ᾽ ἐκεῖνα ὡς σοῖς
Λυσίᾳ.

ΦΑΙ. Ταῦτ᾽ ἔσται· ἀλλὰ ἴωμεν, ἐπειδὴ καὶ τὸ πνῖγος
| ἠπιώτερον γέγονεν.

ΣΩ. Οὐκοῦν εὐξαμένῳ πρέπει τοῖσδε πορεύεσθαι;

ΦΑΙ. Τί μήν;

ΣΩ. Ὦ φίλε Πάν τε καὶ ἄλλοι ὅσοι τῇδε θεοί,
δοίητέ μοι καλῷ γενέσθαι τἄνδοθεν· ἔξωθεν δὲ ὅσα
c ἔχω, τοῖς ἐντὸς εἶναί μοι φίλια. πλούσιον δὲ νομίζοιμι
τὸν σοφόν· τὸ δὲ χρυσοῦ πλῆθος εἴη μοι ὅσον μήτε
φέρειν μήτε ἄγειν δύναιτο ἄλλος ἢ ὁ σώφρων.

Ἔτ᾽ ἄλλου του δεόμεθα, ὦ Φαῖδρε; ἐμοὶ μὲν γὰρ
μετρίως | ηὖκται.

ΦΑΙ. Καὶ ἐμοὶ ταῦτα συνεύχου· κοινὰ γὰρ τὰ τῶν
φίλων.

ΣΩ. Ἴωμεν.

S. He seems to me to be better in his natural aptitude compared with Lysias and his speeches, and furthermore blended with a nobler character, so that it wouldn't be at all surprising if, as his life progresses, in the actual speeches on which he is now engaged, he exceeds those who have ever undertaken to write speeches by a greater margin than if he were to be compared with children, and even greater if this work doesn't satisfy him, and some more divine impulse were to lead him to greater achievements. For there is by nature, my friend, a certain philosophical instinct in the man's mind. This is indeed the b message I'm going to convey to my beloved Isocrates from these gods here, and you announce the other to Lysias as yours.

P. So shall it be. But let's go, especially since the heat has eased off.

S. Then isn't it right to pray to the gods here before we leave?

P. Of course.

S. Dear Pan, and all you other gods here, grant me to become beautiful within and may such things as I have outwardly be in harmony with what is within me. May I c consider the wise man rich, may the amount of gold I have be of the size that none other than a man of sound mind might be able to bear and carry.

Is there still anything else we need, Phaedrus? For me my prayer has been sufficient.

P. Make this prayer for me too. For what friends have, they have in common.

S. Let's go.

INDEX OF NAMES

INDEX OF NAMES

INDEX OF NAMES

INDEX OF SUBJECTS

537

539